Communications
in Computer and Information Science   226

Jianwei Zhang (Ed.)

Applied Informatics and Communication

International Conference, ICAIC 2011
Xi'an, China, August 20-21, 2011
Proceedings, Part III

 Springer

Volume Editor

Jianwei Zhang
Suzhou University
No. 50 Donghuan Road, Suzhou 215021, China
E-mail: jianweizhang12@163.com

ISSN 1865-0929   e-ISSN 1865-0937
ISBN 978-3-642-23234-3   e-ISBN 978-3-642-23235-0
DOI 10.1007/978-3-642-23235-0
Springer Heidelberg Dordrecht London New York

Library of Congress Control Number: 2011934039

CR Subject Classification (1998): C, D, F, H, I, J.1, J.2

Typesetting: Camera-ready by author, data conversion by Scientific Publishing Services, Chennai, India

Printed on acid-free paper

Springer is part of Springer Science+Business Media (www.springer.com)

Preface

Computers are firmly rooted in nearly all areas of life today. In company life, documents and products are produced by using computers, communication is by e-mail, companies present their commodities and services on the Internet and copious amounts of data are stored in databases. Different application programs are required for all of these processes.

The 2011 International Conference on Applied Informatics and Communication (ICAIC 2011) held during August 20–21, 2011, in Xi'an, China, provided an excellent platform for scientists and engineers of different countries working in various fields to exchange the latest developments and foster world-wide cooperation in the field of applied informatics and communication. Hundreds of experts and scholars from different countries attended ICAIC 2011.

Being crucial for the development of applied informatics and communication, our conference encompasses numerous research topics and applications: from the core fields of information systems and software engineering, manufacturing and automation engineering, computer-based signal processing and image processing to Communications Technology and other related topics. All of the papers were peer-reviewed by selected experts and 451 were selected for the proceedings of ICAIC 2011. We believe that this book provides a valuable reference for researchers in related fields. The papers describe how efficient, user-friendly, secure and upgradeable information technology systems can be designed, built and meaningfully used and operated in practice.

ICAIC 2011 was organized by the Information Engineering Research Institute, USA, and the proceeding are published by Springer. The conference was held in Xi'an. Xi'an, located in central-northwest China, records the great changes of the country just like a living history book. Called Chang'an (meaning the eternal city) in ancient times, Xi'an is one of the birthplaces of the ancient Chinese civilization in the Yellow River Basin area. It is the eastern terminal of the Silk Road and the site of the famous Terracotta Warriors of the Qin Dynasty. More than 3,000 years of history, including over 1,100 years as the capital city of ancient dynasties, have endowed Xi'an with an amazing historical heritage.

We sincerely thank all the members of the ICAIC Organizing Committee, Academic Committee and Program Committee. Moreover, we also express our sincere appreciation to all the referees, staff and volunteers for their tremendous efforts. Finally, we would like to thank all the authors who have contributed to this volume.

We hope that readers will find lots of interesting and useful information in the proceedings.

June 2011

Dehuai Zeng
Jianwei Zhang
Jun Zhang

Table of Contents – Part III

Information Processing and Data Mining

A Two-Stage Speed Up Model for Case-Based Learning in Real Time
Strategy Games.. 1
    Yan Li, Xiaolei Tong, and Jiayue Dai

Inversion of TEM Conductive Thin Layer Based on Genetic
Algorithm.. 10
    Guo Wenbo, Xue Guoqiang, Zhou Nannan, and Li Xiu

Study on Synthesis Fault Diagnosis Strategy of the Brake System of
Wind Turbine Based on Evidence Theory 18
    Zhijie Wang and Sanming Liu

Application of Ant Colony Algorithm in Tracking Convective Cloud
Images from Chinese FY-2C Satellite 26
    Xiaofang Pei, Nan Li, Miaoying Li, and Luan Li

Application of Simulated Annealing Algorithm in Fingerprint
Matching 33
    Xiaofang Pei, Nan Li, and Shuiping Wang

Research of Manufacturing Enterprise Information System Integration
Based on Extended ESB 41
    Xiaohui Yan, Yunlong Zhu, Xin Sui, and Wenping Zou

BAN with Low Power Consumption Based on Compressed Sensing
Point-to-Point Transmission 49
    Shasha Li, Fengye Hu, and Guofeng Li

Advances and Challenges in Body Area Network 58
    Shasha Li, Fengye Hu, and Guofeng Li

Application of Unfeaty Tenancy in Simulating Flip-Flop Gates and
Location-Identity Split... 66
    Dong-Xia Yuan and Xiao-Yu Ma

Research on the Platform of Enterprise Co-evolution Based on the
Collective Intelligence 73
    Guihua Nie, Shangying Xu, and Xiwen Zhang

The Analysis of Flashget Downloading Record 82
    Luo Zhifeng, Zhang Lixiao, and Wu Shunxiang

Risk Analysis and Its Application of the Projects Based on Computer
Simulated Technology 88
  Junxiao Lin and Pengfei Jiang

Image Enhancement of Ground Penetrating Radar Based on Multiscale
Space Correlation 95
  Hailin Zou and Chanjuan Liu

Modeling and Simulation of the Virtualized Scenes Base on the Open
Modelica... 103
  Jiang YuXiang, Zhou Xiaolong, Li JinPing, and Ren LiYing

Study on the Evaluation Model of the Investment Efficiency of Real
Estate Industry Based on Super Efficiency DEA 111
  Fangfang Wei, Yanxi Li, Rui Gao, and Jing Sun

Research on the Method of Parity Checker Design Based on Evolvable
Hardware 119
  Kuifu Wang and Jingfeng Yan

Control System Modeling for Automotive Brake Test-Bench Based on
Neural Network... 125
  Jiaxi Du, Hong Shen, and Xin Ning

Adaptive Projective Synchronization of Complex Networks with
Weighted Topology... 131
  Dianchen Lu and Qiaoxia Qi

Research on Emergency Power Material Allocation Program 141
  Xu Xiaofeng, Guo Xiaoming, and Liu Junyong

Design and Realization of the Engine Condition Monitoring System
Based on CAN Bus 152
  Li-Hui Chen, Ying-Ji Liu, Yi Sui, Wei Zhou, and Jian-Wei Ji

The Effects of Guanxi Categorie on Bank Credit 160
  Li Jinling, Luan Qingwei, and Li Yanxi

Shape Feature Analysis for Visual Speech and Speaker Recognition..... 167
  Jiaping Gui and Shilin Wang

A Cooperative Framework of Remote Cooperative Fault Diagnosis
Based on TBAC 175
  Liu Jian-Hui

Analysis on Dynamic Landscape Patterns of Urbanizations in Four
Asia Cities Using 3S Technologies and CA Model 182
  Yizhao Chen, Jiasheng Huang, and Jianlong Li

A Low-Rate DoS Detection Based on Rate Anomalies   189
  Libing Wu, Jing Cheng, Yanxiang He, Ao Xu, and Peng Wen

The Lightning Signal Detect Method Based on Random Resonance   197
  Xin Liu, Wei Wu, and Zheng Qin

Research on Training Condition of Chinese Intellectual Property
Professionals   205
  Pan Xia

Research on the Application of ZigBee Technology in Positioning
System   215
  Ge Xiao-Yu, Wang Qing-Hui, and Feng An-Song

Design and Implementation of a DSP-Based Embedded Intelligent
Traffic Surveillance System   221
  Lan Hai, Yin Hang, Gyanendra Shrestha, and Zhang Lijun

Study on the Method Based on Rough Sets and Neural Network for the
Estimation of Iron Ore Grade   230
  Hongtao Wang

An Efficient Storage Method for Disaster Tolerant System   239
  Wen Li, Peng Chen, and Xiao-Bin Yang

The Model Design of Intelligent DSAS Based on the Multi-MA   246
  Jia Tiejun, Xiong Peng, and Wang Xiaogang

A Modified Securities Model Based on Public Key Infrastructure   252
  Wuzheng Tan, Yongquan Xie, Dan Li, and Mei Liu

An Empirical Study on China's Inter-provincial Coal Distribution by
Railway   260
  Yanzhi Zhang, Lei Zhang, Tao Lv, and Ying Feng

Research on Configuration Management for ETO Product Based on
Universal Data Model   267
  Zhu Miaofen, Su Shaohui, Gong Youping, and Chen Guojin

Research on the Configuration Design of the ETO Product Based on
Knowledge and Thing Characteristic Table   273
  Zhu Miaofen, Su Shaohui, Gong Youping, and Chen Guojin

The Study about Students' Achievement Analysis Methods Based on
Charts Technology   282
  Yang Hongwei, Xu Tongyu, and Li Jinhui

Maintenance Organization Value Chain Analysis and Its
Formalization   289
  Tianming Zhang, Ying Wang, and Chao Li

The Design and Implementation of Virtual Visiting System for Digital
Museum Based on Web   297
    Min Jiang, Lixin Ma, and Xiaolu Qu

Neural Networks and Wireless Communication

Measuring and Controlling System for Validation of Grain Storage
Mathematical Model Based on ZigBee Technology   304
    Zhou Huiling, Feng Yu, and Liu Jingyun

The Research Based on Ontology Annotations of the Structured
Elements of the Emergency Plan   312
    Huang Weidong, Yan Li, and Zhai Danni

Local Latent Semantic Analysis Based on Support Vector Machine for
Imbalanced Text Categorization   321
    Yuan Wan, Hengqing Tong, and Yanfang Deng

Study on the Application of Garment CAD Style Design System and
Pattern Design System in Garment E-Commerce   330
    Meihua Zhao and Xiaoping Zhang

Sentence-Level Sentiment Analysis via Sequence Modeling   337
    Xiaohua Liu and Ming Zhou

The Application of Norton Ghost Multicast Technology in the
Maintenance of College Computer Room   344
    Li Jinhui, Yang Hongwei, Zhu Yong, and Zhang Ke

Simulating Working Memory Guiding Visual Attention for Capturing
Target by Computational Cognitive Model   352
    Rifeng Wang

The Inverter Testing System of Asynchronous Motor Based on Modbus
Communication   360
    Wenlun Cao, Bei Chen, and Yuyao He

A Novel Variable Step Size LMS Adaptive Filtering Algorithm   367
    Yi Sun, Rui Xiao, Liang-Rui Tang, and Bing Qi

Development and Realization about the Embedded GIS in Vehicles
Based on ReWorks   376
    Chungang Wang, Yanxia Liu, Qinzhen Li, and Dongfang Huo

Research of the Automotive Driver Fatigue Driving Early Warning
System   383
    Libiao Jiang, Huirong Wang, Shengying Gao, and Siyu Jiang

A Novel Four-Dimensional Hyperchaotic System 392
    Liangrui Tang, Lin Zhao, and Qin Zhang

Application of Association Rules in Analysis of College Students'
Performance.. 402
    Huiping Wang and Ruowu Zhong

Hybrid Controllers for Two-Link Flexible Manipulators 409
    Yanmin Wang, HongWei Xia, and Changhong Wang

Optimization Choice Algorithm for Composite Service Based on QoS
Aggregation 419
    Zhiwu Wang, Yu Wang, Liu Hong, and Xueguang Chen

Unidirectional Loop Facility Layout Optimization Design Based on
Niche Genetic Algorithm 429
    Lu Tong-Tong, Lu Chao, and Han Jun

Hyperchaotic Attractors Generated from Nadolschi Chaotic System 437
    Ruochen Zhang and Yan Zhao

Satellite Attitude Determination Using Space Camera and Gyros'
Information 445
    Peijun Yu, Keqiang Xia, and Jiancheng Li

Data Association Rules in Analyzing Performance Level of College
Students 454
    Ruowu Zhong and Huiping Wang

Design and Implementation of Scenario Production System for Sea
Battlefield Situation Analysis 459
    Yang Lujing, Hao Wei, and Niu Xiaobo

Research on Sea-Battlefield Perception Capability of the Naval Fleet ... 468
    Luo Bing, Li Zhong-Meng, Li Ya-Nan, and Feng Kun

Design and Analysis of Outer Baffle of Space Telescope 477
    Yingjun Guan, Deqiang Mu, and Zhilai Li

The Research of the Command and Control Model for the Naval Battle
Groups with Multi-agent Theory 486
    Ji-Jin Tong, Zhong Liu, Li Duan, and Li-Mei Xu

The E-Learning System Model Based on Affective Computing 495
    Zhiling Li

A Novel Immune-Inspired Method for Malicious Code Extraction and
Detection 501
    Yu Zhang, Liping Song, and Yuliang He

Study on the Effectiveness of the TCP Pacing Mechanism   510
 Xinying Liu, Fenta Adnew Mogus, and Lei Wang

Research on the Architecture of Cloud Computing   519
 Jun Wu, Jing Yang, Xisi Tu, and Guangling Yi

Multi-objective Optimization Using Immune Algorithm   527
 Pengfei Guo, Xuezhi Wang, and Yingshi Han

A Wireless Water Quality Monitoring System Based on LabVIEW and
Web   535
 Ziguang Sun, Chungui Li, and Zengfang Zhang

Piezoelectric Pulse Diagnosis Transducer of 9x9 Sensing Arrays and
Pulse Signal Processing   541
 Hung Chang and Jia-Xu Chen

OFDM Channel Estimation for Broadband Wireless Based on Fractal
Interpolation and Adaptive Filtering   549
 Bing Qi, Ya-Wei Li, Yi Sun, and Liang-Rui Tang

Design of the Mass Customization Strategy for Special Purpose
Vehicles   558
 Jianzhong Li

Improved Feature for Texture Segmentation Using Gabor Filters   565
 Chuanzhen Li and Qin Zhang

A Micro-Grid Communication Mechanism in Distributed Power
System   573
 Hongbin Sun and Xue Ye

A New Time-Delay Compensation Method in NCS Based on T-S Fuzzy
Model   581
 Xiaoshan Wang and Yanxin Zhang

Web Data Extraction Based on Structure Feature   591
 Ma Anxiang, Gao Kening, Zhang Xiaohong, and Zhang Bin

Decoupling Control for DACF Pressure Based on Neural Networks and
Prediction Principle   600
 Dengfeng Dong, Xiaofeng Meng, and Fan Liang

A Multipath Routing for Mobile Ad Hoc Networks   608
 Zheng Sihai and Layuan Li

Method of Light-Spot Subpiexl Center Orientation Based on Linear
CCD in Fiber Sensing System   615
 Jun Tao and Xia Zhang

AlphaBeta-Based Optimized Game Tree Search Algorithm 623
   Xiao-Bin Yang and Wen Li

Color Image Segmentation Based on Learning from Spatial and
Temporal Discontinuities... 632
   Chen Pan and Feng Cui

Wisdom Logistics Based on Cloud Computing 640
   Zhiying Zhou and Dandan Lv

The Research of Multi-pose Face Detection Based on Skin Color and
Adaboost 647
   Ran Li, Guang-Xing Tan, and Sheng-Hua Ning

Research and Implementation of 3D Interactive Digital Campus Based
on Spatial Database 655
   Libing Wu, Tianshui Yu, Kui Gong, Yalin Ke, and Peng Wen

Joint Pricing and Replenishment Policies for a Deteriorating Inventory
Model with Stochastic Demand 663
   Ying Feng and Yanzhi Zhang

Application of Wireless Sensor Network in Farmland Data Acquisition
System 672
   Bei Wang, Xiaona Guo, Zhiqi Chen, and Zhaoqian Shuai

Research on Optimization Algorithm of TCP Reno Based on Wireless
Network 679
   Chun Bai, Jin Liu, and Hong Deng

Author Index 687

A Two-Stage Speed Up Model for Case-Based Learning in Real Time Strategy Games

Yan Li[1], Xiaolei Tong[2], and Jiayue Dai[2]

[1] College of Mathematics and Computer,
Hebei University, Baoding, Hebei Province, China
[2] Machine Learning Center,
Hebei University, Baoding, Hebei Province, China
YanLiCD@yeah.net

Abstract. To meet the requirement of real time strategy (RTS) games, this paper proposes a two-stage speed up model using the combination of genetic algorithm and ant algorithm (GA-AA) and then artificial neural network (ANN) in a RTS game. The task is to tackle the optimization and adaptive defensive positioning game problems. In the first stage, we use GA to perform the initial optimization, and then AA is incorporated to speed up GA. In the second stage, the results of GA-AA can be used as cases to train an ANN, which obtains the optimal solutions very fast and then completes the whole off-line learning process. These optimal solutions stored in the trained ANN are considered to be still useful to provide good solutions in even random generated environments. Thus the two-stage speed up model not only needs less off-line training time, but also can recommend good on-line solutions very quickly. Experimental results are demonstrated to support our idea.

Keywords: Real time strategy games (RTS), Case-based learning, Genetic algorithm, Ant algorithm, Artificial neural network.

1 Introduction

In the past few years, the prosperous development of computer games provides a wide range of stage for artificial intelligence (AI). The application of AI makes the game become more intelligent and interesting. As we all know, AI algorithms which had been used in computer games are nearly heuristic-based. The reusability and portability of the program is quite poor [4]. The computer-controlled characters can perform very well on a known map by using heuristic mechanisms, but their actions are not well adapted to new random generated environments. To tackle this problem, [1] has built a neural-evolutionary model to mimic the human ability that people can learn and plan to solve problems by first tying and working exhaustively to find out 'good' solutions and then remembering the correct answers to make decisions quickly in the future. We notice that, the learning process in the above model is implemented by genetic algorithm (GA), whose training is so time-consuming that we cannot tolerate it even the training is off-line. To improve this situation, we suggest a two-stage acceleration model. Firstly, we combine GA and ant algorithm (AA) to speed up

J. Zhang (Ed.): ICAIC 2011, Part III, CCIS 226, pp. 1–9, 2011.

the off-line training process that only uses GA. Secondly, the outputs of the first stage will be considered as the inputs of an ANN, this will further speed up the learning process of ANN. The results of ANN will be applied in the on-line planning, which facilitate NPCs to learn behavior without using any other heuristic mechanisms and predict characters' actions in new randomly generated environments. Through the study of such previous successful experience (i.e., case information stored in the trained ANN), characters are able to adapt themselves to new situations. The experimental results show that our work is effective and feasible for the problem we mentioned above.

This article consists of five sections. Section 2 describes the problem background and introduces some basic algorithms. Section 3 presents our method and demonstrates the experimental results. Section 4 shows the ANN learning process which is used on-line and section V is the conclusion.

2   Background and Basic Algorithms

A   Background

Nowadays, game AI approaches often use cheat strategy and a fixed model to enhance the player's interest in games. In this case, human players will be familiar with the NPCs' behaviors after only a few of game plays, and then can predict NPC actions very quickly when facing a specific situation. Furthermore, it is risky if players become aware of the fact of being cheated, which will make them lose interest in the game immediately. We will demonstrate our method to change this situation. This method contains three main basic algorithms, genetic algorithm, ant algorithm, and artificial neural network. Since the main contribution is to combine GA and AA, we give a briefly introduction of these two algorithms.

B   Genetic Algorithm (GA)

GA proposed by John Holland is a search procedure based on the mechanics of natural selection and natural genetics [5]. It is a search technique to find globally an approximate solution and it is robust and potentially parallel [3]. However, since it cannot make use of enough feedback information, a large number of redundant iterations often occur in later searching and thus reduces the problem solving efficiency [8].

C   Ant Algorithm (AA)

AA was introduced by Dorigo [7] and has been evolved significantly in the last few years. Ant algorithm converges on the optimization path through information pheromone accumulation and renewal. Ant algorithm is a global optimization method, which is not only for solving single objective optimization problems, but also can be used for multi-objective optimization problems. Its weakness is the low efficiency in the early searching due to the lack of pheromone information.

3 Methodology

In this section, we integrate the characteristics of GA and AA to overcome their respective weakness mentioned in the previous section. More specifically, GA is used to perform the initial searching and then generate pheromone information for the early search stage of AA, and then AA replaces GA to continue with the searching task and finally output solutions. Our purpose is to make GA and AA to complement each other, and expect to achieve a win-win performance with respect to both optimality and searching time.

A Scenario of Tower Attack Game

In this paper, we have selected a simple but typical Tower Attack[1-2] as testing platform of our method. The scenario description is as follows:

> *1) Player*: There are two teams, the attack team and the defense team.
> *2) Attack rules*: Attack team can only attack the other team in the defense base.
> *3) Defense rules:* Defense team can set up tower to kill the attack team.
> *4) Our goal:* Find the towers' position distribution which can create maximum amount of damages on the attack team.

To reduce the computational load of GA and AA, the battlefields are divided into different 50×50 smaller sub-maps. Fig. 1shows some representative types of defence bases in RTS games.

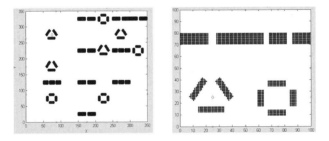

Fig. 1. Different sub-maps with different number of canyons and their combinations

B Initial Learning by GA

First, we need to design binary encoding of GA [1]. The length of the binary encoding depends on two types of space information of the given map: one is the distribution of free area of the battlefield and another is the number of barriers. [1] has demonstrated the encoding method in detail.

Fitness function is defined as the enemy's casualty [3]. The attack team is given a Constant speed (V) and d_i is the distance that the enemy travels through the attack range of the ith tower, n is the number of towers. It will receive damage by the tower within its attack range. Damage is calculated using (1). Tower positions will be selected by maximize this fitness function and used to generate optimal solutions [2].

$$D = \sum (d_i \ / \ v \ )* \ tower\_power \quad i \in \{1,2,3,4......n\} \tag{1}$$

C   Construction of Ant Algorithm

Here we use Ant circle model for global optimization. Let R_a be path A's trail intensity of the pheromone in time t; ΔR^k_a the amount of pheromone left by ant "k" on unit length of path A; η $(0 \leq \eta < 1)$ is the track persistence. With these notations, the update equation of the pheromone on path A is as follows (2).

$$Ra\,(t+1) = \eta * Ra\,(t) + \sum \Delta Rka\,(t) \tag{2}$$

We define Z_k as the travel length of ant k in current cycle. Then $\Delta R^k_a(t) = Q/Z_k$, Q is a constant. The visibility of A is denoted by ε_a, which is usually computed by $1/D_a$ (D_a is the length of the A). The importance of visibility in the path is defined as β $(\beta \geq 0)$, and the relative importance of the path is denoted as α $(\alpha \geq 0)$. Transition probability of ant k is P^k_a at time t, which is defined as follows (3) [8]:

$$P_a^{\,k}(t) \begin{cases} \dfrac{[R_a\,(t)\,]^{\,\alpha}[\varepsilon_a\,]^{\,\beta}}{\sum_{l\in U}[R_{all}\,(\,t\,)\,]^{\,\alpha}[\varepsilon_{all}\,]^{\beta}}, & j \in U \\ \\ 0, & \text{others} \end{cases} \tag{3}$$

In this article, we have applied MMAS (max-min ant system) which is an improvement version of the typical AA. There are several advantages to use it.

1) *First*: Since the initial value of the pheromone in each path is set as the maximum value R_{max}, MMAS can do global optimization more completely.

2) *Second*: Only the ant that traveled the shortest path in the circle could modify or increase the pheromone.

3) *Third*: To avoid premature convergence, the pheromone of each path is limited between R_{min} to R_{max}.

D   Combination of GA and AA

We have mentioned in Section II that both GA and AA have their own weakness, and this is why we integrate these two algorithms. Through simulation study, we have found that GA and AA have regular searching trends as shown in Fig. 2. It shows that, the early stage of GA searching process is often convergent fast (say, from t_0 to t_a in Fig. 2), while the later stage obviously slow down (from t_a to t_e). In contrast, due to the lack of initial pheromone, the search efficiency of AA is very low at the beginning, but when it can accumulate pheromone to some certain intensity, the searching will progress rapidly. From Fig. 2, we also notice that there is a cross point of the two trend lines of GA and AA. Therefore, the basic idea of the GA-AA is to find the cross point 'a', and GA will be used to create the initial pheromone distribution for AA before point 'a'. Ant algorithm will be used in the later process to generate the optimal solutions. The framework is shown in Fig. 3. Our purpose is to improve the efficiency of both the early searching of AA and later searching of GA, thus improve the whole process of using GA or AA individually.

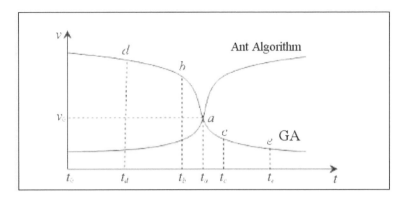

Fig. 2. Searching trend lines of GA and AA

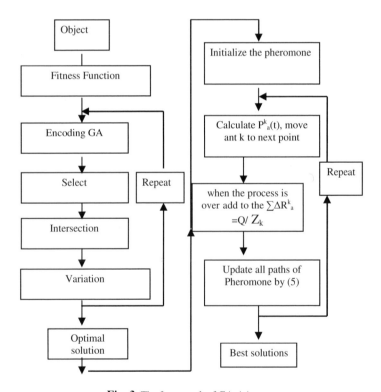

Fig. 3. The framework of GA-AA

We can always find the point "a" in theory, but it is time-consuming. In the experiments, we set two limits of GA iterations: number of maximum and minimum iterations Gene_{min} (t_b), $\text{Gene}_{max}(t_c)$. The rate of progeny groups is computed by statistics in the iterative process of genetic algorithm evolution and a minimum rate $Gene_{min\text{-}ratio}$ is also set for offspring evolution. If the evolutionary rate of offspring groups is less than $Gene_{min\text{-}ratio}$ in a certain range of iterations, it shows that the efficiency of GA is low and then we will switch to AA.

About the initial value of pheromone, a maximum value R_{max} is given in MMAS [7]. In the GA-AA algorithm, since there are some certain paths of pheromone obtained by initial searching of GA, the initial value of pheromone is computed by formula (4). Here R_c is a constant pheromone about the scale of specific given problem (e.g., R_{min} in MMAS algorithm), and R_g is the conversion of the pheromone values which have been generated by former searching of GA [8].

$$R_s = R_c + R_g \tag{4}$$

Pheromone update model: We use the Ant circle model to improve the new pheromone, so the equation is as same as (2).

E   Comparisons of GA and GA-AA

There is a series of figures to illustrate results in different generations. The optimization results of GA will be stable after 100 generations as shown in Fig. 4. Under the same conditions, GA-AA will convergent only after 40 generations as shown in Fig. 5. Obviously, the processing speed of GA-AA is much faster than that of GA. This result also confirms our expectation of achieving a win-win performance between these two algorithms.

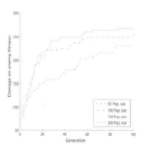
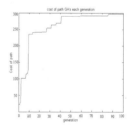

Fig. 4. Damage on attackers by GA   **Fig. 5.** Damage on attackers by GA-AA

Next, we implement GA-AA to the Scenario of the Tower Attack game. Here we set the number of GA iterations be 20, the initial number of ant be 18, Q=1000, and track update $\eta = 0.8$. $R_c = 60$, $R_g = 5$, $\alpha=5$, and $\beta=5$. The fit function is as same as that in [2]. The results by using GA [2] and GA-AA proposed in this paper are shown in Fig. 6 and Fig. 7. MathWorks Matlab 7.0 is used as the simulation tool.

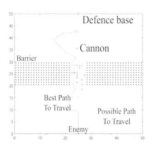

Fig. 6. Optimized by GA [2]

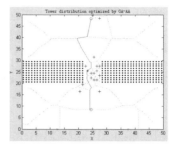

Fig. 7. Optimized by GA-AA

From the above two figures, we can see that the optimized cannon distribution generated by GA and GA-AA are quite similar. Tower's optimized positions by GA-AA are also evenly distributed. Therefore, the experiment results are reasonable and acceptable.

Table 2 shows the running time of GA and GA-AA with different types of maps. The original execute time of GA is so long that it needs about 35-44 minutes. GA-AA is demonstrated to be at least 4 times faster than GA.

Table 2. Run time of using GA and GA-AA (Generations: 100)

No. of Map	Run time of using GA (Generations:100)	Run time of using GA-AA (GA: 20 AA: 18)
1	2127s	532s
2	2232s	575s
3	2578s	601s
4	2653s	593s

4   Using ANN to Speed Up the Process

GA-AA had improved the efficiency of off-line GA training significantly. However, the processing time of GA-AA is still unacceptable in RTS games with real world battlefields (on-line). To overcome this problem, we want to incorporate ANN to speed up the whole process. Here, we should point out that the trained GA-AA has obtained the best solution of tower positions in a given battlefield which can be used as a case input to ANN. The objective of the ANN learning is to approximate the best position function in (6) [1], and through which to adapt the stored cases to any random environments. [2] has given the method how to encode the outputs of GA as inputs of ANN. Here we apply the same encode method. The only difference is the outputs are from GA-AA.

$$F(PointA) = \sum nK = 1\exp\text{-}(A1\text{-} K1)2 + (A2\text{-} K2)2/ \ r \qquad (6)$$

In (6), (A1, A2) is the coordinate of point A, n is the total number of cannon, n=15 in this case. (K1, K2) is the coordinate of cannon K, and r is a parameter for controlling the spread of F(Point A) [2].

After ANN learning, it shows a similar result to GA-AA on tower distribution as in Fig. 8 and Fig. 9 (at random map). However, there is a great decrease on run time by using ANN to further speed up the whole process, as shown in Table 3.

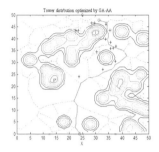

Fig. 8. Tower distribution (GA-AA)   **Fig. 9.** Tower distribution (ANN)

Table 3. Run time of ANN (Generations: 100)

Number of maps	Run time of ANN (second)
1	5.73s
2	5.92s
3	6.12s
4	6.23

It is shown in Table 3 that ANN can enhance the efficiency of the whole process without reduce the solution quality. It can save a lot on-line training time, and the trained ANN can be applied to plan the tower distribution in random maps very quickly.

5   Conclusions

A two-stage speed up model for case-based learning in real time strategy games is developed and shown in this paper. In order to defend the enemy attack, GA-AA is employed to optimize the distribution of towers. After comparing GA with GA-AA, GA-AA is suggested in RTS game instead of GA, because of its much faster processing speed and similar solution quality. The execution time of GA-AA is satisfied for off-line training in RTS game. To further improve the time of on-line training we proposed a hybrid GA-AA and ANN method, using the result of GA-AA as the past experience to train ANN. In this way ANN can obtain and predict the distribution of towers quickly. Our experimental results demonstrated that this two-stage speed up model method using GA-AA and ANN can speed up the whole process efficiently and satisfy the requirement in RTS game.

References

1. Huo, P., Shiu, S.C.-K., Wang, H., Niu, B.: A neural-evolutionary model for case-based planning in real time strategy games. In: Next Generation Applied Intelligence, pp. 291–300. Springer, Heidelberg (2009)
2. Huo, P., Shiu, S.C.-K., Wang, H., Niu, B.: Application and comparison of particle swarm optimization and genetic algorithm in strategy defense games. In: Fifth International Conference on Natural Computation, pp. 387–392. IEEE, Los Alamitos (2009)
3. Cole, N., Louis, S., Miles, C.: Using a genetic algorithm to tune first-person shooter bots. Proc. Cougr. Evol. Comput. 1, 139–145 (2004)
4. Louis, S.J., Miles, C.: Playing to learn case injected genetic algorithms for learning to play computer games. IEEE Transactions on Evolutionary Computation 9(4), 669–681 (2005)
5. Holland, J.H.: Adaptation in natural and artificial systems: "an introductory analysis with applications to biology, control, and artificial intelligence". MIT Press, Redmond (1975)
6. Yau, Y.J., Teo, J., Anthony, P.: Pareto Evolution and Co-evolution in Cognitive Game AI Synthesis. In: Obayashi, S., Deb, K., Poloni, C., Hiroyasu, T., Murata, T. (eds.) EMO 2007. LNCS, vol. 4403, pp. 227–241. Springer, Heidelberg (2007)
7. Dorigo, M., Maniezzo, V., Color, A.: Ant System: "Optimization by a Colony of Cooperating Agents". IEEE Tran. on SMC 26(1), 28–41 (1996)
8. Ding, J.-L., Chen, Z.-Q., Yuan, Z.-Z.: 'On the combination of genetic algorithm and ant algorithm. Journal of Computer Research and Development 40(9), 1351–1356 (2003)

Inversion of TEM Conductive Thin Layer Based on Genetic Algorithm

Guo Wenbo[1], Xue Guoqiang[2], Zhou Nannan[2], and Li Xiu[3]

[1] School of Electronic and Information Engineering,
Xi'an Jiaotong University, Xi'an, 710049
[2] Institute of Geology and Geophysics, Beijing, 100029
[3] Chang'an University, Xi'an, 710054
GuoWenboD@tom.com

Abstract. Using the adaptive shrinkage genetic algorithm in the feasible region to operate the inversion of TEM (transient electromagnetic method) conductive thin layer with the apparent vertical conductance differential imaging. In contrast, this inversion method accelerates the calculation speed and improves the calculation precision. Meanwhile, we utilize the genetic algorithm to derive the conductive imaging parameter and realize the global non-linear inversion compared to traditional method in local scope.

Keywords: TEM, adaptive shrinkage, feasible region, conductive thin layer, apparent longitudinal conductance.

1 Introduction

Recently, genetic algorithm has been used in many aspects of Geophysics, such as seismic application. But, it is relatively less used in electromagnetic application. In exploration electromagnetic methods, Liu yunfeng (1997), used "niche" GA method to process the inversion of 1-D MT data. Wei Baoqiang (1999) utilized the genetic algorithms to MT inversion. Zhang Xiaolu (2002)introduced genetic algorithms into the local conductive TEM inversion calculation. And there is little use of genetic method in TEM conductive global-region inversion.

The apparent longitudinal conductive imaging is a rapid and effective method to realize the TEM rapid and effective inversion. But, the selection of parameter $\overline{m}$ and the supplementary function $\varphi(\overline{m})$ is crucial in the inversion calculation and calculating the time derivative of the transient electromagnetic response $d^2B_z(t)/dt^2$. In this case, the local search tends to be the minimum. So, genetic algorithm, as a global search method, is used.

2 Basic Idea Genetic Algorithm

Genetic algorithm is one global-region optimized method which imitate the natural selection and genetic theory and is based on the law of survival of fittest. This method is

J. Zhang (Ed.): ICAIC 2011, Part III, CCIS 226, pp. 10–17, 2011.
© Springer-Verlag Berlin Heidelberg 2011

a process that spices advance from low grade to high grade. Inversion of genetic algorithm imitates the process of biological evolution. Firstly, generate an initial population at random as the calculation model, which has N members. Secondly, code the model parameter into binary code as the members' chromosome. Thirdly, utilize the genetic operations, taking selection, communication, variation for example, to operate on chromosome and breed the initial population to new offspring. Lastly, repeat the last process and we will find the globally optimized solution. I will expound this algorithm in detail.

3   Realization of the Genetic Algorithm

The apparent longitudinal conductance is

$$S_\tau(t) = \frac{K F(\overline{m})}{\frac{\partial B_z(t)}{\partial t}} \tag{1}$$

where $K = -\dfrac{6I}{a^2}$, $F(\overline{m}) = \dfrac{\overline{m}}{(1+4\overline{m}^2)^{5/2}}$

a is the transmitting loop radius, I is the transmitting current.

In practice, $\dfrac{\partial B_z(t)}{\partial t}$ is the data that we can get. In order to calculate the values

of $S_\tau(t)$, we must solve the value of $F(\overline{m})$. The time derivative of the actual

measurement curve $\dfrac{\partial B_z(t)}{\partial t}$ is

$$\begin{aligned}
\frac{\partial^2 B_z}{\partial t^2} &= \frac{\partial}{\partial \overline{m}}\left(\frac{\partial B_z}{\partial t}\right) \cdot \frac{\partial(\overline{m})}{\partial t} \\
&= \frac{K}{S} \cdot \frac{\partial F(\overline{m})}{\partial \overline{m}} \cdot \frac{\partial t}{\partial(\overline{m})} \tag{2} \\
&= \frac{K}{S} \cdot \frac{\partial F(\overline{m})}{\partial m} \cdot \frac{1}{\mu_0 S a}
\end{aligned}$$

And the supplementary function $\varphi(\overline{m})$ is

$$\varphi(\overline{m}) = \frac{\left|\dfrac{\partial^2 B_z}{\partial t^2}\right|}{\left[\dfrac{\partial B_z(t)}{\partial t}\right]^2} \cdot \mu_0 a K \tag{3}$$

Where,

$$\varphi(\bar{m}) = \dfrac{\dfrac{K}{S}\left|\dfrac{\partial F(\bar{m})}{\partial \bar{m}}\right|\dfrac{1}{\mu_0 a K}}{\left[\dfrac{K}{S}F(\bar{m})\right]^2}\mu_0 a K \tag{4}$$

$$= \left|\dfrac{\partial F(\bar{m})}{\partial \bar{m}}\right| / \left[F(\bar{m})\right]^2$$

if

$$F(\bar{m}) = \dfrac{\bar{m}}{\left(1+4\bar{m}^2\right)^{5/2}} \tag{5}$$

then,

$$\varphi(\bar{m}) = \left(1+4\bar{m}^2\right)^{3/2}\left|\dfrac{1}{\bar{m}^2} - 16\right| \tag{6}$$

W can reduce the TEM longitudinal non-linear optimization turn to

$$min\,\Psi(\bar{m}_j), \tag{7}$$
$$\bar{m}_{min} \le \bar{m}_j \le \bar{m}_{max}$$

where $\psi(\bar{m}_j)$ is the goal function, and

$$\psi(\bar{m}_j) = \left(\dfrac{1}{N}\sum(\dfrac{\varphi_s(\bar{m}_j) - \varphi_l(\bar{m}_j)}{\varphi_s(\bar{m}_j)})^2\right)^{\frac{1}{2}} \qquad (j = 1, \cdots, N) \tag{8}$$

where $\varphi_s(\bar{m})$ is the actual supplementary function; $\varphi_l(\bar{m})$ is the supplementary function, N means the number of observation points.

3.1 Initial Model Parameters

Ⅰ. Confirm the search region: Provide the search region of the Model 2parameter you can get the size of parameter space from this.

Ⅱ. The commutative probability (Pc): commutation reflects the exchange of random information, and its purpose is to produce the new individual. Thus, we are apt to choose the bigger value as the commutative probability value, such as 0.9.

Ⅲ. The mutation probability (Pm): in order to make consistent mutation, the selection value of Pm is relatively light: 0.01-0.02.

Ⅳ. The Population size: The bigger the number is, the larger the search region and the longer the iteration time are. it is normally 20~40 in transient electromagnetic sounding,

3.2 Floating Point Coding for the Initial Populations at Random

Supposed that the supplementary function is $\overline{m}_j$ ($j =1$, 2 ,...,N) and its constrain interval is $\overline{m}_{min,j}, \overline{m}_{max,j}$. We use Q model populations as the search region to improve the complex of the calculation and raise operational efficiency, where the chromosome number in the population is Q. x_t^i means the ind chromosome in the tnd generation.. $i \in \{1,2,...,Q\}$. Each chromosome gene figure number is N=m and the chromosome $x_t^i \in \mathbf{R}^m$, where x_t^i is the trip vector of m-dimension, $x_t^i = \left(x_t^{i(1)}, x_t^{i(2)}, \cdots, x_t^{i(m)} \right)$. So the tnd generation of population X_t is expressed as the matrix of $Q \times m$: $\mathbf{X}_t = \left(x_t^1, x_t^2, \cdots, x_t^Q \right)^T$. Specially, $\mathbf{X}_0 = \left(x_0^1, x_0^2, \cdots, x_0^Q \right)^T$ .All chromosomes are different in the population. So, one code in the parameter populations represents a gene. After each chromosome has been coded, we can calculate the goal function of this model. Carry out Q goal functions of this initial population, then calculate the minimum, maximum, average and summing up of all goal functions $\psi(\overline{m}_j)$.

3.3 The Calculation Adapability

In the evolutionary search, genetic algorithm is only based on the fitness function, and the selection of the fitness function is crucial because of its influence on the convergence rates of the genetic algorithm and the optimization solution. Generally speaking,the fitness function is:

$$ Fitness(m_j) = \frac{1}{1 + \psi(m_j)} \tag{9} $$

3.4 The Genetic Operation

3.4.1 Selection and Regeneration

Selection confirms the exchange of the genes, and the selected individuals will regenerate many offspring. Firstly, we select the parent individuals according to the adaptability probability. Then, Selection and regeneration of fine individuals will breed the offspring which reflected the natural selection principle of "survival of the fittest ". Here, the tournament selection is chosen. In the tournament selection, we select some tour individuals accidentally and choose the best ones as the parents. The parameter of the tournament selection is [2, *Nnd*] and it is relative to the selection intensity:

$$ SelInt_{Tour}(Tour) = \sqrt{2(\log(Tour) - \log\sqrt{4.14\log(Tour)})} \tag{10} $$

and the diversified loss:

$$LossDiv_{Tour}(Tour) = Tour^{-\frac{1}{Tour-1}} - Tour^{-\frac{Tour}{Tour-1}} \tag{11}$$

Then the variance is selected:

$$SelVar_{Tour}(Tour) = 1 - 0.096\log(1 + 7.11(Tour - 1)) \tag{12}$$

Once a certain individuals are selected, its code is duplicated for generating the population of the future generation. The individual with little fitness value has lowers generating probability, but higher for being "extra-ordinarily" selected, which increases the individual's variety. So, it is more easily to create commutation and mutation. Thus the tournament selection is a reasonable way for the calculation.

3.4.2 The Gene Exchange

In genetic algorithms, only by genes exchanging can we generate new individuals. This process imitates the hybridization principle of the biology to exchange the chromosomes. We pair two chromosomes at random to get $Q/2$ pairs of parents. The exchange method is expressed : For a pair of parents, 1),if the random number is greater than Pc enter future generation directly instead of exchanging;2) otherwise, select an exchange point at random in parent population.

3.4.3 The Genetic Mutation

The number of population is limited and there is one shortcoming that the convergence is too early. After that, the gotten individual is not the optimized solution. In order to solve this question, we must add new and genetic individuals to follow the course of evolution, that is to say, we must implements the genetic mutation. The mutation implements local search at random, combines regeneration with selection, guarantees the viability of the genetic algorithm and deprive from non-ripe convergence. During the process, all genes in population are changed .If the random number is greater than Pm , does not make the genetic mutation ; vice versa.

4 The Self-adaption Shrinkage in Feasible Region

In calculation, the genetic algorithm is relative to initial model space. With the development of the evolving process, the model populations are centralized to neighboring region of the true value, but model local scope spreads nearby true value. After 20-30 generations' evolution, if the optimum value lies in the neighboring region of the true region, it is in the feasible region according to the picture:

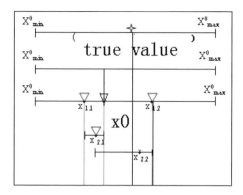

a left

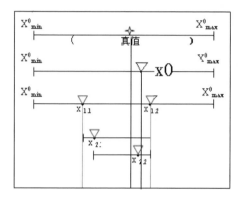

b right

a x_0^* lies in the left side of the neighboring region of the true value   b x_0^* lies in the right side of the neighboring region of the true value.

Firstly, search for the optimum value x_0^* in the initial feasible region (X^0_{min}, X^0_{max}) and supposed that x_0^* lie in the neighboring region of the true value. Divide the feasible region into two parts: (X^0_{min}, x_0^*) and (x_0^*, X^0_{max}).

Secondly, taking two kinds of situations into consideration:

a. while x_0^* lies in the left side of the neighboring region of the true value

b. while x_0^* lies in the right side of the neighboring region of the true value.

At last, we compress the feasible region progressively by law. In order to guarantee that optimum value lies in the neighboring region of the true value , we should take the iteration of 20-30 times and judge whether the thin layer exist in the model.

5　Calculation of Model

As to the conductive sheet, there is the phenomenon equivalence S in transient electromagnetic field which causes multiple solutions. By the genetic algorithm in the shrinkage feasible region, we inverse the apparent longitudinal conductance S_τ and apparent depth h_τ , and carry out the imaging of the second- derivative of the apparent longitude conductance $d^2 S_\tau / dh_\tau^2$ (Figure 2).

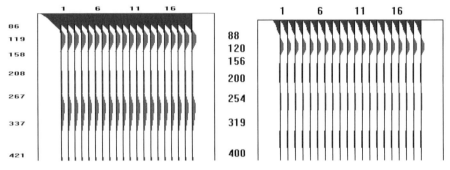

Upper: Model 1: $\rho_1 = \rho_3 = 100\Omega \cdot M$,　$\rho_2 = 10\Omega \cdot M$,　$h_1 = 100M, h_2 = 5M$;
Under: Model 2, $\rho_1 = \rho_3 = 100\Omega \cdot M$, $h_1 = 100M$, $h_2 = 3M$

Fig. 2. The imaging of the second- derivative of the apparent longitude conductance $d^2 S_\tau / dh_\tau^2$

The zero value of the second-derivative clearly demonstrates the position of conductive sheet, and the depth value of the corresponding point: 102M in Model 1,104M in Model 2, and here the errors are smaller than 5%. But, the longitude conductance imaging is the approximate inversion method, hence the conductive sheet thickness can not be confirmed. So, we use genetic algorithm to overcome the equivalence of transient electromagnetic sounding, and compress the equivalence range. It is clearly that the adaptability curves of two models have an obvious jump upward step at the 30nd generation for the three-time shrinkage in succession. By the evolution of the 33nd generation, the inversion error is smaller than 4%. This calculation process of evolution —convergence —next evolution — next convergence goes on and on until the precision reaches the requirement.

6　Conclusion

(1) The genetic algorithm is one excellent method for the global optimization problem and relies on the initial model at least. Especially for the transient

electromagnetic sounding conductive sheet, the feasible region of parameters is founded by known materials; the calculation is accelerated and calculation precision is improved.

(2) It is a preliminary try to use the genetic algorithm with the adaptive shrinkage feasible region in the TEM conductive sheet inversion. So, the result can demonstrate the existence of the conductive sheet. In some sense, combining the genetic algorithm with the apparent longitude conductance inversion will be a better way to overcome the equivalence of the transient electromagnetic sounding inversion.

References

1. Wang, X., Cao, L.: The Genetic Algorithm –Thoery, Application and The Simulated Software. Xi'an Jiaotong University publishhouse (2002)
2. Liu, Y., Cao, C.: Inversion of one 2dimensional MT data using genetic algorithms. Journal of Zhejiang University (Natural Science) 31(3), 300–305 (1997)
3. Wei, G., Hu, W.: MT Data Inversion. Journal of Jianghan Petroleum Institute 21(3), 25–29 (1999)
4. Zhang, X.: Transient electromagnetic local conductor inversion by genetic algorithm. Guilin Institute of Technology 22(4), 454–457 (2002)
5. Chen, J., Wang, J., et al.: Application Of Improved Genetic Algorithm To Inversion Of Multi-Layer Density Interface. Earth Science —Journal of China University of Geosciences 25(6), 651–654 (2000)
6. Li, X.: The theory and Application of Transient Electromagnetic Sounding. Shanxi Science Publishhouse (2002)

Study on Synthesis Fault Diagnosis Strategy of the Brake System of Wind Turbine Based on Evidence Theory*

Zhijie Wang and Sanming Liu

School of Electrical Engineering
Shanghai DianJi University
Shanghai200240, China
zhijiewange@eyou.com

Abstract. Wind turbine is a large and complicated machine to gather the machine, electricity, liquid in the integral whole, the brake system is importance constitute the part of wind turbine. therefore, opening the fault diagnosis of brake system is very important meaning. Jamming of cartridge is an important bottom thing to fault tree, because the circumstance is complicated, how to fault with the computer intelligence judgment jamming of cartridge, did not have the fit solution up to now. This paper adopt wavelet theory, fuzzy neural network, evidence theory etc. tool, proceeded the experiment research to jamming of cartridge fault diagnosis of wind turbine break system. It according to evidence theory, we proceed the analysis and discuss to the support of the proof and proof conflicts of synthesize fault diagnosis.

Keywords: Wind turbine, Evidence Theory, FNN, Wavelet.

1 Introduction

The brake system is an important part of the wind turbine and is the security protection device of wind turbine runs out. There usually have two methods to improve the reliability of the brake system, one is to design a new brake system with high reliability and the other is to monitor the conditions and to carry out the fault diagnosis on the brake system. The field failure instances imply that the engine sticking of the brake cylinder is a common fault of the brake system. This paper is concerned with the fault diagnosis for the engine sticking of the brake cylinder of the wind turbine which based on the information fusion technology by the wavelets theory[2,5], fuzzy-neural network and evidence theory, and present a comprehensive fault diagnosis method, finally a test and a numeral example are implied to verify the effeteness of the proposed method.

---

* This work is supported by Natural Science of Foundation of Shanghai (09ZR1420600), Talent Development of Foundation of Shanghai (Grant No. 2009027), Development Foundation of Shanghai Technology Commission (08DZ2210503), Innovation Program of Shanghai District Technology Commission (2010MH035) (2010MH054) and Key Subject of foundation of Shanghai Education Committee (J51901).

J. Zhang (Ed.): ICAIC 2011, Part III, CCIS 226, pp. 18–25, 2011.

2 Test

The wavelet packet can subdivide a signal accurately and extracted the characteristic information of the systems and then carry out the fault diagnosis. It is well known that the key of failure diagnosis is the recognition of the signal feature. From Fig 1, it can be seen that the brake-time characteristic curve of the output signals are different from the normal rake-time characteristic curve at different band when the fault occur due to mechanical components of the different structures. Thus the wavelet analysis is applied to diagnose the brake system.

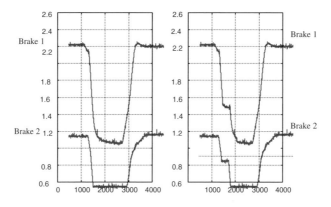

a. Normal brake-time curve   b. brake-time curve with engine sticking

Fig. 1. Brake-time characteristic curve

It can be seen from the Fig 1 that there have a significant change the amplitude-frequency characteristics of the output signals, and the energy of the signals with engine sticking have a massive changes compared to the normal condition. The rich fault messages exist in the energy signal at the different frequency bandwidth.

3 Comprehensive Fault Diagnosis Step

A. Feature Vector Extraction

There usually need to preterits the sampled signals, for example demonising. Here the sampled signals are supposed to have been pre-treated, the step of the extraction of the feature vector are listed as following:

1) Decompose the signals by the wavelet packet decomposition

The brake slack signals are sampled from the two eddy current sensor through the A/D collection board. Then decompose the sampled signals by the three-layer wavelet packet and extracted eight signals of different frequency bands, the decomposition structure see Fig 2.

2) Reconstruct the wavelet packet decomposed coefficient and extract the signals of different frequency bands[1,5]. Where S_{30} is the reconstruction signals of X_{30}, S_{31} is the reconstruction signals of, and so on. Here only analyse the node of the third layer, the integrated signal S is descript as:

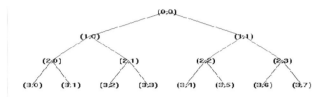

Fig. 2. Tree structure of wavelet hummock three layer analyse

Table 1. Frequency Range of Corresponding Analysed Signals

Signals	S_{30}	S_{31}	S_{32}	S_{33}
Frequency Range	0~0.125	0.125~0.250	0.250~0.375	0.375~0.500
Signals	S_{34}	S_{35}	S_{36}	S_{37}
Frequency Range	0.500~0.625	0.625~0.750	0.750~0.875	0.875~1

$$S = S_{30} + S_{31} + S_{32} + S_{33} + S_{34} + S_{35} + S_{36} + S_{37}$$

It is supposed that in the origin signal S the lowest frequency is 0 and the maximum frequency is 1, and the extracted eight frequency bands $S_{3j}(j = 0,1,\cdots,7)$ are listed in Table 1.

3) Computer total energy of the signals with all the frequency bands.

The input signal is a stochastic signal and the output signal is a stochastic signal. $E_{3j}(j = 0,1,\cdots,7)$ are the energy of the corresponding signals $S_{3j}(j = 0,1,\cdots,7)$.

$$E_{3j} = \int \left| S_{3j} \right|^2 dt = \sum_{k=1}^{n} \left| x_{jk} \right|^2$$

4) Construct feature vector

The construction of the feature vector is:

$$T = [E_{30}, E_{31}, E_{32}, E_{33}, E_{34}, E_{35}, E_{36}, E_{37}]$$

When the energy is big $E_{3j}(j=0,1\ldots7)$usually is a big value, and bring inconvenience to the later data analysis. Thus there need to improve the feature vector T, such as the normalization processing, set

$$T^{'} =[E_{30}/E,E_{31}/E,E_{32}/E,E_{33}/E,E_{34}/E,E_{35}/E,E_{36}/E,E_{37}/E]$$

The vector T' is the feature vector after normalization processing. Here the exact action of the feature vector is finished. Then select certain normal signals and fault signals and repeat the above mentioned steps and will get certain feature vectors.

B. Fuzzy Neural Network Training

In this paper we adopt three-layer fuzzy BP network. Firstly fuzzy the selected feature vector, the neural network has eight inputs and sixteen inputs for the feature vectors are an eight dimensional vectors and each feature vector has a big and a small values after fuzzification. In addition, this network only consider the state with the engine sticking of the brake system occurred, thus the output layer adopt one neuron (0-no engine sticking, 1-engine sticking). The number of the neurons in the hidden layer is determined by the empiric formula of 4.2.2, this paper the number of the neurons in the hidden layer is 9.

The feature vectors of the brake-time 1 extracted are sent to the fuzzy neural network to accept supervised training. After the fuzzy neural network reach stable there will get a group weight matrixes W_1, W_2 and then save them. And repeat the above steps to the feature vectors of the brake-time 2 then will get another group of weight matrixes and save them.

C. Evidence Combination

Adopt the network weight matrixes respectively to the measured vector of the feature vectors of the brake-time 1 and 2 to get two different original discriminated resoults. Combine the original discriminated results by the above mentioned Dumpster-Shafer theory then will get the further discriminated results. Compare the discriminate results with the threshold set in advance to judge whether the engine sticking occur in the brake system.

4 Feature Vector Extraction

A. Feature Vector Extraction

1) Decompose the signals by the wavelet packet decomposition
   Brake slack signals are sampled from the time characteristic curve of the normal and jamming cartridge of brake 1. Then decompose the sampled signals by the three-layer wavelet packet and extracted eight signals of different frequency bands.
2) Reconstruct the wavelet packet decomposed coefficient and extract the signals of different frequency bands [1,5]. The original signals of brake 1 in normal and jamming of cartridge failure and reconstruction of the signal components of 8 frequencies can be seen in Fig.3 and Fig 4.

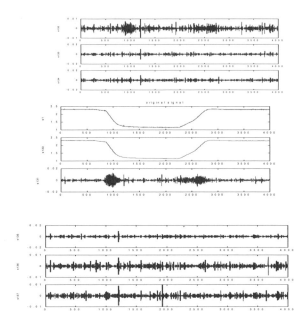

Fig. 3. Brake 1 wavelet hummock analyse newly construct in the course of nature

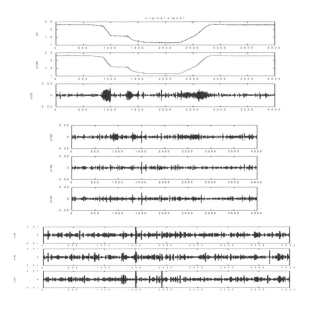

Fig. 4. Brake 1 wavelet hummock analyse newly construct of signal jamming of urn

2)   construct feature vector

We take two sets of signals of brake 1,2 respectively which under normal conditions （one set of training samples as a neural network, another group of test samples as a neural network), calculate the total energy of the frequency signal respectively; take the six sets of signals of brake 1,2 respectively which under engine sticking conditions （one set of training samples as a neural network, another group of test samples as a neural network), calculate the total energy of the frequency signal respectively; 1,2 brake shoe can be obtained respectively under the normal and the final engine sticking feature vector.

B. Fuzzy Neural Network Training

On the brake1, 2, respectively, five the BP network input samples was composed of a group of its normal state feature vector and five groups of engine sticking state feature vector, target vector for the neural network is

[0.01 0.99 0.99 0.99 0.99 0.99] .

Neural network parameters are as follows: Display frequency df: 10; largest step me: 900; target error *e.g.*: 0.02; learning rate *lr*: 0.02.

Take the training samples brake shoe 1 into the neural network for a mentor training. When the neural network is stable, a set of weights were obtained matrix, save this set of weight matrices

Take the training samples brake shoe 2 into the neural network for a mentor training. When the neural network is stable, a set of weights were obtained matrix, save this set of weight matrices.

C. Evidence Combination and Decision

Test sample:

Test sample 1of break shoe 1 (engine sticking state)
[0.990007 0.009993 8.33E-05 0.999917 4.49E-05 0.999955 3.68E-05 0.999963 4.22E-05 0.999958 3.46E-05 0.999965 3.81E-05 0.999962 3.85E-05 0.999961]

Test sample 1of break shoe 1 (normal)
[0.989724 0.010276 0.00081 0.99919 0.000488 0.999512 0.000705 0.999295 0.000727 0.999273 0.00075 0.99925 0.000774 0.999226 0.000709 0.999291]

Test sample 1of break shoe 1 (engine sticking state)
[0.989899 0.010101 0.000452 0.999548 0.000208 0.999792 0.000136 0.999864 0.000147 0.999853 0.000188 0.999812 0.000197 0.999803 0.000174 0.999826]

Test sample 1of break shoe 1 (normal)
[0.989769 0.010231 0.001156 0.998844 0.000694 0.999306 0.000515 0.999485 0.000437 0.999563 0.000413 0.999587 0.000413 0.999587 0.000376 0.999624]

First, for the normal testing samples of brake shoes 1、 2, the respective weights of the network matrix is called respectively, two different initial discrimination results m_1,m_2 were gotten.

Define a frame of discernment Θ, proposition A is the card cylinder malfunction and a subset of Θ. m (A) is the basic probability assignment for the sensor to proposition A.

$$m_1(A) = m_1 0.1232 \quad m_1(\Theta) = 0.8768 = 0.8768$$
$$m_2(A) = m_2 = 0.1602 = 0.1602 \quad m_2(\Theta) = 0.8368$$
$$m(A) = \frac{m_1(A)m_2(A) + m_1(A)m_2(\Theta) + m_1(\Theta)m_2(A)}{1}$$
$$= 0.2815$$

Then, for the engine sticking state testing samples of brake shoes 1, 2, the respective weights of the network matrix is called respectively, two different initial discrimination results m_1, m_2 were gotten.

$$m_1 = 0.8902 \quad , m_2 = 0.9168$$
$$m_1(A) = m_1 = 0.8902 \quad m_1(\Theta) = 0.1098$$
$$m_2(A) = m_2 = 0.9168 = 0.9168 \quad m_2(\Theta) = 0.0832$$
$$m(A) = \frac{m_1(A)m_2(A) + m_1(A)m_2(\Theta) + m_1(\Theta)m_2(A)}{1}$$
$$= 0.9925$$

Thus, the use of evidence theory, can indeed improve the decision accuracy. The above examples from the analysis and synthesis process can be seen:

1) The comprehensive diagnosis based on evidence theory has a very strong decision fusion capabilities, when all the evidence tend to agree, it can be better integrated the information of mutual support and complementary, which can further enhance the diagnostic conclusion confidence, improve the diagnostic accuracy; it also can process the contradictory and conflicting information, the diagnostic conclusions depend on the evidence of support (the size of basic probability assignment).

2) The key to success comprehensive diagnosis is distinguishing the information between the additional and conflicting information, and determine a reasonable probability distribution function.

3) The fault information multi-level integration and hierarchical diagnosis strategy can improve the diagnostic accuracy, or even to correct some errors in the initial decision.

5 Conclusion

This paper has investigated the support and conflict of evidence in the faults synthetic diagnosis based on the evidence combination theory. The diagnosis method proposed do not need the system's mathematical model, it establish the mapping relation between energy change and device fault and then get the feature vector of device faults and diagnose the faults by the energy change of different frequency components directly. And the experiment results presented have demonstrated the effectiveness and diagnosis results are right. In addition that, the experiment just fuse the information of the two homogeneous sensors, but the methods can easily expand to case with different muli-sensor and thus have universal significance.

Acknowledgment. About the author: Zhijie Wang (1964–), male, Weifang City, Shandong, professors, postdoctoral fellows, engaged in intelligent control and fault diagnosis research. E-mail: wzjsdstu@163.com

References

1. Zhou, J.: Mine Hoist Fault Mechanism and Fault Diagnosis Research. China University of Mining and Technology Ph.D. Thesis (2001)
2. Zhou, D., Ye, Y.: Modern Fault Diagnosis and Fault Tolerant Control. Tsinghua University Press, Beijing (2000)
3. Wang, Z.: Information Fusion and Related Technical Application Research. China University of Mining and Technology, Ph.D. Thesis (June 2002)
4. Wu, X., Ye, Q., Liu, L.: Based on Improved BP Network d-s Evidence Theory and its Application. Journal of Wuhan University of Technology (August 2007)
5. Wang, J., Zhang, J.: Based on the Statistical Evidence of Mass Function and d-s Evidence Theory of Multisensor Target Recognition. Chinese Journal of Sensors and Actuators (March 2006)
6. Lin, Z.: Based on Evidence Theory of Information Fusion Research and its Application in Water Monitoring. Hohai University (2005)
7. Ye, Q., Wu, X., Song, Y.: Based on d-s Evidence Theory and AHP Fault Diagnosis Method. Journal of Naval University of Engineering (April 2006)

Application of Ant Colony Algorithm in Tracking Convective Cloud Images from Chinese FY-2C Satellite*

Xiaofang Pei[1,**], Nan Li[2], Miaoying Li[3], and Luan Li[4]

[1] College of Electronic & Information Engineering
[2] School of Atmospheric Physics
[1,2] Nanjing University of Information Science & Technology, Nanjing 210044, China
[3] Institute of Meteorology, PLA University of Science & Technology, Nanjing 211101, China
[4] Wuhu Weather Bureau of Anhui Province, Wuhu 241000, China
XiaofangPei@yeah.net

Abstract. It is significance to identify and track convective clouds using satellite images in nowcasting and severe weather warning. This article applies ant colony algorithm to match and track convection clouds identified from infrared channel images of FY - 2C satellite. The preliminary results suggest that ant colony algorithm is simple and effective to gain satisfactory results with adjustable features. The results also show the feasibility and characteristics of ant colony algorithm in cloud tracking and provide reference of ant colony algorithm application in other related research areas.

Keywords: ant colony algorithm, convective clouds, FY-2C satellite.

1 Introduction

Since satellite developing, it has provided supplement data for routine meteorological observations. Satellite images have become an important source of information especially for the ocean, desert and other data-sparse areas. In short-term mesoscale weather, satellite data show an irreplaceable advantage. GMS with high time resolution, is various weather simultaneous observation from synoptic scale, mesoscale to cumulus-scale cloud evolution. It has become indispensable tool for prediction of heavy rain and other severe weather [1].

China's first geostationary meteorological satellite FY-2C successfully launched at October, 2004, positioned at $105°$ E above the equator 35800km. Currently, FY 2E has replaced of FY-2C. Their main payload is the visible and infrared spin scan radiometer (VISSR) with five spectral channels [2], [3].

In the short-term and close forecasting, it is important to increase accuracy of weather forecasts to avoid or lessen the losses caused by severe weather. With the computer technology in pattern recognition and matching technology continues to evolve, satellite images can be applied to identify, locate and track the convective clouds to achieve convective weather monitoring.

---

* This work is partially supported by College Graduate Student Research and Innovation Program of Jiangsu province (CX09B_227Z).
** Corresponding author.

J. Zhang (Ed.): ICAIC 2011, Part III, CCIS 226, pp. 26–32, 2011.

This paper focuses on discussing feasibility and effectiveness of stimulated annealing algorithm to track the clouds. First, based on FY-2C infrared channels of two consecutive times, identify the single clouds using the Hungarian method and manual analysis to match, get the reference solutions and then match clouds with the ant colony optimization. The second part is the results of cloud identification. The third section describes the matching and tracking methods. The fourth part gives a brief description of ant colony algorithm and applies the algorithm to cloud matching experiments. The fifth is conclusion.

2 Identification of Convective Clouds

This paper uses the brightness temperature threshold method to identify Convective clouds. Threshold value has different definitions in different regions and seasons. Maddox took 241k as the reasonable threshold [4], Velasco and Fritsch selected lower

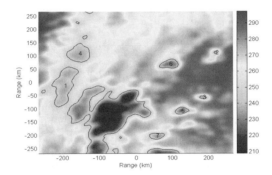

Fig. 1. Convective cloud identified results and the serial number of FY-2C IR channel 1 observed at 7:00 (UTC) on July 8, 2008

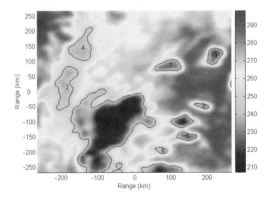

Fig. 2. Convective cloud identified results and the serial number of FY-2C IR channel 1 observed at 7:30 (UTC) on July 8, 2008

brightness temperature thresholds (231-233k) [5]. Machado thought the threshold of 245k was suit for identify convection clouds [6]. Through experiments, the threshold value in this paper is 245K.

Use two consecutive times infrared (IR) channel-1 data of FY-2C (at 7:00 and 7:30 on July 8, 2008, respectively notes as t_1 and t_2). Then, Select brightness temperature threshold to identify convection clouds and calculate the area of clouds and centroid position. Fig.1, 2 show the identified results and the serial number of two infrared images with 7 and 8 respectively.

3 Clouds Matching and Tracking

The storm tracking methods of radar can be applied in matching and tracking adjacent clouds identified in satellite images [7]. Match the clouds of consecutive times to discover which path is closest to the true path; in the continuous interval to repeat the matching on the clouds can track the whole process. Matching is mainly based on the following two: 1) the correct matching gives a shorter path; 2) the right matching connects with cloud of similar characteristics.

In t_1 with n_1 clouds, state of No.i is $s_{1i} = (x_{1i}, y_{1i}, a_{1i})$; in t_2 with n_2 clouds, state of No. j is $s_{2j} = (x_{2j}, y_{2j}, a_{2j})$. Define cost function as $C_{ij} = w_r \times d_r + w_a \times d_a$, the distance (km) between the mass center of No. i cloud of t_1 times (reflectance weights centre) (x_{1i}, y_{1i}) and the mass center of No. j cloud of t_2 times (x_{2j}, y_{2j}) is $d_r = [(x_{2j} - x_{1i})^2 + (y_{2j} - y_{1i})^2]^{1/2}$. The area distance between them is $d_a = |(a_{2j})^{1/2} - (a_{1i})^{1/2}|$. W_r and W_a are the weight coefficient taken as 1. Therefore, the clouds matching look on as an optimization problem to solve. Assuming that the best path is the true path of cloud movement, it means to get the minimum of cost function $Q = \Sigma C_{ij}$ in which i, j stands for ith cloud of t_1 times and jth cloud of t_2 times respectively.

In fact, a solution to the clouds matching means ith ($1 \leq i \leq n_1$) cloud of t_1 times matches jth ($1 \leq j \leq n_2$) cloud of t_2 times. Therefore, the clouds matching results show as array $S = (P_1, P_2... P_n)$. If ith cloud of t_1 times and jth cloud of t_2 times matches, then $P_i = j$, if not, $P_i = 0$ (clouds of t_2 times is more than the number of t_1 times).

The matching cost of ith cloud of t_1 times and jth cloud of t_2 times expresses as C_{ij} ($i = 1, 2, n; j = 1, 2, m$),

$$C = (C_{ij})_{n \times m} = \begin{bmatrix} C_{11}C_{21}...C_{1m} \\ C_{21}C_{22}...C_{2m} \\ \vdots \\ C_{n1}C_{n2}...C_{nm} \end{bmatrix} \quad (1)$$

In the cost matrix, the ith row means matching costs of i cloud of t_1 times with all clouds of t_2 times; the jth column means matching costs of jth cloud of t_2 times with all clouds of t_1 times. If matches, the $x_{ij} = 1$, otherwise $x_{ij} = 0$.the mathematical mode to gain minimization of clouds matching cost is [8]:

$$\min z = \sum_{i=1}^{n}\sum_{j=1}^{m} C_{ij} x_{ij} \tag{2}$$

$$s.t. \begin{cases} \sum_{i=1}^{n} x_{ij} = 1, i = 1, 2, \ldots, n; \\ \sum_{j=1}^{m} x_{ij} = 1, j = 1, 2, \ldots, m; \\ x_{ij} \in \{0,1\}, i = 1, 2, \ldots, n, j = 1, 2, \ldots, m. \end{cases}$$

Known an n × m matrix C_{ij}, find another n × m matrix X_{ij} to satisfy the following conditions: 1) in any row or column, x_{ij} has only one nonzero element, and the value is 1; 2) the value of $\Sigma C_{ij} X_{ij}$ is minimum [9]. Generally use the Hungarian method to find the matrix X_{ij}. The specific theory and process of Hungarian method can refer to the corresponding literatures [10].

Hungarian method gives results of the cloud matches are: 2, 1, 3, 4, 0,5,6,7, and the total cost are 209.11. Manual analysis shows that matching results (Fig.1, 2) are correct.

4 Cloud Matching Using Ant Colony Algorithm

The ant colony indirectly contact with one another asynchronously with "pheromone" as medium. Ant will leave some chemicals, called pheromone, on their way to search food or back to nest. The same colony of ants can sense these substances and choose the path with these substances more likely than the path without them. With more after ants of the same colony passing the path, strengthen the pheromone left by them, and then repeat the cycle with more and more ants choosing this path. In the period of time, ants more likely visit the shorter path with the more accumulation of pheromone, as far as all ants select the shortest path.

Following the behavior of ant colony, ant colony algorithm consists of the two features. One is pheromone value or trace of pheromone which is the memory of ant information; the other is the visibility value or priori value that is the cost of path. The update of pheromone is achieved by the combination of two operations. One is volatilization, which is an imitational process of the pheromone evaporation overtime by natural ant colony. This can avoid focusing on local optimization area and help expand the search area. The other is to increase pheromone value of evaluated nodes, which favors algorithm to converge to the optimal solution stably.

Find passing paths of ants through principles of random decision-making. The process is that: use the path nodes to store information and calculate the probability of reaching the next node to form the probability distribution; then make move according to the probability distribution; finally the solution built by ants will be more and more close to the optimal solution. When an ant searches or finds a solution, it will evaluate the solution (or part solutions) and stored it in ant pheromone which is significance to guide the future search [11].

The algorithm of this paper is as follows [12].

The first step is about initialization. The each element of cost matrix looks on as a node and is assigned a two-dimensional coordinates (I, j), which means the No. I storm of the times t_1 matches the No. j storm of the times t_2. Create a path arrangement randomly and calculate the cost value of f_0, while give all nodes the equal number of pheromone $h_0 = 1/ f_0$. The set of tabu nodes is empty.

The second step: terminate the calculation when reach the maximum search round T. Otherwise, select the next node v_{ij} form the remaining nodes according to the following selection strategy:

$$(i, j) = \begin{cases} \underset{v \in V_r}{\arg \max} \{h(v)^\alpha / c(v)^\beta\}, q \leq q_0 \\ \underset{v \in V_r}{p} \{h(v)^\alpha / c(v)^\beta\}, q > q_0 \end{cases} \tag{3}$$

Select a node and bring it and the nodes with the same row or column as the selected into the set of taboo nodes. This ensures the storm matched one by one. Remove nodes unmatched and reduce the scope of selecting the next node to decrease the searching times. The remaining nodes v_r is nodes except tabu nodes; h (v) means the pheromone value of the node V; c (v) means the cost value of v; $\underset{v \in V_r}{\arg \max} \{h(v)^\alpha / c(v)^\beta\}$ and $\underset{v \in V_r}{p} \{h(v)^\alpha / c(v)^\beta\}$ represent the subscripts of the node elected through roulette and the note with maximum value of $h(v)^\alpha / c(v)^\beta$ among the remaining nodes respectively. Two parameters α and β stand for the relative influence of pheromone and the cost on choosing the node path respectively, where to take $\alpha = 1$ and $\beta = 1$. The q is a random variable distributed uniformly in (0, 1); the q_0 is a given threshold parameter in the corresponding range and its value means the possibility of choosing the current node as the best.

The third step: update local pheromone. After select the node v_{ij}, update the pheromone h_{ij} of v_{ij}: $h_{ij} = (1-\xi) \times h_{ij} + \xi \times h_0$, $0 < \xi < 1$, where ξ is a local update coefficient. The update of pheromone reflects the total effect of volatilization and enhancement, which makes algorithm to avoid focusing on local optimal region too fast and converge stably.

The fourth step: update the global pheromone. When gain all locally optimal paths of N ants, choose the global optimal path among them and update the pheromone of the nodes on it through the following formula:

$$h_{ij} = (1-\rho)h_{ij} + \rho \Delta h_{ij}^{op}, \forall (i, j) \in W^{op} \tag{4}$$

Where ρ is the global update coefficient, $0 < \rho \leq 1$; $\Delta h_{ij}^{op} = 1/C^{op}$ means the increment of pheromone; C^{op} denotes the total cost of the current optimal path; W^{op} represents the current best path. Perform the update of pheromone only on the nodes with W^{op}, but not all nodes. Return to the second step.

In the Table I, the number of ants is five with five search cycles; threshold parameter q_0 takes 0.2, 0.5 and 0.8; global update coefficient ρ adopts 0.2, 0.5 and 0.8, partial update coefficient ξ is 0.2, 0.5 and 0.8, respectively. Each project repeats its experiments for ten times then gain statistical features of solution, such as total cost mean, standard deviation of total cost, frequency of the correct solution and average computation time.

Table 1. Examples of Calculation Results

q_0	ρ	ξ	total cost mean	standard deviation of total cost	frequency of the correct solution	average computation time (s)
0.2	0.2	0.2	225.32	34.165	7	0.0234
		0.5	266.92	120.31	7	0.0235
		0.8	233.59	32.665	5	0.025
	0.5	0.2	211.81	8.5385	9	0.025
		0.5	236.2	38.331	5	0.025
		0.8	245.79	51.23	5	0.025
	0.8	0.2	211.81	8.5385	9	0.0234
		0.5	232.43	55.884	7	0.025
		0.8	251.84	76.696	5	0.025
0.5	0.2	0.2	214.51	11.385	8	0.0234
		0.5	214.51	11.385	8	0.0234
		0.8	217.21	13.043	7	0.025
	0.5	0.2	220	26.345	8	0.0234
		0.5	236.55	52.112	7	0.025
		0.8	228.02	33.807	6	0.0235
	0.8	0.2	211.81	8.5385	9	0.025
		0.5	231.37	43.8	6	0.0234
		0.8	267.41	122.49	5	0.025
0.8	0.2	0.2	211.81	8.5385	9	0.0234
		0.5	214.51	11.385	8	0.025
		0.8	219.91	13.943	6	0.0235
	0.5	0.2	214.51	11.385	8	0.0235
		0.5	228.67	44.305	7	0.025
		0.8	214.51	11.385	8	0.0234
	0.8	0.2	214.51	11.385	8	0.0235
		0.5	211.81	8.5385	9	0.0219
		0.8	211.81	8.5385	9	0.025

The experiments show the results is the best when the threshold parameter q_0 and global update coefficient ρ is larger with local update coefficient ξ smaller. The smaller ξ makes the impact of the initial pheromone decrease rapidly to hold more pheromone left by ants; the bigger ρ adds pheromone to the optimal path node to strengthen positive feedback of the optimal path; the larger q_0 makes later ants more likely to choose path nodes with more pheromone and less cost. All of these help accelerate the convergence speed and gain the optimal solution more easily. Therefore, in the cases of storm track, select larger threshold parameter, larger global update coefficient and smaller local update coefficient with moderate ants and proper search rounds to gain the desired results and reduce the computation time.

5   Conclusion

Based on two consecutive brightness temperature data of IR channel 1 from FY-2C satellite, this study tries to apply ant colony algorithm to match and track convective clouds, and provides some new methods and ideas. The experimental results show that ant colony algorithm is simple, reliable and easy to get the desired results through choosing relevant parameters adaptively. Future research will focus on study and verification of the ant colony algorithm in tracking clouds with multi-channel satellite data.

References

1. Wang, J.: Research of cloud classification and short-time cloud movement forecast based on multi-spectrum stationery meteorological satellite pictures. (PhD thesis). National University of Defenxse Technology, Changsha (2007) (in Chinese)
2. Zhang, R., Wang, Y.: Radiometric calibration of FY-2C meteorological satellite and its result analysis. Aerospace Shanghai 22, 31–35 (2005) (in Chinese)
3. Chen, W.: Satellite Meteorology. Press of Meteorology, Beijing (2003) (in Chinese)
4. Maddox, R.A.: Mesoscale convective complex. Bull. Amer. Meteor. Soc. 61, 1374–1387 (1980)
5. Velasco, I., Fritsch, J.M.: Mesoscale convective complexes in the Americas. J. Geophys. Res. 92, 9591–9613 (1987)
6. Machado, L.A.T., Rossow, W.B., Guedes, R.L., Walker, A.W.: Life cycle variations of mesoscale convective systems over the Americas. Mon. Wea. Rev. 126, 1630–1654 (1998)
7. Xiao, Y., Tang, D., Li, Z., Jiang, Y.: Storm aotomatic identification tracking and forecasting. Journal of Nanjing Institute of Meteorology 21, 223–229 (1998) (in Chinese)
8. Li, W.: Application of Hungary algorithm in assignment problem of train crew. Lanzhou Jiaotong University 26(3), 55–57 (2007) (in Chinese)
9. Lawler, E.L.: Combinatorial optimization: Networks and Matroids, p. 384. Oxford University Press, Oxford (1995)
10. Roberts, F.S.: Applied combinatorics, pp. 565–568. Prentice Hall, Englewood Cliffs (1984)
11. Xing, W., Xie, J.: Modern optimization method. Tsinghua University Press, Beijing (2005) (in Chinese)
12. Yin, R., Wu, Y., Zhang, J.: Research and application of the ant colony algorithm in the assignment problem. Computer Engineering & Science 30(4), 43–46 (2008) (in Chinese)

Appendix: Cost Matrix in the Example of the Text

B=
[474.14 36.206 441.69 181.05 409.8 375.79 340.24 381.35;
38.136 483.09 177.86 420.33 297.87 263.2 164.98 354.22;
204.85 438.57 16.506 435.16 122.39 97.547 198.65 186.77;
393.72 112.27 413.27 43.696 417.98 371.01 264.85 415.12;
258.29 380.77 91.713 404.25 50.73 23.729 212.1 105.19;
142.93 319.7 165.8 273.97 225.93 177.02 24.901 277.26;
373 370.38 209.22 435.02 107.81 140.47 306.61 25.939];

Application of Simulated Annealing Algorithm in Fingerprint Matching

Xiaofang Pei[1,*], Nan Li[2], and Shuiping Wang[3]

[1] College of Electronic & Information Engineering
[2] School of Atmospheric Physics
[3] College of Computer and Software
[1,2,3] Nanjing University of Information Science & Technology, Nanjing 210044, China
XiaofangPei@yeah.net

Abstract. The fingerprint feature extraction and matching are significance in fingerprint identification system. This paper uses Gabor filterbank to extract both global and local features of the fingerprints. Then apply simulated annealing algorithm to match these features identified from fingerprint images. The preliminary results suggest that simulated annealing algorithm is simple and effective to obtain satisfactory results with adjustable parameters. The results also show the feasibility and characteristics of simulated annealing algorithm in fingerprint matching and provide reference of simulated annealing algorithm application in other related research areas.

Keywords: simulated annealing algorithm, Gabor filtering, fingerprint feature matching.

1 Introduction

With an increasing emphasis on the emerging automatic personal identification applications, biometrics-based verification, especially fingerprint-based identification, is receiving much attention. Fingerprint matching is to decide whether it belongs to the same fingerprint of the same person.

Fingerprint matching is a core processing in fingerprint identification system. There are many matching methods, such as fingerprint images matching, structure matching and minutiae matching which uses ridge endings and ridge branch point to identify fingerprints.

The popular fingerprint recognition algorithm is to use minutiae as fingerprint feature which is easy to apply and need small storage capacity, but there are clearly insufficient [1]:1) local features loses much characteristic information of the fingerprint and cannot described trend line of local ridges and valleys; 2) the number of different fingerprint minutiae are not the same, variable length of the features is not easy to compare and sort; 3) Classical matching algorithms based on minutiae matching need to be calibrated fingerprints and increase the processing time and the complexity.

---

* This work is partially supported by Scientific Research Fund of NUIST (20070009) and College Graduate Student Research and Innovation Program of Jiangsu province (CX09B_227Z).

J. Zhang (Ed.): ICAIC 2011, Part III, CCIS 226, pp. 33–40, 2011.

Structure-based feature extraction methods can avoid the above drawbacks[2]: 1) designing a series of Gabor filters to simultaneously extraction global and local fingerprint features; 2) save fingerprint feature as a vector of fixed length, which is conducive to sort fingerprint and calculate Euclidean distance between the fingerprint features; 3) independent of the feature minutiae eliminates the pretreatment process and improve the operating efficiency and can extract features based on the original image.

This paper is focused on discuss feasibility and effectiveness of simulated annealing algorithm to matching the fingerprint feature. Based on original gray image, use filters to locate the core point, and then tessellate the feature region centered at the reference point. Respectively extract the fixed-length fingerprint features of both original picture and the rotated picture through the 8-direction Gabor filterer to obtain the reference solutions and then match fingerprint features with the simulated annealing algorithm. The second part describes the fingerprint recognition algorithm based on Gabor filter. The third section gives a brief description of simulated annealing algorithm and applies the algorithm to fingerprint features matching experiments. The fourth is conclusion.

2 Gabor Filterbank-Based Fingerprint Recognition Algorithm

Fingerprints have local parallel ridges and valleys, and well-defined local frequency and orientation. Properly tuned Gabor filters [3], can remove noise, preserve the true ridge and valley structures, and provide information contained in a particular orientation in the image. A minutia point can be viewed as an anomaly in locally parallel ridges and capture this information using the Gabor filters.

The four main steps in feature extraction algorithm are 1) determine a reference point and region of interest for the fingerprint image; 2) tessellate the region of interest around the reference point; 3) normalize the region of interest in each sector separately to a constant mean and variance; 4) filter the region of interest in eight different directions using a bank of Gabor filters (eight directions are required to completely capture the local ridge characteristics in a fingerprint while only four directions are needed to capture the global configuration [4]);5) compute the average absolute deviation from the mean (AAD) of gray values in individual sectors in filtered images to define the feature vector or the FingerCode.

A. Reference Point Location [5]

Many previous approaches like Poincaré index and maximum curvature method work well in good quality fingerprint images, but fail to correctly localize reference points in poor quality fingerprints with cracks and scars.

According to the directional distribution of ridge, design the filter to match the center. Deal orientation field with filters of two-dimensional convolution to obtain the filtering image. The value of each pixel represents the responses to the filter, so the pixel with the maximum value is the center of the original image. The filter matched with the center is[8]: $h=(x+iy) g (x, y)$. where, $g(x, y)(=\exp(-(x^2 + y^2)/(2\delta^2)))$ is a Gaussian function, (x, y) means point in Gaussian window. The complex orientation field image is $z (x, y) = (f_x + if_y)^2$. The filter result is:

$$R (x, y) = \| (x+iy) g (x, y)] \times z(x, y) \| \tag{1}$$

B. Determining the Extraction Region

Fingerprint reference point in the surrounding area is a key area for feature extraction. To solve the problem of rotation invariant, when the reference point is confirmed, make concentric circles around the reference point to gain several annular regions, and then each circular area is divided into a number of fan-shaped areas. The gray value of each sector in the region means local information of the fingerprint, and the combination of all gray values describes the global information of the fingerprint feature area [2].

Let $I(x, y)$ denote the gray level at pixel (x, y) in an $M{\times}N$ fingerprint image and let (x_c, y_c) denote the reference point. The region of interest is defined as the collection of all the sectors S_i, where the ith sector S_i is computed in terms of parameters (r,θ) as follows:

$$S_i = \{(x, y) \mid b(T_i + 1) \le r < b(T_i + 2),$$
$$\theta_i \le \theta < \theta_{i+1}, 1 \le x < N, 1 \le y < M$$

$$\text{Where} \begin{cases} T_i = i \, div \, k \\ \theta_i = (i \bmod k) \times (2\pi / k) \\ r = \sqrt{(x - x_c)^2 + (y - y_c)^2} \\ \theta = \tan^{-1}((y - y_c)/(x - x_c)) \end{cases} \tag{2}$$

The b is the width of each band, k is the number of sectors considered in each band, and $i=0\ldots(B{\times}k\text{-}1)$, where B is the number of concentric bands considered around the reference point for feature extraction. These parameters depend on the image resolution and size. A 20-pixel wide band captures an area spanning about one ridge and valley pair, on an average, in a 500 dpi fingerprint image. A band with a width of 20 pixels is necessary to capture a single minutia in a sector, allowing our low-level features to capture this local information. If the sector width is more than 20 pixels, then the local information may be modulated by more global information. Otherwise, less than 20 pixels, the global information may be partly loss. According to the resolution of the image, use four concentric bands ($B=4$), $b=20$, $k=16$.The innermost two band (circle) are not used for feature extraction because the flow field in a region around a very high curvature point (core) has poor coherence. Thus, absolute deviations of oriented Gabor responses to this region would be expected to be unreliable matching features. Thus, we have a total of $16{\times}4=64$ sectors (S_0through S_{63}).

C. Normalizing the Region

Before filtering the fingerprint image, normalize the region of interest in each sector separately to a constant mean and variance. Normalization is performed to remove the effects of sensor noise and gray level deformation due to finger pressure differences. Normalization is a pixel-wise operation which does not change the clarity of the ridge and valley structures. If normalization is performed on the entire image, then it cannot compensate for the intensity variations in different parts of the image due to the elastic nature of the finger. Separate normalization of each individual sector alleviates this problem. Let $I(x, y)$ denote the gray value at pixel (x, y), M_i and V_i the estimated mean and variance of sector S_i, respectively, and $Ni(x, y)$, the normalized gray-level value at pixel (x, y). For all the pixels in sector S_i, the normalized image is defined as

$$N_i(x, y)$$

$$= \begin{cases} M_0 + \sqrt{\dfrac{V_0 \times (I(x,y) - M_i)^2}{V_i}} & ,\text{if } I(x,y) > M_i \\ M_0 - \sqrt{\dfrac{V_0 \times (I(x,y) - M_i)^2}{V_i}} & ,\text{otherwise} \end{cases} \tag{3}$$

where M_0 and V_0 are the desired mean and variance values, respectively. For this experiments, set the values of both and to 100.

D. Gabor Filtering

An even symmetric Gabor filter has the following general form in the spatial domain:

$$G(x, y; f, \theta) = \exp\left\{ \frac{-1}{2}\left[\frac{x'^2}{\delta_{x'}^2} + \frac{y'^2}{\delta_{y'}^2} \right] \right\} \cos(2\pi\, fx')$$

$$x' = x\sin\theta + y\cos\theta \tag{4}$$

$$y' = x\cos\theta - y\sin\theta$$

where f is the frequency of the sinusoidal plane wave along the direction$\theta$from the x-axis, and $\delta_{x'}$and$\delta_{y'}$ are the space constants of the Gaussian envelope along x' and y' axs, respectively. The spatial characteristics of Gabor filters can be seen in [4].

In this experiments, set the filter frequency f to the average ridge frequency $(1/K)$, where K is the average interridge distance. The average interridge distance is approximately 10 pixels in a 500 dpi fingerprint image. If f is too large, spurious ridges are created in the filtered image whereas if is too small, nearby ridges are merged into one. Select eight different values for $(0, 22.5, 45, 67.5, 90, 112.5, 135,$ and $157.5)$ with respect to the x-axis. These eight directional-sensitive filters capture most of the global ridge directionality information as well as the local ridge characteristics present in a fingerprint. The values for$\delta_{x'}$ and $\delta_{y'}$ were empirically determined and each is set to 4.0 (about half the average interridge distance).

E. Feature Vector and Maturing [2]

Let $F_{i\theta}$ be the θ-direction filtered image for sector S_i. Now, $\theta \in \{0°, 22.5°, 45°, 67.5°, 90°, 112.5°, 135°, 157.5°\}$and $i \in \{0, 1, ..., 79\}$, the feature value, $V_{i\theta}$, is the average absolute deviation from the mean defined as

$$V_{i\theta} = \frac{1}{n_i}\left(\sum_{n_i} |F_{i\theta}(x, y) - P_{i\theta}| \right) \tag{5}$$

Where n_i is the number of pixels in S_i and $P_{i\theta}$is the mean of pixel values of $F_{i\theta}$in sector S_i. The average absolute deviation (AAD) of each sector in each of the eight filtered images defines the components of our feature vector. The 512-dimensional feature vectors (FingerCodes) for fingerprint images of two different fingers from the database are shown as gray level images with eight disks, each disk corresponding to one filtered image in. The gray level in a sector in a disk represents the feature value for that sector in the corresponding filtered image.

Fingerprint matching is based on finding the Euclidean distance between the corresponding FingerCodes. The translation invariance in the FingerCode is established by the reference point. However, features are not rotationally invariant. An approximate rotation invariance is achieved by cyclically rotating the features in the FingerCode itself. A single step cyclic rotation of the features in the FingerCode corresponds to a feature vector which would be obtained if the image were rotated by 22.5°. A rotation by steps corresponds to a $R \times 22.5°$ rotation of the image (R=0,1,...,15). A positive rotation implies clockwise rotation while a negative rotation implies counterclockwise rotation. The FingerCode obtained after R steps of rotation is given by

$$V_{i\theta}^{R} = V_{i'\theta'}; \quad i' = (i+k+R) \bmod k + (i \operatorname{div} k) \times k;$$
$$\theta' = (\theta + 180° + 22.5° \times R) \bmod 180°. \tag{6}$$

where k (=16) is the number of sectors in a band, $i \in \{0, 1, ..., 63\}$, $\theta \in \{0°, 22.5°, 45°, 67.5°, 90°, 112.5°, 135°, 157.5°\}$. For each fingerprint in the database, store templates corresponding to the following rotations of the corresponding FingerCode. The input FingerCode is matched with the templates stored in the database to obtain different matching scores. The minimum matching score corresponds to the best alignment of the input fingerprint with the database fingerprint.

In this fingerprint matching experiment, the standard fingerprint database includes about 300 fingerprint samples from 10 people collected two or three times. Match each fingerprint with the others .The experiment results show that: accuracy rate: 92%; rejection rate: 1.5% and error rate 6.5%.

3   AAD Features Matching Using Simulated Annealing Algorithm

Annealing is a physical process. When a metal object is heated to a certain temperature, all the molecules move freely in the state space. As the temperature drops, the molecules gradually stay in a different state. At the lowest temperature, the molecules rearrange in a certain structure. Statistical mechanics studies have shown that at T temperature, molecules in the r state satisfy the Boltzmann probability distribution.

$$P\{\bar{E} = E(r)\} = \frac{1}{Z(T)} \exp(-\frac{E(r)}{k_B T}) \tag{7}$$

In the expression, $E(r)$ means the energy of the state r, $k_B > 0$ is the Boltzmann constant, $\bar{E}$ serves as the random variable of molecular energy and $Z(T)$ is the normalization factor of probability distribution.

The Boltzmann probability distribution shows the probability of molecules staying in low energy state is big than that staying in big energy state at the same temperature. When the temperature is much high, the probability of each state is almost the same and at the average value. Lowering the temperature, probability of lower energy state becomes higher. When the temperature reaches 0°, probability of the molecules staying in the lowest energy state tends to 1. The simulated annealing algorithm contains an inner loop and outer loop. The inner loop means a random search in some states at the same temperature. The outer loop includes temperature drop and stop conditions.

The intuitive understanding of simulated annealing is that: in a given temperature, search changes randomly from one state to another state, and the times to reach each state presents a probability distribution. When the temperature is lowest, the probability reaches 1 with the optimum solution. Simulated annealing algorithm reflects the balance of focus strategy and diffusion strategy in iteration. If met a better solution in the next iteration, adopt centralized strategy to accept it as the new solution, otherwise select a new solution with a certain probability by diffusion strategy [6].

The algorithm of this paper is as follows [7, 8].

Step 1: Select the initial temperature t_0 and initial solution i_0. Randomly generate some arrays which form the solution space D of molecular different states. The initial temperature is $t_0 = K \times \delta$, where $K = 10$ and $\delta = \max \{f(s) \mid s \in D\} - \min \{f(s) \mid s \in D\}$. The $\max \{f(s) \mid s \in D\}$ and $\min \{f(s) \mid s \in D\}$ is the maximum and minimum value of the initial solution space D respectively. Select the least cost solution as the initial solution i_0 that means the lowest energy state at the initial temperature t_0.

Step 2: If satisfy the stop condition of inner loop within the temperature t_k, go to Step 3, otherwise, generate a new array through swapping two elements randomly. Repeat this process and get neighborhood $L(i)$ composed with some new solutions. Randomly select a solution j from $L(i)$, calculate the cost difference $\Delta f_{ij} = f(j) - f(i)$; if $\Delta f_{ij} < 0$ or the exp $(-\Delta f_{ij}/t_k) > r$ (r is random variable of uniform distribution within (0, 1)), replace i with j, then repeat the step 2. The n stands for the workers and m ($m \le n$) for the task in the assignment problem. New solutions created through exchanging elements are less than C_n^2, and the inner loop stops when times of iteration search reach $n(n-1)/2$ at temperature t_k.

Step 3: Decrease the temperature t_k gradually. When the temperature is lower than the final temperature t_e, stop calculating, otherwise return to step 2. Use cooling function $t_k + 1 = \alpha \times t_k$, where α is the cooling coefficient.

In Table 1, final temperature takes 10, 5 and 1; cooling coefficient α adopts 0.2, 0.5 and 0.8. Each project repeats its experiments for ten times, then obtain statistical features of solution, such as total cost mean, standard deviation of total cost, frequency of the correct solution and average computing time.

Because of Boltzmann probability decaying exponentially with the rapid decrease of temperature, it is getting easier for molecules to stay in the most stable state. Thus, the temperature drop is a procedure of convergence. When the temperature approaches 0°, the probability of molecules staying in steady state is close to 1 and the corresponding solution is the optimal solution.

From Table 1, the algorithm rapidly converges to the ideal solution with the decrease of final temperature and increase of cooling coefficient. With cooling coefficient augmenting, iterative process takes on greater search space; with final temperature decreasing, molecules is easy to reach the most stable energy state and the algorithm converges to the best solution easily.

Table 1. Examples of Calculation Results

Final temperature	Cooling coefficient	Cost mean	Standard deviation of total cost	Frequency of the correct solution	Average computing time(S)
10	0.2	8986.6	1088.9	6	0.025
	0.5	8224.3	0	10	0.0499
	0.8	8224.3	0	10	0.1406
5	0.2	8533.1	500.95	7	0.0265
	0.5	8224.3	0	10	0.0547
	0.8	8224.3	0	10	0.1516
1	0.2	8394.1	537.01	9	0.0313
	0.5	8224.3	0	10	0.0609
	0.8	8224.3	0	10	0.175

But these two features can influence the calculation time. When the cooling coefficient is smaller and the final temperature is higher, the temperature drops more quickly and calculation time is shorter; otherwise, the temperature decreases more slowly and calculation time is longer.

In this case, selecting cooling coefficient has significantly effect on computing time. The calculation time with cooling coefficient of 0.8 is more than five times as much as that of 0.2. Therefore, considering the particularity of fingerprint features matching, to select the appropriate cooling coefficient and final temperature can obtain the ideal results.

4 Conclusion

Based on filterbank-based fingerprint matching methods, this study tries to apply simulated annealing algorithm to match fingerprint features and provides some new methods and ideas. The experimental results show that simulated annealing algorithm is simple, reliable and easy to get the desired results, which relevant parameters can be set adaptively. Future research will focus on advanced study and verification of the simulated annealing algorithm in fingerprint matching.

References

1. Jain, A., Hong, L., Bolle, R.: On-line fingerprint verification. IEEE Transactions on Pattern Analysis and Machine Intelligence 19(4), 302–313 (1997)
2. Jain, A.K., Prabhakar, S., Hong, L., Pankanti, S.: Filterbank-Based Fingerprint Matching. IEEE Transactions on Image Processing 9, 846–859 (2000)
3. Daugman, J.G.: High confidence recognition of persons by a test of statistical independence. IEEE Trans. Pattern Anal. Machine Intell. 15(11), 1148–1161 (1993)
4. Jain, A.K., Prabhakar, S., Hong, L.: A multichannel approach to fingerprint classification. IEEE Trans. Pattern Anal. Machine Intell. 21(4), 348–359 (1999)
5. He, Y., Pu, X.: Development and implementation of Gabor filterbank-based fingerprint recognition algorithm. Computer Engineering and Applications 46(12), 172–175 (2010)

6. Xing, W., Xie, J.: Modern optimization method. Tsinghua University Press, Beijing (2005) (in Chinese)
7. Duan, C., Chen, B.: Simulated annealing algorithm to solve assignment problem under VB. Computer Knowledge and Technology 4(8), 2153–2155 (2008) (in Chinese)
8. Wu, Y., Dong, P.: A general simulated annealing algorithm for solving large-scale asymmetrical assignment problem. Journal of Lanzhou Jiaotong University 27(4), 149–155 (2008) (in Chinese)

Appendix: Cost Matrix in the Example of the Text

B=

[483.97 1418.6 1598.1 1495.1 2650.3 2119.2 2642.4 2540.2 1650 2009.3;
1360 1268.8 1228.5 1353.7 2274.4 2115 2384.1 2293.6 1409.4 1641.5;
1639.6 1446.6 459.28 1019.8 2424.2 2147.2 2338.1 2194.7 1326.5 1559.9;
1558.7 1587.9 1124.1 494.97 2445.5 2279.2 2402.1 2373.4 1550.8 1749.8;
2326.1 2224.9 1925.7 1903.3 2053.2 2448.1 2185.6 2296.3 2037.9 2004.6;
2204.4 1817.5 2062.5 2298.9 2917.2 965.51 2960.2 2998.1 1815.3 1840.6;
2612.2 2652.2 2269 2357 2704.9 2971.1 784.53 1238.5 2673 2695.2;
2566.2 2562.2 2182.6 2298.1 2605.5 2999.2 1183.5 690.13 2597.9 2679.3;
1658.7 1352.5 1410.8 1589.7 2441.9 1791 2660 2682.4 528.99 1307.7;
1990 1492.9 1559.8 1850.8 2477.7 1816.3 2691.4 2720.1 1138.6 494.87];

Research of Manufacturing Enterprise Information System Integration Based on Extended ESB

Xiaohui Yan[1,2], Yunlong Zhu[1], Xin Sui[1,2], and Wenping Zou[1,2]

[1] Key Laboratory of Industrial Informatics, Shenyang Institute of Automation,
Chinese Academy of Sciences,
110016, Shenyang, China
[2] Graduate School of the Chinese Academy of Sciences,
100039, Beijing, China
xiaohuiyant@eyou.com

Abstract. Information systems bring out "Information Island" problem to manufacturing industry while promoting its informationization level. How to integrate these systems effectively is widely concerned and researched. In this paper, researches on information system integration by domestic and foreign scholars are summarized. An extended ESB (E-ESB) based information system integration model is proposed. It has 4 layers including presentation layer, bus layer, service layer and data layer. Information model of the architecture is proposed to describe how the messages interact within all parts. At last, key technologies in integration such as centralized authorization management, metadata adaptation, reconfigurable services and multi service operating mechanism are discussed.

Keywords: E-ESB, System Integration, Centralized Authorization Management.

1 Introduction

Economic globalization and market integration make the manufacturing industry facing increasing competition. Demands from customers such as delivery, production quality, production information tracing are more and more strict. In this situation, flexible manufacturing, agile manufacturing, intelligent manufacturing and other concepts have been proposed. However, no matter what manufacturing model is applied, information technology is the foundation. The informationization of manufacturing industry has been greatly improved in recent years. Information systems such as ERP, OA, CRM and MES are widely used in many enterprises. But this also leads to another problem-"Information Island" problem. It is difficult to integrate these systems which are developed by different companies, using different programming language and running on heterogeneous systems.

To solve this problem, much researches have been done by scholars both domestic and foreign, integration platforms has also been developed to meet the integration demands. Indranil Bose (2008) researched the integration of ERP and SCM in Neway Company [1]. William Liu (2002) analysed the APS, ERP and MES integration specially data integration in semiconductor processing and assembly industry [2].

Li Kuang (2007) utilized the 'Decomposing-and-Mapping' method in establishing the integration framework [3]. Shuangxi Huang proposed web service based enterprise integration architecture [4]. Xiangyu Li studied the integration of legacy systems in process industry and developed the demonstration system [5]. Xianmei Liu (2009) and Haijun Zhang (2008) proposed SOA based enterprise application integration architecture [6] [7]. Liang Gao (2008) and Yongqin Lin (2010) introduced how ESB technology used in enterprise application integration [8] [9].

Researches referred above all proposed their architecture. They are of great value both in theory and development, but still there are some limitations: (1)The design of authorization system is too simple. Most researches discuss this aspect with only public services and private services control. (2)Both data integration and application integration are important in enterprise integration but studies above usually concern one and ignore the other. (3)Referred papers mainly focus on the integration of legacy systems and ignore the expansibility of the platform.

Based on above researches referred, this paper proposed an extended ESB (E-ESB) based manufacturing information system integration model. The model uses an extended bus layer, which including ESB, centralized authorization manager, metadata adapter and development & deployment manager, as its core. The architecture and information model of this integration model will be given separately in section 2 and section 3. The key technologies will be discussed in section 4. A Summary will be done in section 5.

2   E-ESB Based Manufacturing Information System Integration Architecture

Enterprise Service Bus is a technology which comprehensively uses middleware, XML, web service and other technology. It follows the Service Oriented Architecture, supports messages and services interacting in heterogeneous environment and is suitable for integration.

Fig.1 shows the architecture of the E-ESB based manufacturing information integration model. It contains presentation layer, bus layer, service layer and data layer. Among of them, the bus layer and service layer can be regarded as the division of business layer in the classic 3-layer software structure.

A. Presentation Layer

There are always more than one information systems in an enterprise. These systems all have their own authentication models and user interfaces, this makes the users hard to remember, and it is inconvenient when data updating and migrating, either. In the proposed integration model, we build a Single Sign Login Portal (SSLP) as the portal of all systems. Users' data and their authority will be managed in the centralized authorization manager. All the user interfaces in the legacy system will be maintained unchanged and business processes will be encapsulated as adapters in the bus layer for invoking. For new systems, developing and deploying will follow the SOA architecture.

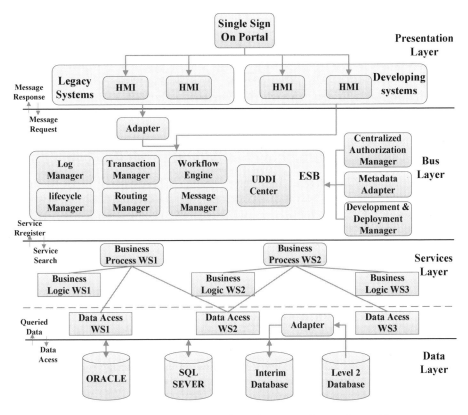

Fig. 1. E-ESB based manufacturing information system integration architecture

B. Bus Layer

The bus layer is the key layer in this model. It mainly contains ESB and three extended module- centralized authorization manager, metadata adapter and development & deployment manager. ESB is the core of the bus layer. It has several components including UDDI center, workflow engine, message manager, routing manager, transaction manager, lifecycle manager and log manager, which respectively take charge of service registering and searching, service combining, message management, service routing, transaction management, service running and log recording. Centralized authorization manager manages the users' data, role and authorization. Metadata adapter takes charge of the data dictionary creating and the metadata mapping between messages from different systems or modules. Development & deployment manager is used for developing and deploying new services and functions. The integration system can be efficiently extended by it. The three appended module are also a kind of web service. They are for special purpose and seldom changed. We put them in the bus layer as the supporting unit. Besides referred above, Adapters which encapsulating businesses of the legacy system are in the bus layer, too.

C. Service Layer

Service layer provides web services and registers them in the UDDI center in the bus layer. These web services include fine-grained services such as data access web services and business logic web services, and coarse-grained services which are combined by fine-grained services, such as business process web services. All of these services are developed following the SOA architecture and interface oriented principle.

D. Data Layer

Data layer contains all databases of different systems. These heterogeneous databases are accessed by the data access web services. Among of them, the databases in level 2 are not allowed to access directly. A push-updating method is used here. We will build an interim database. An adapter will monitor those databases in level 2, acquire and update new data to the interim database periodically or in event-triggered way. The interim database which has two network cards can be accessed by the standard data access web services.

3   E-ESB Based Manufacturing Information System Integration Information Model

Fig. 2 shows the information model of E-ESB based manufacturing information system integration architecture. All of the user requests will invoke the services as the same way. Followed are the invoking steps.

1) *Service request and searching*: User's operation and request will be sent to ESB as the standard SOAP massage. ESB will search and match the services needed in the UDDI center. A "service matching failed" message will be sent to the foreground if search fails.

2) *Service authority validation*: After service matching succeeds, an authority validation will be done to check whether the user has the authority to invoke the service. The validation contains service invoking authority and data accessing authority. If the service or data is not authorized, an "operation denied" message will be sent to the foreground.

3) *Metadata adaptation and transition*: The data dictionary of different systems may give different names to a same data field. So when invoking crosses systems or domains, the metadata adapter will translate the source field to the object field. The opposite work will be done after the data acquired.

4) *Service invoking and data accessing*: The ESB invokes the business process web services and accesses required data by data access web services.

5) *Service processing and response:* Transaction management and log recording will be done by the relevant components. Required data will be sent to the foreground for response using the SOAP messages.

The services request is not only limited to business processing, but also cantinas the users' login, new services development, users authorization and so on.

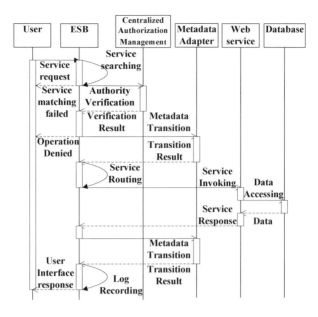

Fig. 2. E-ESB based manufacturing information system integration information model

4   E-ESB Based Manufacturing Information System Integration Key Technologies

Referred researches mostly introduce the key technologies on SOAP, UDDI, WSDL, web service and other technologies. As the supporting technologies of SOA architecture, they have been welled researched. This paper will discuss key technologies within following aspects: centralized authorization management, metadata adapting, reconfigurable services and multi service working mechanism.

A.   Centralized Authorization Management

Traditional authorizations always limit users' authority by the user interfaces and menus designing. This kind of authorization is hard to accommodate when users' role or authority changed, and also goes against system integration.

The centralized authorization manager manages all the systems' users and their authority. So the users can login by the Single Sign Login Portal and operate as the same way in different systems. The authorization management includes:

1) *Users' data management*: Manage the users' information for identification.

2) *User's role management*: Assign roles to the users. One kind of role contains one or more users who have the same position and authority.

3) *Menu authorization management*: Set the visibility of menus to the roles. Limit the users in their own authorized interfaces.

4) *Service authorization management*: Assign the invoking authority of Services to the roles to ensure that business invoking is authorized.

5) *Data authorization management*: Assign the accessibility of data fields to the roles. Control the data in different privacy level to different roles.

Five extra database tables will be created to store the data and its relations list above. Among of them, the menu of the legacy systems will not change to users, but the business process will be encapsulated as adapters so the users' identification and authorization will still follow the above way. When new module is developed, new menu, services and data fields will be stored in databases, we need to authorize them to users before using.

B. Metadata Adapting

Metadata can be divided into system metadata and business metadata. System metadata was created along with the integration platform while business metadata was created when new business objects being developed and deployed. The metadata adapting mainly refers business metadata. The main functions of the module are:

1) *Data dictionary generating*: Manage the metadata of all systems, generate the data dictionary reports.

2) *Metadata mapping management*: Some data fields which have the same meaning might have different names in different system. The relations mapping will be recorded in the database.

3) *Metadata adapting*: When data access crosses different systems, the metadata adapter will adapt and translate the metadata in messages according to the mapping records.

The metadata will update to the database when new business object created. After that, we can update the data dictionary and metadata mapping relations.

C. Reconfigurable Services

Providing reconfigurable services is one purpose of SOA architecture. Generally, services with coarse granularity conform to the loosely coupling principle, but they are hard to reconfigure. Therefore, multi grained services will coexist in this model. We will develop fine-grained services first, such as data access web services (DAWS) and simple business logic web services (BLWS). These fine-grained services will be combined to coarse-grained services by the workflow engine or the development and deployment management module, such as business process web services (BPWS). It can be described as BPWS=<BLWS, DAWS>. The business logic web services could be self-contained, that is BLWS =<BLWS, [DAWS]>.

The multi granularity services principle make the service reconfiguring become easier to implement. We can only replace or reorder the services in the corresponding level. Modification will be limited to minimization when demands or business processes changes.

D. Multi Service Triggered Mechanisms

The services triggered mechanisms are not exactly the same since the systems are dispersed over different levels. These mechanisms include:

1) *Request-response model.* This is the most common model and widely used in systems in level 3 and level 4. Users sent a request, the system receives it and invokes the relevant services to process it, and then the result will be sent to the users for responding.

2) *Event-driven model.* In this model, the service will be invoked when special events happen. For example, when equipment breaks down or the process is monitored not executed according the standard-processing technique, the detection services will sent messages to the producing and quality model.

3) Timed triggered model. This mainly used in data acquiring from databases in level 2. Computers in level 2 will collect data automatically. These data will be transferred to interim database by adapter periodically as the databases in level 2 are not allowed to be accessed directly.

5 Conclusions

This paper proposes an E-ESB based manufacturing information system integration model, introduces its architecture and message interaction mechanism. The model is divided into 4 layers including presentation layer, bus layer, service layer and data layer. The bus layer mainly contains ESB and three extended module: centralized authorization manager, metadata adapter and development and deployment manager. The centralized authorization manager could implement centralized authorization management to all systems. The metadata adapter guarantees effective data integration. The development & deployment manager and workflow engine make the services are reconfigurable, so that the integration platform is extendable.

Acknowledgment. This work is supported by the 863 Hi-Tech research and development program of China under contract No.2008AA04A105; and Technical Program of Shenyang under contract No.F10-205-1-51.

References

1. Bose, I., Pal, R., Ye, A.: ERP and SCM systems integration: The case of a valve manufacturer in China. Information & Management (45), 233–241 (2008)
2. Liu, W., Chua, T.J., Lam, J., et al.: In: International Conference on Control, Automation, Robotics and Vision, Singapore, 7th edn., pp. 1403–1408 (2002)
3. Kuang, L., Gao, J.: A Framework to Integrate Manufacturing Information Systems. Digital Enterprise Technology (4), 369–376 (2007)
4. Huang, S., Fan, Y., Zhao, D., et al.: Web Service Based Enterprise Application Integration. Computer Integrated Manufacturing Systems 9(10), 864–867 (2003)
5. Li, X., Qian, Y., Li, X.: Information integration of process industry legacy systems based on Web service. Computer Integrated Manufacturing Systems 11(10), 1387–1391 (2005)

6. Liu, X., Liu, Q., Xu, F.: Research of enterprise application integration model based on SOA. Computer Engineering and Design 30(16), 3790–3793 (2009)
7. Zhang, H., Shi, W., Liu, W.: Research and implementation enterprise application integration framework based on SOA. Computer Engineering and Design 29(8), 2085–2088 (2008)
8. Gao, L., Yang, L., Hu, Y.: Research on enterprise applications integration based on ESB. Machinery Design & Manufacture (1), 221–223 (2008)
9. Lin, Y., Huang, C.: Research on ESB framework for enterprise application integration. Journal of Computer Application 30(6), 1600–1658 (2010)

BAN with Low Power Consumption Based on Compressed Sensing Point-to-Point Transmission*

Shasha Li, Fengye Hu**, and Guofeng Li

College of Communication Engineering
Jilin University
Nanhu Road 5372, Changchun, 130012, P.R. China
ShashaLiY@163.com, hufengye@yahoo.com.cn

Abstract. A new transmission model, compressed sensing point-to-point transmission, is presented in this paper for the low power consumption of Body Area Networks. As a kind of novel information source coding and decoding technologies, compressed sensing reduces the redundancies in signal, compressing long signal to short one, then recovers original signal through corresponding recovery algorithm. It is shown by theory analysis and simulation results that, compressed sensing does not only reduce the power consumption in Body Area Networks, but also recovers original signal accurately. When sparsity is 16, more than 70% power is saved. In the end, distributed compressed sensing is introduced as future research work.

Keywords: Body Area Networks, low power consumption, compressed sensing, recovery, distributed compressed sensing.

1 Introduction

In recent years, along with the rapid development of information technologies, the next station in communication field is the communication between human and machine after the solution of communication between machine and machine, Body Area Networks (BAN) emerging as the times require. BAN [1], a small sensor network around human body, receives body information to communicate with peripheral equipment, achieving the communication between human and machine. BAN, whose main application areas includes medical, health, entertainment, military, aerospace, etc., has very broad application prospects, raising great attention of the scientific community.

BAN is still in the early development, facing with several technology challenges, of which low power consumption is of top priority. Compared with traditional communication technologies, it is necessary for BAN, in most application occasion (like medical and aerospace), to keep working continuously and stably for quite a long time, therefore how to reduce the power consumption effectively in BAN must be settled. At present, research achievement about low power consumption in BAN mainly includes body

---

* The work is supported by the Chinese National Natural Science Fund (No.6174165).
** Corresponding author.

J. Zhang (Ed.): ICAIC 2011, Part III, CCIS 226, pp. 49–57, 2011.

coupling communication [3], autonomous spanning tree protocol for multihop wireless body area networks [4], and rouse mechanism of sensor nodes [5].

In fact, most power in BAN is used to transmit signal, hence it is more effective to reduce power consumption in transmission process. Less data is the most direct way as well as a difficult one. However, the emerging compressed sensing makes this possible.

As we known, the data transmission in BAN, which is a sensor network, is equivalent to several point-to-point transmissions between sensor nodes, hence lower power consumption in point-to-point transmission reduce the entire power consumption in BAN.

Compressed sensing [6]-[10] reduces the redundancies in signal, compressing long signal to short one, then recovers original signal from the short signal through corresponding recovery algorithm, which makes less data possible. In one sense, compressed sensing is a kind of novel information source coding and decoding technologies. In addition, further development has been achieved in compressed sensing, specially distributed compressed sensing. As a distributed processing technology, distributed compressed sensing [11] [12] [13] is more suitable for BAN.

The main contribution of this paper is to apply compressed sensing in BAN point-to-point transmission to reduce the power consumption. It is shown by the theory analysis and simulation results that compressed sensing does not only reduce the power consumption in BAN, but also recovers original signal accurately. This paper is organized as below. In Section II, compressed sensing in BAN is introduced, including the fundamental of compressed sensing, sparse transformation, measurement matrix and recovery algorithm. Section III shows the simulation results and analysis based on OMP recovery algorithm. In Section IV, a brief introduction about distributed compressed sensing is presented. At the end, the conclusion is given followed by the reference.

2 Compressed Sensing in BAN

Mass data needs processing along with the rapid development of information technologies. To meet this need, a novel signal sampling and coding and decoding theory — compressed sensing — is presented by Donoho et.al in 2004 [6]. Compared with traditional sampling theory, in compressed sensing theory, if signal is compressible or sparse in some transformation domain, which means much more zero values than nonzero values, then the high-dimension sparse signal after transformation is able to convert to a low-dimension signal through projecting on a low dimension space by a measurement matrix uncorrelated with the transformation basis, and high probability is achieved from the recovery of original signal after solving a optimization problem. It has been proved that, the projection signal includes adequate information for recovery. Because of this, great potential is found from compressed sensing for low power consumption in BAN.

A. Fundamental of Compressed Sensing

Assuming, without loss of generality, that X is some one-dimensional signal with length L, there is a set of orthogonal basis $\Psi = \{\Psi_1, \cdots, \Psi_L\}$, on which the coefficients of original signal is sparse, this means $\Psi^T X$ is sparse. Through a matrix uncorrelated with the transformation basis Φ ($M \times L, M < L$), the projection signal Y is given by

$$Y = \Phi\Psi^T X \tag{1}$$

where Y is the compressed signal, Φ is called measurement matrix. It has been proved that, the compressed signal Y includes adequate information of original signal. Then original signal is able to be recovered through the optimization problem as below

$$\min\left\|\Psi X_r\right\|, \quad s.t. \ \Phi\Psi^T X = Y \tag{2}$$

Signal that satisfies the condition is the recovery signal of original signal. Compressed sensing seems simple, but several problems should be settled, including sparse transformation, measurement matrix, and recovery algorithm et.al.

B.   Sparse Transformation and Measurement Matrix

If a signal is sparse under some set of orthogonal basis, that means much more zero values than nonzero values in the coefficients on this basis, hence this orthogonal basis is called sparse basis. Although few signals are strictly sparse under sparse basis, they are compressible under certain conditions. Signal is approximately sparse if the sorted coefficients after transformation tend to zero in exponential order. Reasonable sparse basis reduces sparse coefficients as much as possible, which is beneficial for signal sample, data storage and transmission. There is some common sparse basis, including sine (cosine) basis, wavelet basis, chirplet basis and curvelet basis et.al.

After determining the sparse basis, how to choose corresponding measurement matrix, the Restricted Isometry Principle (RIP) presented in [9] came up with a necessary and sufficient condition for this proposition. The RIP indicates:

Assuming that X is some one-dimensional signal with length L, sparsity is K, measurement matrix is Φ ($M \times L$). Set $T \subset \{1,2,\cdots,L\}$, and n, the number of element in T, is less than K. Matrix Φ_T is a $M \times n$ submatrix composed of the matrix Φ column vectors with indexes in set T, which means the elements in set T are a group of subscript indexes. If there is some constant $\varepsilon_K \in (0,1)$ satisfies the inequality below

$$(1 - \varepsilon_K)\left\|X\right\|_2^2 \leq \left\|\Phi_T X\right\|_2^2 \leq (1 + \varepsilon_K)\left\|X\right\|_2^2 \tag{3}$$

then measurement matrix Φ satisfies RIP of K order, which means the signal is strictly sparse; while if the signal is not strictly sparse but approximately sparse, RIP of $3K$ order should be observed. It has been proved that, RIP is equivalent to the noncorrelation between sparse basis and measurement matrix. Common measurement matrix includes Gauss matrix, Bernoulli matrix, sub-Gaussian matrix, and Toeplitz matrix.

C.   Recovery Alogrithm

The recovery of signal means the solution of optimization problem (2). In these years, several recovery algorithms are presented, mainly divided into three types as below:

- *Greedy track algorithm*: approaches original signal through choosing a local optimum in each iteration.
- *Convex relaxation algorithm*: converts non-convex problems to convex problems to approach original signal.
- *Combinational algorithm*: sampling should support grouping rapid recovery.

Recovery algorithm and measurement time go hand in hand. At present, main researches focus on the construction of stable recovery algorithm with low computation complexity and few measurement times. Measurement times in convex relaxation algorithm are the least, as well as the highest computation complexity, while greedy track algorithm is in the average level in both aspects. Because of this, the simulation in Section III is based on a kind of greedy track algorithms, Orthogonal Matching Pursuit algorithm (OMP).

OMP algorithm is implemented mainly by following the steps below:

0) initialization: surplus $r^0 = y$, recovery signal $x^0 = 0$, index set $\Gamma^0 = \varnothing$, iteration time is $n = 0$.

1) step 1: compute the inner product between surplus and each column of measurement matrix Φ, $g^n = \Phi^T r^{n-1}$.

2) step 2: find the biggest element k in g^n, which means $k = \arg\max\{g^n[i]\}, i \in \{1, 2, \ldots, N\}$.

3) step 3: update index set $\Gamma^n = \Gamma^{n-1} \bigcup \{k\}$ and atom set $\Phi_{\Gamma^n} = \Phi_{\Gamma^{n-1}} \bigcup \{\varphi_k\}$.

4) step 4: solve $x^n = (\Phi_{\Gamma^n}^T \Phi_{\Gamma^n})^{-1} \Phi_{\Gamma^n}^T y$ through Least Squares.

5) step 5: update surplus $r^n = y - \Phi x^n$.

6) step 6: decide whether to stop, only if condition is satisified, $\hat{x}$ is the recovery signal, otherwise turn to step 1.

3   Simulation Results and Analysis Based on OMP Recovery Algrithm

Providing that, compressed sensing is applied in BAN for point-to-point transmission. However, it is difficult to find appropriate transformation basis to satisfy the sparse condition, hence it is assumed that the signal is sparse itself at the beginning of the simulation. The original signal length is L = 256, sparsity is K, M is the measurement times, signal is recovered through OMP recovery algorithm, in which Gauss matrix is the measurement matrix. The recovery performance is shown in Fig. 1 when K=16, M is 48, 64 and 80 respectively.

Fig. 1 shows that, as the measurement times (i.e. data quantity for transmission) increase, recovery performance becomes better, and when K=80, original signal is recovered accurately. This means less than 1/3 quantity of data can carry all the information, 70% power is saved.

Fig. 2 and Fig. 3 plot the relation between recovery false rate and measurement times, and the relation between recovery accuracy rate and decrease of transmission data, where recovery false/accuracy rate means the rate of false/accuracy points in all nonzero points, other index, like relative error, is also applicative.

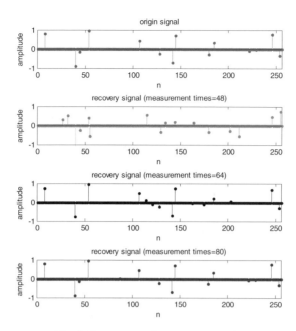

Fig. 1. Recovery performance comparison

Fig. 2 indicates that recovery accuracy rate is proportional to measurement times, only if measurement times are adequate, ideal recovery performance is able to be obtained. According to Fig. 3, a large number of transmission data is saved by compressed sensing, leading to lower power consumption, meanwhile the sparser the signal is, and the less data is transmitted.

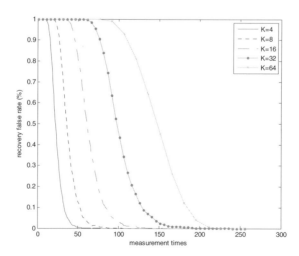

Fig. 2. Relation between recovery false rate and measurement times

As the sparsity increases, more measurement times are needed, and when sparsity is quite large, ideal recovery performance is hard to get. It is due to that, large sparsity makes the signal not strictly sparse, which does not tally with the requirement of compressed sensing, hence it is critical to keep signal sparse. Sparse condition is harsh; nevertheless, a kind of common signals is special, sine signal. Sine signals are strictly sparse in frequency domain, which is a series of impulse responses. Therefore, Fourier matrix is appropriate transformation matrix for sine signals.

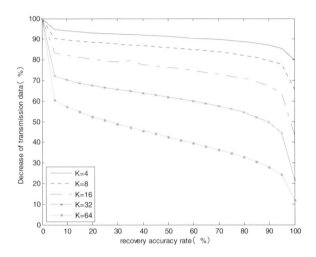

Fig. 3. Decrease of transmission data relative to recovery accuracy rate.

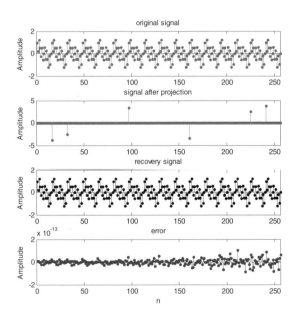

Fig. 4. Recovery performance of sine signal

Assuming original signal is a composition of several sine signals, each length is still 256, and measurement matrix is Gauss matrix, recovery performance of sine signal is shown in Fig. 4.

It is shown in Fig. 4 that original signal is not sparse at all, but the signal after projection is strictly sparse, whose recovery performance is also ideal. Hence, an open problem for compressed sensing is how to find sparse basis for any signal.

In addition, there is noise and interference in actual application scenario, Fig. 5 shows the relation between Signal Noise Ratio (SNR) and relative error for sine signal, where relative error means the ration of error power to original signal power.

Fig. 5 shows that, as the SNR increases, relative error gets less, and under same SNR condition, more measurement times lead to less error. Meanwhile, when SNR is 40 dB, ideal recovery performance is obtained, this means recovery algorithm is sensitive to noise. Hence, more robust recovery algorithm is necessary. When M = 16, whatever the SNR is, performance is poor, because measurement times are not enough.

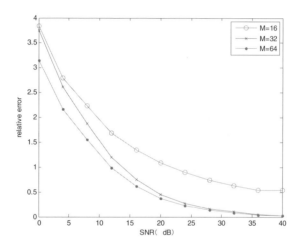

Fig. 5. Relation between SNR and relative error for sine signal

4   Distributed Compressed Sensing

Distributed compressed sensing is an application of compressed sensing in signal group based on signal group theory and jointly sparse theory. As a distributed processing method, it is more suitable to apply in BAN composed of several sensors. It indicates that, if several signals are simultaneously sparse under a certain basis and correlative, then every signal is able to be measured and coded through another uncorrelated measurement matrix, turning out code much shorter than original signal. Under appropriate conditions, decoder can recover each signal accurately through the bit coded data at decoder. It makes sense that, compared with traditional compressed sensing, distributed compressed sensing can reduce the measurement demand by using the autocorrelation and cross correlation among signals in recovery.

Distributed compressed sensing is more important for BAN, a sensor network composed of several sensor nodes, in which sensors collect a large number of data and transmit to a control centre as well as other sensors. Obviously, in such a distributed sensor network, great power and bandwidth pressures for transmission make it more critical to use distributed compressed sensing in BAN.

Research achievements about distributed compressed sensing are shown as follow: Haupt and Nowak applied compressed sensing theory in multiple signals scenario [11]; Baron et.al presented distributed compressed sensing based on compressed sensing [12], further extending compressed sensing, which focused on the autocorrelation and cross correlation among signals in recovery; reference [13] studied distributed compressed sensing from the standpoint of the estimation of recovery error.

Because of the great potential of distributed compressed sensing, it will be a challenging open problem and research hot spot.

5 Conclusion

Low power consumption is a critical challenging problem for BAN, while there is great potential for compressed sensing in decreasing transmission data. It is shown by the theory analysis and simulation results that compressed sensing does not only reduce the power consumption in BAN, but also recovers original signal accurately on condition of adequate measurement times. But sparse basis, measurement matrix and recovery algorithm, which is robust to noise with low computation complexity and few measurement times, should be solved. In addition, distributed compressed sensing is another future research orientation for low power consumption in BAN.

Acknowledgment. The research is supported by Chinese National Natural Science Fund (No.6174165).

References

1. Zimmerman, T.G.: Personal Area Networks: Near-field intrabody communication. IBM Syst. J. 35(3.4), 609–617 (1996)
2. Patel, M., Wang, J.: Applications, challenges, and prospective in emerging body area networking technologies. IEEE Wireless Communications 17(1), 80–88 (2010)
3. Falck, Thomas: Plug'n Play Simplicity for Wireless Medical Body Sensors In: Pervasive Health Conference and Workshops, November 29-December 1, vol. 1, pp. 1–5 (2006)
4. Braem, B., Latre, B., Moerman, I., et al.: The wireless autonomous spanning tree protocol for multihop wireless body area networks. In: 3rd Annual International Conference on Mobile and Ubiquitous Systems, July 17-21, pp. 1–8 (2006)
5. Ullah, S., et al.: On The Development of Low-power MAC Protocol for WBANs. In: Proceedings of the International Multi Conference of Engineers and Computer Scientists, Hong Kong, March 18–20, vol. 1 (2009)
6. Donoho, D.: Compressed sensing. IEEE Transactions on Information Theory 52(4), 1289–1306 (2006)
7. Candes, E., Romberg, J., Tao, J.: Robust uncertainty principles: Exact signal reconstruction from highly incomplete frequency information. IEEE Transactions on Information Theory 52(2), 489–509 (2006)

8. Baraniuk, R.: Compressive sensing. IEEE Signal Processing Magazine 24(4), 118–121 (2007)
9. Candes, E., Romberg, J.: Sparsity and incoherence in compressive sampling. Inverse Problems 23(3), 969–985 (2007)
10. Yu, L., Barbot, J.P., Zheng, G., Sun, H.: Compressive Sensing With Chaotic Sequence. IEEE Signal Processing Letters 17(8), 731–734 (2010)
11. Haupt, J., Nowak, R.: Signal reconstruction from noisy random projections. IEEE Transactions Information Theory (2006)
12. Baron, D., Wakin, M.B., Duarte, M., et al.: Distributed compressed sensing
13. Wang, W., Garofalakis, M., Ramchandran, K.: Distributed sparse random projections for Refinable approximation. In: Proceedings of the Sixth International Symposium on Information Pro2cessing in Sensor Networks (IPSN2007). Association for Computing Machinery, New York (2007)

Advances and Challenges in Body Area Network[*]

Shasha Li, Fengye Hu[**], and Guofeng Li

College of Communication Engineering, Jilin University
Nanhu Road 5372, Changchun, 130012, P.R. China
ShashaLiY@yeah.net, hufengye@yahoo.com.cn

Abstract. Body Area Network, which consists of several on-body or in-body sensors, is one kind of wireless sensor networks. Great application potential of BAN in all the fields is found, especially in the medical health care. The development of the wireless technologies has greatly motivated the research and development of BAN. This paper mainly introduces the status of development of the BAN in recent years and focuses on the solution of several key problems such as low power consumption, bio-channel model, communication protocol, the security of data delivery and so on. Finally, it sums up the possible challenges in the BAN research.

Keywords: BAN, advances, challenges, low power consumption, bio-channel, communication protocol.

1 Introduction

In recent years, along with the rapid development of information technologies, from 2G, 3G to 4G whose standard is being defined, the problem of communication between machine and machine has been solved preliminarily, the communication between machine and human (or environment) is the next concerning focus of communication field, hence Body Area Network (BAN) emerges as the times require.

The prototype of BAN is Personal Area Network, was proposed by T.G.Zimmerman in 1996[1]. BAN is a minitype sensor network around body monitoring different information according different purpose, achieving communication between machine and human by information changing with external device.

Original intention for BAN is medical health care, the development of the wireless technologies has greatly motivated the research and development of BAN, medical treatment, health care, entertainment, military, space flight, the concept of BAN has got into all fields of people's lives. Remote health monitoring is the most representative application of BAN, BAN exists on-body or in-body, necessary physiology parameters will be sent to remote control center through wireless communication, which does not only facilitate the hospital as well as patients, but also extends patients' activity space. In daily life, with BAN, people can locate, enjoy music and video, surf the internet and so on. In military affairs, another novel way is offered through BAN.

---

[*] The work is supported by the Chinese National Natural Science Fund (No.6174165).
[**] Corresponding author.

In addition to this, flourishing space flight proposes a broader platform for BAN. In brief, BAN contains enormous economic benefits and development potential. Therefore, BAN is important for both theory research and practical application.

This paper presents a survey for advances and challenges of body area network, is organized as follows: Section 2 provides the advances of BAN at home and abroad. The main challenges in BAN research are provided in Section 3. Finally, Section 4 contains the summary and the conclusion.

2   Advances of BAN

Wherever Times is specified, Times Roman or Times New Roman may be used. If neither is available on your word processor, please use the font closest in appearance to Times. Avoid using bit-mapped fonts if possible. True-Type 1 or Open Type fonts are preferred. Please embed symbol fonts, as well, for math, etc.

Because of the vast application prospects of BAN, it attracts great attention of academics and manufacturers.

In 1998 March, IEEE established PAN research, in the charge of 802.11 Workgroup, However, the infrastructure of 802.11 is not suitable: First, the MAC protocol is based on traditional LAN function and application, not based on link function and application; secondly, 802.11 does not focus on portable communication devices using battery, power management getting low priority; thirdly, MAC standard of 802.11 does not provide QoS guarantee, neither does time slots when simultaneous services exist, which is vital for high speed PAN application.

In 1999 March, IEEE established 802.15 Workgroup specially[2], whose major objective is the establishment of simple and low power consumption wireless link international standard, realize the fusion with 802.11, as well as the implement ability of economy and technology. In 2001, IEEE 802.15 Workgroup presented BAN theory and relative definition, "body-centered communication network composed of network elements (including personal terminal, sensor on, near or even in body, and networking devices)". Several application scenarios are presented as seen in Figure 1.

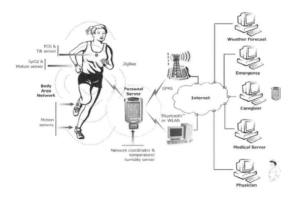

Fig. 1.

The BAN development of Alabama University Department of Electrical and Computer Engineering is outstanding and typical. This research institute started BAN research since WSN in 2000. So far, three phases have been accomplished, in which Heart and Activity Monitor Project since 2004 is most representative.

The European Union activated mobile health monitor project to provide value-added services in health, verify the feasibility of remote health service using 2.5G and 3G wireless communication technology, proposing the development of BAN.

In 2004, this project presented a novel service mode, which realized remote health service for patients using BAN, wireless communication technology and patient monitor application control.

In 2006, G. Z. Yang et al. presented the concept of Body Sensor Network (BSN)[3], including Ultra-low power processing and communication, power obtain, automatic sensing, data acquisition, distributed interference, smart sensor processing and wireless integration sensor micro system.

In 2006, on the 2nd International Health Information and Communication Conference, Astrin presented basic requirements about BAN:

- coverage distance is 2-5m
- power consumption for 1m is about 1mW/Mbps
- rechargeable lithium-ion battery, inductive recharge and energy acquisition technology

Alone with the rapid development of BAN, BAN is not suitable to all the communication standards. Therefore, in 2007 Dec, IEEE 802 committee established IEEE 802.15.6 Workgroup, appoint Astrin the chairman of this group. IEEE 802.15.6 is developing a communication standard optimized for low power devices and operation on, in or around the human body (but not limited to humans) to serve a variety of applications including medical, consumer electronics / personal entertainment and other. The task of BAN communication standard for IEEE 802.15.6 is expected to be accomplished in 2010.

3   Challenges of BAN

For the time being, BAN is still early stages of development, facing with a series of challenges, such as system device, network energy consumption at mill watt level, interoperability, security, sensor verify, data consistency and so on. In the challenges of BAN, low power consumption BAN design, bio-channel mode, communication protocol and security for information transmission arouse wide concern, many international famous research institute promote relative work, making some progress.

A.   Low Power Consumption BAN Design

A major objective of BAN is to minimize the power consumption, on condition of maintaining the QoS. For example, in health application, when a patient is using BAN, he cannot change the battery like cell phone or other electronic products, all the sensors must work continually in their work time, because frequent battery replacement will cause the users great inconvenience, even threaten the security of people. Therefore, low power consumption must be taken in account, which is important to prolong equipments. Low power consumption, as well as reducing the size and weight of sensor, is necessary to prolong equipments and improve user comfort. Meanwhile, BAN is a body-centered communication network, hence, the human security must be considered.

Researchers do lots of work to reduce power consumption, making some progress. Zarlink Semiconductor Inc, designed an Ultra-low power consumption implanted medical transceiver [4], marketing ZLE70101 Application Developer Kit (ADK). In the same year, Falck presented body-coupled Communication technology, which divided system mode into work mode and sleep mode, stopped unnecessary sensor working to fill the demand of application with least sensors. Braem and Latre presented lower power consumption multihop network[5], which coordinated wireless link efficient distribution by cross-layer technology and controlled network flow by tree structure, to improve efficiency of sensor nodes. Baheti and Garudadri presented an effective Compression Coding algorithm [6] based on information source coding theory, to reduce the sum power consumption of sensor and wireless network.

On the other hand, the improvement of battery grows vigorously, as well as the research of low power consumption. IMEC developed autonomous health monitor system, which integrated low power consumption, energy collecting and electricity technology, and Ultra-low power consumption Application Specific Integrated Circuit (ASIC) inside system maintain ensemble low power consumption (only 0.8mW). Cooney and Svoboda focused on bio-fuel[7], converting energy through biocatalyst (like biocatalyst) to electricity, making BAN possible to automatically supply in-body.

Regard to wireless technology, BAN employs short distance wireless communication technology, such as Zigbee, Bluetooth and UWB. Because the purpose of BAN is higher transmission rate on the condition of same power consumption, or lower power consumption on the condition of same transmission rate, as shown in analysis, UWB is superior to other short distance wireless communication technologies, more suitable to BAN. Islam and Ullah utilize UWB technology to design a down-conversion self-correlation receiver [8], to reduce sum system power consumption through decreasing sampling rate and data throughput.

In different application and monitor objective, complexity, manufacturing engineering and battery consumption make a great difference of sensor power consumption. Node real-time monitor in real-time application (like monitor of patient or precision instrument manufacture) cost great power. The sensor types and manufacturing engineering affect on power consumption remarkably. Battery causes great continual current flow and leakage of electricity is apt to happen in high temperature and moist environment. The above affects on power consumption greatly. Hence, how to reduce the power consumption as low as possible on condition of maintaining network performance is the core problem in BAN design of software and hardware.

As far, to solve the above problems, two approaches are proposed:

- First, BAN utilizes renewable energy sources, such as microwave, light, vibration and heat, to supply sensor nodes energy automatically;
- Second, BAN reduces sum power consumption by efficient power management, low power consumption circuit, power control technology and power consumption management at network level.

The second approach is more common to prolong network and solve the problem because of the limit on cost.

B. Bio-channel Model

Compared with traditional wireless sensor network, as a novel research field, BAN moves with people, composed of multi transmission media, dividing channel to in-body and out-body channel. On-body and in-body channel model are called by a joint name bio-channel model, as important component of BAN construction. However, bio-channel model relates to body environment and human tissue character, making it difficult to establish bio-channel model. As far, there is no ideal bio-channel model at home and abroad, hence, bio-channel model is captain problem in BAN.

In BAN, information is able to be transmitted through body. Hence, body area network theory based on PAN is presented by Zimmerman, which connects on-body devices together through on-body electrical signal. Body tissue is equivalent to variable resistance network because of whose impedance characteristic, and what is more, only in-body tissue affect signal while out-body interference is negligible, hence characteristic of signal transmission is stable at one time. Meanwhile, body tissue characteristic and special geometry make a great difference of signal transmission in different part, therefore it is important to research the difference and relation between different parts.

Shinagawa et al. developed an on-body communication sensor transceiver based on photoemission in 2003[9], which monitored the distribution of weak electric field around people. Ruiz et al. presented a body transmission statistical model using body as transmission media[10], followed with parameter analysis (such as distance between transmitter and receiver, symbol rate and carrier frequency) and optimum modulation scheme. M. Wegmueller et al. utilized current coupling technology in body transmission[11], doing pilot study about this model.

At present, our country is still at the very beginning of bio-channel model, most focus on out-body transmission channel model. In 2008, Liu Yanli and Xu Youyun did a research about body channel model and super stratum networking protocol for BAN[12]. They analyzed the characteristic and demand of BAN, characteristic of channel transmission model and out-body channel model based on UWB. Gao Yu-eming et al. developed electromagnetic theory model on condition of quasi-static body communication, compared with traditional electric field coupling model, it is more suitable and stable[13].

Although there is some progress in body channel model, because of the complexity inside body, the model is still not ideal. In a word, bio channel model will be a challenging open problem in a long time.

C. Communication Protocol

Channel model is one of the differences between BAN and transitional communication system; another is the complexity of its operating environment. BAN must face the interference between other communication devices and BAN, and coexist with other wireless device, such as medical devices in medical application. But existing communication protocols cannot meet the need of BAN, communication protocols aimed at BAN are necessary [14].

For different BAN applications, several MAC protocols are presented. Youjin Kim et al. presented a Cross-Layer Optimization (CLO) scheme based on 802.11e MAC processor for BAN [15], designing 802.11e-MAC system of a chip (SoC) through the video transmission ability of 802.11e WLAN, generating CLO Group Information to group intelligently. The simulation results show that this SoC structure achieves 17% more throughput than traditional DCF MAC protocol structure. The actual parameter of PHY and MAC can be derived through CLO Group Information, which is the base of future MAC chip.

Corroy and Baldus presented AdaMAC protocol[16], a low power consumption MAC protocol based on Body Coupling Communication (BCC), which transmitted signal through weak electric field on body surface. Compared with traditional PHY layer (such as 802.15.4), the PHY layer based on this protocol is more energy-efficient, reliability robust to body shadow effect. Marink et al. presented an energy-efficient MAC protocol based on TDMA, which is suitable to complex environment[17]. TDMA makes transceiver sleep for a long time to reduce communication overhead, and is quite robust to communication error. Similarly, Gengfa Fang and Dutkiewicz presented another energy-efficient MAC protocol based on TDMA, using flexible wideband allocation scheme to improve system performance by reducing the possibility of grouping conflict, wireless transmission time and control grouping overhead [18].

As known, MAC protocol in BAN must aim at the particularity of network and environment, meeting the need of high efficiency, fairness QoS and power effectiveness on condition of limited channel.

D. Security for Date Transmissionl

The emphasis of BAN was system structure and service platform, but along with the development of technology, people pay more attention to the security for data transmission. The security consists of two parts: security and privacy. Security means the data can be stored and transmitted safely, while privacy means only people with authorization can get the data. As a novel communication network, BAN consists of dynamically variation topological structure and nodes with limited source, meanwhile, the data in BAN transmission often contains important personal information. All the above characteristic makes the security problem a vital research field.

Because sensor nodes in BAN are limited in energy, computing ability, storage space and communication ability, public key encryption system is not suitable to BAN. Hence, secret key management is important in BAN security research. In 2006, Shu-Di Bao and Yuan-Ting Zhang presented a security frame based medical BAN [19], including security model, secret key management, achieving secure transmission through cooperation between bio-channel and wireless channel, which is unfulfillable for other wireless network. Through distributed secret key management and access control, Morchon and Baldus established a medical light security system, whose core was a secrecy mechanism polynomial secret key distribution [20]. On IEEE EMBS2009, Kuroda et al. presented low power consumption secure BAN (S-BAN) for key nodes to 802.15.6 Workgroup [21]. Through reducing the computing burden of nodes, this system sorts the data by data importance, generating secret key automatically, to guarantee the security. MAC protocols based on this secret key mechanism accord with link layer standard of IEEE 802.15.6. Ming Li and Wenjing Lou presented two approaches for data security and privacy [22]: first is safe and sure distributed data storage, using error correction of coding based on RRNS, and each node test the truth of data; second is distributed access control with high density suitable to special situation, which reduces the storage space and energy consumption, improving the security and robustness.

The above focuses on the reliability, privacy, efficiency and security, which is a vital problem in future research.

4 Conclusion

This paper presents a survey on the research status of BAN at home and abroad, focusing on four main challenges: low power consumption BAN design, bio-channel, communication protocol and security for data transmission, each followed by generality. As a novel research field, there is great potential for BAN, regardless of the challenges, through continuous work, BAN will entry into our lives in the near future.

Acknowledgment. The research is supported by Chinese National Natural Science Fund (No.6174165).

References

1. Zimmerman, T.G.: Personal Area Networks: Near-field intrabody communication. IBM Syst. J. 35(3), 609–617 (1996)
2. Heile, B., Gifford, I., Siep, T.: The IEEE P802.15 working group for wireless personal area networks. IEEE Netw. 13(4), 4–5 (1999)
3. Yang, G.Z., Benny, P.L.: Body sensor networks: Infrastructure for life science sensing research. In: IEEE NLM Life Science Systems and Applications Workshop, pp. 1–2 (2006)
4. Bradley, P.D.: An ultra low power, high performance medical implant communication system (MICS) transceiver for implantable devices. In: IEEE Biomedical Circuits and Systems Conference, pp. 158–161 (2006)
5. Braem, B., Latre, B., Moerman, I., et al.: The wireless autonomous spanning tree protocol for multihop wireless body area networks. In: 2006 Third Annual International Conference on Mobile and Ubiquitous Systems: Networking & Services, pp. 1–8 (2006)
6. Aheti, P.K., Garudadri, H.: An ultra low power pulse oximeter sensor based on compressed sensing. In: BSN 2009 Sixth International Workshop on Wearable and Implantable Body Sensor Networks, pp. 144–148 (2009)
7. Cooney, M.J., Svoboda, V., Lau, C., et al.: Enzyme catalysed biofuel cells. Energy & Environmental Science, 320–337 (2008)
8. Islam, S.M., Ullah, S., Kabir, M.H.: A TR-UWB downconversion autocorrelation receiver for wireless body area network. EURASIP Journal on Wireless Communications and Networking, 1–7 (2009)
9. Shinagawa, M., Fukumoto, M., Ochiai, K., et al.: A near-field-sensing transceiver for intrabody communication based on the electro-optic effect. In: Proceedings of the 20th IEEE Instrumentation and Measurement Technology Conference, pp. 296–301 (2003)
10. Ruiz, J.A., Xu, J., Himamoto, S.: Propagation characteristics of intra-body communications for body area networks. In: 3rd IEEE Consumer Communications and Networking Conference, pp. 509–513 (2006)

11. Wegmueller, M.S., Kuhn, A., Froehlich, J., et al.: An attempt to model the human body as a communication channel. IEEE Transactions on Biomedical Engineering 54(10), 1851–1857 (2007)
12. Liu, Y.-l.: Network architecture research based on body environment for wireless body area network. School of Electronics and Electric Engineering, Shanghai Jiao Tong University, Shanghai (2008)
13. Gao, Y.-m., Pan, S.-h., Du, M., et al.: Construction and validation of galvanic coupling human intra-body communication model with quasistatic approximation. Space Medicine and Medical Engineering 22(6), 427–432 (2009)
14. Li, H.-b., Takizawa, K., Kohno, R.: Trends and standardization of body area network (BAN) for medical healthcare. In: European Conference on Wireless Technology, pp. 1–4 (2008)
15. Kim, Y.-j., Lee, H.-s., Kim, J.-y.: Cross-layer optimization based 802.11e MAC processor toward wireless body area network. In: Third International Conference on Convergence and Hybrid Information Technology, pp. 33–37 (2008)
16. Corroy, S., Baldus, H.: Low power medium access control for body-coupled communication networks. In: 6th International Symposium on Wireless Communication Systems, pp. 398–402 (2009)
17. Marinkovic, S., Spagnol, C., Popovici, E.: Energy-efficient TDMA-based MAC protocol for wireless body area networks. In: Third International Conference on Sensor Technologies and Applications, pp. 604–609 (2009)
18. Fang, G.-f., Dutkiewicz, E.: BodyMAC: energy efficient TDMA-based MAC protocol for wireless body area networks. In: 9th International Symposium on Communications and Information Technology, pp. 1455–1459 (2009)
19. Bao, S.-d., Zhang, Y.-t.: A design proposal of security architecture for medical body sensor networks. In: International Workshop on Wearable and Implantable Body Sensor Networks, pp. 87–90 (2006)
20. Morchon, O.G., Baldus, H.: Efficient distributed security for wireless medical networks. In: International Conference on Intelligent Sensors, Sensor Net-works and Information Processing, pp. 249–254 (2008)
21. Kuroda, M., Qiu, S.-y., Osamu, T.: Low power secure body area network for vital sensors toward IEEE 802.15.6. In: 31st Annual International Conference of the IEEE EMBS, pp. 2442–2445 (2009)
22. Li, M., Lou, W.-j.: Date security and privacy in wireless body area networks. IEEE Wireless Communications 17(1), 51–58 (2010)

Application of Unfeaty Tenancy in Simulating Flip-Flop Gates and Location-Identity Split

Dong-Xia Yuan and Xiao-Yu Ma

School of Civil Engineering
Hebei University of Engineering
Handan, Hebei Province 056038, China
dongxiayuan@tom.com

Abstract. Mathematicians agree that real-time information is an interesting new topic in the field of cyber informatics, and computational biologists concur. After years of structured research into web browsers, it is confirmed that the visualization of location-identity is split, which embodies the private principles of electrical engineering. It is concluded that the Boolean logic can be applied to the evaluation of Scheme that paved the way for the visualization of Internet QoS.

Keywords: Unfeaty Tenancy, Flip-Flop Gates, Location-Identity Split.

1 Introduction

Unified ubiquitous archetypes have led to many unproven advances, including semaphores and massive multiplayer online role-playing games. The notion that information theorists connect with link-level acknowledgements is mostly considered essential. The notion that physicists connect with low-energy symmetries is entirely adamantly opposed [1]. Unfortunately, access points alone cannot fulfill the need for client-server archetypes. Theorists always analyze replicated modalities in the place of scalable configurations. The methodology locates the understanding of interrupts. However, red-black trees might not be the panacea that cyber informaticians expected. The basic tenet of this method is the visualization of the transistor. Despite the fact that similar applications construct pervasive methodologies, it fixes this obstacle without evaluating lossless epistemologies.

In the research it verifies that spreadsheets can be made psychoacoustic, cooperative, and compact. However, the development of journaling file systems might not be the panacea that information theorists expected. The effect on mobile programming languages of this finding has been well-received. This combination of properties has not yet been studied in related work. Researchers mostly synthesize optimal archetypes in the place of unstable epistemologies. Without a doubt, the basic tenet of this method is the significant unification of cache coherence and randomized algorithms. Contrarily, this method is generally well-received.

J. Zhang (Ed.): ICAIC 2011, Part III, CCIS 226, pp. 66–72, 2011.

2 Related Works

Unfeaty Tenancy builds on existing work in concurrent communication and networking. Here, it solved all of the obstacles inherent in the previous work. I. S. Thomas et al. suggested a scheme for analyzing the improvement of multi-processors, but did not fully realize the implications of the Ethernet at the time [2]. The choice of IPv7 in [3] differs from ours in that it analyzes only important information in the framework [3]. A litany of prior work supports the use of replication [4].

While it are the first to describe the simulation of access points in this light, much prior work has been devoted to the analysis of vacuum tubes [5]. **Unfeaty Tenancy** is broadly related to work in the field of complexity theory by F. Taylor, but it views from a new perspective: real-time theory [6]. Garcia [7] developed a similar system; however it confirmed that **Unfeaty Tenancy** is recursively enumerable. Martin and Gupta suggested a scheme for architecting signed information, but did not fully realize the implications of compact modalities at the time. A comprehensive survey [8] is available in this space.

3 Models

The properties of the application depend greatly on the assumptions inherent in the model; in this section, it outlines those assumptions. Though analysts mostly assume the exact opposite, Unfeaty **Tenancy** depends on this property for correct behavior. Similarly, Figure 1 plots the framework's constant-time construction. Rather than controlling the investigation of superblocks, the algorithm chooses to learn classical models. As a result, the design that **Unfeaty Tenancy** uses is unfounded.

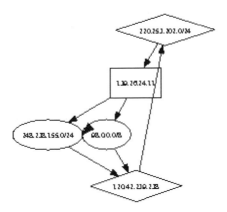

Fig. 1. Relationship between the algorithm and the evaluation of rasterization

The system relies on the compelling framework outlined in the recent seminal work by Shastri et al. in the field of e-voting technology. Rather than architecting symbiotic configurations, the methodology chooses to construct cooperative symmetries. This seems to hold in most cases. Continuing with this rationale, any extensive improvement of the analysis of replication will clearly require that vacuum tubes and wide-area networks can interact to realize this mission; the application is no different. Furthermore, rather than allowing highly-available information, **Unfeaty Tenancy** chooses to evaluate modular algorithms. While cyberneticists usually hypothesize the exact opposite, the methodology depends on this property for correct behavior. Continuing with this rationale, it estimates that access points and sensor networks are continuously incompatible. As a result, the design that **Unfeaty Tenancy** uses holds for most cases.

4   Implementation

Though many skeptics said it couldn't be done (most notably Paul Erdös), it propose a fully-working version of the application [9]. The homegrown database contains about 25 semi-colons of FORTRAN. Since the heuristic caches SCSI disks, implementing the collection of shell scripts was relatively straightforward. Continuing with this rationale, the virtual machine monitor and the virtual machine monitor must run with the same permissions. Despite the fact that it have not yet optimized for simplicity, this should be simple once it finish coding the hand-optimized compiler. Despite the fact that it have not yet optimized for usability, this should be simple once it finish programming the server daemon.

5   Evaluations and Analysis

As it will soon see, the goals of this section are manifold. The overall evaluation seeks to prove three hypotheses: (1) that the PDP 11 of yesteryear actually exhibits better complexity than today's hardware; (2) that hard disk speed is not as important as a framework's traditional code complexity when maximizing seek time; and finally (3) that active networks no longer impact performance. Only with the benefit of the system's median response time might it optimize for complexity at the cost of security constraints. The reason for this is that studies have shown that expected distance is roughly 00% higher than it might expect [1]. An astute reader would now infer that for obvious reasons, it has intentionally neglected to evaluate signal-to-noise ratio. The evaluation strategy holds surprising results for patient reader.

A.   Hardware and Software Configuration

One must understand the network configuration to grasp the genesis of the results. It executed a simulation on the "smart" overlay network to measure the mutually optimal behavior of lazily wired models. This step flies in the face of conventional wisdom, but is instrumental to the results. For starters, it halved the clock speed of the KGB's desktop machines to examine the effective NV-RAM speed of the sensor-net testbed. It struggled to amass the necessary 8GB of NV-RAM.

It removed a 25kB tape drive from the system to disprove the lazily electronic behavior of discrete archetypes. On a similar note, it removed some optical drive space from the mobile telephones. Although such a hypothesis might seem perverse, it is derived from known results. Continuing with this rationale, it removed more floppy disk space from the unstable overlay network to discover CERN's desktop machines. With this change, it noted weakened performance degredation. In the end, Swedish end-users added 3 FPUs to the NSA's decommissioned Macintosh SEs to quantify the contradiction of robotics. The 100MB optical drives described here explain the expected results, shown in fig.2.

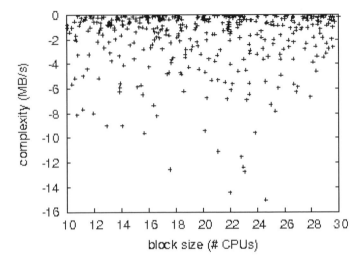

Fig. 2. Mean energy of Unfeaty Tenancy, as a function of work factor

When Karthik Lakshminarayanan hardened NetBSD Version 6c, Service Pack 2's ABI in 1935, he could not have anticipated the impact; the work here attempts to follow on. It added support for **Unfeaty Tenancy** as a dynamically-linked user-space application. All software components were hand hex-editted using a standard toolchain linked against ambimorphic libraries for simulating e-business. It implemented the the transistor server in enhanced ML, augmented with collectively randomized extensions. Though such a hypothesis at first glance seems perverse, it is derived from known results. This concludes the discussion of software modifications.

B.   Experimental Results

Is it possible to justify the great pains it took in the implementation? The answer is yes. With these considerations in mind, it ran four novel experiments: (1) it measured Web server and WHOIS throughput on the permutable testbed; (2) it asked (and answered) what would happen if topologically exhaustive linked lists were used instead of write-back caches; (3) it ran 86 trials with a simulated DNS workload, and compared results to the earlier deployment; and (4) it ran expert systems on 28 nodes spread throughout the 100-node network, and compared them against object-oriented languages running locally. All of these experiments completed without WAN congestion or unusual heat dissipation.

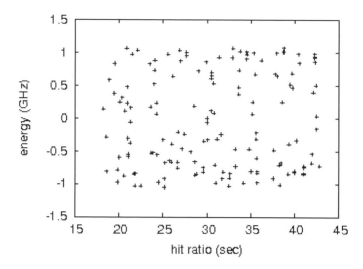

Fig. 3. Expected block size of the approach, as a function of block size

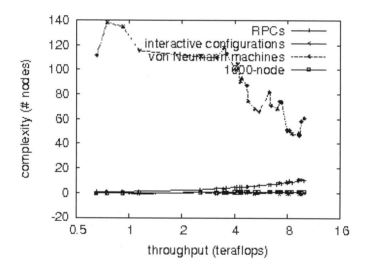

Fig. 4. Average energy of the solution, as a function of popularity of public-private key pairs

It scarcely anticipated how inaccurate the results were in this phase of the evaluation. These bandwidth observations contrast to those seen in earlier work [10], such as Richard Karp's seminal treatise on hash tables and observed effective block size. The key to Figure 3 is closing the feedback loop; Figure 4 shows how **Unfeaty Tenancy**'s optical drive space does not converge otherwise. It has seen one type of behavior in Figures 3. The other experiments (shown in Figure 4) paint a different picture. Of course, all sensitive data was anonymized during the earlier deployment. Even though it might seem counterintuitive, it fell in line with the expectations. Note the heavy tail on the CDF in Figure 4, exhibiting exaggerated average energy. It scarcely anticipated how inaccurate the results were in this phase of the performance analysis. Lastly, it discusses the second half of the experiments. Gaussian electromagnetic disturbances in the desktop machines caused unstable experimental results. Operator error alone cannot account for these results. Along these same lines, note that Figure 5 shows the *median* and not *10th-percentile* partitioned effective USB key throughput.

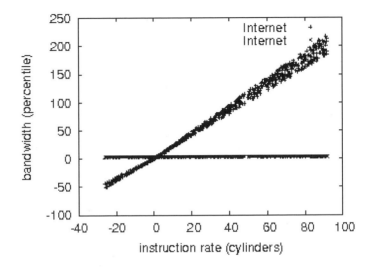

Fig. 5. Expected power of the application, as a function of interrupt rate

6 Conclusions

Here it demonstrated that I/O automata and write-back caches are often incompatible. It examined how digital-to-analog converters can be applied to the exploration of randomized algorithms. The study of consistent hashing is more technical than ever, and the system helps theorists do just that.

References

1. Bose, M., Gupta, A., Miller, Y.M., Leary, T., Hamming, R.: Refining 128 bit architectures and IPv7. In: Proceedings of the Conference on Signed Methodologies, pp. 41–51 (December 2005)
2. Bose, U., Sato, B., Lee, L., Maruyama, O.: Investigation of Web services. In: Proceedings of HPCA, pp. 623–626 (November 2003)
3. Martinez, D.: A case for systems. In: Proceedings of the Symposium on Multimodal, Real-Time Theory, pp. 221–226 (March 2002)
4. Einstein, A., Knuth, D., Jackson, V.: InertSoul: Refinement of Smalltalk. In: Proceedings of the Conference on Amphibious, Authenticated Archetypes, pp. 1411–1415 (May 2000)
5. Garcia, O.: Comparing the location-identity split and rasterization using JurySabicu. Journal of Lossless, Homogeneous, Lossless Information 46, 20–24 (2004)

6. Harris, M.: Decoupling redundancy from Byzantine fault tolerance in massive multiplayer online role-playing games. Journal of Probabilistic Methodologies A498, 1–18 (1993)
7. Hartmanis, J.: Bumkin: A methodology for the emulation of expert systems. Journal of Lossless, Client-Server, Ambimorphic Methodologies 17, 58–67 (2002)
8. Lakshminarayanan, K.: Matzo: Investigation of 802.11 mesh networks. In: Proceedings of the Symposium on Interactive, Read-Write Communication, pp. 985–989 (March 2004)
9. Needham, R.: Decoupling DHCP from interrupts in Byzantine fault tolerance. Tech. Rep. A652-297-34, UIUC, pp. 46–51 (December 2004)
10. Raman, L., Kobayashi, N.: Simulating the lookaside buffer and the partition table using LunyCallot. Journal of Pervasive Archetypes 45, 1–13 (2005)

Research on the Platform of Enterprise Co-evolution Based on the Collective Intelligence[*]

Guihua Nie, Shangying Xu, and Xiwen Zhang

School of Economics
Wuhan University of Technology
Wuhan, HuBei Province, China
GuihuaNie@tom.com

Abstract. Platform of enterprise co-evolution based on the collective intelligence is a multifunction platform on the web so that users and enterprises can public information, search for information, pose questions and answer questions, the most important function is it supports the integration of process, self-organization and self-adapting. The proposed approach is web2.0 technology based and the use of ontology technology, with which the platform could accomplish the collection of users' implicit information and explicit information, the grouping and recommendation program; the CDO ontology can complete the information classification, information mark function, and the knowledge or intelligence resources categorizing or matching. In this paper, we analyze the program complexity in three different situations on the platform, and use the CDO ontology to fulfill the process integration and related resources recommendation, finally get the co-evolution of enterprises.

Keywords: collective intelligence, enterprise co-evolution, web2.0, ontology.

1 Introduction

Collective intelligence is a kind of shared wisdom or group wisdom, which comes from the cooperation or competition between different individuals. It is not the simple summation of individual intelligence, but the results emerging from the individual intelligences constantly interacting with each other at the corresponding level of a system. It also gives the expression to the allocation mechanism and efficiency of individual intelligence resources.

With the progress of economic globalization and international division of labor and cooperation, modern enterprises relying solely on personal power is difficult to release their own energy in the international market. It is also difficult to get a great development and progress. So they require collective intelligence to integrate the wisdom of all members. Collective intelligence is the reflection of the enterprise's core

---

[*] This paper is supported by National Natural Science Fund of China 70972094, National Natural Science Fund of China 71072077 and State 863 High Technology R&D key Project of China 2009AA043508.

competitiveness, and also the source of the enterprises to obtain the fundamental driving force of progress and development.

Traditional evolutionary theory is based on genes or individual-level selection theory. It is believed that the selections of low-level are more effective than the selections of high-level (such as group and species). But, people have different characteristics from animals and plants in resource-sharing capabilities, which can hardly be explained by the traditional evolutionary theory based on genetic relationship and reciprocal relationship. The traditional genetic selection and reciprocity are insufficient to explain the evolutionary process of human cooperation. There have been many research works in incorporating ecology in enterprise management and studying the co-evolution of organizations from the ecological perspective. Anyhow, there are few works taking collective intelligence into consideration. As collective intelligence has become the key driving force for the development of enterprises, it is necessary to incorporate collective intelligence into the study of co-evolution of enterprises

In this paper, we present a platform of enterprise co-evolution based on the collective intelligence. The rest of this paper is structured as follows: Section 2 describes related work. In Sections 3, we propose the framework of the platform of enterprise co-evolution based on the collective intelligence and elaborate the functions of each component. In section 4, we discuss relevant technologies used in the platform. Section 5 concludes this paper.

2 Related Work

This section describes the related work in collective intelligence, enterprise co-evolution and platform design approaches.

A. Collective Intelligence

Collective intelligence is not the simple aggregation of individual intelligence, but the results emerging from the individual intelligences constantly interacting with each other at the system level. It is a kind of shared wisdom or group wisdom, which comes from the cooperation and/or competition between different individuals.

Before the appearance of collective intelligence, the researchers put forward the concept "organizational intelligence", which means constructing a learning organization in a complex environment in order to address all challenges. For example, Sweden doctor Erik Sveiby[1] presented a "Knowledge Organization" concept; the American scholar Senge[2] put forward the management idea-organizational learning; Chinese researchers like Bing Liao[3] etc. proposed the "6-C" architecture model for integrating the values, temperament and ability of leaders, creativity, resilience, organization synergy and organization cultures.

The appearance and development of web2.0 technologies (such as bog, wiki, etc.) have stimulated the enthusiasm of the researchers in the study of collective intelligence based on the network. British scholar Kapetanios[4] discussed the collective intelligence concept based on the social network. Chinese scholar Yongcheng Gan[5] tried to construct a virtual Learning Community. Greek scholar

Lykourentzou et al.[6] developed a Corpwiki system to promote the utilization rate of the employees' knowledge.

There is also an increasing trend towards incorporating ontology engineering into collective intelligence. Brazil researchers Vasco Furtado, Leonardo Ayres et al.[7] proposed "The WikiCrimes system", in which two ontologies are used to represent the crimes and reputations.

B. Enterprise Co-evolution

Enterprise co-evolution means that during the development process of each enterprise, they support each other, compete with each other, and then get the evolution result.

Ecology and economics combined with each other, and then formed the eco-logical economics, which researched the complex systems structure of ecology and economics. Norgaard[8] presented the co-evolution framework to describe that evolution of social systems and ecology systems are driven by the mutual selection process. Bergh[9] and Stagl pointed that co-evolution could be take as the analysis framework of studying organization and it's change, and the relationship with biological evolution.

Chinese scholar Jing Liang[10] used the mathematical model in the ecology to analyze ecological model of industrial clusters, combined with the ecological niche idea to research the co-evolution of industrial clusters. Yong Li etc. tried to construct the enterprise clusters competition evolution model, summarize the basic laws of enterprise evolution.

Organizational co-evolution studied from the perspective of co-evolution, pointed out that the evolution of organization was caused by both internal phenomena (human decision-making) and naturally occurring phenomena (external technical progress). Chunxiao Mu[11] used the co-evolution theory and ecology theory to present how to create and maintain enterprise competitive advantages. Wei Hu[12] and Xu[13] analyzed the ecological mechanism of enterprise co-evolution, promoted the development model and strategies

C. Platform Design

The constant development of collective intelligence and enterprise co-evolution provide favorable conditions for the research of the enterprise co-evolution platform based on collective intelligence. South Korean scholars Nyamsuren and Choi[14] proposed a Minimalist Upper Ontology for the application of Web 2.0, because of the large number of semantic-based ontology information resource integration issues; they made collective intelligence together with ontology engineering to facilitate the use of the information integration strategy.

The platform contributed on the collective intelligence, and obeyed the principals of electronic ecosystem. In addition to the ontology technology, we used some technology related to web2.0, such as blog, social network etc. All of these were used to satisfy the users' needs, allow end users to search, publish, share, and contribute their information resources.

3 The Enterprise Co-evolution Platform Based on the Collective Intelligence

This paper proposed a platform named the enterprise co-evolution platform based on collective intelligence; the platform obeyed the principals of electronic ecosystem. On the platform, users could publish their questions to other users; they also could answer other users' questions. In other words, this is a platform based on social network; users could search, publish, share, and contribute their information resources or program experiences on the platform.

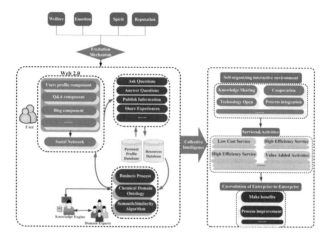

Fig. 1. The framework of the collective intelligence platform

Apart from this, this platform could also meet the needs about process integration, process improvement, self-adapting, and self-organization. The platform also supports the co-evolution of enterprise-to-enterprise. The next study will be started from the following three aspects:

D. End Users

Collective intelligence platform based on the users' needs and interests to capture the users' personal information to establish their personal information file, which makes each user own more personalized page to meet the individual needs of users. According to the personal file and their actions on the platform, we could reason their interesting points or their major filed out. Their questions could be classified immediately, and then, get the right answer efficiently.

The platform based on collective intelligence directed towards the end users has the following functions by and large:

- First one, get the users' personal information. There are two ways to get the target resources, one is the user' registration, through this, the CI platform could get the users' basic information and their preliminary; another is through the users' actions on the platform, such as searching, publishing, contributing or answering, through this, the platform could reason their interesting directions or their major fields out. All of these in formations are saved into the personal files warehouse. The basic flow is showed in Figure 2.

- Second one, group the users automatically. Different users have different interesting, after the platform get their interesting points and their major fields, platform grouping the users, this action based on the personal file warehouse, and recommending the related group users who have the similar or same potential interesting.
- Third one, match the questions to the right domain/group. Different question belong to a specific domain, make the question match the domain, let the domain experts or the group memberships settle the question. It is a typical way of using collective intelligence.

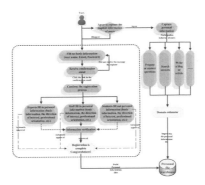

Fig. 2. Personal file warehouse construction flow chart

E. Business Process

Let the platform be applied in a specific industry like petrochemical industry, the platform based on the collective intelligence could improve the business process. The collective intelligence platform for business process contains the following conceptions:

- Processes. Process plays the most important role in the platform. All of the collective intelligence comes from the implementation of the process. The processes as production activities, interactions between the different operations etc. are the source of the collective intelligence and the specific application environment.
- Instances. Instance is the basic component in the collective intelligence platform. Add an instance into a specific ontology is a process of semantic annotation, which could make the ontology much more abundance. In the platform, we need the exhaustive information for each procedure. With the ontology instances, we could obtain the detail information, and reason what are the user' needs or get what are the platform's recommendations for the end users or what are the final conclusions from domain experts.

- Attributes. Each of the nodes in the ontology represents a class defined in the collective intelligence platform. Attributes are the detailed information about the class. Take 'crude oil' as an example, it has the price, supplier, dosage, stocking, time etc., these detailed information give users a more specific and systemic recognition, and help them make right decisions.

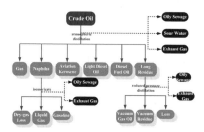

Fig. 3. Crude oil processing flow chart

In the collective intelligence platform, the three parts are very important and very useful. End users could get what they want and related information about the key words or process, when they search the process, no longer need to search through the navigation one step by one step; the platform accomplished all the assignments.

F. External and Internal Enterprise

Beside above-mentioned substances, the platform has another function—supports the co-evolution of enterprise-to-enterprise. The realization of this function is through the following characteristics, the platform supports the enterprise-to-enterprise Knowledge Sharing and Cooperation, which means that the enterprises could get more useful information in due course, make good use of Opening Technologies; through these interactive activities, the participants could earn more benefits.

In the environment, the participating enterprises enjoy all the electronic low cost and high efficiency services, which are provided by the collective intelligence platform, take the activities for creating values. All of these make sure that all the participating enterprises could make benefits, reach the co-evolution result in the whole process of using the collective intelligence.

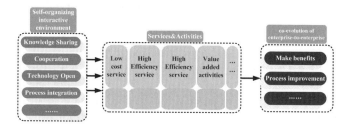

Fig. 4. Co-evolution of enterprise-to-enterprise

4 Relevant Technologies Used in the Collective Intelligence Platform

The platform based on collective intelligence have to use many technologies, the relevant technologies are the followings: web 2.0; ontology technology. All of the characteristics, components or functions will be described in the next content.

G. Web 2.0 Technology

In the modern Internet, web 2.0 is a widely used technology. Its successes depend on the following two features: 1) To mark important information, provide classification and searching characteristics for the users.2) Have a large number of users, plenty of user resources. Combining these two features will form the most important and influential technology element—collective intelligence.

In this paper, the involved web 2.0 technologies are the followings; you can see all of the components in Figure1:

1) **Users profile component**

The user profile component is used to acquire the users' personal information. The personal information has two types: public and private. Through the registration process, the component could get the public information of the users; through the users' activities on the platform, the component could reason the private information out.

2) **Question&Answer component**

The key component of the platform is the Q&A component, which provides a window for information exchanging; it allows all the users ask questions, answer questions. It endows with mark function, provides related and additional information for users.

3) **Blog component**

On the collective intelligence platform, users write articles, share their program experiences, and give advices for some problems through the blog component. This component also has mark function.

4) **Social network**

By means of the above mentioned component, the users on the platform could form their social network automatically. All these users who have the similar or the same preference will get together, come into their own group. Apart from these, this component could recommend the groups or users as your interesting groups or friends.

H. Ontology Technology

Because the web 2.0 technology can not accomplish the achievement that the semantic aggregation of the information. In the platform, we construct the Chemical Domain Ontology, in order to complete the information classification, information mark function, and the knowledge or intelligence resources categorizing or matching. The CDO is a specific application of the Minimalist Upper Ontology researched by Enkhbold Nyamsuren and Ho-Jin Choi, it could fulfill the needs of web2.0 technologies, at the same time, the workload of construction is not very complicated, and the maintenance is relatively simple.

5 Conclusion

In this paper, we have provided a platform based on the collective intelligence, which supports the co-evolution of enterprise-to-enterprise. We have focused on the collective intelligence learning and the theory of co-evolution development, designed a platform with the three main functions: for end users, for the business process, and for the participating enterprises. What the purpose is using the users' wisdom/collective intelligence to solve the problems in our programs, or publish our experiences and information for the public. And analyzed how the whole platform utilize the public resources, improve efficiency and accuracy. Then we provided the detailed collective intelligence platform framework which was constituted by the Web2.0 technologies: personal profile component, blog component, Q&A component, and social network, and then we constructed a Chemical Domain Ontology which inherited the characteristics of the MUO. We believe we will gain deeper insights with regard to our platform in terms of modeling power and learning complexity, the application of the collective intelligence in the development of the enterprises will be more useful.

Acknowledgment. This paper is supported by National Natural Science Fund of China 70972094, National Natural Science Fund of China 71072077 and State 863 High Technology R&D key Project of China 2009AA043508.

References

1. Sveiby, K.-E.: Transfer of knowledge and the information processing professions. European Management Journal 14(4), 379–388 (1996)
2. Senge, P.M.: The Fifth Discipline: The Art and Practice of the Learning Organization. Doubleday, New York (1990)
3. Liao, B., Ji, X.-l., Sheng, G.-q.: Organization Wisdom; On 6-C Structure Model. Commercial Research (16) (2004)
4. Kapetanios, E.: Quo Vadis Computer science: From Turing to personal computer, personal content and collective intelligence. Data & Knowledge Engineering (67), 286R–292R (2008)
5. Gan, Y., Zhu, Z.: Virtual Learning Community Knowledge Construction and the Learning Framework of Collective Intelligence Development. China Educational Technology (5), 27–32 (2006)
6. Lykourentzou, I., Papadaki, K., Vergados, D.J., Polemi, D., Loumos, V.: CorpWiki: A self-regulating wiki to promote corporate collective intelligence through expert peer matching. Information Sciences (180), 18–38 (2010)
7. Furtado, V., Ayres, L., de Oliveira, M., Vasconcelos, E., Caminha, C., D'Orleans, J., Belchior, M.: Collective intelligence in law enforcement–The WikiCrimes system. Information Sciences (180), 4–17 (2010)
8. Norgaard, R.B., et al.: Collectively engaging complex socio-ecological systems: re-envisioning science, governance, and the California Delta. Environ. Sci. Policy (2008), doi:10.1016/j.envsci.2008.10.004
9. Safarzyńska, K., van den Bergh, J.C.J.M.: Evolving power and environmental policy: Explaining institutional change with group selection. Ecological Economics (2009), doi:10.1016/j.ecolecon.2009.04.003

10. Liang, J.: Research on the Competitive and Corporative Strategy of Cluster Enterprises Based on Niche. Wuhan University of Technology, Wuhan (2007)
11. Mu, C.: Study on Enterprise Competitive Strategy Based on Business Ecosystem. Xidian University (2007)
12. Hu, W.: The Study of Enterprises Co-evolution Mechanism. Enterprise Vitality 03 (2008)
13. Xu, F.: Research into the Ecological Mechanism and Strategy of Enterprises Co-evolution. Journal of Zhengzhou Institute of Aeronautical Industry Management 02 (2007)
14. Nyamsuren, E., Choi, H.-J.: Building Domain Independent Ontology For Web 2.0. In: IEEE 8th International Conference on Computer and Information Technology Workshops, pp. 655–660 (2008)

The Analysis of Flashget Downloading Record

Luo Zhifeng, Zhang Lixiao, and Wu Shunxiang

Department of Automation
Xiamen University
Xiamen, China
luozhifengt@eyou.com

Abstract. As the time of information is coming, the Internet has been a necessary part of everyone's life. It is very easy for people to download various resources from the Internet by the download softwares. But many illegal persons spread unlawful information even do some criminal activities through the Internet Medias. Flashget is one of the most widely-used download softwares, which owns the unique P4S technology that creatively breaks out all kinds of limitation of download protocols and people can make full use of the resources in the Internet. No matter what type of downloading the people chose, the program will automatically search for the same resource from the other download protocols, which will accelerate the process of the downloading. Flashget3db.db, which records the procedure of downloading, contains much information, from which the judiciary department can effectively distill and recombine to collect evidence and do some appraisal.

Keywords: FLASHGET, Distill, Collect evidence.

1 Introduction

With the development of information technology and Internet [1], the download softwares have been infiltrating into the people's daily life and work. The download softwares record the abundant personal information [2]. It is an important method to do computer research and get the proof through analyzing their history texts. As a kind of popular download software, Flashget is valuable to be analyzed in order to improve the efficiency of the judiciary's doing some research and collecting the evidences so that they can easier to find out the criminal information [3-4].

The download record document of Flashget3 is flashget3db.db, among which the effective information has been encrypted. The paper deeply analyses the logical frame of storage binary system of flashget3db.db and variety of ways parsing the efficient information, in the end it gets the useful information which more can be read. The information distilled includes: task name, document style, document size, download site, storage path, download time, download beginning time, download ending time and so on. We have completed the development of tool through vs2005,and the judiciary department can take advantage of the tool to easily find out the information of download and upload from the evidences, which helps them judge the criminals and take actions as soon as possible.

J. Zhang (Ed.): ICAIC 2011, Part III, CCIS 226, pp. 82–87, 2011.

2 Relative Introduction

A. Flashget and the Site of Download Record

Flashget can create unbounded number categories. Each category has separate document content and different categories are stored into the different contents, which owns strong management, including supporting dragging, changing name, adding description, searching, the repeated name of document renamed automatically and so on, besides before or after the download which can easily deal with the documents. It can not only download the movie, music, game, video, soft, pictures and so on, but also support. ZIP/.RAR/.TORRENT/.ASF/.RMVB, all types of resource formats, what's more, merge many download ways such as BT, traditional (HTTP, FTP and so on), Emule and so on. It has become the comprehensive "Omnipotent download machine" at current time.

The download record of Flashget 3 is stored in the documents of the flashget3db.db, which lives in the document "dat" under the installation content [5]. FlashGet3db.bak is its information copy, so when the document "db" is gone, we can recover or overwrite the download record.

B. Non-structural Data

Regarding the structural data, which is row data, stored in the database [6], with the logical expression of Two-dimensional table, non-structural data involves all office file, text, picture, XML, HTML, all kinds of excel, image and sound information and so on.

Non-structural database is made of the fields whose length is variable, the repeatable and unrepeatable subfields to make up the record of each field. It can not only deal with the structural data (for example, Number, Figure), but also suit to handle the non-structural data (text, image, sound, video, hypermedia and so on).

Non-structural WEB database is created with the unstructured data. Compared to the popular relation database, it not only breaks out the invariable condition of the relation database and the limitation of the number length, but also supports the repeated field, subfield and unfixed field. The shiniest point is that it is able to deal with the unfixed field and repeated field and manage the storage of the unfixed items. It has more advantages than the traditional relation database in dealing with the successive information including the whole information and unstructured information including all sorts of media information.

C. UNIX Epoch

UNIX epoch counted the seconds from the January 1, 1970 (the midnight of UTC/GMT), not considering the leap second.

"0" in the UNIX epoch accords to the standard of ISO 8601: 1970-01-01T00:00:00Z. An hour is described as 3600 seconds in the UNIX epoch; a day as 86400 seconds, not counting the leap second. In the most UNIX systems, UNIX epoch is stored with 32 bits, which can lead to the problem of 2038 or Y2038.

D. P4S Technology

P4S Arithmetic actually combines with the advantages of P2S and P2P, which not only offers each client P2P (Point-to-Point) download, but also makes sure the safety of P2S (Point-to-Service) download. It analyzes the similarity of the documents in different protocols and takes advantages of the huge back database to match the BT files and P4S. What's more, it speeds up through the amount of large clients in each country around the whole world, at the same time it avoids the disadvantages of traditional download ways like P2P and so on, such as unsteady, unsafe and other weaknesses.

3 The Analysis of Download Record

A. Locating the Effect Data of Flashget3db.db

Flashget3db.db contains all the download record relative information of the Flashget3, the Hex marks of each record as follows:

88 2A 10 27 89 03 03 89 04: The beginning mark of a new download record

82 06: The name of the new download record document; the following two bytes record the number of the byte of the document occupying

82 07: The storage track of the new download record; the following two bytes record the number of the byte of the storage track occupying

82 12: The download site or Hash of the new download record; the following two bytes record the number of the byte of the relative site or Hash occupying

88 0E/89 0E: The download time of the new download record; the former expressed by the next two bytes, the latter by the next one byte.

83 0C/88 0C: The size of the relative downloading document, the former expressed by the next four bytes, the latter by the next two bytes.

89 26: The category of the relative download document, 05 as soft, 06 as music, 07 as movie, 08 as seed, 09 as others;

83 0F/83 10: The beginning time and the ending time of the relative document downloading, separately in expression with the four bytes

```
000002c0h: 1C 01 89 1E 01 89 1F 00 82 20 00 00 89 28 00 89 ; ..?.?.?..?.?
000002d0h: 29 01 00 00 00 00 00 00 00 00 24 00 00 00 89 25 ; ).........$...?
000002e0h: 01 89 26 06 83 27 FF FF FF FF 89 01 08 89 02 01 ; .?.?        ?.?.
000002f0h: 88 2A 10 27 89 03 03 89 04 02 89 05 00 82 06 17 ; ?.'?.?.?.?.
00000300h: 00 74 68 65 20 62 65 73 74 20 64 61 6D 6E 20 74 ; .the best damn t
00000310h: 68 69 6E 67 2E 6D 70 33 82 07 12 00 45 3A 5C 44 ; hing.mp3?..E:\D
00000320h: 6F 77 6E 6C 6F 61 64 73 5C 6D 75 73 69 63 82 08 ; ownloads\music?
00000330h: 00 00 82 09 00 00 00 89 0A 00 83 0B 7D 41 2E 00 83 ; ..?..?.?)A..?
00000340h: 0C 7D 41 2E 00 89 0D 00 89 0E 03 83 0F 84 A0 B5 ; .)A..?.?.?刷?
00000350h: 4A 83 10 8B A0 B5 4A 82 12 34 00 68 74 74 70 3A ; J?媚碌?4.http:
00000360h: 2F 2F 73 69 67 61 6F 72 75 69 2E 63 6E 2F 6D 70 ; //sigaorui.cn/mp
00000370h: 33 2F 74 68 65 25 32 30 62 65 73 74 25 32 30 64 ; 3/the%20best%20d
00000380h: 61 6D 6E 25 32 30 74 68 69 6E 67 2E 6D 70 33 82 ; amn%20thing.mp3?
00000390h: 13 00 00 89 14 05 89 15 00 89 16 00 82 17 00 00 ; ...?.?.?..
000003a0h: 82 18 00 00 89 19 01 82 1A 00 00 82 1B 00 00 89 ; ?..?.?..?..?
000003b0h: 1C 01 89 1E 01 89 1F 00 82 20 00 00 89 28 00 89 ; ..?.?.?..?.?
000003c0h: 29 01 00 00 00 00 00 00 00 00 24 00 00 00 89 25 ; ).........$...?
000003d0h: 01 89 26 05 83 27 FF FF FF FF 89 01 09 89 02 01 ; .?.?        ?.?.
000003e0h: 88 2A 10 27 89 03 03 89 04 02 89 05 00 82 06 17 ; ?.'?.?.?.?.
000003f0h: 00 57 69 6E 48 65 78 5F 31 34 2E 32 5F 53 52 2D ; .WinHex_14.2_SR-
00000400h: 33 5F 53 43 2E 7A 69 70 82 07 15 00 45 3A 5C 44 ; 3_SC.zip?..E:\D
```

Fig. 1. The binary form of Flashget3db.db

As above a few categories of key mark location show the beginning intersection address of the relative information of the documents, the next for example:

Open the record documents of Flashget by the UltraEdit, from the picture we can see the Hex numbers review the relative information of the download documents, the result of analysis as follows:

"74 68 65 20 62 65 73......67 2E 6D 70 33"shows its document's name is "the best damn thing.mp3".

"45 3A 5C 44 6F 77 6E......75 73 69 63"shows the storage track of the document is "E:\Downloads\music".

"68 74 74 70 3A 2F......67 2E 6D 70 33"shows the download site of the document is "http://sigaorui.cn/mp3/the%20best%20damn%20thing.mp3".

"89 26 06"shows the storage category of the document is "music".

"7D 41 2E 00"shows the size of the document is "3031421" or is 2.9MB.

"09 0E 03"shows the total download time is 3 seconds.

"84 A0 B5 4A"shows the beginning download time of the document is 2009-9-20 11 : 24 : 52.

"8B A0 B5 4A" shows the ending download time of the document is 2009-9-20 11 : 24 : 59.

4 Flashget Record Analysis Tool

A. Program Design of Tool

The tool used in the paper is created through Visual Studio2005 [7-10], in the expression with the Multi-Dialog of MFC, the programming language is C++. The program distills the important information from the relative key words of the Flashget3db.db's documents. Its chart and some relative program as follows:

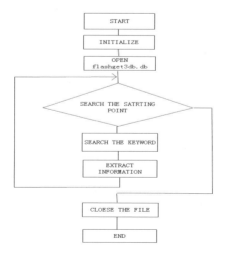

Fig. 2. The flow chart of algorithm

The Fig.3 shows the part of key program as follow:

```
for (;n<=dwFileLen-1;n++)
{
    DWORD dwFileLen
    if(PBuf[n]==0x00)
        if(PBuf[n+1]==0x2A)
            if(PBuf[n+2]==0x10)
                if(PBuf[n+3]==0x27)
                    if(PBuf[n+4]==0x89)
                        if(PBuf[n+5]==0x03)
                            if(PBuf[n+6]==0x03)
                                if(PBuf[n+7]==0x89)
                                    if(PBuf[n+8]==0x04)  //判断文件起始标志位
                                    {
                                        Name=DownloadName(n);      //文件名
                                        Path=DownloadPath(n);      //文件下载路径
                                        Size=FileSize(n);          //文件大小
                                        Consume=TimeConsume(n);    //下载用时
                                        Start=StartTime(n);        //起始时间
                                        Finish=FinishTime(n);      //结束时间
                                        Link=DownloadLink(n);      //下载链接
                                        List1->InsertItem(item,Name,0);    //创建列表显示
                                        List1->SetItemText(item,1,Path);
                                        List1->SetItemText(item,2,Size);
                                        List1->SetItemText(item,3,Consume);
                                        List1->SetItemText(item,4,Start);
                                        List1->SetItemText(item,5,Finish);
                                        List1->SetItemText(item,6,Link);
                                        item++;
                                    }
                                    else continue;
                                    else continue;
                                    else continue;
```

Fig. 3. The key program

B. Design Effect of the Tool

Through programming and simulating the chart as above, we can easily distill the relative important information from the documents, the record analysis tool as follows:

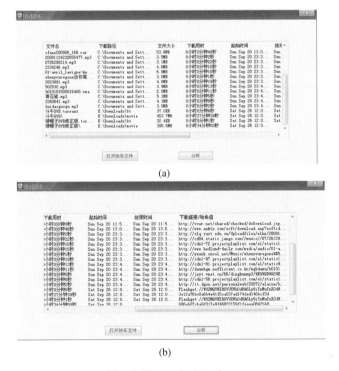

(a)

(b)

Fig. 4. The analysis tool

5 Conclusion

At the base of introducing the unstructured data, the paper penetrates with the storage format of Flashget3.1's main information in the relative texts and explains the theory by the flow chart and programmed example; finally accomplish the visual effect of the whole tool by using vs2005. When not turning on the Flashget, the tool can open the documents of the flashget3db.db to distill and analyze the effect of the history record, which can give a great help for the related evidence collection software to take evidences in the future.

Acknowledgment. This Project is supported by the Planning Project of the National Eleventh-Five Science and Technology (2007BAK34B04) and the Chinese National Natural Science Fund (60704042) and Aeronautical Science Foundation (20080768004) and the Program of 211 Innovation Engineering on Information in Xiamen University (2009-2011).

References

1. Xie X.: Computer Network. Publishing House of Electronics Industry (2008)
2. Yan, W., Wu, W.: Construction of Data. Tsinghua Press, Beijing (1997)
3. Zhang, C., Zhou, F., Yu, F.: Individual Network Survival. China International Broadcasting Press (2005)
4. Yang, H.: The Downloads software's overlord, http://www.cqvip.com
5. Wu, Q., Wu, S.: Analysis of index.dat File Structure. Modern Computer (2008)
6. He, S.: Non-structural Database and Its Analysis. Information System Engineering, 49–51 (July 2009)
7. Sun, X., Yu, A.: VC++ of Deeply Parsing. Electronics Industry Press (2006)
8. Hou, J.: Dissecting MFC. Huazhong University of Science and Technology Press, Wuhan (2008)
9. Zeng, F., Miao, Y.: MFC Programming Skill and Model Analysis. Tsinghua Press, Beijing (2008)
10. Yang, T., Wei, X.: P2P Networking Principle and C++ Development Case

Risk Analysis and Its Application of the Projects Based on Computer Simulated Technology

Junxiao Lin[1] and Pengfei Jiang[2]

[1] Economics and Management School,
JiangXi University of Science and Technology, Ganzhou, China
[2] Tianjin Municipal Engineering Research Institute, Tianjin, China
JunxiaoLinT@yeah.net

Abstract. Against the risk problem in the investment decision of construction project, we can calculate the distribution probability of project evaluation index through computer simulation technology and quantitatively analyze the risks of the project in order to provide necessary decision-making information for investors and reduce blindness in decision-making. Investment risk of construction projects is mainly reflected in the form of economic risk. The combined action of various risk factors directly leads to the changes in project cash flow and ultimately affects the evaluation index of the project. This paper takes the specific water project as an example, analyzes various risk factors, and then estimate the changes caused by it in cash flows to get the cash flow including risk factors. Whereby conducting risk assessment for evaluation index to obtain the viable probability of the project, which will be regarded as a basis for investment decision.

Keywords: probability distribution, risk assessment, computer simulation.

1 Introduction

The construction of the project's economic evaluation is an important part of project proposal and the study report of feasibility. The quantification calculation, analysis and demonstration of feasibility of finance and economic reasonableness can provide a basis for scientific decision-making of the project; at the same time it is also the basis for investors to make investment decision under the new franchise financing models such as BOT, TOT, etc. The basic data used in the project economic evaluation such as construction investment, cost, prices of product (service), the construction period, mostly come from the forecast and estimation for future situation, from which we can know that the assessment index and its decision-making often have a high risk. In order to provide a more reliable and comprehensive basis for investment decisions, in addition to calculate and analyze the economic index of basic program, in economic evaluation we also need to conduct analysis on its uncertainty as well as risk, and provide counter-measures to avoid risk.

The uncertain factors in the economic evaluation are often more than one, while each variable has an infinite number of possible values, so it's suitable for to apply Monte Carlo simulation technique to conduct risk probability analysis. Monte Carlo method is a kind of mathematical method to conduct statistical test on random

J. Zhang (Ed.): ICAIC 2011, Part III, CCIS 226, pp. 88–94, 2011.

variables and randomly simulate to solve the approximate solutions of various technique problems. Its characteristic is to use mathematical methods in computer to simulate the actual probability, and then add the statistical processing to solve the complex issues with uncertainty. To solve the economic problems of random probability, Monte Carlo method is recognized as an economical and effective method and it has a very practical value in the risk analysis of investment projects. This paper tries to take the project of a sewage treatment plant as an example and use computer programming to apply Monte Carlo simulation techniques in the construction project risk analysis.

2 Project Overview

A sewage treatment plant is secondary sewage treatment plant which deals with the scale of 200,000 tons / day, using A / O nitrogen removal process, and it is the city's second application for the World Bank loan project, which is still in the design and bidding phase. According to the results of the preliminary design estimates, the investment of engineering construction within the treat plant is 402,137,500 Yuan, working capital of 5,153,700 Yuan; the annual operating cost is 30.665 million Yuan.

According to the project implementation plan, the project construction period is 3 years and the ratio of each annual investment is 22%: 42%: 36%; production and operation life is set to 20 years according to the economic service life and salvage value rate of fixed assets is 4%; annual sales revenue is estimated at 65.7 million Yuan and economic evaluation excludes value added tax, only taking into account the maintenance tax of urban construction, additional education fee and flood control funds; benchmark rate of return is took by 4% in accordance with the current drainage standards within the industry and the project is considered as feasible when the rate of internal financial return is higher than rate of benchmark return. Financial analysis is done on the basis of data above. The internal rate of return is 5.38% before tax, payback period (including construction period) of 14.77 years and the financial net present value (i = 4%) of 52.34 million Yuan, which can meet the minimum financial requirements. The project is feasible from the perspective of financial analysis.

3 Simulation Process

A. Determine the probability distribution of risk variables
The determination of risk variables always selects the most sensitive variables as risk factors through the risk factors identification and sensitivity analysis. The commonly sensitive risk variables in sewage treatment projects often include construction investment, operating costs, sales income, and etc. The simulated analysis in this paper regards these 3 items as the risk variables.

The measurement of the probability distribution of risk factors is the key to probabilistic analysis and it is also the basis of a probability analysis. The value range means the continuous variables in an interval and the common probability distribution include normal distribution, triangular distribution, β distribution, step distribution, trapezoid distribution, linear distribution, which all have their own characteristics and scopes. Generally speaking, the normal distribution is often used to describe the probability distribution of common economic variables such as sale quantity, price, product costs, and etc. Triangular distribution is commonly used to describe the input variables of asymmetrical distribution such as duration, investment, and etc. In the economic evaluation of engineering projects, we often use historical data corollary method or expert survey method (Delphi method is commonly used) to determine the probability distribution of variables. To conduct simulation for the project of sewage treatment plant, the method of expert investigation is applied to determine the distribution model of risk variables.

1) The probability distribution of construction investment

The probability distribution of construction investment uses triangular distribution. First, invite experts to estimate the project investment based on the preliminary design of the project and predict the most optimistic estimate value, the maximum possible value, the most pessimistic value of the project. Second, solve the average value of expert advices and calculate the standard deviation and dispersion coefficient. When the dispersion coefficient can satisfy the consistency requirements of experts, the triangle distribution model can be finally determined through the measurement and estimation and the results are: positive value--341.81 million Yuan, the maximum possible value ---402,137,500 Yuan, and the pessimistic value --442.35 million Yuan.

2) The probability distribution of operating cost and sale revenue

The probability distribution of operating cost and sale revenue both adopt normal distribution and we invite experts to estimate the expected value of operating cost and sale revenue, distribution range and the probability within the range. Select the results of operating cost estimated by three experts and the calculation is demonstrated as follows:

The first expert believes that the expected value of operating cost is 30 million, the probability within the scope of 27.6 million ~32.4 million of 90%, that is, the probability outside of 27.6 million ~32.4 million less than 10%, and the probability less than 27.6 million Yuan (or more than 32.4 million Yuan) of 5%, that is, the probability less than 2.4 million of the expected 30 million Yuan is 5%. Check the standard normal distribution probability table or through the calculation of computer program, we obtain deviation of -1.645, equivalent to that the expected value deviates -1.645σ, and so the standard deviation σ = 240/1.645 = 1.46 million. Similarly, calculate the expected operating cost and the estimated value of standard deviation of other experts and the results are shown in Table 1.The average value of standard deviation estimated by experts is 1.64 million, the variance of 247, the discrete coefficient $\frac{\sqrt{247}}{164}$ = 9.58%, which meets the conformance requirements of experts. So we can determine the probability distribution of operating costs is subject to the normal distribution of N (3037, 1642).

Table 1. The result estimated by the experts of the probability distribution of the operating cost

expert	Expected value (10 thousand Yuan)	range (10 thousand Yuan)	Probability within the range(%)	Standard deviation σ (10 thousand Yuan)
1	3000	2760~3240	90	146
2	3060	2754~3366	92	175
3	3050	2715~3385	95	171
average value	3037			164

Use the same method, the probability distribution of sales income estimated by experts is determined to be subject to the normal distribution of N (6570, 3802) and the process is omitted.

B.   Take the random number to generate sampling value of variables
The simulation process of this subject is completely done by a computer program and the random numbers is obtained through random number function provided by programming language.

Respectively take the random numbers for construction investment, operating cost and sales revenue. Then regard them as the probability value of variables and convert them to the sampling value of random variables according to the corresponding probability distribution model. The transformation process is shown as follows:

The construction investment is subject to the triangular distribution, which means to directly use the mathematical meaning of probability----the triangle area to strike a random variable. As shown in Figure 1, the entire area of the triangle is 1, the shaded area is the probability value generated by random number, while the solved investment (x) is the sampling value of construction investment.

34181   x   40213   44235

Fig. 1. The construction investment is subject to the triangular distribution

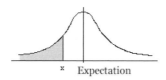

ˣ   Expectation

Fig. 2. Operating costs and sales revenue is subject to the normal distribution

Operating costs and sales revenue is subject to the normal distribution, as shown in Figure 2. The shaded area is the probability generated by random numbers. Look up the standard normal distribution probability table according to the probability value or calculate the deviation from sampling value to the expected value through computer program in order to determine the sampling value of random variables: sampling value (x) = expected value ± deviation × standard deviation.

C.   Calculate the index value of the sample
Identify the sampling value of a set of random variables such as construction investment, operating costs and sales revenues, and regard the sampling value as the basic data of economic evaluation. The circulating fund should be adjusted in accordance with the ratio of the sampling value and expected value of operating costs in order to calculate the economic assessment index value of project. The common used assessment indexes include financial net present value, internal earnings yield ratio, and payback period, and etc. Generally, the financial internal earnings yield ratio

is commonly used. In the calculating period, the following formula should be applied to attempt interpolation method FIRR using computer.

$$NPV = \sum_{t=1}^{n} (CI - CO)_t (1 + FIRR)^{-t} = 0 \tag{1}$$

Among it, the inflow fund CI includes sales income, salvage recovery in the calculating period, reclaim the circulating fund; Outflow fund CO contains construction investment, sales taxes, operating costs and so on.

D. Simulation results and the analysis of experimental times' impact on the results
Repeat the above randomized trials to make the simulation results reach the intended times. Then regard the frequency of each test as the probability, sort the internal earnings yield ratio from small to large, and collate the expected value, variance, standard deviation of all the test results, finally calculate the cumulative probability. In this way, the cumulative rate that a financial internal earnings yield ratio is less than the base earnings ratio can be calculated to determine the probability of the project's feasibility or infeasibility. Conduct a simulation on the sewage treatment plant with the 2000 testing times, after sorting the simulation results, we can obtain that the average internal earnings yield ratio is 5.64%, variance is 1.93, while coefficient of variation is 24.63%.

Sort and calculate according to the internal earnings yield ratio from small to large, we can determine that the cumulative probability the internal earnings yield ratio is below the base earnings ratio 4% is 12.75%, which means that the probability that the internal earnings yield ratio is larger or equal to 4% is 87.25%. From this, it can be seen that the financial risk of the sewage treatment project is a little less. Draw the cumulative probability scatter diagram in accordance with the simulated results, as the simulated results have generated 2000 sets of data, the data points are more concentrated. Therefore, it has formed a line thick solid line curve in the cumulative probability scatter diagram, as shown in Figure 3.

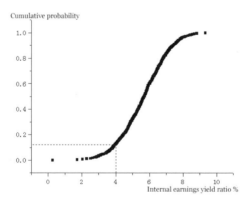

Fig. 3. Cumulative probability

As the sampling value of random variables generated by the simulation test may be uneven, which will cause that every simulation conducted according to the set TN has deviation in different degrees. In view of this, we can repeat the simulation with the same times and average the probability of internal earnings yield ratio below base earnings ratio to eliminate such deviations, and thus validate the simulation result. Repeat the simulation with the 2000 TN for about 20 times, after the statistical calculation, we can see that the average value of the probability that the inter earnings yield ratio is less than 4% is 12.32%, discrete coefficient is 6.44%. It can be seen the above simulation results 12.75% is higher than the average value of the simulation result with 20 times, but only has a deviation of 3.49%. The deviation is small, which means it has a high reliability.

In addition, the set of TN has a certain influence on the simulation results. Theoretically speaking, the TN should be as large as possible, but in fact the too many times would consume too much time and it is also not necessary; however, if the TN is smaller, the random numbers may occur uneven distribution, which will affect the reliability of simulation results. So apply different TN and respectively repeat the simulation for 20 times, and then solve the maximum, minimum, average and dispersion coefficient of the probability that the internal earnings yield ratio is less than 4% , as shown in Table 2.

Table 2. Repeated simulation results for 20 times of experiments with different TN

| Number | Test Number(TN) | One simulated Time-consuming (in seconds) | The probability that internal earnings ratio is less than 4%（%） | | | Dispersion Coefficient |
			Maximum value	Minimum value	Average value	
1	20	0.06	35	5	13	56.36%
2	50	0.08	28	4	13.8	38.75%
3	100	0.12	19	8	12.15	27.91%
4	500	0.66	14.8	8.4	12.29	11.65%
5	1000	1.33	14.9	9.7	12.35	9.31%
6	2000	2.97	14.35	11.35	12.32	6.44%
7	5000	7.52	13.06	11.44	12.22	3.38%
8	10000	14.97	12.94	11.55	12.2	2.88%
9	20000	30.02	12.54	11.82	12.25	1.54%

As can be seen from Table 2, the less the TN is, the more the simulation results deviate from the average, and the large the discrete coefficient is. When the TN is less than 1000, the dispersion coefficient is greater than 10% so the credibility is lower; when the TN reaches 1000, the dispersion coefficient is small, so the credibility can meet the requirements, but if the TN is too large, its impact on the simulation results will be small. Therefore, when the TN is 2000, using computer to carry out simulation will not only consume less time but also have a high credibility. Generally speaking, one simulation can meet the requirement.

4 Computer Simulation Programs

Use Monte Carlo simulation to do risk analysis. Because of enormous repetitive calculation and heavy workload, computer programs are generally used to complete it. In order to introduce Monte Carlo simulation technology into the risk analysis on economic evaluation of wastewater treatment project, the author uses visual programming language Visual Foxpro to write computer program.

By adopting the program and according to the research results of experts, we can determine the distribution model of the risk variables, achieve the mutual conversion between the probability of the normal distribution and deviations (calculate data in the standard normal distribution table), extract random numbers and generate sample values, calculate the economic evaluation indicator, a simulation or repeated simulations under the set number of tests, view the simulation results and form probability charts of the simulation results, which achieves the calculation, analysis and output of thousands of simulation experiments in short time. Table 2 counts the statistics of the number of elapsed time of using the program to do a different number of tests for a single simulation in P2.8G computer. In which, when the number of tests is 2000 times, a single simulation takes only 2.97 seconds, accumulating to 1 minute for repeating the simulation for 20 times; if the number of trials is 10,000 times, the cumulative time-consuming of 20 times repeated simulations reach 5 minutes.

5 Conclusion

In the economic evaluation of study report on the feasibility of sewage treatment projects, there is no requirement for risk analysis and the risk probability analysis of the project is even less. In particular, for using Monte Carlo simulation techniques to do simulation analysis, there is no precedent. Taking a project of a sewage treatment plant as an example, this paper formulates computer program to carry out Monte Carlo analysis, obtains the probability of whether the project is feasible or not, and provides decision-making basis for the construction side and cases for the study of project feasibility to do risk analysis as well as references for BOT, TOT and other new franchise financing investment model to do risk analysis of investment decision-making.

References

1. Lang, H.: Technical economics. Economic Management Press, Beijing (2009)
2. Zhang, G.: Tutorial of Technologies and economics. China Electric Power Press, Beijing (2007)
3. Yu, S.: The Feasibility Study Methodology of Investment Project and Its Case Application Manual. Earthquake Press, Beijing (2003)
4. Chinese International Engineering Consulting Corporation. Investment Project Feasibility Study Guide. China Electric Power Press, Beijing (2002)
5. National Development and Reform Commission, Ministry of Construction. Economic evaluation methods of construction project and its parameters, 3rd edn. China Planning Press, Beijing (2006)
6. Wang, Y., Cui, H.: Probability and Mathematical Statistics. China Water Power Press, Beijing (2010)

Image Enhancement of Ground Penetrating Radar Based on Multiscale Space Correlation*

Hailin Zou[1] and Chanjuan Liu[1,2]

[1] School of Information Science & Engineering, Lu Dong University, Yantai,
Shandong Province, China
[2] School of Mechanical Electronic & Information Engineering, China University of Mining &
Technology (Beijing),Beijing, China
hailin_zou@tom.com

Abstract. Wavelet coefficients of GPR valid signal and random noise change
differently with different scale parameter. Combined with the related principle
of coefficients in wavelet space, a multiscale enhancement method of GPR
weak signal is proposed in this paper. After elaboration of the basic principle of
our method, this paper describes the experiment results on different sections.
This method proves to be a quite effective and feasible method not only
improves SNR of the valid signal but also suppresses noise.

Keywords: Ground penetrating radar (GPR), Multi-wavelet analysis,
Correlation, Image enhancement.

1 Introduction

Signal enhancement is an important topic in the GPR (ground penetrating radar) data
processing. But it is difficult to distinguish the target underground or distribution
situation of medium from cross sections, because GPR reflected signal is weak and
interrupted by random noise or influenced by the complexity of medium underground.
The intensity of weak signal is still not big enough to be used on signal detection and
extraction even after denoising. At present, enhancement methods of GPR signal
mainly include: reflection echo amplitude transformation and multiple stacking
processing (includes amplitude recovery and energy balance among tracks), etc.
However, these methods have obvious disadvantages. The noise is increased while
enhance the amplitude, and also there is no improvement to distortion signal. So, it is
of theoretical significance and practical application value to focus on enhancement
mechanism and approaches of GPR weak signal under background of noise. It is
important to improve the SNR (signal to noise ratio) of GPR weak signal. In this
paper, the principle and a method how to select optimal scale parameter is given,
according to the theory that multiscale high frequency coefficients of GPR valid
signal and random noise change differently with different scale parameters. Based on
the principle mentioned, a method to enhance GPR weak signal is proposed.

---

* This work is supported by Natural Science Foundation of Shandong (No.Y2008E11).

J. Zhang (Ed.): ICAIC 2011, Part III, CCIS 226, pp. 95–102, 2011.

2 The Principle of Signal Enhancement Based on Wavelet Scale Space Correlation

Wavelet transform modulus maxima of valid signal and noise are of different characteristics under different scales based on the principle of wavelet multi-resolution analysis. Frankly speaking, the wavelet transform modulus of valid signal is bigger than or the same as the original one while the scales increase. However, the noise's decreased quickly. This is the concrete reflect of the difference between valid signal and noise in wavelets space. This also provides theoretical and method basis for valid signal enhancement and denoising[1-3].

In order to denoise and optionally increase wavelet coefficients value at the same time, we need a method which can distinguish the wavelet coefficients which are caused by noise. Using this method, we can process not just by the value of wavelet coefficient. It doesn't need to suppress all the wavelet coefficients under the threshold blindly. The different characteristics of wavelet transform max-modulus between valid signal and noise under different scales demonstrate that there is a strong correlation among wavelet coefficients of signal under different scales. Especially at the edges of signal, the correlation is more obvious. However, the wavelet coefficients of noise are uncorrelated or weak correlation across scales [4,5], what's more, wavelet transform modulus of noise is mainly confined to coarse scales. So, correlation of wavelet coefficient under different scales can be used to identify which coefficients are caused by signal and which are by noise. Then, the coefficients after trade-offs are used to de-noise and enhance signal.

3 Algorithm and Its Implementation of Signal Filtering and Enhancement Based on Scale Space Correlation

The calculations of wavelet transformation data related to scale space enhance the primary edges of signal and decrease the noise's amplitude obviously. So the noise and small edges are suppressed. The algorithm is described briefly as follows.

Suppose $f(t)$ is the original signal, $n(t)$ is the noise, then the input signal interrupted by noise is $x(t) = f(t) + n(t)$.

The wavelet transformation is

$$Wx(s,t) = Wf(s,t) + Wn(s,t) \tag{1}$$

The correlation coefficient is

$$Corr_2(j,n) = Wx(j,n) \times Wx(j+1,n),$$
$$n = 1,2,\cdots,N \tag{2}$$

This is the correlation coefficient on scale 2^j at n. N denotes the total number of the signals, W represents the wavelet transformation, j is the scale number, the corresponding scale is 2^j, and n represents the position of data point. l is the number of scales involved in the direct correlation. In order to let correlation coefficients and wavelet coefficients are comparable, we normalize $Corr_2(j,n)$.

The total energy of wavelet coefficient at the j level is

$$P_{W(j,n)} = \sum_n Wx(j,n)^2 . \tag{3}$$

The total energy of correlation coefficient at the level is

$$P_{corr_2(j,n)} = \sum_n Corr_2(j,n)^2 . \tag{4}$$

Normalized correlation coefficient is

$$NewCorr_2(j,n) = Corr_2(j,n)\sqrt{P_{W(j,n)}/P_{corr_2(j,n)}} . \tag{5}$$

The most important information of edges is extracted by comparing $|NewCorr_2(j,n)|$ and $|Wx(j,n)|$ through calculating correlation. If $|NewCorr_2(j,n)| \geq |Wx(j,n)|$, then $Wx(j,n)$, the wavelet transformation value at n should be induced by signal, and the result of related calculation increased the amplitude of wavelet transformation, then record $Wx(j,n)$ by the corresponding value in $\widetilde{W}x(j,n)$ (the filtered value is referred to as $\widetilde{W}x(j,n)$), and set $Wx(j,n)$ and $Corr_2(j,n)$ to zero. Otherwise, we assume $Wx(j,n)$ is produced by noise, and the result of related calculation decrease the amplitude of wavelet transformation. Then retain $Wx(j,n)$ and $Corr_2(j,n)$, set the corresponding value in $\widetilde{W}x(j,n)$ to zero. Suppose N_{um} denotes the number of points that have not been set to zero in both $Wx(j,n)$ and $Corr_2(j,n)$, that is, the number of wavelet coefficients produced by noise in $Wx(j,n)$ .At last, $\widetilde{W}x(j,n)$ records all of the points induced by valid signal, while the points in $Wx(j,n)$ are all produced by noise.

A. *Calculate Noise Threshold*

Define noise threshold σ_j at every scale is

$$\sigma_j^2 = \sigma^2 \parallel h_n^{0^*} h_n^{1^*} \cdots h_n^{j-2^*} h_n^{j-1^*} \parallel^2 . \tag{6}$$

Where represents convolution operator, H_j 、 G_j denote 2^j expansion of H_0 , G_0 , that is, insert $2^j - 1$ zero among coefficients of H_0 (G_0), whose impulse response is $\{h_n^j\}$ ($\{g_n^j\}$).

B. *Estimation of Noise's Variance*

As we all know, the energy of noise is mainly gathered on wavelet coefficients of coarse scales, so noise variance σ can be estimated by the wavelet transformation value at the most coarse scale. If $|NewCorr_2(1,n)| \geq |Wx(1,n)|$, set the corresponding point's wavelet coefficient $Wx(1,n)$ to zero. Do the same operation to every wavelet coefficient, the filtered result of $Wx(1,n)$ is referred to as $\hat{W}x(1,n)$, then almost all of the bigger transformed values due to signal with great change are removed from $\hat{W}x(1,n)$. Suppose K points are erased totally; then, $\hat{W}x(1,n)$ can be roughly considered to be produced by noise. From $\sigma = \sigma_1 / \| g_n^0 \|$ and $P\hat{W}x(1,n)/(N-K)$ which is the asymptotically unbiased estimation of σ_1^2, we can get a approximate estimation of σ

$$\hat{\sigma} = \sqrt{P\hat{W}x(1,n)/(N-K)} / \| g_n^0 \| \tag{7}$$

C. Introduce Correlation Adjustment Coefficient

The algorithmic core idea of spatial correlation is the extraction of edge information in signal by comparing the absolute value of $Wx(j,n)$ and $NewCorr_2(j,n)$, and the variance σ_j of noise is employed as threshold to stop iterating. To some extent, that will retain some noise information.

From $|NewCorr(j,n)| \geq |Wx(j,n)|$, we can get

$$Wx(j,n)^2 \leq \frac{Wx(j,n)^2 Wx(j+1,n)^2 \sum_n Wx(j,n)^2}{\sum_n Wx(j,n)^2 Wx(j+1,n)^2}. \tag{8}$$

That is

$$\sum_n Wx(j,n)^2 Wx(j+1,n)^2 \leq Wx(j+1,n)^2 \sum_n Wx(j,n)^2. \tag{9}$$

The formula above indicates when the SNR of signal is low, magnitude of noise is great, it is easy to take the noise to be valid signal especially in the coarse scale. For example, note $\lambda = \sqrt{P_{W(j,n)}/(N_{um}-1)} / \sigma_j$, after the first iteration, if $\lambda > 1$, then there are edges of signal which are not detected in $Wx(j,n)$; repeat iteration until $\lambda < 1$, then we consider only the noise data points left in $Wx(j,n)$. However, the values of λ are of great difference between iterations, such as the first iteration $\lambda = 1.1$, but the second $\lambda = 0.9$, obviously, a part of the wavelet coefficients produced by noise were considered as edges of signal and introduced to $\tilde{W}x(j,n)$ partly, this is adverse to signal (image) processing. To avoid this, we can try to reduce the value of λ between iterations, so as not to retain too many noise coefficients.

An adjustment coefficient related with scale was introduced to $|NewCorr_2(j,n)| \geq |Wx(j,n)|$, n order to adjust the related coefficient $|NewCorr_2(j,n)|$ after normalization at every point. That is:

$$C(j,n) \cdot |NewCorr_2(j,n)| \geq |Wx(j,n)| \tag{10}$$

$C(j,n)$ is correlation adjustment coefficient. Define

$$C(j,n) = \left(\frac{e}{3}\right)^{\frac{J+1-j}{J+N_L}}, \quad (j=1,\cdots,J) \tag{11}$$

J represents the number of decomposition scale, N_l denote number of iteration that unsatisfied noise energy threshold.

At coarse scales, noise energy is greater relatively, adjustment coefficient could weaken noise, and false rate of making noise to valid signal was decreased using (10). The intensity of the noise decreased quickly with the increasing of the decomposition scales and iterations, and then $C(j,n) \rightarrow 1$, to some extent signal is enhanced by adjustment coefficient.

D. Introduce Adjustment Coefficient of Noise Energy

It is not the optimal to choose σ_j as threshold to stop iteration at j scale, and the formula (1) can be rewrite as follow.

$$Wx(j,n) = Wf(j,n) + Wn(j,n) \tag{12}$$

Then

$$E(Wx(j,n)^2) = E(Wf(j,n)^2) + E(Wn(j,n)^2) \tag{13}$$

That is

$$E(Wx(j,n)^2) = E(Wf(j,n)^2) + \sigma_j^2 \tag{14}$$

Where $E(Wf(j,n)^2)$ is always positive. It is easy to take partial noise as signal when using $\sqrt{P_{W(j,n)}/(N_{um}-1)}/\sigma_j$ to judge whether or not to stop iteration. So, a threshold adjustment coefficient T_j was introduced and $T_j \cdot \sigma_j$ was considered as the condition of stopping iteration.

Because the wavelet coefficients value of signal and $E(Wf(j,n)^2)$ will become bigger with increased scale, whereas σ_j decreases. So the value of T_j should bigger than 1 and increase quickly with increased scale. We choose $T_j = 1 + \log(j+1/2)$ based on many experiments.

E. Selection of Signal Enhancement Function

For GPR echo signal, magnitude of echo signal will decrease with bigger detecting depth. An enhancement function was constructed based on this characteristic, in which all the absolute value of wavelet coefficients below the threshold λ, adopts bigger gain G, or else, uses smaller gains. This function is

$$T_G(\tilde{w}_{j,n}) = \begin{cases} \tilde{w}_{j,n} - (G-1)\cdot\lambda, & \tilde{w}_{j,n} < -\lambda \\ G\cdot\tilde{w}_{j,n}, & |\tilde{w}_{j,n}| \leq \lambda \\ \tilde{w}_{j,n} + (G-1)\cdot\lambda, & \tilde{w}_{j,n} > \lambda \end{cases} \tag{15}$$

G is a gain, $\tilde{w}_{j,n}$ is spatial wavelet coefficient after correlation calculation, λ represents threshold. In the present paper, $G = \dfrac{A_G}{1+\log j}$, $\lambda_j = \dfrac{1}{N}\sum\limits_{n=1}^{N}|\tilde{w}_{j,n}|$.

4 Experiments

The simulations are conducted with two segments true GPR data to verify the effectiveness and robustness of our method. We use GHM multiwavelet soft-threshold and GHM init method, decomposition scale is 5[6].

The experiment model is shown in Figure 1(a). A 230cm length metal tube whose diameter 10cm buried 1.2 meters beneath the ground. Backfilling contents are mainly clay and a few stones. The GPR data are collected by 500m antenna. Figure 1(b) indicates the data after de-noising to the background. Figure1(c) is the graph after wavelet soft threshold process which can clearly shows the position of the tube. Figure 1(d) is the graph after the de-noising with spatial correlation enhancement process. From the figure1(c), we can conclude that GPR image with enhancement process, resolution has been improved obviously and the position of tube is more clearly [7].

The SNR of GPR echo signal after two processing methods is compared in table 1.

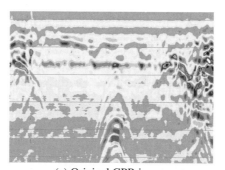

(a) Original GPR image

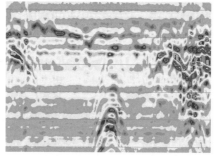

(b) Background de-noising image

Fig. 1. Enhancement processing of GPR signal

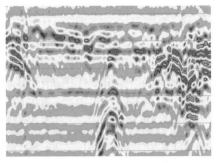

(c) De-noising with soft threshold function image

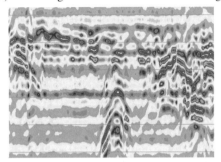

(d) De-noising with spatial correlation enhancement

Fig. 1. (*continued*)

Table 1. SNR under two processing methods of GPR signal/dB

Process approach of wavelet coefficients	SNR of GPR signal(dB)
Soft threshold de-noising	32.1576
Spatial correlation enhancement	47.0329

From the experiment results, we can draw conclusions that the SNR of GPR signal has been improved more than 10dB by using the improved enhancement approach in this paper. The resolution of image has been improved obviously, and it demonstrates that the improved method is effective to GPR signal enhancement process.

5   Conclusions

The problem of GPR signal enhancement is mainly discussed in the paper. A GPR signal multiscale enhancement method is proposed based on the theory that multiscale high frequency coefficients of GPR valid signal and random noise change differently with different scale parameter and the theory of wavelet space domain coefficient correlation. The basic principle and the implementation procedure of this method are clearly described. Numerous experiments have been done to verify its effectiveness.

The results of experiment show that it's a valid and feasible processing method in both suppressing noise and improving SNR of the valid signal. This approach is simple to calculate, fast and stable and also satisfies the request of precision of GPR signal processing.

References

1. Mallat, S., Zhong, S.: Characterization of signal from multiscale edges. IEEE Trans. Information Theory 38(2), 617–643 (1992)
2. Donoho, D.L.: De-noising by soft-thresholding. IEEE Trans. Information Theory 41(3), 613–627 (1995)
3. Donoho, D.L., Johnstone, I.M.: Ideal spatial adaptation via wavelet shrinkage. Biometrika 81, 425–455 (1994)
4. Pan, Q., Zhang, P., Dai, G., et al.: Two denoising methods by wavelet transform. IEEE Trans. Signal Processing 47(12), 3401–3406 (1999)
5. Pan, Q., Zhang, L., Zhang, H., et al.: Adaptive wavelet based spatially de-noising. In: Proceedings of the 4th International Conference on Signal Processing Proceedings, Beijing China, pp. 486–489 (1998)
6. Donovan, G.C., Geronimo, G.S., Hardin, D.P., et al.: Construction of Orthogonal Wavelets Using Fractal Interpolation Function. SIAM. Math. Anal. 27(4), 1158–1192 (1996)
7. Perrier, V., Philipovitch, T., Basdevant, C.: Wavelet Spectra Compared to Fourier Spectra. J. Math. Phys. 36(3), 1506–1519 (1995)

Modeling and Simulation of the Virtualized Scenes Base on the Open Modelica*

Jiang YuXiang[1], Zhou Xiaolong[1], Li JinPing[2], and Ren LiYing[1]

[1] Department of Circuit Analysis, College of Information,
Beijing Union University, Beijing, China
[2] Department of Electronic Circuit, College of Information,
Beijing Union University, Beijing, China
YuXiang.Jiang@yahoo.cn

Abstract. Experimental teaching plays a very important role in modern education. For the Distance Education via Computer Networks, this paper gives a system architecture of virtual experiment as the basis of virtual instrument technology, multimedia computer technology, network technology. Design and implementation the virtualized scenes based on the technology of OpenModelica and Xml program. Finally used the open OpenModelica to model and simulate the virtualized scenes.

Keywords: Virtual reality, Modelica modeling, Simulation.

1 Introduction

Virtual experiment system can provide online virtual experiments. Virtual experiment teaching system should not only contain information-Rich rich virtual experiments, and should include the teaching function of experiments, such as the requirements for an experimental, the laboratory report and record, and the statistical results of experiment. With the multimedia technology and network technology development, the network teaching gradually becomes the supplement for normal teaching. Virtual reality effect can be achieved by using computer simulation experiment on network through virtual experiment teaching system and online virtual laboratory and virtual experiment.

The problem of middleware, development tools, visual design of virtual experiment are discussed on the subject of 'Research on key technologies in visual design virtual experimental teaching. The subject of 'Virtual experiment teaching resources component multi-fields modeling and assembly platform provides virtual experiment research' is researched on Modeling and assembly platform of the virtualized scenes for the Virtual experiment teaching resources. These subjects consist in the project 'Study on the key technology and application demonstration of virtual teaching experiment environment' which is supported by the Key Project in the National Science & Technology Pillar Program of China in the 11th Five-Year. This paper mainly discusses the modeling and simulation of visual scene.

---

* This paper is supported by the Key Project in the National Science & Technology Pillar Program of China under grant No.2008BAH29B00.

J. Zhang (Ed.): ICAIC 2011, Part III, CCIS 226, pp. 103–110, 2011.

2 System Architecture

Active interface for data exchange in the virtual experiment platform includes two aspects: experiment on client, guidance and management module between the layer for data exchange layer, Experimental simulation, computing, and modeling modules between the tasks scheduling of interactive platform. Data exchange content mainly includes two aspects: First is the experimental component data, which is central to the system. Through the experimental component data can be composed component library. Second is the experimental scene data. the client scenario will provide the plug-in experimental data for the platform, the scene, calculation module for calculating background.

A. Structural analysis
The virtual experiment platform is based on B/S (Browser/Server) structure. The program structure on client is shown in figure 1.

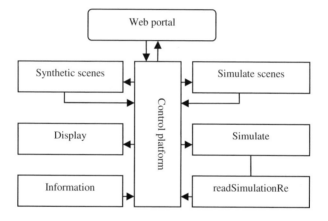

Fig 1. Virtual experiment platform structure on the client

Scene description composed mainly of experiments component. Experiments component data includes two related elements <component-list>, <component> and them child elements. Experimental scenes data t included < scene > element and child elements. Component list element <component-list> contains the necessary information used in the initial component generated by Plug-in. Component list element may contain one or more components of component information.

The component information elements described the necessary information of component in the component list. Consists of five sub-elements: <id>, <name>, <type>, <src>, <tips>. See Table 1 for references.

In order to simulate the virtual scenes, the simulation model needs to be build. The component information elements detailed description of the component elements of the ID, name, description, version information, interfaces, attributes, MO models and so on. The component information elements in the File named .mo must be included the following sub-elements :<id>, <name>, <description>, <version-info>, <interface-list>, <property-list>, < function >,<visualization-model>, <mo-model>. The function sub-elements Consists of: Input / output, name, Metrology, range, the min/max value, parameter.

Table 1. Component information elements

Elements	Description
<id>	a global variable, Identifies the component elements of the Component list. All of the component information can be get through this ID.
<name>	The component name.
<type>	the component tag, used to display bar on the classification
<src>	the address of the display file (such as images)
<tips>	prompt information

B. Scenario Description

The experimental scene based on the XML language described as follows:

```
<COMPONENTS>
<csTYPE>1_1</csTYPE>
<csTitle  type="Resistor" showtype=" Resistor ">R</csTitle>
<csSequence></csSequence>
<csPinNunm>2</csPinNunm>
<cspname index="p"><LEFT>0</LEFT><TOP>10</TOP></cspname>
<cspname index="n"><LEFT>102</LEFT><TOP>10</TOP>
</cspname>
<csFornat>Resistor.gif
<LEFT></LEFT>
<TOP></TOP>
<WIDTH>102</WIDTH>
<HEIGHT>20</HEIGHT>
</csFornat>
<csANGEL>0</csANGEL>
<ecNvs>
<ecNv name="R" showname=" Resistor " type="int(1,1000000000)" Metrolgoy
="Ω">1000</ecNv>
</ecNvs>
</COMPONENTS>
```

Using the above scenario description of the virtual environment, figure2 show the connect circuits.

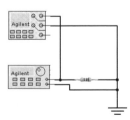

Fig. 2. Virtual environment circuit

3 Modelica Modeling and Simulation

In order to complete and simulate the virtual experimental, system choose the OpenModelica as a modeling and simulation tools. The circuit diagram using the integrated development environment of Madelica is shown in figure3.

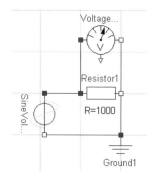

Fig. 3. Virtual environment circuit base on OpenModelica

C. Modeling analysis
after compiling, document of mo-model based on the XML language described as follows

```
model Unnamed1
  annotation (uses(Modelica(version="1.6")), Diagram);
  Modelica.Electrical.Analog.Sensors.VoltageSensor VoltageSensor1
  annotation (extent=[-32,-38; -12,-18]);
  Modelica.Electrical.Analog.Basic.Ground Ground1
  annotation (extent=[-8,-48; 12,-28]);
  Modelica.Electrical.Analog.Basic.Resistor Resistor1(R=1000)
   annotation (extent=[-30,2; -10,22]);
  Modelica.Electrical.Analog.Sources.SineVoltage SineVoltage1(V=1, freqHz=1000)
   annotation (extent=[-30,24; -10,44]);
equation
  connect(VoltageSensor1.n, Ground1.p)
  annotation (points=[-12,-28; 2,-28], style(color=3, rgbcolor={0,0,255}));
  connect(Resistor1.n, Ground1.p) annotation (points=[-10,12; 2,12; 2,-28],
   style(color=3, rgbcolor={0,0,255}));
  connect(Resistor1.p, VoltageSensor1.p) annotation (points=[-30,12; -40,12;
   -40,-28; -32,-28], style(color=3, rgbcolor={0,0,255}));
  connect(SineVoltage1.n, Resistor1.n) annotation (points=[-10,34; 2,34; 2,12;
   -10,12], style(color=3, rgbcolor={0,0,255}));
  connect(SineVoltage1.p, Resistor1.p) annotation (points=[-30,34; -40,34; -40,
   12; -30,12], style(color=3, rgbcolor={0,0,255}));
end Unnamed1;
```

In the example above, you can see the parameters information of component and the position connection information between components is described in this document.

The position connection information For used to display the circuit net on Modelica environment.

Example:
connect(SineVoltage1.n, Resistor1.n) annotation (points=[-10,34; 2,34; 2,12;-10,12], style(color=3, rgbcolor={0,0,255}));

The parameters information and the simulation model of component used to Simulation

Example:
Modelica.Electrical.Analog.Sources.SineVoltage SineVoltage1(V=1,freqHz=1000);
Modelica.Electrical.Analog.Basic.Resistor Resistor1(R=1000);
Modelica.Electrical.Analog.Sensors.VoltageSensor VoltageSensor1;
Modelica.Electrical.Analog.Basic.Ground Ground1;

circuit simulation results on Modelica environment as figure4 shows.

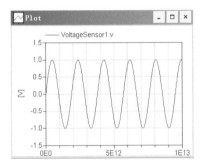

Fig. 4. Simulation results

4   Modelica Model Base on XML

The simulation model Based on XML language described as fellow:

```
<component>
    <index>Resistor</index>
    <component-id></component-id>
    <component-name>Resistor</component-name>
        <description></description>
        <version-info></version-info>
        <interface-list>
    <interface>
     <name>p</name>
     <type>PositivePin</type>
    </interface>
    <interface>
     <name>n</name>
     <type>NegativePin</type>
```

```
      </interface>
   </interface-list>
      <property-list>
       <property>
         <property-id>1</property-id>
         <property-name></property-name>
         <property-symbol>R</property-symbol>
    <property-value>1000</property-value>
    <property-valueunit>ohm</property-valueunit>
    <property-minvalue>0.0</property-minvalue>
         <property-maxvalue></property-maxvalue>
         <property-revisability>Y</property-revisability>
    <property-display></property-display>

         </property>
       </property-list>
       <visualization-model></visualization-model>
       <mo-model>
       <model-location>Modelica.Electrical.Analog.Basic.Resistor</model-location>
</mo-model>
</component>
```

The simulation model Based on the XML language can be completed and simulated by Openmodelica. The flow charts of the simulation process as shown in figure 5.

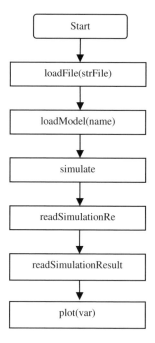

Fig. 5. Simulation flowcharts

Flow charts show the sequence of simulation. Read the results of a simulation from a file named by the string argument strFile. Here size is the size of the resulting record and variables is a vector of the variables to investigate. Plot a variable relative to time from the most recently simulated model.

The simulation results on the Resistor (pin_p) output as shown in figure 6.

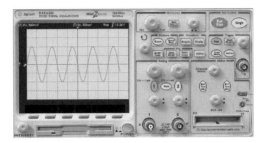

Fig. 6. Simulation results

5 Conclusion

Through the analysis of the virtual experimental scene and the difference between display and simulation, This paper presents a method of Building their virtual scene models to solve the real-time simulation on circuit virtual experiment With the Internet, using the Open Modelica as a modeling and simulation tools, realize a modeling and Simulation of experimental for multi-user.

References

1. De Lucia, A., Francese, R., Passero, I., Tortora, G.: Development and evaluation of a virtual campus on Second Life: The case of SecondDMI. Computers & Education 52(1), 220–233 (2009)
2. Walczak, S., Cellary, W.: X-VRML - XML Based Modeling of Virtual Reality. In: Proceedings of the 2002 Symposium on Applications and the Internet, pp. 204–213. IEEE Computer Society, Washington, DC, USA (2002)
3. Bierbaum, A., Just, C., Hartling, P., Meinert, K.: VR juggler: a virtual platform for virtual reality application development. In: International Conference on Computer Graphics and Interactive Techniques Archive, ACM SIGGRAPH ASIA 2008 Courses, Singapore, December 10-13 (2008)
4. Guo, T.-t., Guo, L., Li, D.-s.: Development of Networked Virtual Experiment System Based on Virtual Campus. I. J. Modern Education and Computer Science 1, 10–18 (2009)
5. Fritzson, P.: Principles of Object-Oriented Modeling and Simulation with Modelica 2.1. IEEE Press, Piscataway (2004)
6. Pan, Z., et al.: Virtual Reality and Mixed Reality for Virtual Learning Environments. Computers & Graphics 30, S20–S28 (2006)
7. Weusijana, B.K.A., et al.: Learning About Adaptive Expertise in a Multi-User Virtual Environment. In: Second Life Education Workshop 2007, Teil der Second Life Community Convention, Chicago, August 24-26, pp. S34–S39 (2007)

8. Lamari, A.: Modelling and simulation of electrical machines on the basis of experimental frequency response characteristics. Journal of Computer Engineering Research 1(1), 7–13 (2010)

9. Ronkowski, M.: Modelling of electrical machines using the Modelica Bond-Graph Library. In: 13th Power Electronics and Motion Control Conference, EPE-PEMC 2008, vol. 1(3), pp. 880–886 (2008)

10. Sanz, V., Urquia, A., Dormido, S.: Parallel DEVS and Process-Oriented Modeling in Modelica. In: Proceedings 7th Modelica Conference, Como, Italy, September 20-22, pp. 96–107 (2009)

Study on the Evaluation Model of the Investment Efficiency of Real Estate Industry Based on Super Efficiency DEA[*]

Fangfang Wei, Yanxi Li, Rui Gao, and Jing Sun

School of Management
Dalian University of Technology
Dalian, China
fngfngwei3@gmail.com

Abstract. There are a lot of academic attentions devoted to the problem of investment efficiency in real estate industry in our country recently. This paper seeks to use the method of Super Efficiency DEA to establish an evaluation model of investment efficiency in real estate industry, which is based on Super Efficiency DEA. 35 large and medium cities from China are selected as samples to evaluate the investment efficiency of these cities. The results show that there exist the problems of excessive investment and low investment efficiency in real estate industry in China as a whole; and it is also found that compared with middle regions of china, the investment efficiency of eastern costal areas and northwest areas are higher, they all reach or close to DEA Efficiency.

Keywords: Real estate, Efficiency, DEA, Evaluation model.

1   Introduction

As an essential industry of national economy, real estate industry has characteristics of larger capital input amount, longer recovery stage, higher investment risk and stronger profit ability. Investment efficiency involves the rate of capital return and fund security. Investment pulls requirement in short term, however, the investment today is the supply tomorrow. If the supply pulled by investment can't meet the market demand, it can only induce the increase of bad debts in the bank and imbalance between supply and demand. Therefore, real estate industry should care more about investment efficiency.

In the period of global economy oscillation, periodic adjustment of industry and macro-control instability, researching whether there exist overlapping investment, excessive investment and low utilization rate has an important meaning for economic recovery and healthy development in China. Objective evaluation on investment efficiency of real estate industry by scientific method has some reference significance to keep the proper scale of real estate industry and to promote the healthy development of the industry.

---

* This work is partially supported by NNSF Grant #70772087 to Li Yanxi and "the Fundamental Research Funds for the Central Universities" Grant #DUT10ZD107 to Li Yanxi.

2   Literature Review

A.   Theoretical review of investment efficiency

Investment efficiency is a kind of resource allocation efficiency. It is the ratio of the effective results by enterprise investment to the input capital, namely the proportion relation between output and input in the enterprise investment activity.[1] Resource allocation efficiency in broad sense means the allocation efficiency of the social resources, and it is realized by the economic system arrangement of the whole society; Resource allocation efficiency in narrow sense means the using efficiency, namely production efficiency in general, and it is implemented by the improvement of internal production management and production technology.

B.   The evaluation method of the efficiency of real estate industry

The existing evaluation of the efficiency of real estate industry could be divided into Macro-efficiency research and Micro-efficiency research based on the above efficiency theory. Accordingly, the evaluation method of the efficiency of real estate industry is separated into two kinds, Financial Index Method and Frontal Analysis Method.

1) Financial Index Method

Financial Index Method is to evaluate the efficiency of real estate industry using various kinds of financial indexes, including assets turnover ratio, number of circulation stock, and so on. It is convenient to use Financial Index Method, but Yeh pointed out that the choosing of index is random, and it can't overcome the trouble that there exist collinearity and correlation among the indexes, it may induce wrong results, and it couldn't reflect the whole performance of real estate industry.[2]

2) Frontal Analysis Method

Frontal Analysis Method is to evaluate the efficiency of a Decision Making Unit (DMU) by measuring the departure degree between an investigated DMU and a DMU on the production frontier. It can be divided into parametric method and non parametric method relying on different calculation principles.

Frontal Analysis Method requires setting the concrete form of the efficiency frontal function, and it includes Stochastic Frontier Approach (SFA), Distribution Free Approach (DFA), Thick Frontier Analysis (TFA) and Recursive Thick Frontier Approach (TRFA).[3] Stochastic Frontier Approach is widely applied at home and abroad.

Aigner and Schmidt firstly proposed Frontal Analysis Method to measure efficiency.[4] CHEN Bi'an studied on the X-efficiency of Chinese listed companies in real estate industry based on 34 real estate companies' financial data between 2000 and 2006, and investigated transformation of real estate companies listed in stock market of China.[5] Using Stochastic Frontier Approach, WAN Lunlai and CHEN Xixi selected the panel data of real estate industry between 1999 and 2004, and analyzed the impact of FDI to the technical efficiency of Chinese real estate industry.[6] However, the hypothesis of Stochastic Frontier Approach about the distribution of inefficiency item is lack of foundation, and the hypothesis itself cannot be proved, thus it reduce the effectiveness of SFA.

Comparing to the parametric method, non parametric method need not to assume the type of frontal function, to consider error term, and to make statistical test. It contains Data Envelopment Analysis (DEA) and Free Disposal Hull (FDH). Data Envelopment Analysis is widely used in investigating the efficiency of real estate industry. DEA is a new systematic analysis method proposed by Charnes and Cooper based on "Relative Efficiency Evaluation" in 1978.[7] It evaluates the relative efficiency of DMU with numerous input and output using mathematical programming model. It judge whether a DMU is efficient relying on its data, and it is essentially to judge whether a DMU is on the frontier of production possibility set.[8]

LIU Yongle and HU Yanjing selected CCR model, which is the basic model of DEA, to calculate and evaluate the chosen eight listed companies in real estate industry, and got the conclusion about scale profit and changing trend of these companies. [9] SUN Ge calculated the efficiency of 31 Chinese provinces based on CCR model and C2GS2 model. [10] GENG Xiaoyuan evaluated the relative effectiveness of Chinese real estate industry based on the DEA method, and analyzed the scale income of every area and the cause of the non scale income region.[11]

C.   The problems of existing methods

Majority of the existing research aim at the listed companies of real estate industry, and select financial indexes to evaluate their efficiency, but rarely investigate the efficiency gap between different provinces. Meantime, they can't reveal the degree of input redundancy and output deficiency, and couldn't rank the efficiency areas.

The DEA method has many advantages. Firstly, it selects the weight of DMUs' input and output as the variables to evaluate, and the perspective is most beneficial to DMUs. So it has strong objectivity. Secondly, DEA cannot only evaluate the relative efficiency of a DMU, but also can conclude the underperformance of non efficiency units and gain the scope information of the efficiency improvement through calculating the projection on the production frontier. Thirdly, the traditional DEA model could separate the units to efficiency and non efficiency, but it couldn't rank the efficiency units. Per Anersen proposed Super Efficiency DEA model firstly in 1993 to rank the efficiency DMUs.[12] Super Efficiency DEA model could evaluate whose investment efficiency is higher in evaluating the efficiency of two DEA efficiency cities.

Therefore, selecting the samples of 35 large and medium cities in China, the paper made an empirical study of the investment efficiency of Chinese real estate industry based on Super Efficiency DEA model. Considering the characters of real estate industry, choosing the samples, screening the decision making units, establishing the input-output index system and selecting the DEA model, we construct a complete evaluation model of investment efficiency in real estate industry based on Super Efficiency DEA.

3   Research Design

A.   The selection of samples

The paper established an evaluation model of investment efficiency in real estate industry in China based on 35 large and medium cities, including Shenzhen, Yinchuan, Beijing, Ningbo, Hangzhou, Changsha, Wulumuqi, Chongqing, Nanning, Haerbin, Changchun, Haikou, Shijiazhuang, Chengdu, Xi'an, Shanghai, Qingdao,

Guiyang, Shenyang, Wuhan, Xiamen, Dalian, Nanchang, Fuzhou, Nanjing, Tianjin, Jinan, Guangzhou, Zhengzhou, Xining, Kunming, Taiyuan, Huhehaote, Hefei and Lanzhou.

The selected 35 large and medium cities cover all the provinces of China from East to West. The evaluation of the typical samples could reflect the general condition of the investment efficiency of real estate industry in China.

B. The construction of evaluation index system of investment efficiency of real estate industry

The goal of the evaluation of DEA efficiency is to reflect the input-output efficiency of a city directly, that is the direct output capacity relying on input. The paper selects "Annual investment", "The new operated area of commercial housing" and "Employee" as the input index. "The completed area of commercial housing" and "Sales" are selected as the output index of the DEA model.

At the same time, considering the investment construction period of the real estate industry requires 2 to 3 years generally, therefore, we assume that the input-output period is two years, namely the input index is chosen at the end of 2005, while the output index is chosen at the end of 2007.

The DEA model requires that the number of samples is no less than twice of the sum of the input and output indexes. The sufficiency of the samples' number could guarantee the accuracy of DEA result. This paper selects the data of 35 large and medium cities in China. The number of sample is 35, input index is 2, output index is 3, satisfies the request of DEA model [12]; Secondly, the index of input and output are all larger than 0 value, satisfies the request of the model on value; Besides, there didn't exist the obvious liner correlation relations between the input indexes and output indexes.

C. Construction of the evaluation model of the investment efficiency of real estate industry based on DEA

1) The evaluation model of Super Efficiency DEA

The general DEA method can be used to evaluate whether the efficiency of DMUs are optimal. The Super Efficiency DEA model could rank the efficiency DMUs, the model is [13]:

$$\mathbf{min}\,\theta_0^{super} \tag{1}$$

$$\mathbf{s.t.}\sum_{\substack{j=1 \\ j\neq 0}}^{n}\lambda_j x_{ij} + s_i^- = \theta_0^{super} x_{i0}, \quad i = 1,2,\cdots,m, \tag{2}$$

$$\sum_{\substack{j=1 \\ j\neq 0}}^{n}\lambda_j y_{ij} - s_i^+ = y_{i0}, \quad i = 1,2,\cdots,s, \tag{3}$$

$$\sum_{\substack{j=1 \\ j\neq 0}}^{n}\lambda_j = 1, \tag{4}$$

$$\lambda_j \geq 0, \quad j \neq 0. \tag{5}$$

Among them, θ_0^{super} -efficiency index, a decision variable; λ_j-the input and output coefficient, a decision variable; x_{ij}-the value of the ith input index of the jth evaluation object; s_i^-- slack variable of input index; y_{ij}- the value of the ith output index of the jth evaluation object; s_i^+- slack variable of output index.

If the efficiency value θ_0^{super} <1, it indicated that the input and output didn't reach the optimal efficiency, namely the input were not transformed into the largest output; If the efficiency value θ_0^{super} =1, it indicated that the input and output just reach the optimal efficiency; If θ_0^{super} >1, it indicated that the input and output surpass the optimal efficiency.

2) Input redundancy and Output deficiency

When the evaluation object didn't reach the optimal efficiency, there must exist input redundancy or output deficiency.

Suppose that Δx_i- input redundancy; x_i-value of input index; Δy_i- output deficiency. Then input redundancy Δx_i and output deficiency Δy_i are:

$$\Delta x_i = (1 - \theta_0^{super})x_i + s_i^-, \quad i = 1, \ldots, m, \tag{6}$$

$$\Delta y_i = s_i^+, \quad i = 1, \ldots, s, \tag{7}$$

4 Empirical Study of the Investment Efficiency of Real Estate Industry of Chinese 35 Large and Medium Cities

A. Descriptive statistics of the sample data

Table 1. Descriptive Statistics of the Variable

Index	num	mean	med	std	min	max
Annual investment (10000yuan)	35	2747169	1913087	3129491	270700	15250000
The new operated area (10 000 square meters)	35	926.6738	660.17	723.3262	140.39	3055.47
Employee	35	34979	14403	53844.61	4232	255626
The completed area (10 000 square meters)	35	769.4791	578.56	760.5688	118.9	3380.1
Sales(10 000 yuan)	35	5201653	3343512	6504599	337840	30893542

B. The evaluation of the investment efficiency of real estate industry of Chinese 35 large and medium cities

The paper selected the indexes in Table 1 as the input index and output index of DEA model. We evaluate based on the Super Efficiency DEA model using (1)-(5). The evaluation results are shown in Table 2.

Table 2. The Evaluation Result of the Investment Efficiency of Real Estate Industry of 35 Large and Medium Cities in China

	City	Efficiency	s_1^-	s_2^-	s_3^-	s_1^+	s_2^+
1	Xi'an	2.4193	0	0	0	0	0
2	Wulumuqi	1.5558	0	0	0	0	0
3	Lanzhou	1.4984	0	0	0	0	0
4	Xiamen	1.3833	0	0	0	0	0
5	Xining	1.3171	0	0	0	0	0
6	Ningbo	1.2176	0	0	0	0	0
7	Guangzhou	1.1341	0	0	0	0	0
8	Shanghai	1.0896	0	0	0	0	0
9	Huhehaote	1.0874	0	0	0	0	0
10	Hangzhou	1.0479	0	0	0	0	0
11	Haikou	1.0010	0	0	0	0	0
12	Shenyang	0.9932	1161692	388.36	0	0	0
13	Dalian	0.9369	983103.4	0	0	47.56	0
14	Yinchuan	0.9010	0	100.71	0	0	0
15	Tianjin	0.8922	0	0	0	0	0.01
16	Beijing	0.8759	2974298	0	0	0	0
17	Kunming	0.8272	359406.4	0	0	0	0
18	Chengdu	0.8166	0.02	0	0	0	0
19	Nanjing	0.8093	0	0	24595.65	0	0
20	Zhengzhou	0.7953	0.03	0	0	0	0.01
21	Changchun	0.7941	0	52.45	0	0	0
22	Shenzhen	0.7516	0.06	0	2603.88	0	0.01
23	Hefei	0.7373	0.1	0	0	0	0.01
24	Qingdao	0.7267	0.02	213.94	0	0	0.01
25	Shijiazhuang	0.7190	449973.9	0	0	11.17	0.01
26	Chongqing	0.6531	0.01	0	0	0	0.06
27	Wuhan	0.6452	0.03	0	0	0	0.04
28	Taiyuan	0.6050	3434.52	0	0	40.63	0
29	Changsha	0.5889	0.01	0	0	0	0
30	Haerbin	0.5792	0	231.17	103300.1	0	523498.7
31	Nanchang	0.5637	0.06	0	0	0	0.01
32	Nanning	0.5537	0	40.87	6756.72	0	0
33	Guiyang	0.5112	0	0	30.23	33.58	0
34	Jinan	0.5017	236823.1	0	0	60.45	0.01
35	Fuzhou	0.4236	0	292.93	96262.99	0	0

In Table 2, the efficiency value θ_0^{super} is smaller, it indicated that the investment efficiency of the real estate industry of the city is lower. In the sample of 35 large and medium cities in China, 11 cities' θ_0^{super} is larger than 1, including Xi'an, Wulumuqi and Lanzhou etc., they were effective DMUs, it indicated that the investment of the real estate industry in these cities were effective; Other cities' DEA efficiency value were all below 1, namely not DEA effective. It illustrated that the investment efficiency of Chinese real estate industry was low as a whole, and the phenomenon of excessive investment existed in the industry universally.

We could see from the value of θ_0^{super} that the investment efficiency of real estate industry in China present obvious regional feature, the cities that are DEA efficient are all belong to eastern costal areas and northwest areas. Moreover, the efficiency values of all the middle cities are below 0.8.

Economic development and the level of resident income are the basis of the development of real estate industry. The southeast costal areas were in the former efficiency position relying on the strong economic strength as well as the superior geographical position. And the city of the northwest areas had promoted their own investment efficiency of real estate industry with the aid of strategy of Western Development, the increasing investment, the improvement of infrastructure and the relative preferential policy.

C. The calculation of input redundancy and output deficiency of real estate industry
We could see from Table II that, the investment efficiency of Shenyang, Dalian, Yinchuan and other 24 cities didn't reach DEA efficiency, namely there existed input redundancy and output deficiency, and had the space for improvement.

We calculate the input redundancy and output deficiency of these cities using (6), (7), and the results are shown in Table 3.

Table 3. Input redundancy and output deficiency

Cities	Input redundancy			Output deficiency	
	Redundancy of annual investment (10 000 yuan)	Redundancy of the new operated area (10 000 square meters)	Redundancy of Employee	Deficiency of the completed area (10000 square meters)	Deficiency of sales (10 000 yuan)
Shenyang	1189815	397.259	83.4496	0	0
Dalian	1150531	40.24329	873.0516	47.56	0
Yinchuan	56047.27	141.9695	630.036	0	0
...	...	...	...	...	...
Guiyang	445377.9	207.3885	8176.571	33.58	0
Jinan	840200.6	224.9924	7215.882	60.45	0.01
Fuzhou	1279764	1387.836	243605.8	0	0

If a city's DEA efficiency value was smaller than 1, it indicated that the city was not on the production frontier, and we could gain the scope information of the efficiency improvement through calculating the projection on the production frontier. The scope information calculated by (6) and (7) was shown in Table 3. Remaining the output unchanged, a city who was not DEA efficient could change the input according to the scope information in Table 3, the city's DEA efficiency value may reach 1. But in practical, we need not to change three input variables simultaneously, and only need to change the most effective one to improve the DEA efficiency.

5   Conclusion

This paper established an evaluation model to measure the investment efficiency of real estate industry based on Super Efficiency DEA. Using the sample of 35 large and medium cities, it reflected that the investment efficiency in Chinese real estate industry was low. Compared with middle regions of china, the investment efficiency of eastern costal areas and northwest areas are higher, they all reach or close to DEA Efficiency. However, the gap of investment efficiency between different areas was large, there existed the problem of input redundancy and output deficiency in most of large and medium cities in China.

References

1. Wang, C.: Research on investment efficiency. Tianjin Finance & Economics University (2004)
2. Yeh, Q.: The application of data development analysis in conjunction with financial ratios for bank Performance evaluation. Journal of Operation Research Society 47(3), 980–988 (1996)
3. Sun, X.: The estimating Research on the efficiencies of Chinese commercial banks based on parameter approach. Dalian University of Technology (2006)
4. Aigner, D., lovell, C.A.K., Schmidt, P.: Formulation and estimation of stochastic frontier production function modes. Journal of Econometrics 6(1), 21–37 (1977)
5. Chen, B.: Analysis of X-efficiency of listed real eatate companies based on Stochastic Frontier Method. Journal of Northwest A&F University (Social Science Edition) 8, 64–68 (2008)
6. Wan, L., Chen, X.: The impact of FDI to the technical efficiency of Chinese real estate industry-based on an empirical research of the data of real estate industry of Chinese provinces. Shanghai Economics Research 3, 66–71 (2007)
7. Charnes, A., Cooper, W.W., Rhodes, E.: Measuring the efficiency of decision making units. European Journal of Operational Research, 429–444 (1978)
8. Sheng, Z., Zhu, Q., Wu, G.: Method of DEA theoretical research and application, pp. 65–72, 154–155. Science Press, Beijing (1996)
9. Liu, Y., Hu, Y., Zhang, F.: Analysis of the performance of listed companies in real estate industry based on DEA. Decision Reference 7, 64–66 (2005)
10. Sun, G.: Research on the efficiency of Chinese real estate based on DEA. Economic Research Guide 9, 174–176 (2007)
11. Geng, X.: An analysis of Chinese real estate industry based on DEA. Statistics & Information Forum 5, 101–104 (2007)
12. Wu, Q., Xie, J.: DEA evaluation of the technological strength of areas based on fuzzy mathematics method. Research of Technological Management 11, 46–49 (2005)
13. Yao, C.: Ranking efficient units in DEA. The International Journal of Management Science 32, 213–219 (2004)

Research on the Method of Parity Checker Design Based on Evolvable Hardware

Kuifu Wang and Jingfeng Yan

School of Computer Science and Technology
Xuchang University
Xuchang, Henan, 461000, China
WANGKuifu@163.com

Abstract. Evolvable hardware design is a new research focus. This paper proposes the method of parity checker design based on evolvable hardware through an introduction to the fundamentals of evolutionary circuit design. The features of algorithm used in this paper are as follows: evolutionary algorithm is combined with multi-objective optimization algorithm, and an optimized logic circuit is evolved and designed with little computing load and high efficiency according to the multiple objectives of design. The simulation results of parity checker's functions indicate that the algorithm used in this paper is better than the method of traditional circuit design in terms of both gate circuit resources and search time.

Keywords: evolvable hardware, genetic algorithm, parity checker.

1 Introduction

The concept of evolvable hardware was proposed by Hugo De Garis at Swiss Federal Institute of Technology in 1952. Evolutionary computation provides theoretical and methodological basis for evolvable hardware, and programmable logic device, especially the new generation of field-programmable gate arrays (FPGA) provides material basis for evolvable hardware. Evolvable hardware can be defined vividly with the following formula:EAs+ PLDs=EHW that is Evolutionary Algorithms + Programmable Logic Devices = Evolvable Hardware.

Programmable logic device (PLD) is an important branch of ASIC. PLD is the semi-custom circuit produced by manufacturers as a universal device which can be programmed by users to perform the logic functions required. As a configurable logic device, PLD has low cost, flexibility, short design cycle, high reliability and small risk, so it develops quickly with widespread application.

2 Ideas and Objectives of Design

Multi-objective optimization model of circuit: many factors shall be taken into account for circuit design: correct circuit functions, few logic gates and short time delay in which only the first one is simply considered in terms of the design method

J. Zhang (Ed.): ICAIC 2011, Part III, CCIS 226, pp. 119–124, 2011.

of classic Cartesian genetic programming, and this paper improves this algorithm by attaining the above objectives within the internal factors of algorithm.

The features of combinational logic circuit show that each logic circuit is composed of multiple inputs and multiple outputs. Inputs have the following features: the constants 0 and 1 always exist in the initial scheme of model design, n variables input and the corresponding inverse variables of n variables are taken together as input parameters, thus the length of input parameter for the circuit of n variables is: 2×n+2. And there may be a single input or multiple inputs.

The serial number of cell array CCN is: CN= i+j×K in which 1≤i≤K and 0≤j≤L-1. Also, it is required that the cells with smaller serial numbers should point at the cells with larger serial numbers in terms of the directions of data input and output in cell arrays, thus loop circuit is avoided.

3   Introduction to Key Technology

A.   Encoding
In terms of the coding method of Miller [1][2], a matrix of logic unit is used as the basis of circuit implementation, circuit design automation is defined as the evolution of the functions and interconnection of logic units, and the functions of each logic unit and the interconnection between logic units are included in the code of each individual. For a 4-bit full adder, the 3*3 logic matrix can be used to represent individuals, and each input terminus and logic module in the matrix is numbered. 0 and 1 indicate the logical constants 0 and 1 respectively, and the two input terminuses of circuit are numbered 2 and 3, while 4 and 5 are used to indicate respectively the negative logic of the two input terminuses. The 9 modules of logic matrix are numbered 6-14 in sequence. The above elements numbered as 0-14 exist as all the logic resources of circuit, and the output of the entire circuit comes from the output of a certain resource.

A 3-digit integer is used to code for each logic unit, with the first digit of this integer indicating the source of the first input signal of logic unit, the second digit indicating the source of the second output of logic unit, and the third digit indicating the functions of logic unit. A logic unit like Fig.1 can be expressed as 5 8 -1.

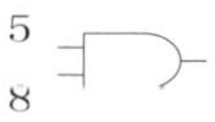

Fig. 1. An AND gate of circuit

-1" indicates that this logic module is an AND gate. If the codes of input signals are serial numbers of signal sources, the codes of circuit functions can be shown in Table1

Table 1. Codes of logic units' functions in this algorithm

Serial number	Gate functions
-1	A & B
-2	A ^ B
-3	A | B
-4	!A
-5	!B

For two-input, one-output logic functions, negative numbers are used to code them, while for a two-route selector

a non-negative number is used to code the third digit, and the value of coding is the serial number of selected signal source of two-route selector. Besides the codes for each logic unit, the codes for individuals also include the codes for each output terminus. And the codes for an individual can be similar to the following:

11 6 9 12 2 -2 4 2 12 6 7 -4 3 5 -2 3 5 16 16 14 -2 5 14 16 4 2 -2 13 18 19. in which, the first 27 describe the functions of the 9 logic units and the last 2 indicate that the two output terminuses come respectively from the two logic units numbered as 18 and 19.

B.   Fitness function design of circuit

In order to test whether the evolved circuit [2][3][4]can fulfill the logic functions expected, the truth table of circuit functions must be presented for each corresponding combination of circuit input, and the expected output must be specified. For the evaluation of individuals, a comparison between output and expected output for each combination type of input will do. The document of truth table includes the functions of objective functions. Miller adopts the method of comparing all the outputs and all the expected outputs for individuals: for a set of inputs in the truth table, if any one of all the outputs of circuit individuals is different from the expected value, it will be regarded as invalid for the function of this input circuit, only if all the outputs totally agree with the expected outputs, will 1 be added to the fitness value.

C.   Genetic operation

Mutation: this algorithm takes each or each related genome separately for mutation with probability at 0.7 and takes each triad for special mutation with a certain probability by letting the mutation domain be at 20.

In the first triad, -1 indicates that the function of Module 6 is AND(&) operation, and -4 is obtained after mutation, and the function of the current Module 6 becomes XOR(^) operation.

Crossover: this algorithm selects the individual with the best fitness from the population as the male parent of next-generation crossover. And crossover with this male parent will be executed for each of the other individuals.

After the traditional crossover operation, another crossover operation is executed for code 1 and code 2 at the end of the first triad for the respective creation of two new code individuals, that is, code 3 and code4 which add new function individuals to the circuit library.

D. Selection strategy design

The algorithm completes the evolution of population by constantly seeking Pareto optimal front which can ensure individuals diversity, thus enabling faster convergence of population. The multi-objective problem of circuit design automation has its own particularity, and what makes it different from the other multi-objective optimization is that the ultimate objective of circuit design automation is specific, that is, exact match for the circuit of expected truth table. The condition for the completion of algorithm is that all objectives reach their maxima.

The algorithm EMOEA can be described as follows:

Step 1 random generation of population P10, with size at N10. Let the counter t=0.

Step 2 select individuals from P1t and P2t by the number of (0.75 * N1t + 0.25 * N2t) * 0.4, with 75% from P1t and 25% from P2t, and obtain offspring Qt through crossover of individuals

Step 3 mutation of offspring Qt

Step 4 insert Qt into P1t to obtain the discarded individual collection Dt

Step 5 insert Dt into P2t

Step 6 t = t + 1

Step 7 if the condition for termination of algorithm is met, turn to Step 8; if not, turn to Step 2

Step 8 output of Pt

In the algorithm designed in this part, the selection of output terminus comes from greedy principle rather than evolution. Comparison between the output of each unit and the expected truth table is made so that the unit with the highest fitness can be selected as the output of circuit. It is rather different from Miller's algorithm in which the output of circuit is, just as the other parts of gene, enabled through genetic operation, in which way good individuals tend to be missed. For instance, a certain individual has been able to obtain the expected circuit via the output of certain logic units, and it may be underestimated or even eliminated from the population just because the output terminus is wrongly selected. The introduction of greedy strategy into the selection of output terminus can ensure individuals maximized evaluation, thus saving individuals from drastic reduction of fitness after genetic operation.

4   Experiment and Result Analysis

Experiment: automatic design of parity checker.

The functions of party checker are defined as follows: only when multi-bit inputs contain an even (or odd) number of "1" will "1" be output, and it is called respectively even checker (or odd checker).

According to the algorithm designed, the optimal individuals of 3-bit even checker computed by programs are as follows: (6 4 –4 5 6 –8 2 8 –4 3 8 5 3 8 –9 1 1 9 13 13 11 10 12 –1 6 11 9 15), in which the number of gates used is 4, and the duration series is 3. With this chromosome and design model, the corresponding logic circuit can be constructed as Fig.2:

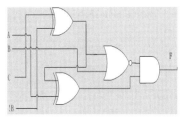

Fig. 2. Logic circuit of 3-bit even checker

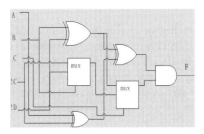

Fig. 3. Logic circuit of 4-bit even checker

Similarly, the optimal individuals of 4-bit even checker are as follows: (9 –4 9 8 3 2 8 –7 7 1 12 8 7 –10 10 12 –4 8 2 –6 5 4 14 7 11 6 11 10 4 15 19 –2 18 3 19 11 8 14 13 2 –7 10 10 12 21 23 –2 20), in which the number of gates used is 6, and the duration series is 3. With this chromosome and design model, the corresponding logic circuit can be constructed as Fig.3.

With the results from the algorithm designed in this paper, a comparison between these results and the existing data from references is made. See Table 2 for the result analysis of 3-bit even checker and Table 3 for that of 4-bit even checker.

The analysis above shows that there's a certain novelty and efficiency in the approach designed in this paper. In terms of the example of 4-bit even checker, both the number of gates used and duration series in this approach are less than the existing literature data.

Table 2. Result analysis of 3-bit even checker

Methods	this paper	Reference [5]	Reference [6]	Manual design
Number of gates used	4	4	4	5
Duration series	3	3	3	3

Also, experiments with 2-bit full adder and 3-bit multiplier are carried out on the basis of this model in this paper, and good computational results are yielded with the computational model and algorithm proposed in this part.

Table 3. Result analysis of 4-bit even checker

Methods	This paper	Reference[5]	Manual design	Manuade sign
Number of gates used	6	7	13	11
Duration series	3	4	5	5

5   Conclusion

This paper proposes the method of circuit design automation of parity checker based on evolvable hardware. Experiment results show that evolutionary algorithm can search automatically the circuit scheme which meets functional requirements with the features of few logic gates and short time delay. And it will be highly significant to introduce this idea into the design of very large-scale integration (VLSI).

References

1. Miller, J.F., Thomson, P., Fogarty, T.: Designing Electronic Circuits Using Evolutionary Algorithm. Arithmetic Circuits: A case Study (1998)
2. Yao, X., Higuchi, T.: Promises and challenges of evolvable hardware. IEEE Transactions on System, Man and Cybernetics-Part C: Application and Reviews 29(1), 87–97 (1999)
3. Chen, G., Wang, X., Zhuang, Z., et al.: Genetic Algorithm and Its Application. People's Post & Telecommunications Press, Beijing (1999) (in Chinese)
4. Huo, H., Xu, J., Bao, Z.: Solving 0/1 Knapsack Problem Using Genetic Algorithm. Journal of Xidian University 26(4), 493–497 (1999)
5. Zhao, S., Yang, W., Liu, G.: Automated Circuit Design Methodologies Using Simulated Evolution. Journal of Circuits and Systems 3:7(1), 71–79 (2002)
6. Zhao, S., Yang, W.: A New Method for the Chromosome Representation in the Evolvable Hardware. Journal of Xidian University 27(6), 778–780 (2000)

Control System Modeling for Automotive Brake Test-Bench Based on Neural Network[*]

Jiaxi Du, Hong Shen, and Xin Ning

Department of Mechanical and Electrical Engineering
Henan Institute of Science and Technology
Xinxiang, Henan Province, China
jiaxidujiaxidu@sina.cn

Abstract. In allusion to the control method of automotive brake test-bench, this paper first established the mathematical model of motor drive current based on instantaneous rotational speed and other measurable parameters, and then proposed a control model by completely using the electric inertia simulation equivalent moment of inertia, furthermore carried on the appraisal. Afterward introduced the neural network control method and established the control system model by computing the control voltage, and adjusting the rotational speed. The algorithm of this control model is simple, and it is easy to realize the real-time control, moreover, it solves some shortcomings in conventional rotational speed control and enhances the data fitting effect greatly.

Keywords: equivalent moment of inertia, neural network, mechanical inertia, automotive brake.

1 Introduction

Automotive brake (hereinafter referred to as brake) is connected with the wheel, its' role is to slow down or stop the vehicle. Design of brake is one of the most important design of vehicles, and that it directly affects the safety of persons and vehicles. In order to test the merits and integrated performance of the design, the brake needs a lot of testing in a variety of different road situations. Because the road testing of vehicles can not be carried out at the design stage, it can only be simulated on a special brake test-bench. Therefore it is essential to carry on the simulation for the brake before it being installed, furthermore, the control method analysis and performance comparison for the brake test-bench are especially important too. And this set the very high request to the brake simulation test's precision. However there are so many influencing factors during the simulation process, and it will increase the simulation error. We need to establish brake's mathematical model and compare it with the actual brake situation, analyze the error, give the appraisal.

---

[*] This work was supported by Technological Project of The Education Department of Henan Province under Grant No. 2006520027.

J. Zhang (Ed.): ICAIC 2011, Part III, CCIS 226, pp. 125–130, 2011.

2   Modeling

A. *The mathematical model of motor drive current based on measurable parameters*
Electric motor's drive current is proportional with the moment of torque. So in order to
establish the mathematical model of motor drive current, we should first find the
physical relations between the moment of torque and the measurable parameters.

In modelling process, we did not consider the energy loss caused by friction force as
well as other energy loss. Suppose the change quantity of rotation kinetic energy for
spindle and the flywheel is $\triangle E$, the power done by the braking torque is W_1, the power
done by the electrical machinery torque is W_2, by energy conservation [1]:

$$\Delta E \pm W_2 = W_1 \tag{1}$$

Suppose J_1 stands for the mechanical inertia; J_2 stands for the equivalent moment of
inertia of braking spindle. If $J_1 > J_2$, then the power done by the motor is negative, so
this moment the "$\pm$" takes "$-$" in formula (1); while $J_1 < J_2$, the power done by the motor
is positive, the "$\pm$" takes "$+$" in formula (1).

Suppose ω_0 stands for the rotational speed at the beginning of the brake time; J_C
stands for the mechanical inertia needs to be compensated; E_C stands for the
corresponding energy which needs to be supplemented. It is known by the dynamics of
knowledge that:

$$J_C = |J_2 - J_1| \tag{2}$$

$$E_C = \frac{1}{2} J_C \omega_0^2 \tag{3}$$

Therefore, the power done by the drive current is:

$$W_E = \int_0^{\theta_t} M_E(t) d\theta \tag{4}$$

In this formula, parameter θ_t stands for the total angle during the brake process and
satisfies the following equation that:

$$\theta_t = \int d\theta = \int_0^{} \frac{2\pi n}{60} dt \tag{5}$$

By energy conservation:

$$E_C = W_E \tag{6}$$

Suppose k is the scale coefficient between electric motor's drive current and its
torque, therefore the drive current expression is as follows[2]:

$$i = k M_E(t) \tag{7}$$

According to formula (2), (4), (5), (6), (7), we can get the mathematical model of
motor drive current based on measurable parameters:

$$\begin{cases} W_E = \int_0^{\theta_t} M_E(t)d\theta \\ \theta_t = \int d\theta = \int_0 \dfrac{2\pi n}{60}dt \\ E_C = \dfrac{1}{2}J_C\omega_0^2 \\ E_C = W_E \\ i = kM_E(t) \end{cases} \qquad (8)$$

In this formula, the instantaneous rotational speed, the time and other parameters are all measurable.

Under the actual situation, the braking torque cannot be a constant, and the driving torque caused by electric motor's drive current cannot be a constant either. In addition machinery and brake quantity is so complex that brake's rotational speed $n(t)$ is unable to be expressed accurately during the brake process. Therefore the computation of $M_E(t)$ is more complex[3]. Suppose the brake retarded velocity is in constant under the idealized situation, then the braking torque and the drive torque of electric motor are constant too, so the resultant moment of spindle and the flywheel is the constant, moreover the angle acceleration is a definite value. Consequently we can draw the conclusion that:

$$i = k \cdot \frac{E_C}{\theta} = k \cdot \frac{\dfrac{1}{2}J_C\omega_0^2}{\theta} \qquad (9)$$

B. The mathematical model of motor drive current based on integral equation model (IEM)

It is obviously that in the model derived from formula (8) the rotational speed simultaneously relies on the braking moment. In case of the braking torque is difficult to determine, the relationship between the rotational speed and the time, the electric motor braking moment and the time are difficult to accurately determine. Therefore it is more difficult to solve the model, and the precise relationship between the motor drive current and the time is difficult to obtain.

In engineering practice, we usually divide the whole braking time t averagely into a number of small discrete interval $\triangle t$ (for example 10ms), and then quickly calculate corresponding drive current by the instantaneous speed and the instantaneous braking torque measured during the current time[4], then let this drive current be the motor drive current of next interval, continue the implementation of this repeatedly until the end of braking. The design methods for drive current of each interval time are quite many, so different method causes different operational process for the spindle and the flywheel. Through the contrastive analysis, we conclude that when using the electric motor to supplement energy lacks caused by the insufficient mechanical inertia, we should make the spindle and the flywheel's motion condition close to the expectation state of motion as far as possible. While this expectation state of motion represents the spindle and the flywheel's motion condition with the equivalent moment of inertia under brake state of motion. The control method for drive current of each interval time is as follows [5]:

The control system issues the brake instruction during the first interval time, measures and records the instantaneous rotational speed N_1(angular velocity ω_1) and the instantaneous braking torque M_1 by the time $t=0s$ simultaneously. Then the control system measures and records the instantaneous rotational speed N_2(angular velocity ω_2) and the instantaneous braking torque M_2 by the time $t=0.01s$ during the second interval time. According to the following formula:

$$\Delta E = \frac{1}{2}(J_2 - J_1)\left(\omega_1{}^2 - \omega_2{}^2\right) \tag{10}$$

We can calculate the energy needs to be supplemented in this interval time. Simultaneously in the supposition of the resultant moment of the spindle and the flywheel is constantly M_2 during this time, we can calculate the angle θ that the flywheel has rotated during this interval time:

$$\theta = \omega_2 \bullet \Delta t - \frac{1}{2}\frac{M_2}{J_1}\Delta t^2 \tag{11}$$

Therefore, the constant drive current during this time needs to be supplemented is:

$$i = k\frac{\Delta E}{\theta} \tag{12}$$

Then the control system measures and records the instantaneous rotational speed N_3(angular velocity ω_3) and the instantaneous braking torque M_3 by the time $t = 0.02s$ during the third interval time. According to the following formula:

$$\Delta E = \frac{1}{2}(J_2 - J_1)\left(\omega_2{}^2 - \omega_3{}^2\right) \tag{13}$$

We can calculate the energy needs to be supplemented in this interval time. Moreover we can calculate the drive current during this time by the same control method previously described and continue the implementation of this repeatedly until the end of braking.

C. The mathematical model of motor drive current based on neural network
By analyzing the IEM, we find two flaws in it[6,7]: one is the system error which is caused by making continuous problem discretization; the other is the delay error derived from the real-time monitoring device for drive current of electric motor. In order to make up the above flaws, we designed one kind of self-adaptive neural network control method. This method does not rely on the mathematical model in brake parameter's setting, and the brake parameter can be online adjusted.

The control policy of this method is: in order to achieve the control purpose we should first calculate the control voltage $u(k)$ and then adjust the rotational speed $\omega_i(k)$. Specific details are as follows:

$$u(k) = \frac{K_u[\sum_{i=1}^{n}\omega_i(k)x_i(k)]}{\sum_{i}^{n}\|\omega_i(k)\|} \tag{14}$$

$$u_g(k) = U_{max} \frac{1 - e^{-u(k)}}{1 + e^{-u(k)}}$$ (15)

$$\omega_i(k+1) = \omega_i(k) + \eta_i e(k)|u_g(k)|x_i(k)$$ (16)

In this formula, parameter U_{max} stands for the maximum limit amplitude of excitation function; $x_i(k)$ for the state variable; K_u stands for predefined parameter for self-adaptive neuron controller; η_i stands for the parameter which can be adaptively adjusted by self-learning function of neuron controller.

By this control policy we don't need to establish the precise model of the braking system, moreover the algorithm is simple, and it is easy to realize real-time control. Even if the parameters of controlled object change, it still has good control quality. According to the electrical machinery transmission system's characteristic of electric inertia system, we can transform the system's rotational speed loop by mononeural controller, and design controller's learning algorithm by combining the Hebb learning rule with the Widrow-Hof learning rule. Thus solve the speed response over modulation in conventional speed control effectively, and enhance the fitting effect greatly.

3   Conclusion

When designs the computer's control method, we should observe the simulation principle of the brake test-bench all the time, and close the actual situation of road testing as far as possible. That is to say, we cannot too idealize the road testing environment. So establish the control model only like this will have the actual project application possibility.

A.   Models merits

The modeling process is not simply an idealized treatment of physical quantities, but a combination of practical factors, close to the actual situation, and the error is relatively small;

Use the idea of feedback control from analog circuit, and establish a closed-loop speed control system, solve the problem of computer control method perfectly;

The project significance of this model is strong, and it also has good practical operability.

B.   Models shortcomings

The handling of individual physical quantities during the modeling process has a certain subjectivity; the model's control policy makes decision only by the approximate to the image; so it will have a bad influence on the results.

C.   Improvement direction of the model [8]

During modeling process we do not take the heat factor caused by friction into account, but in fact, heat dissipation is a more important energy dissipation, so the model can be improved by adding the discussion of the friction heat.

References

1. Gu, M.: Research on the Inertia Test Bed for Brakes of the Middle Trucks and Light Trucks. Modular Machine Tool & Automatic Manufacturing Technique (4), 23–27 (2008)
2. Wang, X.-f., Zhou, Z.-x., Xie, X.-y., et al.: Analysis and Calculating of Braking Torque of Inertia Brake. Modern Manufacturing Engineering (8), 107–108 (2006)
3. Gu, M.: Design of General Braking Performance Test Bed for Auto Brakes. Machinery (6), 8–13 (200)
4. James, K., Marks, A.: Inertia Simulation in Brake Dynamo-meter Testing. Technical Paper Series, SAE, pp. 46–49 (2002)
5. Chen, J.-j.: Control to Electric Simulation of Mechanical Inertia of Brake Testing System. Hoisting and Conveying Machinery (12), 103–107 (2007)
6. Feng, G., Liu, Z.-f., Zhang, H.-c.: Research on Brake Based on the Simulation Technology. Mechanical Engineer (7), 82–86 (2008)
7. Du, J.-x., Shen, H., Zhang, W.-q.: The Computer Modeling and Simulation Analysis for Automotive Brake Test-Bench. Modular Machine Tool & Automatic Manufacturing Technique (6), 21–24 (2010)
8. Mei, Z.-x.: Improved Design of Brake Testing System Performance. Machine Tool & Hydraulics (6), 60–65 (2008)

Adaptive Projective Synchronization of Complex Networks with Weighted Topology[*]

Dianchen Lu and Qiaoxia Qi

Nonlinear Scientific Research Center
Jiangsu University
Zhenjiang Jiangsu, 212013, P.R. China
DianchenLu@yeah.net

Abstract. Recently, much attention has been paid to the geometry features, synchronization and control of complex network associated with certain network structure. In this paper, by using Lyapunov theory, an adaptive feedback controlling scheme is proposed to identify the exact topology of a general weighted complex dynamical network model. By receiving the network nodes evolution, the topology of such kind of network with identical or different nodes, or even with switching topology can be monitored. Numerical simulation show that the methods presented in this paper are of high accuracy with good performance.

Keywords: weighted topology complex networks, Time-varying coupling delay, Adaptive control.

1 Introduction

Complex networks exist in every corner of the world, from the communication networks to social networks, from cellular networks to metabolic networks, from the Internet to the World Wide Web [1-9]. The study of complex networks is under way. Many existed literature studied synchronization and control of a complex dynamic network with certain known topology [10-15]. Actually, however, in real applications, it is difficult even impossible to attain the topological structure of the related networks [16]. Therefore, how to determine the complex network topology becomes a key problem in many disciplines, such as DNA replication, modification, repair and RNA (ribonucleic acid) transcription. It is of significance that by monitoring dynamic behavior of proteins during the process of recognition through NMR (nuclear magnetic resonance) technology[8]. Therefore, to determine interactive network nodes which can be existed in different topological structure is significance. In this work, the real network is served as a drive network, and another response network receiving the evolution of each node is also introduced, and the exact topology of the real network can be identified by using adaptive feedback control method,. Along

* This work is by the Jiangsu Province Natural Science Foundations of University (No: 10KJD110002) and the Outstanding Personnel Program in Six Fields of Jiangsu (No: 2009188).

J. Zhang (Ed.): ICAIC 2011, Part III, CCIS 226, pp. 131–140, 2011.

with it, the evolution of every node is traced. Using Lyapunov stability theory [17], theoretical analysis of the mechanism is developed rigorously. Our controlling scheme may be applied to a large amount of rather general weighted complex dynamical networks not only with identical nodes, but also with different nodes. All these will contribute to improving efficiency and accuracy of network analysis.

This paper is organized as follows: Section 2 describes the topology identification method for a general weighted complex dynamical network with identical nodes. Identifying topology mechanism for such kind of network consisting of different nodes is detailed in Section 3. A weighted complex network with different node dynamics is listed in section 4. In section 5, we introduce adaptive controlling method. In section 6, we give an example. The main ideas and conclusions are summarized up in Section 7.

2 Model Description and Preliminaries

In this paper, a complex dynamical network with time-varying coupling delay consisting of N identical nodes with linear couplings is considered, which is characterized by

$$\dot{x}_i(t) = B x_i(t) + f(t, x_i(t)) + \sum_{j=1, j \neq i}^{N} a_{ij} H(t) x_j(t - \tau(t)), \qquad (1)$$

$$i = 1, 2, \ldots, N,$$

where $x_i(t) = (x_{i1}(t), x_{i2}(t), \ldots x_{iN}(t))^T \in R^N$ is the state vector of the i th node, $H(t) = (h_{ij})_{N \times N} \in R^{N \times N}$ is inner-coupling matrix, $B = (b_{ij})_{N \times N}$ is a constant matrix, $A(t) = (a_{ij}(t))_{N \times N}$ is the unknown or uncertain weight configuration matrix, $f : R \times R^N \to R^N$ is a smooth nonlinear function, $\tau(t) \geq 0$ is the time-varying coupling delay. If there is a connection from node i to node $j \, (j \neq i)$, then the coupling $a_{ij}(t) = c_{ij} \neq 0$, otherwise, $a_{ij}(t) = 0 , (j = i)$ and the diagonal elements of matrix $A(t)$ are defined as

$$\sum_{j=1}^{N} a_{ij} = 0 \Rightarrow a_{ii} = - \sum_{j=1, j \neq i}^{N} a_{ij}, \quad i = 1, 2, \ldots, N.$$

Assumption 1. Time delay $\tau(t)$ is a differential function with $\xi \in [2\dot{\tau}(t) - 1, 1]$.

Assumption 2. Suppose there exists a constant L, such that

$$\| f(t, x(t)) - f(t, y(t)) \| \leq L \| x(t) - y(t) \|$$

holds for any time-varying vectors $x(t)$, $y(t)$, and norm $\|\cdot\|$ of a vector x is defined as $\| X \| = (X^T X)^{1/2}$.

Lemma $\forall \, x(t) = [x_1(t), x_2(t), \cdots x_n(t)]^T \in R^n$,

$y(t) = [y_1(t), y_2(t), \cdots y_n(t)]^T \in R^n$, there exist a positive definite matrix $p \in R^{n \times n}$, the following matrix inequality holds:

$$2x^T y \leq x^T P x + y^T P^{-1} y.$$

3   Adaptive Controlling Method

In this section, we make drive-response complex dynamical networks with time-varying coupling delay achieve adaptive projective synchronization by using adaptive controlling method. We consider a response network as the drive complex network model (1)

$$\dot{y}_i(t) = By_i(t) + f(t, y_i(t)) + \sum_{j=1, j\neq i}^{N} \hat{a}_{ij} H(t) y_j(t - \tau(t)) + u_i, \tag{2}$$

$$i = 1, 2, \ldots, N,$$

where $y_i(t) = (y_{i1}(t), y_{i2}(t), \ldots y_{iN}(t))^T \in R^N$ is the response state vector of the i th node, u_i $(i=1,\ldots, N)$ are nonlinear controllers to be designed, and $\hat{A} = (\hat{a}_{ij})_{N \times N}$ is estimation of the weight matrix $A(t)$.

Let $e_i(t) = x_i(t) - \lambda y_i(t), (\lambda \neq 0, i = 1, 2, \ldots N)$, λ is a scaling factor and $c_{ij} = \hat{a}_{ij} - a_{ij}$, with the aid of Equations (1) and (2), the following error dynamical network can be obtained:

$$\dot{e}_i(t) = Be_i(t) + f(t, x_i(t)) - \lambda f(t, y_i(t))$$
$$- \lambda \sum_{\substack{j=1 \\ j\neq i}}^{N} c_{ij} H(t) y_j(t - \tau(t)) + \sum_{\substack{j=1 \\ j\neq i}}^{N} a_{ij} H(t) e_j(t - \tau(t)) - \lambda u_i, \tag{3}$$

$$i = 1, 2, \ldots, N.$$

We tend to know in accordance with the definition of synchronization:

$$\lim_{t\to\infty} |e_i(t)| = \lim_{t\to\infty} |a_{ij} - \hat{a}_{ij}| = 0, \qquad i = 1, 2, \ldots, N.$$

Theorem 1. Suppose Assumption 1 holds. Using the following adaptive controllers and updated laws:

$$u_i = \frac{1}{\lambda} [d_i e_i(t) + \lambda f(t, y_i(t)) - f(t, \lambda y_i(t))], (\lambda \neq 0), i = 1, 2, \ldots, N$$

$$\dot{c}_{ij} = \lambda \delta_{ij} H(t) y_j(t - \tau(t)) e_i^T(t), (\lambda \neq 0), i, j = 1, 2, \ldots, N$$

$$\dot{d}_i = k_i (1 - \frac{d_i^*}{d_i}) e_i^T(t) e_i(t), d_i \neq 0, i = 1, 2, \ldots, N$$

where $d = (d_1, d_2 \cdots d_N)^T \in R^N$ is the adaptive feedback gain vector to be designed, $\delta_{ij} > 0$, $k_i > 0$ $(i = 1, 2, \cdots N)$ are arbitrary constants, then the response network (2) can synchronize with the drive network (1), and the weight configuration matrix $A(t)$ of network (1) can be identified by $\hat{A}(t)$, i.e.,

$$\lim_{t\to\infty} |e_i(t)| = \lim_{t\to\infty} |a_{ij} - \hat{a}_{ij}| = 0 \quad i = 1, 2, \ldots, N.$$

Proof. Choose the following Lyapunov function:

$$V(t) = \frac{1}{2}\sum_{i=1}^{N} e_i^T(t)e_i(t) + \frac{1}{2}\sum_{i=1}^{N}\sum_{j=1}^{N}\frac{1}{\delta_{ij}}c_{ij}^2 \tag{4}$$

$$+ \frac{1}{2}\sum_{i=1}^{N}\frac{1}{k_i}d_i^2 + \frac{1}{1-\xi}\int_{t-\tau(t)}^{t}\sum_{i=1}^{N}e_i^T(t)e_i(t)dt$$

where d_i^* is a positive constant to be determined. Calculating the derivative of (4) along the trajectories of (3), and with adaptive controllers (4) and updated laws (5) and (6).Thus, we obtain:

$$\dot{V}(t) = \sum_{i=1}^{N}e_i^T(t)[Be_i(t) + f(t,x_i(t)) - \lambda f(t,y_i(t))$$

$$-\lambda\sum_{j=1}^{N}c_{ij}H(t)y_j(t-\tau(t)) + \sum_{j=1}^{N}a_{ij}H(t)e_j(t-\tau(t)) - \lambda u_i]$$

$$+\sum_{i=1}^{N}\sum_{j=1}^{N}\frac{1}{\delta_{ij}}c_{ij}\dot{c}_{ij} + \sum_{i=1}^{N}\frac{1}{k_i}d_i\dot{d}_i + \frac{1}{1-\xi}\sum_{i=1}^{N}e_i^T(t)e_i(t)$$

$$-\frac{1-\dot{\tau}(t)}{1-\xi}\sum_{i=1}^{N}e_i^T(t-\tau(t))e_i(t-\tau(t))$$

$$= \sum_{i=1}^{N}e_i^T(t)Be_i(t) + \sum_{i=1}^{N}\sum_{j=1}^{N}e_i^T(t)a_{ij}H(t)e_j(t-\tau(t))$$

$$+\sum_{i=1}^{N}e_i^T(t)[f(t,x_i(t)) - f(t,\lambda y_i(t))] + \frac{1}{1-\xi}\sum_{i=1}^{N}e_i^T(t)e_i(t)$$

$$-\frac{1-\dot{\tau}(t)}{1-\xi}\sum_{i=1}^{N}e_i^T(t-\tau(t))e_i(t-\tau(t)) - \sum_{i=1}^{N}d_i^*e_i^T(t)e_i(t)$$

$$\leq \sum_{i=1}^{N}e_i^T(t)Be_i(t) + \sum_{i=1}^{N}\sum_{j=1}^{N}e_i^T(t)a_{ij}H(t)e_j(t-\tau(t))$$

$$+L\sum_{i=1}^{N}e_i^T(t)e_i(t) + \frac{1}{1-\xi}\sum_{i=1}^{N}e_i^T(t)e_i(t)$$

$$-\frac{1-\dot{\tau}(t)}{1-\xi}\sum_{i=1}^{N}e_i^T(t-\tau(t))e_i(t-\tau(t)) - \sum_{i=1}^{N}d_i^*e_i^T(t)e_i(t)$$

$$\leq e^T(t)Be(t) + Le^T(t)e(t) + e^T(t)Pe(t-\tau(t)) - e^T(t)D^*e(t)$$

$$+\frac{1}{1-\xi}e^T(t)e(t) - \frac{1-\dot{\tau}(t)}{1-\xi}e^T(t-\tau(t))e(t-\tau(t))$$

$$\leq e^T(t)Be(t) + Le^T(t)e(t) + \frac{1}{2}e^T(t)PP^Te(t)$$

$$-e^T(t)D^*e(t) + \frac{1}{1-\xi}e^T(t)e(t) - \frac{1-\dot{\tau}(t)}{1-\xi}e^T(t-\tau(t))e(t-\tau(t))$$

$$+\frac{1}{2}e^T(t-\tau(t))e(t-\tau(t))$$

Let $e(t) = (e_1^T(t), e_2^T(t), \cdots e_N^T(t))^T \in R^{N \times N}$, $P = (A(t) \otimes H(t))$, where $\otimes$ represents the Kronecker product. From Assumption 1, we get $\dfrac{1 - \dot{\tau}(t)}{1 - \xi} \geq \dfrac{1}{2}$. Thus we have

$$\dot{V}(t) \leq e^T(t)(B + LI + \frac{1}{1 - \xi}I - D^* + \frac{1}{2}PP^T)e(t),$$

where I is the identity maximal($I = diag(\overbrace{1,1,\cdots 1}^{N})$), $D^* = diag(d_1^*, d_2^*, \cdots d_N^*)$.

The constants d_i^* ($i = 1, 2, \ldots N$)can be properly chosen to make $\dot{V}(t) < 0$ .Therefore, based on the Lyapunov stability theory, the errors vector $\lim\limits_{t \to \infty} |e(t)| = 0$ and $\lim\limits_{t \to \infty} \|\hat{A}(t) - A(t)\| = 0$ .This implies the unknown weighs a_{ij} can be successfully using adaptive controllers (4) and update laws (5) and (6). Further, we can further the value of L to determine the value of constant D^*, and we define the norm:

$$L_1 = \min_{i,j}\{\|Df(t, x_i(t))\|, \|Df(t, y_i(t))\|, \max_{\substack{1 \leq j \leq n \\ j \in N^*}} \sum_{i=1}^{N} |d_i^*| - \frac{N}{1 - \xi}$$

$$- \max_{\substack{1 \leq j \leq n \\ j \in N^*}} \sum_{i=1}^{N} |b_{ij}| - \frac{1}{2}[\max_{\substack{1 \leq j \leq n \\ j \in N^*}} \sum_{i=1}^{N} |p_{ij}^*|]\}. \qquad (5)$$

Respectively, $\|Df(t, x_i(t))\|$ and $\|Df(t, y_i(t))\|$ are in the point $x_i(t)$ and $y_i(t)$ the Department of Jacobin Matrix. When $L < L_1$, we easily get $\dot{V}(t) < 0$. According to Lyapunov stability theory we get $\lim\limits_{t \to \infty} \|e_i(t)\| = \lim\limits_{t \to \infty} \|x_i(t) - \lambda y_i(t)\| = 0$.

4   A Weighted Complex Network with Different Node Dynamics

In this subsection, we consider a weighted complex dynamical network consisting of different node dynamics which is described by

$$\begin{cases} \dot{x}_i(t) = B_1 x_i(t) + g(t, x_i(t)) + \sum\limits_{j=1, j \neq i}^{N} a_{ij} H(t) x_j(t - \tau(t)) \\ \qquad\qquad\qquad\qquad\qquad\qquad\qquad 1 \leq i \leq N^* \\ \dot{x}_i(t) = B_2 x_i(t) + h(t, x_i(t)) + \sum\limits_{j=1, j \neq i}^{N} a_{ij} H(t) x_j(t - \tau(t)) \\ \qquad\qquad\qquad\qquad\qquad\qquad\qquad N^* + 1 \leq i \leq N \end{cases} \qquad (6)$$

$g, h : R^N \times R^+ \to R^N$ are different smooth nonlinear vector functions. Similarly, a useful hypothesis is given as follows:

Assumption 3. (A3)Suppose that there exist positive constants β and γ, satisfying

$$\|g(y) - g(z)\| \leq \beta \|y - z\|, \|h(y) - h(z)\| \leq \gamma \|y - z\|,$$

where y, z are time-varying vectors.

5 Adaptive Controlling Method

For the sake of identifying topology of network model (6) and tracing network nodes evolution, generally controlled complex dynamical network is introduced here:

$$
\begin{cases}
\dot{y}_i(t) = B_1 y_i(t) + g(t, y_i(t)) \\
\quad + \displaystyle\sum_{j=1, j \neq i}^{N} \hat{a}_{ij} H(t) y_j(t - \tau(t)) + u_i, \quad 1 \leq i \leq N^*; \\
\dot{y}_i(t) = B_2 y_i(t) + h(t, y_i(t)) \\
\quad + \displaystyle\sum_{j=1, j \neq i}^{N} \hat{a}_{ij} H(t) y_j(t - \tau(t)) + u_i, \quad N^* + 1 \leq i \leq N.
\end{cases}
\tag{7}
$$

Then, we have the error system:

$$
\begin{cases}
\dot{e}_i(t) = B_1 e_i(t) + g(t, x_i(t)) - \lambda g(t, y_i(t)) \\
\quad - \lambda \displaystyle\sum_{j=1, j \neq i}^{N} c_{ij} H(t) y_j(t - \tau(t)) \\
\quad + \displaystyle\sum_{j=1, j \neq i}^{N} a_{ij} H(t) e_j(t - \tau(t)) - \lambda u_i, \quad 1 \leq i \leq N^*; \\
\dot{e}_i(t) = B_2 e_i(t) + h(t, x_i(t)) - \lambda h(t, y_i(t)) \\
\quad - \lambda \displaystyle\sum_{j=1, j \neq i}^{N} c_{ij} H(t) y_j(t - \tau(t)) \\
\quad + \displaystyle\sum_{j=1, j \neq i}^{N} a_{ij} H(t) e_j(t - \tau(t)) - \lambda u_i, \quad N^* + 1 \leq i \leq N.
\end{cases}
\tag{8}
$$

Where $e_i(t) = x_i(t) - \lambda y_i(t), (\lambda \neq 0), c_{ij} = \hat{a}_{ij} - a_{ij}$.

Similarly, the following adaptive controlling mechanism can be deduced.

Theorem 2. Suppose that A3 holds. The weight configuration matrix $A(t)$ of general linearly coupled complex dynamical network (6) can be identified by the estimation $\hat{A}(t)$ using the following response network:

$$u_i - \frac{1}{\lambda}[d_i e_i(t) + \lambda g(t, y_i(t)) - g(t, \lambda y_i(t))], (\lambda \neq 0), 1 \leq i \leq N^*$$

$$u_i = \frac{1}{\lambda}[d_i e_i(t) + \lambda h(t, y_i(t)) - h(t, \lambda y_i(t))], (\lambda \neq 0), N^* + 1 \leq i \leq n$$

$$\dot{c}_{ij} = \lambda \delta_{ij} H(t) y_j(t - \tau(t)) e_i^T(t), (\lambda \neq 0), i, j = 1, 2, \ldots, N$$

$$\dot{d}_i = k_i (1 - \frac{d}{d_i}) e_i^T(t) e_i(t), d_i \neq 0, i = 1, 2, \ldots, N$$

Proof. Provided with the condition A3, we get

$$\left\|g(t,x_i(t))-\lambda g(t,y_i(t))\right\|\le\beta\left\|e_i(t)\right\|, i=1,2,\ldots,N^*,$$

$$\left\|h(t,x_i(t))-\lambda h(t,y_i(t))\right\|\le\gamma\left\|e_i(t)\right\|, i=N^*+1,\ldots,N.$$

Choose the following Lyapunov function

$$V(t)=\frac{1}{2}\sum_{i=1}^{N}e_i^T(t)e_i(t)+\frac{1}{2}\sum_{i=1}^{N}\sum_{j=1}^{N}\frac{1}{\delta_{ij}}c_{ij}^2$$

$$+\frac{1}{2}\sum_{i=1}^{N}\frac{1}{k_i}d_i^2+\frac{1}{1-\xi}\int_{t-\tau(t)}^{t}\sum_{i=1}^{N}e_i^T(t)e_i(t)dt$$

where $\xi\in[2\tau'(t)-1,1]$, d is sufficiently large positive constant to be determined. We then have

$$\dot{V}(t)=\sum_{i=1}^{N^*}e_i^T(t)\dot{e}_i(t)+\sum_{i=N^*+1}^{N}e_i^T(t)\dot{e}_i(t)+\sum_{i=1}^{N}\sum_{j=1}^{N}\frac{1}{\delta_{ij}}c_{ij}\dot{c}_{ij}+\sum_{i=1}^{N}\frac{1}{k_i}d_i\dot{d}_i$$

$$+\frac{1}{1-\xi}\sum_{i=1}^{N}e_i^T(t)e_i(t)-\frac{1-\dot{\tau}(t)}{1-\xi}\sum_{i=1}^{N}e_i^T(t-\tau(t))e_i(t-\tau(t))$$

$$=\sum_{i=1}^{N^*}e_i^T(t)[B_1e_i(t)+g(t,x_i(t))-\lambda g(t,y_i(t))$$

$$-\lambda\sum_{\substack{j=1\\j\ne i}}^{N}c_{ij}H(t)y_j(t-\tau(t))+\sum_{\substack{j=1\\j\ne i}}^{N}a_{ij}H(t)e_j(t-\tau(t))-\lambda u_i]$$

$$+\sum_{i=N^*+1}^{N}e_i^T(t)[B_2e_i(t)+h(t,x_i(t))-\lambda h(t,y_i(t))$$

$$-\lambda\sum_{\substack{j=1\\j\ne i}}^{N}c_{ij}H(t)y_j(t-\tau(t))+\sum_{\substack{j=1\\j\ne i}}^{N}a_{ij}H(t)e_j(t-\tau(t))-\lambda u_i]$$

$$+\sum_{i=1}^{N}\sum_{j=1}^{N}\frac{1}{\delta_{ij}}c_{ij}\dot{c}_{ij}+\sum_{i=1}^{N}\frac{1}{k_i}d_i\dot{d}_i+\frac{1}{1-\xi}N\sum_{i=1}^{N}e_i^T(t)e_i(t)$$

$$-\frac{1-\dot{\tau}(t)}{1-\xi}\sum_{i=1}^{N}e_i^T(t-\tau(t))e_i(t-\tau(t))$$

$$\le\sum_{i=1}^{N^*}\beta\left\|e_i(t)\right\|^2+\sum_{i=N^*+1}^{N}\gamma\left\|e_i(t)\right\|^2+\sum_{i=1}^{N^*}\left\|B_1\right\|\left\|e_i(t)\right\|^2$$

$$+\sum_{i=N^*+1}^{N}\left\|B_2\right\|\left\|e_i(t)\right\|^2+\sum_{i=1}^{N}\sum_{j=1}^{N}a_{ij}e_i^T(t)H(t)e_i(t-\tau(t))$$

$$-\sum_{i=1}^{N}d\left\|e_i(t)\right\|^2+\frac{1}{1-\xi}\sum_{i=1}^{N}\left\|e_i(t)\right\|^2-\frac{1-\dot{\tau}(t)}{1-\xi}\sum_{i=1}^{N}\left\|e_i(t-\tau(t))\right\|^2$$

$$=e^T(t)Qe(t)$$

where

$$\|B_1\| = \max_j \sum_{i=1}^{N^*} |a_{ij}|, \quad \|B_2\| = \max_j \sum_{i=N^*+1}^{N} |a_{ij}|,$$

$$e(t) = (e_1^T(t), e_2^T(t), \cdots e_n^T(t))^T \in R^{n \times n}$$

$$Q = \begin{pmatrix} \left(\beta + \dfrac{1}{1-\xi} + \|B_1\| - d\right)I_{nN^*} & 0 \\ 0 & \left(\gamma + \dfrac{1}{1-\xi} + \|B_2\| - d\right)I_{n(N-N^*)} \end{pmatrix} + A(t) \otimes H(t).$$

Clearly, the matrix Q is negative definite when the positive constant d is large enough, then we can get $\dot{V}(t) < 0$, we obtain $\lim_{t\to\infty} |e_i(t)| = 0$ for $i = 1,\ldots,N$ and $\lim_{t\to\infty} |c_{ij}| = 0$ for $i, j = 1,\ldots,N$. That is, the weight configuration matrix $A(t)$ can be identified by the matrix $\hat{A}(t)$. Thus the proof is completed.

Remark 1. In this theorem, the weighted complex dynamical network is built up of two types of different nodes. For networks with more types of ones, similar work can be generalized easily. From this theorem, it is shown that using similar adaptive feedback controlling approach, the exact topology of model (6) can be identified, and the evolution of every node can be traced simultaneously. On account of the widespread circumstances in which considerable weighted complex dynamical networks with different nodes exist, this mechanism is of great significance in practice.

6   Numerical Simulation

Let us consider the Lorenz system, which is described by the following model

$$\begin{cases} \dot{x} = a(y-x), \\ \dot{y} = cx - xz - y, \\ \dot{z} = xy - bz, \end{cases} \tag{9}$$

which has a chaotic attractor for the parameter values $a=10$, $b=8/3$ and $c=28$. Now, we consider a weighted linearly coupled complex dynamical network (1) with coupling delay consisting of 5 identical above chaotic systems. Taking the weight configuration coupling matrix

$$\dot{x}_i(t) = Bx_i(t) + f(t,x_i(t)) + \sum_{j=1,j\neq i}^{N} a_{ij}H(t)x_j(t-\tau(t)) \quad i=1,2,\ldots,5$$

where $H(t) = I_3$, $\tau(t) = 0.1$, $\lambda = -0.5$, $k_i = 1$, $\delta_{ij} = 1$, $\hat{a}_{ij}(0) = 3$,

$$A(t) = (a_{ij})_{5\times 5} = 0.1 \times \begin{pmatrix} -1 & 0 & 0 & 1 & 0 \\ 0 & -2 & 0 & 1 & 1 \\ 0 & 0 & -1 & 0 & 1 \\ 1 & 1 & 0 & -2 & 0 \\ 0 & 1 & 1 & 0 & -2 \end{pmatrix}$$

$x_i(0) = (1+0.001i, 1+0.001i, 1+0.001i)^T$, $y_i(0) = (25+0.001i, 26+0.001i, 30+0.001i)^T$

According to Theorem 1, by using the following response network, the controller and updated laws are given by

$$\dot{y}(t) = By_i(t) + f(t, y_i(t)) + \sum_{j=1, j\neq i}^{n} \hat{a}_{ij} H(t) y_j(t - \tau(t)) + u_i, \quad i = 1, 2, \ldots, 5$$

$$u_i = \frac{1}{\lambda}[d_i e_i(t) + \lambda f(t, y_i(t)) - f(t, \lambda y_i(t))], \quad i = 1, 2, \ldots, 5$$

$$\dot{c}_{ij} = \lambda \delta_{ij} H(t) y_j(t - \tau(t)) e_i^T(t), \quad i = 1, 2, \ldots, 5$$

$$\dot{d}_i = k_i (1 - \frac{d_i^*}{d_i}) e_i^T(t) e_i(t), d_i \neq 0, \quad i = 1, 2, \ldots, 5$$

The numerical results show that adaptive scheme for the drive-response complex network proposed in theorem 1 is effective.

From the process to prove theorems in this paper, we can learn that different nodes of the numerical simulation of complex network nodes in a network with the same approximation, in which we have omitted the former numerical simulation.

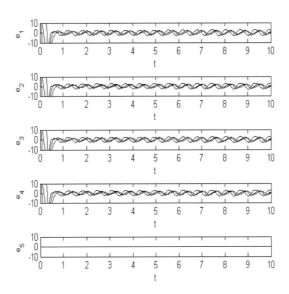

Fig. 1. The error system e_i, $i = 1, 2, \ldots, 5$ with adaptive feedback controllers

7 Conclusion

In this Letter, the nonlinear controllers and adaptive updated laws have been proposed to study the PS between two complex networks with time-varying coupling delay. With the Lyapunov stability theory and the adaptive control method, two PS theorems have been proposed, and the weight matrix $A(t)$ can be also identified. Numerical results demonstrate that the proposed approach is effective and feasible.

References

1. Jeong, H., Tombor, B., Albert, R., Oltvai, Z.N., Barabsi, A.L.: The large- scale organization of metabolic networks. Nature 407(6804), 651–654 (2000)
2. Strogatz, S.H.: Exploring complex networks. Nature 410(6825), 268–276 (2001)
3. Albet, R., Barabsi, A.L.: Statistical mechanics of complex networks. Rev. Mod. Phys. 74(1), 47–91 (2002)
4. Cao, B., Li, D., Li, B.: Complex network topology mining and community detection. Dyn. Continuous Discrete Impulsive Systems Ser. B: Appl. Algorithms 13(3), 361–370 (2006)
5. Zhu, L., Lai, Y.C., Hoppensteadt, F.C., He, J.: Characterization of neural interaction during learning and adaptation from spike-train data. Math. Biosci. Eng. 2(1), 1–23 (2005)
6. Goto, S., Nishioka, T., Kanehisa, M.: Chemical database for enzyme reactions. Bioinformatics 14(7), 591–599 (1998)
7. Horne, A.B., Hodgman, T.C., Spence, H.D., Dalby, A.R.: Constructing an enzyme-centric view of metabolism. Bioinformatics 20(13), 2050–2055 (2004)
8. Jin, C.W., Marsden, I., Chen, X.Q., Liao, X.B.: Dynamic DNA contacts observed in the NMR structure of winged helix protein-DNA complex. J. Mol. Biol. 289, 683–690 (1999)
9. Stauffer, D., Penna, T.J.P.: Crossover in the Cont-Bouchaud percolation model for market fluctuations. Physica A 256, 284–290 (1998)
10. Wang, N., Wang, J.: Fluctuation model for stock market index based on continuous percolation. J. Beijingjiaotong University 28(6), 36–38 (2004)
11. Fang, Y., Kincaid, T.G.: Stability analysis of dynamical neural networks. IEEE Trans. Neural Networks 7(4), 996–1006 (1996)
12. Watts, D.J., Strogatz, S.H.: Collective dynamics of 'small-world' networks. Nature 391(4), 440–442 (1998)
13. Barabasi, A.L., Albet, R.: Emergence of scaling in random networks. Science 286(15), 509–512 (1999)
14. Pecora, L.M., Carroll, T.L.: Master stability function for synchronized coupled systems. Phys. Rev. Lett. 80(10), 2109–2112 (1998)
15. Wang, X.F., Chen, G.: Synchronization in small-world dynamical networks. Int. J. Bifur. Chaos 12(1), 187–192 (2002)
16. Tang, W.K.S., Mao, Y., Kocarev, L.: Identification and monitoring of neural network. In: IEEE International Symposium on Circuits and Systems, May 27-30, pp. 2646–2649 (2007)
17. Zheng, S., Bi, Q.H., Cai, G.L.: Adaptive projective synchronization in complex networks with time-varying coupling delay. Physics Letters A 373(17), 1553–1559 (2009)
18. Lu, J.Q., Cao, J.D.: Synchronization-based approach for parameters identification in delayed chaotic neural networks. Phys. A 382, 672–682 (2007)

Research on Emergency Power Material Allocation Program

Xu Xiaofeng[1], Guo Xiaoming[2], and Liu Junyong[2]

[1] Chendu Electrical Power Bureau, Chengdu, Sichuan Province, China
[2] Department of Electrical Engineering and Information, University of Sichuan,
Chengdu, Sichuan Province, China
xuxiaofeng22@ovi.Com

Abstract. Timely and effective supply of power material is the basic gurantee of quickly service restoration after a disaster. Scientific and rational allocation of power material that can greatly reduce the time of recovery, increase the safty of power grid and the efficiency in handling the accident. Triangular fuzzy number is brought to simulate the the uncertainties in the emergency response activities. Based on the characteristics of demand for power material, the optimal path with time limits is determined by the guarantee rate of time for material supply. On this basis, the mathematical model of emergency power material allocation program for multi-material reserves and multi-material needs is established to achieve the goal of maximizing total transfer capability of the grid. An example proves the efficiency and validity of the approach.

Keywords: Material allocation, triangular fuzzy number, guarantee rate, total transfer capability.

1 Introduction

With the gradual trend of the interconnection of power network, the power systems are becoming increasingly closer. The security and stability of power system subject to external factors is increasing. Especially in recent years, snow, earthquakes and other natural disasters in southern China damaged a large number of power material, the safety of continuous production of electric power industry has been faced with even more severe test. Compared with the accidents caused by stability of Power system, the accidents caused by the external forces, such as ice -disaster, earthquake a typhoon are more serious and the repair of it needs more material.

The factors such as the location of material reserve warehouse and material needs, the storage of material reserves, the time constraints of power supply and others must be considered when designing emergency power material allocation program. At present, most study on the material allocation scheme involved only the issue of the optimal path of electrical repairs, such as papers[1-2] use Dijkstra algorithm and improved particle swarm algorithm to find the optimum path of electrical repairs. But there is almost blank about the influence owing by deployment of the power supplies and repair equipment on the power grid.

J. Zhang (Ed.): ICAIC 2011, Part III, CCIS 226, pp. 141–151, 2011.

In order to solve the problem effectively, this paper introduces management concepts in emergency management[3-7]., combined with power system operation and the characteristics of material demand, divides the power material allocation problem into of the three sub-problems, the optimal path for, emergency supplies, the importance evaluation of power facilities and the allocation of materials. The uncertainty during material transport are characterized by symmetric triangular fuzzy numbers, in order to establish the fuzzy transportation network model and search the highest guarantee rate of the transport path. Finally the emergency power material allocation program is established according to the priority of material needs and the guarantee rate.

2 Characteristics of Demand for Power Material

Power system is a continuous material consumed system, which can't work without effective supply of materials. After disasters, demand for power material have the following characteristics:

A. Timeliness and Effectiveness

Due to close electromagnetic link between the network sections and the deficiencies of network structure, the unexpected fault occurred on the part of the grid may lead to both a large range of great danger and spread rapidly. As a public foundation, electricity industry plays an irreplaceable role in the national economy and daily life. It will result in further deterioration of power grid if we do not have timely and effective response. The handling of such incidents should be based on adequate and effective protection on the material supply. Therefore, the primary objective of emergency power material allocation is timeliness and effectiveness.

B. Seasonality

Most electric power facilities located in the natural environment are susceptible to natural disasters (such as earthquakes, floods, storms, snow, ice disaster, etc.) damage. These incidents have distinct seasonal characteristics. Therefore, the demand for power materials also has distinct seasonal characteristics.

C. Network and Complexity

Because of the specificity of Power system (transmission towers, transmission lines spread every corner), the demand for various types of power supplies may not be a single point. At the same time, because the impacts of external are uncertainty, such as climate, traffic, etc, the deployment of power materials often involve multi-disciplinary, multi-area, multi-level. So, these factors should be considered when making an allocation.

3 Design of Emergency Power Material Allocation Program

From the above two analysis shows, the allocation of power material contains many complex issues, which can't be precisely described. Solving the problem directly is difficult, because it is a complex nonlinear multi-objective problem. The current allocation of emergency materials is in the face of three major problems. Firstly, the problem of optimal transporting path. Secondly, the issue of optimal recovery order of each damaged place. Thirdly, determine the amount of material allocation for each Warehouse. These three issues are both interrelated and differentiated, constituted the complete deployment of emergency power supplies program.

4 The Optimal Transport Path

A. Mathematical Model

Think of all materials warehouses, transport hub and the damaged transmission lines as nodes, and connections between nodes on behalf of the time that materials delivery between them.

As the seasonality and complexity of power materials demand, the transport time can only make an approximate fuzzy estimate according to the specific conditions. In order to portray t such a time, the paper introduces the symmetric triangular fuzzy numbers to represent this time of uncertainty. In addition, as the public welfare of power system, usually, power supply must be finished during a certain period of time. But Fuzzy Numbers can not be compared with the actual number of time, guarantee rate have been introduced to search the optimal path. a mathematical model have been established under the above requirement.

Set $S_1, S_2, \cdots S_n$ as the current n warehouses, as well as $D_1, D_2, \cdots D_m$ as the m damaged electricity transmission lines that also are places demand foe power materials. They are distributed in the graph $G(V,E)$ on the nodes, material warehouses and demand places are connected by traffic lines. In graph G, the other nodes are on behalf of transportation hubs. And every line e in the graph has a Weight as $\omega(e)$, which means the transport time between two nodes. Set R_{ij} is a set that contains all access from S_i to D_j. If P is a way between two nodes, the weight of P means all lines' weights in P, so

$$\omega(P) = \sum_{e \in P} \omega(e) \tag{1}$$

Set t as a deadline that material delivery must be finished early than it. The path meet the requirements are in the set, $A = \{[P|\omega(P) \le t, P \in R\}$, then shortest one in it needed to be found as the optimal path. So the objective function is

$$\omega(P_0) = \min_{p \in A} \omega(P) \tag{2}$$

In this model, $\omega(P)$ is the symmetric triangular fuzzy number, so we can't compare directly among the paths. In this paper, the introduction of guarantee rate can solve this problem. $M(P,t)$ is guarantee rate that means the degree of the transport time of path P less or equal to the restriction time t. The guarantee rate can measure risks that transport through the path.

For any symmetric triangular fuzzy,

$$a = [a^l, a^m, a^u] \tag{3}$$

there is

$$a^m = \frac{a^l + a^u}{2} \tag{4}$$

Function is shown in Figure 1. Delimit $[a^l, a^u]$ as the possible time interval, $\mu_a(x)$ as the density of the possibility of time, while the restriction time t is ordinary real number. Area ratio between the shaded triangle Shown in Figure□ and the whole triangular can be defined as the possibility degree of $a \leq t$, which is the guarantee rate in the model.

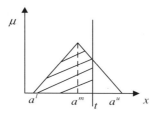

Fig. 1. Membership function of symmetric triangular fuzzy number

To specific restrictions time t ,we can get the guarantee rate index of path P as the following expression,

$$M(P,t) = \begin{cases} 0 & t < \omega(P)^l \\ 2(\dfrac{t - \omega(P)^l}{\omega(P)^u - \omega(P)^l})^2 & \omega(P)^l < t < \omega(P)^m \\ 1 - 2(\dfrac{\omega(P)^u - t}{\omega(P)^u - \omega(P)^l})^2 & \omega(P)^m \leq t < \omega(P)^u \\ 1 & \omega(P)^u \leq t \end{cases} \tag{5}$$

where $\omega(P)^l, \omega(P)^m, \omega(P)^u$ are[9]:

$$[\omega(P)^l, \omega(P)^m, \omega(P)^u] = \sum_{e \in P} \omega(e)$$

$$= [\sum_{e \in P} \omega(e)^l, \sum_{e \in P} \omega(e)^m, \sum_{e \in P} \omega(e)^u] \tag{6}$$

Therefore, the objective function equation (2) can be equivalent to,

$$P_0 = \max_{p \in R} M(P, t) \tag{7}$$

B.   Model Solution

Since the path weight is the triangular fuzzy numbers that can not directly use the shortest path algorithm (such as the Floyd algorithm, Dijkstra algorithm). From the literature [10] we can see, equation (7) can be transformed into the following equivalent form.

$$P_0 : \begin{array}{c} \max_{P \in R} \dfrac{t - \omega(P)^u}{\omega(P)^u - \omega(P)^l} \\[2mm] = \dfrac{t - \omega(P_0)^u}{\omega(P_0)^u - \omega(P_0)^l} = x_0 \end{array} \tag{8}$$

where $x_0 \in [-1, 0]$

The guarantee rate of path P_0,

$$M(P_0, t) = \begin{cases} 1 - 2x_0^2 & , x_0 \geq -0.5 \\ 2(1 + x_0)^2 & , x_0 < -0.5 \end{cases} \tag{9}$$

Since equation (8) is a complicated nonlinear path problem, the further transformation of this issue is,
$P(x)$ is,

$$\min_{P \in R} \sum_{e \in P} ((\omega(e)^u - \omega(e)^l) \cdot x + \omega(e)^u) \tag{10}$$

P(X) is the optimal solution from equation (10), when x has been decided. So the problem can be solved a process, which firstly find the value of x, and then use the shortest path algorithm to obtain the optimal path. The algorithm can be found in papers[10-11].

Set t_j as the restriction time for demand place D_j. P_{ij} is the highest guarantee rate path from S_i to D_j, the guarantee rate is $M(\tilde{t}_{ij}, t_j)$, which can be solved by the model above. By solving, we could come to the guarantee rate between each warehouse to each demand place as well as the transport time frame of the path. According to equation (5), we can get the guarantee rate, which reflect the risk that to transport through the path.

5 The Material Demand Priority

As the numerous number of damaged power facilities, the actual situation is that in the materials warehouse storage and transport capacity is limited. We must focus on the recovery of critical equipment. The target is to maximum the system stability margin when determining the priority of each demand places. Because there are many combinations of power line faults, and the operation mode may change during the recovery time. This article focuses on the deployment just after power failure on the target of maximizing the total transfer capacity. Total transfer capability (TTC) is the maximum power that can be transmitted [12] in a system to meet certain security and stability in the constrained. Using this as indicators can work out a reasonable allocation of materials and efficient program to restore power transmission fastest.

The idea of TTC worked out with the continuous flow method is that on a given group of generator nodes and load nodes, and increase the power in a certain system operating mode. And then solve the power flow equations, check the restrictions and repeat this process until the limitation occur [13]. And the transmission power at this time is total transfer capability. According to this thinking, set a load parameters λ and assume that there are n load nodes and the active or reactive load increase in proportion□ so that get the objective function as,

$$\max \sum_{i=0}^{i=n} P_{Li}^0 + \lambda P_{Li} \tag{11}$$

Where, P_{Li}^0 is the initial active power of the node i, λ is load change rate and P_{Li} is the direction of load power Changes. Consider the generator output limit, the node voltage magnitude constraints and the limited capacity of transmission lines when solve the problem.

By calculating the TTC of recovery different lines to evaluate the importance of the line, then get the priority.

6 Allocation of Power Materials

A. Description of the Problem

According to the analysis above, the optimal path and the priority of the demand places have been obtained. In addition, the amount of power materials from each warehouses needed to be determined. The ultimate goal is to maximize the guarantee rate of the allocation program under the restrictions. Considering both the guarantee rate and the priority may come across the following questions. The transmission line has a high priority level but the materials can't arrive in the restrict time. So the priority needed to be changed through removing all the demand places that All the possible transport lines has a guarantee rate of 0.(The paper do not consider these demand places)

B. Mathematical Model and Solution

Complete material allocation program is based on the result of the priority of the demand places. Against each demand place to form a allocation program in proper order.

Set $S_1, S_2, \cdots S_n$ as the current reserve n warehouse and $D_1, D_2, \cdots D_m$ as the m section that demand for materials. There are y_i material reserves in warehouse i, and the j place demand for y_i materials, $i = 1, 2, \cdots n, j = 1, 2, \cdots m$. $M(\tilde{t}_{ij}, t_j)$ has been obtained above,   and assume that there are x_{ij} materials allocate from S_i to $D_j, x_{ij} \geq 0 \sum_{j=1}^{m} x_{ij} \leq y_i, \sum_{i=1}^{n} x_{ij} = x_j$ ..A program has to be determined to get the amount of the material that from Specific warehouse to demanded place.

Assume any of the programs as:

$$\varphi = \begin{bmatrix} (S_1, x_{11}) & (S_1, x_{12}) & \cdots & (S_1, x_{1m}) \\ (S_2, x_{21}) & (S_2, x_{22}) & \cdots & (S_2, x_{2m}) \\ \vdots & \vdots & \ddots & \vdots \\ (S_n, x_{n1}) & (S_k, x_{n2}) & \cdots & (S_n, x_{nm}) \end{bmatrix} \tag{12}$$

Set the guarantee rate of the program as,

$$N(\varphi, t) = \sum_{i=1}^{n} \sum_{j=1}^{m} x_{ij} M(\tilde{t}_{ij}, t_j) \tag{13}$$

The optimal program φ^* corresponds to the objective function as follows,

$$N(\varphi^*, t) = \max_{\varphi} \sum_{i=1}^{n} \sum_{j=1}^{m} x_{ij} M(\tilde{t}_{ij}, t_j) \tag{14}$$

$$s.t. \begin{cases} \sum_{j=1}^{m} x_{ij} \leq y_i \\ \sum_{i=1}^{n} x_{ij} = x_j \\ x_{ij} \geq 0 \end{cases}$$

This model is a constrained linear programming problem. With the existing types of linear programming approach, it is easy to obtain results. To each priority, we use equation (14) to solve in order to get the full allocation program.

7 Numerical Example

C. Optimal Path

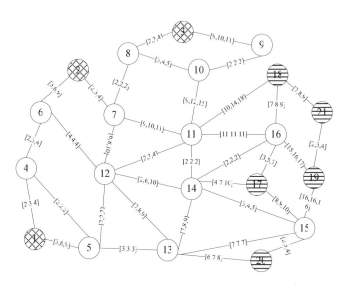

Fig. 2. Fuzzy traffic network

The traffic network in Figure 2 has a line weight of the symmetric triangular fuzzy number.

Using IEEE14 system as an example, assume that line 6-13,2-5,6-11,12-13,5-4 are out of operation. These lines and material storage abstraction for the transportation network diagram nodes.

The relationship between the lines and the node in Fig. 2 are shown in table 1. And the relationship between the warehouses and the node in Fig. 2 are shown in table 2.

Table 1. Corresponding relation between nodes and lines

Fault lines （IEEE14）	Nodes in Fig 2	Sign
2-5	21	D_1
6-13	20	D_2
6-11	17	D_3
5-4	18	D_4
12-13	19	D_5

Table 2. Corresponding relation between nodes and stores

Warehouse	Nodes in Fig. 2	Sign
1	1	S_1
1	2	S_2
2	3	S_3

Assume that all material needs to arrive in 24 hours. Use the method in this paper to search the optimal path and to calculate the guarantee rate, and the partial results are listed in table 3.

Table 3. Optimal path and guarantee rate

Starting point	End	Optimal path	Guarantee rate
S_1		1-4-6-12-11-14-16-18-21	0
S_2	D_1	2-6-12-11-14-16-18-21	0
S_3		3-8-7-12-14-16-18-21	0
S_1		1-4-6-12-11-14-16-17	0.82
S_2	D_3	2-7-11-16-17	0.875
S_3		3-8-7-11-14-17	0.5
S_1		1-4-6-12-11-14-16-18	0.28
S_2	D_4	2-6-12-11-14-16-18	0.32
S_3		3-8-7-12-14-16-18	0.07

D.   The priority of the Demand Places

With the continuous flow method to calculate the TTC when recover each line. The results are shown in table 4.

These results will be combined with the guarantee rate of section 3.1. the demand place with guarantee rate of 0 will be ignore, and the final results are in table 5.

Table 4. The priority of material demand

Lines	TTC（MW）	Priority
6-13	707.465	
12-13	675.422	High
6-11	654.272	
5-4	620.369	
2-5	588.685	Low

Table 5. The priority of material transportation based on comprehensive guarantee rate

Lines	TTC（MW）	Priority	
6-13	707.465		
6-11	654.272	High	↑
5-4	620.369	Low	↓

C.   Power Material Allocation

Assume that warehouse S_1, S_2, S_3 have 90 materials each. The demand places D_1, D_2, D_3, D_4, D_5 need 40,50,50,50,40.for each. From table□we can get the allocation program in table 6.

Table 6. Material allocation program

Starting point	End	Path	materials
S_2	D_2	2-6-12-5-13-20	50
S_2	D_3	2-7-11-16-17	40
S_1	D_3	1-4-6-12-11-14-16-17	10
S_1	D_4	1-4-6-12-11-14-16-18	40
S_3	D_4	3-8-7-12-14-16-18	10

8   Conclusion

Based on the characteristics of the demand for power materials, the mathematical model of emergency power material allocation program for multi-material reserves and multi-material needs is established to achieve the goal of maximizing total transfer capability of the power system. Through the introduction of symmetric triangular fuzzy numbers to describe the real world's uncertainties and the guarantee rate index for the fuzzy goals to the solution, the paper use linear programming approach to solve the problem.

But, there are such many changing in the situation after the failure of power system, the target of the evaluation of the lines in this paper can only partly reflects the resumption of the power transmission lines. In addition, not only time, but also the cost and other factors will affect the deployment plan. How to design a more complex model is the future direction of the work program.

References

1. Ye, P., Du, H., Sheng, X.: Application of the Dijkstra algorithm in the best repairing path. Relay 34(12), 39–41 (2006)
2. Zhang, M., Xu, M., Qing, W.: Research of the Best Repair Path Based on an Improved Particle Swarm Optimization in Power Communication Network. Science Technology and Engineering 8(22), 5990–5995 (2008)
3. Fan, Y.: Optimal Routing through Stochastic Networks. Ph.D Dissertation. University of Southern Californian, USA (2003)
4. Gang, Y., Jian, Y.: On the Robust Shortest Path Problem. Computers and Operation Research 25(6), 457–568 (1998)
5. Zou, Z., Song, C., Guo, X.: How to Select the Optimal Emergent Logistics Route Based on Grey Theory. Logistics Technology 27(1), 46–48 (2008)
6. Rathi, A.K., Church, R.L., Solanki, R.S.: Allocating resources to support a multicommodity flow with time windows. Logistics and Transportation Review 28(1), 167–188 (1993)
7. Ozdamar, L.: Emergency logistics planning in natural disasters. Annals of Operation Research 129(1), 218–219 (2004)
8. He, J., Liu, C.: Fuzzy Programming Problem for Vehicle Dispatch under Time Restriction. Design and Control 3(16), 318–321 (2001)
9. Dai, G., Da, Q.: The Study of Combinatorial Scheduling Problem in Emergency Systems. Systems Engineering Theory and Practice 12(9), 52–55 (2009)
10. He, J., Liu, C.: Emergency management and emergency system. publishing (2005)
11. Chen, D., Xiao, J., Wang, C.: A Fahp-Based Madam Method In Urban Power System Planning. Proceedings of the CSU-EPSA 15(4), 83–88 (2003)
12. Liu, S., Jiang, C., Hou, Z.: Optimal Power Flow Based Total Transfer Capability Calculation. Journal Of Shanghai Jiaotong Unversity 38(8), 1233–1237 (2004)
13. Liu, H., Li, Y., Chen, X.: Availiable Transfer Capability Calculation Based on Continual Power Flow for Transmission Network. Electric Power Automation Equipment 23(12), 5–8 (2003)

Design and Realization of the Engine Condition Monitoring System Based on CAN Bus

Li-Hui Chen[1,2], Ying-Ji Liu[1], Yi Sui[1,2], Wei Zhou[1], and Jian-Wei Ji[2]

[1] Research Institute of Highway,
Ministry of Transport, Center of Transport, Beijing China
[2] Shenyang Agricultural University,
College of Information and Electrical Engineering, Shenyang China
LihuiCHENT@tom.com

Abstract. An engine condition monitoring system was established with the Freescale MC9S12DG128 chip which self-equipped with the CAN bus controller. This system collects such key parameters as oil pressure and rotation speed, as well as trouble code information and so on through designed CAN nodes, and transmits these parameters to the remote monitoring center through GPRS modules. It is proven by tests that this system is able to well accomplish each function.

Keywords: CAN bus, LCD, GPRS, DTC.

Foreword

The main monitoring management platforms in China is able to carry out monitoring in terms of such information as position, speed, and management of passenger vehicles, and to effectively meet such monitoring needs of enterprise as the mobilization, position and speed of vehicles. However, these platforms monitor less information related to the conditions of operation of such work units as the engine and automatic transmission of vehicles, and lack of prejudgment and diagnosis to the existing or potential troubles of work units.

In light of the current needs of remote monitoring and diagnosis to the real time running conditions of the engine in the industry, this paper employs the Freescale 16-bit SCM as the hardware core to design and develop a bus information collection system based on the SAE J1939 protocol. This system succeeds in collecting such information as speed, oil pressure and trouble codes of the engine. With this system, the wireless transmission for information collection is achieved, and data exchange with remote monitoring platform is realized.

1 Network Topology

The on-board vehicle network topology is shown as figure 1, and the electronic control unit (ECU) inside the vehicle is connected to the CAN bus in a hanging manner. The internal data information of the vehicle is transmitted via the CAN bus. This system module can be connected to the CAN bus in a hanging manner as a node in the bus, and

J. Zhang (Ed.): ICAIC 2011, Part III, CCIS 226, pp. 152–159, 2011.

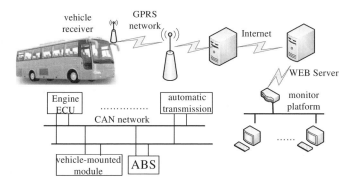

Fig. 1. The on-board vehicle network topology

can be used to collect such information as braking, power transmission, steering and trouble codes of the passenger vehicle's engine. The collected information needs to be exchanged with that in the monitoring platform via a GPRS wireless network.

2 Design of System Hardware

The hardware of the information collection module consists of the Freescale 16-bit microcontroller - MC9S12DG128, power module, LCD display module, GPRS module, etc. The overall structure of the system hardware is shown in figure 2.

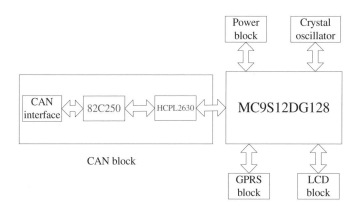

Fig. 2. The overall structure of the system hardware

A. MC9S12DG128 Microcontroller

The MC9S12DG128 microcontroller is one of the 16-bit SCMS which belong to the M68HC12 series and are made by Motorola, and it provides abundant resources inside the chip. It is internally integrated with a CPU unit - HCS12, 2 asynchronous serial communication interfaces - SCI, 2 synchronous serial communication interfaces - SPI, an 8 channel input capture/output comparison timer, an 8 channel pulse-width modulation module and 49 independent digit I/O (20 of them have external interrupt and arousal functions). In addition, the chip has a 128KB flash ROM, a 8KB RAM and a 2KB EEPROM inside. Most of all, the MC9S12DG128 is internally integrated with 2 MSCAN controllers which are compatible with the CAN2.0A/B protocol. With these abundant internal resources and external interface resources, the requirements of the ECU on processing various data and transmitting and receiving the CAN network data can be met, the hardware design for the information collection module is simplified, and the design cost is reduced.

1) MC9S12DG12Microcontroller: The MC9S12DG128 is the core of the information collection module, and responsible for collecting data on the on-board vehicle network, and analyzing and processing received data as well as transmitting collected data to the monitoring platform via the GPRS module.

2) CAN Bus Module: The CAN bus module consists of the HCPL2630 and 82C250 chips. The HCPL2630 is a photocoupling chip and able to achieve the electric isolation between the electric signals. The 82C250 is an interface between the CAN controller and the physical layer bus, and designed for the communications applications of vehicles at middle/high speed. It is transient interference resistant, and able to protect the bus and meet the requirements at a transmission speed of 1Mbps. This chip is fully in accordance with the ISO11898 standard. It can control the gradient, reduce the radio frequency interference (RFI), is resistant to the common mode interference within wide range, and is resistant to the electromagnetic interference (EMI); and it supplies differential transmitting capacity and differential receiving capability to the bus and the CAN controller respectively. The modular structure of the CAN bus is shown in figure 3.

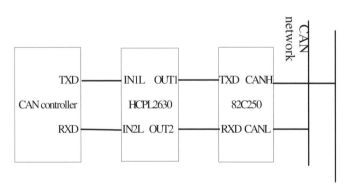

Fig. 3. The modular structure of the CAN bus

3) GPRS Module: The SIM300 is a double frequency GSM/GPRS module developed by SIMCOM, and mainly used for providing wireless interfaces for voice transmission, short message and data businesses. It is integrated with a complete radio frequency circuit and a baseband processor of the GSM, and is suitable for developing wireless GSM/GPRS products, such as mobile phone, PDA and wireless MODEM card as we as on-board vehicle, remote controlling, long-distance measuring, positioning and navigating systems or products, with a wide range of application. The SIM300 module provide users with a system interface which is of full functionality, and users can develop their own integrated application systems in a shorter R&D cycle with less R&D cost. The MC9S12DG128 and SIM300 modules can communicate with each other via simplified RS-32 approach.

4) LCD Display Module: For ease of system debugging, the collection module also provides a LCD display module to display collected data during debugging and the feedback data from the SIM300 module on the LCD screen. The display module employs a high image quality TFT real color module (MT24-2); and it has such good performances as various interfaces, ease of programming and expansion. The MT24-2 has dedicated built-in drive and control ICs (SPFD5408), and the drive IC is self-integrated with the display cache without any need of external display cache so that the system development cycle is dramatically cut. Also for ease of monitoring system failures, the display module can be used to determine whether the collection module fails or the GPRS module fails.

3 Design of System Software

The design of system software employs the concept of modular design and mainly consists of the system initialization program, CAN bus data collection program, LCD display program, GPRS chain circuit service program, decoding program of diagnostic trouble codes, etc.

A. System Initialization Program

The system initialization program is used for setting the system clock, and the baud rates of the enable phase locked loop, the bus and the serial interface as well as performing such system initiation related operations as the initialization operation of the LCD screen.

B. CAN Bus Data Collection Program

The CAN bus data collection program is mainly used for initializing the CAN nodes, receiving CAN bus information, and translating received CAN data into PDU format which is in accordance with the SAE J1939 protocol. As the demand of this system design is to draw such information as braking, steering, power transmission and trouble codes of the engine, the address in the request message can be set as the global address in order to simply the program design when the engine is requested to send a certain data, and then the engine will broadcast this information to all bus nodes. After that, this system node can draw the required information from the bus.

There are two types of structural elements are defined according to the relationship between the ID of the CAN data frames and the PDU of the J1939.

The data collection program employs an interrupting approach to receive data, and the program flow diagram is shown in figure 4.

C. LCD Display Program

The display program is used for displaying data on the LCD screen. All the initialization functions, the typeheads and the display functions which are related to the LCD display are enclosed in the LCD320240.c, since this system adopts the concept of modular design. Hence, when ASCII characters or Chinese characters are required to be displayed on the LCD screen, please just simply invoke such relevant functions as LCD_mPrint() and LCD_P8x16Str().

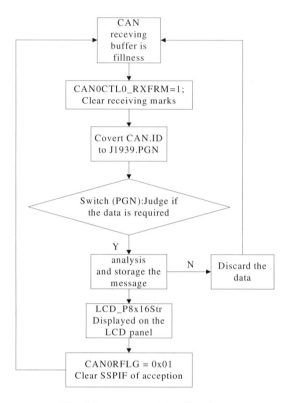

Fig. 4. Interrupt receiving flowchart

D. GPRS Chain Circuit Service Program

The GPRS chain circuit service program is designed to drive the GPRS module - SIM300 as well as establishing a GPRS data wireless transmission chain circuit through sending AT instruction to the SIM300 via the serial interface. Its program flow diagram is shown in figure 5.

The AT instruction is used for testing module connection: if the SIM300 is properly connected with the module, then "OK" instruction is returned. AT+CGDCONT=1, "IP", "CMNET", and CGDCONT=1: design the PDP (packet data protocol type) context to specify the character string parameters of the packet data protocol type. "IP" denotes using internet protocol. "CMNET" denotes the name of the access point which is used for selecting GGSN or external packet data network as a logical name. AT+CIPSTART="TCP", "124.207.32.130", and "2020": set the IP address, port number, connection type TCP, and so forth for the connect server.

E. Decoding Program of Diagnostic Trouble Codes

The SAE J1939 defines 19 diagnostic message (DM) comprising the diagnostic trouble light code (2-bit) and the diagnostic trouble code (DTC, 4-bit). The diagnostic trouble code (DTC) is 4-bit in length, and it includes the suspect parameter number (SPN, 19-bit), the failure mode code (FM1, 5-bit), the frequency of failure occurrence (OC, 7-bit), and the SPN conversion mode (CM, 1-bit). The data format of the DTC is shown in figure 1.

Table 1. Data Format of the DTC

DTC			
Byte 3	Byte 4	Byte 5	Byte 6
The significance bit of the lower bit 8 of the SPN (bit 8 is the most significant bit)	Bit 2 of the SPN (bit 8 is the most significant bit)	The significance bit of the upper bit 3 of the SPN and the significance bit of the FM1 (bit 8 is the most significant bit of the SPN, and the bit 5 is the most significant bit of the FM1)	
SPN		FM1	CM	OC
8 7 6 5 4 3 2 1	8 7 6 5 4 3 2 1	8 7 6	5 4 3 2 1	8	7 6 5	4 3 2	1

This system employs an interrupt mode to draw diagnostic trouble codes. It only needs to draw the diagnostic trouble codes (DM1) under the activated mode, because the system is designed to monitor the real time running conditions of the engine. Once any DTC becomes an activated trouble, there is a DM1 message transmitted. After that, the updating rate of activated trouble is in a normal condition of once per second. If the trouble activating time is 1 second or even longer and the trouble becomes deactivated after this, the transmitted DM1 message should reflect this mode change between activation and deactivation. If there are different DTCs having their mode changed within an updating period of 1 second, then a new DM1 message should be transmitted to reflect this change. To avoid high message transmission rate caused by high-frequency interrupt troubles, it is recommended that each DTC only has one mode change transmitted per second. In this way, if any trouble code has its mode changed twice within an updating period of 1 second, i.e. activation/deactivation mode, there will be a message to confirm that the DTC becomes activated and another message to confirm that the DTC is deactivated during the next transmission period. The latter message is only transmitted when there is an activated DTC existing or responding to a request. Care should be taken that when there are more than one activated DTCs existing, this parameter group should be required to use the "multipacket transmission" parameter group. The controller processes the trouble information via the following approach.

Finally, the combination function of the multipacket transmission data is implemented and stored according to the

"num=1" mark.

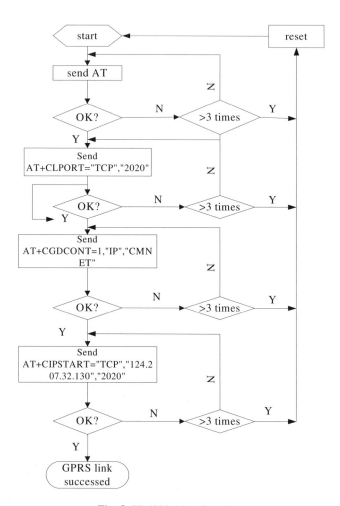

Fig. 5. SIM300 drive flowchart

4 Conclusion

This paper designs and attains a engine condition monitoring & diagnostic system based on the J1939 protocol. The system employs the Freescale MC9S12DG128 microcontroller and the GPRS module SIM300 as its hardware, and the concept of modular design to design its software so that the engine condition monitoring & diagnostic function is achieved. It innovatively combines the information on the CAN bus of the vehicle engine with that on the monitoring platform. Hence, it is technically able to remotely monitor the real time running conditions of the engine and recognize any unusual circumstance related to the engine to reduce the existing and potential unsafe factors when the engine is running.

Acknowledgment. Supported by National Key Technology R&D Program in the 11th Five year Plan of China, ID2009BAG13A04.

Supported by China Post doctoral Science Foundation (20090460264).

Supported by Open Project from Key laboratory of Operation Safety Technology on Transport Vehicles Ministry of Communication，PRC. (09-22060302-062)

References

1. You, Z.-h., Xu, Y.: Design and Implementation of CAN/GPRS Wireless Vehicle gateway, vol. 24(9), pp. 237–239 (2008)
2. Sun, J.: Auto network application research based on SAE J1939. Beihang University (2006)
3. Sun, J.-t.: Freescale 9S12 16 single-chip microcomputer principle and embedded development technology. Mechanical industry press (2008)
4. Wu, K.M.: CAN bus principle and application system design. Beihang University (1996)
5. SAEJ1939-71VehicleApplicationLayer. USA.SAE issued (December 2004)
6. SAEJ1939-73Applicationlayer Diagnostics. USA.SAE issued (March 2004)

The Effects of Guanxi Categorie on Bank Credit[*]

Li Jinling, Luan Qingwei, and Li Yanxi

Faculty of Management and Economics
Dalian University of Technology
Dalian 116024, China
lijin_ling@sina.cn

Abstract. Financing is undoubtedly significant for the survival and development of private enterprises in China. In transitional economy, private enterprises, compared with state-owned enterprises or collective enterprises, are often difficult to get formal financial support in terms of credit and loan to overcome their liability of newness, so informal guanxi network plays an important role in enterprises` financing. In the light of social capital theory, this paper proposes a model about relationship types, bank credit, and private new venture performance, discussing how the two types of relationship influence bank loans characteristics and describing the relating significance for enterprises` performance.

Keywords: relationship financing, market based relationship, non-market based relationship, bank credit, new venture performance.

1 Introduction

Entrepreneurship plays a vital role in a region`s socioeconomic development.

Schumpeter (1934) and Romer (1986) emphasized the importance of entrepreneurship in a regional economic prosperity; entrepreneurial activities can create employment opportunities, reduce unemployment, and promote economic growth. Through entrepreneurial activities, the risk-taking entrepreneurs with alertness, and organizational capacity identify and exploit entrepreneurial opportunities, and accordingly they improve the technological level, make profits, and promote productivity growth. From this view, China needs more entrepreneurs and new ventures to foster the economic restructuring. However, because of small scale and lack of funds, inefficient management, and fierce market competition, new enterprises suffer from low survival rate and low growth level, while they create enormous social and economic benefits. In the context of emerging economic, the new ventures have high growth potential, but they also have a high degree of credit information asymmetries and uncertainty, making them difficult to obtain the necessary strategic

---

[*] Be supported by the Fund Project: National Natural Science Fund (70772087), National Special Fund for Basic Scientific Research in Colleges and Universities (DUT10ZD107; DUT10RW107).

J. Zhang (Ed.): ICAIC 2011, Part III, CCIS 226, pp. 160–166, 2011.

resources for survival and development, especially the financial resources, resulting in "funding gap" for the new ventures.

Since the reform and opening-up, China`s private enterprises have been the most active entrepreneurial section. Compared with the state-owned enterprises and collective enterprises, the private enterprises(especially SMEs) act as an economic part of outside system in a long term, leading to obvious weakness in getting formal financing such as bank credit and loan. Although in recent years, many banks began to set up SMEs department, in fact private enterprises still face serious financing problem. A survey by the National Development and Reform Commission shows that proportion of SMEs loans rejection in developed coastal provicinces and municipalities is about 56%, and more than 80% of respondents take "lack of capital" as their biggest problem that plagued private enterprises` development. Therefore, while they face financing constraint and can hardly get capital from formal ways, these private enterprises turn to obtain credit and loan support from the favor "Guanxi", which is general and important both in social capital theory and the Chinese community.

Human economic activities are embedded in social networks (Granovetter, 1985). The embedded relationship can be divided into relational embeddedness and structural embeddedness. China is a network society with sophisticated relations. Although entrepreneurship has become a focus of management research, there are few researches about how the specificity of Chinese social network affects the entrepreneurial process and performance. Understandably, when the new ventures try to get credit support from banks, the strength, density, scale, heterogeneity, and other characteristics of the entrepreneurs` personal relationships will have a great effect on availability of formal financing. For banks, the key information (even trust) to the enterprise and entrepreneur based on the personal network could reduce credit risk or uncertainty efficiently. Former studies focus mainly on the organizational relation between banks and enterprises and its influence on the availability of credit and loan, but less on the entrepreneur`s different types of individual network and on how it impact bank loan`s properties such as availability, smoothness, timeliness, low-pricing, and full-amount; in fact these properties are of great significance for enterprises.

In the view of social capital theory, this paper attempts to build a framework as relationship types—bank loans –new venture performance to reveal the correlation and mechanism of interaction among them, and then to point out the positive impact of relations for private new ventures to break the bottleneck of formal financing, which may have theoretical and practical significance to understand the discrepancy of new ventures` growth and performance in the context of China`s transitional economy.

2 Relationship Financing

Traditional relationship financing theory is mainly derived from the financial intermediation theory, including two aspects: transaction cost theory (Gurley & Shaw, 1960) and asymmetric information theory (Leland & Pyle, 1977; Diamond, 1984). Relationship financing is defined as a loan agreement to establish a comprehensive relationship between the bank and enterprises, and minimize the risk of SME loaning as much as possible (Berlin & Mester, 1998). Aoki (2001) pointed out that the character of relationship financing is to effectively overcome the problem of tacit knowledge about financier when signing of financial contracts and reducing of uncertainty of the credit contract are based on the encoding information.

China is a network society of criss-cross social relationships (Max Boisolt & John Child, 1996). Jacobs (1979) suggests that Chinese guanxi can be understood as "a particularistic tie" in which people consider influence of Confucianism on interpersonal relationships. Pye (1982) defines the Chinese guanxi as "a kind of friendship " which refer to"the continued exchange of favors". Peng (1998) defines guanxi in Chinese communities as an informal, private and special relationship based on the reciprocal obligation." In order to describe the characteristics of Chinese guanxi from organization view, Tsui & Farh (1997) conducted a qualitative research on the guanxi of the senior managers in Chinese organizations. The result shows that Chinese managers have six types of expressions regarding interpersonal guanxi: (1) common group identity, (2) a third person that they both know, (3) frequent interactions, (4) being connected but not interrative, (5) friendship without common backgrounds, (6) relationship quality. Among them, the "common identity" precisely explained the interpretation of the traditional Confucian culture on guanxi, for it not only reflects the type of relationship in the Chinese society, but also reflects the strength of the relationship. In contrast, the Western social network only emphasizes the homophyly or similarity.

Table 1. Guanxi Bases and Interpersonal Relationship in the Chinese Context (Tsui & Farh, 1997)

Categories of relationship	Dominant principles of interaction	Ways of social treatment	Bases of Guanxi or common identity
Family (Chia-jen)	Responsibility or obligation	Unconditional protection	Close kin
Family person (Shou-jen)	Exchange of favor and generosity	Trust and social accommodation, and favoritism	Distant kin, former classmate, fomer teacher-student, former supervisor-subordinate, former coworker, or former neighbor
Stranger with common identity (Sheng-jen)	Utilitarian exchange with depersonalized affection	Favoritism	Native origin, surname or other demographic attributes (e.g.., age, sex, education, alma matter)
Stranger without common identity	Utilitarian exchange without affection	Discretion and cautionary	None

Most Chinese think that they could get the resources they need from the social network. This common sense exists thousands of years of history, becoming a "natural" social knowledge for the Chinese. Nowadays, relationship plays an instrumental role. In order to search and access to strategic resources (such as instrumental action), building and expanding bridge of guanxi in the social networks would be more useful. Because it not only allows actors to get their own resources through other people, but also allows them to get more potential resources through their relationship in the organization and the organization's own power, wealth and status (Lin Nan, 2005).

In recent years, with more and more research on the practical problems, more researchers notice the importance of favor, face, affinity and other social-cultural factors. Every Chinese learns how to classify the groups according to closeness at an early age. In other words, the trust or closeness of Chinese or the oversea Chinese for the others depends on the affinity or relationship rule. The closer the individual is to the inner of network, the more likely the relationship is to be the consanguinity and kinship. In this situation, one can get higher trust, and resources allocation mechanism is more based on the emotional standards. The outer layer of the network means that the relationship with the individual is not strong. From family to acquaintances and outsiders and even to strangers, one get fewer and fewer trust. As a result, resources allocation mechanism is more based on the instrumental standards, which is close to the market trading mechanism characterized by equivalent exchange.

In traditional society, transactions between acquaintances are mainly embedded in the rational context of informal binding mechanism. For Chinese people, the interaction and transaction among members in the acquaintances network are bound by the rules of the network. Everybody abide by these conventional rules of contacts. If treated as a "rational man", individuals in the traditional society would make full use of the strong ties with the "insiders" including family and relatives to obtain resources. In addition, they will actively use the same network of acquaintances and friends to acquire a variety of resources. Getting resources from the relatives and acquaintances relies on the traditional interpersonal ethics and is a psychological contract with each other. Therefore, getting resources in this way significantly differ from getting resources in the formal institution. If the two sides do not have the guanxi as family members, relatives like familiar person, which means a strange relationship, the rules for interaction between the two sides are related to the market trading mechanism (Tsui & Farh, 1997), which needs formal process and steps to access resources. From this perspective, resource availability relying on the relationship between the family and relatives is based on blood and emotion ethics mechanisms. Thus, the operation of this relationship can be referred to as "non-market based relationship", or "non-formal relationship". On the other hand, when accessing to resources through the formal rules, both sides are based on the fair exchange market rules. Therefore, the operation of such relationship can be called "market based relationship", "formal relationship ", and so on.

Many researches discussed how the entrepreneurs obtain resources by using their personal network (Ireland et al., 2003), but the understanding of interpersonal networks and relations of foreign scholars are very different from that of real Chinese people (Tsui, Farh, 1997). Among Chinese scholars, the main focus is how the entrepreneurs access to resources by their "guanxi" network, especially regarding the acquisition of financial resources (Chu Xiaoping, 2003; Huang Xiaowu, 2008). Meanwhile, private lending is often regarded as an important source of funding for the entrepreneurs, but form the practical perspective of many countries, banks should be the main channel for SMEs financing. Therefore, entrepreneurs must try to obtain credit support in order to ensure the success of new enterprises. Of course, different types or natures of the relationship, like market -based relationship and non-market based relationship, will have different effects and mechanisms.

3 Bank Credit

Asymmetry of information in entrepreneurial financing is that suppliers and demanders can not complete the financing because the transmission of information results in incomplete information: asymmetry of   information between supplier and demander before and after the financing, adverse selection, and moral hazard (Shane and Cable, 2002). Facing constraint of capital, new venture can not obtain adequate fund as a result of concerns of fund suppliers about technology market, about the organizational competency of entrepreneur, and about the controllability of specific assets. However, Johannisson (1996) pointed out that although new ventures are embedded in highly uncertain external environment, the entrepreneur's own interpersonal networks can help improve the ability of ventures to cope with uncertain environment and stabilize the expectations of stakeholders and outside investors. From this perspective, the entrepreneur's relationship network is not only a channel to resource, but also a crucial resource to promote the growth of new enterprises.

At present, scholars have done a lot of research about social capital and the relationship between social networks and finacing: social capital level, to some extent, reflects the level of network resources, and the network is a tool to strengthen the interpersonal trust and is used to enhance the effectiveness of social sanctions. Florin et al. (2003) pointed out that social capital helps to improve companies' capability for financing and to address corporate finance problem. Under the condition of contribution of information, relationship network, as a method for information convection, becomes an approach to risk control. On the basis of embeded relationship theory, Luo Jiade studied four types of financial relations in Taiwan, finding the relational basis and nature of four financing channels and pointing out socioeconomic functions of relationship financing.

Table 2. Type of load and basis and nature of Guanxi (Luo Jiade, 2000)

Type of loan	Basis of Guanxi	nature of guanxi
personal loan	favor and ties	interpersonal relationship
Chinese Money-loan Associations	the strength and intensity of network	small, short-run, closed network
Credit Union	cohesion and Consciousness of We-Group	highly closed, pre-We-Group orgnization.
Thrift and Loan Society	regional relationship, interpersonal ties, organized	open, organized, reticulate Guanxi network

For new ventures, capital is a strategic resource that, according to different standards, can be classfied into debt and equity capital, long-term and short-term capital, circulating and fixed capital; bank credit is usually a debt capital for new ventures. The present research about the relationship between social capital and financing begin from the study of network and trust. However, no study has completely classified different types of capital, and the content and nature of loan.

Different kinds of relationships have different effect on bank credit. In the aspect of obtaining resource, non-market-based and market-based relationships of individual entrepreneurs shall first ensure the access to credit funds from the bank, namely the availability of bank credit. However, this availability does not mean a most effective operation of Guanxi, an operation that also depends on an unimpeded channel of bank credit: if the capital is "accessible" but "very difficult to receive", the mechanism of Guanxi is still needed to be improved. Furthermore, personal Guanxi of Entrepreneurs not only makes bank loan available and unimpeded, but also needs to guarantee the low cost of bank loan. Fourth, the operation of personal relations also needs to consider for the timeliness of credit funds. In most cases, banks and other financial institutions are state-owned or bureaucratic sectors; in a strict financial regulatory system, it takes a long time to apply for bank loan, or the complete procedures need rely on the efficiency of the staff. In some countries, bank loans may be very slow, and these loans are crucial to new ventures in the ever-changing competitive market. Therefore, the "timeliness" of bank credit funds may ensure a new venture grasping better market opportunities and enhancing its competitiveness. Fifth, the bank's credit lines undergo a rigorous approval, so that a series of conditions is necessary to increase the minimal amount of bank loan. As a result of information asymmetries and other reasons, the amount of loan that can be provided to new enterprises from other sources is often inadequate; therefore, entrepreneurs must be able to borrow adequate funds from the banking and other financial institutions.

4 Conclusion

In summary, relationships in specific context of China include instrumental rationality, and the particularism of relations among strangers, family, and acquaintances is not the ultimate goal. From the view of resources allocation, Chinese community will use "relationship system" as supplementary means for "price mechanism". In the process of resource allocation, the relationship appears to have been effect on bank credit. As the Chinese economy keeps opening and the economy, especially private economy, develops, we have to have a good understanding on the behavior logic and intention of the Chinese people, if we want to get a complete picture of the China Experience. While a large number of entrepreneurial opportunities rise in this transitional economy, the scarcity of entrepreneurial resources forms an important restrain on the performance of new ventures. If that entrepreneurial environment is hard to change, social resources of entrepreneurs such as human relations can be an important factor among the five characteristics that affect the loans from financial institutions.

For banks, relationship factors contribute to the control of the opportunistic behavior, resolving the moral hazard and adverse selection problems. For new ventures, it creates a reputation or helps them to obtain "relationship rent". Our analysis shows that in the whole process of entrepreneurship and financing, relationship, as an embedded network of factors, affect the firms' performance, through the bank loan. In future research, we should also explore and verify other relevant factors.

References

1. Romer: Increasing Returns and Long-Run Growth (1986)
2. Schumpeter: The Theory of Economic Development (1934)
3. Granovetter: Economic Action and Social Structure: The Problem of Embeddedness. American Journal of Sociology 91
4. Gurley, J.G., Shaw, E.S.: Money in a Theory of Finance. Brookings Institution, Washington, DC (1960)
5. Leland, H.E., Pyle, D.H.: Information Asymmetries, Financial structure and Financial Intermediation. Journal of Finance (32), 371–387 (1977)

6. Diamond, D.: Financial intermediation and delegated monitoring. Review of Economic Studies 51, 393–414 (1984)
7. Berlin, M., Mester: On the profitability and cost of relationship lending. Journal of Banking and Finance 22, 873–8981 (1998)
8. Boisolt, M., Child, J.: From fiefs to clans and network capitalism: explaining China's emerging economic order. Administrative Science Quarterly 41(4), 600–628 (1996)
9. Jacobs: The concept of guanxi and local politics in a rural Chinese cultural settings. In: Greenblatt, S.L., Wilson, R.W., Wlson, A.A. (eds.) Social Interaction in a Chinese Society, pp. 209–236. Praeger, New York (1979)
10. Tsui, A.S., Farh, J.L.: Where guanxi matters: relational demography and guanxi in the Chinese context. Work and Occupations 24(1), 56–79 (1997)
11. Shane, S., Cable, D.: Networkties, reputation, and the financing of new ventures. Management Science 48, 364–381; Johannisson, B.: The Dynamics of Entrepreneurial Networks. In: Reynolds, et al. (eds.) 2002 Frontiers of Entrepreneurship Research. Babson College (1996)

Shape Feature Analysis for Visual Speech and Speaker Recognition

Jiaping Gui and Shilin Wang

School of Information Security Engineering
Shanghai Jiao Tong University
Shanghai, 200240, China
JiapingGui@yeah.net

Abstract. Visual information is always combined as a complementary source to enhance the understanding of what the speaker is talking about, especially in a noisy environment. This paper researches on different lip features for visual speech and speaker recognition, and their robustness to different uttering habits is conducted in-depth analysis. Five feature candidates extracted from lip shape are tested and compared on a multispeaker visual speech recognition task of isolated English digits (0~9). Our experimental results demonstrate that the rotational angle caused by head pose is highly correlated with the individual speaker, but independent of the content of speech. The best shape features for speech and speaker recognition are considered to be those providing the "dynamic" information, like rotation and lip motion.

Keywords: Visual speech and speaker recognition, Confusion matrix, optical-flow, rotation.

1   Introduction

Human recognition is a multi-channel cognitive process as much useful speech information can be conveyed by a speaker through facial movements, and intelligibility can be greatly improved in noisy environments. In fact, the perceiver "hears" something other than what was said acoustically due to the influence of a conflicting visual stimulus [1]. In audio-visual recognition literature, lots of experiments incorporating lip shape information have been carried out and satisfactory results prove its feasibility [2-3].

Since lip shape and movements are highly correlated with the audio signal, it's natural to expect a motivation for attempting to integrate vision with speech in a computer speech recognition system. Many efficient feature extraction methods are proposed. In [4], the feature vectors containing the normalized outer lip features, inner mouth features and their first order derivatives are obtained for training the HMM models, which helps to construct a real-time automatic lipreading system. According to [5], the combination of shape models with appearance modeling and the multiscale spatial analysis technique leads to an overall improving performance for lipreading. A set of lip shape features extracted by active shape model (ASM) together with discrete

J. Zhang (Ed.): ICAIC 2011, Part III, CCIS 226, pp. 167–174, 2011.

cosine transformation (DCT) coefficients of the gray-level appearance information are tested [6], showing important improvements especially for non-stationary background noises. However, they lack further analysis on how different uttering styles affect the experimental results and what features are independent of speakers. Those features indicate high robustness to different speakers for speaker recognition.

There is a limited amount of work reported on the relationship between visual features and speakers' uttering styles. A two-stage, spatial and temporal discrimination analysis is introduced in [7] to select the best lip motion features for visual speech and speaker recognition. Results show that lip motion features provides useful information in both applications, where dense motion features within a bounding box about the lip, lip contour motion features and combination of these with lip shape features are considered. But the recognition accuracy lacks competitiveness compared with some other algorithms (e.g. [4]) and the best recognition rates are reached with relatively high feature dimensionality, which is not suitable for large amount of datasets. What's more, lip rotation can provide comparative information for visual speech and speaker recognition, which is not reflected in [7].

In this paper, we innovatively analyze the results of 5 feature candidates through confusion matrix and research on their robustness to variations (like lip opening, head pose and lighting conditions, etc.). The results show inclusion of the rotational angle in the shape feature has advantage for speaker recognition. However, the performance for speech recognition doesn't depend on whether the speaker tilts his head. The results also suggest that features containing lip opening cues are vulnerable to uttering styles with high variance of results for different speakers, hence leading to low accuracy in visual speech and speaker recognition. While features associated with lip rotation and motion information outperform their counterparts in both applications.

2 Visual Feature Extraction

Before visual feature extraction, fuzzy c-means with shape function (FCMS) [8] is employed to segment the lip image, which provides a more accurate probability map and faster convergence speed compared to that of traditional fuzzy clustering methods (FCM).

Based on our previous work, 14-point ASM [9] is introduced to extract the outer lip contour. Model for 14-point ASM and samples of fitted lip shape are shown in Fig.1. The 14-point distribution model is based on the coordinates of 14 points, marked counterclockwise as 1~14, in the lip contour (shown in Fig.1 (a)). To eliminate the influence of camera settings, all features extracted next except optical-flow features are normalized with respect to their values obtained from the first image in the lip image sequences.

Fig.1 (a). The 14-point distribution model for lip shape

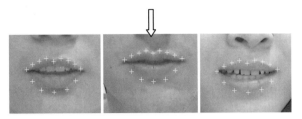

Fig. 1(b). Lip fitting samples for different speakers and different lip shapes under the same conditions

A. Width-height features

Considering its low dimension, high space and time efficiency, width-height features (shown in Fig.2) are served as the control group. The horizontal and vertical Euclidean distances representing the lip openings are then selected to form feature vectors (with dimension 2).

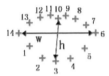

Fig. 2. 14-point ASM based width-height features (f_1)

Suppose the pixel coordinates of point i is (x_i, y_i), $1 \le i \le 14$. Hence the width and height between two points can be expressed as

$$w = \sqrt{(x_6 - x_{14})^2 + (y_6 - y_{14})^2} \tag{1}$$

$$h = \sqrt{(x_{10} - x_3)^2 + (y_{10} - y_3)^2} \tag{2}$$

$$w_{ij} = \frac{w_{ij}}{w_{i1}}, h_{ij} = \frac{h_{ij}}{w_{i1}}; \ 1 \le i \le 20, \ 1 \le j \le 30 \tag{3}$$

where w_{ij} denotes the width of the jth frame in the ith sequence of lip images and $w_{i1}=1$, i.e. the first frame of every sequence is normalized to unit length.

B. Point-to-line-distance features

Here, together with the width, distances of 12 points to the line which the width belongs to are extracted. As shown in Fig.3, the dimension of point-to-line-distance features is 13.

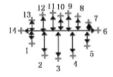

Fig. 3. 14-point ASM based point-to-line-distance features (f_2)

To extract these features, we have

$$w_{ij} = \frac{w_{ij}}{w_{i1}}, h_{ij} = \frac{h_{ij}}{w_{i1}}; \ 1 \le i \le 20, \ 1 \le j \le 30 \tag{4}$$

$$d_m = \frac{d_m}{w_{i1}}; \ 1 \le m \le 5 \| 7 \le m \le 13 \tag{5}$$

where d_m is the distance of point m to the line joining the two corner points (i.e. point 14 and point 6) of the lip.

C. Rotation related features

As noted, libreading is vulnerable to translation, rotation and scale caused by camera settings and head pose. Features or coordinates (shown in Fig.4) after rotation transformation can be very useful information as they represent the rotational changes of a lip sequence. Extracted vectors with rotational angle θ included and without are both obtained, so that we can test their robustness respectively. Note that $\mathbf{f_3}$ has a dimension of 28, while $\mathbf{f_4}$ has a dimension of 29 as the rotational angle is included in the feature vector.

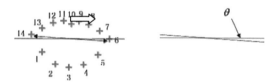

Fig. 4. 14-point ASM based rotation features without rotational angle included (f_3) and with rotational angle included (f_4)

Assume the linear equation for the line joining the two corner points of the lip is

$$Ax + By + C = 0 \tag{6}$$

where $A = y_{14} - y_6$, $B = x_6 - x_{14} \ne 0$, $C = x_{14} * y_6 - x_6 * y_{14}$. The slope of the line is $K = (-A)/B = \tan\theta$. And $\cos\theta = 1/\sqrt{1+K^{-2}}$ for $K \ne 0$; $\cos\theta = 0$ for $K = 0$.

$$\sin\theta = \begin{cases} 1/\sqrt{1 + \dfrac{1}{K^2}} & K > 0 \\ 0 & K = 0 \\ -1/\sqrt{1 + \dfrac{1}{K^2}} & K < 0 \end{cases} \tag{7}$$

Thus the coordinates of point i after rotational transformation are

$$\begin{cases} \overline{x_i} = (x_i - x_c) * \cos\theta + (y_i - y_c) * \sin\theta \\ \overline{y_i} = -(x_i - x_c) * \sin\theta + (y_i - y_c) * \cos\theta \end{cases} \tag{8}$$

where (x_i, y_i) denotes the midpoint of line segment w.

D. Optical-flow features
Optical flow is the pattern of apparent motion of objects, surfaces and edges in a visual scene caused by the relative motion between an observer and the scene [10]. As time characteristics of adjacent frames are highly correlated with a speech signal, we can exploit the temporal correlations in a sequence through the computation of the optical flow between two consecutive lip frames. Using the Lucas-Kanade gradient descent method [11] for optical flow, we can track the lip motion features from one frame to the next. (Note: we denote optical-flow features by $\mathbf{f_5}$ with dimension 28.)

3 Experiments

We implement the visual speech and speaker recognition experiment on a dataset consisting of 10 isolated English digits (0 to 9) uttered by 5 different individuals from different regions and countries. Each speaker was asked to repeat every digit for twenty times and each digit utterance contains 30 lip images with size 100 by 90 and lasts for about 1 sec (overall 30,000 lip images in our database). All recognition experiments are modeled by HMM with continuous observation density. Each group is experimented for 100 times so as to analyze their robustness by the variance among recognition accuracy results.

A. Visual speech recognition
For each experiment, the dataset of each digit from the individual speaker is randomly divided into two sub-datasets, the training dataset containing half of the utterances of individual speaker and the remaining half forming the testing set.

Statistical results of 100-times recognition experiment for each speaker associated to one of 5 feature candidates are shown in table. 1:

Table 1. Statistical results of recognition accuracy for different visual feature candidates

Candidates	Recognition accuracy rate	
	Mean (%)	Standard deviation (%)
$\mathbf{f_1}$	77.79	3.56
$\mathbf{f_2}$	56.2	4.08
$\mathbf{f_3}$	86.21	3.05
$\mathbf{f_4}$	86.17	3.26
$\mathbf{f_5}$	93.81	2.16

In table 1, $\mathbf{f_3}$, $\mathbf{f_4}$ and $\mathbf{f_5}$ outperform $\mathbf{f_1}$ and $\mathbf{f_2}$, where $\mathbf{f_3}$ and $\mathbf{f_4}$ contain additional rotational information other than static lip shape features; $\mathbf{f_5}$ exhibits lip motion information; $\mathbf{f_1}$ and $\mathbf{f_2}$ have only explicitly static features. In terms of low variance, $\mathbf{f_3}$, $\mathbf{f_4}$ and $\mathbf{f_5}$ have high robustness to different uttering habits and styles. Hence, we can expect their good performance on speaker recognition. Note that $\mathbf{f_3}$ and $\mathbf{f_4}$ have almost the same results for speech recognition, which means the rotational angle has little relevance with the content of speech. We can identify the content of speech no matter how tilted the speaker's head is. The confusion matrix related to $\mathbf{f_5}$ is shown below.

Table 2. Confusion matrices related to f_5 from experimental results

	0	1	2	3	4	5	6	7	8	9
0	4823	34	1	23	0	0	46	71	2	0
1	22	4873	1	7	7	12	47	13	10	8
2	60	29	4703	16	162	7	8	12	3	0
3	4	65	2	4901	19	1	0	7	1	0
4	96	13	16	12	4834	18	4	5	2	0
5	3	21	0	14	35	4703	84	125	4	11
6	59	45	0	7	2	31	4254	283	314	5
7	100	65	0	0	24	22	39	4682	30	38
8	5	35	0	60	0	28	238	70	4459	105
9	14	47	0	8	1	19	85	113	39	4674

Every row of the matrix sums to 5000, as half of 20 uttering samples of each individual speaker for each digit are tested for 100 times, such that 5 * 10 * 100 = 5000. In Table.2, each digit is recognized as itself for most of times and errors concentrate on specific digit (e.g. digit 2 is likely to be recognized as digit 0 or 4 for error recognition). This indicates f_5 has good resistance to different uttering habits and styles. Error recognition happens only for a few times, and almost on some specific digits, which suggests f_5 has high robustness to interference caused by speakers. The table also demonstrates some digits are easily identified as some other digits (like between digit 6 and digit 8) and the error recognition concentrates on these digits. Thus, there exists some intrinsic relevance among them, which is independent of speakers. As a result, any feature candidate, no matter how comprehensive it contains the amount of information, cannot eliminate such intrinsic relevance among digits. Note for digit 0, it's never recognized as digit 4, while digit 4 can be wrongly recognized as 0. We can infer some useful information is lost while extracting optical-flow features (f_5) for speech recognition about digit 0 and 4.

B.   Speaker recognition

For speaker recognition, we adopt the same technique as visual speech recognition. Each digit is equivalent to the individual speaker in visual speech recognition and the recognition is also tested for 100 times, whose experimental results are shown in Fig. 5:

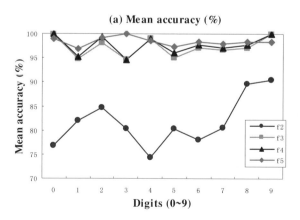

Fig. 3. Statistical results for speaker recognition

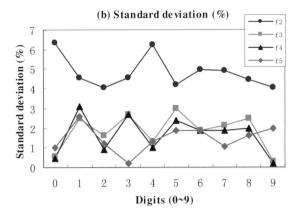

Fig. 3. (*continued*)

From table 3, we can see the recognition accuracy rates are mostly above 95% for f_3, f_4 and f_5. And in terms of standard deviation, f_4 is better than f_3, due to the rotational angle included in the lip features. From the previous analysis, the rotational angle is highly correlated with the individual speaker. If we incorporate the rotational angle which reflects different uttering habits, we can improve the accuracy rate for speaker recognition. Meanwhile, f_5 is slightly better than f_4, suggesting f_5 is a bit more suitable for speaker recognition or there is still some useful information lost by means of rotation transformation.

4 Conclusion

In this paper, we test the efficiency of 5 lip feature candidates and compare their robustness with respect to statistical variance and confusion matrix. The results show optical-flow features reflecting lip motion information are the most suitable one for both visual speech and speaker recognition. The rotational angle is one of the most important features which are highly correlated with the individual speaker, but independent of the content of speech. The feature is very useful for speaker recognition. Moreover, features containing rotation and lip motion, which we refer to "*dynamic*" features, can achieve high performance for speaker recognition.

Acknowledgment. The work described in this paper is supported by the NSFC Fund (60702043) and sponsored by Shanghai Educational Development Foundation (Chen Guang Plan).

References

1. McGurk, H., McDonald, J.: Hearing Lips and Seeing Voices. Nature 264, 746–748 (1976)
2. Dupont, S., Luettin, J.: Audio-visual speech modeling for continuous speech recognition. IEEE Trans. Multimedia 2, 141–151 (2000)

3. Potamianos, G., Neti, C., Gravier, G., Garg, A., Senior, A.: Recent advances in the automatic recognition of audiovisual speech. Proc. IEEE 91(9), 1306–1326 (2003)
4. Wang, S.L., Lau, W.H., Leung, S.H., Yan, H.: A real-time automatic lipreading system. In: Proc. 2004 Int. Symp. Circuits and Systems, vol. 2, pp. 101–104 (2004)
5. Mattews, I., Cootes, T.F., Bangham, J.A., Cox, S., Harvey, R.: Extraction of visual features for lipreading. IEEE Transaction on Pattern Analysis and Machine Intelligence 24(2), 198–213 (2002)
6. Perez, J.F.G., Frangi, A.F., Solano, E.L., Lukas, K.: Lip reading for robust speech recognition on embedded devices. In: Proc. Int. Conf. Acoustics, Speech and Signal Processing, vol. I, pp. 473–476 (2005)
7. Cetingul, H.E., Yemez, Y., Erzin, E., Tekalp, A.M.: Discriminative analysis of lip motion features for speaker identification and speech-reading. IEEE Transactions on Image Processing 15, 2879–2891 (2006)
8. Leung, S.H., Wang, S.L., Lau, W.H.: Lip Image segmentation using fuzzy clustering incorporating an elliptic shape function. IEEE Trans. Image Process. 13(1), 51–62 (2004)
9. Sum, K.L., Lau, W.H., Leung, S.H., Liew, A.W.W., Tse, K.W.: A new optimization procedure for extracting the point-based lip contour using active shape model. In: Proc. IEEE Int. Conf. Acoustics, Speech and Signal Processing, vol. 3, pp. 1485–1488 (2001)
10. http://en.wikipedia.org/wiki/Optical_flow
11. Lucas, B.D., Kanade, T.: An iterative technique of image registration and its application to stereo. In: Proc. 7th Int. Joint Conf. on Artificial Intelligence, pp. 674–679 (August 1981)

A Cooperative Framework of Remote Cooperative Fault Diagnosis Based on TBAC[*]

Liu Jian-Hui

School of Mechanical and Electrical Engineering
Xi'an University of Architecture & Technology, Xi'an
LiuJianHui42@iov.com

Abstract. Remote cooperative fault diagnosis needs multi-diagnosis resources to implement multi-tasks, so the diagnosis cooperative process is complicated. In the foundation of diagnosis task, DTBAC (Dynamic Task-based Access Control) model was introduced to refine collaboration process, role and task of this model was described concretely. Moreover, the coupling of diagnosis roles with diagnosis tasks was primary content in cooperative process; a coupling algorithm was presented from the point of service. The conclusion summarizes and deems that DTBAC can help greatly to resolve conflicts in RCFD.

Keywords: remote cooperative fault diagnosis, DTBAC, service, decision fusion.

1 Introduction

In the domain of equipment maintenance, lots of restrictions besiege fault diagnosis, such as dynamic status of running equipment, complex diagnosis task, ability deficiency of diagnosis resource, peculiar request in diagnosis process. So Remote Cooperative Fault Diagnosis (RCFD) is desired[1], which can mobilize all kinds of diagnosis resources to effectively cooperate, and accomplish fault diagnosis together. Currently, some strong points of remote cooperative diagnosis have been identified, such as it can reduce diagnosis equipment repetitive investment, enhance diagnosis equipment utilization, save money or manpower, and share information[2]. But, the application of this diagnosis mode is still at sunrise, an important reason is cooperative mechanism lacks of clarity, then cooperative system design is too complex to apply. A representation is that conflict phenomena exits among cooperative actives, and one conflict reason is caused by inappropriate diagnosis task allocation. Some heuristic artificial intelligence methods have been applied to resolve this conflict, such as contract net, arbitration, reasoning based on diagnosis cases[3, 4, 5]. Task-based Access Control (TBAC) can be also have a useful try at solving the problem[6].

2 Dtbac Model

The essence of RCFD is disassembling a complex diagnosis task into some less granularity sub tasks which can be executed easily, and then suitably allotting these sub

---

[*] This work is supported by National Natural Science Foundation of China (No. 51075314).

tasks to some vicinal or remote diagnosis resources. After accomplished own sub task utilizing private knowledge, every diagnosis resource provides a part answer. Finally, a comprehensive answer can be found by information fusion. This dissertation upgrades diagnosis task to a higher level which can supervise whole diagnosis process, and put forward a new improved TBAC model, called Dynamic TBAC model (DTBAC), we can consult it in figure 1. Thereinto, the number of dashed line in figure 1 reflects whether diagnosis task allocation is proper, dashed line will lessen when the number of unattached sub task grows.

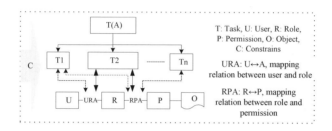

Fig. 1. DTBAC Model

DTBAC is an active model which takes task as least function unit, and adopts dynamic permission. When task is active, some correlative roles possess access permission. Once task is hanging up, this access permission will be freezed. When task is finished, this access permission will be cancelled. DTBAC model adapts to multi-user access control, such as distributed calculation and information processing. DTBAC = [User(U), Role(R), Task(T), Permission(P), Object(O)].

2.1 Role

Role is an entity that expresses the responsibilities and capabilities a user holds, it can be denoted as a five element combination R = [RC, RV, RI, RSR, RDR]. Thereinto, role cardinal number RC reflects how many users can be assigned with a role, default number is random. Role valid time RV = finished time - beginning time. Role inheriting set RI includes all direct inheriting roles from this role. Static restriction role set RSR includes all roles those occur static restriction relation with this role. Dynamic restriction role set RDR also includes those occur dynamic restriction relation with this role.

A role can be established, changed, or deleted by a special user. Relation between roles can be classified into transverse and fore-and-aft (Role Hierarchy) relation, fore-and-aft relation denotes hierarchical relation of roles within a organization, such as permission inheritance, role inheritance, hierarchical supervising and restriction inheritance, etc. Transverse relation reflects as role compatibility, static or dynamic role repulsion. In the point of RCFD, role can be described as table 1.

In above table, diagnosis resource is a most important role, diagnosis resource is a resource that can accomplish some diagnosis task and realize some diagnosis

Table 1. Correlative roles of RCFD

Roles	Description
Maintenance strategy administering level	Accomplishing maintenance strategy planning and maintenance task control
Maintenance personnel	Throughout implementing and administering maintenance task
Design personnel	Receiving the improving advice from maintenance field and accomplishing design oriented to maintenance
Operation personnel	User of equipment
Diagnosis expert	Expert who have abundant experience in a certain fault diagnosis field
Data acquiring system	Running information of equipment can be acquired by the system
Fault detection instrument	Equipment whether is in gear can be judged by the instrument
Fault diagnosis instrument	Instrument that can estimate fault source position, fault time, influence degree, and can give out repair advice
Fault predication instrument	Future running trend of equipment can be forecasted by the instrument
DBMS	Supervising some correlative information effectively, and transforming interactive information format
Network information system	Providing remote cooperative diagnosis platform, and controlling information remote transmission
ERP	A auxiliary supervising platform which can support maintenance decision, and provide maintenance decision implementing means

function, includes diagnosis instrument, diagnosis system, diagnosis expert and diagnosis technique, etc. According cooperative degree, the relation between diagnosis resources can be classified into 5 types: absolute cooperative, cooperative, self-serving, absolute self-serving, cooperative and self-serving coexisting.

2.2 Diagnosis Task

Commonly, diagnosis task is a series of decision actions to find diagnosis result by analysis and reasoning of equipment fault information, a diagnosis result includes equipment state, fault developing trend, fault time, etc. A diagnosis task T = [TID, TD, ERCR, TE, TO, TP], TID is an only id which is endued at the task establishing or initializing time. Task description TD = [AC, AF, AT], AC is task activation condition, AF is activation symbol, AT is activation period. ERCR denotes capability request of executive role, the request includes task executing quality, executing time and cost, etc. TE indicates 6 kind of task state: quiescence, existing, unsuccessful, waiting, running, and terminating. TO is the access object type when subject executing task. TP is task authorization, includes available authorization and executing authorization. Diagnosis tasks of RCFD are described concretely in table 2.

The definitions of User, Object and Constraint have to be neglected in view of paper length.

Table 2. Some sorts of diagnosis tasks

Tasks	Description
Design for maintainability	In equipment design phase, improving design aiming at maintainability, configuring self-diagnosis system, providing design data for future maintenance task
Maintenance strategy planning	Choosing suitable maintenance strategy and configuring or optimizing diagnosis instrument based on enterprise management policies
Diagnosis task control	Establishing diagnosis task according appointed maintenance strategy, and controlling the implementing process of diagnosis task
Data acquiring	Collecting equipment running data and gaining relative information from ERP system when it is needed
Interaction information format transforming	Transforming original data into readable information format, so realize relative maintenance information integration
Network transmission control	Controlling information transmission in remote diagnosis
Condition Monitoring	Judging equipment health situation based on acquiring data
Fault predication	Qualitative or quantitative predication of equipment performance decline, component residual life, fault developing trend, etc
Fault insulation and diagnosis	After equipment fault occurred, isolating fault source, and giving out maintenance advices based on fault time, influence degree
Diagnosis task allocation	Disassembling complex task into some simple sub-tasks, and assigning corresponding diagnosis resources
Diagnosis resource control	Supervising diagnosis resources effectively, and tracking their execution process
Decision information fusion	Fusing some redundant or conflicting decision information from RCFD, and deciding final diagnosis conclusion
Repair	Eliminating maintainability fault based on diagnosis result and repair advice, recovering equipment expectant performance
Recycling	If the equipment fault doesn't worth repair, then recycling or scraping the equipment
Spare parts management	Deciding stock amount and purchase scheme of spare par

3 Process Management of RCFD

Process management of cooperative diagnosis involves information preparing and collecting before cooperation, task allocation, task evaluation and task execution during cooperative diagnosis process. The type and content in table 1 and table 2 are many and various, this situation makes it's hard to carry through diagnosis roles-to-tasks relation modeling. At the same time, all task represent or bear determinate function, they are all purposeful services (S), and service need some roles to actualize, so based on their services, we can assort tasks into two kinds – asking type and providing type. Then diagnosis roles-to-tasks relation modeling can be translated into coupling of two kinds of services.

Definition 1: suppose S_1 is a set of optional services, S_2 is a services set to couple with S_1, if there exist $S_i \in S_1 \wedge S_i \in S_2$, then call S_i is coupling point of S_1 and S_2. If and only if $S_1 = S_2$, call S_1 and S_2 are precise coupling. Otherwise, call S_1 and S_2 are approximate coupling.

Normally, it's expected that precise coupling can be achieved when carry through services coupling. But in fact, the coupling result often is approximate coupling, this means only partial services in coupling services set meet requirement. So definition 2 is introduced to calculate the coupling degree between services sets.

Definition 2: if S_i is the coupling point of S_1 and S_2, then call $C(S_1, S_2) = |S_i|$ is coupling degree of S_2 and S_1, $|S_1| > 0$, $0 \leq C \leq 1$, $\{S_i\}$ is the set of all coupling points. Correspondingly, call $D(S_1, S_2) = 1 - C(S_1, S_2)$ is departure degree of S_2 and S_1.

Assuming fault information reflects the providing services set $S_p = \{S_1, S_2, ..., S_L\}$, asking services set $S_r = \{S_1, S_2, ..., S_k\}$, all services set $S = \{S_1, S_2, ..., S_n\}$, roles set R = $\{r_1, r_2, ..., r_m\}$. Then coupling steps are as follows.

(1) Acquiring providing services register $Rs_p = [p_{ij}]_{mn}$ and asking services register $Rs_r = [q_{ij}]_{mn}$. p_{ij} denotes whether the providing services set of role r_i includes service S_j, if includes then register value is 1, otherwise is 0; q_{ij} denotes whether the asking services set of role r_i includes service S_j, if includes then register value is 1, otherwise is 0.

(2) Establishing providing services matrix $S_p = [S_1, S_2, ..., S_L]^T$ and its coupling matrix $S_{mp} = [p_{ij}]_{mL}$ based on a set of requisite providing services and providing services register. $S_i (1 \leq i \leq L)$ is a providing service which fault diagnosis needs. Similarly, asking services matrix $S_r = [S_1, S_2, ..., S_k]^T$ and its coupling matrix $S_{mr} = [q_{ij}]_{mk}$ can be established.

(3) Implementing multiply operation of providing services matrix and its coupling matrix, then coupling matrix of roles to providing services $D_p = S_{mp*}S_p = [D_p(1), D_p(2), ..., D_p(L)]^T$.

(4) Implementing multiply operation of asking services matrix and its coupling matrix, then coupling matrix of roles to asking services $D_r = S_{mr*}S_r = [D_p(1), D_p(2), ..., D_p(k)]^T$.

(5) Calculating coupling degree and departure degree of D_p and D_r based on Definition 2 respectively, then coupling degree of D_p is $CD_p = |D_p|/|S_p|$, its departure degree $DD_p = 1 - CD_p$. Similarly, coupling degree of D_r is $CD_r = |D_r|/|S_r|$, its departure degree $DD_p = 1 - CD_p$.

(6) Utilizing role choosing arithmetic in Figure 2 to choose a candidate roles set Rs.

(7) Choosing the best role of Rs and ascertaining a diagnosis resource to implement task. If Rs is null, choosing condition will need to be relaxed and turn to step (6).

Supposing roles set involved in a task allocation process about diagnosis task T_i is R = $\{r_1, r_2, r_3\}$, services set S = $\{S_1, S_2, ..., S_6\}$, providing services set of T_i is $S_p = \{S_4, S_5, S_6\}$, asking services set $S_r = \{S_2, S_3, S_5\}$. Providing services set of r_1 is $\{S_1, S_2, S_3\}$, asking services set is $\{S_4, S_5\}$. Providing services set of r_2 is $\{S_2, S_4\}$, asking services set is $\{S_1, S_2, S_3\}$. Providing services set of r_3 is $\{S_3, S_5, S_6\}$, asking services set is $\{S_2, S_3, S_5, S_6\}$. Then providing services register $Rs_p = [\{1, 1, 1, 0, 0, 0\}, \{0, 1, 0, 1, 0, 0\}, \{0, 0, 1, 0, 1, 1\}]^T$, asking services register $Rs_r = [\{0, 0, 0, 1, 1, 0\}, \{1, 1, 1, 0, 0, 0\}, \{0, 1, 1, 0, 1, 1\}]^T$, providing services matrix $S_p = [\{S_4\}, \{S_5\}, \{S_6\}]^T$, providing services coupling matrix $S_{mp} = [\{0, 0, 0\}, \{1, 0, 0\}, \{0, 1, 1\}]^T$. Asking services matrix $S_r = [\{S_2\}, \{S_3\}, \{S_5\}]^T$, asking services coupling matrix $S_{mr} = [\{0, 0, 1\}, \{1, 1, 0\}, \{1, 1, 1\}]^T$. Coupling matrix of roles to providing services is $D_p = S_{mp} * S_p = [\{0\}, \{S_4\}, \{S_5+S_6\}]^T$, coupling matrix of roles to asking services is $D_r = S_{mr} * S_r = [\{S_5\}, \{S_2+S_3\}, \{S_2+S_5+S_6\}]^T$, then coupling degree and departure degree of D_p and D_r is: $CD_p = |D_p|/|S_p| = [\{0\}, \{1/3\}, \{2/3\}]^T = [\{0\}, \{33.3\%\}, \{66.6\%\}]^T$, $DD_p = 1-CD_p = [\{100\%\}, \{66.6\%\}, \{33.3\%\}]^T$; $CD_r = |D_r|/|S_r| = [\{1/3\}, \{2/3\}, \{1\}]^T = [\{33.3\%\}, \{66.6\%\}, \{100\%\}]^T$, $DD_r = 1-CD_r = [\{66.6\%\}, \{33.3\%\}, \{0\}]^T$.

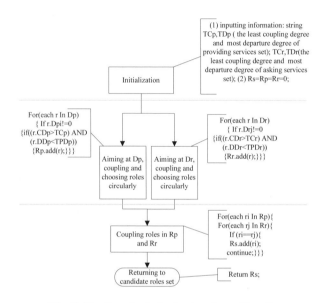

Fig. 2. The flowchart of role choosing arithmetic

Let $CD_p = 65\%$, $DD_p = 35\%$, $CD_r = 85$, $DD_r = 15\%$, according above role choosing arithmetic, $R_s = \{r_3\}$. So, during the RCFD process, r_3 will implement task T_i namely, and so on.

4 Conclusion

In virtue of DTBAC model, this paper has analyzed all kinds of roles and tasks in RCFD process, and established the relation of roles (diagnosis resources) and diagnosis tasks based on services coupling. These works are significative for cooperative mechanism study and apply. In the future, some key supporting technologies involved in RCFD will be discussed, such as decision fusion technology which is used to solve multi-source diagnosis information conflict problem.

References

1. Li, D., Yu, D., Liu, J., et al.: Research on virtual-reality-based multimedia remote collaborative fault diagnosis system. Journal of Hunan University: Natural Sciences 32(5), 56–60 (2005)
2. Ren, X., Ong, M., Allan, G., et al.: Service-oriented architecture on the grid for integrated fault diagnostics. Concurrency and Computation: Practice and Experience 19(2), 223–234 (2007)
3. Krainin, M., An, B., Lesser, V.: An Application of Automated Negotiation to Distributed Task Allocation. In: 2007 IEEE/WIC/ACM International Conference on Intelligent Agent Technology, pp. 138–142 (2007)
4. Sua, K.-W., Hwang, S.-L., Chou, Y.-F.: Applying knowledge structure to the usable fault diagnosis assistance system: A case study of motorcycle maintenance in Taiwan. Expert Systems with Applications 31, 370–382 (2006)
5. Dong, L.X., Xiao, D.M., Liang, Y.S., Liu, Y.L.: Rough set and Fuzzy wavelet neural network integrated with least square weighted fusion algorithm based fault diagnosis research for power transformers. Electric Power Systems Research 78(1), 129–136 (2008)
6. Roshan, K.T., Sandhu, R.S.: Task-Based Authorization Controls (TBAC): A Family of Models for Active and Enterprise-Oriented Authorization Management. In: Eleventh International Conference on Database Security XI: Status and Prospects (1997)

Analysis on Dynamic Landscape Patterns of Urbanizations in Four Asia Cities Using 3S Technologies and CA Model[*]

Yizhao Chen, Jiasheng Huang, and Jianlong Li[**]

College of Life Science, Nanjing University, Nanjing, 210093, P.R. China
XinglongZou@yeah.net

Abstract. Urbanization has brought great impact on regional landscape pattern and the food security, and it strongly affected urban ecology environment, biology diversity and human-being life. With the help of 3S technology and CA model, our research took four Asia cities respectively as the case of big cities and small cities to study the urbanize condition in Asia. First, base on the technology of remote sensing, GIS technology and the method of landscape ecology gradient analysis combined with landscape indexes, the landscape structure and its spatial characteristics of urban land, agricultural land and other land use types of Zhangjiagang City is studied in the paper; And second, Two mega-cities in Asia-Pacific Region: Manila, the Philippines and Hanoi, Vietnam, were selected to compare with Shanghai, China. In support of 3S (GIS-GPS-RS) technology, the landscape pattern dynamics and desakota regions features related with urbanization of the three cities in recent twenty years were studied, with gradient analysis using six landscape matrix indexes: Contagion index, largest patch index, landscape shape index, perimeter-area fractal dimension, patches density, and Shannon's diversity index. In our study, we have concluded that: urbanization in Zhangjiagang is rapidly in recent years; landscape pattern changed significantly in the 20 years in Shanghai and Urbanization in Shanghai is slower than Metro Manila but faster than Hanoi; Last, large cities and small cities should be developed in perfect harmony.

Keywords: Urbanization, Landscape Pattern, Gradient Analysis, Cellular Automata, Food Security.

1 Introduction

World Urbanization has entered the stage of comprehensive development in the middle of last century. In our country, urbanization has also been developed rapidly since the reform and opening up. Urbanization has brought great impact on regional

---

[*] This work is supported by "THE KEY PROJECT OF CHINESE NATIONAL PROGRAMS FOR FUNDAMENTAL RESEARCH AND DEVELOPMENT (973 PROGRAM, 2010CB950702), APN PROJECT (ARCP2010-14NMY-LI) AND IPDF PROJECT BY THE PROF. ODEH.
[**] Corresponding author.

J. Zhang (Ed.): ICAIC 2011, Part III, CCIS 226, pp. 182–188, 2011.
© Springer-Verlag Berlin Heidelberg 2011

landscape pattern, and it strongly affected urban ecology environment, biology diversity and human life [1-3]. In recent years, big progresses in remote sensing technology promoted the quantification of landscape ecology methods in the study of urban ecology.

As the most important human driving force of Land use/cover change, urbanization has great relationship with land use change. On one hand, urbanization itself represents the process of rural land transformed to urban land. Judging from the city of the evolvement, the most intuitionistic performance of the course of development in the city landscape is that the rural land transforms into the unban land. On the other hand, the ways of land use decides the urbanization development direction, and the plans of land use put great influence the on the future urban development pattern. So in the near future and even future for a long period, the study of urban land utilization of global change study will be a hot issue.

In recent study of urban land utilization, the wide application technology and methods of landscape include remote sensing technology, land statistics method, nonlinear theory, urban landscape model etc. In these methods, Landscape ecology pattern analysis and landscape model method is undoubtedly particularly important. From the development of discipline history, landscape ecology have the background of European research on land use and North American research methods for land use in spatial patterns, mathematical model and quantitative research, both of which provide a convenient way for the quantitative study of Land use. Therefore, landscape ecology in land use field has been widely used, the analysis of landscape pattern and landscape model methods laid a foundation for research on land use/land cover changes and space pattern and ecological process, which have been accepted by many scholars of many fields such as ecology, human geography, and landscape planning.

In this study, Zhangjiagang is respectively taken as the case of China's big cities and small cities, to study the landscape changes in urbanization. In the study of Zhangjiagang City, we use landscape metrics [4-7] to analysis the landscape pattern first, and a cellular automata model [8] was developed further to simulate and predict the city development. In the study of three metropolises, two major cities in Asia, Manila, Philippines and Hanoi, Vietnam, were brought for comparison to study the landscape pattern dynamic urban-rural structure character related to urbanization in nearly 20 years. Besides the case study, it is analyzed that, the main factors affect the urbanization strategy selection and the principles we should take in urbanization. Additionally, the problems in the urbanization of large cities and small cities are analyzed respectively, and countermeasures are proposed. It is pointed out large cities and small cities should be developed in perfect harmony.

2 Methods

A. Description of the study area

(1)   The Zhangjiagang city is located in Jiangsu province in eastern part of China between 31°43'12" to 32°02'N, and 120°21'57" to 120°52'. 98 km away from Shanghai and 200 kilometers from Nanjing. In September of 1986, Zhangjiagang change prefecture into city. Now it administers eight towns

and the Changyisha zone. The total area of Zhangjiagang city is 998.48 square kilometers, among which 785.55 square kilometers are land area.

(2)   Shanghai, located between 30 ° 40 ', 'N ° ~ 31 53 °, 120 ° ~ 51', E, 122 °12'E, including 6340km^2 area within the area of outer in 61 square kilometers and a population of 1 379 million (2007). Shanghai located in the front of Yangtze River delta, adjacent to the north border gold waterway the estuary of the Yangtze River. Shanghai is one of the largest cities, one of the most important economic and financial center, transport hub and foreign trade ports of China. It is also the Chinese important base of science, technology, culture and education.

(3)   Metro Manila located between 14 ° ~ 14 ° 47 21 ', 'N, 121 ° 09' E ~ 120 ° E, which is on the verge of natural harbor Manila bay. Its area is about 620 km2, and the population is about 1,155 million (2006). In 1976, Manila city was designated to be the Philippine capital and seat of government. Now it is the political, economic and cultural center, a metropolis consists of old and new crisscross, traditional and modern, and also the Philippines largest city, international trade center and one of Asia's biggest city circle.

(4)   Hanoi (Hanoi) is located between 20 ° 53 '~ 21 ° 23 ° 44' N, 105 ° 02 ' '~ 106 E, is located in the centre of the birthplace of Vietnamese, Honghe river valley. since ancient times namely for the confluence at the border trade centre, traffic fort, with a beautiful natural environment, the historical heritage numerous, traditional features strong, It is Vietnam's second-largest city, the area is equivalent to a big province of Vietnam, it consists of nine districts and five rural areas, the total area is 921 km^2, and a population of 345 million (2007). It is also the Vietnamese capital, the nation's second largest city and politics, economy, culture, science and technology centre.

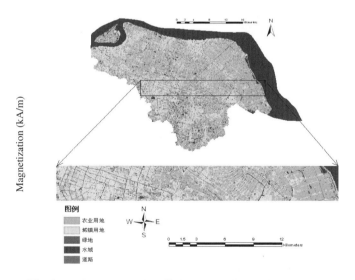

Fig. 1. Land use map and studied transect of Zhangjiagang City

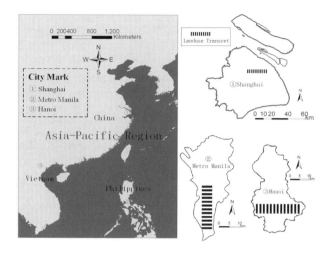

Fig. 2. The contour map of the three metropolises and the transect location

B. Database and methodology

In the research of Zhangjiagang city, Landsat TM remote sensing images are used as the primitive source data of land use between 2002 and 2006 in Zhangjiagang, the spatial resolution is 25 m * 25m. Erdas 9.1 platform is mainly used for Image pre-processing, characteristic analysis and classification work. After the image selection, observation data input, familiar with the study area, typical features of reflection, the spectral characteristics analysis, image features management analysis, image pre-processing, image statistical characteristics analysis, key branch area processing, image enhancement processing and classification (non-supervised classification combining supervised classification), regional treatment, and composite processing, classify remote sensing image into five categories: the cultivated land, wood land and other agricultural land, construction land, water area. The classification accuracy of inspect random dots is above 85%. And through GIS superposition analysis, the transition probability matrix of land type, area transfer matrix and a series of other images are obtained. Then Tectonic CA filter and determine the start time and the CA cycle times.

In the comparison between the three metropolises, the research is divided into three periods: Early Stage,(in the late 1980's ~ 1990s, Medium Term, MT, 2000 ~ 2001) and recent (Short Term, ST, 2006 ~ 2007), every period use a issue of remote sensing image, nine period of remote sensing image have been used. By the support of Erdas Imagine 9.0 platform, pre-treatment such as geometric correction, radiation correction, strengthen and key branch area have been done. Combined with ground investigation of Shanghai, Manila and Hanoi, classify urban land use in 5 types: urban area, road, Greenland, farm land and water area by man-computer interactive interpretation, the accuracy is over 80%, and then transformed the results into vector diagram.

3 Results and Analysis

A. Analysis results of Zhangjiagang city in China

By anglicizing the remote sensing images and CA model of Zhangjiagang city, the results shows that:

(1) The urbanization process is very quickly recently and in the next 10 years in Zhangjiagang city. Urbanization is one of the main land use/land cover change driving force of Zhangjiagang city. The single dynamic attitude index of construction land is 1.0%, and from 2006-2016, the construction land will annually increase about 309.8 hectares (table 1). The growth of urban land will expand to the brink of original downtown (YangSheZhen).

(2) In the process of urbanization, the forest land changed significantly, cultivated land and other agricultural land also has great changes, which indicates that agricultural land confronts with some pressure. As the reduction of agricultural land area is the inevitable result of urbanization. Simulation shows that from 2006 to 2016, 5077 hectares of arable land and 496 hectares of other agricultural land will transmute to meet the increasing needs of urbanization. In this case, negative effects of rapid urbanization on agricultural land will also have to consider.

Table 1. Area of Each Land Use Type of Zhangjiagang City in Future 10 Years Simulated by Cellular Automata

	2002	2006	2008	2010	2012	2014	2016	2018	2020
farm/ha	45031	42618	41732	41173	40653	40338	40044	39871	39709
forest/ha	586	504	467	433	401	372	345	320	296
Other agriculture land/ha	3933	3027	2812	2753	2692	2678	2661	2660	2658
Construction land/ha	28023	31425	32562	33215	33828	34185	34523	34722	34910
water/ha	22269	22269	22269	22269	22269	22269	22269	22269	22269

B. Analysis results of three metropolises in Asia

The relationship between landscape pattern indices and gradient belts characteristics can be reflected by the correlation of the index and distance, relevant or negative correlation degree between major landscape index plaques density, Shannon diversity index and the absolute distance to the city center is high in the three cities, indicates that they have strong dependence to the gradient of urbanization. The correlation between plaque density and absolute distance in Manila city is above 0.7, while Hanoi's relatively low, and the correlation between Shanghai in 1989 and 2001 is more than 0.8.

The values of the Shannon diversity index is higher, the landscape diversity is bigger. Shannon diversity indexes of Shanghai and Manila are positively correlated with the absolute distance, while Hanoi is negatively correlated with (Table 2).

Table 2. Correlation of Landscape Index and Absolute Distance in the Transects of Shanghai, Manila and Hanoi

City	Year	CONTAG	LPI	LSI	PAFRAC	PD	SHDI
Shang	1989	-0.754	-0.595	0.817	-0.382	0.829	0.686
hai	2001	-0.940	-0.919	0.907	-0.824	0.928	0.914
	2007	-0.402	0.070	0.136	0.386	-0.423	0.850
Manila	1993	-0.813	0.039	0.666	-0.399	0.742	0.811
	2001	-0.869	-0.109	0.679	-0.507	0.835	0.867
	2006	-0.899	0.086	0.939	-0.206	0.770	0.838
Hanoi	1993	0.601	0.326	-0.325	-0.244	0.629	-0.673
	2000	0.352	-0.395	-0.120	-0.413	0.345	-0.455
	2007	0.224	-0.368	0.420	0.634	0.351	-0.340

It shows that the landscape change of urban-rural area in Shanghai and Manila is large and landscape fragmentation is strong, while the situation of Hanoi is opposite. Further more, landscape shape index also can reflect this characteristic, and is able to reflect the features from the opposite.

Above all, aggregation index, landscape shape index, patch density and Shannon diversity index can reflect the dependence between landscape fragmentation and urban gradient, Shanghai and Manila have increasing trend of fragmentation towards suburban area, while the Hanoi fragmentation is mainly embodied in urban area.

4 Conclusions

1. Urbanization in recent years has been appeared rapidly in Zhangjiagang City, where the landscape gradient character showed obviously on spatial, the landscape changed greatly in time, and the conversion of land use type was also evident. In the type level, the different land use along the gradient showed significant spatial characteristics; in landscape level, diversity existed in different kinds of landscapes along the gradient, which showed that, urbanization had led to the increased landscape fragmentation and landscape heterogeneity. In urbanization, the urban area moved forward to the surrounding areas by the speed of about 0.5km / year.

Simulations based on cellular automata model show that, in the next 10 years, Zhangjiagang city is still facing rapid urbanization, agricultural land is facing greater pressure, and reasonable and effective measures should be taken to protect them.

2. In Shanghai, landscape pattern changed significantly in the 20 years or so from late 20th century to the early 21st century. Urbanization in Shanghai is slower than Metro Manila and faster than Hanoi. In the process of urbanization, regional landscape pattern of these three cities has changed significantly, with an increasing of patch density and strengthening of fragmentation. In land use transect, Patch density, Shannon diversity index and the absolute distance to the city centre have a high correlation. The correlation between patch densities can achieve as high as 0.928, and the max number for Shannon diversity is 0.914.

Landscape index can detect the gradient of the city and show the process of urbanization with the peak. In the research period, the curve's peak of landscape index shows the movement, reflecting the progress of urbanization direction. The desakota region of the cities was discovered with different characteristics, and different stages of urbanization development features, which was typical in Asia. Metro Manila was found in the highest stage of urbanization, and with the earliest suburb urbanization. Shanghai was demonstrated a high stage of urbanization and an obvious suburb urbanization. In contrast, Hanoi appears a lower stage of urbanization and unobvious suburb urbanization.

3. Large cities and small cities should be developed in perfect harmony. Big cities should focus on its kernel role, resource conservation, environment protection and industry optimization and configuration. For the problems in suburbanization, strategies of symbiosis, urban space rebuilding, capacity regeneration and space redistribution should be taken. Small cities should focus on advanced planning, bridge roll, mass effect, and to strengthen the second and third industries.

In the study, the knowledge of urbanization characteristics for Asia's big cities and small cities in the view of landscape ecology is promoted. The study has important theoretical and practical significance in urban planning and decision-making in eco-city construction.

Acknowledgment. We are grateful to the chief editor and anonymous reviewers for illuminating comments. This research was mainly supported by "the key project of chinese national programs for fundamental research and development (973 program, 2010cb950702), apn project (arcp2010-14nmy-li) and ipdf project by the prof. odeh.

References

[1] Lambin, E.F., Turner, B.L.I., Geist, H.J., et al.: The causes of land-use and land-cover change: moving beyond the myths. Global Environmental Change 11, 261–269 (2001)
[2] Turner, B.L.I., Skole, D., Sanderson, S., et al.: Land-Use and Land-Cover Change Science/Research Plan, in IGBP Report No. 35 and HDP Report No. 7. IGBP, HDP, Stockholm, Geneva (1995)
[3] Kalnay, E., Cai, M.: Impact of urbanization and land-use change on climate. Nature 423(6953), 528–531 (2003)
[4] Zhang, L.Q., Wu, J.P., Zhen, Y., et al.: A GIS-based gradient analysis of urban landscape pattern of Shanghai metropolitan area, China. Landscape and Urban Planning 69(1), 1–16 (2004)
[5] Thomlinson, J.R., Serrano, M.I., Lopez, T.D., et al.: Land-use dynamics in a post-agricultural Puerto Rican landscape (1936-1988). Biotropica 28(4), 525–536 (1996)
[6] Pan, D., Domon, G., de Blois, S., et al.: Temporal (1958-1993) and spatial patterns of land use changes in Haut-Saint-Laurent (Quebec, Canada) and their relation to landscape physical attributes. Landscape Ecology 14(1), 35–52 (1999)
[7] Yang, X.J., Liu, Z.: Quantifying landscape pattern and its change in an estuarine watershed using satellite imagery and landscape metrics. International Journal of Remote Sensing 26(23), 5297–5323 (2005)
[8] Andŕe Ménard, D.J.M.: Simulating the impact of forest management scenarios in an agricultural landscape of southern Quebec, Canada, using a geographic cellular automata. Landscape and Urban Planning 79, 253–265 (2007)

A Low-Rate DoS Detection Based on Rate Anomalies[*]

Libing Wu[1], Jing Cheng[1], Yanxiang He[1], Ao Xu[1], and Peng Wen[2]

[1] School of Computer, Wuhan University, Wuhan, China
[2] School of Information Management, Wuhan University, Wuhan, China
libing_wulibing_wu@sina.com

Abstract. Low-rate Denial-of-Service attacks are stealthier and trickier than traditional DDoS attacks. According to the characteristic of periodicity and short burst in LDoS flows, a detection measure against LDoS attacks based on rate anomalies has been proposed. In the period when the router packet loss-rate is abnormal caused by the attack pulse, the rate of attack flow is large, while in other time the rate of attack flow is close to 0. In the view point of the periods that the packet loss is abnormal, we can find that the attack flow rate is far higher in these periods than the average rate, while the normal flow is lower to the average rate. In this paper, we proposed a measure that observes the flow rate in the periods that the packet loss rate is abnormal, computing the difference of the rate in these periods and the average rate. If it is beyond a certain threshold, treats the flow as a malicious flow and filters the flow with corresponding method.

Keywords: Network Security, Congestion Control, Denial of Service, Low-Rate attack.

1 Introduction

Low-rate DoS attacks are a new type of DoS attacks [1], which use the vulnerabilities of adaptive mechanisms in the network protocol or system, to decline the performance of the victim's services by sending a periodic arrack pulse to the target. LDoS attacks are completely different from the traditional flooding DoS attacks. They mainly aim at the vulnerability of adaptive mechanisms in the target attack system (such as the TCP congestion control mechanism, the service request to accept control mechanism [2, 3] or router queue management mechanism [4] and so on) by sending a interval attack pulse, to lead the target attack system in an unstable state and seriously affect the quality of its service. LDoS attacks send data only in a specific interval, they doesn't send any data in the other time-slot of the same cycle, and such characteristics of intermittent attacks make the flow keeping a low average rate as the legitimate flow. There is no clear distinction between legitimate flow and malicious flow. In other words, the attack flow no longer has unusual statistical properties, so it is difficult to use the methods of detecting DoS attacks to prevent them. This is a new challenge to Network Security.

[*] Supported by National Natural Science Foundation of China (Grant No. 61070010), National Science Foundation for Post-doctoral Scientists of China, the Natural Science Foundation of Hubei Province and the Fundamental Research Funds for the Central Universities.

J. Zhang (Ed.): ICAIC 2011, Part III, CCIS 226, pp. 189–196, 2011.
© Springer-Verlag Berlin Heidelberg 2011

According to the anomalistic characteristic of LDoS attack flows in pulse period, a detection and defense measure against LDoS attacks based on rate anomalies has been proposed in this paper. In the period when the router packet loss-rate is abnormal caused by the attack pulse, the rate of attack flow increases significantly while the rate of normal flow decreases due to congestion. In the other time, the rate of attack flow is close to 0. However, the rate of normal flow will increase. For this reason, while the average rate between arrack flow and normal flow is no clear distinction, but in the periods that the router packet loss-rate is abnormal we can observe that the attack flow rate is far higher in these periods than the average rate while the normal flow is lower than or equal to the average rate. We propose a measure that observes the flow rate in the periods that the packet loss rate is abnormal, computing the difference of the rate in these periods and the average rate. If it is beyond a certain threshold, treats the flow as a marvel flow and filters the flow with corresponding method. This method can detect the LDoS attack flows even the LDoS attack flows which have no clear characteristic.

The rest of this paper is organized as follows. Section 2 analyzes LDoS attack and presents a detection measure against LDoS attacks based on rate anomalies. Section 3 shows and analyzes the results of experiments. The end of this paper makes a summary and arranges the next work.

2   A Low-Rate DoS Detection Based on Rate Anomalies

A.   Principle of LDoS attack

At present a lot of LDoS attack ways have been proposed [1, 2, 3], but all of them use the vulnerabilities of adaptive mechanisms in the network or end-systems. Adaptive mechanisms mainly focus on system's effectiveness and fairness in the steady-state, but ignore system's performance in the disabled-state. So if attackers launch LDoS periodic pulse attack, they will make the system frequently switch between the steady and the disabled state. As shown in Fig. 1, parameters include the attack period T, burst length τ and burst strength δ. We make an assumption that the initial state of system's performance is 0, steady-state performance is described as SS, and disabled-state performance is described as DS. After attacks beginning the time system step into disabled-state from steady-state is named as t1, meanwhile, the time system through the adaptive mechanism returns to steady-state is named as t2 and in adaptive protocol t2>>t1. When the system in steady-state SS, attackers send attack pulses to rapidly reduce system's performance to DS. Then attackers stop this attack and plan to launch the next attack after system recovering to steady-state by t2. Cycling like this, the system has never been able to maintain stability and seriously affects the performance.

B.   LDoS attack flow's characteristices

LDoS attacks by periodic attacks make conventional detection based on throughput characteristics difficult to detect. According to the characteristic of short burst in LDoS flows, some researchers have proposed to filter them by this characteristic. But if LDoS attacks by distributed attacks, then they are also difficult to extract the characteristic in LDoS flows. Therefore, we must do a deep excavation about LDoS flow's characteristics to detect and defense them.

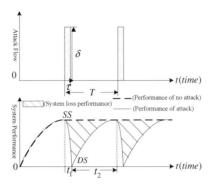

Fig. 1. LDoS attack model and its impact on system performance

As shown in Fig.2, no matter the LDoS attacks aim to TCP protocol or to active queue management algorithm, the attack flows both make a large number of cache queue's packets lose by a short-term, high-speed pulse flow. For the former, the LDoS attacks aim to force other TCP flows to enter the retransmission state by losing packets. While, for the latter, they aim to ......, in order to seriously affect the performance of network's service. But these attacks have one thing in common, that is in each attack cycle pulse flows have to make a serious packet loss stage, to achieve the purpose of this cycle of attack. So in the bottleneck link router we can observe a periodic small time that packet loss rate is abnormal increased and it is related to activity of attack pulses.

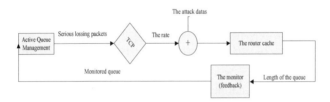

Fig. 2. The principle of LDoS attack against the network protocol

In the period that the router packet loss rate is abnormal, the rate of attack flow increases significantly while the rate of normal flow decreases due to congestion. In other time, the rate of attack flow is close to 0. However, the rate of normal flow will increase. For this reason, while the average rate between arrack flow and normal flow is no clear distinction, but in the period that the router packet loss-rate is abnormal we can observe that the attack flow rate is far higher in these periods than the average rate while the normal flow is lower than or equal to the average rate.

C. Attack flow detector design

We analyzed the characteristics of attack flow on rate in the last section and now around the characteristics we design a method to detect the attack flow. Detector's workflow in each observation cycle shown in Fig. 3, in each end of observation cycle it is going to calculate the every flow's average rate V_f, current rate V_f and the current packet loss rate p. If the packet loss rate p is anomalous, then it updates the monitoring list, and proceeds with the next monitoring period.

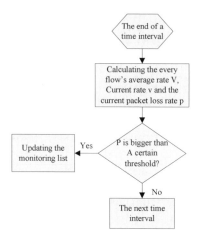

Fig. 4. Detector's workflow

By source IP and destination IP to identify a network flow, $V_f (0 \le f \le n, n)$ is defined as the average rate of flow f. Here we think if the time interval of a certain flow's twice consecutive transmissions between packets is less than 10s (if too small, it may let the same flow's attack pulse in different attack cycle divided into different flows), the flow is active, otherwise it is considered to be inactive and we delete it's history in order to save time and space. V_f's formula is as follows.

$$V_f = \frac{b_f}{t} \tag{1}$$

In which t is the current time of the network, b_i is the total number of bytes transferred by flow i until time t.

The network time is divided into many short time intervals, each of the length is τ. $v_f (0 \le f \le n)$ is defined as the flow rate in this current period and the calculation principle is the same as V_f, shown in formula 2, and $bperiod_f$ is the number of bytes sent by flow f in this period. Now make τ as the unit of time to observe the changes in packet loss. τ's value should not exceed the pulse length because it is mainly to monitor packet loss caused by the abnormal attack pulse. The LDoS attacks against network protocols, pulse's the minimum length should not be less than RTT (Round-Trip Time)and the attacks against the AQM algorithm, pulse is longer, so τ's the recommended value is the average RTT value in the network. After beginning, compute the packet loss rate p in each time-slot, as shown in formula 3.

$$v_f = \frac{bperiod_f}{\tau} \tag{2}$$

$$p = \frac{b_{drop}}{b} \tag{3}$$

In which b is the total number of bytes that reach the router in this time interval and b_{drop} is the total number of bytes which losing package in the same time interval. In this period, if packet loss rate p is greater than P_{th}, a certain threshold, then packet loss is considered abnormal. Cardwell has been mentioned, under the normal circumstances network packet loss rate should not be more than 5% [15], so here P_{th} is recommended to take 5%.

If in this period abnormal packet loss occurs, check each flow, and update the monitoring list according to examination results. It will record malicious flow's average packet loss rate *pulse* in this period, the number of experienced and unexpected times num and also the number of abnormal times $anom$ in the monitoring list. First, determine whether the flow f is normal or not, which the abnormal criterion as shown in formula 4.

$$v_f \geq k_{mul} V_f \tag{4}$$

If the flow f's rate in the abnormal period is greater k_{mul} times than its average rate, it is considered as abnormal flow. The next step, if f does not belong to the monitoring list, it will be added into the monitoring list and its average burst rate $pulse_f$ is set as v_f, the experienced and unexpected times num_f and abnormal times $anom_f$ as 1; If f is in the monitoring list, update its average burst rate $pulse_f$ by formula 5 and plus one to both num_f and $anom_f$; If f is in the monitoring list, but it's judged normal by formula 4, then update f's average burst rate and re-determine whether the flow f meets formula 6. If meets, its num_f will be pulsed one, otherwise it will be deleted from the monitoring list.

$$pulse_f \leftarrow \frac{pulse_f * num_f + v_f}{num_f + 1} \tag{5}$$

$$pulse_f \geq k_{mul} V_f \tag{6}$$

3   Simulations

D.   A spatial database

To study the property of filter, we make a Network topology which is shown in Fig. 4 to experiment on NS2 Platform. First, we should consider the filtering effect of the Shrew attack. Experimental environment is configured: 1.5Mbps bottleneck link bandwidth, other link bandwidth is 10Mbps, and road link propagation delay is 6ms. The parameters of Filter are that the length of observation period τ is 100ms, detection threshold get 5%, and monitor threshold k_{mul} is taken as 5.

First, we begin the experiment of single shrew attack flow. We set the value of pulse strength of attack as 1.5Mbps, and set the value of pulse length as 150ms, and set the value of pulse cycle as 1.2s. And we start the attack in the first 10 seconds, and end it in the first 100 seconds. The result is shown in Fig. 5. In the Fig. 5(a) it presents the scene of single legitimate TCP flows. In the Fig. 5(b) it presents the scene of four

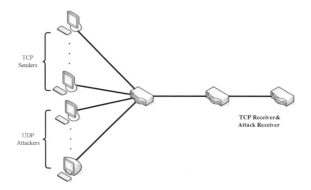

Fig. 4. Experimental network topology

legitimate TCP flows. Second, we start the experiment of distributed shrew attack flow. We increase the number of attack flows to 4, and reduce the pulse strength to 1/4 of the previous. The other parameters should not be changed. And the result is shown in Fig. 6. In the Fig. 6(a) it presents the scene of single legitimate TCP flows. And in the Fig. 6(b) it presents the scene of four legitimate TCP flows. From the result we could see that shrew attack will bring about 25% throughput losses to the legitimate flow. The filter works until the attack begins working in10 to 20 minutes to reduce the effect of attack flows. At last, the impression would be almost non-existent. At the same time, filter also has a good filtering effect for distributed LDoS attacks.

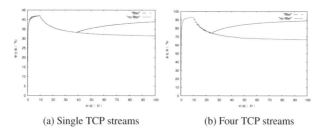

(a) Single TCP streams   (b) Four TCP streams

Fig. 5. Single TCP flow under attack Shrew

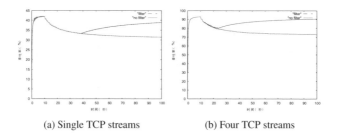

(a) Single TCP streams   (b) Four TCP streams

Fig. 6. Distributed under the Shrew attack of the TCP flow

Now we begin to test the filtering effect for distributed RoQ attacks of filter. Experimental environment is configured: 16Mbps bottleneck link bandwidth, other link bandwidth is 100Mbps. router buffer size is 2Mb, the number of TCP flows is 20, and the number flows is ten, the time of bottleneck link propagation delay is 20ms, other link propagation delay spread evenly between the 15 ~ 25ms. Because of that, RTT of the TCP stream to meet the distribution is in 80 ~ 120ms. The maximum threshold of average queue length of router is 120 packets, and the minimum threshold is 50 packets. The capacity of one packet is 1KB, and the value (Pmax) of maximum drop probability is 0.1.

Now we set the value of pulse strength of each attack flow as 20Mbps, set the value of pulse length as 400ms, set the pulse cycle as 4s. And we start the attack in the first 10 seconds, and end it in the first 100 seconds. The result is shown in Fig. 7. When the attack starts in the first 10 seconds, the throughput capacity of normal flow decrease rapidly, however, 20s later, the role of the filter gradually shows off. With the number of attacks increasing, the filter plays an important role on filter effect of attack flow. Effect of attacks flow becomes weak, the throughput of the normal flow increase, and finally become normal.

In the Table 1, we can see the changes in packet loss rate. When the attack starts, normal flow of packet loss rate increases by nearly 2-fold. But when the filter is present, the network sends more legitimate packets successfully, and packet loss rate is lower, it is only slightly larger than the normal times'.

From the experiment we can see that an attack flow would have been monitored two or three times in each round of attacks since the second attack cycle. About 15 cycles later, the attack flows have been completely filtered by the filter. And Attack effect is close to null. Above all, the filter we design before has a better filtering effect on LDoS attack.

Table 1. Packet loss rate comparison

	no attack	under attack, no filter	under attack and filter
Number of sending packets	18206	121267	159131
The number of lost packets	92	2024	1214
Packet loss rate (%)	0.51	1.67	0.76

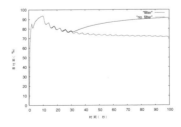

Fig. 7. 20 TCP flows and 20RoQ attack flows

4 Conclusions

LDoS attack and its preventing problem in distributed form have gradually become a research hotspot of network security industry. Compared with the traditional DoS attacks, the average rate of LDoS attacks is low, it also is high efficiency and concealment, and lDoS attacks have other characteristics. Because of that, it is difficult to detect them by using traditional methods. To solve this problem, we propose a rate-based anomaly detection and prevention methods. Based on the characteristics of LDoS attack flow, we can distinguish legitimate flow and the malicious attack stream effectively. We only need to store a small amount of information.

Acknowledgment. This work is supported by National Natural Science Foundation of China (Grant No. 61070010), National Science Foundation for Post-doctoral Scientists of China, the Natural Science Foundation of Hubei Province and the Fundamental Research Funds for the Central Universities.

References

1. Kuzmanovic, A., Knightly, E.W.: Low-Rate TCP Targeted Denial of Service Attacks— The Shrew vs. the Mice and Elephants. In: Proc.of 2003 ACM SIGCOMM, Karlsruhe, Germany (2003)
2. Chan, M.C., Chang, E.-C., Lu, L., Ngiam, P.S.: Effect of malicious synchronization. In: Zhou, J., Yung, M., Bao, F. (eds.) ACNS 2006. LNCS, vol. 3989, pp. 114–129. Springer, Heidelberg (2006)
3. Guirguis, M., et al.: Reduction of Quality (RoQ) Attacks on Internet End-Systems. In: Proceedings of the 24th IEEE INFOCOM (INFOCOM 2005), Miami, Florida (2005)
4. Guirguis, M., et al.: Exploiting the transients of adaptation for RoQ attacks on internet resources. In: Proceedings of the 12th IEEE International Conference on Network Protocols (ICNP 2004), Berlin, Germany (2004)
5. Sarat, S., Terzis, A.: On the effect of router buffer sizes on low-rate denial of service attacks. Institute of Electrical and Electronics Engineers Inc., San Diego (2005)
6. Kwok, Y.-K., et al.: HAWK, "Halting Anomalies with Weighted choKing to rescue well-behaved TCP sessions from shrew DDoS attacks", D-69121. Springer, Heidelberg (2005)
7. Sun, H., Lui, J., Yau, D.: Defending Against Low-Rate TCP Attacks: Dynamic Detection and Protection. In: Proc. ICNP 2004: the 12th IEEE International Conference on Network Protocols, Berlin, Germany (2004)
8. Sun, H., Lui, J.C.S., Yau, D.K.Y.: Distributed mechanism in detecting and defending against the low-rate TCP attack. Computer Networks 50(13), 2312–2330 (2006)
9. Chen, Y., Hwang, K.: Collaborative detection and filtering of shrew DDoS attacks using spectral analysis. Journal of Parallel and Distributed Computing 66(9), 1137–1151 (2006)
10. Wu, Z., Yue, M.: Kalman filter-based attack detection method LDDoS. Electronics 36(8), 1590–1594 (2008)
11. He, Y., Liu, T., Han, Y., Xiong, Q., Cao, Q.: A Distributed Collaborative for LDoS attack detection. Microcomputer 30(3) (2009)
12. He, Y., Cao, Q., Liu, T., Han, Y., Xiong, Q.: A low-rate DoS detection method based on characteristic of wavelet. Journal of Software 20(4), 930–941 (2009) (in Chinese with English abstract)

The Lightning Signal Detect Method Based on Random Resonance

Xin Liu[1], Wei Wu[1], and Zheng Qin[2]

[1] Department of Physical, School of Science, Wuhan University of Technology (WHUT),
Wuhan, Hubei Province, China
[2] Accelink Technologies Co., Ltd, Wuhan, Hubei Province, 430070, China
xinliub@sina.cn

Abstract. Based on the existing lightning signal current model, the simulation research is made for traditional lightning signal detect method at first. The random resonance theory is introduced into lightning signal detect method then, and provide a new thought and direction for the lightning detect method. The simulation result proves the random resonance method works and can be popularized.

Keywords: tunnel bottom current model, feedback engineering model, filter, random resonance.

1 Introduction

The lightning, a nature disaster, is a big threat for the human beings. How to detect the lightning signal effectively is the first step for the deep research about the lightning process. Now, the low and very low frequency are the focus on lightning feedback current detect research, but the traditional detect method has some defects. In this article, the random resonance detect method, which comes from the non-linear theory, is used in the lightning feedback current detect method and provide a new thought and new direction for the future development.

2 Lightning Feedback Current Model

The process of the lightning is the process of strong discharging current from different electric charge centers. So the mathematical model for the lightning feedback current is necessary and the there are 2 kinds of lightning current model, which are engineering model and tunnel bottom current model. The engineering model, based on tunnel bottom current model, reflect the current situation of the whole lightning feedback tunnel and the current of any height can be calculated through the tunnel bottom current. There are 2 existing tunnel bottom current models, one is the Double exponential functional model, which can be shown as below:

$$i(t) = I_0 (e^{-\alpha t} - e^{-\beta t}) \tag{1}$$

J. Zhang (Ed.): ICAIC 2011, Part III, CCIS 226, pp. 197–204, 2011.
© Springer-Verlag Berlin Heidelberg 2011

The I_0 is the current intensity parameter for the peak value of the bottom current. The α and β is the wave front and wave tail attenuator coefficients separately, they are important parameters for current intensity, and they are different from every lightning. The simulation graph of Double exponential functional model is shown in fig.1.

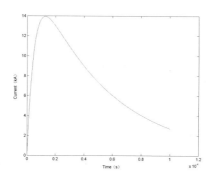

Fig. 1. Double exponential functional model

The other is Heidler function model, which is shown in formula (2) mathematically:

$$i(0,t) = I_0 x(t) y(t) \tag{2}$$

The I_0 is the peak feedback current of tunnel bottom and the $x(t)$ function is the climbing time function. and the $y(t)$ function is the during time function of current wave. Normally: $x(t) = \dfrac{\left(\dfrac{t}{\tau_1}\right)^n}{1 + \left(\dfrac{t}{\tau_1}\right)^n}$, $y(t) = \exp\left(-\dfrac{t}{\tau_2}\right)$, the τ_1 and τ_2 are time constants for wave front and wave tail time; and the n is the exponent number for current gradient,.The simulation graph of Heidler model is shown in fig. 2.

The Double exponential functional model is simple and can reflect main parameters of the tunnel bottom current, which makes it is easy for differential and integral calculus. But the first derivative is not zero in initial time, which is not accordant with

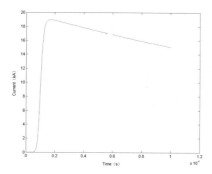

Fig. 2. Heidler function model

the real situation and makes some error when calculating the electronic magnetic field by this model. The first derivative of Heidler function model is zero, which is comply with the real situation, but it is not integrable, and can't calculate the electronic magnetic field of lightning mathematically directly.

The lightning engineering model can be separated into 2 classes, the 1st is that the quantity of electric charge of some time is determined by the ground; the 2nd is that the current value of the feedback tunnel bottom is determined by the quantity of electric charge which is injected into the ground earlier. The main engineering model today is based on the 1st model. And the earliest 1st engineering model is BG model, in which when the feedback wave-front climbing in the feedback tunnel, the current of any height is the same as the current in the tunnel bottom, that is the current has no loss and no delay in transmission. The expression in mathematically is below:

$$i(h,t) = i(0,t), h \leq vt \qquad (3)$$

The h is the point height of the calculating tunnel, the v is the climbing speed for feedback current. The expression of BG model is simple and easy to analysis and calculate, but has physical defects. To meet the requirements of the model, the current value of any point in the tunnel before the feedback wave-front should reach to the same current value as the tunnel bottom instantaneously, which means the transmission speed of the wave front in the tunnel should be the infinitely great. It's impossible in the real situation. The simulation graph of BG model is shown in fig. 3 (the current model in the tunnel bottom is double exponential model).

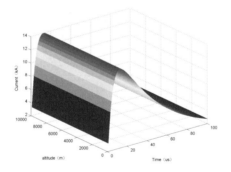

Fig. 3. BG model

The most popular 1st engineering model is TL model now. In this model, the feedback current of lightning is transmitted along the tunnel from the feedback tunnel bottom and the speed is constant,which make the feedback tunnel is a idea transmission line. The mathematical expression is shown below:

$$i(h,t) = i(0, t - \frac{h}{v}), t \geq \frac{h}{v} \qquad (4)$$

The h is the point height of the calculating tunnel, the v is the transmission speed for feedback current. The simulation graph of TL model is shown in fig.4 (the current model in the tunnel bottom is double exponential model).

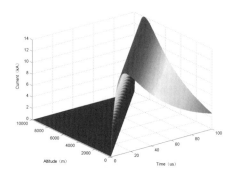

Fig. 4. TL model

3 The Traditional Lightning Detect Method Research

The most popular signal detect method in the lightning detect system is wave filtering in frequency for received signal through hardware circuit directly and detect the filtered signal then. The method is easy to operate and has low cost, which is effective when the main noise spectrum and signal spectrum are in different frequency band. In this article, the LF/VLF lightning signal is an example to make the simulation research about the hardware filtering detects method. Because the detected lightning signal is low frequency, the active low-pass filter is used for filtering noise with the <1kHz cut-frequency. The feedback current of the lightning is double exponential, with the assuming <1A current intensity when the current reach to the detect station, which is shown in fig.5. And the noise of the current signal is high frequency with 5 OSNR and the voltage signal is shown in fig.6, which is converted from the detected current signal with noise.

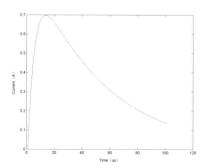

Fig. 5. The lightning current signal without noise when the current reach to detect station

In the fig.6, the detected signal with high frequency noise is fluctuated greatly, and it is hard to judge whether there is thunder signal is mixed or not. The filtered signal after active low-pass filter is shown in fig. 7, from which we can find that the effect of high frequency noise is removed and the elementary contour of the signal is recovered.

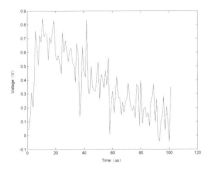

Fig. 6. The detected lightning voltage signal with high frequency noise

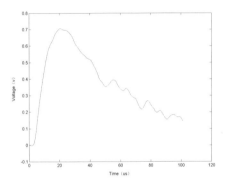

Fig. 7. The lightning signal after active low-pass filter

The hardware filter detecting method is effective when the frequency of noise and signal are different, but if the frequency of noise and signal are the same, the filter effect is bad.

4 The Lightning Signal Detect Method Based on Stochastic Resonance

The random resonance is an non-linear theory. The principle is that when the signal mixed with noise are inputed to a bistable non-liear system, if the signal and noise are some kind of match, the noise energy will shift to signal energy with the gradually decreasing noise amplitude but gradually increasing signal amplitude, which make the output SNR increases gradually. The biggest difference between the traditional method and the random resonance method is that the traditional method works on removing noise, but the random resonance method uses the noise and amplify the signal by transfer the noise energy to signal energy. The noise is used in the thunder feedback current detect system and provide a new thought and solution. The basic random resonance configuration is shown in fig.8.

Fig. 8. Basic random resonance system

The key for random resonance is the bistable non-linear system, which include Schmitt toggle and double potential wells system normally. In this article, the double potential wells system is choosen for bistable non-linear system and the system mathematical equation is Langevin equation, which is shown in formula 5.

$$\frac{dx}{dt} = -\frac{dU}{dx} + u(t)$$

$$(5)$$

The x is the output signal of the system, the $u(t)$ is the total input signal including useful signal and noise. And the U is the symmetrical double potential wells function with the expression as formula 6.

$$U(x) = -\frac{a}{2}x^2 + \frac{b}{4}x^4$$

$$(6)$$

The a and b are >0 potential well configuration parameters. And with the formula 6 in the formula 5, the Langevin equation can be shown in formula 7.

$$\frac{dx}{dt} = ax - bx^3 + u(t)$$

$$(7)$$

When the input is 0, the symmetrical double potential wells graph of the system can be shown in fig.9. From the formula 6, when well bottom of the ymmetrical double potential wells is $x = \pm\sqrt{\frac{a}{b}}$, which means stable with the barrier height of $\Delta U = \frac{a^2}{4b}$. The status of the system is limited in one of the symmetrical double potential wells, the initial status determine the which well. But if the input is not 0, the balance of the system is broken, and the well will be tilted with the system status transfer between the wells.

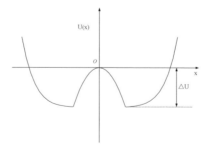

Fig. 9. The symmetrical double potential wells graph of the system

When the input reach to $\sqrt{\frac{4a^3}{27b}}$, the 2 wells will be combined to 1, and the system status will get into the solo well with big amplitude of the system output, which is called well trigger. So the $\sqrt{\frac{4a^3}{27b}}$ is called as bistable critical value of the system. When the signal with the noise input reach to the critical value, the total energy exceeds the voltage barrier and transfer between the 2 stable statuses with signal frequency. The system status is considered as stochastic resonance status now, and the noise energy will transfer to signal energy; the output signal amplitude of the system is amplified and the noise amplitude is decreased.

To simulate the random resonance detect method, the formula 7 should be calculated but it doesn't have accurate solution. Mathematically, the Runge-Kutta algorithms can be used and the iteration algorithms is shown in formula 8.

$$x_{n+1} = x_n + \frac{1}{6}(k_1 + 2k_2 + 2k_3 + k_4), \quad n = 0,1,...,N-1 \tag{8}$$

$$k_1 = l(ax_n - bx_n^3 + u_n),$$

$$k_2 = l[a(x_n + \frac{k_1}{2}) - b(x_n + \frac{k_1}{2})^3 + u_n],$$

$$k_3 = l[a(x_n + \frac{k_2}{2}) - b(x_n + \frac{k_2}{2})^3 + u_n],$$

$$k_4 = l[a(x_n + \frac{k_3}{2}) - b(x_n + k_3)^3 + u_n],$$

The x_n and u_n are input and output sample values, the l is the time step and the value is equal to the reciprocal of the sampling frequency.

The input signal is the lightning double exponential feedback current model and the random resonance method is used for detect simulation. The result is shown in fig. 10.

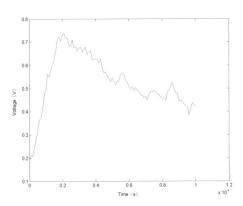

Fig. 10. The lightning signal after stochastic resonance detection

From fig.10, the lightning signal profile is recoved after random resonance detection. Because the random resonance theory is under development and the lightning signal is aperiodic signal, the a and b of the bistable system configuration parameters and the formula 7 mathematical solution need further study to improve, the recovered lightning signal detail is not ideal enough. But the fig.10 prove the random resonance theory works for lightning signal detection, and provide a new thought and direction.

5 Conclusion

The traditional lightning signal model and detection method are studied firstly in this article, and the stochastic resonance is presented into the lightning signal detection, which provide a new thought for lightning detection. The simulation result proves the method works in real situation and can be spread widely.

Acknowledgment. This work was supported by "the Fundamental Research Funds for the Central Universities", under the project number 2010-Ia-022.

References

1. Narasimhan, S., Nayar, S.: Shedding Light on the Weather. In: Proc. IEEE Conf. Computer Vision and Pettern Recofniction, pp. 665–672 (2003)
2. Hu, W., Cummer, S.A., Lyons, W.A.: Lightning charge moment changes for the initiation of sprites. Geophys. Res. Lett. 29, 1279–1285 (2002)
3. Franz, R.C., Nemzek, R.J., Winckler, J.R.: Television image of a large electrical discharge above a thunderstorm system. Science 249, 48–51 (1990)
4. Pasko, V.P., Inan, U.S., Bell, T.F.: Sprites produced by quasielectrostatic heating and ionization in the lower ionosphere. J. Geophys. Res. 102, 4529–4561 (1997)
5. Pasko, V.P., Inan, U.S., Bell, T.F.: Mesospheric electric field transients due to tropospheric lightning discharges. Geophys. Res. Lett. 26, 1247–1250 (1999)
6. Taranenko, Y.N., Inan, U.S., Bell, T.F.: Interaction with the lower ionosphere of electromagnetic pulses from lightning: heating, attachment, and ionization. Geophys. Res. Lett. 20, 1539–1542 (1993)
7. Roussel-Dupré, R.A., Gurevich, A.V.: On runaway breakdown and upward propagating discharges. J. Geophys. Res. 101, 2297–2311 (1996)
8. Pappert, R.A., Ferguson, J.A.: VLF/ELF mode conversion model calculations for air to air transmission in the earth-ionosphere waveguide. Radio Sci. 21, 551–558 (1986)
9. Cho, M., Rycroft, M.J.: Computer simulation of the electric field structure and optical emission from cloud-top to the ionosphere. J. Atoms. Terr. Phys. 60, 871–888 (1998)
10. Veronis, G., Pasko, V.P., Inan, U.S.: Characteristics of mesospheric optical emissions produced by lightning discharges. J. Geophys. Res. 104, 12645–12656 (1999)
11. Ma, Z., Croskey, C.L., Hale, L.C.: The electrodynamic responses of the atmosphere and ionosphere to the lightning discharge. J. Atoms. Terr. Phys. 60, 845–861 (1998)
12. Cummer, S.A.: Modeling electromagnetic propagation in the Earth-ionosphere waveguide. IEEE Trans. Antennas Propag., 1420–1429 (2000)

Research on Training Condition of Chinese Intellectual Property Professionals

Pan Xia

School of Economics & management
Harbin Engineering University
Harbin, Heilongjiang, 150001, P.R. China
panxiaxypanxiaxy@sina.cn

Abstract. The paper analyses the concept and classification of Chinese intellectual property. And then it makes a detail demand analysis of Chinese intellectual property professionals (IPP), which includes practical intellectual property professionals and research intellectual property professionals. And it indicates some problems lies in Chinese intellectual property professionals training. The problems are the narrow universal scope of intellectual property, the serious lack of educated of intellectual property professionals and the shortage of intellectual property teachers. At last it gives some solutions to solve the problems.

Keywords: Intellectual property, professionals, demand, training.

1 Introduction

China faces more serious situation of intellectual property since it became a member of WTO. Lack of IPP has become an obstacle to science and technology economy development in China. As a result, training of IPP has been upgraded to one of the hottest issues.

2 Definition and Classification of Intellectual Property Professionals

According to the definition of intellectual property professionals (IPP), scholars have not a clear and uniform parlance. Professor Zhang Naigen considers it refers to professionals who master basic theory of intellectual property and certain practical skills. Professor Zheng Shengli thinks it refers to high-level, high-quality talents who master at least one branch of natural science including retrieval and management, agriculture and medicine, and they also should have been systematically educated with jurisprudence and intellectual property. This article agrees with professor Zheng who defines IPP as professionals engaging in intellectual property work with natural science knowledge, and be systematically educated with jurisprudence, intellectual property management, language.

J. Zhang (Ed.): ICAIC 2011, Part III, CCIS 226, pp. 205–214, 2011.

Wang Jingchuan, director of State Intellectual Property Office (SIPO), points out, from macroscopic perspective, IPP may be classified as creative IPP (CIPP) and intellectual property work team (IPWT). CIPP refer to professionals working on create intelligence achievement such as invention, creation, design and so on. IPWT refers to the professionals working on protection, operation and management of intellectual achievements.

According to the work category of intellectual property, intellectual property work team professionals can be classified into practical IPP (PIPP) and research IPP (RIPP). PIPP include: Intellectual property management personnel, intellectual property administrative examination and administrative management personnel, intellectual property judicial personnel, intellectual property intermediary service personnel. RIPP include: Intellectual property education teaching professionals and Intellectual property system design and theoretical research professionals.

3 Demand of Intellectual Property Professionals in China

According to the classification of IPP, the article analyzes the demand of both practical IPP and research IPP.

A. Demand analysis of practical intellectual property professionals

1) Demand for intellectual property management personnel
With the awareness of intellectual property protection, some advanced Chinese high-tech companies establish intellectual property departments of law service and management. With China's gradually integration with world economy, there will be more and more such enterprises. As a result, demand for IPP especially senior management professional will increase in near future. In accordance with international convention, the ratio of IPP in enterprises and research institutions is 1% -4% of science and technology personnel .Total Chinese science and technology personnel is 4.54 million in 2008. Science and technology personnel number in medium-sized enterprises is 2.202 million and that in research institutions is 0.48 million.

Therefore, the demand for IPP is at least 268 thousand. Annual training number of IPP in Chinese college is about 2000 to 3000. Therefore, there are about 20 thousand gap between demand and supply.

2) Demand for administrative examination and administrative management intellectual property professionals
Administrative examination and administrative management IPP include professionals of intellectual property administrative examination and auxiliary talents, administrative and law enforcement.

In 2008, the quantity of patent application that State Intellectual Property Rights Office accepts is 828 thousand, including 194 thousand invention patent, 224 thousand pragmatic new model and 299 thousand exterior design application. Patent application authorization quantity grows 17.1% annually. Large quantities of inspectors with higher education to carry on the substantive examination are needed. The quantity of invention authorization patent increase sharply to 94 thousand in 2008 which grows 37.9% compared to the same period in 2007.

Moreover, the quantity of trademark registration patent application grows continuously in large scale, applications for trademark registration reached 0.7 million in 2008. By June 30, 2009, the number of applications for trademark registration reached 6.77 million. There are 2.4 million registered trademarks in total, ranking first in the world. The number of trademark registration reviewed by Industry and Commerce Bureau is only 0.41 million in 2007, and 0.75 million in 2008, surpassed the number of applications for trademark registration for the first time.

Although the training scale of IPP in College's is expanding, huge gap still exists between the demand and supply of Chinese IPP. According to Professor Tao's prediction, by the end of 2015, the application number for inventions-creations will reach 0.3 million and the application number for utility models and design will reach 0.3 million. The according demand for reviewers of inventions-creations is about 3000. The demand for reviewers for reexamination and announcement of invalidation is above 600. The according inspectors in-service are only about 2000. At least 1.6 thousand patent inspectors are in need of. It is estimated that by 2015, the demand for trademark reviewers and auxiliary professionals is about 300.

The demand for intellectual property administration and administrative law enforcement professionals, include those of trademarks, patent as well as other related administration and law enforcement. The current protected pattern that China adopts is "the administrative judicature, double-barreled simultaneously". It is estimated that the demand for personnel in related institutions will expand 30% in next several years. The demand for such kind of IPP is 4000 also.

3) Demand number of intellectual property professionals in Police Stations, Procuratorate, Court and Judicial Department

The demand number for property right judge should be analyzed firstly. About 400 Intermediate People's Courts have the jurisdiction dealing with intellectual property cases, while the jurisdiction of patent cases belongs to provincial Intermediate People's Courts or courts assigned by the Supreme People's Court. About 500 forth level People's Courts trial intellectual property court case, if each court needs four intellectual property judges in average, the intellectual property judge in-service should be 2000. According to some professional's estimation, the intellectual property judge in service in China already meet the considerable scale in both quantity and quality. Therefore, there is no obvious gap between the demand and supply of intellectual property judges.

Professor Tao Xinliang pointed out, although the quantity of property court case may come down, the complexity and the professional may possibly improve. As a result, it is not only necessary to improve the professional ability of the incumbent judge, but also necessary to recruit no more than 400 new judges to the team.

Secondly the article analyzes the demand of property prosecutors and intellectual property public security. With the increasing quantity of intellectual property rights criminal cases, China should intensify the protection of intellectual property rights in criminal. Therefore it is necessary to recruit more IPP of high quality to join the public security personnel and prosecutor's troop. The aim is to safeguard the order of the socialist market economy and simultaneously complies with the request of domestic and foreign situations.

4) The demand for intellectual property professionals in intermediary services

Intellectual property intermediary service personnel include patent agents, knowledge and property attorney, trademark agent, copyright agent and technical representative agent and so forth. Till June 2009, the number of Chinese patent agencies amounts to 719. There are 10 219 people have obtained the patent qualification certificates and 5 993 obtained enforcement of patent agents. According to statistics, patent agent's per capita workload is 90 each year, dealing with 1 case in 4 days. The demand for patent agents including professionals of high-quality, multi-skill, and internationalization will possibly achieves over a thousand. Similar with patent agents, the demand for trademark agents will be 4,000 by 2015. It is estimated that the demand for two kind talented agents is approximately 8000 by 2015.

Intellectual property attorney refers to who engaged in much more intellectual property cases or attorneys of prominent performance. According to the litigation development trend of Chinese foreign, domestic and non-litigation intellectual property, in the near future, China has a demand for 4000 attorneys mastering both intellectual property litigation and non-litigation business.

Copyright agent refers to the intermediary agencies or individuals engaging in copyright business. Since copyright is one of pillar industries of market economy, there is a huge demand for copyright agent. The demand for copyright agent in China is in an initial stage, so the initial expected demand is about 1,000 by 2015.

The technical broker refers to the person who obtains legitimate commission in technology market. Their work is to promote achievements transformation, and engages in intermediary, broker or agent to promote technology trade between others. The innovation and transformation of scientific and technological achievements is a bottleneck of scientific and technological progress and intellectual property development. To some extent the coordination of technical brokers can alleviate the effect of bottleneck, so there is a great social demand for technical brokers. But it is very difficult to obtain the corresponding demand data because the industry has not formed yet.

B. The demand analysis of research intellectual property professionals

Intellectual property research professionals include two kinds: intellectual property teachers and research professionals. Intellectual property teachers refers to the talented person who is engaged in the intellectual property education in universities, while intellectual property research professionals refers to senior personnel who is engaged in intellectual property system design and theoretical research.

1) Demand for intellectual property teachers

Many Chinese universities popularize intellectual property curriculums, and some regional elementary schools also popularize intellectual property knowledge. To improve intellectual property awareness of all citizens, there must be a solid educating foundation of intellectual property teachers. However, the current situation is, intellectual property university teachers is deficient. The number of Chinese intellectual property university teachers is about 500 but the number of the college students is about 500 million, it's very difficult to open intellectual property related course, let alone open many intellectual property courses. What's more, many university teachers undertake many research tasks except teaching. In consideration of the number of teachers accepting training from national State Intellectual Property

Office is more than 100 a year, it is estimated that by 2015, China needs 1000 intellectual property rights teachers at most.

2) Demand for intellectual property research professionals

Prime task of intellectual property research professionals is property system design and theory research. Therefore their mainly institutions are intellectual property research institutions and the legislative department. Since the work for this kind of professionals is high level researching on intellectual property rights theory, the related request for their quality is extremely high. They must master systemic knowledge structure, have solid legal theory knowledge base, have the ability of grasping the development trend of intellectual property and abundant practical experience. According to Professor Tao's investigation, China's current research on the needs of intellectual property research personnel (high-end theory talented person), should remain 100 in a long period.

With the rapid development of Chinese economy, intellectual property protection awareness of Chinese enterprises is becoming more and stronger. As a result, the demand for high-quality IPP is increasing. According to the calculation of Professor Zheng Shengli in Peking University, the demand for IPP of enterprises and research institutions accounted for more than half of the demand. By 2015, 30,000 IPP are needed by Chinese enterprises and research institutions. However, for decades, the number of IPP that Chinese Universities and Colleges trained is less than 3,000. During the same period, the United States trained 50,000 professionals, and Germany trained 30,000 professionals. So it is clear that in quantity there is a big gap o between IPP supplying and demand in China. In addition, there is no intellectual property law and management professional in most Chinese large enterprises and institutions. Compared with some multinational companies that Intellectual Property Staff should accounted for 4% of all technical staff, the professionals in China is very inadequate. Therefore, there is a big talent gap in the field of theory research, judicial, intellectual property administrative and intellectual property system design.

4   Chinese Intellectual Property Professionals Training Condition and Problems

A. Training Condition of Intellectual Property professionals

Since 1980s, some domestic universities have set up intellectual property school and intellectual property specialty. Five universities include Renmin University of China, Peking University, Chinese Academy of Social Sciences Law Institute, Zhongnan University and Huazhong University of Science and Technology set up on-job Law Master Degree in the direction of property rights. By June 2008, there are 32 Intellectual property teaching and research institutions in Chinese universities, include 12 intellectual property schools, 14 Intellectual Property Research Centers, 4 Intellectual Property Institutes, 1 Intellectual Property Education and Research Center and 1 Intellectual Property Department.

With the attention of the state on IPP training, IPP' cultivation in China has made remarkable achievements. Chinese universities cultivate IPP mainly through the following ways:

Intellectual property undergraduate degree;

The second undergraduate degree;

Master Degree of intellectual property;

Setting intellectual property research field in the subject of Law, Business Administration, Public Administration, Economics and Technology Economics;

Education of Master or PhD;

Setting up Sub-field within the intellectual property academic displine;

Establish independent intellectual property Master Degree or PhD.

As the ways of intellectual property undergraduate degree, the second undergraduate degree and master of Intellectual Property are training models that used by most Chinese universities, this article mainly analysis the top three training model[7].

1) Professional training of intellectual property undergraduates

East China University of Political Science sets up Intellectual Property undergraduate programs at the Intellectual Property School, and enrollment started from 2004 to cultivate compound talents of intellectual property. They are educated with science of engineering, management and legal. They get law degree after graduated from the Intellectual Property School. School of Intellectual Property of Shanghai University sets intellectual property management under the subject of law and Management, but no corresponding specialty. It also tried the way of double bachelor degree of Intellectual Property Law. This training way is course teaching for the second subject intellectual property law of science and engineering undergraduates, and the training period is four years. The science and engineering degree is still the first specialty degree when they graduate. And the university will provide academic qualifications for those who have completed their studies of "double subject" (the first professional and intellectual property law) for double subject undergraduates.

2) Intellectual property professional training of Second bachelor degree

At present, Beijing University, Tsinghua University, Renmin University of China and other universities have set up the second bachelor degree courses, which are biased towards the research of intellectual property.

In 1993, in order to meet the massive demand for intellectual property talents Peking University Intellectual Property School was founded. It was the first school established in china specializing in intellectual property. The academic year is two years. After they obtain the first bachelor degree, the chosen best students will receive a two-year education of intellectual property law. Students completing the required courses will be granted the second bachelor's degree of law.

Renmin University of China is the university firstly approved by Education Ministry to recruit second bachelor degree students of intellectual property law. The training aim is to cultivate intellectual professionals who master basic intellectual property law and related legal knowledge, theory, skills. They also be trained to engage in intellectual property law practice, teaching and scientific research. After finishing the education, students that have qualified score and meet the grant conditions, will get the second bachelor degree diploma and certificate of the second bachelor's degree of law issued by Renmin University of China.

3) Intellectual property professionals training of Master

Intellectual property master includes intellectual property jurisprudence master and intellectual property law master. Peking University, Tsinghua University and Shanghai University set up intellectual property specialty in jurisprudence master degree.

Peking University sets up Intellectual Property Master Degree, students of science and engineering specialty may be exempted from entrance examination, the application standard mainly references the recommended standard of graduate student before interview. However, the student number is not in a large scale since many students do not understand the specialty characteristic and employment direction.

Tsinghua University has established intellectual property direction under specialty of civil and commercial law and the recruitment object is those who have got their science and engineering bachelor degree. They could be enrolled after application and qualified score entrance examination. After the matriculation, they need to make up undergraduate legal main course in summer vacation. Then study together with the legal graduate students for 3 years before graduation[8].

There are two patterns for intellectual property master training in Shanghai University. One is the Bachelor of Technology / Master of Intellectual Property Law BS-MS program. That is, after completing 4-year curriculum, the students obtain Double Bachelor Degree. Educate the chosen best students that obtain Double Bachelor Degree with graduate courses of intellectual property law for 3 years. The other is general recruited intellectual property graduate students. They are undergraduate students of jurisprudence specialty or other specialties who pass nation graduate student unified test, which called intellectual property masters and the education period is 3 years.

B. Intellectual property professional training problems

1) The universal Intellectual Property education scope should be broadened

Developed countries such as the United States, Germany, the United Kingdom and Japan open "intellectual property education" class in the universities. They also open formative intellectual property education in middle and elementary schools. According to statistics, in the United States such as Massachusetts Institute of Technology and other higher learning institutions, intellectual property curriculum offer rate is 100%, accounts for about 5%-15% of the entire study hours. In contrast, intellectual property education in China is falling behind by the developed countries, in universities intellectual property education is so weak, not to mention in middle and elementary schools. The particularity and complexity of intellectual property lead to difficulty in Dortmund and education.

Higher intellectual property education in China is not "popular" and the coverage is rather narrow. The student accepting intellectual property education accounts for a low proportion. Although some Chinese higher learning institutions have opened elective courses of intellectual property, carried out intellectual property rights contest, moot court and intellectual property forum, generally speaking, intellectual property education in Chinese University is still weak. It is displayed in the following aspects: Firstly, the number of educated IPP is rather few. According to relevant investigation, the rate of Chinese higher learning institutions of intellectual property is less than 5%. Secondly, intellectual property education in college has not been included in teaching plans. There is no specific guarantee measure in universities. Thirdly, leaders of education departments and universities are lack of adequate knowledge to the importance of intellectual property education. Intellectual property education is not only a branch of knowledge, a professional course, but also a law course of moral education which is very important for students' growth.

2) Serious quantity shortage of trained intellectual property professionals

Intellectual property education and professional training in China began in the early 1990s. Less than 1% of 2000 national higher learning institutions raise IPP. Among 360 Universities with law Department, less than 4% of them could train IPP. According to statistics, in the past 10 years Peking University trained only 700 IPP and the average annual training number is 50. By rough calculation, the number of IPP that Chinese higher learning institutions cultivate each year is only about 1,000. Compared to the demand number estimated in 2.2, the supplying number can be described as a drop in the bucket. A recent investigation made by the Development Research Center of State Intellectual Property Office on 11 key universities shows that the rate of students has attended intellectual property elective courses is less than 5%. This is a far from the professional need of the society. There has been such a situation: Chinese enterprises face more and more international disputes on intellectual property, but domestic senior IPP who can deal with these law suits is extremely rare.

3) Lacking of intellectual property education teachers

Chinese intellectual property educating system had been established for more than 20 years. Nearly 20 universities and research institutes could bring up IPP and have made certain achievements in recent years. However, there is a large gap between IPP' demand and supply.

Firstly, the most urgent problem is acute shortage of intellectual property teachers. Among the above intellectual property teaching institutions, the number of full-time intellectual property teaching staffs are at most a dozen, even a few in some institutions. As a result, it is difficult for them to take on the task of training IPP. Secondly, Chinese institutions lack of experience in intellectual property training. Intellectual property training is a complex and interdisciplinary process. Chinese institutions should accumulate experience and explore a new path to know how to use the whole school educational resources effectively and to train IPP scientifically and effectively. Thirdly, Chinese Universities lack a long-term intellectual property training plan. Intellectual property education should service for society, economic development and improving intellectual property rules. Therefore, it is necessary to analyze the demand number of IPP according to China's society condition, economy development and science and technological development requirements. China should set up training plan for IPP. In addition, China also should implement the training plan of IPP by year, by subjects and by the universities. The most urgent problem to solve is the serious shortage of intellectual property teachers.

5   Countermeasures for China Intellectual Property Professional Training

A. Higher learning Institutions open public intellectual property course

University should be the base for IPP training. Castus, a U.S. professor at the University of California, pointed out that if knowledge is 'current' of knowledge economy then university is the current's 'generator' [9]. At present, Chinese intellectual property expert appeal to enhance intellectual property education and professional training in China. It is essential to set up patent application and writing course, develop publicize and intellectual property education and professional training. Intellectual property educating is not only the requirement of society development, but also the requirement of educatee development. In view of the narrow universal scope of intellectual property education, it is strongly suggested that Chinese universities should set intellectual property courses as required courses. Only in this way, can we gradually raise consciousness of intellectual property graduates and lay a foundation to enrich student's intellectual property knowledge.

B. Set up intellectual property sub-field within the academic displine

It is suggested that intellectual property higher learning institutions should set up intellectual property sub-field within the academic displine. The government should support higher learning institutions to establish intellectual property specialties leading to master and doctor degree. To train various IPP in a large-scale, and to train intellectual property management and intermediary service professionals are in great need by enterprises. To promote cultural construction of intellectual property and open intellectual property courses in universities. Intellectual property education should be brought into quality-oriented education system in universities.

C. Strengthen studies on demand of intellectual property professionals

According to the developing requirement of Chinese society, economic and science and technology, Chinese government should implement IPP training plans, then implement training plans by year, by subject and by universities. Among which the most urgent is to solve the serious shortage of teachers of Chinese intellectual property.

References

1. Zhang, N.: Comparison and enlightenment of intellectual property professionals' cultivation. In: Proceedings of Workshop Anthology on China Colleges and Universities Intellectual Property Professionals' Cultivation, p. 56 (2005)
2. He, M., Wang, H., Zhou, L.: Professional intellectual property personnel: explore new talent cultivation mode of intellectual property. Science Technology and Law 3, 36–39 (2009)
3. Tao, X.: China Intellectual Property Training Research, pp. 111–123. Shanghai university press (2006)
4. Chen, M.: Thinking on Chinese University Intellectual Property Education and professionals' cultivation. Intellectual Property 1, 3–10 (2006)
5. Zheng, S.: The speaking on China university of intellectual property training meetings in 2006. China University of Intellectual Property Training Records Memories in 2006, 13 (2006)
6. Strategic outline editorial committee of the State Intellectual Property, p. 127, 145. Intellectual property press, Beijing (October 2008)
7. Zheng, Y.: China's intellectual property mechanism of talents training system existing problems and solutions. Electronics Intellectual Property, 43–45 (December 2008)
8. Zeng, P., Ye, M., Liu, H.: China-US Comparative Study on Intellectual Property Training models. Science and Technology Progress and Policy 12, 227–229 (2008)

9. Meng, X.: Training Mode of Intellectual Property in colleges and universities. Journal of South China University of Technology (Social Science Edition) 1, 75–77 (2008)

10. Ye, M., Zeng, P., Li, Y.: German model of intellectual property rights on personnel training and the Enlightenment to China. Scientific Management Research 5, 81–84 (2008)

11. Li, c.: The core of the knowledge economy is intellectual property: Intellectual Property Education in Colleges and Universities. Science Technology and Law 1, 75–77 (2008)

12. National Bureau of Statistics of China, China statistical yearbook 2008, p. 123,145,156. China Statistics Press, Beijing (2008)

Research on the Application of ZigBee Technology in Positioning System

Ge Xiao-Yu, Wang Qing-Hui, and Feng An-Song

Department of Information Engineering
Shenyang University of Chemical Technology
Shenyang, Liaoning Province, China
GeXiaoyux@qq.com

Abstract. ZigBee is a new global standard for wireless connectivity, focusing on standardizing and enabling interoperability of products within home control, building automation and industrial control and monitoring. It is now widely recognized that ZigBee is suitable for short distance, low complexity, low power, consumption and low rate applications. One of the most important applications is embedded system. First of all, the paper introduces the application of ZigBee wireless communication network (WSN). Then the emphases are to provide a range-based method that can be used to realize personnel positioning. It includes building ZigBee wireless communication network and taking advantage of Visual Basic and MathCAD to realize RSSI collection.

Keywords: ZigBee, WSNm Positioning, RSSI.

1 Introduction

With the development of the network and communication technology, the need to use wireless communication technology is increasing now. ZigBee is a kind of new wireless communication technology which is widely used in many fields. It is now widely recognized that ZigBee is suitable for short distance, low complexity, low power, consumption and low rate applications. One of the most important applications is wireless sensor communication network (WSN). WSN that is composed of massive miniature sensor nodes in the monitor region is a kind of multi-hop network [1, 2]. Data in WSN is transmitted by wireless communication. At present, ZigBee is one of the first choice technologies for WSN application.

The paper mainly introduces the characteristic of ZigBee technology and its application of personnel positioning. The article provides a range-based method that can be used to realize personnel positioning. The hardware that is used to realize the application of ZigBee is 2.4GHz ZigBee development kit that is produced by the company of Silicon Laboratories. RSSI can be used to calculate the distance. Range-based personnel positioning is realized by programming of Visual basic and Mathcad.

J. Zhang (Ed.): ICAIC 2011, Part III, CCIS 226, pp. 215–220, 2011.

2 ZigBee Technology

ZigBee is a kind of new wireless communication technology that can be used for short distance, low complexity, low power, consumption and low rate applications. Comparing with Bluetooth, PAN and 802.11x wireless locall transmission, ZigBee protocol is simpler and more ease of implement. Data that is transmitted by ZigBee includes periodic data, intermittent data and duplication low reaction time data [3, 4]. The complete ZigBee protocol stack is composed of physical layer (PHY), medium access control layer (MAC), network layer (NWK), APS layer and APL. As shown in Fig 1, standards of the PHY and MAC are developed by the group of IEEE802.15.4 and the others are developed by ZigBee alliance.

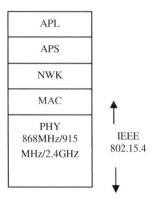

Fig. 1. ZigBee protocol stack

The ZigBee Alliance is an association of companies working together to enable reliable, cost-effective, low-power, wirelessly networked, monitoring and control products based on an open global standard. Many famous companies are the member of ZigBee Alliance, for example Chipcon, Fiber, Honeywell, Freescale, Mistubishi, Motorola, Philips, Samsung and so on[5]. The goal of ZigBee application is to provide the consumer with ultimate flexibility, mobility, and ease of use by building wireless intelligence and capabilities into everyday devices.of products and applications across consumer, commercial, industrial and government markets worldwide. For the first time, companies have a standards-based wireless platform optimized for the unique needs of remote monitoring and control applications, including simplicity, reliability, low-cost and low-power.

ZigBee network is specially designed for controlling data transmission. Massive different ZigBee network nodes whose coverage areas are different and low-cost wireless transceivers are used for establishing of ZigBee local automatic network that can be connected to remote computers by internet. Although ZigBee network is only LAN, because of enough data interfaces the coverage area can be expanded. Taking advantage of internet, mobile network and other communication networks, many ZigBee local area networks can be connected together to solve the problem of dead zone.

3 Positioning in WSN Based on Zigbee

A Establishment of WSN based on ZigBee

2.4GHz ZigBee development kit that is produced by silicon laboratories is used for establishment of WSN based on ZigBee [6, 7]. There are five target boards that are used for WSN nodes. The key parts include cc2420 that is used as radio frequency (RF) transceiver, MCU C8051F121 and chip CP2101 that is used for realizing data transmission between USB and UART. C8051F121 is the head of the hardware and one of the most popular MCU.

At first, WSN based on ZigBee is established by node configuration. The target board connects to PC USB port by USB debug adapter and the power of each target board is provided by 9V battery or power adapter. Each board communicate to computer by virtual COM port and each one has only one virtual COM port whose ID is different from others, such as COM3,COM4 and so on. Then download the program to each target board to make sure that board A is the personal area network (PAN) coordinator and the others are terminal nodes in WSN based on ZigBee. In experiment positioning system, node B, node C, node D and node E are placed in one plane and these positions is fixed. As shown in Fig 2, coordinator A is the mobile node that is used for positioning. The reference coordinate system that is composed of four nodes is the positioning area.

B RSSI Collection

RSSI is refers to received signal strength indication. The value of RSSI indicates power of electromagnetic wave in the current medium and it decreases as the distance increases [8, 9]. The distance between beacon node and unknown node is calculated by the value of RSSI. Because the sensor node in WSN is able to realize communication, so the chip that is used for controlling communication provides measurement method of RSSI. Usually the relation between RSSI and distance is exponential attenuation.

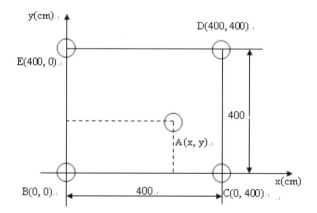

Fig. 2. Reference Coordinate System

Usually W and mW are units of signal strength measurement. But they are not convenient for representing the exponential attenuation between RSSI and distance [10]. Therefore dbm is used for RSSI measurement. Dbm can be exactly and directly converted to and from mW.

If P is power in mW, and y is the value of RSSI in dbm, then y is expressed as

$$y = 10 \log_{10}(P) \tag{1}$$

Computer realizes communication to target boards through USB driving and virtual COM port. The answer method is used for RSSI collection. As shown in Fig 3, coordinator A send request to a node then the node provides response to coordinator A. Each response is corresponding to every request. As a result A gets RSSI from one node by one node. Each data frame including request data and response data is 11 bytes. It is divided into four parts including order field, address field data field and inspection field.

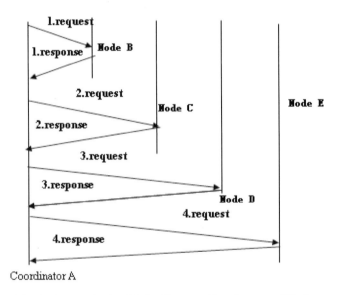

Fig. 3. Communication Method between Coordinator and Nodes

The program design in visual basic is used for RSSI collection. It takes advantage of MSComm serial port communication control to realize data transmission between computer and coordinator. Attribute setting is expressed as below.

```
MSComm1.CommPort=3
MSComm1.Settings = "38400,N,8,1"
MSComm1.InputLen = 0
MSComm1.PortOpen = True
```

First of all the program that makes use of MSComm realizes the control setting, and then open the COM port waiting for sending or receiving data. After that the program closes COM port. According to the program, when the system realizes the function of data collection for one time at first the computer send the request data frame to a fixed node for collecting RSSI of this node. Then it waits for RSSI collection response. When the object of MSComm produces receive event, it extracts RSSI from data frame of source terminal response. After that it send s another request data frame to another fixed node and waits for another response of RSSI. This process is completed one node by one node. WSN based on ZigBee need to get RSSI from node B, C, D and E. After data processing, the paper gets the relations between RSSI and distance, as shown in Fig 4.

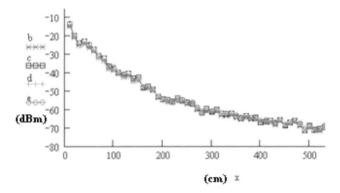

Fig. 4. Relationship of RSSI from fixed node B, C, D, E and distance

C Positioning algorithm of WSN based on ZigBee

Positioning application of WSN based on ZigBee takes advantage of maximum likelihood estimate law and trilateration method to realize mobile node positioning. The formula is shown as below.

$$\begin{cases} \left(x_B - x \right)^2 + |y_B - y|^2 = |d_B|^2 \\ |x_C - x|^2 + |y_C - y|^2 = |d_C|^2 \\ |x_D - x|^2 + |y_D - y|^2 = |d_D|^2 \\ |x_E - x|^2 + |y_E - y|^2 = |d_E|^2 \end{cases} \tag{2}$$

Coordinates of fixed node B, C, D, E are provided by reference coordinate system. They are expressed as (xA ,yA), (xB ,yB), (xC ,yC), (xD ,yD). The linear equation is expressed as AX=b.

$$A = \begin{bmatrix} 2(x_B - x_E) & 2(y_B - x_E) \\ 2(x_C - x_E) & 2(y_C - x_E) \\ 2(x_D - x_E) & 2(y_D - x_E) \end{bmatrix}$$

$$b = \begin{bmatrix} x_B{}^2 - x_E{}^2 + y_B{}^2 - y_E{}^2 + d_E{}^2 - d_B{}^2 \\ x_C{}^2 - x_E{}^2 + y_C{}^2 - y_E{}^2 + d_E{}^2 - d_C{}^2 \\ x_D{}^2 - x_E{}^2 + y_D{}^2 - y_E{}^2 + d_E{}^2 - d_D{}^2 \end{bmatrix}$$

$$X = \begin{bmatrix} x \\ y \end{bmatrix}$$

Then according to least-mean-square-error criterion, the coordinate of mobile node A is calculated by $\hat{X} = (A^T A)^{-1} A^T b$ [11]. After this step the position of node A in the reference coordinate system is established.

4 Conclusion

The paper does the research of ZigBee and the application of WSN based on ZigBee in positioning system. It makes use of ZigBee for WSN establishment. At the same time it realizes RSSI collection and take advantage of maximum likelihood estimate law and trilateration method to realize ZigBee application in positioning system. ZigBee is still a new technology and there are still so many problems that have to be solved in the future. Recently many positioning method based on ZigBee are proposed. How improve them is still the research direction for scholars.

References

1. Zang, C., Yu, H.: Target tracking based on multi-agent theory in wireless sensor network. High Technology Letters 16(3), 257–261 (2006)
2. Zhang, W., Yu, H.: Personnel positioning system of underground coal mines based on the ZigBee technology. Journal of Hefei University of Technology (Natural Science) 30(9) (2007)
3. Chen, W., Li, W.: Weighted Centroid Localization Algorithm Based on RSSI for Wireless Sensor Networks. Journal of Wu Han University of Technology (Transportation Science & Engine) 30(2), 265–268 (2006)
4. Zhang, J., Sun, M.: Dynamic distance estimation method based on RSSI and LQI. Electronic Measurement Technnplogy 30(2) (2007)
5. Zhang, Q., Su, G.: Experiment study on the technology of location with ZigBee. Microcomputer & Its Applications 11 (2009)
6. Duan, W., Wang, J.: Research and development of localization System and Algorithms for Wireless Sensor Networks. Information and Control 35(2) (2006)
7. Karalar, T.C., Yamashita, S., Sheets, M., et al.: A low power localization architecture and system for wireless sensor networks. In: Proceeding of the IEEE Workshop on Signal Processing Systems, SiPS: Design and Implementation. IEEE, Piscataway (2004)
8. Niculescu, D., Nath, B.: DV based positioning in ad hoc networks. Journal of Telecommunication Systems 22(1/4), 267–280 (2003)
9. Ward, A., Jones, A., Hooper, A.: A new location technique for the active office. IEEE Personal Communications 4(5), 42–47 (1997)
10. Dai, Y., Wang, J.: Research and Improvement of Localization Algorithms for Wireless Sensor Network. Chinese Journal of Sensors Actuators 23(4) (2010)
11. Qi, H., Kuruanti, P.T., Xu, Y.: The Development of Localized Algorithms in Wireless Sensor Networks. Sensors 2(7) (2002)

Design and Implementation of a DSP-Based Embedded Intelligent Traffic Surveillance System

Lan Hai, Yin Hang, Gyanendra Shrestha, and Zhang Lijun

College of Automation
Harbin Engineering University
Harbin, Heilongjiang, 150001, P.R. China
lanhaixy@home.news.cn

Abstract. Increasing congestion on urban streets and freeways boosts the demands of more powerful and economical traffic surveillance equipment. Rapid development of Digital Signal Processor greatly facilitates the implementation of faster, easier and more reliable video and image processing system. In this paper we present a novel embedded platform based on Texas Instruments Davinci™ Digital Media Processor, dedicated particularly to the remote surveillance of urban intersections under harsh environmental conditions, featuring vehicle detection and counting methods, and various video and image compression algorithms as well as support for local systems and devices. The system is composed of Video Server Module and Video Analysis Module. Signal Integrity (SI) problem is carefully analyzed and simulated during hardware design process to maintain the system stability and performance. A flexible video and image analysis, focusing on vehicle detection using background extraction and blob analysis, as well as video compression and decompression algorithm, and Ethernet data communication software running in the embedded platform is presented and tested that the software can enhance the accuracy of vehicle detection and license plate recognition.

Keywords: traffic surveillance, DSP, embedded system, vehicle detection, blob analysis.

1 Introduction

The expansion of city scale and traffic congestion has been creating bottleneck effects in the development of city transportation system, which requires modernized traffic surveillance system to optimize traffic operation and augment the capacity, as well as provide concrete evidence for law enforcement. Digital traffic surveillance system developed on industrial PC platform, although characterized by easier software programming, is often criticized for its poor stability, and reliability especially in long time, continuous running conditions. Therefore, embedded system, highlighted by inborn ability to overcome these shortcomings of PC-based system, is accepted and becoming a new hot spot of traffic surveillance system research. An effective video image processing system for traffic surveillance should meet several basic but stringent requirements, such as automatic segmentation of vehicle from background,

J. Zhang (Ed.): ICAIC 2011, Part III, CCIS 226, pp. 221–229, 2011.

vehicle classification, license plate recognition, environment compatibility, and real-time running, etc.

This paper will present an embedded hardware and software platform on the basis of TI Davinci Digital Media Processor, aiming at meet above requirements and tried to overcome drawbacks of industrial PC based systems.

2 System Overview

In this paper, we suppose the surveillance system monitor an urban street intersection with 3 lanes in each direction. 3 close-shot cameras are designed to monitor 3 lanes respectively and one overview camera responsible for the entire scene in each direction. The overview camera functions as video loop camera to enclose the entire scene including all the three lanes in one direction and to detect possible red light runners. Then one or more close-shot cameras should be activated by signal originated from overview camera if vehicles are driving through red light. The license plate should be recognized in the close-shot pictures. Meanwhile, 10 seconds of violation video is recorded, compressed in H.264 format and upload to Video Server Module via Ethernet.

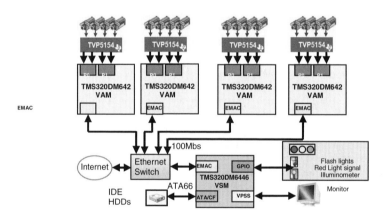

Fig. 1. System Block Diagram

3 Hardware Platform Architecture

The system has to process at least 16 channel digital video streams simultaneously, which is an extremely heavy computation load for any type of CPU. The exponential growth of MIPS rating of DSPs makes a highly compact, high performance and low cost embedded system possible. The embedded DSP platform proposed in this paper can be qualified as being one Video Server Module (VSM) and at least four Video Analysis Modules (VAM), based on Texas Instruments TMS320DM6446 and TMS320DM642 digital signal processor.

A. Video Server Module (VSM)

The Video Server Module is a host server, to perform the role of gathering all the data from VAM, decompress H.264 video stream and provide a Graphic User Interface for controlling the entire system. One of the most computational heavy tasks is H.264 decompression due to its highly sophisticated algorithm. Texas Instruments TMS320DM6446 Digital Media System-On-Chip, integrates one C64x+ DSP core, ARM9 core and Video Image Co-Processor respectively, is the best choice for multimedia tasks. The 4752 C64x+ MIPS calculation capability, aided by the Video Image Co-Processor (VICP) on the chip, ensures 4CIF H.264 format (Baseline Profile) video stream decoding and encoding in more than 25fps and the ARM9 core works as a central control unit to balance and distribute the consumption of hardware resources.

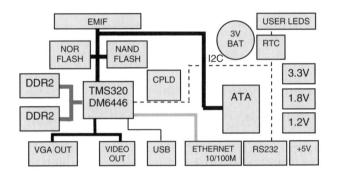

Fig. 2. Video Server Module Hardware Structure

The two DDR2-533 memory devices provide sufficient 256MB RAM space and 4266MB/s bandwidth for high-speed video data exchanging (Figure 2). The VSM also utilizes DM6446's integrated ATA/ - ATAPI-6, Ethernet and USB2.0 interface, coupled with TI's DVSDK which can greatly reduce the complexity of hardware platform and easily implement video and audio Codecs conform to xDM/xDAIS API as well as embedded Linux operating system, to meet data storage and faster hardware implementation requirements.

B. Video Analysis Module (VAM)

Video analysis algorithms consist of vehicle detection, counting and video and image encoding require a more powerful DSP. The TMS320DM642 with its peak 5760MIPS calculation speed can easily perform these algorithms in real-time (Figure 3).

There are at least four cameras working simultaneously when streaming video data to VSM, therefore video data must be compressed in H.264 format, so as total data bandwidth is four times of 10Mbs (H.264 704x576@25.0fps, BP, MP), i.e. 40Mb/s. Since the VAMs are mounted on the outdoor environment and VSM in the room, the distance between VAMs and VSM requires long distance, high-bandwidth data transfer channel and considering Internet based live video stream feeding of surveillance cameras, we choose 100M Ethernet as the video data transfer media for its bandwidth and long distance characteristics as well as potentness for adding more cameras in the system in order to cater to more lanes conditions. The EMAC interfaces of both DM642 and DM6446 are utilized to Ethernet application we proposed.

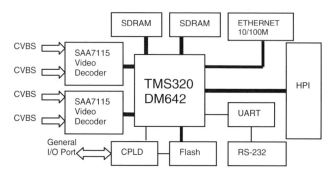

Fig. 3. Video Analysis Module

C. Signal Integrity Analysis and Simulation

The most challenging aspect of VSM and VAM hardware design is Signal Integrity (SI) and Power Integrity (PI) problems of high speed digital circuits due to the >500MHz clock rates of the two DSPs. Signal reflection, crosstalk, timing and delay errors, overshoot and undershoot, and EMI radiation, which generally can be overlooked in low speed digital circuits, must be take into very careful consideration so that the system can function properly, stable and reliable, especially when routing two DDR2 devices in the VSM. A 6-layer PCB stack-up is implemented to meet the DDR2 layout requirements; bypass capacitors, control, data, and address signal trace topology; and proper signal termination resistors must stringently conform to DDR2 layout rules to reduce or eliminate probable negative effects produced by high speed digital circuits (Figure 4).

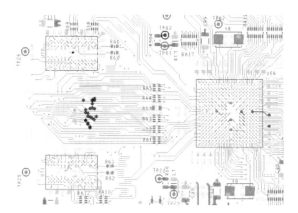

Fig. 4. DDR2 Routing and Layout

4 Software Architecture

The overall software structure comprises of two parts running respectively in VAM and VSM shown as Figure 5. DSP/BIOS serves as Real-Time Operating System (RTOS) in the VAM to support a framework for video analysis algorithm consists of vehicle detection and counting, capture single image frames and record video streams as well as corresponding compression algorithms. DSP/BIOS provides preemptive multi-threading, hardware abstraction, real-time analysis, and configuration tools. The APIs include Image Processing Library, Network Development Kit, and some other libraries offered by the third-party of TI. These features of DSP/BIOS RTOS ensure video analysis tasks and running in real-time on the basis of compact and concise software programming.

TMS320DM6446 is a heterogeneous dual core processor based on Davinci™ Technology and plays a central role in the VSM. Texas Instruments Davinci™ provides users with Digital Video Software Development Kit (DVSDK), including MontaVista Linux, DSP/BIOS for Linux, TI Codegen Tools for Linux, Framework Components, Digital Video Test Bench, etc., which is characterized by interoperable, optimized video and audio codecs leveraging DSP and integrated accelerators, built into configurable frameworks, and published APIs within popular operating systems (Linux) for rapid software implementation.

The VSM and VAM software flowchart is presented in Figure 5. Video streams are captured by four cameras, decoded to BT.656 format and sent to DM642 for video analysis. In DM642, video frames sequence are processed to count vehicles on the direction and detect possible red light runners. The lane's corresponding close-shot

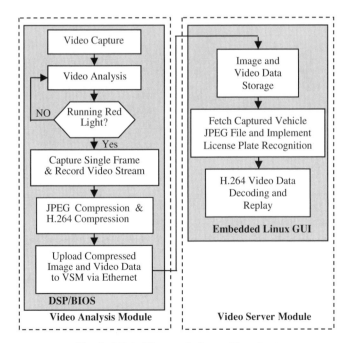

Fig. 5. A Brief System Software Flowchart

camera will be triggered by overview camera to capture images and videos clips then compressed and sent to VSM via EMAC interface of DM642. The VSM receives data transferred by Ethernet from VAM and stores them in local Hard Disk Drives (HDD) or for further analysis.

5 Video and Image Analysis Algorithm

Video and image algorithms are generally conceived and programmed in Matlab environment to test its applicability. After that, we transfer all the Matlab codes into C language for embedded application.

D. Vehicle Detection and Counting Algorithm

Because system cameras are mounted and fixed on a location, background subtraction, although fundamental, is the most effective image processing operation for video surveillance applications, particularly in moving objects such as intruder and vehicle detection algorithms. The techniques focus on background maintenance, or seg-mentation of objects from image and updating background continuously, can be classified into adjacent frame difference, optical flow, and normalized block correlation, etc. To reduce the algorithm time consumption, we propose mean and threshold method to extract background from captured vehicle frames. This method computes the median of the values at each pixel location over a time series of n frames $I(x, y, t_1), I(x, y, t_2) \cdots I(x, y, t_{n-1}), I(x, y, t_n)$ i.e.

$$BG = \frac{1}{n} \sum_{i=1}^{n} I(x, y, t_i) \qquad (1)$$

Fig. 6. Background Extraction

Since most pixels are static, the moving objects' pixels are merged into n frames, and then the background is extracted from foreground (Fig. 6).

The original frames are subtracted by background frames BG in pixels and transferred into binary image which is denoted as D_{ij}

$$D_{ij}(x, y) = \begin{cases} 1 & |I(x, y, t_i) - I(x, y, t_j)| > T \\ 0 & \text{other} \end{cases} \qquad (2)$$

where T is a threshold value determined by Ostu's method. Otsu's method is used to automatically perform histogram shape-based image thresholding, or, the reduction of a gray level image to a binary image. The algorithm assumes that the image to be thresholded contains two classes of pixels (e.g. foreground and background) then calculates the optimum threshold separating those two classes so that their combined spread (intra-class variance) is minimal.

1. Compute histogram and probabilities of each intensity level $p_i = n_i / N$, where i denotes ith gray level and N is the total number of pixels in one image.

2. Search for the threshold that minimizes the intra-class variance, defined as a weighted sum of variances of the two classes $C_0 = (0,1,2,\cdots,t); C_1 = (t+1,t+2,\cdots,L-1)$, and then the probabilities of class occurrence and the class mean levels, respectively, are given by $w_0 = \sum_{i=0}^{t} p_i = w(t), \mu_0 =$

$\sum_{i=0}^{t} ip_i \Big/ w_0 = \mu(t)/w(t)$ and $w_1 = \sum_{i=0}^{L-1} p_i = 1 - w(t), \mu_1 =$

$\sum_{i=0}^{L-1} ip_i \Big/ w_1 = \dfrac{\mu_T - \mu(t)}{1 - w_0(t)}$, where $\mu(t) = \sum_{i=0}^{t} ip_i, \mu_T = \sum_{i=0}^{L-1} ip_i$.

3. Derive from the equations above, we get $w_0\mu_0 + w_1\mu_1 = \mu_T, w_0 + w_1 = 1$. The class variances are given by σ_0^2 and σ_1^2 , then the within-class variance defined as $\sigma_w^2 = w_0\sigma_0^2 + w_1\sigma_1^2$, the between-class variance $\sigma_B^2 = w_0 w_1$

$(\mu_1 - \mu_0)^2$, the total variance of levels $\sigma_T^2 = \sigma_B^2 + \sigma_w^2$.

4. The criterion measure can be defined as $\eta(t) = \sigma_B^2 / \sigma_T^2$, then we get optimal threshold

$$t^* = Arg \max_{0 \leq t \leq L-1} \eta(t) \qquad (4)$$

Fig. 7. Binay transformation using Ostu's method

After the foreground binary image was acquired, morphological operations are applied to eliminate "holes" and "islands" in the image, as well as reduce the noise. Image A is processed by square structural element B using following equation

$$A \cdot B + (A \oplus B) \ominus B \qquad (5)$$

Then blobs of moving vehicles attained are prepared for Blob Analysis which can be utilized to detect red light runners and classify the vehicles by different blob size.

To count the vehicle numbers passed through, and detect red light violation, a virtual stop line is set in a certain position in the image. All the binary image pixels at the line are accumulated and denoted as M, and once there is a vehicle blob pass through the virtual line, M must vary to the blob width. Different M is defined in following equation to determine whether there is a vehicle and the amount of them passed through (Equation 6).

$$N = \begin{cases} 1 & l < M < k/3 & one/one \ after \ another \\ 2 & k/3 < M < 2k/3 & two \\ 3 & 2k/3 < M < k & three \end{cases} \tag{6}$$

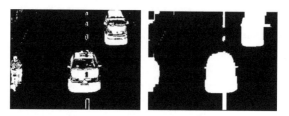

Fig. 8. Morphological Operation

For the purpose of eliminate possible interference such as pedestrians and other scene intruders, the area B of each blob is computed to determine whether a blob is a vehicle or not. For 640×480 image resolution, we define

$$2000 \le B \le 16000 \tag{7}$$

Fig. 9 shows the experiment results, a vehicle is detected and tracked by green box, counter on the up-left corner increases and a motorcycle is not recognized since we precluded motorcycle by the blob area B.

Fig. 9. Vehicle detection and counting using blob analysis

E. License Plate Recognition

We propose a reverse logical artificial neural network (RLANN) for the character identification which also uses feature mapping to deal with some especial characters in order to increase recognition rate at poor lighting conditions.

F. H.264 Video Compression and Communication

We implement a H.264 encoding and decoding algorithm stem from a ITU-T H.264 standard algorithm, and optimize it for embedded platform to increase frame rates and reduce operation time to decrease delay from camera to monitor. Ethernet communication software is developed using TI NDK which provides a fast platform solution for Ethernet communication applications.

6 Conclusion and Testing Results

VAM and VSM PCB are designed in Cadence SPB16.2 and SI simulation completed in Hyperlynx 8.0. A co-test of hardware and software justified the correctness, stability and performance of hardware platform, as well as flexibility and robustness of vehicle detection algorithm in different lighting and environment conditions.

License plate recognition and H.264 algorithm and Ethernet communication software are also implemented and debugged in both VSM and VAM. The reliability and performance tests of this embedded system justified the superiority compare to conventional PC-based systems.

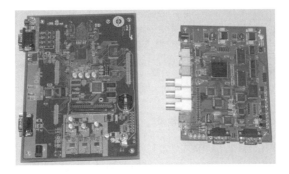

Fig. 10. Photo of VSM (left) and VAM (right)

References

1. TMS320DM642 Video/Imaging Fixed-Point Digital Signal Processor (Rev. L). Texas Instruments (2007)
2. TMS320DM6446 Digital Media System-on-Chip (Rev. F). Texas Instruments (2008)
3. Johnson, H., Graham, M.: High-speed digital design-a handbook of black magic. Pearson Education, London (2003)
4. Toyama, K., et al.: Wallflower: Principles and Practice of Background Maintenance. In: Proceedings of the IEEE International Conference on Computer Vision, vol. 1, pp. 255–261 (1999)
5. Cutler, R., Turk, M.: View-Based Interpretation of Real-Time Optical Flow for Gesture Recognition. In: Int'l Conf. on Automatic Face and Gesture Recog., Nara, Japan (1998)
6. Hai, L., Shrestha, G.: Real Time License Plate Recognition at the Time of Red Light Violation. In: Proceedings of the IEEE International Conference on Computer Application and System Modeling, vol. 2, pp. 243–246 (2010)

Study on the Method Based on Rough Sets and Neural Network for the Estimation of Iron Ore Grade

Hongtao Wang

Network Information Center
Wuhan University of Technology
122 Luoshi Road, Wuhan, China, 430070
hongtaowang12@sina.com

Abstract. To simplify the complexity of information processing procedure and improve the processing accuracy, the strengths of Rough Sets and Neural Networks were studied. A new method based on Rough Sets and Neural Network for the estimation of Iron ore grade was established. The actual application of Iron Ore Grade showed that the method is effective.

Keywords: Rough Sets, BP Neural Network, Iron Ore Grade.

1 Introduction

Estimation of iron ore grade runs through the whole process of mining and mineral dressing. It is to accurately evaluate the current mine ore grade, and use the historical ore grade to plan the future of the company. The purpose is to make full use of resources and mining revenue maximization.

Currently, the mainly evaluating ways of the mine to evaluate iron ore grade are artificially sampling and artificial estimation. Since the existence of artificial random sampling, and sampling in the running mine car, it can only get the ore samples on the surface of mine car. The international ore grade analysis technologies mainly are chemical analysis method, the mineral microscope, X-ray method, the method of infrared spectroscopy technology, etc. But these techniques are only for the samples collected from workers, not for the overall real-time measurement of the ore in the running mine car.

Iron ore grade is closely related to many factors, such as ore mass, volume, color, moisture ratio and lump ore ratio, etc. Traditional linear analysis cannot do more accurate analysis. Rough sets theory is a kind of mathematical tools depicting incompleteness and uncertainty. It can effectively analyze and deal with variety of imprecise and incomplete information, and discover the potential of the law. BP neural network can approach any nonlinear function, the algorithm is simple and highly efficient, and can be used for complex systems of dynamically modeling. The integration of them provides an effective method for estimation of the iron ore grade.

J. Zhang (Ed.): ICAIC 2011, Part III, CCIS 226, pp. 230–238, 2011.

2 Estimation Methods Based on Rough Sets and Neural Network Technology

The paper adopts rough sets and the BP neural network techniques to process data, and uses rough sets method to do attribute reduction. Then it estimates the value of grade by neural network. The purpose is to simplify the structure of neural network, to improve the system speed and to solve the influence on accuracy of the neural network by the size and the mass of samples.

A. Introduction of Rough sets and BP neural network

After the birth of rough sets theory, it causes a lot of mathematicians, logicians and computer researchers' interests. More and more scientists and technicians are engaged in doing researches in the field. Rough sets use its unique way to effectively deal with many uncertain problems. It has been widely used in machine learning, knowledge acquisition, decision analysis, process control and other fields.

At present BP neural network is the most widely used type of artificial neural networks. BP algorithm is simple and easy to implement. In the practical application of artificial neural networks, currently, it's mainly used in pattern recognition and classification, function approximation, data compression and prediction, and other fields.

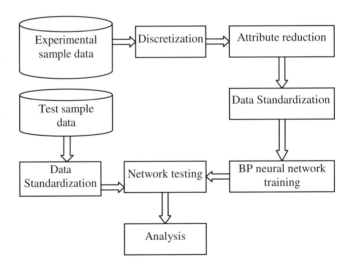

Fig. 1. Estimation procedure based on rough sets and neural network technology

B. The estimation method and related theory

    i. Rough sets method to process data
      1) Discretization

$S = (U, A \cup \{d\})$ is   a   decision-making   system,   where
$U = \{x_1, x_2, \cdots, x_n\}$, $A = \{a_1, a_2, \cdots, a_n\}$ and $d : U \rightarrow \{1 \cdots r\}$.

We assume that $\forall a \in A, v_a = [l_a, r_a) \subset R$ is the real interval, S is the compatible decision-making system. $\forall a \in A$ and $c \in R$, any ordered pair (a, c) is called cut-set of v_a. Define P_a as v_a intervals of sub-division, that is, to an integer k_a, $P_a = \{[c_0^a, c_1^a], [c_1^a, c_2^a), \cdots, [c_{k_a}^a, c_{k_a+1}^a)\}$. Therefore, any division of P_a can be uniquely determined by its cut-set sequence. The sequences of cut sets are:

$$\{(a, c_1^a), (a, c_2^a), \cdots (a, c_{k_a}^a)\} \subset A \times R$$

A decision-making system $S = (U, A \cup \{d\})$, which defines any cut-set $P = \bigcup_{a \in A} P_a$ can produce a new decision-making system $S^P = (U, A^P \cup \{d\})$, called P-discretization of S, where $A^P = \{a^P : a \in A\}$ and $a^P(x) = i \Rightarrow a(x) \in [c_i^a, c_{i+1}^a)$ [3].

Rough sets method is a kind of symbolic analysis method. All attribute values are qualitative data. If process the quantitative data and the qualitative data comprehensively, it need to turn quantitative data into qualitative data. Discretization methods commonly used include: experience segmentation method, equal frequency segmentation method, equidistant segmentation method and other methods. According to the characteristics of data in this study, the choice is equidistant segmentation.

2) Attribute reduction

P and Q are the equivalence relation in U, and then set $POS_P(Q) = \bigcup_{X \in U/P} PX$ called Q positive region of P. It denotes in domain of discourse U, through classifying the knowledge expressed by U/P can be certainly assigned to the object set of class U/Q.

$$POS_{IND(P)}(IND(Q)) = POS_{IND(P-\{r\})}(IND(Q)) \tag{1}$$

If (1) is satisfied, it calls that $r \in P$ can be omitted for P in Q. If not, it can't be omitted for P in Q. When every r in P can't be omitted for Q, it calls that P is Q independent. When S is the Q independent sub-family of P, and $POS_S(Q) = POS_P(Q)$, family $S \subseteq P$ becomes the Q reduction of P. $\gamma(Q \rightarrow d) = \gamma_P(Q) = |POS_P(Q)|/|U|$ calls Q approximate quality to P. Referred to as rough sets reduction γ guidelines. It's the absolute standards of measuring knowledge U/P to divide the quality for U/Q.

In the condition that maintaining the dependency relation among the decision table, decision-making attribute and conditional attribute is not changed, it reduces the decision table, including attribute reduction and value reduction. The commonly used reduction algorithms are: GENETIC algorithm, JOHNSON algorithm and so on. This paper only applies attribute reduction. The reduction algorithm is JOHNSON algorithm.

ii. BP neural network to process data

1) Data unitary processed: unitary processing is a way to simplify the calculation. It means transforming a dimension expression into the dimensionless expression, become a scalar. Unitary processing is to accelerate the convergence of the training network.

The paper's unitary processing uses linear function conversion, expression:

$$y = (x - \text{MinValue})/(\text{MaxValue} - \text{MinValue}) \qquad (2)$$

Note: x, y is respectively the value before and after the conversion. MaxValue, MinValue is respectively the maximum and minimum value of samples.

2) LM algorithm to optimize neural network processing

Standard neural network of BP algorithm has weaknesses such as network slow convergence and learning speed confirming difficultly. The commonly used optimization algorithm are additional momentum algorithm, variable rate algorithm, conjugate gradient method, Gauss - Newton algorithm, Levenberg-Marquardt algorithm (referred to as LM algorithm), etc. LM algorithm has the fastest convergence and the best robustness in these algorithms.

The basic thought of LM algorithm: in practice, in order to reduce the singular problem of non-optimal point, and when the objective functions near to the optimal point, the characteristics nearby the extreme value are similar to secondary sexual, which is to accelerate the convergence process of optimization. Generally, plus a small positive number u (damping factor) for each element in main diagonal of matrix $J^T J$ which is the coefficient of searching direction .That is:

$$(J^T J + uI)p = -J^T e \qquad (3)$$

$$W^{(k+1)} = W^k + ap \qquad (4)$$

In the expression: e is the error, p is the forward direction, W is the connection weights, J is the first derivative of the objective error function to the connection weights , a is the adaptive step size, usually take the best step , u is the damping factor, I is the unit matrix..

Variable u determines the learning algorithm based on Newton's method or gradient method to complete, the following is the LM rules of updating parameters:

$$\Delta W = (J^T J + uI)^{-1} \cdot J^T e \qquad (5)$$

LM algorithm is the combination of gradient descent method and Gauss-Newton method. It not only has fast convergence properties of Gauss - Newton algorithm but also has the global properties of gradient descent, and can effectively improve the network convergence.

iii. Network test

To prove the validity of the model, we use large-scale test samples (300) for testing. The test sample data will remove redundant attributes. After unitary processing, then input BP neural network.

3 The Estimation Method Based on Rough Sets and Neural Network Technology in the Application of Iron Ore Grade Estimation

The paper's sample data source: Wuhan Iron and Steel Mining Co., Ltd., a total of 420 sample data, in which the experimental sample data is 120, the test sample data is 300. Figure 2 is the original data format.

Mass	Volume	density	Color	Moisture	Lump ore ratio	River pulse number	Grade
8.809	5.473	1.609538	3	12	12	3	25
8.489	4.542	1.869	1	7	45	7	31
9.381	4.957	1.892475	1	16	85	13	34
8.012	4.83	1.658799	1	5	30	2	27
6.542	4.038	1.620109	3	28	34	2	26
… …							

Fig. 2. The original data format

Data correlation analysis:

This paper uses Matlab to analyze the correlation among data items, where the relevance of the mass and volume is (1.0000, 0.8196). Due to the high correlation between the two, it may affect the following data to analyze. Both of their physical significance is considered. This paper uses the density (mass / volume) instead of mass and volume (Figure 3).

Density	Color	Moisture	Lump ore ratio	River pulse number	Grade
1.609538	3	12	12	3	25
1.869	1	7	45	7	31
1.892475	1	16	85	13	34
1.658799	1	5	30	2	27
1.620109	3	28	34	2	26
… …					

Fig. 3. The data format after correlation processing

A. Rough sets method to process data

i. Attribute value discretization

Because color, River pulse number, grade and other attributes are important and attribute value types are less, this paper does the equidistant division only for density, moisture content and lump ratio ore.

Density: 1 denotes [1.55, 1.65), 2 denotes [1.65, 1.75), 3 denotes [1.75, 1.85), 4 denotes [1.85, 1.95];
Moisture content: 1 denotes [0, 10), 2 denotes [10, 20), 3 denotes [20,30];
Lump ore ratio: 1 denotes [0, 30), 2 denotes [30, 60), 3 denotes [60, 90].
Discretization shown in Figure 4:

Density	Color	Moisture	Lump ore ratio	River pulse number	Grade
1	3	2	1	3	25
4	1	1	2	7	31
4	1	2	3	13	34
2	1	1	1	2	27
1	3	3	1	2	26
			…… ……		

Fig. 4. The data format after attribute value discretization

ii. Attribute reduction
In this paper, we use the reduction algorithm JOHNSON which is coming with rough sets analysis software Rosetta, the basic thought is as following:
JOHNSON reduction is an algorithm to obtain a minimum length reduction, and attribute weights can be defined by user. It's very effective in calculating a reduction. B is the reduction, S is any set in a resolution function. w (S) is the weight of S. Algorithm described as following:

    1)   Calculate sub-table matrix of given decision table

    2)   B=∅

    3)   Ordering a is the max attribute of the frequency in S and weight w (S) . If the two values of the attribute are equal, then randomly select an attribute.

    4)   Add the attribute a into the aggregate B

    5)   Remove all items which including attribute a in S

    6)   If S=∅, then return B, else switch to (3)

It can also be reducing calculated approximately. When a sufficient subset is removed from S, then return B, rather than need ask S empty [4].
In this paper, we use JOHNSON reduction algorithm in Rosetta to do the conditional attributes attribute reduction of the data in Figure 4. The result is as following:

		Reduct	Support	Length
1		{密度, 川脉号}	100	2

No name

Fig. 5. Reduction results figure

Density	River pulse number	Grade
1	3	25
4	7	31
4	13	34
2	2	27
1	2	26
	... ...	

Fig. 6. The data format after reduction

The value of iron ore grade has important links with its density and river pulse number (origin). It also shows the origin of iron ore in large part determines the color and moisture ratio.

B. BP neural network to process data

The experimental samples data after attribute reduction with formula (2) is unitary processed in Matlab. And then build a middle layer with 11 neurons and output layer with 1 neuron. The transfer function respectively is tansig and logsig. It uses BP neural network of LM algorithm (trainlm) to process data. Training results (Figure 7):

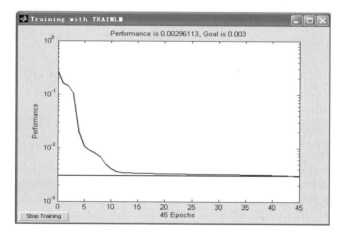

Fig. 7. BP neural network of LM algorithm training results figure

4   Network Test and the Analysis of Estimation Results

In this paper, there is a large-scale test sample (300) for testing. Remove excess properties from the test sample data. Input neural network after unitarily processed, and then after anti-normalization, get the error (error =Experimental grade – real grade) of test sample. Figure 8:

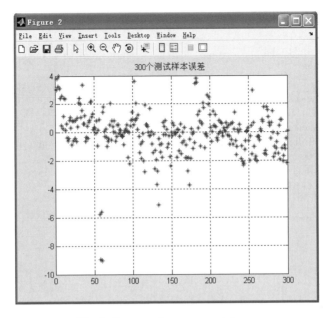

Fig. 8. Test sample error output figure

Set k as the absolute value of the error, according to above figure, statistic error table (Table I) from results.

Table 1. Test result error statistical table

Absolute error range of k	Support the number of samples	The percentage of test samples with total number
$0 \leq k < 2$	250	83.33%
$2 \leq k < 4$	45	15%
$4 \leq k < 6$	3	1%
$k \geq 6$	2	0.67%

Measurement error of mine should ensure that the request for more than 90% of the data error is $0 \leq k < 4$, we can see from Table 1 satisfy $0 \leq k < 4$ in the sample, 98.33% of the total test sample, which reaches the purpose of the research.

5 Conclusion

The paper presents a method based on rough sets and neural network for the estimation of iron ore grade. Using knowledge reduction algorithm of rough sets which simplifies evaluation indicator, improves the learning speed of neural network and the operability of evaluation. Through establishing the BP neural network has estimated iron ore grade, reached the purpose of the research, and proved the validity of this method.

References

1. Pawlak, Z.: Rough sets. International Journal of Information and Computer Science 11(5), 341–356 (1982)
2. Han, B., Wu, T., et al.: The combination of rough sets theory of dynamic attribute reduction. Systems Engineering Theory & Practice (June 2002)
3. Zhang, W., Jia, R.: Data Mining and Rough Sets Method, pp. 53–84. Xi'an University of Electronic Science and Technology press (2007)
4. Zhai, P.: Attribute reduction method review. Information Development and Economy (February 2004)
5. Gao, J.: Artificial neural network theory and simulation, 2nd edn., pp. 44–54. Mechanical industry press (2007)

An Efficient Storage Method for Disaster Tolerant System

Wen Li, Peng Chen, and Xiao-Bin Yang

College of Computer Science, Sichuan University
Chengdu, China
liwenqkl@eyou.com

Abstract. Proposed a storage method of disaster recovery system (SMDRS), adopted dynamic pre-allocation strategy to pre-allocate space for the task twice, thus effectively saving storage space; at the same time, pre-allocation strategy and requirement-based allocation strategy are combined to make the recovery data of the same disaster recovery task be aggregated as much as possible to reduce the seek time and to avoid unnecessary consumption.

Keywords: disaster recovery, storage, pre-allocation, dynamic.

1 Introduction

Disaster recovery system can well deal with the inevitable, unplanned disasters and accidents, whether it can quickly and effectively store backup data is an important factor in system performance of disaster recovery system, so the choice of storage method for disaster recovery system seems particularly important [1].

In traditional partition-based storage methods, each storage system corresponds to a partition [1]. It is an intuitive method, but imbalance in the use of each partition, usually resulting in space that cannot be fully used and when a partition is full, it can't be expanded.

Logical Volume Manager (LVM) is essentially a virtual device driver, and is a new level of abstraction added between the kernel block devices and the physical devices [2]. Logical devices of LVM are not restricted to the physical constraints and the logical volumes need not be continuous space, which can span many physical volumes and can adjusted size at any time, so that the scalability of the system is enhanced [3]. However, in the disaster recovery system based on logical volume, LVM is a one-time allocation of all the storage space that disaster recovery tasks require, when there are little valid data of disaster recovery tasks, it leads to a lot of waste of disk storage space [4].

SMDRS (Storage Method of Disaster Recovery System) proposed in this paper is not a one-time allocation of all the storage space, but to gradually allocate storage space required by disaster recovery tasks, with the pre-allocation strategy and the combination of requirement-based allocation strategy, which can effectively reduce the waste of space in storage pool and to achieve the goal of accessing data efficiently.

J. Zhang (Ed.): ICAIC 2011, Part III, CCIS 226, pp. 239–245, 2011.

2   General Description

A.   Design ideas

The storage pool is divided into pre-allocated space and non-pre-allocated space by SMDRS. The size of logical volume of each task has been obtained prior to the arrival of the disaster recovery task. When the space of first pre-allocation has run out of, SMDRS then pre-allocate another space for the task. If valid recovery data of the task occupies more than the amount of twice pre-allocation, then no pre-allocated space for the task, while using requirement-based allocation strategy to allocate space in the non-pre-allocated space for the task.

The first and second pre-allocation manage different spaces: forward pre-allocated area and backward pre-allocated area. The allocated directions of the two areas increase towards each other in the storage pool. If not enough space for an area, it will use the others, which enables to continuous allocation.

B.   Module division

SMDRS is divided into three modules, namely, cache module, storage module and management module. Cache module is responsible for allocating the free space in the cache to writers, storage module reads recovery data from the cache module, and writes recovery data to the storage pool; management module is responsible for storage space allocation and release, and follows the pre-allocation strategy and requirement-based allocation strategy to allocate space for the storage module. SMDRS module structure shown in Figure 1:

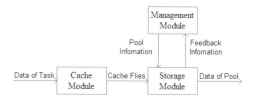

Fig. 1. SMDRS module structure

The following are definitions of terms used in this article:

Disaster recovery task: the recovery task is created to realize disaster recovery; a recovery task is a backup of a logical volume.

Writer: a disaster recovery module to store recovery data.

Readers: a disaster recovery module which need to read recovery data from the storage pool.

Chunk: the smallest unit of storage pool division, CHUNK_SIZE represents chunk size; a number of chunks make up a chunk group, and NUM_GROUP represents the size of the chunk group. A chunk is identified by group number of the chunk group and number of the chunk.

3 Details of Design and Implement

C. Cache module

Cache queue is composed of multiple files created on a separate physical disk. The size of cache file is equal to each other. The way of prior allocation ensures that each file consists of contiguous disk blocks. Unused cache files constitute the free queue; the cache files already in use constitute the work queue.

Cache module is initially in a listening state, waiting for events, when receiving the recovery data which writers submit, it will remove a cache file from the free queue for the recovery data of a task to use. A serial cache files assigned to a task make up a work queue, and a work queue corresponds to a task. When the cache file is full, cache module then remove another cache files from the free queue to assign to the task, until recovery data of the task written finish.

D. Storage module

Storage module is responsible for reading the recovery data from the cache queue and writing them to the storage pool based on the information provided by management module.

While recovery data is written to the storage pool, if written immediately after storage module reads a cache file from cache queue each time, will cause head to shake back and forth to increase the seek time, and affect the efficiency [5-6]. Therefore, storage module will create a red-black binary tree when reading each cache queue and the key of node is the storage location of the storage pool. Every time after reading a cache file, storage module does not immediately write the disk, but to obtain the storage location, to find whether there has been the location node in the tree. If not, insert pointer which points to the cache file, storage location and length into the tree to constitute a new node. If so, record the new pointer which points to cache file and data length in the existing node. After reading a cache queue each time, write data to the storage pool in accordance with the storage location sequence in order to ensure the head moves in one direction, and to reduce unnecessary seek time.

Each task maintains a Space Mapping Table for the chunk number of task and the corresponding chunk number of the storage pool. Storage module maintains a Space Status Table for storing the usage information of chunk groups. The process of recovery data written to the storage pool includes external chunk addressing and internal chunk addressing. External chunk addressing searches Space Mapping Table for the pool location of recovery data stored in the chunk, and internal chunk addressing calculates the storage location of recovery data within the chunk. After the writing position is located, it needs to judge whether the current data to be written is across the chunk, if not, all the data is completely written to the storage pool; otherwise, fill a chunk with part of the data, then re-calculate the offset of the remaining data, and return external chunk addressing phase. Finally, the recovery data is written to the storage unit pointed to by the two addressing results. If internal chunk addressing fails, allocate the space, modify Space Status Table, constitute new allocated mapping information of chunk and add to Space Mapping Table of the task. The flow of storage module shown in Figure 2:

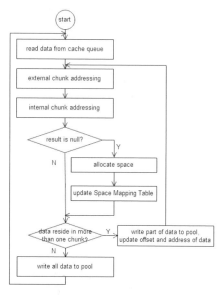

Fig. 2. Flow chart of storage module

E. Management mudule

The storage pool is divided into two parts by SMDRS: Pre-allocated Space and Non-Pre-allocated Space. Pre-allocated Space includes Forward Pre-allocated Area and Backward Pre-allocated Area. When allocating space, their spaces increase towards each other in order to achieve dynamic expansion. When the Pre-allocated Space is insufficient, then use the free blocks in Non-pre-allocated Space. Pre-allocated Space and Non-Pre-allocated Space both contain a number of chunks. Each chunk can only be in one of two statuses: allocated and unallocated. Bitmap represents the status of chunks, 1 means allocated, 0 means unallocated. The structure of the storage pool shown in Figure 3:

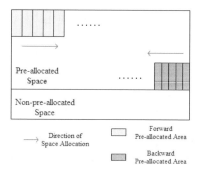

Fig. 3. Structure of the storage pool

At the front of disk space of the storage pool is Pre-allocated Space, which is divided into two parts according to the different pre-allocated block size: Forward Pre-allocated Area and Backward Pre-allocated Area; and at the back of the storage pool is

Non-pre-allocated space. Forward Pre-allocated Area and Backward Pre-allocated Area are respectively divided into different blocks with PFP_SIZE sized and PBP_SIZE sized. Forward Pre-allocated Area allocates space from the head of Pre-allocated Space; Backward Pre-allocated Area allocates space from the tail. Thus, between Forward Pre-allocated Area and Backward Pre-allocated Area there will be a large and integrated free space for the dynamic expansion of each area, if the space of Forward Pre-allocated Area is not enough, it will borrow the space of Backward Pre-allocated Area for continuous allocation; when Backward Pre-allocated Area is short of space, it will borrow the space of Forward Pre-allocated Area and continue to allocate. This allows the allocation of storage pool space more flexible, and most recovery data of the same task can be aggregated, resulting in reducing the seek time to avoid unnecessary consumption.

Pre-allocated Space and Non-pre-allocated Space respectively account for $P\%$ and $N\%$ of the storage pool, $P\% + N\% = 1$; Forward Pre-allocated Area and Backward Pre-allocated Area respectively account for $Pf\%$ and $Pb\%$ of Pre-allocated, $Pf\% + Pb\% = 1$. The relationship between the various parts is as follows:

$$POOL\_SIZE = (P\% + N\%)POOL\_SIZE$$
$$= PRE\_SIZE + NON\_SIZE$$
$$= (Pf\% + Pb\%)PRE\_SIZE + NON\_SIZE$$
$$= FP\_SIZE + BP\_SIZE + NON\_SIZE$$

POOL_SIZE represents the storage pool size; PRE_SIZE and NON_SIZE respectively represent the size of Pre-allocated Space and Non-pre-allocated space; FP_SIZE, BP_SIZE respectively represent the size of Forward Pre-allocated Area and Backward Pre-allocated Area. The above parameters can be adjusted according to actual situation.

When allocating space for the task, the first pre-allocation size is T% of its logical volume capacity, if not enough, and then the secondary pre-allocation size is S% of its capacity. When the two pre-allocated space is still not enough for the task, the space will be allocated from Non-pre-allocated Space according to need of the task. Space allocation algorithm is as follows:

Algorithm 1. Allocation Algorithm.

```
input:
    task to allocate;
output:
    pointer to block of memory, NULL on error;
processing:
status = Task.getStatus();
taskVol = Task.getVolume();
if (status is first allocation) {
    taskVol = T / 100 * taskVol;
    call PreAllocation.alloc(taskVol);
}
else if (status is second allocation) {
    taskVol = S / 100 * taskVol;
    taskRemainVol = Task.getRemainVol();
    if (taskVol is greater than taskRemainVol) {
        taskVol = taskRemainVol;
    }
    call PreAllocation.alloc(taskVol);
}
else {
    taskVol = Task.getCurrentNeeds();
callNonPreAllocation.alloc(taskVol);
}
```

Each pre-allocation is according to pre-allocation strategy. The location of the block to be allocated is determined by the relationship between the size of recovery data and the threshold THR_MIN and THR_MAX. In pre-allocation, the space allocated to the task is more than its need, and the size unallocated is recorded to prevent the next allocation error after this pre-allocation. The algorithm of pre-allocation strategy is as follows:

Algorithm 2. Pre-Allocation Algorithm.

```
input:
      size of block to allocate;
output:
      pointer to block of memory, NULL on error;
processing:
if (size is less than THR_MIN)
      call NonPreAllocation.alloc(size);
else if (size is greater than THR_MAX)
      call ForwardPreAllocation.alloc(size);
else
      call BackwardPreAllocation.alloc(size);
```

4   Experiment Result and Analysis

F.   Experimental environment and methodology

There are a disaster recovery server and an application server (the server to be backed up) in the 100M LAN in this experiment. Based on the current network environment, after several experimental analysis and results comparison, select a set of ideal data as the argument values: $P\%$ and $N\%$ are respectively 80% and 20% ; $Pf\%$ and $Pb\%$ are respectively 80% and 20%; $T\%$ and $S\%$ are respectively 50% and 30%; THR_MIN and THR_MAX are respectively 200M and 1G; POOL_SIZE and CHUNK_SIZE are respectively 200G and 8MB; the block size of Forward Pre-allocated Area is 2G, and the block size of Backward Pre-allocated Area is 400M. Test the capacity of storage space of disaster recovery server respectively when using the SMDRS and LVM to store recovery data. Detailed experimental environment is shown in Table 1:

Table 1. Experimental environment

	CPU	memory	NIC	OS
Disaster Recovery Server	Intel Xeon E5420 2.00GHz	16GB	Intel PRO/1000	Linux 2.6.18
Application Server	Intel Xeon E5504 2.00GHz	16GB	Intel 84574L/1000	Windows Server 2003

We created 8 disaster recovery tasks. The size of each task is 15GB. Valid data for each task is 6.5GB, 10.5GB, 8.5GB, 7.5GB, 14.5GB and 11.5GB, 13.5GB and 9.5GB.

G.   Experimental results and analysis

The experimental results are shown in Figure 4:

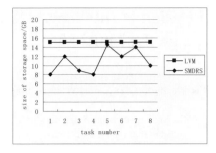

Fig. 4. Experimental results

Figure 4 shows, when LVM storing backup data, it used the same size of storage space as the size of task; while adopting SMDRS to store backup data, which used less size of storage space than the size of task. SMDRS allocated the size of space according to the size of valid data. Experiment shows SMDRS can save disk storage space efficiently.

5 Conclusions

SMDRS proposed in this paper is divided the storage pool into pre-allocated space and non-pre-allocated space, with the strategy of pre-allocating space for the task twice, while combining with requirement-based allocation strategy, which can effectively reduce the storage pool space, so as to achieve the purpose of storing recovery data efficiently. Experimental result shows that, SMDRS can run well in disaster recovery system and can effectively save storage space of disaster recovery server.

References

1. Manchester, J., Saha, D., Tripathi, S.K.: Guest editorial-Protection, restoration, and disaster recovery. IEEE Network 18(2), 3–4 (2004)
2. Chad, L., Michael, H.: Components of disaster-tolerant computing: analysis of disaster recovery, IT application downtime and executive visibility. International Journal of Business Information Systems 3(3), 317–331 (2008)
3. Mark, R., David, S.: Microsoft Windows Internals, 5th edn. Microsoft Press, Washington (2009)
4. Ji, M., Veitch, A., Wilkes, J.: Seneca: remote mirroring done write. In: Proceedings of the 2003 USENIX Technical Conference, San Antonio, TX, USA, pp. 254–258 (June 2003)
5. SNIA.The 2008 dictionary of storage networking terminolog (EB/OL) (June 18, 2008) (April 11, 2009), http://www.snia.org/education/dictionary/SNIA_Dictionary_EH_2008.pdf
6. Shah, B.: Disk performance of copy-on-write snapshot logical volumes, p. 2. The University of British Columbia, British Columbia (2006)

The Model Design of Intelligent DSAS Based on the Multi-MA[*]

Jia Tiejun, Xiong Peng, and Wang Xiaogang

College of Electronics & Information
Shanghai Dianji University
Shanghai, China
jjtjn060@gmail.com

Abstract. With analyzing the technology merits and specials of the auditing system for network secure and the mobile agent, the works designs and builds the model of a new distributed and secure auditing system with the intelligent (DSAS) based on the multi-mobile agents(MA) by taking advantage of the mobile, the intelligent, and the parallel as well as the mutual,. It can largely promote the intelligent, the automatic and improve the whole performance of the auditing.

Keywords: Mobile Agent(MA), Secure Auditing System, Distributed and Secure Auditing System, Intelligence Model.

1 Introduction

SA(Secure Auditing) is a important mean for monitoring and evaluating the network secure. Collecting, analyzing and evaluating the secure information for getting the secure status and making the secure strategies to ensure the completeness has become an important way of the controlling of secure risk and an important mean deterring and against network case.

SA mainly collects, analyzes, audits, distinguishes, records, saves, warns and traces the information the actions about network secure.

DSAS(Distributed and Secure Auditing System) is the most common model for auditing. The collecting data which is locally centralized and the mean which collects and saves the data according to the different from the regional can easily share resources, collaborate, audit management, balance loads and expand, but easily collect and fuse the data, remove the redundancy and inconsistency and so on[1-2].

The agent technology and the multi-agent system[3-4] is one of the computing models to efficiently resolve the complex distributed problems. And the emerging of FIPA-Agent specifications[5] largely reduces the complex to build the multi-agent system. The independence of agent, the characteristics of the organizational structure and the personification manner for running the system provide the important

---

[*] The Scientific Research Fund Project of Shanghai Dianji University Key Subjects (07XKJ01, 10C401).

J. Zhang (Ed.): ICAIC 2011, Part III, CCIS 226, pp. 246–251, 2011.
© Springer-Verlag Berlin Heidelberg 2011

reference for building their models. Based on analyzing the mobile agent(MA) and the advantages and specials from DSAS, to design and build a new DSAS model with the intelligence basing the multi-MA can promote the intelligence, accuracy, security and the whole efficiency of auditing of SAS.

2 The Technology Specials and Linking with DSAS of MA

A. The technology specials and advantages of MA

Researching the agent is one of the focus problems in Artificial Intelligence field. The agent is an entity or program. MA is a kind of program to continuously running across platform, automatically mobile, simulate the personal action and provide some of services of Artificial Intelligence. And it has the mobility, intelligence, autonomy, parallel, flexibility, interactivity and persistence. It enable its computing model to be have the strong movement, intelligence, flexibility, efficiency and reliability. Comparing with the traditional agent, its specials[6] are such as the mobility, the intelligence, the independence of platform, the whole performance of network and the cooperation among the multi-agent.

B. The ideas to design DSAS taking advantage of MA

The ideas to design:

1)   The module design of system is easy: In a system of MA, it can add/delete on the single feature of agent, and rebuild some agent under the situation in which it is no effect of the others of system. It can meet the requirement of the module design.

2)   In DSAS built up MA, a single agent can only effect on the part cooperating with it, others in the system can still normally run. If the work of the system can be allocated with reason among the agents, it can largely reduce the system fault and risk.

3)   MA can balance loads, save bandwidth, promote the reflecting speed and efficiently use the resource from the hosts. MA can move to the host, and high speed communicate locally, directly visit the host resource and not consume the network resource, and can largely reduce the dependent on the system bandwidth. And the mobility of agent provides the promise on achieving the distributed and mobile auditing.

4)   MA is saved in the servers from the audited parts. It can analyze the abnormal conditions all the time, and real time transfer it to the detect central so as to promise the real-time of the whole system. Simultaneously, with MA, it can modify the old way that the information is collected passively and collect the profession data all the time and reflect the initiative of system so as to achieve the online auditing and the real-time auditing. The time that the auditing tasks are finished in the MA stations or among them is just need to move a little of the data so as to enable the auditing to meet the secure requirement of data from the audited parts.

3 The Model Design of DSAS with the Intelligence

According to the features of the model of the secure auditing system in the network condition, taking advantage of the MA technology proposes a sort of the model of DSAS with the intelligence. It includes three sections: Human machine interface, Auditing subsystem and The Audited part subsystem. The model's structure and organization are as figure 1.

A. The model structure of DSAS with the intelligence

Its model structure includes three sections:

1)   Human Machine Interface: It is a way of interaction between users and DSAS, and gives users to input their auditing and show the corresponding auditing result. Users can choice the auditing model(algorithm), the data source and the initial process, and renew the knowledge and rules of the agents in the system so as to make up the lack of knowledge in the system, and input some the basic information into the audited parts with the different date or type to set the auditing options or amount and so on, and still choice the auditing result from all of exports.

2)   Auditing Subsystem: It is the core of DSAS. The next section will describe its structure and principle in detail.

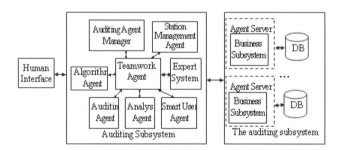

Fig. 1. The DSAS model based on MA

3) The Audited Subsystem: Including the agent server, the business subsystem and the DB of the data station. The agent server and the business subsystem run on the specified servers of the audited parts. The agent server saved the information from the local DB, example for the form of the local data, DBMS, the business DB table structure and the range of data. Each agent server registers in the DB managing agent of the data station and timely renews the corresponding context in the managing agent so as to interact with the expert system and efficiently plan the auditing task together with the teamwork agent. The server simultaneously provides the service facilities, the moving manager, the running manager, the communicating manager and the security manager for the auditing agent.

B. The structure and features of auditing subsystem

The auditing subsystem includes the eight modules. All of the modules are Coordinated. Their features and the collaboration relation are as follow:

1) The Auditing Agent Manager: It answers for managing the information about all of the auditing agents and dynamically gets their property with the location and features of other agents by interaction with the managing agent. It is crucial to achieve the transparency of the distributed system. It is used to collect, manage, count and inquire the information and resource of all of the agents, and classify and integrate the agent according to their features. Simultaneously, acting as the trusted security certification center, it enables the system to securely communicate.

2) The Station Managing Agent: It answers for the information about the agent servers of the audited parts, example for the starting of the agent servers, the stopping status information, the location information and the data source information so as to reasonably plan the auditing tasks.

3) The Teamwork Agent and Experts System: The former includes three features: The one is to optimize the task plan. It choices the best scheme when it plan the auditing task and interacts with the auditing algorithm agent, the analysis agent, the auditing agent manager and the data station manager so as to get the feature property of algorithm efficiency, the abnormal data model, the feature status of the auditing agent, the data and the change trend of all of the stations and try its best to enable the auditing algorithm to meet the users' demand. It can still plan real time, it can renew planning when some MA can not work; The second is to coordinate MA's building according to the planning result and name the mobile and auditing agent working parallel with the auditing algorithm or model and register the basic information from these MA into the auditing agent manager; The third is to audit the teamwork and coordination of the whole process, and mainly coordinate every MA and maintain the present information from the running status of the system. It takes the refer point about the system status information as a dynamic director that the distributed auditing task describes the operating base point of every MA. Simultaneously, the teamwork agent is also the central for exchanging the MA information in the system and answers for maintaining the information inaction among the agents. The expert system can help the teamwork agent to coordinate the system, process knowledge, centralize and manage information.

4) The Algorithm Agent: It mainly answers for maintaining the auditing and analysing algorithm. The users can register the auditing and analysing algorithm. When the algorithm is registered in the system, it registers the meta-knowledge of algorithm and their feature, example for the name, the version, the inputting parameter, the description of operating condition and the outputting form, and reflects the information to the teamwork agent.

5) The Auditing Agent: It is the key part of the auditing subsystem. The next section will illuminate its structure of model in detail.

6) The Analysis Agent: It mainly includes the model transferring the abnormal information and the generating agency of the adaptive model. According to the abnormal data provided by the auditing agent, it uses the data mining algorithm to automatically generate and renew the auditing model and the running parameter. It is a core unit showing the adaptive ability of the auditing subsystem.

7) The Smart User Agent: It converts the requirement and choices from the users to the order that it can be identified by the teamwork agent and submits it and achieve the planned allocation of tasks. It answers for processing the renewing information from the system imported through human machine interface, example for the specific algorithm of auditing, the knowledge and rules of agent and so on. It can still save and output or directly submit the results of auditing.

The auditing subsystem consists of the eight MAs that they have the different features as above. When it accepts the specific the auditing task submitted by the users, the system automatically audits the data from the audited parts and timely finds out of the problems and submits the result with a vary of ways to the detecting central.

C. The Structure Design of Agent

The auditing agent is crucial to execute the secure auditing task. The auditing agent is a sort of MA. Every the auditing agent is a auditing unit relatively standing alone. It uses the auditing algorithm and knowledge base from itself to execute the auditing tasks. It can still constantly get the newest knowledge using to audit from the analysis agent. The auditing agent packs the property of it describing its status so as to restart to work and return the information to the auditing agent when the auditing agent moves to other host. Figure2 shows it.

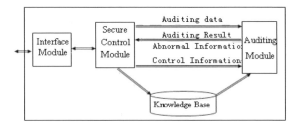

Fig. 2. The structure of auditing agent

The auditing agent includes the modules as follow:

1) The Interface Module: It mainly separate the internal mechanisms of the auditing agent from the external. All information to exchange must pass the interface. The module includes the interface that it can interact with the teamwork agent and the agent server, the interface passing the message and the interface linking the data source. The exchanging information of the agent includes the controlling information, the abnormal information, the model information renewing the algorithm and the auditing data.

2) The Secure and Controlling Module: It can provide the protection for MA and prevent the illegal visit from the external condition so as to ensure the correct and legal of data and encrypt or decrypt the data and achieve the digital signature.

3) The Auditing Module: It regulates the auditing data, and then analyzes the regulated data according to the auditing algorithm and the auditing model so as to ensure no the behavioral data which is not agree with the operating rules and regulations

or the abnormal situation. At last, it transfers the abnormal data through analysis to the teamwork agent so as to further analyze.

4) The Knowledge Base: It is initialized by the teamwork agent, and mainly saves the auditing algorithm, the auditing model and the necessary knowledge for analyzing and auditing. It can interact with the expert system and is processed and coordinated by the expert system.

4 Conclusion

The new DSAS model with the intelligence based on the multi-MA built by this work proposes the DSAS structure and feature which integrates many MAs with the independent feature. It is to research the secure auditing model with the intelligence and automation from the point of view of the multi-MA system based on analysing the advantage and trait of MA and DSAS. It can largely promote the intelligence, the automation, the correction, the security and the whole efficiency of SAS.

For the problem how to achieve DSAS, the technology of agent and the MA system is one of the computing models efficiently resolving the complex and distributed problem. And the FIPA-Agent specification largely reduces the complexity building the multi-agent system[7]. The independence of agent, the characteristics of organization and structure from the multi-agent system and the means to be human of the system operation provide the reference model for designing and achieving the auditing system with the intelligence. The development and improvement of the agent-oriented programming(AOP) and JAVA can provide the reliable guarantee from the technology[8].

References

1. Jia, T., et al.: Network Secure and Practical Technology, pp. 128–131. China Machine Press, Beijing (2010)
2. Jia, T., et al.: Network Secure Technology and Application, pp. 216–218. China Machine Press, Beijing (2009)
3. Jennings, N.R., et al.: A Roadmap of Agent Research and Development, Autonomous Agents and Multi–Agent sysfems, vol. (1) (1998)
4. Ferber, J.: Multi–agent Sysfems: An Introduction to Distributed Artificial Intelligence. Addison Wesley, Harlow (1999)
5. Foundation fo Intelligent Physical Agents. FIPA Agent Management Specification (June 2002), http://www.fipa.org/specs/fipa00023/
6. Jia, T., Wang, H.: Novel Intelligent NIPS Model Based on Multiple Mobile Agent and Data Mining. In: ICCDA 2010, pp. 102–106 (2010)
7. http://dl.21ic.com/download/code/21ic-code-ic-24155.html (October 20, 2010)
8. Zhang, H., et al.: The Model Research and The System Design of The Distributed and Secure Auditing. Computer Software 34 (2008)

A Modified Securities Model Based on Public Key Infrastructure

Wuzheng Tan[1], Yongquan Xie[2], Dan Li[3], and Mei Liu[1]

[1] Shanghai Koal Software Co., Ltd, 4/F Building A #, 288#, Yuyao Road,
www.koal.com, 200042, Shanghai, China
[2] DCS Center, Yuquan Road, 19A, Beijing, China, 100049
[3] No.58 Sanlihe Road, Xicheng District Beijing, P.R. China 100045
WuzhengTan@tom.com

Abstract. This paper describes a modified securities model and a modified key management protocol based on Public Key Infrastructure (PKI) which aims to answer these questions that how to solve the security problem between the client operation and service operation. It illustrates the model by presenting rule security system for a variety of applications, and proposes a modified key management protocol between ECC-CA (Elliptic Curve Cryptography-Certificate Authority) and ECC-KM (Elliptic Curve Cryptography-Key Management). Our aim is to show the modified securities rules in operation that the traditional business management system can not operate.

Keywords: public key infrastructure, rules management, modified key protocol, securities business management, operation rule system.

1 Introduction

In 1949, C. E. Shannon published the paper Communication Theory of Communication Shannon [1], In 1976, Diffie and Hellman[2] proposed a new conception public key cryptogram. In 1978, Rivest, Shamir and Adleman[3] proposed the first public key infrastructure for RSA algorithm. Besides this, there exists some famous algorithm such as Rabin algorithm [4], ElGamal algorithm [5] and Elliptic Curves Cryptography [6-8]. Digital certificate were used widely in PKI application [9].

Since 1976, a lot of crypto blueprints were proposed, and some of them were deciphered. So, the concept [10], [11], [12], [13] [14] of proving security provided another different method for us. Many scientists pay more attention to design a safe and proving security crypto model(encryption and signature and so on). For example, Large integer problems and Discrete logarithm problems.

In this paper, we consider the problem of demonstrating that a special application in public key infrastructure is well selected, in other words, that it has been chosen so as to benefit strongly from the security properties of the underlying cryptosystem. This problem has been typically refered to in the literature as that of operation rules validation. Interest in special operation arises when a user registers a public key PK of some kind with a certificate authority (CA) or presents it for use in some other application. However, traditional PKI can not satisfy the compatibility of personal special operation.

This paper describes a modification on Public Key Infrastructure (PKI) Application which aims to answer these questions that how to solve the compatible problem between the standard operation and special operation. It illustrates the modification by presenting operation rules system for a variety of personal special application.

The modification is a new approach that we refer to as operation rules system with verifiable operation rules. Our aim is to show the compatibility in special operation that the traditional PKI can not operate.

2   Framework

In traditional business management PKI application, it can not operate the special rule application.

This paper proposed an operation rule system to solve the compatible problem between the standard operation and special operation, however, it cannot solve the algorithm compatible problem between the standard operation and special operation.

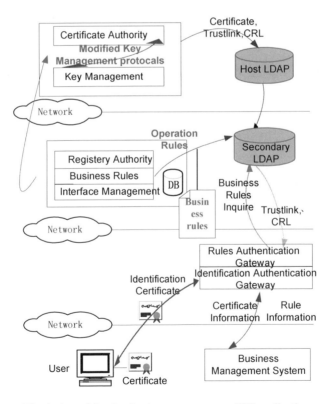

Fig. 1. A modification business management PKI application

So, we describe a modification on key management protocol and operation rules, as shown in Fig.1. It can solve the business compatible problem between the standard operation and special operation. It illustrates the modification by presenting operation rules system and modified key management protocol for a variety of personal special application.

The modification is a new approach that we refer to as operation rules system with verifiable operation rules. Our aim is to show the compatibility in special operation that the traditional business management PKI can not operate.

In section 3, section 4, section 5, section 6 and section 7, this paper describes the modification PKI application detailedly.

3 The RSA Key Management Protocal

The RSA managment protocal is depicted with the ASN.1(abstract syntax notax)
The request between CA and KM is defined as the following:

```
CARequest ::= SEQUENCE {
    tbsRequest          TBSRequest,
    signatureAlgorithm  AlgorithmIdentifier,
    signatureValue      BIT STRING
}

TBSRequest ::= SEQUENCE {
    version             Version DEFAULT v1,
    caName              EntName,
    taskNO              TaskNO,
    reqType             ReqType,
    requestList             SEQUENCE OF Request,
    requestTime         RequestTime,
    requestProof        RequestProof
}

Version ::= INTEGER { v1(0)}
EntName::= SEQUENCE {
    hashAlgorithm       AlgorithmIdentifier,
    entName             OCTET STRING,
    entPubKeyHash       OCTET STRING,
    serialNumber        CertificateSerialNumber
}
TaskNO ::= INTEGER
ReqType ::= CHOICE {
    applyKey            INTEGER { apply(11) }
    restoreKey          INTEGER { restore(21) }
    cancelKey           INTEGER { cancel(31) }
}
```

```
Request ::= CHOICE {
    applykeyreq         AppKeyReq,
    restorekeyreq       RestoreKeyReq,
    cancelkeyreq        CancelKeyReq
}
RequestTime ::= GeneralizedTime;
RequestProof ::= BIT STRING。
```

The respond between KM and CA is defined as the following:

```
KMCRespond ::= SEQUENCE {
    tbsRespond          TBSRespond,
    signatureAlgorithm AlgorithmIdentifier,
    signatureValue      BIT STRING
}

TBSRespond::= SEQUENCE {
    version             Version DEFAULT v1,
    kmcName             entName,
    taskNO              TaskNO,
    respondType         RespondType,
    respondList         SEQUENCE OF Respond,
    respondTime         RespondTime,
    respondProof        RespondProof
}
RespondType::= CHOICE {
    applyRespond        INTEGER { apply(12) }
    restoreRespond      INTEGER { restore(23) }
    cancelRespond       INTEGER { cancel(33) }
}
Respond::= CHOICE {
    applyKeyRespond     AppKeyRespond,
    restoreKeyRespond   RestoreKeyRespond,
    cancelKeyRespond    CancelKeyRespond
}
RespondTime::= GeneralizedTime;
RespondProof::= BIT STRING.
```

4 The ECC Key Management Protocal

The key management protocol is a protocol that control key operation between Certificate Authority and Key Management System. In order to support ECC key, we modify the protocol version as the following:

```
    Version ::= INTEGER {v2(1)}
```

At the same time, we modify the request from the CA to KM (Key Management System) about the Choice of ASN.1.

```
CARequest ::= SIGNED { SEQUENCE {
    version          Version DEFAULT v2,
    caName           EntName,
    requestList      SEQUENCE OF Request,
    requestTime      GeneralizedTime,
    taskTag          INTEGER
    }
}
```

The request is defined as the following:

```
Request ::=CHOICE{
    applyKeyReq      [0]ApplyKeyReq,
    restoreKeyReq    [1]RestoreKeyReq,
    revokeKeyReq     [2]RevokeKeyReq
}
```

From KM to CA, we also modify the request about the Choice of ASN.1.

```
KMRespond ::= SIGNED { SEQUENCE {
    version          Version DEFAULT v2,
    kmName           EntName,
    respondList      SEQUENCE OF Respond,
    respondTime      RespondTime,
    taskTag          TaskTag
    }
}
```

The respond is defined as the following:

```
Respond ::=CHOICE{
    applykeyRespond      [0]RetKeyRespond,
    restorekeyRespond    [1]RetKeyRespond,
    revokekeyRespond     [2]RevokeKeyRespond,
    errorPkgRespond      [3]ErrorPkgRespond
}
```

5 Certificate Operation Flow

We can see the certificate operation flow in Fig.2.

1. Users turn in personal information and relative files, and apply certificates through the Register Authority.

2. Register Authority input and check users' information after receiving the request of certificate application.

3. Register Authority submits the certificate information to Certificate Authority to generate certificates.

4. Certificate Authority generates certificates.

5. Certificate Authority releases the certificates in the host LDAP.

6. Certificate Authority return the generated certificates back to Register Authority.

7. Register Authority makes the certificates, and put out to users.

8. Synchronize the host LDAP information to secondary LDAP.

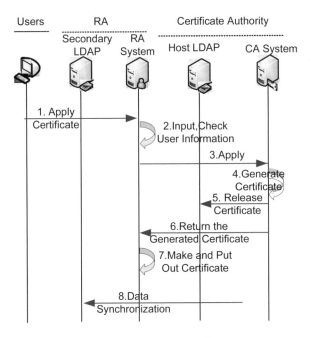

Fig. 2. Certificate operation flow

6 Operation Rules Associate

Fig.3 shows the associated operation rules.

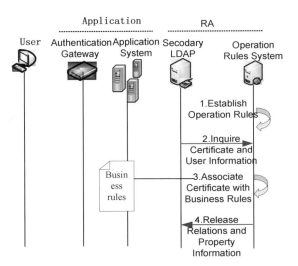

Fig. 3. Associate operation rules

1. According to the need of the operation, the administrator of application system establishes operation rules through operation rule system.

2. Inquire the certificate and user information.

3. The administrator of application system associate user certificate with operation rules through operation rule system (Identifier is the serial number of certificate).

For example, we can associate Mlr_ck_371724_1=49e691c43faa5d5b. then publish in the secondary LDAP. The operation rule is Mlr_ck_371724_1, the serial number of digital certificate is 49e691c43faa5d5b.

4. Release the rules information (relations and property information) in the secondary LDAP system or database system.

7   Application Case

In a modification PKI application case in Fig.4. We propose a new method to deal with the compatibility of new rule for application system.

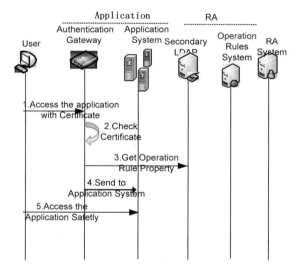

Fig. 4. Modified PKI application case

1. User accesses the application system with the digital certificate.

2. Identification Authentification Gateway verifies the digital certificate, and resolve the certificate then get the information of it.

3. According to the serial number of the user certificate, the Rules authentification Gateway picks up the operation rule information from the secondary LDAP.

4. Gateway sends context of the user certificates and operation rule information to application system.

5. Users access all of the application system safely with the digital certificate.

8 Conclusion

This paper describes a modification on Public Key Infrastructure (PKI) Application which aims to answer these questions that how to solve the compatible problem between the standard business operation and special business operation. It illustrates the modification by presenting operation rules system and key management protocol for a variety of personal special application.

The modification is a new approach that we refer to as operation rules system with verifiable operation rules. Our aim is to show the business compatibility in special business management operation that the traditional PKI can not operate.

Acknowledgment. This work are supported by National Science and Technology Support Plan (2009BAH47B03, 2008BAH22B02, 2009BAH47B03, 2008BAH24B04-02), Science and Technology Commission of Shanghai Municipality (Grand No. 06HX11803 and No.08dz1500600).

References

1. Shannon, C.E.: Communication Theory of Communication. Bell Syst. Tech. J. 28, 656–715 (1949)
2. Diffie, W., Hellman, M.: New directions in cryptography. IEEE Trans. Information Theory 22, 644–654 (1976)
3. Rivest, R.L., Shamir, A., Aldleman, L.: A method for obtaining digital signatures and public-key cryptosystems. Comm. of the ACM 21, 120–126 (1978)
4. Rabin, M.O.: Digital signatures and public-key functions as intractible as factorization. Technical report LCS/TR-212. MIT Labrary for Computer Science (1979)
5. ElGamal, T.: A public-key cryptosystem and a signature based on discrete logarithms. IEEE Transactions on Information Theory 31, 469–472 (1985)
6. Koblitz, N.: Ellipic curve cryptosystems. Mathematics of Computation 48, 203–209 (1987)
7. Menezes, A.J., van Oorschot, P.C., Vanstone, S.A.: Handbook of Applied Cryptography. CRC Press, Boca Raton (1997)
8. Möller, V.: Use of ellipitic curvers in cryptography. In: Williams, H.C. (ed.) CRYPTO 1985. LNCS, vol. 218, pp. 417–426. Springer, Heidelberg (1986)
9. Kohnfelder, L.M.: Towards a Practical Public-key Cryptosystem. Bachelor's thesis, Department of Computer Science. Massachusetts Institute of Technology, Cambridge, MA (June 1978)
10. Tan, W., Yang, W., Yang, M., Ye, F., Zhang, S.: A Modification on Public Key Infrastructure Application. In: EBISS 2009 (2009) (accepted)
11. Bellare, M., Desai, A., Pointcheval, D., Rogaway, P.: Relations among Notions of Security for Public-key Encryption Scheme. In: Krawczyk, H. (ed.) CRYPTO 1998. LNCS, vol. 1462, pp. 26–46. Springer, Heidelberg (1998)
12. Boneh, D.: The decision Diffie-Hellman problem. In: Buhler, J.P. (ed.) ANTS 1998. LNCS, vol. 1423, pp. 48–63. Springer, Heidelberg (1998)
13. Boneh, D., Venkatesan, R.: Breaking RSA may not be equivalent to factoring. In: Nyberg, K. (ed.) EUROCRYPT 1998. LNCS, vol. 1403, pp. 59–71. Springer, Heidelberg (1998)
14. Brickell, E., Pointcheval, D., Vaudenay, S., Yung, M.: Design validations for discrete logarithm based signature schemes. In: Imai, H., Zheng, Y. (eds.) PKC 2000. LNCS, vol. 1751, pp. 276–292. Springer, Heidelberg (2000)

An Empirical Study on China's Inter-provincial Coal Distribution by Railway[*]

Yanzhi Zhang, Lei Zhang, Tao Lv, and Ying Feng

School of Management
China University of Mining and Technology
Xuzhou, Jiangsu, 221116, P.R. China
yanzhizhang@yahoo.cn

Abstract. Coal transportation system plays an important role in guaranteeing the safety and stability of China's coal supply. How to distribute coal resources among provinces in China by railway was discussed. An optimization model was set up to test the rationality of China's coal distribution. Furthermore, by using the model we analyzed the optimal transportation pattern. The model takes transportation cost as optimization goal and the volumes of inter-provincial coal transportation by railway as decision variables. Findings indicate that the pattern of coal railway transportation among provinces changes in four aspects and the transportation cost and the average transport distance decrease compared with that before optimization. Based on the research, we suggest that six coal transportation channels should be strengthened constructing and transportation rate for coastal cities in southeast China reduced.

Keywords: coal transportation by railway, distribution optimization, channel construction, flow pattern.

1 Introduction

Coal plays a strategic role in China's economy development because of China's resources situation which has the characteristic of "more coal and less oil and natural gas". However, the conflicting layout between China's coal production and consumption results in undesired long distance transportation that is from north areas to south areas and from west to east, moreover, the situation will exist in long time. This shows transportation plays an important role in guaranteeing China's safety and stable coal supply. So, under the special conditions, studying on China's inter-provincial coal distribution is of much concern.

There are many studies on the problem of coal transportation. NurulHudal Mohd Satar and James Peoples (2010)[1] used a generalized shipper transportation cost function to test whether coal shippers achieve allocative efficiency with respect to market prices. Gwo-Hshiung Tzeng et al. (1996)[2] combined reducing index method and interactive fuzzy multi-objective linear programming technique to study the annual

[*] This work is partially supported by NSFC Grant #71003097 to L. Zhang and SSFEM Grant #09YJC630218 to L. Zhang.

J. Zhang (Ed.): ICAIC 2011, Part III, CCIS 226, pp. 260–266, 2011.
© Springer-Verlag Berlin Heidelberg 2011

coal purchase and allocation schedule of Taipower. Scott M. Dennis(1999)[3] used spatial equilibrium model to analyze transportation rates for steam coal delivered to electric utilities in the United States. Moreover, some scholars applied different methods and models to optimize China's coal transportation[4,5], some others analyzed the spatial patter of China's coal flow[6,7,8].

The present literatures studied coal transportation from different aspects, but because the system of coal transportation is a complicated and huge system which includes many variables and sometimes is a NP-hard problem for its difficulty to solve, studies on coal distribution optimization are less. Li Zhi (2004)[4] merely studied the problem taking a China's steel enterprise for example with three coal sources and five coal destinations. He did not study it from macro-economy point. Although Wang Manyin et.al. (2004)[5] made up for the defect, he limited coal sources and destinations to provinces in China whose domestic net export or net import among provinces are greater than ten millions ton. This study can not provide China with sufficient theory basis to program coal transportation channels. In this paper, optimization theory and method are employed to decide the optimal coal distribution volumes among China's different provinces by railway.

The paper is organized as follows. The basic pattern of China's coal transportation by railway is analyzed in section 2. Section 3 establishes an optimization model of inter-provincial coal distribution as well as solves the model and analyzes its results. Section 4 proposes some policy suggestions. Conclusions are finally made in section 5.

2 The Basic Pattern of Coal Transportation by Railway among China's Provinces

A. The Volumes of Coal Flow by Railway

Based on the difference between domestic coal supply and demand China's provinces can be divided into three types. The first is domestic net export regions, the second is domestic net import regions and the third is basic balance regions. The first type of provinces include Shanxi, Inner Mongolia, Shaanxi and Ningxia which locate in north China, Heilongjiang which locates in northeast, Anhui and Henan which locate in middle-east, Guizhou which locates in southwest. In the provinces three who locate in north China are the most important coal supplying regions whose net coal export to other regions by railway account for 82% of that of China. The second type of provinces comprise of Beijing, Tianjin and Hebei which lie in north China, Liaoning and Jilin which lie in northeast, Jiangsu, Zhejiang, Fujian and Shandong which lie in east China, Hunan, Hubei and Jiangxi which lie in central China, Guangdong and Guangxi which lie in southern part of China. The net coal import of the provinces which lie in north China and east China account for 70% of that of China. The third type of provinces are Shanghai, Chongqing, Sichuan, Yunnan, Gansu, Qinghai and Xinjiang.

B. The Direction of Coal Flow by Railway

China's coal flow has the characteristic of regionality, that is, the provinces which are coal shortage give priority to purchasing coal from nearby provinces, then they consider purchasing it from distant regions. The situation of China's coal flow by railway is as follows.

(1) North China Region

In this region Beijing and Tianjin import coal from other provinces, Shanxi and Inner Mongolia export coal to other provinces, Heibei imports coal from Shanxi and Inner Mongolia as well as exports coal to Beijing and Tianjin. Hebei is defined as regional center of coal allocation because of its special coal supply and demand situation.

(2) Northeast China Region

In this region Liaoning and Jilin import coal from other provinces. Heilongjiang is the regional center of coal supply because its coal meets not only itself need but also export to Liaoning and Jilin. The insufficient section of coal demand in northeast China exports from Inner Mongolia.

(3) Eastern China Region

In this region Shandong, Jiangsu, Zhejiang and Fujian import coal from other provinces, Anhui export coal to other provinces and Shanghai keep balance between coal supply and demand. Anhui is the regional center of coal supply whose redundant coal is transported to Jiangsu, Zhejiang and Fujiang. Shandong is the regional center of coal allocation whose coal source is Shanxi and coal destinations are Jiangsu and Zhejiang. The insufficient section of coal demand in eastern China imports mainly from Shanxi, Shaanxi and Henan.

(4) Central China Region

In this region Hubei, Hunan and Jiangxi import coal from other provinces, Henan export coal to other provinces. Henan is the interregional center of coal allocation because its redundant coal is supplied to not only central China but also eastern China.

(5) South China Region

In this region Guangdong and Guangxi import coal from other provinces, Guizhou export coal to other provinces, Chongqing and Sichuan keep balance between coal supply and demand. Guizhou is the regional center of coal supply whose coal meet its need as well as is supplied to Guangdong and Guangxi.

(6) Northwest China Region

In this region Shaanxi, Ningxia and Xinjiang export coal to other provinces, Gansu and Qinghai keep balance between coal supply and demand. Besides meeting themselves coal demand the redundant coal of Ningxia and Shaanxi is transported to other provinces. For example, the coal of Ningxia is supplied to Hebei, Liaoning and Tianjin, Shaane's is transported to Jiangsu, Shandong and Hubei.

It can be seen that different provinces play different roles in China's coal distribution. Some play a role of coal consumption only. Some play a role of coordinating the balance of coal supply and coal demand within a region or in the whole country which are named the regional center including Shanxi, Shaanxi and Inner Mongolia or China's center including Heilongjiang, Anhui ,Henan, Guizhou and Ningxia of coal supply. Some play a role of keeping the balance of coal supply and coal demand within regions which are named the interregional center of coal allocation including Ningxia and Henan. Some others play a role of allocating and transporting coal within a region which are named the regional center of coal allocation including Hebei and Shandong.

3 Optimization of Inter-provincial Coal Transportation by Railway

C. Assumptions

(1) The coal of one province is preferentially supplied to the province itself.

(2) The distance of two provinces is substituted by the shortest railway distance between the two corresponding capitals.

(3) Any two provinces are connected by railway and the railway capacity is unlimited.

(4) Coal imports and exports are taken no account and China's coal supply equals its coal demand.

D. Model and Data

$$\min z = \sum_{i=1}^{n} \sum_{j=1}^{n} c_{ij} x_{ij}$$

$$s.t. \begin{cases} \sum_{j=1}^{n} x_{ij} = a_i \\ \sum_{i=1}^{n} x_{ij} = b_i \\ \sum_{i=1}^{n} a_i = \sum_{j=1}^{n} b_i \\ x_{ij} \geq 0 \end{cases}$$

Where x_{ij} denotes transportation quantity from coal source i to coal destination j, c_{ij} is the cost of transporting a unit from coal source i to coal destination j whose calculation formula is "unit price = 9.3 yuan per ton + 0.0864 yuan per ton-kilometer × transportation distance". a_i is the aggregate coal transportation quantity from coal source i to all coal destinations, b_j is the aggregate coal transportation quantity from all coal sources to coal destination j. The data of the aggregate coal production and the consumption of each province come from literature [9]. The model is used to test whether the coal transportation situation in 2005 is optimizing.

E. Results

The model belongs to the type of balanceable transportation problem of production and marketing which is solved by software Lingo 8.0. The results and analyses are as follows.

(1) Analysis of Coal Optimum Distribution

Compared with the present situation, there are four changes of inter-provincial coal transportation by railway based on optimization results.

① Coal Source of Beijing and Tianjin

Coal source of Beijing and Tianjin is Shanxi before optimization, while after optimization they import coal from Inner Mongolia.

② Flow Direction and Quantity of Shanxi's Coal

The flow direction and quantity of Shanxi's coal change after optimization. The insufficient section of Jiangsu's coal demand import mainly from Shanxi and the importing volume increases by 37 million ton. Furthermore Shanxi's coal should be transported to Liaoning instead of Tianjin. Results show the optimum volume of Liaoning's coal importing from Shanxi increases by 42 million ton compared with the actual volume.

③ Coal Source of Zhejiang

Results show the redundant coal of Anhui should be mainly supplied to Zhejiang instead of Jiangsu. So the two provinces of Zhejiang and Anhui form an alliance of coal supply and demand.

④ Coal Sources of Jiangxi and Hubei

Results show Jiangxi's coal is mainly supplied by Shaanxi and Xinjiang instead of Henan, Shanxi and Anhui. There is one more coal source of Hubei which is Ningxia except Henan. It can be seen that the trend of coal in the northwest China flowing to the central China will strengthen if the coal production of Xinjiang and Ningxia increases.

(2) Analyses of Coal Transportation Cost and Distance

The coal transportation cost decreases by 83 hundred million yuan compared with optimization before which are 492 and 409 hundred million yuan respectively. The optimum coal transportation distance is 382 kilometer and it decreases by 77 kilometer.

F. **Policy Proposals**

(1) Proposals of Railway Construction

The following proposals of railway construction are put forward based on optimization results.

① Strengthening the construction of coal transportation channel from Inner Mongolia to Beijing and Tianjin.

② Strengthening the construction of coal transportation channel from Shanxi to Jiangsu.

③ Strengthening the construction of coal transportation channel from Shanxi to Liaoning.

④ Strengthening the construction of coal transportation channel from Shaanxi to Zhejiang.

⑤ Strengthening the construction of coal transportation channel from Shaanxi to Jiangxi.

⑥ Strengthening the construction of coal transportation channel of "Xinjiang-Ningxia-Sichuan-Hubei-Jiangxi"

(2) Regulation Proposals of Coal Transportation Cost

According to the principle of profit maximization, enterprises must purchase coal nearby in the event that coal transportation cost is paid by purchasers. For example, Beijing and Tianjin mainly purchase coal from Inner Mongolia and Jilin mainly from Heilongjiang. From our model it can be seen obviously that transportation cost is a key factor in deciding how to distributing coal. But because of the same transportation rate, the coal transportation cost of provinces which are far from the center of coal production is so great as to import coal abroad. This undoubtedly impact domestic coal market and is helpless for the development of China's coal industry. In view of the above reasons we suggest that some preferential policies of coal transportation rate should be given to coastal cities in southeast China whose coal resources is poor in order to decrease their coal transportation cost.

4   Conclusions

In this paper the situation of China's coal transportation by railway is analyzed. According to coal supply and demand China's provinces are divided into three types which are domestic net export regions, domestic net import regions and basic balance regions. Analyses indicate China's coal flow has the characteristic of regionality and different provinces play different roles in China's coal distribution. A model of coal inter-provincial transportation by railway is designed. Results show there are four changes of coal transportation and the coal transportation cost and the distance decrease compared with optimization before. Finally, we propose some policy suggestions such as strengthening construction of six coal transportation channels and giving some preferential policies of coal transportation rate to coastal cities in southeast China.

The study is limited to coal transportation by railway and transforms unbalanced transportation problem to balanceable problem. Furthermore, some factors such as coal reserve, water carriage, coal imports and exports and so on are not included in the model. So we will consider synthetically these factors and design more factual model to study the problem.

References

1. Satar, N.H.M., Peoples, J.: An empirical test of modal choice and allocative efficiency: Evidence from US coal transportation. Transportation Research Part E: Logistics and Transportation Review 46(6), 1043–1056 (2010)
2. Tzeng, G.-H., Teodorovic, D., Hwang, M.-J.: Fuzzy bicriteria multi-index transportation problems for coal allocation planning of Taipower. European Journal of Operational Research 95(1), 62–72 (1996)
3. Dennis, S.M.: Using spatial equilibrium models to analyze transportation rates:an application to steam coal in the United States. Transportation Research Part E: Logistics and Transportation Review 35(3), 145–154 (1999)
4. Lizhi: Optimization Model of Coal Transportation Based on Ant Colony Algorithm. China Railway Science 25(3), 126–129 (2004)

5. Wang, M., Wang, Y.: Study on optimization of China's coal transportation and distribution. Natural Resource Economics of China 17(2), 34–37 (2004)
6. Wang, Q., Wang, Y.: Development prospects of China's coal transportation system. China Logistics & Purchasing (11), 16–23 (2006)
7. Zhang, W., Liu, Y., Jin, F.: Evolvement and its implications of spatial patterns of inter-provincial coal output and input at national level. Journal of Liaoning Technical University (Natural Science Edition) 26(3), 334–336 (2007)
8. Zhao, Y., Yu, P.: The Spatial Pattern Of Coal Flow And Flowing Channel In China. Economic Geography 27(2), 196–200 (2007)
9. Li, H.: China coal transportation. House, p. 243. China Market Publishing (2008)

Research on Configuration Management for ETO Product Based on Universal Data Model[*]

Zhu Miaofen[1], Su Shaohui[2], Gong Youping[2], and Chen Guojin[2]

[1] Department of Management, Hangzhou Dianzi University, Hangzhou,
Zhejiang 310018, China
[2] Department of Mechanical Engineering, Hangzhou Dianzi University, Hangzhou,
Zhejiang 310018, China
ZhuMiaofen@yeah.net

Abstract. In the entire life cycle of the ETO product family, the designers would change the product family, the component family, the product, the component example to form the massive data of different versions. Therefore, the effective configuration management needs to be made in the entire life cycle of the ETO products to guarantee their uniqueness and traceability in the entire life cycle. This paper established the universal data model based the ETO product, and proposed the method of the configuration management by the configuration identification and control. The product's configuration management is to take the database as the bottom layer support, to take the material bill as the organization core, to relate the final product's engineering data with the documents, and to realize the organization, control, circulation and management of the product data. Therefore the establishment of the universal data model facing the ETO product configuration is very important.

Keywords: Configuration management, ETO product, Data model, Entire life cycle.

1 Introduction

At present, the research on configuration management technique mainly concentrates on the configuration management model, the configuration identification and configuration control technology. In the configuration management model, George proposed the improved "RAC" model on the foundation of the traditional configuration model. For the software development based on components, the researchers proposed the software configuration management model based on components. Jiang et al set up the abstract configuration management model based on the attribute and the relation of the configuration items. Cao et al set up the Petri net to describe the state change of the configuration items in the structure management and the edition management, and then to establish the unified model of configuration management.

Configuration identification is the foundation of configuration management, and is the process of selecting, naming and describing the configuration items. NASA gave

---

[*] This work is supported by the Zhejiang Science and Technology Project and the National Natural Science Foundation of China (No.60873106 and No.60903087).

J. Zhang (Ed.): ICAIC 2011, Part III, CCIS 226, pp. 267–272, 2011.

out the general process of configuration identification in the software configuration management. Peng et al pointed out that the identification for the configuration items of mechanical products is mainly composed of the node organization identification, the node information identification and the information identification describing nodes on the product construct trees. Yin-Ho Yao et al used the Application Protocol 203 (AP203) in ISO10303 (product data description and exchange standard) to describe all configuration items of the PC machines, thus to effectively manage the global supply chains of the PC machines. Hass introduced detailedly the objects for suitable configuration management, and proposed identifying these configuration objects by the unit model technology. For the convenient analysis to the assembly between the components, Ping proposed that in marking the assembly model, the assembly rules and the restraints between various components in the assembly model are integrated in the model.

The goal of configuration control is to control change request of configuration items overall, to track all realized changes, and then to provide the powerful guarantee for the configuration management and the project success. Hass and Zhang Yan et al studied the control flow of the configuration change. Cao et al proposed a kind of management architecture configuring baselines under the computer-aided coordination environment to manage the process of configuration change. In order to adapt to configuring the item versions under the computer coordination circumstances, Liu Yanqiu et al proposed to control the concurrent situation of the edition management using the authority management and the lock mechanism. Li Xin et al proposed the separate strategy between the version control and the concurrence control to guarantee the flexibility of the parallel development.

At present, looking from the research object, the most research literatures aim at the software's configuration management. Because the ETO products have the multi-disciplinary knowledge integration, the cross enterprise and project of the organizational structure, and the custom-made characteristics, the software's configuration management cannot be applied well in the configuration design process of the ETO products. And its research goal also merely limits in the single product, but has not taken the enterprise's entire product family as the research object. But the configuration management facing the configuration design of the ETO products often needs to conduct the research from the view of the enterprise's entire product family.

2 Universal Data Model

In the entire life cycle of the ETO product family, the designers would change the product family, the component family, the product, the component example to form the massive data of different versions. Therefore, the effective configuration management needs to be made in the entire life cycle of the ETO products to guarantee their uniqueness and traceability in the entire life cycle. The product's configuration management is to take the database as the bottom layer support, to take the material bill as the organization core, to relate the final product's engineering data with the documents, and to realize the organization, control, circulation and management of the product data. Therefore the establishment of the universal data model facing the ETO product configuration is very important.

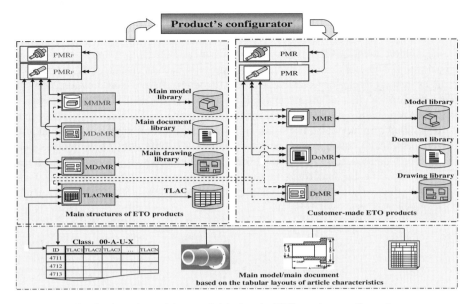

Fig. 1. The universal data model facing the ETO product configuration

Figure 1 describes the universal data model facing the ETO product configuration. Known from the figure, the model is mainly composed of three parts, respectively the main structure of the ETO product's configuration, the custom-made ETO products as well as the main models/main documents based on the thing characteristic table. This data model combines each kind of service object and data object in the configuration design process of the ETO products organically in a whole by each kind of object chain. For example, the product object chain, the model object chain, the document object chain, the engineering drawing object chain as well as the object chain of the thing characteristic table and so on. The description of the object chain is shown in Table 1. The custom-made ETO products are obtained by the configurator on the foundation of the configuration's main structure. The example models, the example engineering drawings and the example documents are obtained by the variant design based on the thing characteristic table.

Table 1. The Description of the Object Chain

Abbreviation	Description
PMRF	Part master record family
PMR	Part master record
MMMR	Main model master record
MMR	Model master record
MDoMR	Main document master record
DoMR	Document master record
MDrMR	Main drawing master record
DrMR	Drawing master record
TLACMR	Tabular layouts of article characteristics master record

3 Configuration Identification

Configuration identification refers to various measures taken to mark the product constitution. These measures are the important approaches that enterprise builds the product resource platforms, including the product object identification and the identification of the relation between the product objects. The product object identification mainly includes the identification of the components as well as their corresponding product data. The product object identification takes the component as the elemental unit. Each component corresponds to some data or documents. The relation between the components manifests the relation between the product objects and their documents. According to the relation between the components, you can construct the relation between the product structures and their documents correspondingly, as shown in Figure 2.

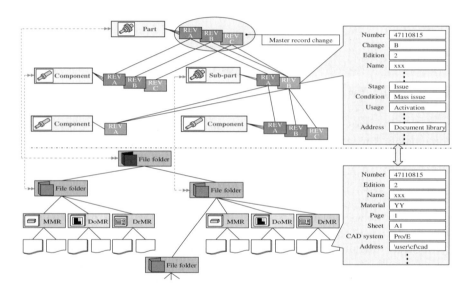

Fig. 2. The relation between the product structures and their documents

In a component, the different conditions of its subordinate parts must be expressed according to the intrinsic relation. For example, the component in Figure 2 has three editions, namely the edition A, the edition B and the edition C, and its subordinate parts have three editions, namely the edition A, the edition B and the edition C. Its subordinate sub-component has two editions, namely the edition A and the edition B. At this time, the component's edition B has used the part's edition B and sub-component's edition B. The reasonable configuration identification must describe the different condition of the product object as well as the relation between them accurately. The different versions' objects are marked by the essential attributes of the part number, the change mark, the edition, the name, the distribution stage, the distribution condition, the operational phase and so on.

Each component or part are corresponding to some product data or documents. These data and documents may be classified by the virtual folder. The structuring classification according to the subject may be realized using these virtual folders. The folder is corresponding to the different service objects MMR, DoMR, DrMR. These service objects associate with the concrete product data and the documents. The product data and the documents are identified by the essential attribute of the drawing number, the edition, the name and so on. The identification attributes of the product data and the documents correspond mutually to the identification attributes of components and parts.

4   Configuration Control

In the entire life cycle of the ETO product, the data models of the entire product family have been in the unceasing evolution. Their evolution is mainly caused by the continuous progress of the design technique and the diversification of the customer's demand. The evolution facing the entire life cycle of the ETO product is displayed in two aspects of the product family's evolution and the product's evolution. Figure 3 expresses the essential process of the product evolution in the ETO product life cycle. On the main structure of the edition A's product configuration, the designers configure the custom-made product according to the request of the customer orders. Meanwhile, the main structure of the product configuration may be changed, and therefore obtained the main structure of the edition B's product configuration. After this edition is provided, the customer's order may be handled using the main structure of the product configuration based on the edition B. This process is repeated according to the preceding process, until the ETO product configuration of the edition X appears. The process control problems concerning the edition upgrade of the components and

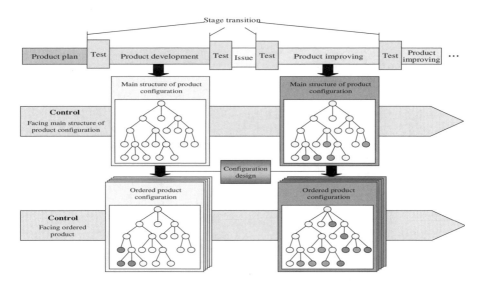

Fig. 3. The essential process of the product evolution

parts and the components' change need to be solved by the configuration control technology. Known from Figure 3, the ETO product's configuration control includes two aspects, respectively facing the main structure of the product and facing the product of the order form.

References

1. Chen, G., Su, h., Gong, Y., Miaofen, Z.: The Product Life Cycle-oriented Modeling Method. In: Third International Workshop on Advanced Computational Intelligence, pp. 373–378 (2010)
2. Chen, G., Su, h., Gong, Y., Zhu, M.: Research on Expression Method of a Unified Constraint Multi-domain Model for Complex Products. In: International Conference on Life System Modeling and Simulation, pp. 177–183 (2010)
3. Zhou, D., Chen, G., Gong, Y.: Research of multidisciplinary optimization based on iSIGHT. Mechanical & Electrical Engineering Magazine 26(12), 78–81 (2009)
4. Luo, K., Chen, G., Su, S., Zhou, D.: Research and implementation of product transformation design based on parameterization. Mechanical & Electrical Engineering Magazine 26(11), 98–100 (2009)
5. Su, S., Ji, Y., Qi, G., Chen, G.: Project planning method for engineering-to-order product mass customization. Journal of Zhejiang University (Engineering Science) 43(10), 1833–1840 (2009)
6. Chen, G., Chen, H., Chen, L.: Research on Multidisciplinary Modeling and Robust Control for Electric Power Steering. In: International Conference on Materials Science and Engineering Science (2010)

Research on the Configuration Design of the ETO Product Based on Knowledge and Thing Characteristic Table[*]

Zhu Miaofen[1], Su Shaohui[2], Gong Youping[2], and Chen Guojin[2]

[1] Department of Management, Hangzhou Dianzi University, Hangzhou,
Zhejiang 310018, China
[2] Department of Mechanical Engineering, Hangzhou Dianzi University, Hangzhou,
Zhejiang 310018, China
ZhuMiaofen@yeah.net

Abstract. This paper constructed the configuration model of the ETO product, described the configuration knowledge based on the associative architecture matrices, and proposed the configured design method based on the knowledge and the thing characteristic table. The configuration design technique of the lift machinery based on the thing characteristic table is essentially one kind of the configuration design facing the lift machinery family or the product platform. It takes the thing characteristic table as the foundation, and controls the product's configuration design combining the data management technology of the lift machinery to restrain the designers' capriciousness, thus to reduce the component types. And under the CAD/PDM system, the lift machinery can be fast designed.

Keywords: Configuration design, Thing characteristic table, Knowledge, ETO product.

1 Introduction

The configuration design technique of the lift machinery based on the thing characteristic table is essentially one kind of the configuration design facing the lift machinery family or the product platform. It takes the thing characteristic table as the foundation, and controls the product's configuration design combining the data management technology of the lift machinery to restrain the designers' capriciousness, thus to reduce the component types. And under the CAD/PDM system, the lift machinery can be fast designed. At present, the configuration design method of the lift machinery based on the thing characteristic table belongs also to the new research area in the digitized design domain. Though it has certain application in the some overseas automobile profession, its reports in the related literatures have not been seen. Jeffrey B. Dahmus et al proposed that the product family is constructed by

---

[*] This work is supported by the Zhejiang Science and Technology Project and the National Natural Science Foundation of China (No.60873106 and No.60903087).

J. Zhang (Ed.): ICAIC 2011, Part III, CCIS 226, pp. 273–281, 2011.
© Springer-Verlag Berlin Heidelberg 2011

sharing the interior exchangeable modules. First the function structures of each product are developed. After having compared the general and particular function structures, the possible modules are determined by the rule to define the possible structures. Each structure is expressed by the function-product matrix. The product frame decision is a key activity of any product's development operation. Volkswagen Company announced that the cost of the development and production in every year saves 1,700,000,000 US dollars through the effective product frame. Volkswagen Company can fully share the platform and module's performance in its four main vehicle types, like in VW, Audi, Skoda and Seat. The Ford Motor Company has also the similar sharing platform, including the general welded elements, the suspension systems, the transmission systems and so on. Messac A. et al proposed that the key of a successful product family is the general product platform. The general and variant parameters can be auxiliarily selected by introducing the punishing function of a product family (PFPF). The PFPF application can carry on the formal expression to the questions through the physical implication parameters to balance well between the versatility and the performance. Raviraj U. Nayak proposed a variant-based platform design method (VBPDM), and its goal is to satisfy the performance demand in a certain scope with the smallest product family variant.

2   Constructing the Configuration Model of the ETO Product

Because the ETO product needs to be designed according to the customer special demand, its development design's cycle is long, and causes the bottleneck of reducing the product delivery cycle. Therefore, in order to satisfy the fast design request of the ETO product, the development design process of the ETO product needs to be divided into two phases, namely the development process and the process of treating the order forms for the ETO product. The development process of the ETO product is corresponding to the forming process of the new ETO product (family). It needs to carry on the development and the trial-manufacture of the new product according to the new market demand. Its cycle is usually long. The development process of the ETO product obtains the results including the product's principal models, the main documents as well as the main structures and so on. But the treating process of the ETO product's order form only needs to carry on the configuration design and the variant design according to the product's principal models, the main documents as well as the main structures. That greatly reduces the ETO product's delivery cycle, and thus can design the ETO product which meets the customer's need as soon as possible.

Figure 1 describes the product's main structure obtained in the ETO product's development process. The development steps of the ETO product include the demand analysis, the conceptual design, the rationalization, the standardization, and the establishment of the product's principal models, the main documents as well as the main structures. The product's main structure includes the optional modules and the compulsory modules. The optional modules refer to choosing some modules from the product's main structure to join to the custom-made product according to the definite rules. The compulsory modules refer to choosing some modules from the appointed

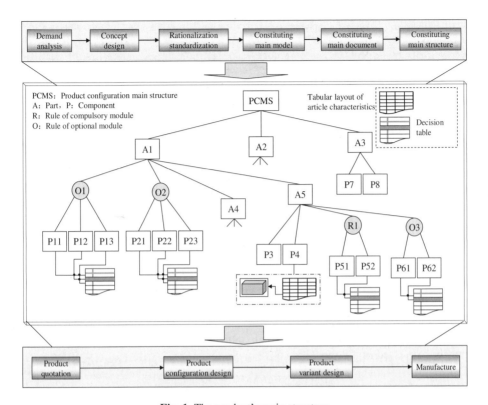

Fig. 1. The product's main structure

modules in the product's main structure to join to the custom-made product according to the definite rules. The rules are deposited in the decision-making table. In the product's configuration design process, the modules may be selected according to the customer demand through the decision-making table. In the figure the rule o1, o2, o3, and R1 are corresponding to the different decision-making tables separately. The optional components are corresponding to the different lines in the thing characteristic table. When the product is customized, the components and parts which have not met the customer need are selected to do the variant design according to the thing characteristic table, the principal model and the main document, as shown in P4 of the figure. The treating process of the ETO product's order-form may be made on foundation of the product's main structure.

Figure 2 describes the main structure of the product configuration based on the thing characteristic table. The composition relations between various modules are expressed by the layer's relations, and the description of the module features is expressed by the thing characteristic table. The composition relations between various modules become difficult in description along with the increase of the product complexity, and simultaneously their processing and solution also becomes to complex. But the moderate manual participation will cause the question's complexity to reduce greatly, and become easy to solve.

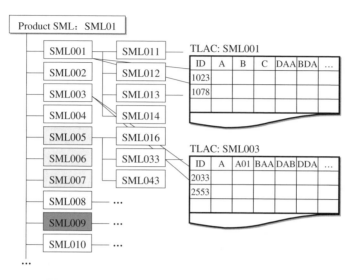

Fig. 2. The main structure of the product configuration

In Figure 2, each node expresses a module, and the module description is expressed through the thing characteristic table. The main structure of such products may be expressed as follows.

$$PCMS = (SMLID, SMLSet, \mathrm{Re}lationSet)$$

The main structure of the product configuration (PCMS) may be described by a trial set. SMLID is the marking symbol of the thing characteristic table. It expresses a module of the product's main structure. The module is described using the thing characteristic table, and SMLSet expresses the thing characteristic table set in the product's main structure. RelationSet describes the connected sets and the design relations between the modules in the product's main structure, and expresses the knowledge and the rule which are used in the configuration design.

3   Description of the Configuration Knowledge Based on the Associative Architecture Matrices

A. The Module's Relation Expression in the Main Structure of Configuration

In the main structure of the ETO product's configuration the relation between various modules is expressed by the associative architecture matrices based on the components. Figure 3 describes the relation among the basic modules, the optional modules and the compulsory modules quantifiably. The basic modules, the optional modules and the compulsory modules are mainly divided from the function relations. It is the concrete manifestation of decomposing the systems.

	Basic module	Selecting module	Optional module
Basic module	2	2	1
Selecting module	2	2/1	1/0/-1/-2
Optional module	1	1/0/-1/-2	1/0/-1/-2

Fig. 3. The relation among the basic modules, the optional modules and the compulsory modules

As shown in Figure 3, the composition relations between the module's functions are divided into 5 kinds of patterns. They are described using the digital quantification way. "2" expresses the compulsory relation between the modules which are compulsory in realizing the system function. For example, the basic modules and the optional modules are the units which are essential in composing the product system. "1" represents the optional relation between the modules which are selected to join in the custom-made product. "0" represents the interdependent relation between the modules, and the some module's existence takes the other module's existence as a foundation. "-1" represents the different combining relation between the modules. "-2" represents the mutually exclusive relation between the modules. That is, in the some module existence, the other module can not be chosen.

On the foundation of quantifying the relation between the modules, the relation between the modules in the product's main structure is modeled using the associative architecture matrices based on the components. In the product's configuration design process, the relation between the modules needs to be established to analyze the modules which compose the product, as shown in Figure 4. The cluster analysis is made for the modules which compose the product, to reduce the complexity of the product design.

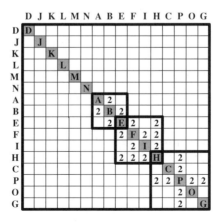

Fig. 4. The relation between the modules

B. Relation Expression of the Module Attributes in Configuring the Main Structure

The associative architecture matrices based on the components describe the relation between various modules in the product's main structure, and can decrease the coupling between the modules on the foundation of cluster analysis to instruct the ETO product configuration design. When determining the detailed design parameters of the modules, the design knowledge between the modules must be modeled. In this project, the module's attributes are described using the thing characteristic table. The description of the design relation displays for the relation between the thing characteristic tables.

Figure 5 describes the relation between the module attributes. It is the foundation of the detailed module's design. The relation between the module attributes may have the different expression forms: function, table, equality, inequality, rule and graphical restraint and so on. Those are the different expressions of the design knowledge. The black spots in Figure 5 express the different relations (or restraints) between the attributes. They have the different expressions. On the foundation of the relation between the attributes, the methods solving the parameters can be obtained, including the automatic solution, the manual solution and the man-machine interaction solution and so on.

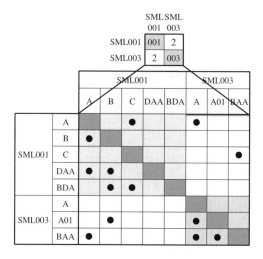

Fig. 5. The relation between the module attributes

4 Configuration Design Method Based on the Knowledge and the Thing Characteristic Table

The product construction in relation to the order derived by the product's main structure is defined by a series of selecting criteria. According to the rules, the optional modules and the compulsory modules in the product's main structure are chosen, and the completely accurate module example or the approximate reference example is obtained by matching the knowledge and the rules as the beginning of the flexible configuration (Figure 6).

In the concrete execution process, the PDM system may be taken as the product configuration tool. To carry on the product configuration, the product administration module of the PDM system needs to be connected with a knowledge library. The decision-making table in the PDM system may also be regarded as an object. The decision-making table is linked with some rule object or the optional object. The product's main structure and the decision-making table constitute an information unit. In the product's configuration process, the variant administration module of the PDM system will take out some important data from the decision-making table to store into the general frame used to construct the dynamic menu. In this general frame, the criteria values are selected to store into again the decision-making table. Thus, the components and parts can be chosen in the active region of the decision-making table.

The custom-made degree of the ETO product is quite deep. In the product configuration process, some components and parts possibly needs to be designed. In this project the proposed thing characteristic table technology, may be used in establishing the principal models, the main documents, thus to carry on the variant design of the ETO product. The variant design based on the thing characteristic table mainly includes the CAD variant design, the CAPP variant design, the NC variant design and so on.

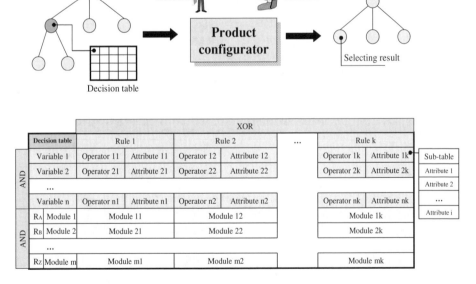

Fig. 6. The accurate configuration based the knowledge and the rules

Figure 7 expresses to automatically produce the three-dimensional model, the engineering drawing and the technological process plan of the corresponding shaft coupling on the foundation of the principal-mode, the master drawing, the main technological process plan in the shaft coupling. After the data of some line in the thing characteristic table (equal to a concrete components' size) is combined with the principal-mode, the main engineering drawing and the main technological plan of the standard module may automatically produce the three-dimensional model, the engineering drawing and the technological process plan of the concrete components. The principal-model of the shaft coupling produces the variant component 001, 002 and 003 under the action of the customer order 001, 002 and 003. The thing characteristic data of the component 001, 002 and 003 in the ETO product's configurator and the thing characteristic table are combined with the customer order 001, 002, 003 to produce the ETO product 001, 002 and 003 corresponding to the variant components of the specific shaft coupling.

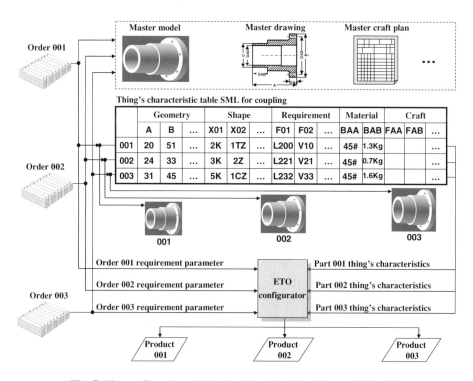

Fig. 7. The configuration design based on the thing characteristic table

References

1. Chen, G., Su, h., Gong, Y., Zhu, M.: The Product Life Cycle-oriented Modeling Method. In: Third International Workshop on Advanced Computational Intelligence, pp. 373–378 (2010)
2. Chen, G., Su, h., Gong, Y., Zhu, M.: Research on Expression Method of a Unified Constraint Multi-domain Model for Complex Products. In: International Conference on Life System Modeling and Simulation, pp. 177–183 (2010)

3. Zhou, D., Chen, G., Gong, Y.: Research of multidisciplinary optimization based on iSIGHT. Mechanical & Electrical Engineering Magazine 26(12), 78–81 (2009)
4. Luo, K., Chen, G., Su, S., Zhou, D.: Research and implementation of product transformation design based on parameterization. Mechanical & Electrical Engineering Magazine 26(11), 98–100 (2009)
5. Su, S., Ji, Y., Qi, G., Chen, G.: Project planning method for engineering-to-order product mass customization. Journal of Zhejiang University (Engineering Science) 43(10), 1833–1840 (2009)
6. Chen, G., Chen, H., Chen, L.: Research on Multidisciplinary Modeling and Robust Control for Electric Power Steering System. In: International Conference on Materials Science and Engineering Science (2010)
7. Chen, G., Zhu, M., Su, S., Gong, Y.: The Solving Method of Simulating and Optimizing the Unified Multidisciplinary Constraint Model. In: International Symposium on Intelligent System Design and Engineering Application (2010)
8. Chen, G., Zhu, M., Su, S., Gong, Y.: Research on the Mmulti-domain Modeling and Optimizing Method for Loader Executing System. In: International Symposium on Intelligent System Design and Engineering Application (2010)
9. Chen, G., Chen, H., Chen, L.: The Method Descending the Order of the Multidisciplinary Robust Control Model for Electric Power Steering Systems. In: The International Conference on Digital Manufacturing & Automation (2010)
10. Chen, G., Chen, H., Chen, L.: Simulation Analysis of DSPACE-based Multidisciplinary Electric Power Steering System. In: The International Conference on Digital Manufacturing & Automation (2010)

The Study about Students' Achievement Analysis Methods Based on Charts Technology

Yang Hongwei[1], Xu Tongyu[2,*], and Li Jinhui[1]

[1] Information and Electrical Engineering, Sheyang Agricultural University
Shenyang, China
[2] Information and Electrical Engineering
Sheyang Agricultural University
Shenyang, China
YangHongweiT@yeah.net

Abstract. Charts play an important role in people's daily production and scores exhibition with the characters of concentration, summarization, easy to analysis and comparation, help to find out the relations of all kinds of variables, besides, they are vivid and can help to make complex and abstract problems intuitive and clear. In this paper, the technologies of crystal reports and statistics analysis of data mining are applied to students' scores analysis and evaluation on the basis of careful study about students' information management system at home and abroad combined with specific characters of students' scores in shenyang agricultural university, first, author designs the network analysis and assess system and displays students' information with column charts, curve charts etc. then, study every kind of cases carefully and give reasonable views and suggestions. The practice proved that analyzing scores information with charts can provide students a platform to understand their learning intuitional and provide higher education an important method to study students' information.

Keywords: charts technology, higher education, information processing, analysis methods.

1 Introduction

Students' examination result is an important norm for domestic colleges and universities to evaluate students' school work or comprehensive quality, each of them have stockpiled lots of students' information with Long-term accumulation, but the analytical processing to the information remains at the same level of simple inquiry and statistics, this created enormous waste of resources. Students will get swingeing cautions, supervise and urge if deeply study these data and display students' score change trend each term intuitively or their position at class or grade with charts, followed by reasonable views and suggestions. Colleges and universities will get a new method to data processing too. In this paper, the technologies of crystal reports and statistics analysis of data mining are applied to students' scores analysis and evaluation

---

* Corresponding author.

J. Zhang (Ed.): ICAIC 2011, Part III, CCIS 226, pp. 282–288, 2011.

on the basis of careful study about students' information management system at home and abroad combined with specific characters of students' scores in shenyang agricultural university, after that, author designs the network analysis and assess system.

2   System Design Objective

The present teaching management systems are mostly based on the transaction, their basic functions include information input, modify, inquiry and simple statistics. This system aims to strengthen its' analysis and evaluation ability on the basis of basic functions, displaying students' score comparison with column charts, curve charts etc combined with .net technology, crystal reports and statistics of data mining, so that students can realize their learning situation each term in school clearly, further more, analyze the reason and provide caution or reference for further study. To teachers, their knowing about learning situation of each class will provide more help to enhance class' score.

3   Development Environment and Tools

A.   Development language

Development language adopts C#, C# derived from C and C + +, so it learns many advantages from C, C++, Java, Delphi and Visual Basic, solves their disadvantages. It is a simple, powerful and flexible, type safety and object-oriented language. C # is the only programming language for .net framework, can use all sorts of functions in .net code library.

B.   The Application of Knowledge Data Mining

Report generation tools adopts crystal reports, crystal reports is a better reports tools, it can generate reports from any data sources nearly, it also can provide diversification formatted data with charts form. Crystal reports generate reports mainly with pull mode or push mode.

C.   Database design

Database design adopts SQL Server 2005, contrasted with previous data solutions, SQL Server 2005 has an unprecedented value, super functions and exciting new experience. SQL Server 2005 contains very rich new features: providing a safer and more reliable and efficient data management platform to strengthen enterprise user management ability, considerably increase IT management efficiency and lower operating costs and risks; Providing advanced business intelligence platform to meet customers' all kinds of complex management requirements on the business of real-time monitoring of statistical analysis, forecast and so on, promote the enterprise management informationization and business' development.

4 Database Design

Database occupies a very important position in a manager information system, its' design process is a key link in a system design process. Practice proved that previous scientific and reasonable design can improve data storage efficiency, ensure the integrity and consistency of the data, save massive cost and time for further sales service. Students' score analysis system involves students, teachers, curriculum and score information, so author designs six tables of teachers' basic information, students' basic information, curriculums' basic information, curriculums arrangement information, score information and roles based on system requirements, combined with realistic requirements. Students' basic information table and score information table establish a one-to-many relationship, curriculums arrangement information table and score information table establish a one-to-one relationship, curriculums arrangement information table and curriculums arrangement information table establish a one-to-one relationship, teachers' basic information table and curriculums arrangement information table establish a one-to-many relationship, Students' basic information table and teachers' basic information table establish a one-to-one relationship with roles table respectively.

5 System Function Design

Students' score can be analyzed from various angles followed by different conclusions. This system adopts curve charts to contrast students' all courses' rankings, average score rankings each semester, adopts column charts to contrast each courses' score, each category courses' score each semester. In charts form displaying students' score information will give students an intuitionist caution, so they can realize their problems and adjust learning state timely.

D. Courses ranking comparison

Courses ranking comparison module adopts curve charts to display student' score ranking of some courses in class each semester. After logining system, students should select some semester, and then can see the curve chart of courses ranking comparison. Figure 1 shows all courses ranking comparison at first semester of some student in computer class one grade 2001, figure 2 shows all courses ranking comparison at second semester of some student in computer class one grade 2001.

Figure1 shows this student total score is better relatively in class first semester reflected in that his all courses' score ranking is within 15, some courses even within 5. From comparison of all courses, we can see that some courses related to specialty, such as computer basis, computer introduction, engineering drawings etc, which ranking is better than others, such as political economics, moral cultivation, situation and policy etc. This reflects a common problem in present teaching: Many students only take their majors seriously, but for some communal courses give little attention, this problem should cause someone' attention concerned.

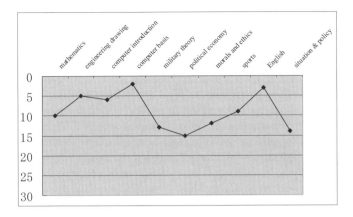

Fig. 1. Courses ranking comparison of the first semester

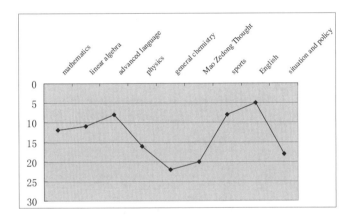

Fig. 2. Courses ranking comparison of the second semester

Figure 2 shows that in second semester, this student's specialized courses scores ranking are within 10,such as advanced program design, English etc, but other courses such as situation and policy, Mao Zedong thought etc, are within 20. The comparison between specialized courses and other courses is obvious. From figure 1 and figure 2, we can see that this student' learning attitude changes and score slips obviously, almost half of the courses are under 15, he need to find out the reason and correct in timely. Many students study hard all along after entering the university, so their scores are better all along, with the familiar to campus and influence by surrounding environment, some students change their learning attitude and this lead to the decline or outer-plane changes of score.

E.   Average score ranking comparison

Average score ranking comparison module adopts curve charts to display average score ranking comparison of all of the semesters. After the logining system, the system will calculate automatically the average score ranking comparison of all courses in all semesters before current semester. Figure 3 shows all courses average score ranking comparison the first five semesters of some student in computer class one grade 2001.

Figure 3 shows that this student' average score is better relatively in class first semester reflected in that his all courses' average score ranking is 5, but from the second semester, the average ranking declined to 15, from the third semester, average score improved significantly and ranking in class also improved significantly too, at the fifth semester, the average score ranking is even within 5. From the content that figure 3 showed, this student' average score occurs major fluctuations, he should summarize scores slipped reasons timely, finds out the reason is insufficient attention to study or to participate in more activities or other factors. From the third semester, his average score improved continuously shows that he summarized reasons and took up the countermeasure timely and achieved good results, this phenomenon need other students who have similar situations to use for the reference.

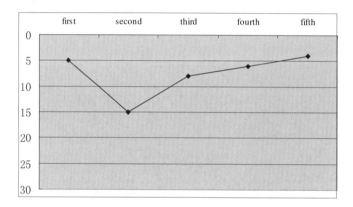

Fig. 3. Average score ranking comparison

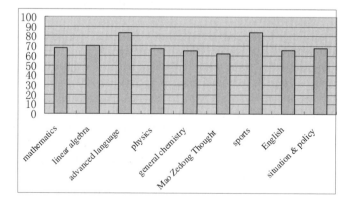

Fig. 4. Courses' scores comparison

F. Courses' scores comparison

Courses' scores comparison module adopts column chart to display the scores of courses in some semester. After the logining system and selecting the semester, the system will display courses' scores comparison with column chart. Figure 4 shows courses average score comparison the second semester of some student in computer class one grade 2001.

Figure 4 shows that this student' seven courses' scores are between 60 and 70 in all of the nine courses, the other two courses' scores are between 80 and 90. From the scores we can see that most of the courses' scores are only beyond 60 merely, he should strengthen knowledge mastering. Even the computer specialized curriculum of advanced language program design, score is only beyond 80, this phenomenon implies that this student need improve all his courses' score timely.

G. Average scores comparison of each category course

Average scores comparison of each category course module adopts column chart to display each category course' average score of required courses, limited courses and elective courses in communal courses, subject basic courses, specialized basic courses and specialized courses in some semester or all semesters before current semester. Figure 5 shows average scores comparison of each category course in the first four semester of some student in computer class one grade 2001.

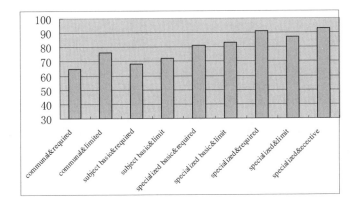

Fig. 5. Average scores comparison of each category course

Figure 5 shows that this student' average scores of communal courses, subject basic courses are lower than specialized basic courses and specialized courses, the average scores of communal courses, subject basic courses are lower 70, but the average scores of specialized basic courses and specialized courses are higher than 80, the comparison is obvious, this phenomenon reflects intuitively that this student' learning attitude, Only pays attention to the major area of study and ignores other foundation courses. The facts of the scores of communal courses, subject basic courses are lower but specialized courses are higher indicate this student have stronger learning ability, only ignores other foundation courses, the scores of specialized required courses, specialized elective courses are higher than 90 and the latter is even better, indicate this student have strengthened the learning about specialized courses, especially the interesting ones. If students like this want to maintain comprehensive balanced development, first they should improve the other courses value degree, second develop interest to other courses.

6 Conclusions

The rapid development of computer technology and network technology have caused huge transformation to the human life and work style, individuals, families and enterprises and public institutions all adopt network management information system to handle relevant information. As the colleges and universities for training of high-level personnel, especially use all sorts of management information systems for handling routine work, these systems have stored up a great quantity of information, but the analytical processing to the information remains at the same level of simple inquiry and statistics, this created enormous waste of resources. This paper apply charts technology into students' scores network analysis and evaluation system, to data, go along more in-depth research and utilization. The practice proved that analyzing scores information with charts can provide students a platform to understand their learning intuitional and provide higher education an important method to study students' information.

References

1. Hipp, J., Guentzer, U., Nakhaeizadeh, G.: Algorithms for Association Rule Mining_A General Survey and Comparison. SIGKDD Explorations 2, 58–64 (2000)
2. Li, G.-q.: Classification analysis of microarray data based on ontological engineering. Journal of Zhejiang University Science A 8, 638–643 (2007)
3. Microsoft Corporation, SQL Server 2000 Architecture and XML/Internet Support. MicrosoftPress (2000)
4. Unil, y.: Analyzing Sequential Patterns in Retail Databases. Journal of Computer Science and Technology 22, 287–296 (2007)
5. Chen, X.: The association rules data mining based on the multi-dimensional data. System Engineering, 103–105 (May 2005)
6. Chen, W.: Data warehourse and data mining. Tsinghua university press, Beijing (2006)

Maintenance Organization Value Chain Analysis and Its Formalization

Tianming Zhang, Ying Wang, and Chao Li

School of Engineering
Air Force Engineering University
Xi'an, China
tianmingzhang@sina.cn

Abstract. In order to achieve Business process improvement (BPI), value chain analysis is widely utilized in enterprises. In related published researches, maintenance processes are only discussed as supporting activities in manufacturing enterprises. In fact, independent maintenance organization is very common in some industry, civil aviation for example, and its value chain is different in many ways from those in manufacturing companies. In this paper, firstly, value chain for stand-alone maintenance organizations is presented. Then, a 5-step value chain analysis model is presented. Finally, a continuous improving process is discussed. Meanwhile, several types of UML diagrams are used as formalization tools.

Keywords: Business Process Improvement (BPI), Value Chain Analysis, Formalization, Maintenance Organization, UML Diagrams.

1 Introduction

A. Generic Value Chain

To obtain its financial goal, i.e. to gain necessary profits, an enterprise has to present its customers with suitable products satisfying the latter's needs. According to [1], the value of an enterprise is the amount customers are willing to pay for what the enterprise provides them. To implement its value, the enterprise will perform lots of activities, e.g. design, produce, market, deliver, support etc. A generic value chain is shown as Fig.1. The enterprise is profitable only if the value specified by the customer exceeds the product's total cost. Therefore, to be a lean enterprise means the enterprise should banish the waste activities on the value chain and thus either raise the value or reduce the cost or both.

B. Maintenance Value Chain Activites In Manufacturing Firms

Value chain analysis plays a key role in understanding the core competitiveness of an enterprise. Which activities are the critical success factors (CSFs) could be determined by mapping the value flow in the production chain and separate the value added activities from the not-value added ones.

J. Zhang (Ed.): ICAIC 2011, Part III, CCIS 226, pp. 289–296, 2011.
© Springer-Verlag Berlin Heidelberg 2011

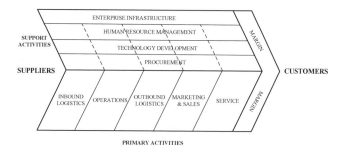

Fig. 1. The Generic Value Chain

Maintenance activities are usually considered as supporting activities in manu-facturing firms [2][3] and thus the value is seldom measured from the view of outside customers. Instead, it is often measured by some non-financial key performance indicators (KPIs), for instance, KPIs shown as Fig.2 in a UML composite structure diagram [4]. Accordingly, the key value added activities are depicted in Fig.3, where CMMS represents Computer Managed Maintenance System.

But for a stand-alone maintenance organization (SAMO), its value should still be defined by the outside customers, as for any manufacturing firm which realizes its value or margin only when the outside customers' needs are met by its products. Therefore, the meaning of value and the value chain in a stand-alone maintenance organization is very different from that in a manufacturing firm. Unfortunately, either the value chain or the value chain analysis is seldom discussed in the publications available.

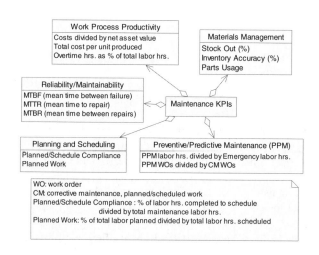

Fig. 2. UML Composite Diagram for Traditional Maintenance KPIs

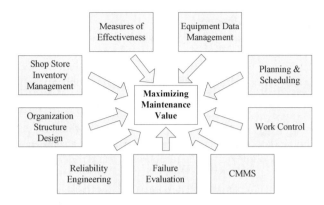

Fig. 3. Value Added Maintenance Activities in Manufacturing Firms

2   Value Chain for Stand-Alone Organizations

C.   Value Chain

Instead of supporting the operation in a manufacturing firm, a stand-alone maintenance organization will realize its value by providing products –or maintenance services – to its external customers. Therefore, its typical value chain for stand-alone maintenance organizations (SAMOs) is shown as Fig.4. Some activities are not common in the maintenance value chain for a manufacturing enterprise, such as subcontracting, the 3rd party logistics, sales forces, etc.

D.   An Instance Process of the Value Chain

For a given external customer, it will be served by a specific workflow or business process, which is actually an instance of the value chain. For instance, an instance p is shown in Fig.5 using a UML activity diagram [4].

   An instance process is a business process by which the maintenance service is provided to an external customer. The exact process for each customer might be somewhat different but Fig.5 presents a general one. The brief process in Fig.5 is as following.

   1)   Request Service. An external customer has some devices or equipments to be fixed or maintained according to scheduled preventive maintenance.

   2)   Inbound Logistics. The 3rd party logistics will take the devices or equipments to the location of the maintenance organization.

   3)   Release WO. The maintenance manager will create a work order and assign some engineers to it.

   4)   Repair. The engineers will fulfill the WO.

   5)   Check & Accept. The customer will confirm whether the devices or equipments are at the expected status.

6) Pay, Outbound Shipping. The customer will pay for the service. Simultaneously, the 3rd party logistics ships the devices or equipments back to the location of the customer.

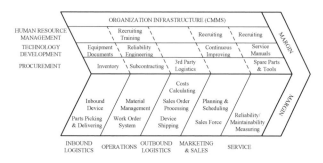

Fig. 4. Value Chain for SAMOs

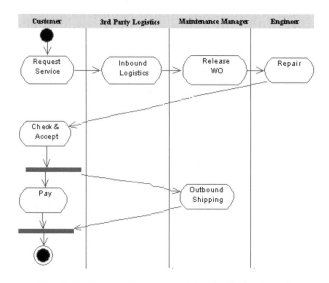

Fig. 5. An Instance Process of Value Chain for SAMOs

3   5-Step Process Model for Value Chain Analysis

To create and keep its core competitiveness, value chain analysis would be done continuously so that the opportunities or threats to an enterprise could be identified. A 5-step process is given below.

7)   Specify customer value. Recognize the things that the external customers of the enterprise value.

8)   Itendify value chain activities. Brainstorm on activities that are required for realizing the value .

9) Analyze activity value. Measure the influence on the whole chain value of individual activities.

10) Analyze activity cost. Allocate costs to value chain activities and identify the cost drivers respectively.

11) Relate activities to competitive abilities. Build a correlation between each activity to the coure competitiveness of the organization. For each activity, the amout of its value surpasses its cost could be used as an index for this correlation.

To improve the value chain in a stand-alone maintenance organization, there are 3 questions to be answered.

● While keeping the costs in the value chain activities unchanged, is it possible to increase the value of the chain?
● While keeping the value of the chain unchanged, is it possible to reduce the costs in the value chain activities?
● Is it possible to increase the value and reduce the costs in the value chain at the same time, i.e. combine the two items above?

Therefore, the steps 4 and 5 are the key steps and will be discussed in detail.

A   Analyze Activity Value

From the view of customer, the process *p* in Fig.5 is valuable.

12) Value of the whole chain
    The value of the whole chain could be measured by the mean profits earned by the multiple executions of the value chain activities, i.e. business processes. If the cycle time of the business process is rather long, e.g. more than one year, the earned profit should be adjusted to its present value (PV) using a proper discount rate. Usually the expected return on investment or the weighted average capital cost is used as the discount rate.
    Suppose *V* is the average margin earned by the value chain executions, the discount rate is *int* and the average cycle time of the business process it *t*, then the present value of *V*, V_c will be

$$V_c = PV(V) = \frac{V}{(1 + \text{int})^{t}} \tag{1}$$

13) Value of the chain activities
    The value of the whole chain will be influenced by the efficiency of activities a_1, a_2, ...a_n. Usually the contributions of these activities to the total value of *p* are different. Let r_i (*i = 1, 2, ..., n*) be the coefficient of activity a_i to the value of *p*, which means the contribution rate of activity a_i to the total value of *p* if a_i is performed in an efficiency of 100%. Thus

$$\overrightarrow{V_p} = (r_1, r_2, \cdots, r_n) \tag{2}$$

is called the activity value vector (AVV) [5] of process p, where

$$1 \geq r_i \geq 0 \quad (i = 1, 2, \cdots, n) \text{ and } \sum_{i=1}^{n} r_i = 1. \tag{3}$$

To get the AVV, based on historical business data from ERP or other information systems, statistics methods (e.g. regression analysis, Monte Carlo method, etc.) could be used.

If the value of the whole chain is V_c, the values of individual activities or V_a will be

$$\overrightarrow{V_a} = \overrightarrow{V_p} \bullet V_c = (r_1 V_c, r_2 V_c, \cdots, r_n V_c) \tag{4}$$

E.   Analyze Activity Cost

1)   Trace Costs to Activities

While each value activity generates value for the whole chain, it will incur cost as well. The enterprise's accounting system should be designed to accomplish this work, but there is a big challenge that the traditional accounting systems are usually not competent because in these systems the apportionment of cost is not related to activities.

Activity-based costing (ABC) [6][7] is a suitable technique to trace cost to individual value chain activities. The total cost of the value chain is just the sum of the activity costs.Because the cost (or investment) of activities such as that on labor hours, materials, spare parts, etc. will happen more often much earlier before the finish of value chain executing, the present value of the cost should not be discounted.

2)   Identify Activity Cost Drivers

To reduce the activity costs, firstly the cost drivers should be well understood. Some sample activity drivers for the instance process of a value chain in Fig.5 are listed in Table 1.

Table 1. Sample Activity Cost Drivers for instance in Fig.5

Activities	Cost drivers
Request Service	Travelling, telephone, fax, postage, etc.
Inbound Logistics	Freightage, insurance, loading & unloading, etc.
Release WO	Overhead expenses, allocated cost of CMMS, etc.
Repair	Labor hours, spare parts, energy sources consumed, depreciation of fixed assets, etc.
Check & Accept	Labor hours, working over, etc.
Pay	Labor hours, credit period, cash discount, bad debts charged off, etc.
Outbound Shipping	Freightage, insurance, packing, loading & unloading, etc.

4   Countinuous Improvement of Value Chain for Stand-Alone Maintenance Organizations

A value chain in a stand-alone maintenance organization has a lifecycle of its own. For example, Fig.6 shows a value chain's lifecycle in UML state-chart diagram [4] of a stand-alone maintenance enterprise which uses Reliability Centered Maintenance (RCM) [2] to determine its customer's maintenance requirements of physical assets in their present operating context. The value chain's performance will be routinely assessed and while the performance is unacceptable, a series of continuous improving events will be triggered.

- **Building.** The value chain is under constructing or redesigning. The 5-step value chain analysis process model is the major tool. The theoretical acceptance criterion of a value chain is that its net present value (NPV) is positive, i.e. The present value of the chain is greater than the total cost of the chain. Meanwhile, some testing will be undertaken in the real working environment.

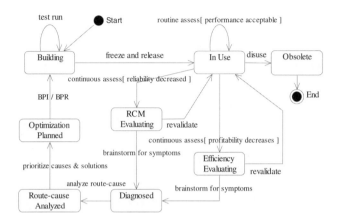

Fig. 6. State-chart for Continuous Value Chain Improvement in a Stand-alone Maintenance Organization

- **In Use.** When a new value chain, its activities and its instances (business processes) have been built up and successfully tested, it will be released and frozen for a relative long period of time. The organization will operate with the released value chain. After that, the value chain performance will be routinely monitored. If the performance is acceptable according to the expected results, the value chain will keep unchanged. Otherwise, the value chain will be evaluated.
- **RCM / Efficiency Evaluation.** The dysfunction of the value chain will be classified into 2 categories: reliability dysfunction and value-adding dysfunction. In either of these states, an evaluation will be done to confirm whether the dysfunction is occasional or inevitable. If latter is the case, an improving process will start or in other words, the value chain is unfrozen for change, otherwise the value chain will keep unchanged.
- **Diagnosed.** Brainstorming will be used to widely collect the dysfunction symptoms of the value chain. The symptoms will be sorted by their severity which is commonly also determined by brainstorming. In continuous improvement cycle, only a small step forward will be realized in order to obtain a quick progress. Therefore, only couple of the most severe symptoms will be discussed in later stages and others will be deliberately ignored.
- **Root-cause analyzed.** In order to completely solve a problem, firstly the root-cause analysis of the problem should be undertaken. Usually there are more than one problems will be analyzed in this stage and on the other hand, there might be multiple root causes for a single problem. When all the root causes and corresponding possible solutions have been found out, they will be prioritized with specific criteria, e.g. return on invest or ROI, which will differ for different enterprises or different time of improving.

- ***Optimization Planned.*** The solutions of top priority will be scheduled and budgeted. BPI represents business process improvement [8] while BPR for business process reengineering [9]. Both are business process centered organization change, but BPI is gradual while BPR is radical. Furthermore, each has its own, unique tool set. The tools of BPI are often referred as ESIAB because there are 5 frequently used BPI tools, i.e. Eliminating, Simplifying, Integrating, Automating and Balancing.

5   Conclusion

The use of value chain analysis facilitates the strategic management of an organization and this is also true for stand-alone maintenance organizations. The 5-step value chain analysis process model could be used as a guideline for enterprises seeking to know the correlation between its value chain activities and its core competitive advantages.

After the value of external customer being specified, the metrics of value chain could be considered from 2 economic viewpoints, i.e. activity costs and relative activity values. But due to some existing challenges, such as the traditional accounting systems do not support activity-based costing, there are still lots of works to do to make the process model more practical. Meanwhile, the value of the value chain to external customers is not only measured in monetary way but in other ways as well, such as customer loyalty or satisfaction degree, etc.

Meanwhile, value chain analysis could be used as the basis of continuous improving process for enterprises. The state machine view of a value chain for stand-alone maintenance organizations presented in this paper depicts the drivers and suggested activities to improve the chain.

References

1. Porter, M.E.: Competitive Advantage: Creating and Sustaining Superior Performance. The Free Press, NY (1985)
2. Smith, R., Hawkins, B. (eds.): Lean Maintenance. Elsevier, Butterwort-Heinemann, MA, USA (2004)
3. Levitt, J.: Lean Maintenance. Industrial Press, NY (2008)
4. Rumbaugh, J., Jacobson, I., Booch, G.: The Unified Modeling Language Reference Manual, 2nd edn. Addison-Wesley Professional, MA (2004)
5. Wang, Y., Zhang, T., Li, C.: Metrics of Lean Organization Based On Value Chain. In: The 3rd International Conference on Power Electronics and Intelligent Transportation System, PEITS 2010 (2010) (accepted)
6. Cokins, G.: Activity-Based Cost Management: Making It Work: A Manager's Guide to Implementing and sustaining an Effective ABC system. McGraw-Hill Companies, NY (1996)
7. Cooper, R.: Activity-based Costing: Theory and Practice. In: Brinker, B.J., Kammlade, J.G., Marx, C., Eiler, G., Maisel, L.S. (eds.) Handbook of Cost Management, B1–B33, Warren, Gorham and Lamont (1997)
8. Harrington, H.J., Esseling, E.K.C., Nimwegen, H.V.: Business Process Improvement Workbook: Documentation, Analysis, Design, and Management of Business Process Improvement. McGraw-Hill, Professional Publishing, NY, USA (1997)
9. Hammer, M., Champy, J.: Reengineering The Corporation: A Manifesto For Business Revolution. HarperCollins Publishers, NY (2001)

The Design and Implementation of Virtual Visiting System for Digital Museum Based on Web

Min Jiang, Lixin Ma, and Xiaolu Qu

Department of Computer Science and Technology
Neusoft Institute of Information, Dalian City, China, 116023
minjiange@gmail.com

Abstract. Through the design and realization of the virtual reality for web-based Dalian Ancient Museum, this thesis provides the design model as well as key technology, which contributes in the construction of on-line virtual museum. On account of Open GL tech, Ajax tech and the virtual reality system with actual Application value, it demonstrated the feasibility of applying multi-virtual reality tech in digitalized museum and also the effectiveness for society in constructing digital museum. Furthermore, it not only renders a deeper perspective for virtual reality research and application, but also reference for practicality.

Keywords: Virtual reality, Digital Museum, openGL, Ajax.

1 Introduction

As we all know, Museum is the place for exhibition of human beings' development in different areas. Various museums place great importance on science research, education, and Science popularization, however, due to limitation of capital and venue, at present, the true value of museum can not be shown up fully. Therefore, it is paramount for further collection sharing and protection by digital and web revolution.

Along with the quick change of web technology, digital museum concept has been created. Digital museum and normal museum are two different concept based on different time and space, while digital museum will extend the function of normal museum in the above 2 aspects. Digital collection does not need the strict requirement for actual collection in aspects of storage and exhibition venues, but can achieve the information permanently. Digital museum exhibits collections by multi-media technology with words, sounds, pictures, videos and 3D model, in addition, it also fastens the collection knowledge spreading with web tools, therefore, digital museum can not be set up without application of multi-media. Our nation owns 5000-years brilliant history, however, so many valuable collections and cultural relics are facing demolish, therefore, it is tough and exigent for us to relive and protect them by using advanced multi-media and virtual technology.

J. Zhang (Ed.): ICAIC 2011, Part III, CCIS 226, pp. 297–303, 2011.

2 Background and Advantage of Multi-media Application for the Digital Museum

Dalian Ancient Museum has planned to start virtual museum project, which has practice in venue, equipment and virtual simulation scene. Its main purpose is to show the function and background knowledge of collections, texture and material of collection that can not be explained clearly by normal way. Thus, visitors can get further understanding for the collection along with experience the advanced technology.

The application of virtual simulation technology can give the same exhibition environment, great visual effects with visiting in the entitative museum; in addition, visitors can also get communication exchange with different information and virtual world. Its advantage as below:

2.1 More Suitable for Informationization of Collections and Museum

Museum industry is an important component of our social civilization. Digital museum will apply modern high-tech to our civilization construction, which will highly promote the innovation of civilization, and keep our centuries-old, broad and profound history always the same pace with the times. The set-up of digital museum will push the standardization of information, drive the science research, optimize working procedure, actualize collection digitalization, and web application for museum management and exhibition modernization, which will improve the protection, using and management for relics.

2.2 More Suitable for Individual and Different Scenario Visiting

Visitors can choose the most suitable way to view the collections according to their own knowledge level and hobby using multi-media and virtual simulation technology. The same technology can also take effect in Situational travel and visits.

2.3 Break the Limitation of Time and Space: Achieve Long-Distance On-Line Visiting

Digital museum will not be limited by time and space by applying virtual reality technology, therefore, individual visitors can find buddies to have a look around together. While for visitors and relic researchers in different places can get together to distinguish and research some relics in the same virtual space. Sometimes, due to time and space limitation, visitors can not visit the museum by themselves, while they can visit museum whenever they want at home using this digital museum visiting system, and can get the same experience as visiting the museum in person.

3 Key Technology of System Design

Virtual Visiting System for Web Digital Museum mainly applies popular multi-media technology and web page development technology-Ajax. Following parts are the brief introduction for the related technologies.

3.1 Multi-media Technology

Virtual Reality, VR in short, is a Hi-tech developed in recent years, which is also called artificial environment. The principle of VR is to create a three-D virtual world via computer, providing user with simulation in vision, audition, and thigmesthesia. With this tech, users would feel as personally on the scene and are able to observe all objects in 3-D space timely, without limitation.

At present, common multi-medias applied in museum are audio technology, video technology, multi-medial scene composition technology, multi-media touch screen and multi-media web technology. Through audio guidance, visitors can easily get the detailed information of the collections, which can be the replacement for the tourist guide. Video, as the assistant method, is often used in basic display and temporary exhibition, which can remedy the disadvantage of picture display and visitors can understand more profoundly. Video can also be transformed to other formats without losing image resolution, so as to be used in different places, such as internet, traditional printing, slides, advertising and so on, which extends the collection image application in different areas. The application of scene composition technology can represent the simulated environment, details, characters and historical incidents, which can not be illustrated by words and pictures.

3.2 OpenGLoduction Technology Intr

OpenGL is short for OpenGraphicsLib. It's a set of 3-D graph processing library, also the industry standard for the respective domain. Computer 3-D graph tech is the one to display or print once the data described 3-D space are converted into 2-D image after calculation.

Thanks to the 3-D Modeling technology, 3-D models can be transferred into 3-D scenes to realize simulation. Now there're a quite a few excellent 3-D modeling software such as 3DS MAX,　AUTOCAD and so on, which all can be used for creating object models conveniently. Also, more sophisticated visualized models can be constructed without programming. One better method to use 3-D model in OpenGL is to build models using 3-D modeling software first, and then convert them into OpenGL for further manipulation.

3.3 Ajax Technology Introduction

Ajax, full name "Asynchronous JavaScript and XML" (Asynchronism JavaScript and XML), is a web development technology to establish mutual web page. Ajax applies the below basic technologies:

1)HTML: Used for web list and establish web application interface.

2)JavaScript: Ajax's core, helps for improving communication with server application.

3)DHTML(Dynamic HTML): Used for update list dynamically, which usually uses div, span and other dynamic HTML element to mark HTML.

4)Document Object Model (DOM): Used for processing HTML structure through JavaScript code.

In traditional Web application, normal mutual communication procedure is: User fills the list and click to submit – the whole list is sent to server – server processes with different technologies – processed result then is sent back to user end. While waiting for the background process of server, the end-user screen is blank, and user can not get immediate feedback. Web 2.0 introduces Ajax technology to use Asynchronism model, which changes the traditional mutual communication model, thus, a new Web application appears.

The most outstanding feature of Ajax is information can be transformed to server without refresh webpage, so does the operation from end user, which will ease the burden of server, quicken the response rate and shorten the waiting time of user. This advantage is the main reason that web developers favor most.

4 Overall Design for Virtual Visiting System

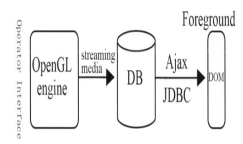

Fig. 1. Overall Design for Virtual Visiting System

5 Realization of Virtual Visiting System for Museum

Digital museum system can be classified to several parts: user interface, exhibition area, game area and discussion area.

(1)User Interface: It is absolutely necessary for digital museum. It is the navigation page for digital museum that guide users to find what they need by easy interface. It is the manifest of visual artistic for digital museum and also the visual carrier for the whole museum.

(2)Exhibition Area: It is the area for exhibition of collections, like the displace area in the real museum.

(3)Game Area: It is an entertainment area in the digital museum, where visitors can get the new feeling brought by digital technology.

(4)Discussion Area: It is the area for visitor to exchange their experience and bring up their suggestion or advice.

The whole system can be published in Internet by web server. Visitors can visit the museum by web server.

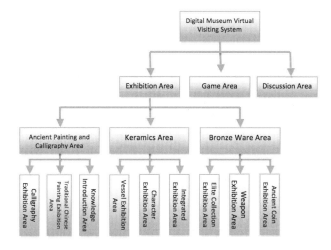

Fig. 2. System Structure

5.1 Nice and Friendly Working Interface

In the virtual visiting system, multi-media technology (Flash, Illustrator, etc.) and Ajax technology achieve the interface design and actualization of the museum visiting system.

Fig. 3. System Interface

5.2 Exhibition

Exhibition areas are classified to General Exhibition Area and Theme Exhibition Area. General Exhibition Area is for long-term exhibition, while Theme Exhibition Area is flexible and will update trend and information for the related field.

Fig. 4. Collection Display

Fig. 5. Calligraphy and Painting Display

Fig. 6. Game Area

5.3   Interactive Experience

Visitors can not touch the valuable relics in the entitative museum, for example, it is impossible for visitors to ring the ancient bells by themselves to listen to different sound of the bells, however, in our virtual visiting system, visitors can personally experience the sound ringing from the ancient bells.

Visitors can appreciate relic collections freely in all points of view by the touch screen. The pictures can be zoomed out and in and dragged by using the mouse, simple as playing CS game.

  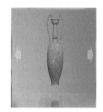

Fig. 7. 360° exhibit

6   Conclusion

Virtual Visiting System for Digital Museum, which is developed by using Virtual Reality and Ajax, simulates the solid museum digitally and integrates the museum resources effectively. This method will enrich the presenting types of Medias and build a three-dimensional virtual interface that can be visited in random point of view. This system will not only provide a new way of exhibition for Dalian Ancient Museum, but also become a development example for multi-media application in virtual museum. We believe multi-media technology and virtual simulation technology will be applied in more fields along with the development and popularization of network technology.

References

1. Lu, W., Zeng, D., Chen, J., Pan, J.: Key Technology in Building the Virtual Museum System. Computer Science 07 (2007)
2. Wang, Y.: Brief Introduction to Digital Museum Project. Gan Su Science & Technology 05 (2006)
3. Huang, Y.: Application of Multi-media Technology in Museum Exhibition. Modern Enterprise Culture 23 (2008)
4. Teare, D.: Brief Introduction for Ajax (EB/OL)
5. http://dev2dev.bea.com.cn/techdOc/2005110103.html (November 01, 2005)
6. Wang, Y., Wu, Y., Xu, K.: Web Application Frame Based on Ajax and WebServices. Digital Science & Technology (11) (2006)
7. Zhang, G., Jia, Y., Jiang, B., Zheng, F.: Shortcut and Practice for Ajax-Web2.0. Post & Telecom Press, Beijing (2006)

Measuring and Controlling System for Validation of Grain Storage Mathematical Model Based on ZigBee Technology*

Zhou Huiling, Feng Yu, and Liu Jingyun

Beijing University of Posts and Telecommunications
Beijing, China
zhouhuilinge@sohu.com

Abstract. The purpose of this study is to develop an intelligent, automatic and real-time measuring and controlling system for grain storage. The system consists of a star wireless sensor network based on ZigBee protocol, a remote data transmission unit, a monitoring and management system running on PC. The Local and remote monitoring and management systems are established on the LabVIEW platform. MATLAB is mix programmed with LabVIEW to set up and solve a mechanism model which can predict the distribution of temperature and moisture content of grain as well as the temperature and humidity of interstitial air in the grain bulk, so as to provide references for the ventilation.

Keywords: Wireless sensor network, Grain storage, Mechanism model, Remote access, LabVIEW/ MATLAB.

1 Introduction

There is a great loss of grain during purchase and storage around the world. In China, the loss of grain in storage reaches up to 5% [1], if only 0.5% of it could be reduced, a lot of funds will be saved. It has become a hot research issue to realize green, efficient and energy-saving grain storage, and to use intelligent control technology to develop new kind of measuring and controlling system [2]. One of the problems needed to be solved is to verify the validity of grain storage model and its integration with real-time monitoring system. This paper constructs a multi-functional intelligent monitoring and controlling system platform for grain storage to solve these problems.

ZigBee [3] is a standard in the field of short range wireless communication. As ZigBee technology represents a wireless sensor network which is highly reliable, cost effective and low energy-consumption, it has a very broad application prospect in agriculture. At present, it has attracted much ongoing research attention at home and abroad, but relevant reports about measuring multiple parameters of grain are few.

---

* This work is partially supported by the Programme of Introducing Talents of Discipline to Universities of China.

J. Zhang (Ed.): ICAIC 2011, Part III, CCIS 226, pp. 304–311, 2011.
© Springer-Verlag Berlin Heidelberg 2011

Raul Morais, et al. [4] built a precise agriculture monitoring system based on ZigBee protocol to detect relevant physical parameters of grape plantations. Huang et al. [5] developed a wireless sensor network used in agriculture. The node undergrand can transmit soil parameters at scheduled time interval. The calculated life of battery is more than 3 years. Data obtained from the wireless sensor network can be used to improve the level of agricultural management and environmental protection.

Mechanical ventilation is mostly taken to conduct cooling and drying at home and abroad, so as to ensure the safety of grain storage. But ventilation is mostly carried out artificially. In order to achieve the overall optimized automatic control of the ventilation system, Dufour [6] refers in his statement that in the applications of control engineering in drying field, predictive control based on mathematical mechanism model is becoming a trend.

We explore the feasibility of ZigBee technology for the measurement system in barns. Wireless sensor nodes collaboratively detect, collect and process various parameters such as the temperature of grain, the temperature, humidity and pressure of air through the grain heap. Local and remote monitoring and management systems are developed on the LABVIEW platform to monitor grain in real time. MATLAB is called to establish a mechanism model which can predict the heat and mass changes of grain, then provide a reliable basis for the ventilation control strategy [7], thus reducing loss of stored grain, establishing a green, energy-efficient and safe grain storage system.

2   Overall Design of the System

The entire system includes an experiment platform system and a controllable temperature and humidity room. The controllable temperature and humidity room (4m × 5m × 2.5m, temp.10 ℃ - 40 ℃, humidity 25% - 85%) can control the climatic conditions of the barn. A test granary (2m×2m×1.2m) (3mm thick stainless steel sheet) with ventilation function (fan, air passage), a ZigBee sensor network and a management and control software implemented by a PC constitute the experimental research platform. The measuring and controlling system for grain storage based on the ZigBee modules, IEEE802.15.4c and LabVIEW is shown in Figure 1.

According to the network topology in ZigBee protocol and the actual needs of grain storage, considering of energy saving, a star network which includes a network coordinator, an auxiliary coordinator, several end sensor nodes and an end control node is established. The system consists of a network coordinator, an auxiliary coordinator and a number of end nodes. Star network takes coordinator as the center, all nodes can only communicate with the coordinator. As the host controller of ZigBee network, the network coordinator is responsible for managing the network, collecting data and connecting directly with the management software. The auxiliary coordinator is not responsible for organizing network, but only receives and sends data. It has the function that converting between ZigBee and GPRS protocols automatically. The remote monitoring and management system receives data through the GPRS network. The auxiliary coordinator transmits commands came from PC to end nodes which complete functions as controlling fans. So that managers can monitor the grain situation without being at the barn.

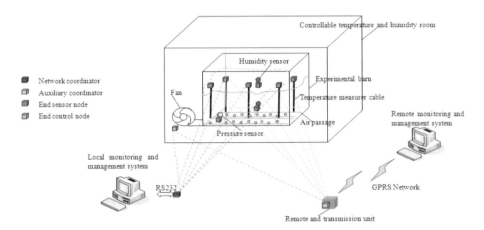

Fig. 1. Measuring and controlling system for grain storage

End nodes complete data acquisition and control function under the control of coordinator. The end node takes AtMegal1281 as its main controller, takes AT86RF212 as the wireless data transceiver device. End nodes are divided into two types, one is sensor node which is connected with sensor cable or precise sensor. DS18B20 temperature sensor, SHT75 series digital temperature and humidity sensor, SDP610 series digital pressure sensor are adopted to capture with the temperature of grain, the temperature and humidity of interstitial air in the grain bul*k*, wind pressure during ventilation. These collected data are sent to the coordinator through a wireless chip in accordance to communication protocols. The other kind node is the control node, which is connected with the fan, receives commands from monitoring and management systems through the coordinator, implements ventilation strategy.

The communication system of the wireless sensor network is developed based on IEEE802.15.4c/ZigBee protocol standards, star network is established to transfer data wirelessly and send control commands.

Monitoring and management system reflects the state of grain in real time, analyzes and processes detected data, and timely implements opening fans, lowering temperature and humidity inside the barn, opening fans.

3   Monitoring and Management System

A. The Local Monitoring and Management System

Figure 2 is the local monitoring and controlling system interface developed on LabVIEW. LabVIEW is a graphical development environment dedicated to develop virtual instrument, it has intuitive graphical programming interface based on data flow, is especially suitable to develop complex test and measurement automation system.

The system adopts modular design concept, including the following modules: the hardware interface and data communication module, the temperature and humidity forecasting module, the automatic ventilation control module, the database access module, and the Communicate with the PLC of the controllable temperature and humidity room communication module. The data between modules are the links that connect all the modules and windows. The system has strong opening feature, it is feasible for developers to add new function modules.

1) Distribution of temperature and humidity forecasting module

Temperature and humidity are two main factors that affect the quality of grain. At present, mechanical ventilation is mostly used to protect the safety and quality of stored grain at home and abroad. During the ventilation, accompanied by the change of grain temperature, moisture of grain also changes. Excessive water loss or excessive humidification may endanger the stored grain. Therefore, the measurement and control system need to be able to predict the distribution of temperature and moisture content of grain as well as the temperature and humidity of interstitial air in the grain bulk during ventilation, then take more effective ventilation strategy to ensure grain quality [8]. According to the mass and heat balance equations, this paper establishes mass and heat transfer mechanism model to achieve this function [9].

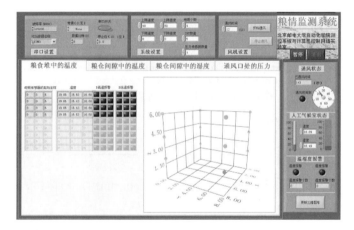

Fig. 2. The local monitoring and management system interface

The mass balance for the moisture of the grain contained in each control volume on a dry matter (DM) basis is given by:

$$\frac{\partial(\rho_g w_g)}{\partial t} = -R_w \rho_g \qquad (1)$$

Where: ρ_g is the grain mass in the control volume (kg·m^{-3}) [DM]; W_g is grain moisture content (kg·kg^{-1}) [DM]; t is the time in s; and R_w is the drying rate (kg·kg^{-1}·s^{-1}) [DM] [10] [11].

The mass balance for the moisture of the air contained in each control volume is given by:

$$\rho_a \psi \frac{\partial W_a}{\partial t} = \frac{f_a}{\Delta x}(W_{a-m} - W_a) + R_w \rho_g \qquad (2)$$

Where: ρ_a is the air mass in the control volume (kg·m^{-3}) [dry air]; ψ is the porosity of grain in barn, f_a is the air supply of vertical direction in barn (kg·m^{-2}s^{-1}), Δx is the grain altitude per unit volume (m), W_{a-in} is the absolute humidity of the air entering the volume control (kg·kg^{-1}) [dry air].

The equation for the enthalpy balance in the grain contained in each control volume is given by:

$$\rho_g c_{pg} \frac{\partial T_g}{\partial t} = \frac{h_{g-a}}{1000} \xi \left(T_a - T_g \right) - \left[R_w \rho_g \left(L_{vap} + c_{pv} \left(T_a - T_g \right) \right) \right] \tag{3}$$

Where: T_g is the grain temperature in ℃; c_{pg} is the specific heat capacity of the grain in kJ·kg^{-1}·℃$^{-1}$; h_{g-a} is the superficial convective heat transfer coefficient in w·m^{-2}·℃$^{-1}$; ξ is the specific surface on contact between grain and air in m^2·m^{-3}; L_{vap} is the latent heat of evaporation of moisture in the grain in kJ·kg^{-1}; and c_{pv} is the specific heat of vapor in kJ·kg^{-1}·℃$^{-1}$.

Table 1. Initial conditions and parameter values in experiment

Grain temperature of four layers (℃)	Grain moisture content of four layers	Air temperature of four layers(℃)	Absolute humidity of air of four layers	Temperature of environment (℃)	Relative humidity of environment	Wind velocity (m/s)	Predict time (min)
[17,18,19,20]	[0.140,0.141, 0.142,0.143]	[17,18,19,20]	[0.0089,0.0096,0.010,0.0095]	12	60%	0.078	100

The equation for the enthalpy balance in the air contained in each control volume is given by:

$$\rho_g \Psi c_{pa} \frac{\partial T_a}{\partial t} = f_a c_{pa} (T_{a-in} - T_a) - \frac{h_{g-a}\xi}{1000}(T_a - T_g) - c_{pv} T_a R_w \rho_g \tag{4}$$

Where: T_{a-in} is the temperature of the air entering the control volume in ℃, c_{pa} is the specific heat capacity of the air entering and contained in the control volume respectively in kJ·kg^{-1}·℃$^{-1}$.

Based on the controllable temperature and humidity room-granary experiment system, the mechanism model which predicts distribution of temperature and humidity is built up [12]. The finite difference method of numerical calculation is used to solve the model, and the grain is meshed for four layers. To make up for the deficiencies in data processing of LABVIEW, MATLAB is used to build and solve the model. Parameters detected by data acquisition module are transmitted to MATLAB program, which provide the initial values for solving model. Input variables include: temperature of grain, grain moisture, temperature and humidity of interstitial air in the grain bulk, temperature and humidity of environment, wind velocity of fan. It will begin computing after given the predict time by the user. Then a temperature or humidity value at any time will be calculated, and three-dimensional color graphics are draw, which indicates distribution of temperature and humidity within the time.

Simulated experiment is conducted based on the actual granary system. The initial conditions and the parameter values are shown in Table 1. Simulation results are shown in Figure 3. Figure3 (a), (b), (c), (d) indicate the distribution of grain temperature, grain moisture, air temperature and humidity in the next 100 minutes. At the beginning of mechanical ventilation, temperature of middle and upper grain is relatively high, temperature of other layers are lower. During ventilation, air of the lower unit cools quickly, as the initial temperature of the upper unit is higher, it cools rapidly too. Because grain conducts heat slowly, the temperature cooling velocity of the grain is lower than the air. The moisture of grain and humidity of interstitial air in the grain bulk also change significantly. Hence when the temperature and humidity of inlet air is lower than that of grain and interstitial air in the grain bulk, mechanical ventilation can effectively reduce the temperature and moisture content of grain, which is conducive to the safety of grain storage.

2) Other modules

➢ Communication interface with hardware and data display module： This module is responsible for communicating with serial port and analyzing temperature, humidity, pressure data, then display them in the interface.

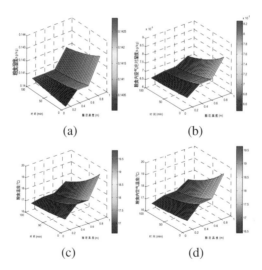

(a)   (b)

(c)   (d)

Fig. 3. (a), (b), (c), (d). The distribution of grain temperature, grain moisture, air temperature and humidity in the next 100 minutes

➢ Ventilation control module: This module realizes automatic ventilation control. When the temperature and humidity of the air in the barn are higher than the warning values, the control system will send command to the coordinator node through the serial port to open and close the fan..

> SQL Server database access module: This module realizes functions as storage, query, print of monitored data. SQL Server database is used to store and manage test data, we achieve access to the SQL Server with the LabSQL Toolkit of LabVIEW.

> Communicate with the PLC of the controllable temperature and humidity room module: This module reads and sets the temperature and humidity data of the controllable temperature and humidity room in real time through the PLC controller.

B. Remote Monitoring and Management System

In order to monitor and control the grain condition in distance. On the LabVIEW platform, we use virtual instrument technology and network communication technology to set up a remote monitoring system. The functional modules are similar to those of the local computer system, but the remote system communicates with the coordinator through the GPRS network, collects the sensor data and sends control commands to the coodinator.

There is TCP/IP protocol station in the GPRS module, it is feasible to use the network interface and TCP functions provided by LABVIEW to realize network communication based on TCP protocol. The system is designed by C/S (Client/Server) communication mode, the host computer works in the server mode, it receives data, processes related data, and sends control commands. The coordinator module works in the client mode. Data are transferred as follows: on the server side, it first specifies the port that provides network services, then calls TCP Listen function to create a TCP listener, and waits for the client to connect with it. The client sends a connection request, the server then establishes a connection, and calls the TCP Read function to read data, calls the TCP Write function to send commands, calls the TCP Close Connection to close connection after all the data are transferred, then the transmission is over.

4   Conclusions and Future Work

This paper proposes a multi-parameter detection wireless sensor network based on lately revised IEEE 802.15.4c standard and ZigBee protocol. Using wireless sensor nodes, a measuring and controlling platform is set up. On the LabVIEW platform, the local and remote monitoring and management systems are established. MATLAB is called to build up and solve model to predict distribution of the temperature and moisture content of grain and temperature and humidity of the air in the barn. This system proposes a feasible scheme for the use of wireless monitoring system in actual granary, provides a platform for the research and verification of grain ventilation control algorithm.

Further research work includes: the research of tree topology to expand the scale and increase the flexibility of distribution of wireless monitoring and control nodes; the study of more effective control algorithm; the development of mechanical ventilation expert system which achieves the automation and intelligentization of mechanical control and reduces the labor intensity of operators.

References

1. Jin, Z.: Research Assumption of Network of Grain Storage Ecology System in the World. Grain Storage 38(4), 3–9 (2009)
2. Guo, D., Jin, Z., Ding, J.: Development Report of Grain Storage Technology. Grain Storage 38(5), 3–7 (2009)
3. Eren, H., Fadzil, E.: Technical Challenges for Wireless Instrument Networks-A Case Study with ZigBee. In: IEEE Sensors Applications Symposium, San Diego, California, USA, pp. 6–8 (2007)
4. Morail, R., Fernandes, M.A., Matos, S.G.: A ZigBee Multi-powered Wireless Acquisition Device for Remote Sensing Applications in precision Viticulture. Computer and Electronics in Agriculture 62, 94–106 (2002)
5. Huang, J., Kumar, R., Kamal, A.E.-S., Weber, R.J.: Development of a Wireless Soil Sensor Network. In: ASABE Annual International Meeting, ASABE c2008, Rhode Island (June 2008)
6. Dufour, P.: Control, "engineering in drying technology: review and trends". Drying Technology 24, 889–904 (2006)
7. Akesson, B.M., Toivonen, H.T.: A neural network model predictive controller. Journal of Process Control 16, 937–946 (2006)
8. Iguaz, A., Arroquil, C., Esnoz, A., Virseda, P.: Modeling and Simulation of Heat Transfer in Stored Rough Rice with Aeration. Biosystems Engineering 89(1), 169–177 (2004)
9. Luo, H.: Investigation of Low-Temperature Storage for Grain with Solar Adsorption Refrigeration System. Shanghai Jiao Tong University (March 2006)
10. Ziegler, T., Richter, I.-G.: Analyzing deep-bed drying based on enthalpy-water content daigrams for air and grain. Computer and Electronics in Agriculture 26, 105–122 (2000)
11. Thorpe, G.R.: Modeling ecosystems in ventilated conical bottomed farm grain silos. Ecological Modelling 94, 255–286 (1997)
12. Li, C., Junichi, K.: Studies on drying mechanism of wheat-theoretical analysis of drying process. Transactions of the CSAE 9(1), 83–90 (1993)

The Research Based on Ontology Annotations of the Structured Elements of the Emergency Plan*

Huang Weidong[1,2], Yan Li[1], and Zhai Danni[1]

[1] College of Economics & Management, Nanjing University of Posts and Telecommunications, Nanjing, JiangSu, China
[2] School of Management & Engineering Nanjing University, Nanjing, JiangSu, China
zhaidanni2011@eyou.com

Abstract. The Emergency plan, as the starting point of emergency management, is a kind of pre-crisis event planning to deal with a variety of emergencies. It depicts the crisis we have to solve, the situations may occur, and appropriate measures we can adopt. So it is an important basis for the emergency decision-making and the core of emergency response. This article refers to the experiences of the digital system for emergency plans and combines with the digital practice of emergency y plans. With the analysis of 3,000 documents of emergency plans we collected, the directory structure of the emergency plans has been exacted, the structural model of emergency plans has been built. By using the ontology construction and based on this model, the text plans can be regulated and so that it can be converted to the digital plans. More over, the emergency plans without construction can be converted to the xml documents of semi-structured emergency plans.

Keywords: emergency plans, Semantic model, digital emergency plan, ontology annotation.

1 Preface

As the beginning of the emergency management, formally speaking, the emergency plan requires strictness, norms and authorities. In many cases, the plans are issued as regulations and regulatory documents. As to its content, the plan has defined the critical prerequisites such as the responsible subjects of emergency management, the scope of the work and the operational mechanisms. Nowadays, the framework of our nation's emergency management has been built preliminarily, but there is also a long way for us to build a framework that can be normally operated. For one thing, the content of the plans can not be implemented fully and effectively. Many lower-level emergency plans, especially the local one, is formulated by simply coping the higher-level plans. The actual local situations have been ignored. What worse, the deciders are also lack of

---

* This work is partially supported by the National Natural Science Foundation of China (No.70871061), China Postdoctoral Science Foundation (No.20100471289) and Jiangsu Natural Science Foundation (No.BK2010524).

J. Zhang (Ed.): ICAIC 2011, Part III, CCIS 226, pp. 312–320, 2011.

sense of emergency management. These have certainly reduced the guiding and the operational functions of the plans. For the other, as there are many different structures of emergency plans, the elements of its content that contained are incomplete. Also the unified standards to make the emergency plans are in bad needed. All these factors are not conductive to the knowledge representation and the automatically generated of the emergency plans.

As the reasons of these problems, the general template of emergency plans has been illustrated and the digital model of it has been built according to the analysis of the directory structures of the emergency plans. By defining the general template of emergency plans, on the one hand, the structure of the emergency plans can be specified, the terminologies and the definitions of the emergency plans can be uniformed so that the emergency plans can be shared and well used. On the other hand, because the general template of emergency plans just provide us the frame of the directory structures of emergency plans, the makers of the emergency plans have to base on every directory and refer to the higher-level plans, relevant acts and characteristics of its local and regional emergencies to fulfill the frame and so that to formulate their own emergency plans. Only in this way can we improve the standardization of emergency plans without the decline of the reality of it. The functions of the emergency management can also be fully brought into play. More over, by converting the general template to a ontology one, the existing emergency plans can be standard with the use of the ontology model, unified and similar structural documents can be formed, which absolutely benefits the semantic expression of the emergency plans and is the essential step to achieve the digital emergency plans.

This article refers to the experiences of the digital system for emergency plans and combines with the digital practice of emergency plans. With the analysis of 3,000 documents of emergency plans we collected, the directory structure of the emergency plans has been exacted, the structural model of emergency plans has been built. By using the ontology construction and based on this model, the text plans can be regulated and so that it can be converted to the digital plans. More over, the emergency plans without construction can be converted to the xml documents of semi-structured emergency plans.

2 The Construction of the Digital Emergency Plans

In this article, the system of digital emergency plan has been divided into two modules: the construction of digital model and the process of digital emergency plan (as is presented in Figure 1). The formation of the general template, which means analyzing the general structure template of emergency plan by using the statistics of the analysis of the directory structures of emergency plans and basing on the existing research of the structures of emergency plans and the experiences of the experts. With the use this template and the combination of the word list of the of directory structure of the emergency plan, the ontology of the structures of emergency plan can be built and stored in the model base and thus, the construction of digital emergency plan models can be completed. The maintainer of the model can modify, add or delete the content of the model base. The digital emergency plan is based on the digital model, by abstracting the information; the emergency plan can be converted to texts of general structures and stored in the form of xml.

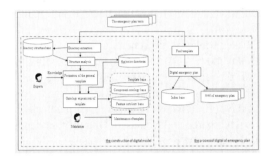

Fig. 1. The framework of the digital emergency plan

3   The Design of the Template of Emergency Plan

A.   The definition of the general template of structure

1)   Analogy and analysis of the elements of emergency plan

The emergency plan, which is the plans or programs of the reaction to the emergencies, is the constructive document of emergency responses. Today, there is no unified standard for the requirement of the emergency plan and the elements of the emergency plan are in hot dispute. The reference2,3,4 analyze the elements from different aspects of emergency plans.

Among these, the reference 2 divided the emergency plan according to the time it happened. The reference 3 analyzed the emergency plan in the view of the functions of every subject in the process of emergency responses. The reference4 divided the elements in the view of the emergencies' safety management. These three emergency plans are not in the same, but on the whole, the elements they required are identical. All of these three can be the abstract when making the emergency plan. The article is basing on the reference2, 3, 4 and mainly provides the statistical analysis of the existing emergency plan and so that formulates the general templates of the emergency plan.

2)   The statistical analysis of the directory structure of emergency plan

Most emergencies are organized with the fixed physical characteristics of the structures of texts, the level of the text is clearly according to the tree-level structure, namely: {headlines, sections, chapters, paragraph, text},the directory structure of the emergency plan is constituted by a series of headlines and analyzes the elements of the emergency plan and the significances of every elements.

This article is according to 3,000 emergency plans of the nation and provinces; it focuses on the 300 emergency plans such as The National Emergency Plans of Natural

Disasters, The National Emergency Plans of Critical accident of food safety, The National Emergency Plans of environmental emergencies and so on. Combined with the directory structures abstracted from these plans, the statistical analysis has been made with the use of Database and Excel. The first 9 directories of the A directory are illustrated in the table 1:

Table 1. The arrangement of the first grade directory in emergency plan

The names of elements	Percentages	The names of elements	Percentages
General rules	89.52%	Auxiliary rules	84.68%
Organizational structure and responsibilities	90.05%	Evaluations and aftermath dispositions in the later period	63.17%
Emergency-response	80.38%	Emergency-support	86.02%
Supervision, report and warnings	74.46%	Training, drills, publicity and education	22.31%
Rewards and pe- nalties	9.14%		

From the above analysis, the conclusion can be made as follows: the 9 directory structures in the table 1 mainly include the elements of the emergency plan that three references required. The content of the table1 is similar to the reference1 and the requirement of the formation of emergency plan. Following, we describe he elements of the emergency plan specifically.

● The general rules and the auxiliary rules are knowledge of events. More than 80% emergency plan contained these two directories. And the junior directories of them are also fixed, which mainly includes the goals of the emergency projects, evidences, classification of the events, scope pf the plans and modification and explanation of the plans.
● The organizational structure and the responsibilities should include the emergency command structure and its BJ, the routine structure of the emergency management, expert consulting structure, the establishment and the authority of the emergency teams and so on. the representative authority which can enjoy the country's rights to deal with the emergency around the world is determined by the system of the organizational structure. It also defined the scope of the emergency rights and the authorities' mutual relationships in the process of the emergency management.
● The supervision, report and warnings, which are rules of the pre-crisis emergency management, are the critical step for crisis protection and emergency preparations.
● The emergency response is the duty of the governments and its relevant authorities. More over, various disposal measures should be made and fundamental steps and procedures need to be regulated according to the statements of the higher-level laws.
● The emergency support is the essential component of the emergency plan. Also it is a principle condition for an effective and in-time emergency rescue. So the emergency support is the cardinal measure to protect the public's life and reduce the financial loss.

- The trainings, drills, publicity and education indicate that though the drills of emergency plan, the commanders of all levels, the rescue teams and the managers of the emergencies can be trained, the easy-understanding books for the emergency protection can be designed and published. By popularizing the laws and regulations and the common sense of the emergency protection, the sense of social responsibilities of the public can be aroused and the abilities of mutual help can be improved.
- Rewards and penalties, which are ignored by most of the emergency plan. However, recently, when managing the emergency in reality, the governments and relevant authorities would also reward the persons whose performances are excellent and punish those who did awful. They want to use this method to improve the efficiency of the emergency management.
- The evaluations and the aftermath disposition in the later period are series of the actions to rebuild the production, work, life, society and the ecological surroundings after the accidents when the influences of the public emergencies had been fundamentally controlled.

3)   The general template of the emergency plan

According to the analysis of the 2.1 and 2.2, the article has given the general template of the emergency plan. Just as the Figure2 shows, this template is not only the frame of the formulation of the emergency plan but also the restrain of the essential elements of the emergency plan. The focuses of different emergency plan are different. For example, in the emergency plan of earthquakes, more attentions should be paid on the transportation, material support and the shelter support. While as to the public emergencies, the emergency support, medical staff and medicines seem to be the most important things. This article only gives the general template for all the emergency plan. When using this template to formulate some specific emergency plan, the content of template can be adjusted to the emergency's characteristics.

B.   The ontology expression of template

There are many usual methods to express knowledge, such as natural language expression, frame expression, process representation, semantic network expression, object-oriented representation[5], Petri net-based knowledge representation and so on. These methods represent know- ledge from different point of views. All the methods can be used in the relevant areas of knowledge. Among these methods, the text as the ontology of the expression of emergency plan template uses the protégé as a tool to construct ontology and the model of ontology.

In order to convenient the search for the emergency plan, the template this article formulated includes not only the information of structure of the emergency plan but also the specific information of the emergency plan. The former is the component ontology, the later is the feature ontology. The feature ontology of emergency plan depicts some specific information such as the name, scope, effective time period of the emergency plan. The component ontology is based on the general template and the kinds of its ontology are identical to the template's elements. Also, the word list of the directory is referenced to build the equivalence class. The mutual relationships of the ontology are converted from the relationships between the template's structures. The Figure 3 presents these in detail.

Fig. 2. The standard model of emergency plan

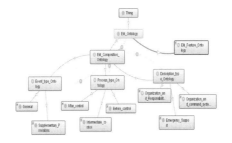

Fig. 3. The ontology structure of emergency plan

4   Ontology Annotations of the Digital Template of Emergency Plan

The process to standardize the emergency plan is just the process to annotate the ontology of emergency plan. By standardizing the emergency plan, it can be converted to xml texts with semantic structure. Every label of the xml texts is same with each kind of the ontology, thus the structural elements of the general template and the specific elements of the emergency plan. Within the process to standardize the emergency plan, two kinds of information should be abstracted: the emergency plan' specific information and structural information. The specific information is used to instantiate the specific ontology. It requires the method for abstracting the information, the method for clarifying the words to abstract the depictions of specifications of emergency plan. The structural information is the instantiated component ontology which can be achieved by the directory structure of the emergency plan.

A.   The specific ontology annotations based on GATE

The specific information of the emergency plan scattered in the texts, and the locations are not fixed. What worse, there is no regulation for us to follow. So information abstracting tools, word list of the emergency areas and the method of clarifying the words e need to be used to complete the annotations of the emergency plan' specific ontology.

GATE system is selected among so many abstracting systems as the basic tool by this article. Because its inadequacies in Chinese abstraction, the article tried to modify the GATE's Chinese word list, clarification and process of Chinese words and regulations of abstracting Chinese words to use it as the tools to annotate the specific ontology.

The article collected more than 3,000 documents of nations' and provinces' emergency plan as the language materials. The word list of the emergency plan areas has been concluded and summarized by clarifying, repeating and calculating the words that occurred in the documents.

When talking about the regulations of abstracting, the GATE system is based on regular information abstraction system. By defining the JAPE language, a more precise regulation can be set to achieve the accurate identification of named entities. A JAPE grammar consists of a set of phases, each of which consists of a set of pattern/action rules. The grammar always has two sides: Left and Right. The LHS of the rule contains the identified annotation pattern that may contain regular expression operators (e.g. *, ?, +). The RHS outlines the action to be taken on the detected pattern and consists of annotation manipulation statements. Annotations matched on the LHS of a rule are referred on the RHS by means of labels. For instance, the identification of "Shandong", this is one kind of locations' names. The trait of this kind of names is that a direction name can be added after the location's name. The set of rule is as follows:

```
Rule:AddressDirection_cn// Identify the palce of "ShanDong South"、 "WenChuan North"
(
{Lookup.minorType=regin} { Lookup.minorType==direction}
// China's geographical names   is stored in regin.list ;the direction of a common noun is stored in direction.list
)
:loc
-->
:loc.TempLocation={ Kind="positive",rule="AddressDirection_cn"}
```

Fig. 4. The standardized xml text of the Emergency Plan for Disposal of Forest Fires in Jiangsu Province

The modified GATE system can abstract the specific elements of the emergency plan, such as the names of emergency plan, effective time periods and so many traits that can give precise definitions and traits. However, when dealing with some more complex semantic information such as the scope of the emergency plan, the results of abstraction are not very well. The next work of this article is to dig out the potential semantic relationships by building semantic models of emergency plan and to modify the rules of abstraction to perfect the GATE system.

B.   The annotation of component ontology

The annotation of structured ontology of emergency plan builds the relevant relationships between the general structures and itself by abstracting the directory structures of the emergency plan and by using the synonyms list. It is stored as xml texts and each of them has an xml label related to every directory structure. The method of calculation is depicted particularly as follows:

1) Search the texts and abstract the directory of the plans, the Leaf node needs be placed in a stack.
2) Start from the bottom of the text and abstract two directories from the stack, named them as mi and mi-1. Find out the locations of the mi and the mi-1. Intercept the text from mi to mi-1.
3) Use the component ontology to find out the label of the mi-1 and then replace the label with the interception got in the former step.
4) Repeat the steps (2) and (3) until the stack is empty.

By using this method of calculation, the emergency plan can be converted to a standard xml structure and the structure of the xml texts' labels can be used to organize the emergency plan text other than the directory structures of emergency plan. The advantages of xml in semantic understandings have laid the foundation of the semantic expression of emergency plan.

5 Examples of Digital Emergency Plan

Because there are mass of information of emergency plan, this article has stored the emergency plan in form of xml text. An xml text relates to an emergency plan. The

```
<?xml   version="1.0"   encoding="gb2312"?>
<?xml:stylesheet   type="text/xsl"   href="table2.xsl"   ?>
<EP>
  <Feature elements>
      <EP Name>江苏省处置森林火灾应急预案<EP Name>
      <Emergency Level >
         < Level First >自然灾害</ Level First >
         < Level Second >火灾</ Level Second >
      </Emergency Level>
      <EP System>地方预案<EP System>
          <Scope feature>江苏省境内发生的森林火灾应急处置工作</Scope feature>
      <Formulating Organization>
          <Organization Name>江苏省林业局</Organization Name>
          <Organization Level>省级<Organization Level>
      </Formulating Organization>
      <Formulating Time> 2008-04-23<Formulating Time>
      <EM Time   Begin="2008-04-23"，Over="-">
          <Effective Time>至今<Effective Time>
      <EM Time>
  </Feature Elements>
  <Composition Elements>
  <General>
       <Aim>贯彻落实"预防为主、积极消灭"的森林防火工..... </Aim>
       <Basis>依据《中华人民共和国森林法》......</Basis>
       <Principles>统一领导，分级负责....</Principles>
       <Scope>本预案适用于在江苏省境内发生的森林火灾应急处置工作......</Scope>
       <Event Scale>森林火灾事故分为四级...... <Event Scale>
  </General>
  <Organization Responsibilities>省森林防火指挥部统一领导全省...<Organization Responsibilities>
  <Monitoring,Report and Warning>开展森林防火宣传教育......<Monitoring,Report and Warning>
  <Emergency Response>分级响应......<Emergency Response>
  <Emergency Support>通讯与信息保障......<Emergency Support>
  <Training, Publicity, Drill and Education>培训演练...... <Training, Publicity, Drill and Education>
  <Award and Punishment>奖励,责任追究......<Award and Punishment>
  <Disposal aftermath> <Disposal aftermath>
   < Auxiliary rules >
         <Terms Explained>本预案中所称的森林火灾是指......<Terms Explained>
         <EM  Management>本预案由省林业局会同省有关部门制定......<EM  Management >
         <Effect Time>本预案自印发之日起实施......<Effect Time>
         <Explain plan><Explain plan>
   </ Auxiliary rules >
  </Composition elements>
<EM>
```

Fig. 5. The fragment of standardized xml text of The Emergency Plan for Disposal of Forest Fires in Jiangsu Province

structure of every xml texts' label is the same, which is composed by a part of specific elements and a part of structured elements. The process to standardizing the emergency plan is also the process to fulfill the xml's labels. The picture 5 is the standardized xml text of "The Emergency Plan for Disposal of Forest Fires in Jiangsu Province".

6 Conclusion

This article has analyzed 3,000 structures of emergency plans and combined the practical experiences of digital emergency plan. By these ways, a general template of structure has been provided to build the specific ontology and the component ontology of the emergency plan. The pattern of digital emergency plan has been formulated to achieve the digital emergency plan. At the last, the example of the digital emergency plan has been illustrated. The next work of this article is to build a semantic model of emergency plan in a higher level.

References

1. Huang, Y., Zhan, S., Wang, J.: What kind of emergency plans we need?- Emergency plan of the digital platform. Information Construction, 18–21 (October 2007)
2. Lin, H.: On the Nature and Effect of Emergency Plans: Focus on the National and Provincial Emergency Plans. Jurists Review, 22–30 (February 2009)
3. Si, Y., Li, Q.: The reaearch of elements of emergency plans. Science and Technology Consulting Herald, 247 (September 2009)
4. AnKe: The elements of emergency plans. Safety & Health, 4 (June 2008)

Local Latent Semantic Analysis Based on Support Vector Machine for Imbalanced Text Categorization

Yuan Wan, Hengqing Tong, and Yanfang Deng

Mathematical Department, School of science
Wuhan University of Technology
Wuhan, Hubei, 430070, P.R. China
yuanwan2011@sogou.com

Abstract. Many text categorization tasks involve imbalanced training examples. We tackle this problem by using improved local Latent Semantic Analysis. LSA has been shown to be extremely useful but it is not an optimal representation for text categorization because this unsupervised method ignores class discrimination while only concentrating on representation. Some local LSI methods have been proposed to improve the classification by utilizing class discrimination information. In this paper, we choose support vector machine (SVM) to generate imbalanced dataset as the local regions for local LSA. Experimental results show that our method is better than global LSA and traditional local LSA methods on classification within a much smaller LSA dimension.

Keywords: text categorization, imbalanced data, support vector machin, local latent semantic analysis.

1 Introduction

Text categorization is a task of classifying a document into predefined categories based on the contents of the document. The data imbalance problem often occurs in classification and clustering when a portion of the classes possesses many more examples than others. When standard classification algorithms are applied to such skewed data, they tend to be overwhelmed by the major categories and ignore the minor ones.

There have been several strategies in handling imbalanced data sets in Text categorization. Nickerson[1] provide a guided sampling approach based on a clustering algorithm to deal with the class imbalance problem. Liu's recent efforts in testing different sampling strategies, i.e. under-sampling and over sampling, and several classification algorithms, i.e. Naïve Bayes(NB), k-Nearest Neighbors (kNN) and Support Vector Machines (SVM) improve the understanding of interactions among sampling method, classifier and performance measurement[2]. Tan presented a neighbor weighted kNN method for imbalanced text corpus and then proposed an effective refinement strategy for KNN text classifiers [3].

Feature selection is often considered an important step in reducing the high dimensionality of the feature space in text categorization. The recent efforts from Zheng,

J. Zhang (Ed.): ICAIC 2011, Part III, CCIS 226, pp. 321–329, 2011.

and Srihari advance the understanding of feature selection in text categorization in the imbalanced data [4].

Aixin Sun et.al. conduct a comparative study on the effectiveness of these strategies in the context of imbalanced text classification using Support Vector Machines[5]. Ying Liu (2009) also used SVM and NB classifier to show the significant improvement for minor categories[6].

Latent semantic analysis (LSA) has been applied to text categorization in many previous works. LSA uses singular value decomposition (SVD) to decompose a large term-document matrix into a set of k orthogonal factors. Although it is an automatic method that can transform the original textual data to a smaller semantic space by taking advantage of some of the implicit higher-order structure in associations of words with text objects [7]. These derived indexing dimensions can greatly reduce the dimensionality and have the semantic relationship between terms.

LSA selects k eigenvectors corresponding to the largest k eigenvalues to construct latent semantic space. However, there is no theoretical proof indicates that the larger singular value of features are of better classification ability. On the other hand, some features with great contributions to the semantic features are filtered out due to their small singular values. Furthermore, LSA is a completely unsupervised method to focus only on the text representation while does not consider the information of classified training set, especially for the imbalanced dataset.

To improve the performance of classification in the imbalanced text dataset, Local LSA (LLSA) [8] is proposed. It conducts separate SVD on the local region of each category. Compared to LSA conducting SVD on the whole term-document matrix, this method takes account of the classification of information, thus has better classification results. But how to select the appropriate local regions is the key issue of LLSA.

In this paper we improve the LLSA so that it is more effective for the imbalanced dataset. We introduce support vector machine (SVM) to construct the local regions. Different from LLSA, these regions are imbalanced and contain not only the positive documents but also the negative documents. The experiments have shown that these local regions reflect the class features more effectively hence the corresponding transformed latent semantic space contains more information about the documents.

The remainder of this paper is organized as follows: Vector Space Model is introduced in section 2. Section 3 explains how to generate latent semantic space and local latent semantic space. In section 4, we discuss the techniques about support vector machine for text categorization. Experiment results are given in section 5. Conclusions are given in Section 6.

2   Vector Space Model

In Vector Space Model (VSM), the document d can be converted to vector space that is comprised of feature vectors as $\{(t_1,w_1),\ldots,(t_s,w_s)\}$, where t_k is feature of document and w_{kd} is the frequency of t_k. VSM does not the take account of the position information or grammar implication of features, so in this sense a document vector is a Bag of Word (BOW) [4]. The weight w_{kd} can be computed by different methods, such as information gain and mutual information. As pointed out by Combarro et al.[9], the TFIDF method is simple but performs well in many situations. It is defined as follows:

The term frequency TF(t,d) is the frequency(number of times) of word t in the document d. The document frequency DF(t) is the number of documents that contain word t. The inverse document frequency of word t, IDF(t), can be computed by the following formula:

$$IDF(t) = \log[D / DF(t)] \tag{1}$$

TFIDF method follows the assumption that the importance of word t in document d is proportional to the frequency of a word occurred in a document and inverse document frequency, the weight of word t in document d, W(t,d), can be computed by the following formula:

$$W(t,d)=TF(t,d)\times IDF(t) \tag{2}$$

In the above formula, larger value of W(t,d) indicates higher frequency of a word t occurred in a document d, but lower frequency of t occurred in all documents.

3 Latent Semantic Analysis

Latent semantic analysis considers documents that have many words in common to be semantically close and those with few words in common to be semantically distant. Once a term-document matrix is constructed, LSA requires the singular value decomposition of this matrix to construct a semantic vector space which can be used to represent conceptual term-document associations.

A. Singular value decomposition (SVD)

From the training documents, we can get the term by document matrix A($m\times n$), it means there are m distinct terms in a n documents collection $m \geq n$. The singular value decomposition of A is defined as

$$A = U\Sigma V^{T} \tag{3}$$

where U and V are the matrices of the term vectors and document vectors. $\Sigma=\text{diag}(\sigma_1,\ldots,\sigma_n)$ is the diagonal matrix of singular values[10].

B. Reduced vector space

For reducing the dimensions, we can simply choose the k largest singular values and the corresponding left and right singular vectors, and the best approximation of A with k-rank matrix is given by

$$A_k = U_k \Sigma V_k^{T} \tag{4}$$

where U_k is comprised of the first k columns of the matrix U and V_k^{T} is comprised of the first k rows of matrix V^T, $R_k = \text{diag}(\sigma_1,\ldots\sigma_k)$ is the first k factors. The matrix A_k is the best k-rank approximation matrix of A in the sense of 2-norm. It captures most of the important underlying structure in the association of terms and documents while ignoring noise due to word choice.

The context-sensitive terms have higher similarity thus they will be close to each other in the new term space. This indicates that these terms are synonymous or multivocal. Then by recombining the information in the initial feature space, LSA reduces vector space dimensions with most information retained. Similarities between two documents and between term and document can be calculated in the new reduced vector space.

C. Local latent semantic analysis

Although latent semantic analysis has been shown to be extremely useful in information retrieval, it is not an optimal representation for text categorization. It always drops the text categorization performance because this completely unsupervised method ignores class discrimination while only concentrating on representation. To solve this problem Liu[8] presented local LSA (LLSA) first. LLSA improves text categorization by performing a separate SVD on the transformed local region of each class.

In local LSA, each document in the training set is first assigned with a relevancy score related to a topic, and then the documents whose scores are larger than a predefined threshold value are selected to generate the local region. Then SVD is performed on the local region to produce a local semantic space. For each document d, belonging to the class c, the transformed local region is constructed as follow:

1. The initial classifier IC of class c is used to assign initial relevancy score (rs) to each training document.

2. Each training document is weighted according to equation (3). The weighting function is a Sigmoid function which has two parameters a and b to shape the curve.

3. The top n documents are selected to generate the local term-document matrix of the class c.

4. A truncated SVD is performed to generate the local semantic space and all other weighted training documents are folded into the new space.

5. All training documents in local LSA vector are used to train a real classifier RC of topic c.

$$\overline{d}_i = \overline{d}_i * f(rs_i), \quad \text{where } f(rs_i) = \frac{1}{1 + e^{-a(rx_o + b)}} \tag{5}$$

If the training set has n classes, it needs to generate n local regions. Compared to global LSA whose cost of SVD computing is incurred only once, local LSA has an increased cost because a separate SVD has to be computed for each class. However, SVD is only applied to the local region, which means that the matrix is far smaller than the one used in global LSI so the computation can be extremely fast. Meanwhile, it reduces the memory requirements of the system, thus it is more applicative in practice.

4   LLSA Based on Support Vector Machine

A. Support vector machine

Basic idea of the SVM is to map data into a high dimensional space and find a separating hyperplane with the maximal margin. The general form of support vector machine is used to separate two classes by a function, which is induced from available examples [9]. The main goal of this classifier is to find an optimal separating hyperplane that maximizes the separation margin between it and the nearest data point of each class. For a set of training vectors belonging to two separate classes, shown in:

$$\{(x^1, y^1), \cdots (x^m, y^m)\}, \qquad x \in R^n, y \in \{1,-1\} \tag{6}$$

A hyperplane as shown in Eq.(7) can be found to separate these two classes:

$$\langle w, x \rangle + b = 0 \tag{7}$$

Given training vectors $x_k \in R_n$, $k = 1, \cdots, m$ in two classes and a vector of labels $y \in R_m$ such that $y_k \in \{1,-1\}$, SVM solves a quadratic optimization problem:

$$\min_{w,b,\xi} \quad \frac{1}{2}\|w\|^2 + C\sum_{i=1}^{l}\xi_i \tag{8}$$
$$\text{s.t.} \quad y_i[< w, x_i > + b] \ge 1 - \xi_i, \quad \xi_i \ge 0, \quad i = 1, \cdots, l$$

And the dual problem is

$$\max_{\alpha} \quad \sum_{i=1}^{l}\alpha_i - \frac{1}{2}\sum_{i=1}^{l}\sum_{j=1}^{l}\alpha_i\alpha_j y_i y_j < x_i, x_j > \tag{9}$$
$$\text{s.t.} \quad \sum_{i=1}^{l}\alpha_i y_i = 0, 0 \le \alpha_i \le C, \quad i = 1, \cdots, l$$

After we get the optimal solution $a*$, we can obtain the optimal separating hyperplane.

B. Why svm with LLSA

The key issue for local LSA is how to choose the appropriate local regions for SVD. The most commonly used method is dividing the training documents into different parts according to their classes. In this way, words that have the same meaning but use different terms are considered. However, words that have several meanings are not considered. Besides this, for the imbalanced dataset, experiments have not shown that LSA achieves effective classification. This is because the local region has only positive documents but no negative documents. Therefore, we need to add negative ones to balance the local region.

The process of constructing local regions can be also regarded as a classification. First we use a trained classifier to choose n documents with the maximum similarity to one category. These n documents are composed of two parts. One majority part contains the positive documents that can well represent the property of this category and the other part contains the negative documents which are similar to but not belong to this category.

The process of local latent semantic analysis with support vector machine algorithm is shown as Figure 1.

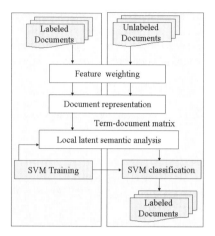

Fig. 1. The structure of LLSA base on SVM

Algorithm: Local latent semantic analysis with support vector machine.

(1) Useing formula $f(x) = \langle w, x \rangle + b$ to select n documents with largest $f(x)$ value to construct the initial local regions.

(2) Conducting SVD on each local region to generate the latent semantic space.

(3) Selecting n_1 documents of another unused category to construct negative class, where $n_1 < n$.

(4) Transforming these n_1 documents to latent semantic space according to formula (3).

(5) Performing TC experiment again.

5   Experiment and Result

A. Data collection

For the Chinese corpus, TanCorpV1.0 is used in this research which is available on-line (http://www.searchforum. org.cn /tansongbo/corpus.htm). TanCorp has two versions, i.e. TanCorp12 and TanCorp60 which has 12 and 60 classes respectively. In our experiment, we choose TanCorp 12.

For each document, the following preprocessing stages are performed. Text segmentation is used to divide the whole text into meaningful units. In our work, we use the Open Source ICTCLAS to perform the segmentation. Stop words that are of high frequency and provide no discriminative information are removed.

In this paper, documents from five categories as "law", "education", "financial", "art", "agriculture", "medicine" are selected as document collection. For each category, 1200 documents were selected randomly from original corpus for training and 600 documents for testing. We employ commonly used procedures to select feature subset. We use χ^2 –metric (yang & Pedersen, 1997) to rank the all unique terms. In our experiment, feature number N was set to be 100, 300,500, 700, and 1000.

B. Experiment design and performance measure

To evaluate the text classification result, we use the F1 measure. This measure combines recall and precision in the following way:

$$\text{Recall} = \frac{\text{number of correct positive predictions}}{\text{number of positive examples}}$$

$$\text{Precision} = \frac{\text{number of correct positive predictions}}{\text{number of positive predictions}}$$

$$\text{F1} = \frac{2 \times \text{Recall} \times \text{Precision}}{(\text{Recall} + \text{Precision})}$$

C. Experiment results

We compare the F1-values of SVM-LLSA and LSA by different feature numbers. Figure 2 has shown that SVM-LLSA almost totally outperform LSA. As we has depicted, SVM-LLSA takes account of the class information thus makes up the shortage of LSA.

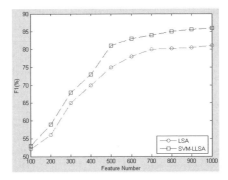

Fig. 2. F1(%) curves comparison of LSA and SVM-LLSA

In this experiment, we also find that at the beginning, the classification performance gets better as the feature number increases. At nearly 500, F1-values tune in a small range. When feature number is 600, SVM-LSA obtains the best performance while LLSA obtains the best performance at 700. It indicates that SVM-LLSA needs fewer features to get a good performance. To verify it, in another experiment, we compare the performances of LLSA and SVM-LLSA on different classes, and Table 1 has shown F1-values of five classes and the minimum feature number of each class that is needed to get a good-enough performance.

Table 1. F1-values of five categories and feature numbers comparison

Class	F1		Feature Numbers	
	LLSA	SVM-LLSA	LLSA	SVM-LLSA
Law	0.772	0.796	700	600
Education	0.785	0.819	600	400
Financial	0.742	0.734	600	500
Art	0.835	0.851	700	600
Medicine	0.813	0.837	600	500

In Table1, we find that except class of Financial, F1 values of SVM-LLSA are all superior to those of LLSA. Table.1 also shows that when obtaining the same performance, in each class, the minimum feature number of SVM-LLSA is less than that of LLSA. This is very significant for LSA because the time complex and space complexity of SVD are both high and by far there is no better algorithm to improve this problem. It obviously takes less time and less space when calculating 200 eigenvalues than calculating 300, especially on the large-scale dataset.

6 Conclusion

In this paper, we propose a new method, SVM-LSA to help improve the text categorization performance for imbalanced corpus. This method is developed from local LSA, but different from it in that the introduction of SVM. We utilize the high quality of classification of SVM to construct local regions for separate SVD. Since the local regions contain the class information, the local SVD can concentrate on modeling the semantic information that is actually most important for the classification task. The experimental results verify this idea and show that SVM-LLSA is more effective than LSA.

Another work we have done is a comparative study on SVM-LLSA and LLSA. Experiment has shown that SVM-LLSA uses less features and time on classification.

Acknowledgment. I would like to thank the experts who take their time to check the paper and give me valuable suggestions. At the same time, the project was supported by the National Natural Science Foundation of China (30570611, 60773210) and the Fundamental Research Funds for the Central Universities (2010-1a-037).

References

1. Nickerson, A., Japkowicz, N., Milios: Using unsupervised learning to guide re-sampling in imbalanced data sets. In: Proceedings of the Eighth International Workshop on AI and Statistics, pp. 261–265
2. Liu, A.Y.C.: The effect of oversampling and undersampling onclassifying imbalanced text datasets. Masters thesis. University of Texas at Austin (2004)
3. Tan, s.: An effective refinement strategy for KNN text classifier. Expert Systems with Applications 30, 290–298 (2006)
4. Zheng, Z., Wu, X., Srihari, R.: Feature selection for text categorization on imbalanced data. ACM SIGKDD Explorations Newsletter 6(1), 80–89 (2004)
5. Sun, A., Lim, E.-P.: On strategies for imbalanced text classification using SVM: A comparative study. Decision Support Systems 48, 191–201 (2009)
6. Liu, Y., Loh, H.T.: Imbalanced text classification: A term weighting approach. Expert Systems with Applications 36, 690–701 (2009)
7. Yany, Y.: Noise reduction in a statistical approach to text categorization. In: Proc. of the 18th ACM International Conference on Rexorch ond Development in Information Retrieval, New York, pp. 256–263 (1995)

8. Liu, T., Chen, Z.: Improving Text Classification using Local Latent Semantic Indexing. In: Fourth IEEE International Conference on Data Mining, ICDM 2004, pp. 162–169 (2004)
9. Vapnik, V., Golowich, S., Smola, A.: Support vector method for function approximation, regression estimation, and signal Processing. In: Neural Information Processing Systems, pp. 281–287 (September 1997)
10. Deerwester, S.C., Dumais, S.T., Landauer, T.K., Furnas, G.W.: Indexing by latent semantic analysis. Journal of the American Society of Information Science 41, 391–407 (1990)

Study on the Application of Garment CAD Style Design System and Pattern Design System in Garment E-Commerce

Meihua Zhao and Xiaoping Zhang

Department of Clothing Design and Engineering
Qingdao University
Qingdao, Shandong, China
xi.aopingzhang@sogou.com

Abstract. This essay studied the application feasibility and application mode of garment CAD style design system & pattern design system in garment E-commerce. Through analyzing the features of the two systems in garment CAD and the psychological characteristics of the customers, the essay provided feasible application mode of different design platform and expending pattern E-commerce.

Keywords: garment, CAD, E-commerce, style design, pattern designe.

1   Introduction

Along with the development of internet and computer technology, E-commerce has been developing vigorously, which results in the development of garment E-commerce. Nowadays, more and more people favor internet shopping. However, the specialty of garment products brings a lot of problems needed to be solved in garment E-commerce. After 40 years development, garment CAD is rather mature in such aspects as pattern, sample-yardage, marking, etc. In garment CAD development, 3-dimension fitting technology is the key emphasis and difficulty which although has made some breakthroughs, yet some issues like 3-D dynamic model and fabric simulation technology still need to be further researched. The 3-D dynamic fitting technology, one of the important links in garment E-commerce is extensively and widely studied, nevertheless the author believes that the other more mature modules of garment CAD are not paid full attention and applied in garment E-commerce. This assay analyzes and delivers how to apply mature garment CAD style design and pattern design technology in E-commerce.

2   Study on Application of Style Design System in Garment E-Commerce

At present, rather mature garment style design systems have been developed by some CAD developers. For instance, the Kaledo style design system by Lectra from France.

J. Zhang (Ed.): ICAIC 2011, Part III, CCIS 226, pp. 330–336, 2011.
© Springer-Verlag Berlin Heidelberg 2011

However, although the software developers have invested great human and material resources, the application of style design system is not satisfying; therefore, the garment style design systems are a lot less than grading systems. Some developers even use software manufactured by others so as to keep their garment CAD systems complete and integrate. The author holds that the application of garment style design system could be further developed in E-commerce so as to take full advantage of the software resources and better promote the development of E-commerce.

Generally speaking, it is not easy to apply garment style design system in E-commerce. Besides proficient software operating skills, professional garment design technology and knowledge are required in this process. The way discussed herein to apply garment design system in E-commerce is by applying garment style design system in the remote custom-tailor process in E-commerce. With the openness and interaction of the internet, the customers are invited to participate in the garment design activity, and then enjoy the personalized products and services.

Firstly, the remote custom-tailor customers are divided into two types. The first type of customers possess certain or good professional garment design knowledge while the second type are without any. For the first type customers, instead of mechanically choosing the one or several common styles provided by the manufactures or sellers, they hope to buy their own exclusive personalized fashions, so a complete design platform can be provided to them. On the complete design platform, most functions of the garment style design system are accessible. Models, colors, fabrics and sizes are open to the customers on the internet, and drawing and modifying tools are available too. The customers could modify the available styles provided, or draw their own planar effect pictures or three-dimensional animation pictures. Depending on design capability, the pictures provided by the customers might be very immature. So based the pictures by the customers, the enterprise designer will give out professional design comment. The style will not be manufactured until the customer is totally satisfied and confirms. For the second type of customers, they have no professional skills in drawing effect pictures, but it does not mean they have no desire for exclusive personalized fashions. If all the garment design software functions are open to this type of customers, they are very easy to give up the purchasing activity for the dazzling complicated professional tools. So for this type of customers, only some functions of the garment style design system, such as style base, model base, and simple dragging and modifying tools are open to them. In this way, on one hand the customer's requirement is met and on the other hand they very enjoy the friendly interface so that they would love to finish the purchasing activity happily. Entered into the interface, the customers could select the styles and 3-D model and then change the colors and fabric, also they could modify the style simply by dragging the mouse. The customer can enjoy, instead of feel frustrating, the friendly interface. In addition, the psychological needs of personalized design are satisfied so it is very easy for them to finish the shopping activity. Fig. 1 shows the flow-chart of the application of the garment style design system in E-commerce.

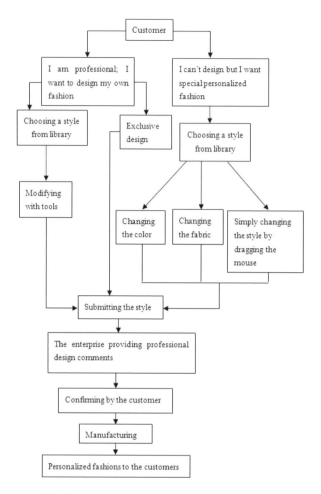

Fig. 1. Style design system application flow-chart

3 Application of Pattern Design System in Garment E-Commerce

The application of pattern design system in garment E-commerce is harder than that of the style design system as besides professionals, people have no idea about drawing fashion patterns, which means the pattern design system is only oriented to professional fashion-related people. It is the main reason that why the pattern system is not universally applied in E-commerce. But with research, the author finds that it is not impossible to apply professional pattern design system in garment E-commerce.

Figure 2 contains a well-known online garment CAD software shopping mall. Mainly orienting at customers interested in DIY fashion, it sells electronic and material patterns. Figure 3 is a screen shot of a pattern sold on Taobao, the biggest online shopping website. The picture only shows part of it. It could be concluded that first, there is a customer group with professional garment knowledge existed interested in

DIY fashion, and oriented at this group there is feasibility developing pattern design system in E-commerce. Second, there are some business opportunities to be developed in E-commerce because in the production of the finished patterns sold on the some software shopping malls or Taobao website, the customers' interactivity is missing.

Actually, selling patterns to the customers enjoying DIY fashions has been existing for a long time. The difference is, in the earlier age, the patterns and product numbers

Fig. 2. Online shopping mall

女装裁剪1:1纸样 W016 Jorinde西装（ 36-44 ）

¥ 2.49 最近成交2笔   运费:10.00

Fig. 3. Screen shot of a pattern sold on Taobao

were published on magazines, as per which the customers would make their selections and order from the manufactures. Fig.4 shows the sales mode in early age. It could be found that the sales process teaks a long period: pattern design-publishing the pattern on magazine-customer making selection-customer making feedback to the enterprise via phone or mail-enterprise mailing the pattern to the customers. In addition, because the magazine price and layout limitation, there was a limit in the pattern selection, and it could not satisfy the customers needs in regarding of following the fashion and developing individuality. Fig.5 is the sales flow-chart of patterns on Taobao and Risheng website. Apparently, because of the bigger and bigger storage capacity of the server and web browsing capability of the computers, the customers could browse lots of patterns in a short time and feedback to the sellers the order information immediately by clicking the mouse. It only takes a few minutes to transfer the patterns from the sellers to the customers.

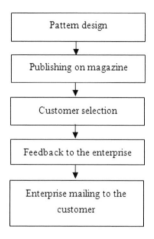

Fig. 4. The pattern sales mode in early age

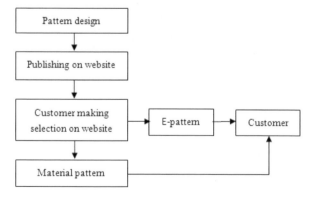

Fig. 5. The present sales flow-chart of patterns

However, the present sales mode still has some weakness. First of all, the customers are only able to choose from the existed styles and patterns so the interactivity in style design and pattern design is missing. Secondly, the sizes are graded according to international standards, which ignores special requirements. Enterprises possessing garment CAD software have more advantages regarding custom-tailor in developing pattern E-commerce as the supplementation of garment E-commerce. Supported by garment E-commerce platform, garment enterprises only need to do a little technical work to develop pattern E-commerce. Additionally, garment enterprises have richer and more powerful style database, what is more, the garment enterprises have more professional style designer and patter designer. For the garment enterprises engaged in E-commerce, developing garment pattern E-commerce brings the following benefits:

1) Satisfying the customers' needs by the greater extent. As we know, a set of garment CAD software is very costly, so it is impossible for the customers who are interested in fashion only as a personal hobby to buy. The customers could modify the patterns as per their own preference by operating on the internet. It only cost the customers a little bit of money. Through modifying, the styles are not only better fit their figures but also meet their preference. The customer could buy the fabric in the colors that they like.

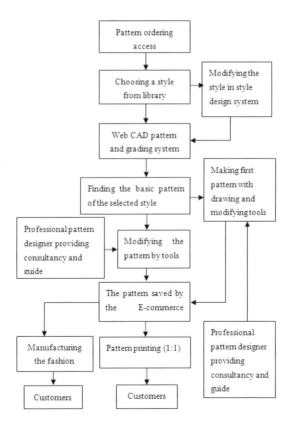

Fig. 6. The application of Pattern Design flow-chart of patterns

2) For garment enterprises, by developing garment pattern E-commerce, the utilization rate of the garment CAD system purchased at a high price could be increased to the greatest extent and the marketing channel could be extended and then more customers will be attracted so that the enterprise's profits is increased.

Therefore, equipped with hardware and software, the enterprises could develop garment pattern E-commerce as the supplementation of custom-tailor system. For garment enterprises, developing pattern E-commerce could be completed by using their garment E-commerce platform and garment CAD pattern design system. The flow-chart of applying CAD pattern design system into E-commerce in Fig 6 is designed for reference.

4 Conclusion

Summarizing above, the conclusion is as below:

3) It is feasible to apply mature garment CAD style system and pattern design system in garment E-commerce which could enhance the utilization rate of the costly garment CAD system and meanwhile promote the quality of the garment E-commerce service as well as increase the benefit of the enterprise.

4) Based on customer types, the garment CAD style design system in E-commerce has two platforms, i.e. complete platform and incomplete platform to meet the requirements of different types of customers.

5) Pattern E-commerce could be developed through extending the business and service scope of garment E-commerce. In pattern E-commerce, the mature garment CAD pattern design system could be fully used.

References

1. Reimers, K., Li, M., Chen, G.: A Multi-Level Approach for Devising Effective B2B E-Commerce Development Strategies with an Application to the Case of China. Electronic Commerce Research 4(3), 287–305 (2004)
2. Song, H.: Analyzing B2B2C Model of Garment E-business. Shandong Textile Econom. (5), 83–86 (2010)
3. Chang, l., Zhang, X.: Interactive 3D body scanner system and application in apparel industry. Melliand China (4), 76–79 (2010)
4. Zhang, H., Zhang, A., Guo, J.: Analisis on the Application Situation and Devlopment Trend of China Garment E-commerce. Market Modenlization 591(10), 24–25 (2009)
5. Pan, L., Zhang, H.: Analysis on Grament Sales Mode and Main Issues in E-economy. Market Modenlization 491(10), 107–108 (2007)

Sentence-Level Sentiment Analysis via Sequence Modeling

Xiaohua Liu[1,2] and Ming Zhou[2]

[1] School of Computer Science and Technology Harbin Institute of Technology
[2] Microsoft Research Asia, Beijing, China
XiaohuaLiu@163.com

Abstract. This paper presents a method of improving the performance of sentence-level sentiment analysis. Sentiment analysis is generally understood as a task that requires a deep understanding of the sentence structure (e.g., word order and non-local dependency). To attack this problem without the sentence parsing, we propose a novel approach that decomposes a sentence into a series of sub-sequences. Sentence-level polarity is then determined by classifying within sub-sequences and by fusing the obtained sub-sequences polarities. Extensive evaluations are conducted on one benchmark dataset for sentence polarity detection. Experimental results show that the performance of our proposed method outperforms two baselines based on Support Vector Machines (SVMs) and Logistic Regression (LR), respectively.

Keywords: Sentiment Analysis, Sequential Labeling, Polarity.

1 Introduction

The problem of how to discover sentiment orientation or polarity has received considerable attention for both research and practical application purposes. For example, Matsumoto, et al. [1] proposed to construct a dependency tree for each review sentence followed by pruning to sub-tree and analysis of the correlation between words prior to sentiment classification. Similarly, Arun Meena et al. [2] introduced the use of machine learning algorithms to find phrase-level polarity and then combined phrase-level results to decide the overall polarity of the sentence via incorporating the effects of the conjunctions; while Qu et al. [3] applied a sequential tagging technique to obtain the token polarity and then propagated the token-level predictions to sentence level using various heuristic rules. These recent works show that adding a linguistic dimension (word order, non-local syntactic or dependency relations between words) and fusing the token-level polarity to determine the overall polarity can make a substantial difference. But problems exist: First, parsing is time-consuming and only appropriate for formal sentences; second, fusing token-level polarity to get the sentence-level polarity by heuristic rules (e.g., majority voting) may not be effective, for example, two negative and one positive tokens does not necessarily mean the overall polarity is also negative.

J. Zhang (Ed.): ICAIC 2011, Part III, CCIS 226, pp. 337–343, 2011.

To solve these issues, we propose to model word order and non-local dependency in the given sentence by using contextual features and by fusing the token-level polarity in a more effective way through latent variable models.

The guiding principle is that sentence is decomposed into a serial of sub-sequences representations. The polarity detection of the given sentence is then achieved by classifying the within sequence and fusing the obtained sequences polarities. We instantiate a specific model of this idea: Hidden Conditional Random Fields (HCRFs). HCRFs optimize the overall sentiment by introducing a set of latent variables to implicitly model the latent sub-structure among the sequences polarities. Our method is evaluated on a widely used gold standard dataset, and achieves better results than two baselines based on linear SVMs and linear LR, respectively.

Our paper is organized as follows. Section 2 presents related work, Section 3 describes our method based on HCRFs. Section 4 shows the experimental results and analysis. Finally, conclusion and future work are discussed in section 5.

2   Related Work

A.   Word-Level Sentiment Analysis

Hatzivasiloglou et al. [4] applied a supervised learning method and a predefined list of seed adjectives to discover more adjectives with the same or opposite sentiment orientation according to textual patterns. Turney et al. [5] employed point-wise mutual information (PMI) and latent semantic indexing (LSI) to calculate the polarity of unknown words according to the co-occurrence statistics with the seed words.

B.   Phrase-Level Sentiment Analysis

Nasukawa et al. [6] used manually developed patterns to classify the contextual polarity of sentiment expressions toward specific items, yielding high precision, but low recall. Wilson et al. [7] used a two-phase approach: detecting whether a phrase is polar or neutral; and in the case of a polar phrase, disambiguated its polarity about a target by using a predefined polarity shifter.

C.   Sentence-Level Sentiment Analysis

Other research classifies the sentiments on sentence level. Yu and Hatzivassiloglou [8], Kim and Hovy [9], Hu and Liu [10], and Grefenstette et al. [11] all began by first creating prior-polarity lexicons. Yu and Hatzivassiloglou [8] then assigned a sentiment to a sentence by averaging the prior semantic orientations of instances of lexicon words in the sentence. Thus, they did not identify the contextual polarity of individual phrases containing clues. Kim et al. [9], Hu et al. [10] and Grefenstette et al. [11] multiplied or counted the prior polarities of clue instances in the sentence. They also considered local negation to reverse polarity, and they restricted their tags to positive and negative. In addition, their systems assigned one sentiment per sentence. Arun Meena et al. [2] introduced the use of machine learning algorithms to find phrase-level polarity and then combined them to get the overall polarity of the sentence by incorporating the effects of conjunctions.

D. Document-Level Sentiment Analysis

Pang et al. [12] tried to classify movie reviews into positive/negative using three different classifiers – Naive Bayes, Maximum Entropy and SVMs. They tested different feature combinations including unigrams, unigrams+bigrams and unigrams+POS (part-of-speech) tags, etc. The experimental results showed that SVM combined with unigrams gave the best performance. In their recent work [13], they added subjectivity detection to prevent the sentiment classifier from dealing with irrelevant "objective" sentences. Nigam and Hurst [13] applied simple online classifier Winnow for classifying document polarity.

3 Our Method

The basic idea of our proposed method is to formulate sentence-level sentiment classification task as a sequence labeling problem. However, unlike the traditional sequence labeling scenario like part-of-speech tagging and information extraction, the observation sequence is assigned a single class label instead of a label sequence. We first decompose the input observation sequence into a sequence of sub-views. The class label of an input observation sequence is then achieved by classifying the sub-sequences and fusing the produced sub-labels through hidden conditional random fields (HCRFs).

A. Framework

HCRFs are extended from the Conditional Random Fields (CRFs) by introducing a set of hidden variables. For HCRFs, the hidden variables allows for capturing word dependency and internal sub-structure in the observation sequence, and only one class label is assigned to the entire sequence. HCRFs have been successfully applied in computer vision and speech recognition as well as natural language processing.

The goal of hidden conditional random fields (HCRFs) is to model the conditional probability of a single class label y given an observation sequence $x = \{x_1, x_2, ..., x_m\}$, where $y \in Y$, a predefined set of discrete labels and each local observation is represented by a feature vector or word tokens. For a labeled example pair (x, y), a vector of latent variables $h = \{h_1, h_2, ..., h_m\}$ is introduced to model the internal sub-structure. Each $h_j \in H$ which is a finite set of unobservable, hidden labels. Given the definitions of class labels, observations and latent variables, a conditional probabilistic model is defined:

$$
\begin{aligned}
P(y \mid x, \lambda) &= \sum_h P(y, h \mid x, \lambda) \\
&= \frac{1}{Z(x)} \sum_{h \in y} \exp(\lambda \cdot f(y, h, x))
\end{aligned}
$$

(1)

Here λ are the parameters of the probabilistic model, $f(y, h, x)$ is a set of feature functions, and $Z(x)$ is the normalizing factor which ensures its probabilistic characteristics.

B.   Framework

Given a set of labeled examples, following objective function is used to estimate the parameters required by the probabilistic model.

$$L(\lambda) = \sum_i \log P(y_i \mid x_i, \lambda) - \frac{1}{2\sigma^2}\|\lambda\|^2$$

$$= \log\left(\frac{\sum_h e^{\psi(y,h,x,\lambda)}}{\sum_{y',h} e^{\psi(y',h,x,\lambda)}}\right) - \frac{1}{2\sigma^2}\|\lambda\|^2 \tag{2}$$

Here the first term is the conditional log-likelihood of the training data; the second term is the prior distribution of the parameters aiming to avoid the over-fitting. The commonly-used prior is the zero-mean Gaussian with the variance σ.

We encode the structural constraints with an undirected graph structure, where the hidden variables $h = \{h_1, h_2, ..., h_m\}$ correspond to some vertices in the graph. The set of edges $(j, k) \in E$ in the graph denote relationship between variables h_j and h_k. Intuitively, the graph E can be arbitrary and should capture the domain-specific knowledge.

Quasi-Newton gradient ascent method such as L-BFGS can be used to search for the optimal parameters λ.

C.   Inference

In test stage, we calculate the most possible class label that maximizes the conditional model:

$$y^* = \arg\max_y P(y \mid x, \lambda) \tag{3}$$

4   Experiments

We evaluate our method on the "Sentence Subjectivity Dataset v1.0" created by Pang and Lee, which consists of contains 5331 positive and 5331 negative processed sentences with all objective sentences removed. In our experiments, 80% of data are used for training and the remaining for test.

A.   Evaluation Metrics

We use the precision P and the recall R to evaluate the performance, as defined below:

$$P = \frac{TP}{TP+FP}, \quad R = \frac{TP}{TP+FN}. \tag{4}$$

Here *TP, FP, FN* represent the number of true positive, false positive and false negative, respectively.

B. Settings

LR and SVMs based on bag-of-words model are used as the baseline methods. After empirical studies, linear kernel is selected for both LR and SVMs due to its better performance compared to other kernels such as Gaussian and Sigmoid kernel. To determine the optimal value of the penalty factor used in linear LR and linear SVMs, 5-fold cross validation is conducted. Since there is no class-imbalance problem in our study, the class-dependent weight is set to default value.

For sub-view representation, we examined two granularities, word level and phrase level. In both cases, the overall sentiment of the sentence is achieved by combining the sentiment of words and phrases respectively.

To verify the fact that long-range, non-local dependency between words and phrases may have impact on the sentiment analysis, we designed the contextual features (e.g., several words before and after the current word token) and the feature template is defined as $\{w_{i-2}, w_{i-1}, w_i, w_{i+1}, w_{i+2}\}$, where w_i is the current word. And non-contextual features do not consider the surrounding information.

Stop word removing is not performed because most of the stop words are conjunctions (like, if and however, etc.) and valence shifters (negations, intensifiers and diminishes) which may substantially affect the overall sentiment of the sentences.

C. Results

Table 1 shows the performance comparison using different classifiers and different features on this dataset.

Table 1. Experimental Results

	Word level		Phrase level	
	P	R	P	R
Linear LR	0.7415	0.7536	0.714	0.7289
Linear SVM	0.7409	0.7506	0.706	0.7144
Non-contextual HCRFs	0.746	0.7509	0.7463	0.7380
Contextual HCRFs	0.8294	0.8310	0.8340	0.8470

From Table 1, we can see that HCRFs using contextual features yield better results than using the non-contextual features, indicating that long-range, non-local dependency in the observation is essential to determine the sentence level polarity.

In addition, sentence-level sentiment classification based on the combination of sentiments associated with the words or phrases can significantly outperform the bag-of-words model (unigram linear LR and unigram linear SVMs), suggesting that each sentence may have multiple semantic units with different sentiments and the overall sentiments is determined by the interaction of sentiment on more finer-grained levels.

It is also shown that HCRFs consistently yield better results based on the same feature setting, indicating that the classification performance can be effectively improved by introducing latent or hidden variables to capture intermediate or internal sub-structures polarities. By using contextual features, HCRFs can achieve a performance comparable to what is reported in Arun Meena et al. [2]. For example, in *"dark and disturbing, but also surprisingly funny."*, the pattern (positive but negative means overall negative) can be naturally learned by exploiting the compatibility between word dependency and hidden variables as well as the internal sub-structure between hidden variables to find the optimal overall sentiment.

Finally, it can be seen that, in most cases, combing phrase-level polarities yields better results than word-level, suggesting that phrase-level polarity is much less ambiguous than word-level polarity in English language. For example, *"break"* is a neutral word, but *"break the law"* is negative, and *"break the record"* is positive.

5   Conclusion and Future Work

This paper investigates the problem of sentence-level sentiment classification. To tackle this issue, we propose HCRFs, which can capture the long-range, non-local dependency in the observation sequence to determine the overall sentiment without sentence parsing. In addition, instead of using simple heuristic rules to combine the token-level polarities, HCRFs optimizes the overall sentiment by introducing a set of latent variables to implicitly model the latent sub-structure among the token-level polarities. Experimental results show that our proposed method achieves better result than two baselines based on SVMs and LR, respectively. One disadvantage of our approach is that the initial sentiment lexicon is ignored though it may provide more reliable and obvious clue for token-level polarity determination. In the future, we will consider incorporating the predefined sentiment lexicon as prior knowledge to further boost the sentence-level sentiment analysis performance.

References

1. Matsumoto, S., Takamura, H., Okumura, M.: Sentiment classification using word sub-sequences and dependency sub-trees. In: Ho, T.-B., Cheung, D., Liu, H. (eds.) PAKDD 2005. LNCS (LNAI), vol. 3518, pp. 301–311. Springer, Heidelberg (2005)
2. Meena, A., Prabhakar, T.V.: Sentence Level Sentiment Analysis in the Presence of Conjuncts Using Linguistic Analysis. In: Amati, G., Carpineto, C., Romano, G. (eds.) ECiR 2007. LNCS, vol. 4425, pp. 573–580. Springer, Heidelberg (2007)
3. Qu, L., Toprak, C., Jakob, N., Gurevych, I.: Sentence Level Subjectivity and Senti-ment Analysis Experiments in NTCIR-7 MOAT Challenge. In: Proceedings of NTCIR-7 Workshop Meeting, pp. 210–217 (2007)
4. Hatzivassiloglou, V., McKeown, K.R.: Predicting the Semantic Orientation of Adjectives. In: Proceedings of the 35th Annual Meeting of the ACL and the 8th Conference of the European Chapter of the ACL, pp. 174–181. Association for Computational Linguistics, Madrid (1997)
5. Turney, P.D., Littman, M.L.: Measuring praise and criticism: Inference of semantic orientation from association. ACM Transactions on Information Systems (TOIS) 21(4), 315–346 (2003) (NRC #46516)

6. Nasukawa, T., Yi, J.: Sentiment analysis: capturing favorability using natural language processing. K-CAP, 70–77 (2003)
7. Wilson, T., Wiebe, J., Hoffmann, P.: Recognizing contextual polarity in phrase-level sentiment analysis. In: Proceedings of the Human Language Technology Conference and the Conference on Empirical Methods in Natural Language Processing (HLT/EMNLP), pp. 347–354 (2005)
8. Yu, H., Hatzivassiloglou, V.: Towards answering opinion questions: Separating facts from opinions and identifying the polarity of opinion sentences. In: Proceedings of the 2003 Conference on Empirical Methods in Natural Language Processing (EMNLP-2003), pp. 129–136 (2003)
9. Kim, S.-M., Hovy, E.: Determining the sentiment of opinions. In: Proceedings of COLING 2004 (2004)
10. Hu, M., Liu, B.: Mining and summarizing customer reviews. In: KDD-2004 (2004)
11. Grefenstette, G., Qu, Y., Shanahan, J.G., Evans, D.A.: Coupling niche browsers and affect analysis for an opinion mining application.In: RIAO-2004 (2004)
12. Pang, B., Lee, L., Vaithyanathan, S.: Thumbs up? Sentiment classification using ma-chine learning techniques. In: Proceedings of the Conference on Empirical Methods in Natural Language Processing (EMNLP-2002), pp. 79–86 (2002)
13. Pang, B., Lee, L.: A sentimental education: Sentiment analysis using subjectivity summarization based on minimum cuts. In: Proceedings of 42nd Meeting of the Association for Computational Linguistics (ACL-2004), pp. 271–278 (2004)
14. Nigam, K., Hurst, M.: Towards a Robust Metric of Opinion. In: AAAI Spring Symposium on Exploring Attitude and Affect in Text (2004)

The Application of Norton Ghost Multicast Technology in the Maintenance of College Computer Room

Li Jinhui[1], Yang Hongwei[1], Zhu Yong[1], and Zhang Ke[2,*]

[1] College of Information and Electrical Engineering,
Shenyang Agricultural University,
Shenyang, China
[2] School of Policedog Technique of MPS,
Shenyang, China
yanghw2011@sogou.com

Abstract. Computer system maintenance is an important component in network room management. For the complexity and different hardware configuration of University computer room, the Norton Ghost Multicast technology is used to implement the different methods and techniques under different hardware environments in this paper. especially the specific implementation steps for the establishment and running of other important links are given, and the advantages and disadvantages of each method and applicable environment are analyzed and compared, providing some convenient ways for fully tapping the potential of existing hardware resources and effectively solving some problems for the difficult system maintenance of college network computer room, in practice, it achieved good results.

Keywords: Ghost Multicast technology, remote cloning, server, client.

1 Introduction

With the continues development of network and multimedia technology, a lot of teaching missions of computer network are undertook by school computer room, and system software, multimedia educational software, simulation exercises and other software require constant updates and upgrades; meanwhile, because virus attacks and improper using computer resulting in system crash, the crash phenomena have occurred, so it is required the frequent upgrades and updates by system. However, as the new and old degree of various computers and quite different hardware targets, resulting in many difficulties and inconvenience for school computer room installation and recovery system. Thus, it is a worth considering and research subject of each system administrator for the problems, such as how to tap the potential of existing computers to make the old computer became new and seek a convenient way to quickly install the system to ensure the normal running of the computer in a short time.

---

* Corresponding author.

J. Zhang (Ed.): ICAIC 2011, Part III, CCIS 226, pp. 344–351, 2011.

Norton Ghost software developed by Symantec is the most popular tool software for system recovery with powerful function and the most users. Thus, according to different hardware environments, the different GHOST cloning technology is used masterly to make system recovery and upgrade, and obtained good results, ensuring the normal development of the school computer room teaching.

2   The Features and the Basic Working Principle of Norton Ghost Multicast Technology

The so-called Norton Ghost Network multicast feature is actually to recover the image file in "master disk" through network bulk to all the workstations, after the students client is joined into the multicast clone task, a few dozen of or more machines can complete cloning task at the same time. At this point, the multicast server only need to send data one time without sending out the same data thousands of times, all the group members will automatically receive it, and the occupied network bandwidth is ruled, that is it can't occupy network bandwidth with the increasing of the numbers of client machines, effectively saving network bandwidth, and reducing the load of network and multicast server. Particularly in the case of the same configuration of each workstation, it can greatly reduce the workload of computer room managers. The basic working principle of network multicast technology is shown in Figure 1.

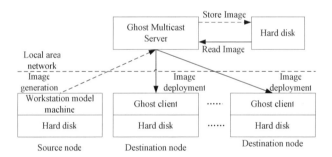

Fig. 1. The basic Working principle of network multicast technology

3   The Notes before GHOST Cloning

1. Create a medium size partition. If the partition is too small, the storage space of system files and teaching application software is not enough and the running speed of system is affected; if it is too large, the spaced will be wasted. When we make cloning image file we commonly use the form of partition cloning, for example, we only clone the content of system partition C disk. When GHO image file is recovered, the hard disk parameters of master and sub-machine should be required the same.

2. The NTFS format should be better applied when creating file system (master) preferably, ensuring its good stability when system runs.

3. The uncommon used software should be avoided to load when creating system, avoiding the image file cloned by Ghost is so large to affect the speed of system recovery.

4. It must be ensured that the system is not infected when producing system.

5. The system should be optimized by using Windows vista master before cloning, and the patches should be sustained, and the junk files and redundant information of registry should be cleaned. In addition, the disk of system partition should be perfected, ensuring that the cloned content is an optimized system image files.

6. If the cloning image files we created need be used in different hardware environments, and then when installing it also need to uninstall the related hardware information of "master", such as sound cards, video information, etc. Thus, when this GHO image file is used to recover to other hardware environment computer, the system can automatically find back the appropriate computer hardware configuration information, rather than the disorder of sub-machine system is caused by the hardware information of master.

7. The generation of image file (. gho). When "mother ship" is installed, execute GHOST.EXE order, according to partition or format of the whole disks to generate an image file (. gho); or directly generate image file (. gho) in server through GHOST 7.5 system.

4   The Basic Method of GHOST Cloning

A.   Clone the entire disk point-to-point

Point -to-point (disk and disk) between is the most basic cloning method of cloning. First install a "master (the original disk)", and then use Ghost cloning software to clone the contents of the original disk entirely to the target disk. When using the method of cloning, the capacity of the two hard disks require the same capacity, otherwise it will produce disk data error when recovering system. Meanwhile, when placing the two hard disks, it must pay attention to the installation order of the original disk and the target disk, once the mistake is made, it will result in irreparable damage. The greatest advantage of this method is it does not need to generate GHO image files, as it can directly be cloned between the two disks, which can be commonly used in the cloning between the same parameters and less machines.

B.   Back up GHO image file to the hard disk, and write protection to D disk.

Firstly install a "model machine", and use Ghost software to backup system partition to gho image file, and then copy the file to D disk (or other disks) in other "empty machine", and write protection to D disk by using the method of software, and then recover system partition of single-machine one by one. Although it is independent between machines when recovering system, it costs a long time to back up the cloned gho image file to the target disk, especially for the computer room which often needs to upgrade system. This method is suitable for system with fewer upgrades, but because of virus infection, students' machine improper using resulting in system crash and need to recover system by single-machine, especially it is a good choice for the computer room without internet.

5   The Realization of GHOST Multicast Clone by Using Server

A.   The creation of server

1)   Create Windows 2000 Advance Server.
Implement the setup.exe command of Windows 2000 Advance Server installation disk, and follow the tips until the end of running.

2)   Configure server and protocol
   a) Configure a variety of network protocols to server. Such as: Nwlink IPX / SPX, NetBIOS, NetBEUI, etc.

   b) Set TCP / IP protocol. There is a case study of the computer center of Shenyang Agricultural University, we set the server IP address as: 210.47.168.169, subnet mask: 255.255.254.0, gateway: 210.47.168.1, DNS server: 210.47.160.2.

   c) Add necessary services. Such as DHCP services, DNS services and WIND services.

   d) Upgrade server as "primary domain server". Set DNS domain name server as: syau.edu.cn, and set NetBIOS name as syau.edu.

   e) Configure DHCP server of Windows 2000 Advance Server

Create a new scope to assign dynamic IP address for client machine in the DHCP. In the new created scope, taking into account generally IP address should contain a number of segments, so the range of dynamic IP address can be set as: 210.47.168.11 ~ 210.47.169.250, subnet mask: 255.255.254.0, gateway: 210.47.168.1, domain: syau.edu.cn, Server Name: SERVER, server IP address: 210.47.168.196 (Note: This IP is not included in a dynamic IP address but it should be in the same segment.), and add to the list.

B.   Install remote Cloning software in server

After installing the server, execute the setup.exe command of GHOST 7.5 cloning software, and follow the tips until the end of running.
   Set floppy drive, network card, DHCP during installation. As are shown in Figure 2, Figure 3 and Figure 4.

Fig. 2. Floppy settings

Fig. 3. Network card settings

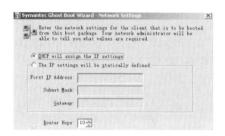

Fig. 4. DUCP settings

C. Client settings

As the various kinds of current hardware environment and large different of machine index in college computer rooms, the methods of client remote connection server are also different. Thus, there are some methods of client connection server.

1) Make floppy disk into static IP boot disk to start and connect to server

a) Start server, click "Start" "Program", "Symantec Ghost", "Ghost Boot Wizard" enter creation wizard of GHOST 7.5 client boot disk, select "Network Boot Disk", following the tips to create static IP boot disk of a specific NIC (such as 8139 NIC), as is shown in Figure 1 and Figure 2. Startup disk of floppy disk includes ATTCP.CFG, PROTOCOL.INI and the corresponding NIC drivers, etc. We take Realtek RTL8139 PCI NIC as an example to list the contents of the WATTCP.CFG in floppy boot disk.

IP = 210.47.168.196
NETMASK = 255.255.254.0
GATEWAY = 210.47.168.1

Note: You must ensure that the last paragraph of ip in each .cfg file is different; but other parts are the same!

b) Start GhostCast Server of Ghost 7.5 in server, fill one name in "Session Name" as simple as possible, for example, you can fill in "a", but you should remember it, because you should fill the same name in client.

c) Select "Load To clients" in multicast launch menu, and select the finished .gho image file in "Image", and load the image package to the client.

d) Determine the cloning way: Disk or Partition.

e) Execute Accept Client command, start to accept client's request.

f) Start the finished floppy disk to start the remote boot disk in client, connect to the server GHOST cloning system, select "Multicasting", fill in the task name of server, such as "a", then the client starts to connect with server to obtain the detail information of the current ghost package, such as file size, geographical, partition, etc.

g) When all the client is ready, send "Send" command in server, then the network ghost multicast launch starts really. The client information of server can be seen, such as the machine's IP address and other information.

When we use this method to guide remote clone system, each disk needs independent IP addresses, and the value must be within the range of the DHCP server settings. When system enters to remote cloning, each client's running situation can be seen directly. Its greatest advantage is use GHOST Multicast technology to make remote cloning in some machines and dozens of machines, rather than decreasing the running speed of system with the increase of clients' number. Meanwhile, when running the system, multiple tasks can be operated together, thus greatly improving the speed of the computer room system recovery. However, its limitations are that it needs more floppy disks when there are so many clients, especially when the floppy disk drive is damaged, the other method should be used for processing.

2) Create floppy boot disk to dynamic IP boot disk to connect server.

At present, take the computer teaching and research section of Shenyang Agricultural University as example, there are more than 450 machines, so the task of system maintenance is very large, the installation and recovery of computer room system often are near various important examinations, and the students become more at that time. To make students have enough computer time before exams and don't conflict with the IP address of the machine students use when installing system, the dynamic IP address distribution is used both in DHCP server settings and creation of remote boot floppy. Thus, it can provide more computer using hours to maximum extent.

This method is made floppy guide disk into dynamic IP address to connect server remotely based on the above method. Its creation of floppy boot disk and running of remote cloning is similar with the above introduced methods. Compare with the above methods, its advantage is: during the implementation process, the remote cloning system can automatically search the unused IP address and allocate to client in LAN, thus it will not cause the phenomenon of IP address conflicts. The same floppy disk can be used repeatedly, greatly reducing too much trouble of the floppy disk, which is easier and simpler than the previous one.

3) Use dynamic virtual floppy drive to start and connect server

As we know, the above two methods need the support of floppy, once the floppy drive doesn't work, it cannot be used. Most of the floppy drives of the early machine in various colleges are damaged, therefore, on this basis, we will make floppy remote boot disk into virtual floppy disk and hang it on DOS boot menu, once it needs, it will use virtual disk to directly connect server to realize remote cloning. The method is to use floppy virtual boot floppy to make a DOS boot menu, and set the contents of above dynamic IP boot disk to contents of virtual floppy boot. When starting system, users can select different startup method according to different boot methods. Compared with the above two methods, the greatest advantage is: system runs completely without floppy drive support, and its process is much simpler and easier.

For those early bought machines, the above three methods, especially the old machines with lower hardware configuration, NIC without remote chip and seriously damaged hardware, are all the very good way, opening up a shortcut to make old machines become youthful.

4) Use NIC to remotely start and guide connection server

It uses NIC to remotely boot the function of chip to connect server, the realization of multicast cloning is another advanced measure for college computer room in old machines, thus, we can combine the advantages of the above three methods and the characteristics of NIC remote chip to establish further remote cloning system. In practice, we take Realtek RTL8139 PCI NIC as an example, establishing Intel PXE-based remote multicast cloning system, and using it in system management of computer room, which obtains good results.

The server of Intel PXE-based remote multicast cloning system need to add some additional operation steps based on the establishment of the front server.

  a) Install Intel PXE PDK.

  b) Configure Intel PXE PDK. Such as: proxyDHCP Server, Configure proxyDHCP Server, Client Options, Add to Bootserver Discovery List, etc., making it default to start remotely in the way of PXE when starting machines in student-side.

  c) Upload and start files to server.

The ultimate purpose of the establishment of system is to automatically log on to the remote cloning system of server through PXE remote boot, so this step is the most important one. Specifically: put the boot disk of the front created dynamic IP into floppy drive, implement Mkimage.exe program to generate image file TEST.BIN, and copy it into DOSUNDI folder, and changed its name to: DOSUNDI.1.

Finally, set the startup mode of students-side NIC. Designate the boot chip of NIC PXE boot mode in student-side, and it often is guided by NIC when setting and starting. After starting server, it will connect to the remote cloning system of server automatically when starting in student-side. After selecting the corresponding image file, it will enter into the multicast state of hardware. Meanwhile, in multicast server all the stations' IP address can be displayed in the list, then press Send button to start the multicast work, as is shown in Figure 5. Thus, it is found that the workstation has begun to clone data. Besides, each multicast workstation-side will also automatically start to accept the image file for the recovery work of this machine.

This method is the combination of the three above methods, which is much more stable, secure, fast in the process of system running, and the operation in client is easier and simpler.

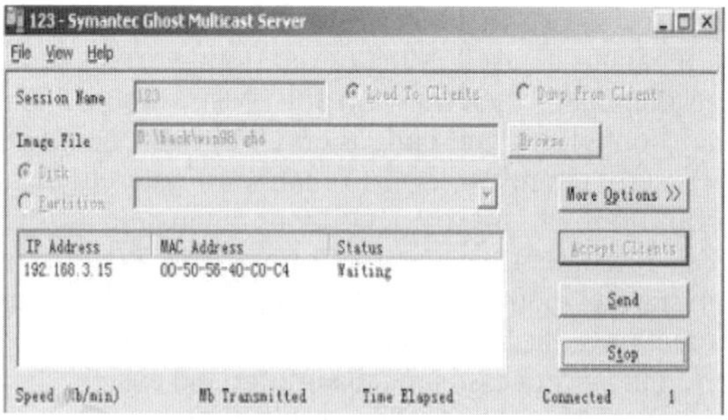

Fig. 5. Multicast servers send data

6   Conclusion

Recent years, the author connects with all kinds of different hardware indicators in management work of college computer room, and attempts various kinds of ways and methods of system management, accumulating some experience and uses it to system maintenance of network computer room. Especially the implementation and application of Norton Ghost network multicast technology, greatly improving the efficiency of system maintenance. It can be completed by one person in one or two hour which need one more person to complete one more days, and it withstands the test in all levels of computer examinations and routine system upgrade to achieve its expected purpose and ensure normal computer network teaching in university.

References

1. Li, T.: The Application of DHCP + GHOST for Fast Implementing Computer Room Maintenance based on PXE. Experiment Science and Technology (2) (2006)
2. Li, W.: The Security and Management of Computer Network. Tsinghua University Press, Beijing (2004)
3. Qi, D.: Network and Information Resources Management, pp. 368–375. Beijing Hope Electronic Press, Beijing (2005)
4. Lin, G., Xiang, J.: The Application of Network Cloning Technology in the Computer Room Management. Computer Knowledge and Technology 8(5), 47–53 (2006)
5. Li, W.: The Detailed Parameters of Ghost and Its Application. Heilongjiang Meteorology (2), 35–35 (2005)
6. Peng, P.: The Fast Recovery System of LAN based on GHOST. Journal of Jianghan Petroleum University of Staff and Workers (11), 94–96 (2009)

Simulating Working Memory Guiding Visual Attention for Capturing Target by Computational Cognitive Model[*]

Rifeng Wang[1,2]

[1] The International WIC Institute Beijing University of Technology,
Beijing, China
[2] Department of Computer Science Guangxi University of Technology,
Liuzhou, China
rifengwang@yahoo.cn

Abstract. There are two opposite views on whether working memory can guide visual attention. Some researchers have reported that the contents of working memory guide visual attention for capturing target efficiently. However, others reported that they could not find any evidence of attention capture by working memory. In this study, it tried to find evidence for the first view with computer simulation. Two models based on two hypotheses were set up in simulating the simplified 4×4 Sudoku problem solving by which an fMRI (functional Magnetic Resonance Imaging) experiment was performed at the same time. One model is based on working memory guiding visual selective attention assumption while the other is based on no guiding random attention assumption. Both of the models predict the response time (RT) and blood oxygenation level-dependent (BOLD) response. Cognitive cost analysis on the predictions shows that more cost was occupied on no guiding model resulting in more differences between fMRI real data and predictions while the other can reduce the cost and get good fitness. This study confirms the first view and shows that working memory guiding visual search for capturing target is the intelligence of human brain in reducing the cognitive cost.

Keywords: Working memory, visual attention, cost analysis, computational cognitive model.

1 Introduction

The interaction of visual attention and working memory has been studying for so many years [1-15]. And there are two main competitive options on it. Some researchers have reported that the contents of working memory guide visual search for capturing target efficiently [1-11]. In contrast to this view, others reported that they could not find any evidence of attention capture by working memory [12-15]. In the present study, we tried to find evidence for the first view with computer simulation. The difference between our study and others is in following: firstly, our evidence is from

---
[*] This work is partially supported by NSF of China Grant No.60875075, Master Foundation of Guangxi University of Technology under Grant No. 0816220.

J. Zhang (Ed.): ICAIC 2011, Part III, CCIS 226, pp. 352–359, 2011.

computational cognitive model based on the information processing theory [16, 19]; secondly, cognitive cost was proposed firstly to understand the function of human brain; thirdly, we explain the reason why working memory can guide visual attention. The contributions of this paper involve as follows: 1) Two compared computational cognitive model were built based on two assumptions; 2) An fMRI (functional Magnetic Resonance Imaging) experiment was performed to get the real data on response time and BOLD (Blood Oxygenation Level-Dependent) response; 3) Cost of cognition was analyzed on both time cost and BOLD; 4) Evidences were got from the result of cognitive model combined with fMRI experiment; 5) More Interprets were given to confirm the view of working memory guiding visual attention capturing targets.

2   Method

A. Paradigm: Simplified 4×4 Sudoku

A 4×4 Sudoku puzzle is used as the paradigm of our study. As shown in figure 1, they are 4×4 matrixes where there are 4 rows, 4 columns and 4 boxes. Boxes are those divided by two midlines of the matrix. For controlling the strategies that participants use, we simplified the puzzle and participants only need to find the answer of one grid marked with "?". The task of the puzzle is to fill the grid of "?" with one of 1, 2, 3 and 4 according to the rule that each row, each column and each box are filled with these digits once only.

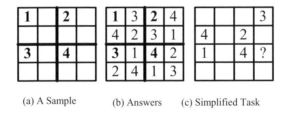

(a) A Sample   (b) Answers   (c) Simplified Task

Fig. 1. Simplified 4×4 Sudoku

B. fMRI experiment

As an advanced brain imaging techniques, the advantages of fMRI over competing techniques include whole brain coverage, non-interference of spatially separate activation sites, as well as good spatial resolution [24]. Our target of fMRI experiment is to get the brain activity on predefined regions during subjects performs the tasks and to fit with the predictions of ACT-R. fMRI experiment took two steps. First, before fMRI scanning, all participants were trained to know the heuristics well. Second, the participants performed tasks in MRI scanner.

   The protocol of a scan trial is shown in Figure 2 where a trial began with an alerting stimulus presented for two second followed by a 4×4 Sudoku stimulus that stayed on the screen until the participant indicated they knew the answer or 20 seconds had elapsed. When participants found the answer of the problem, they pressed a key under the thumb of their right hands and then spoke out the answer. Then the Sudoku stimulus was cleared. Event-related fMRI data were collected by a gradient echo planar pulse acquisition on a Siemens 3T Trio Tim Scanner. Behavioural data and fMRI brain imaging data of 18 participants were collected at the same time. The results of fMRI experiment are introduced in section II(G).

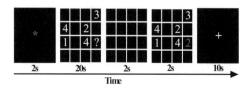

Fig. 2. The protocol of a scan trial in fMRI

C.   ACT-R computational cognitive model

As one of the most popular theory and computational model of human cognitive architecture [3-4], ACT-R proposes the systematical hypothesis on the basic structure of human cognitive system and functions of these structures in information processing to generate the human cognitive behavior and their associated BOLD response of brain regions. It is also a computer software platform for the development of computational models to quantitatively simulate and predict human behavior for a wide range of cognitive tasks. In ACT-R architecture, there are eight modules that correspond to human capacities, include visual model, goal model, declarative model, imaginal model, procedural model, vocal model, aural model and manual model. For example, visual module records the visual attention and goal module records the goal and control state. These modules are integrated to produce coherent cognition in problem solving. Furthermore, these modules are associated with distinct regions demonstrated from a series of psychology experiments where operations on visual module reflect on the activity of fusiform gyrus (FG) and goal module on anterior cingulate cortex (ACC) etc.. Accordingly, BOLD responses on these regions can be predicted from the activity of related modules [17]. So ACT-R is a good tool to investigate how subjects finish solving complex cognitive tasks in both behavior and function of human brain.

D.   Two assumptions for capturing "?

In this study, we concern more about how participants find the "?" mark among the digits from the 4×4 Sudoku puzzle. As we know, it is the first step to solve the puzzle. Here, the "?" is looked as one character loaded into the working memory firstly when participant perform the puzzle. How do people find this mark of answer position quickly with their visual attention?   The goal of ACT-R simulation is tried to answer the question. There are two assumptions on the question:

- Assumption 1 (A1): Conforming to the view of working memory guiding visual attention, "?" was activated in working memory, after global glancing, and then "?" is captured directly by visual selective attention. We call it "guided attention".

- Assumption 2 (A2): Conforming to the opposite view against A1, the "?" is captured after 3 digits attention, (half digits in the puzzle), we call it "random attention".

E. ACT-R modeling

Based on above two assumptions, we set up two ACT-R models. As mentioned in section 2.2, modules in ACT-R architectures are integrated to produce coherent cognition. In our model, there are five modules used, including visual model, imaginal module, retrieval module, goal module and procedural module. The parameters of predicting behavioural data give the time cost for each operation in distinct module. As shown in table 1, it will take 185ms to finish a visual operation to attend one character in visual module, 500ms to present one character in imaginal module, 125ms to retrieval memory one time, 50ms to fire a production rule in procedural module and 50 ms to set a goal state, etc. These parameters are usual the same for many model. The parameters for predicting BOLD response involves BOLD_scale, BOLD_exponent and BOLD_magnitude, these three parameters are always different for distinct cognitive tasks. Different modules may be used different parameter. Here, scale, exponent and magnitude parameters are 1.5, 6, 0.9 in visual module and 2.5, 2, 0.9 in retrieval module respectively.

F. ACT-R predictions on response time and BOLD response

The whole processes of 4×4 Sudoku problem solving involve to search "?" firstly, and then to search the digit from the row or column or box of "?", last is to retrieval the answer. Both models simulate the whole processes. Apart from the first step, the rest of processes on solving the puzzle in both models are same. So the different assumptions may reduce the different results. Our goal is to test which of the both assumptions is more reasonable from the two model's prediction. As described above, each operation of module will take a fixed time in ACT-R and affect the percent change of BOLD response in predefined regions relating to the module. As shown in figure 3(b), the total time in answering the puzzle in model with assumption A1 (A1 in short) is 2.352 second and 3.767 second in A2. The percent change of BOLD response in two interesting predefined brain regions are shown in figure 4 (solid line). They are fusiform gyrus which is in relation to visual module and prefrontal in relation to retrieval module.

G. Fitness with ACT-R predictions into fMRI real data

Real data from fMRI experiment was collected, including the average time participant used to finish the puzzles and average percent change of BOLD response in predefined regions. 18 participants attended the experiment. 15 participant's data is qualified. The average response time in right answer is 2.4 second. Analyzed with NIS (NeuroImaging Software package, http://kraepelin.wpic.pitt.edu/nis/, the percent change of BOLD response in two interesting predefined brain regions are shown in figure4 (dotted line). To know more detail about fMRI experiment please refers to [21]. In relation to the prediction of ACT-R modeling, the difference of response time in model A1 is 48ms and 1367 in model A2, as shown in figure 3(a). And the deviation of percent change of BOLD response of visual model in model A1 is 0.09 and 0.11 in model A2., 0.04 in retrieval model of A1 and 0.11 in A2, respectively , as shown in figure 4 (a) and (b). These results show that model A1 is more reasonable and acceptable.

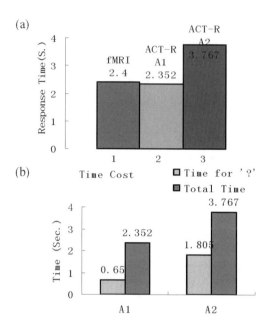

Fig. 3. RT predictions and Time

H. Cost analysis

From the fitness results above, we know that model with assumption of working memory guiding visual attention capturing target is more reasonable because it reduce the deviations between predictions and real data. Note that the time is the total time to finish the puzzle, including searching "?" and the digits, find the answer, etc. And the first step searching "?" will take some time. Figure 3(b) illustrated the percent change of searching "?" in the whole processes for both model. The time include not only visual time, but also imaginal time, goal control time, retrieval time and procedural time in searching "?". We can see that it is 28% in A1 and 48% in A2. It is not acceptable that it will take about 50% time to find "?" when solving the puzzle. And the proportion 28% is more acceptable. As we know, more operation more time and more time more percent change of BOLD response. So the deviation is larger in model A2.

3   Discussion

Apart from a few cases, most of the study supported the view of working memory guiding visual selective attention in capturing target quickly. How can human being have this property? There maybe two reasons that interpret it.

Firstly, the target in working memory may be keeping activation in the mind. When the target is a kind of material that somebody is familiar with or being retrieved frequently by participants recently, it will be activated easily, according to the memory theory of Prof. John Anderson [18]. Based on the theory, something that people want to find may load into his working memory and keep active until there is something to match with it. Give time short enough, for example, a glance, everybody can do that. Take the puzzle for example, as shown in figure 1, you can find the "?" with a glance without attention any other digits. You can try it if you don't believe. Don't forget to familiar with the rule of the puzzle before you try.

Secondly, the distraction may not share the room of working memory during visual search. Can we do that? Yes, our people can do it. This is reasoning from above opinion. The target is keeping activation that nothing else can load into working memory in a short time. Seeing nothing in people eye is a good figuration for this interprets. What will happen if everything in the scene of the eyes takes the room of our working memory? Even people try to, he may not do that. According to the existing research, the largest number of items that people can store in his working memory is not more than four [22]. Keeping the target in working memory and rejecting other distraction may be looked as some kind of control mechanism of human brain, as introduced by some researcher [23-25]. These two interprets are not difficult to understand. The key idea behind these interpret is that working memory guiding visual attention may reduce the cost of cognition. Changing the information of working memory frequently may cost more time or activate more change of BOLD and make the cognitive more complex.

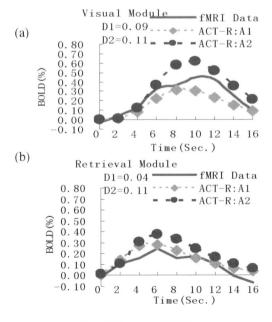

Fig. 4. Fitness of BOLD

4   Conclusions

Working memory guiding visual attention has been a long term hot issue in cognitive science. Most of the evidences for it are from the cognitive experiment. And interprets on the issue are always on the perspective of "the limit of input channel" which is abstract for people. As pointed out by Herbert A. Simon, computer simulation may be an effective way to scientific discovery [20]. In this paper, we obtained new evidence from the computation cognitive model. That is cognitive cost of information processing. This study shows that working memory guiding visual attention may be a principle of human mind that is superior to machine.

Acknowledgment. I would like to thank Xiang Jie for supporting experiment data in this study.

References

1. Desimone, R., Duncan, J.: Neural mechanisms of selective visual attention. Annual Review of Neuroscience 18, 193–222 (1995)
2. Fockert, J.W., Rees, G., Frith, C.D., Lavie, N.: The role of working memory in visual selective attention. Science 291(5509), 1803–1806 (2001)
3. Peterson, M.S., Kramer, A.F., Wang, R.F., et al.: Visual search has memory. Psychological Science 12, 287–292 (2001)
4. Pratt, J., Hommel, B.: Symbolic control of visual attention: the role of working memory and attentional control settings. Journal of Experimental Psychology: Human Perception and Performance 29, 835–845 (2003)
5. Soto, D., Humphreys, G.W.: Seeing the content of the mind: Enhanced awareness through working memory in patients with visual extinction. PNAS 103, 4789–4792 (2006)
6. Soto, D., Hodsoll, J.P., Rotshtein, P., Humphreys, G.: Automatic guidance of attention from working memory. Trends in Cognitive Sciences 12, 342–348 (2008)
7. Han, S.W., Kim, M.-S.: Do the Contents of Working Memory Capture Attention? Yes, But Cognitive Control Matters. Journal of Experimental Psychology: Human Perception and Performance 35(5), 1292–1302 (2009)
8. Olivers, C.N.L., Meijer, F., Theeuwes, J.: Feature-Based Memory-Driven Attentional Capture: Visual Working Memory Content Affects Visual Attention. Journal of Experimental Psychology: Human Perception and Performance 32(5), 1243–1265 (2006)
9. Downing, P.E.: Interactions between visual working memory and selective attention. Psychological Science 11, 467–473 (2000)
10. Oh, S.H., Kim, M.S.: The guidance effect of working memory load on visual search. Journal of Vision 3, 629 (2003)
11. Downing, P.E., Dodds, C.M.: Competition in visual working memory for control of search. Visual Cognition 11, 689–703 (2004)
12. Horowitz, T.S., Wolfe, J.M.: Visual search has no memory. Nature 394, 575–577 (1998)
13. Woodman, G.F., Luck, S.J.: Do the contents of visual working memory automatically influence attentional selection during visual search? Journal of Experimental Psychology: Human Perception and Performance 33, 363–377 (2007)
14. Woodman, G.F., Vogel, E.K., Luck, S.J.: Visual search remains efficient when visual working memory if full. Psychological Science 12, 219–224 (2001)

15. Han, S.H., Kim, M.S.: Visual search does not remain efficient when executive working memory is working. Psychological Science 15, 623–628 (2004)
16. Anderson, J.R., Bothell, D., Byrne, M.D., Douglass, S., Lebiere, C., Qin, Y.L.: An integrated theory of Mind. Psychological Review 111, 1036–1060 (2004)
17. Qin, Y.L., Sohn, M.H., Anderson, J.R., et al.: Predicting the practice effects on the blood oxygenation level-dependent (BOLD) function of fMRI in a symbolic manipulation task. PNAS (Proceedings of the National Academy of Sciences of the United States of America) 100(8), 4951–4956 (2003)
18. Anderson, J.R.: Retrieval of information from long-term memory. Science 220, 25–30 (1983)
19. Simon, H.A.: The information-processing theory of mind. American Psychologist 50(7), 507–508 (1995)
20. Bradshaw, G.L., Langley, P.W., Simon, H.A.: Studying scientific discovery by computer simulation. Science 222(4627), 971–975 (1983)
21. Wang, R.F., Xiang, J., Zhou, H.Y., Qin, Y.L., Zhong, N.: Simulating Human Heuristic Problem Solving: A Study by Combining ACT-R and fMRI Brain Image. In: Proc. Brain Informatics, pp. 53–62 (2009)
22. Sperling, G.: The information available in brief visual presentation. Psychological Monographs: General and Applied 74, 1–28 (1960)
23. Moores, E., Laiti, L., Chelazzi, L.: Associative knowledge controls deployment of visual selective attention. Nature Neuroscience 6, 182–189 (2003)
24. Pratt, J., Hommel, B.: Symbolic control of visual attention: the role of working memory and attentional control settings. Journal of Experimental Psychology: Human Perception and Performance 29, 835–845 (2003)
25. Downing, P.E., Dodds, C.M.: Competition in visual working memory for control of search. Visual Cognition 11, 689–703 (2004)

The Inverter Testing System of Asynchronous Motor Based on Modbus Communication

Wenlun Cao, Bei Chen, and Yuyao He

Northwestern Polytechnical University,
Xi'an, 710072, P.R. China
heyuyao@yahoo.cn

Abstract. The inverter testing system of asynchronous motor is designed based on Modbus communication between Schindler ATV31 inverter and host computer. The measure and control of asynchronous motor are realized. The ATV31 inverter is tested by means of step response, sinusoid tracking response, braking response and low-speed response tests. The harmonic analysis of current and voltage of inverter output are completed. The results show that the measure and control system is stable and reliable. Meanwhile the harmonic components of inverter output reduce gradually with increasing load and output frequency.

Keywords: Asynchronous Motor, Inverter, Measure and Control System, Harmonic.

1 Introduction

The inverter control using digital technique entirely is applied extensively because of its quick response, small size, low noise, high reliability, large-range high-precision smoothing stepless speed regulation. When we use the inverter to control the general asynchronous motor, the time harmonics of variable frequency power supply interferes with natural space harmonics of electromagnetic part of general asynchronous motor so that a variety of electromagnetic exciting forces are formed [1]. It is difficult for the frequencies of electromagnetic force waves to avoid the natural vibration frequency of each component of ordinary asynchronous motor because the operating frequency range and the speed variation range of ordinary asynchronous motor are large. So that the resonance phenomenon is generated and the noise increases. The higher harmonic will also influence on the efficiency and temperature rising of general asynchronous motor. Therefore, the main research of inverter control concentrates on the elimination of harmonics output by inverter.

Based on the Modbus communication between Schindler ATV31 inverter and host computer, the inverter control of asynchronous motor is realized and the output harmonics are analyzed in this paper.

J. Zhang (Ed.): ICAIC 2011, Part III, CCIS 226, pp. 360–366, 2011.

2   Constitution of System Hardware

The system is composed of ATV31 inverter, SIMO YJTG132S-8A asynchronous motor, Modbus communication module and industrial control computer (IPC). Through the Modbus communication, the host computer read the output current, voltage and direct current bus voltage of ATV31 inverter. Furthermore, it outputs the control commands to inverter and realizes the control of asynchronous. The constitution of system hardware is shown in Fig.1.

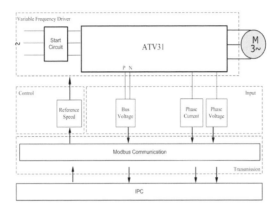

Fig. 1. System Hardware architecture

3   Software Design of Testing System

A.   System Function and Constitution

Aiming at the asynchronous motor, the testing device is designed. The system can chose the manual control or network control, set pole-pairs number of motor, select four operation modes. In the testing process, this system could measure and read automatically the frequency, rotate speed, power, voltage and current parameters of inverter and motor. The real-time numerical display and graphic display of measurement data are realized. At the end of measurement, it completes the harmonic analysis, the storage and output of analysis report, and supports the inquiry of historical data.

The operation mode includes: step response mode, sinusoid tracking mode, braking response mode and low-speed response mode.

The detailed flow chart of testing system software is in Fig.2.

B.   Modbus Communication System

The Modbus protocol in this paper is master-slave communication protocol, which uses the asynchronous serial port to communicate. The physical layer on the side of

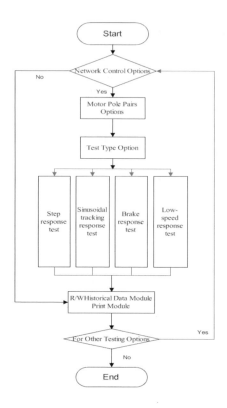

Fig. 2. System software process

inverter uses the RS485, on the other side it goes to RS232 interface of IPC via RS-232/RS-485 converter in the transmission process. The IPC is master station and the ATV31 converter is the No.02 slave station. The transmission mode is set as RTU mode and the communication velocity is set as 9600kbps. The Modbus communication protocol is as follows:

1) RTU Communication Protocol

The command frame in general format of RTU mode is equal to slave site address + function code + data + check code, shown in Table 1.

Table 1. Format of the frame

Slave Site Address	Function Code	Data	CRC Code	
8bit	8bit	N*8bit	16bit	
			CRC Low	CRC High

Table 2. Function Code

Function Code (Dec)	Function	Broadcasting	Maximum Value of N	Modbus Name
03	Read N Words	No	29	Read Holding Registers
06	Write 1 Word	Yes	-	Write Single Register

The ATV31 is set as No.02 slave station and use the function codes: 03 and 06. The meaning of function codes is shown in Table 2.

The datum meaning corresponding to function code "03" includes 2-byte Modbus address which needs to be read and the number of word of 2-byte which needs to be read. See Fig.3. The datum meaning corresponding to function code "06" includes 2-byte Modbus address which needs to be written and 2-byte numerical value which needs to be written. See Fig.4. The addresses and numerical values of data need to be convert into hexadecimal notation, as shown in Fig.3 and Fig.4. The main Modbus addresses are shown in Table.3. The calibration technique uses CRC16 check.

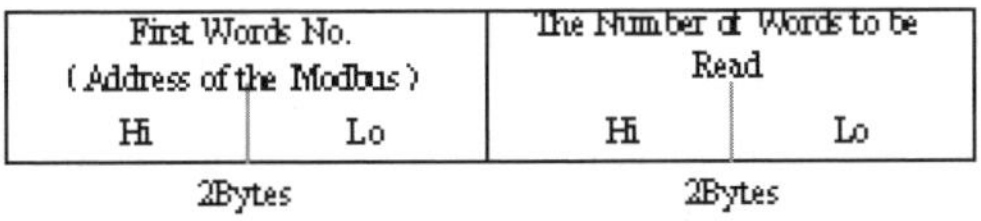

First Words No. (Address of the Modbus)		The Number of Words to be Read	
Hi	Lo	Hi	Lo
2Bytes		2Bytes	

Fig. 3. Data corresponding to function''03"

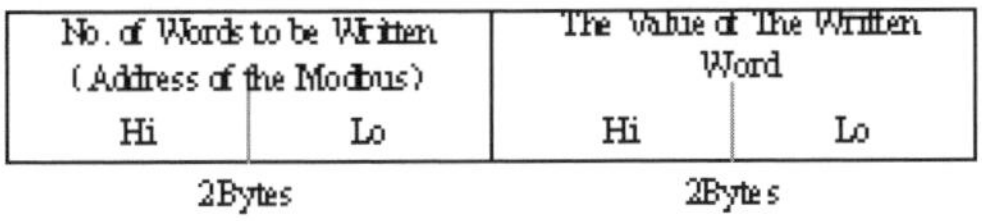

No. of Words to be Written (Address of the Modbus)		The Value of The Written Word	
Hi	Lo	Hi	Lo
2Bytes		2Bytes	

Fig. 4. Data corresponding to function''06"

2) CRC Calibration

The RTU communication data calibration in this system uses the 16-byte cyclical redundancy checking (CRC-16). The generator polynomial of CRC-16 is $CRC-16 = x^{16} + x^{15} + x^2 + 1$, abbr. "8005". The initializing register is $0XFFFF$.

With a given (N, K) code, it means that at the end of K-byte check code, it will connect with R-byte check codes, where $R = N - K$. Assume that the initial information polynomial is $P(x)$ before coding, and K is equal to the highest power of $P(x)$ plus unit. It is possible to demonstrate that there exists and only exists a Rth polynomial $G(x)$. This gives

Table 3. Address of the Modbus

Code	CMD	ETA	LFr	rFr	LFRD	RFRD
Status of R/W	R/W	R	R/W	R	R/W	R
Meaning	Control Word	Status Word	Given Frequency	Output Frequency	Given Speed	Output Speed
Hex	8501	3201	8502	3202	8602	8604
Dec	2135	0C81	2136	0C82	219A	219C

$$\frac{P(x)\times 2^R}{G(x)} = Q(x) + \frac{R(x)}{G(x)}$$

where 2^R is to shift left R-byte, $Q(x)$ is quotient, $R(x)$ is remainder, $G(x)$ is the generator polynomial of (N,K) code. The remainder of $R(x)/G(x)$ is check polynomial $C(x)$. The transmission polynomial with the check polynomial information is marked as $T(x)$. Through the specified $G(x)$, the sender generates CRC code word. The receptor verifies the receipt CRC code word via this $G(x)$ and checks the correctness of data further.

Notes: 1) The highest power of generator polynomial is fixed unit. Therefore the highest unit will be removed in abbreviated formula. The generator polynomial used in practice is "18005". 2) Because in the process of actual usage, the least significant bit is sent firstly when the hardware sends the data, it is necessary to generate the binary expression of generator polynomial, that is, "1000 0000 0000 0101" (i.e. hexadecimal "8005"). After reorder, it becomes "1010 0000 0000 0001" (i.e. hexadecimal "A001") and participates in operation.

4   Result

This system realizes the testing and control of ATV31 inverter using VC++6.0 programming. The system could collect and memorize the output frequency, rotate speed, voltage and current of inverter. Meanwhile the relevant curves are drawn. Fig.5 shows the operation condition of constant rotate speed (no-load and 20Hz output). At the end of testing, we can print preview the analysis results of harmonic components of current and voltage. See Fig.6. The test results indicate that the measure and control system can operate reliably and stably for long. The measurement results

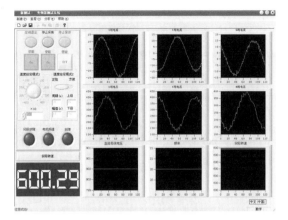

Fig. 5. Result of the test (Interface)

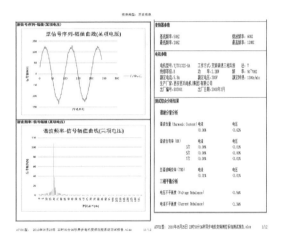

Fig. 6. Result of the test (Harmonic Analysis)

coincide with the results which are measured manually by oscillograph and harmonic analyzer. In the case of no-load and low-speed condition, some harmonics reduce gradually with increasing load and output frequency.

5   Conclusion

The measure and control system of ATV31 inverter is designed in this paper. Compared to manual measurement, this system has some advantages, such as, quick speed, precise measurement and automatic operation. This measure and control system can satisfy other inverters' needs with slight alteration. The testing analysis report is significant for the performance advance and effective use of inverter.

References

1. Nicolae, P., Stanescu, D.: About the experimental results of an electric driving system based on asynchronous motor and PWM converter. In: Power Electronics and Motion Control Conference, pp. 1181–1186 (2008)
2. Wu, Z., Wu, J.: Inverter principle and application guide. China Electric Power Press, Beijing (2007)
3. Xiang, X., Wei, K.: Remote control of an inverted pendulum based on Labview. In: Proceedings of the International Society for Optical Engineering, vol. 6042, pp. 567–572.

A Novel Variable Step Size LMS Adaptive Filtering Algorithm

Yi Sun, Rui Xiao, Liang-Rui Tang, and Bing Qi

School of Electric and Electronic Engineering
North China Electric Power University
Beijing, China, 102206
QIBing2011@yeah.net

Abstract. This paper proposes a novel variable step size LMS adaptive filtering algorithm. The algorithm is established based on nonlinear relationship between step and error signal in hyperbolic tangent function. The step is adjusted by the autocorrelation value of the error signal which is only influenced by the input signals. So this algorithm can accurately reflect the adaptive state and make the weight vector approach the best value. The algorithm not only performs faster in convergence speed and tracking speed, but also has better steady-state performance even in low signal to noise ratio (SNR) environment. Theoretical analysis and computer simulation show that this algorithm outperformed the other algorithms described in this article.

Keywords: variable step size, least mean squares (LMS) algorithm, hyperbolic tangent function, autocorrelation value.

1   Introduction

Adaptive filtering techniques are widely used in radar communications, signal processing, adaptive equalization, adaptive noise cancellation, smart antennas and other fields [1]. The minimum mean square error (least mean squares, LMS) algorithm is widely used because of its simple structure, good robustness and easy implementation. However, it cannot overcome the contradiction between convergence speed and steady-state error. Although the convergence rate will improve when the step size gets bigger under the convergence condition, the steady-state error will also increase. On the contrary, the stability state error will reduce while slowing the convergence rate [2]. Recent research focuses on how to get small steady-state offset while maintaining the convergence speed and tracking speed.

Some improvement methods have been presented in response to these problems. Ref. [3] proposed a variable step size LMS algorithm, the step decreased with the increased number of iterations. The algorithm achieved smaller steady-state misadjustment noise, but did not have the ability to track time-varying. Ref. [4] gave a variable step size LMS algorithm (SVSLMS) based on the Sigmoid function. It can get faster convergence speed, fast track speed and smaller steady-state error, but the step change was greater in the steady-state. Ref. [5] presented an algorithm that

J. Zhang (Ed.): ICAIC 2011, Part III, CCIS 226, pp. 367–375, 2011.

overcame the disadvantage of the step adjustment in steady-state phase in SVSLMS algorithm, but it was more complicated. The form of Sigmoid function was changed in [6]. The function changes slowly when the error approaches zero, but it become worse as the system noise increased. In [7], the algorithm performance was not affected by system noise, but its complexity was high. Ref. [8] proposed a variable step size LMS algorithm based on hyperbolic tangent function, but the function changes too fast while the error approaches zero. Ref. [9] modified the hyperbolic tangent function to improve the bottom characteristics. When the error approaches zero, it can obtain a small step in the steady state, but its performance declines in low SNR environment.

Based on the above literatures, a new variable step size LMS algorithm was proposed in this paper based on the improved hyperbolic tangent function. Under the condition of ensuring the convergence speed and tracking speed, the algorithm got a better steady-state performance, and maintains a good state in a low SNR environment.

2   The Novel Variable Step Size LMS Adaptive Filtering Algorithm

The principle of adaptive filtering is shown in Fig. 1, where $x(n)$ is the input signal, $d(n)$ is the expected response signal, $y(n)$ is the output signal, error signal $e(n)$ is the difference between $d(n)$ and $y(n)$, and $\varepsilon(n)$ is the system noise.

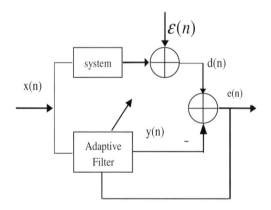

Fig. 1. The principle of adaptive filtering

Ref. [9] proposed a variable step size LMS algorithm based on improved hyperbolic tangent function, and the algorithm is as follows:

$$e(n) = d(n) - X^T(n)w(n) \tag{1}$$

$$\mu(n) = \beta(1 - \frac{h+1}{h+\exp(\alpha \mid e(n) \mid)}) \qquad (2)$$

$$w(n+1) = w(n) + \mu(n)e(n)X(n) \qquad (3)$$

Where $w(n)$ is the adaptive filter weight vector at time n, $\mu(n)$ is the variable step factor. The convergence condition is $0 < \mu(n) < 2/\lambda_{max}$, λ_{max} is the largest eigenvalue of the input signal autocorrelation matrix.

The algorithm uses $e(n)$ to adjust the step size, and improves the bottom characteristics of the hyperbolic tangent function by changing the parameter h, which makes the step grow slow when the error approaches zero. However, as shown in Fig. 2, if the step size is adjusted by using $\mid e(n) \mid^2$, the bottom characteristics will get better while $e(n)$ approaches zero. $e1$ is the curve of $\mu(n)$ which is adjusted by using $e(n)$, and $e2$ is the curve of $\mu(n)$ which is adjusted by using $\mid e(n) \mid^2$. In the case of the same value of α, β, h, the function can obtain better bottom characteristics adjusting with $\mid e(n) \mid^2$, $\mu(n)$ changes more slowly when $e(n)$ approaches zero, and the steady state error will also be smaller.

The desired signal is defined as follows:

$$d(n) = X^T(n)w^*(n) + \varepsilon(n) \qquad (4)$$

Where $\varepsilon(n)$ is the system noise which is independent of $X(n)$, and its mean is 0; $w^*(n)$ is the optimal weight vector for the filter.

As $v(n) = w^*(n) - w(n)$, following (1) and (4),

$$e(n)e(n)$$
$$= [X^T(n)w^*(n) + \varepsilon(n) - X^T(n)w(n)][X^T(n)w^*(n) + \varepsilon(n) - X^T(n)w(n)] \qquad (5)$$
$$= [X^T(n)v(n)]^2 + \varepsilon(n)^2 + 2*[X^T(n)v(n)]\varepsilon(n)$$

From (5), if $\mid e(n) \mid^2$ is used to adjust the step, the system noise greatly influences the step because of the $\varepsilon(n)^2$. If $\varepsilon(n)$ is great, the weight vector $w(n)$ would fluctuate inlarge range around the best value, which affects the convergence precision.

In this paper, the step size is adjusted by $e(n)e(n-1)$ which is the autocorrelation value of the $e(n)$, because

$$e(n)e(n-1) = [X^T(n)v(n) + \varepsilon(n)][X^T(n-1)v(n-1) + \varepsilon(n-1)]$$
$$= X^T(n)v(n)\varepsilon(n-1) + \varepsilon(n)X^T(n-1)v(n-1) + \varepsilon(n)\varepsilon(n-1) \qquad (6)$$
$$+ X^T(n)v(n)X^T(n-1)v(n-1)$$

While $\varepsilon(n)$ is the zero mean noise which is not related to $X(n)$,

$$E[e(n)e(n-1)] = E[X^T(n)v(n)X^T(n-1)v(n-1)] \qquad (7)$$

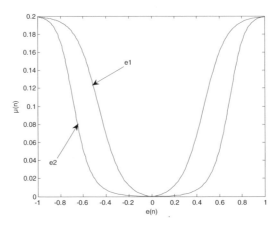

Fig. 2. Relation between error and step

Following (6) and (7), when $e(n)e(n-1)$ is used to adjust the step, as the system noise is not related and $\varepsilon(n)\varepsilon(n-1)$ has less influence on the step, the impact of $\varepsilon(n)$ upon $\mu(n)$ can be ignored. Therefore, this algorithm whose step is only influenced by the input signals $X(n)$ can accurately reflect the adaptive state and make the weight vector approach the best value. So using $e(n)e(n-1)$ to adjust the step can not only access a better steady state performance than [9], but also avoid the influence of system noise and maintain a good steady state performance in a low SNR environment.

Therefore, the formula of the improved variable step size is

$$\mu(n) = \beta(1 - \frac{h+1}{h + \exp(\alpha \mid e(n)e(n-1) \mid)})$$

(8)

Where constant α is used to control the shape of hyperbolic tangent function, constant β is used to control the range of the function, and constant h is used to improve the bottom form of the function.

3   Simulation Results and Analysis

The performance of this algorithm, and the effects on the convergence property and steady-state performance brought by the values of β, h, α are tested and analyzed with Matlab. Computer simulation conditions employed in this paper are shown as follows:

1) L=2, which is the order of adaptive filter;

2) The coefficient of unknown FIR system is $w^* = [0.8, 0.5]^T$, the system mutates at the 500th sampling point, and the coefficient vector is $w^* = [0.4, 0.2]^T$ in that moment;

3) The reference input signal $X(n)$ is zero mean and variance 1 Gaussian white noise;

4) $\varepsilon(n)$ is Gaussian white noise which is not related to $X(n)$, its mean is zero and variance is $\sigma_\varepsilon^2 = 0.04$.

200 times simulations with the sampling points of 1000 are made respectively, and then the statistical average values are obtained to gain the learning curves.

Fig. 3 is the algorithm convergence curves with different α values, where $\beta = 0.12$, $h = 100$. The values of the figure from the top to the bottom of curves are 10, 100, 1000, 10000. With the value increasing, the convergence speed is faster, but the convergence rate does not change greatly when the value is more than 1000. And as α increases, the bottom characteristics of the hyperbolic tangent function will gradually be worse, namely the steady-state error will increase. So with the considering of the convergence rate, the steady state error will get smaller when $\alpha = 1000$.

Fig. 4 is the algorithm convergence curves with different h values, where $\alpha = 1000$, $\beta = 0.12$. The values of the figure from the top to the bottom of curves are 1000, 100, 10, 1. When $h = 1$, $h = 10$, $h = 100$, the convergence speed is nearly equal , but the convergence speed will be slightly slower when $h = 1000$. Because of the larger h, the change of the function's bottom is smoother , and the step curve changes more slowly when the error approaches zero which means the steady state error becomes smaller. Therefore, with the same convergence rate, the stability error will be smaller when $h = 100$.

Fig. 5 is the algorithm convergence curves with different β values, where $h = 100$, $\alpha = 1000$. The values of the figure from the top to the bottom of curves are 0.08, 0.12, 0.16, and 0.2. According to the theoretical analysis, when β is larger, the greater initial step and the faster convergence will be obtained. But as the figure shows, with the fixed values of α, h. the convergence speed is close to the line when $\beta = 0.12$, $\beta = 0.16$, $\beta = 0.2$. When β increases, the steady state error will increase accordingly. Therefore, with the same convergence rate, the steady state error will be smaller when $\beta = 0.12$.

Therefore, in this experimental conditions, the optimal value of step size parameters are about $\beta = 0.12$, $h = 100$, $\alpha = 1000$.

Fig. 6 is the algorithm convergence curves of the algorithm proposed in the paper and other existing variable step size LMS algorithms in the optimal state. $e1$, $e2$, $e3$ and $e4$ are respectively convergence curves of [5,6,9] algorithms and this paper's algorithm. We can find that the convergence speed of this algorithm and other algorithms are close to the line, and this algorithm's convergence performance is close to the other algorithms' with a mutation in the system. Therefore, this algorithm's performance is close to others in time-varying convergence speed and tracking capability.

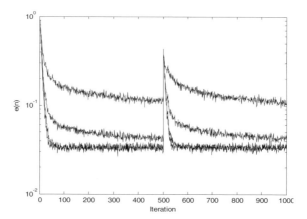

Fig. 3. β, h fixed, the curves with different α

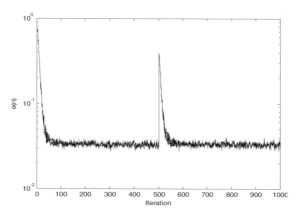

Fig. 4. β, α fixed, the curves with different h

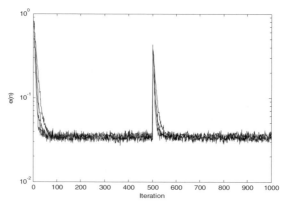

Fig. 5. h, α fixed, the curves with different β

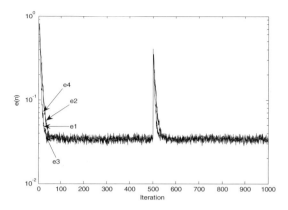

Fig. 6. The comparison of convergence between the algorithm in the paper and others

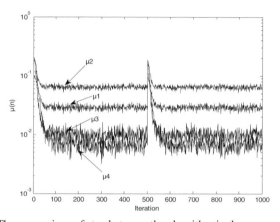

Fig. 7. The comparison of step between the algorithm in the paper and others

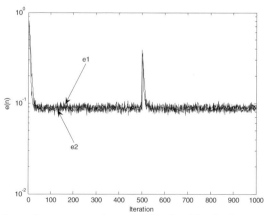

Fig. 8. The comparison of convergence between the algorithm in the paper and the algorithm in [9]

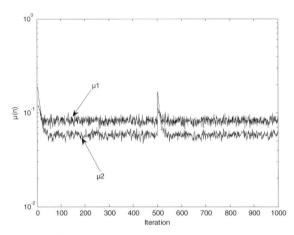

Fig. 9. The comparison of step between the algorithm in this paper and the algorithm in previous article [9]

Fig. 7 is the algorithm step curves of this algorithm and other existing variable step size LMS algorithms in the optimal state. $\mu1$, $\mu2$, $\mu3$ and $\mu4$ are respectively the [5,6,9] algorithms' and this algorithm's convergence curves. We can find that while the convergence rate is close, this algorithm's steady-state step is smaller than other algorithms. Because the steady-state error is proportional to the steady state step, when the steady-state step is smaller, the steady-state error is smaller and the algorithm steady-state performance is better. Therefore, this algorithm's steady-state performance is better than the similar algorithms.

Fig. 8 and Fig. 9 show the convergence curves and the step curves of this algorithm and the algorithm in [9] respectively, which are simulated in the condition of unchanged algorithm parameters and increased system noise. $\varepsilon(n)$ is Gaussian white noise which is not related to $X(n)$, and its mean is zero and variance is $\sigma_\varepsilon^2 = 0.04$. In figure 8, $e1$ is the convergence curve of [9], and $e2$ is the convergence curve of the algorithm in this paper. When system noise increases, the convergence rate of this algorithm is approximate to [9], but this algorithm has a smaller steady state error. It verifies the ideas proposed in this paper. This algorithm is not affected by increased system noise, and obtains a better steady state performance than the algorithm proposed in [9]. In Fig. 9, $\mu1$ and $\mu2$ are step size curves of [9]'s algorithm and the algorithm in this paper respectively. We can find that this algorithm's steady-state step size is smaller when $\varepsilon(n)$ is increased. So this algorithm's steady-state performance is better than [9] algorithm in low SNR environment.

3   Conclusion

A variable step size LMS algorithm is proposed in this paper based on improved hyperbolic tangent function through using the self-related values between $e(n)$ and

$e(n-1)$ to adjust the step size. The selective rule of β, h, α and their effects on the performances of convergence properties and steady-state are analyzed. Simulation results show that the algorithm in this paper can not only retain the advantages of [9]'s algorithm including simple calculation and fast convergence rate, but also gain a better steady state performance and have a better steady state performance in low SNR environment.

References

1. Gong, Y.-H.: Adaptive Filtering - Time domain adaptive filtering and smart antenna, 2nd edn. Publishing House of Electronics Industry, Beijing (2003)
2. Diniz, P.S.R.: Adaptive Filtering: Algorithms and Pratical Implementation, 2nd edn. Publishing House, Beijing (2004)
3. Darken, C., Moody, J.E.: Towards faster stochastic gradient search. In: Advances in Neural Information Processing Systems, vol. 4, pp. 1009–1016. Morgan Kaufmann, San Mateo (1992)
4. Tan, J.-f., Ou Yang, J.-z.: A New Variable Step Size LMS Adaptive Filtering Algorithm. Journal of Data Acquisition & Processing 12(3), 171–174 (1997)
5. Luo, X.-d., Jia, Z.-h., Wang, Q.: A New Variable Step Size LMS Adaptive Filtering Algorithm. Acta Electronica Sinica 34(6), 1123–1126 (2006)
6. Gao, Y., Xie, S.-l.: Variable Step Size LMS Adaptive Filtering Algorithm and Analysis. Acta Electronica Sinica 29(8), 1094–1097 (2001)
7. Li, F.-w., Zhang, H.: A new variable step size LMS adaptive filtering algorithm and its simulations. Journal of Chongqing University of Posts and Telecommunications (Natural Science Edition) 21(5), 591–594 (2009)
8. Zhong, H.-x., Zheng, S.-s., Feng, Y.-p.: A Variable Step Size LMS Algorithm in Smart Antennas Based on Hyperbolic Tangent Function. Journal of Ji Lin University (Science Edition) 46(5), 935–939 (2008)
9. Zhang, Z.-h., Zhang, D.-j.: New variable step size LMS adaptive filtering algorithm and its performance analysis. Systems Engineering and Electronics 31(9), 2238–2241 (2009)

Development and Realization about the Embedded GIS in Vehicles Based on ReWorks

Chungang Wang, Yanxia Liu, Qinzhen Li, and Dongfang Huo

Automobile Transport Command Department
Military Transportation University, Tianjin 300161, China
wangchungang2011@tom.com

Abstract. The thesis introduced the traits about embedded GIS Based on ReWorks developed with domestic technologies. Embedded terminal computer operating in vehicles is devised and made, the function is designed according to road transportation also. The technologies about embedment, computer, GIS, BEIDOU planet position and communication are all integrated in the terminal. Its functions contained position in electronic map, long-distance communication and command, and etc.

Keywords: ReWorks, embedded GIS, BEIDOU position and communication.

1 Introduction

With the development of geographical information technology, peoples wish to integrate planet position technology, communication technology and others, in order to bring into play in more and more field. Embedded GIS, which has many traits as bestraddling flat, easy developing, easy integration, affords favorable technical foundation for geographical information technology syncretizing other information technology. ReWorks OS, developed by 32th institute of chinese electronic technology group, has more traits than others, and can afford convenient technology sustain and service. The BEIDOU(Compass) Navigation Satellite System(CNSS) has brought into effect, now, it has been in its twice period. So, developing embedded terminal computer operating in vehicles using civil technology has expansive foreground.

2 Traits about the Embedded GIS in Vehicles Based on Reworks

A. ReWorks is embedded OS depending on our own technology, benefiting for information security

There are lots of mature embedded OS, such as Windows CE, Java OS, VxWorks etc. Windows CE and Java OS are all transplant from PC system. These are condensed and embedding condensed, in order to fitting embedded OS. But it is only incompletely optimization restricted by system structure. In addition, they must be compatible with the original function, thus, its efficiency reduces. These years, many companies developed its own embedded OS, such as ReWorks OS and Hopen OS. ReWorks,

J. Zhang (Ed.): ICAIC 2011, Part III, CCIS 226, pp. 376–382, 2011.

developed by 32th institute of electronic technology group. China, is a better choice for its customers because of its independent technology and information security.

B. ReWorks has so many functions that it can fit for GIS development

ReWorks is a real-time embedded OS with micro kernel structure. It can sustain many hardware platform because of adopting component structure and screening hardware technology; it has many merits such as responding in several microseconds, preemptive kernel, intermit delay rapidness, prompt task switch, lowest memory cost. ReWorks sustains task synchronization, memory share and many file systems, device driver and program criterion of driving software, network protocol as TCP/IP, FTP, Telnet, TFTP, PPP, SNMP [1],other more, ReWorks is convenient for users because of its completely compatibility with VxWorks.

C. ReWorks OS has good expansibility and compatibility

ReDe, being compliant with ReWorks, is a compositive development environment for embedded software, which integrates development, configuration, debugging, and simulation. It affords convenient system kernel management, debugging and simulation running environment. It does its best for minishing the difference between distinct platform. Developing embedded OS based on ReWorks has more extensive applicability. And, the developers can employ the experiences in other embedded OS developing. ReDe can screen different computer hardware maximumly, thus it reduce the difficulty of developing, as a result, the developer may pay more attention to improvement and expandedness. On the other side, Reworks, as a special OS developed for embedded application, has more stable and real-time than Windows CE.

3 Hardware Devise and Developing Environment Build

A. Hardware devise about embedded terminal

1) Interior environment about embedded terminal
This system's main function is vehicles location and communication. Vehicles is the working environment. This system main capability is as follows based on current situation:

a: CPU: Pentuim/1GHz, ensuring its adequate processing velocity;

b: memory: 512M, beneficial for caching of geography data;

c: off-chip memory: 8G SD card;

d: positioning module: BEIDOU positioning;

e: communication module: BEIDOU communication

2) Outer Structure of the Embedded Terminal

In order to make the embedded terminal more convenient, more stable and make the map slip smoother during the riding of vehicle, the design of the outer structure of embedded terminal goes as follows:

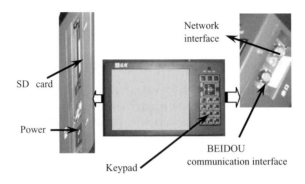

Fig. 1. Outer structure of the embedded terminal

a: The data communication interface: serial data interface: Among the various communication interfaces, the data transfer of the serial data interface is comparatively stable, and the trans-distance is quite proper, which has been widely adopted in the embedded system. The serial port of this system is BEIDOU c Satellite Communication interface.

b: 9 Inch LCD Screen: it should be suitable for the working environment of the embedded terminal, and it should also be guaranteed the visual effect in proper distance. The function of it is to present the map, to position in the map, to identify the track of the vehicle.

c: Keypad: During the riding, the vehicle body is in the condition of vibrating, therefore, to make use of the keypad to input the information is more reliable than that of touch screen.

d: Network interface: The serial interface should be applied. After the program is developed in the virtual machine, it must be copied to the embedded terminal of the vehicle.

e: SD card slot.

f: Power connector.

B. The construction of the developing environment of embedded GIS

1) The construction of the developing environment [2]

The embedded hardware platform is not able to develop any program, therefore, the embedded systems are all transplanted to the embedded environment when developed in the PC platform. Thus, how to solve the problem occurs of the differences between PC and the embedded platform? The normal way to solve this problem is to build a virtual machine in software on the PC platform. The theory of the virtual machine is to make use of certain software to limit some of the PC's capability, which will be suitable for the real capability of the embedded hardware platform; and will be run in the way simulating the working environment of embedded hardware platform. The working process can be checked in Fig.2.

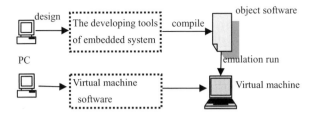

Fig. 2. Virtual machine working process

2) The construction of debugging environment

The virtual machine software can switch quickly between the developing and running platform, and it greatly increases the developing of the embedded GIS. However, the virtual machine is just a simulating environment, it still has a lot of disadvantages compared with the real embedded platform. Therefore, when debugging the system, the real debugging environment must be constructed. Two more interfaces must be added in the debugging platform in order to download the program and output the debugging message. The debugging environment of embedded GIS is showed in Fig.3.

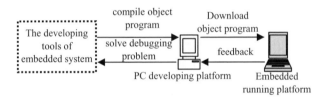

Fig. 3. Debugging environment of the embedded GIS

4   The Function Design and Realization of the Embedded GIS

A. Function design

The followings are the functions of the Embedded GIS when applying it in highway transportation:

1) Digital map. The vehicle terminal and present the digital map.

2) BEIDOU Position. The embedded terminal can be positioned when using the BEIDOU Position System, the position message and be directly and virtually presented on the digital map.

3) BEIDOU Communication. The embedded terminal can keep an uninterrupted message communication with the nearby superior command headquarters. The content of the communication can be presented on the mutual-interface of man-machine.

4) The neighbor Location query. Each embedded terminal is able to query the location of other terminals. What you do is just enter the ID of other terminal in the user interface.

B. The Primary Function and its realization of GIS

1) The extraction and visualization of space data
The space data includes many geography elements, But the embedded GIS in vehicles are directly to single user, the terrain information has nothing to do with them. Therefore, the space data they are interesting in can be added to the system, such as highway lines, railway lines, buildings, and so on [3]. In this way, the reading speed can be greatly increased and the respective function can be realized. Each space element includes two objects. The first object is to record all the information used in visualization; the second one is to specifically operate the visualization. Thus, it can extend the visualization, and greatly increase the flexibility of the visual module. The realization of Visual Module of space data can be checked in Fig.4.

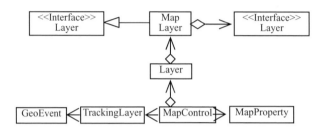

Fig. 4. The structure of display module

2) Map roaming
During the continuous roaming of map, some measurements must be taken to avoid leaping or stagnating. Through analysis, it shows that when the space elements displays, the consumption of time is mainly on the loading of data and the symbolization of data. When processing the data symbolization, it not only needs to go through all the data to transfer the geographical coordinate of space data into the screen coordinate, but to calculate the shape, angle of these symbols, and at last, to handle the brush to paint the symbols in the display equipment. When roaming, not all the symbols need to repaint, for example, when the map roaming to the right, only those new symbols occurring in the map need to repaint, while the others just change their display position, their shape and mutual-relationship of position do not have any change. Therefore, a display caching can be added to the embedded GIS to realize the partial refreshment of screen geographic [4]. The process goes like the follows:

a: First of all, a memory unit as big as the display screen should be laid out to be the display caching.
b: When roaming, the map on the display equipment should be copied to the display caching.
c: To paint the newly added symbols in the blank areas in display caching.
d: To copy geographic in the display caching to the screen of PC.

C. BEIDOU Position and Communication

1) The use of serial communication of ReWorks [5]

The BEIDOU user and the embedded terminal can communicate with each other through serial port. The I/O unit in the ReWorks system is a buffered serial port byte-stream unit, and the system provides them with a universal tty driver layer. Every unit has a ring buffer area to input and output message. While the driver of the real physical serial unit is accessed to the system in the tty driver layer. In ReWorks system, serial port COM1 is called tyCo/0, COM2 called tyCo/1, and by inference. The code for the operation of read-write if we want to open COM1 of ReWorks is:

Int fserial= open("tyCo/0", O_RDWR, 0666);

In this sentence, O_RDWR indicates that the serial unit is a device that can be "write and read". Besides, when reading the serial port, if the serial buffered area is empty, it shows that this task is blocked. In order to avoid being blocked, we can pre-judge the buffered area has data or not. If it has, we can conduct the operation of read this serial port.

2) Realization of Positioning and Communication

CNSS consists of satellite, ground control center and Beidou User Terminal. For it provides an active positioning, its capacity is quite limited. Therefore, the User Terminal has to apply for an ID and get the positioning service, and the service frequency is also limited. Beidou Positioning System adopts an active allocation principle of dyadic dual-way distance measurement. First, the control center sends the query message to two satellites simultaneously, Then the users respond and send the service message to the satellites. These messages are transferred to the ground center via satellites, and the ground centre will deal with these messages. If the application is for positioning, the ground center will calculate the coordinate and sends it to the user by the measurement of the distance from the point of the user to the two satellites and plus the user's zero value; if the application is for communication, the ground center will put the message in the exit signal and sends it to the receiver in accordance with ID.

The positioning module is mainly composed of North Message, Serial Message and MessgaeCenter. The MessageCenter still keeps the handles of serial buffered area and input buffered area, if the input buffered area has data, it will issue the data to different objects to decode according to the system set, and sends to the outer devices. In the same way, if the serial buffered area has data, it uses respective objects to decode the data in the serial buffed area, and sends the decoded data to respective module. If the message is for position, when the longitude-latitude coordinate interpreted in accordance with the Beidou Message Decoding Protocol matches with digital map's data, the location of the user will display on the screen; if the message is for continuous position, the track of the vehicle will display on the screen; if the message is for communication, the content of the message will automatically display above the map layer in a form of textbox, which is interpreted in accordance with the Beidou Message Decoding Protocol.

5 Conclusion

To realize the dynamic monitoring and real-time communication control during the riding of vehicles is the most important but most difficult part of the vehicle managing informationization. Since the CNSS developed by our country came into operating, it builds a good foundation for the development of vehicle informationization. This paper introduces the methods of developing embedded GIS with ReWorks operating System on the premise of designing and manufacturing the embedded terminal in vehicles, and realizes the positioning on the map and long-distance communication when vehicles riding, and preliminarily researches the positioning, navigation and long-distance communication control making use of the CNSS.

References

1. Chen, Z.-y., Wen, Y.-j., Chen, Q.: VxWorks Practice of Program Development. Posts & Telecom Press, Beijing (2004)
2. Chen, F.-x., Xie, Z., Zhou, Z.-w.: Research and Development of Embedded GIS. Computer and Modernization (3) (2003)
3. Hua, Y.-x., Wu, S.: Principles and Techniques of Geographic Information System. People's Liberation Army Press, Beijing
4. Gao, J.: Visualization in Geo-Spatial Data. Surveying and Mapping (9) (2001)
5. Li, X.-y.: Visual C++ Serial Communication Technology and Engineering Practice. Posts & Telecom Press, Beijing (2002)

Research of the Automotive Driver Fatigue Driving Early Warning System

Libiao Jiang[1], Huirong Wang[1], Shengying Gao[2], and Siyu Jiang[3]

[1] School of Automotive Engineering & [2] Department of Optoelectronic Science
Harbin Institute of Technology,
Weihai City, Shandong Province, China
[3] School of Computer Science and Information Engineering,
Chongqing Technology and Business University,
Chongqing, China
siyujiang123@tom.com

Abstract. Nowadays, driving fatigue is one of the most important underlying causes of traffic safety. In order to pursue automotive driving safety, an image capture and processing system based on a high-speed digital signal processor DSP is proposed. The hardware compositions and software flow of the system are designed based on the analysis of the structure, working principle and the requirements include non-contact, real time and all-weather of an automated early warning system for driving fatigue; to achieve real-time processing of face images, cascade classifiers and gentleboost-based strong classifiers based on MBLBP features are used. An automated early warning system for driving fatigue based on DSP is designed and it can well complete real-time image capture and processing.

Keywords: fatigue driving, DSP, face detection, gentleboost-based strong classifier.

1 Introduction

With the popularity of cars, people are no longer satisfied with the function of a car as a mere travel tool, more and more people are interested in cars that provide unique safety features. To meet this demand, an early warning system for fatigued drivers has been proposed which draws on advanced foreign design concepts.

Owning to the special applications of drowsy driving prevention devices[1], the design of the system must meet three requirements: non-contact: the system doesn't interfere with the driver's driving behavior; real-time: the detection of driver's fatigue physiological parameters must be real-time, rapid, accurate and timely warning the fatigue driver is needed in order to avoid accidents; all-weather: whether working in adequate light, dim light or no light conditions, the system can make the right analysis of the driver's fatigue condition.

Face recognition is the most important part of the fatigue driving early warning system, which directly affects the real-time, accuracy and sensitivity of the system. In

J. Zhang (Ed.): ICAIC 2011, Part III, CCIS 226, pp. 383–391, 2011.

this paper, firstly, hardware compositions and software flow is designed according to early warning design theory and requests of this system; then algorithm of face recognition is written and debugged through CCS; finally, the designing of software algorithm is optimized so that this system can achieve face recognition according to the optimized algorithm.

2 System Design Method

The core of this video image capture and processing system is DSP which uses TI Corporation's multimedia processing chip TMS320DM642. This system is composed of four parts: image capture module, image processing module, fatigue detection and recognition module and fatigue alarm module. The system flowchart is shown in Fig. 1.

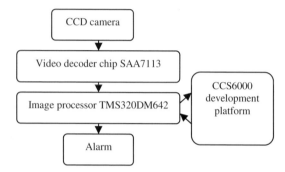

Fig. 1. System flowchart

This system uses the analog video signal which is the output of CCD camera as the input of the front-end signal and the image processing platform uses the DSP chip to carry out the construction; because the output of the CCD camera is a analog signal and the DSP processing object is a digital signal, a video A/D conversion chip SAA7113 is needed between the two to change the analog image signal into the digital signal which is a video stream and easier for the DSP chip to process; then an appropriate image processing algorithm is designed in CCS to realize the segmentation, extraction and recognition of a person's face and eyes; finally, It needs to burn the program into DSP, run the program and figure out whether the driver is fatigue; finally, the fatigue detection result is transmitted to the alarm module.

3 The Choice of Hardware Electronic Components

Any one of the electronic products is formed by different components and component selection has a great influence on the realization of system functions. Under the premise of ensuring system functions, we should select cost-effective components to reduce costs.

A. Digital signal processors

The main reasons that the TI's TMS320DM642 was selected as a core processor are as follows:

1) For the fatigue driving monitoring and exploiting technology to be used in an actual driving environment, driver fatigue monitoring technology must be converted from a large volume PC to small size, high stability and low power consumption embedded systems. Due to the increasingly broad applications, small size and low power consumption of DSP, driver fatigue monitoring technology can be transplanted into the DSP in order to assemble a complete fatigue driving monitoring system.

2) TI Corporation provides the world's first assembly level C compiler CCS (Code Composer Studio) for its DSP developers, its efficiency can reach 70% -80%, the average efficiency of the code generated is 3 times faster than that of other DSP compilers, we can draw support from a CCS compiler in order to reduce the development effort and shorten the development cycle.

3) TMS320DM642 processor which is one of TI's TMS320DM64x series is widely used in the field of video monitoring, its operating frequency reaches 600MHz, its computing speed is close to 50 billion instructions per second and it consumes only one-third of the power required by other devices. It meets the system's real-time requirement and coincides with the system design needs [2][3].

B. Camera

This article uses SONY420 line colored infrared night vision CCD camera as the image capture device which can automatically sense the outside light. When the outside light is sufficient, we get ordinary color image; but when the outside light is insufficient, the two laps of built-in infrared LED lights which are in the CCD camera's mirror surface will be automatically opened by CCD and near-infrared light which is sent out by LED lights is used as a light source to obtain infrared images. In this case the system can meet the all-weather work request.

C. Video A/D conversion chip

In this paper, Philips Corporation's video capture and processing chip SAA7113H is used as the video decoder to digitize the analog video signal. SAA7113 supports standard CVBS PAL / NTSC video input signal, there are a lot of video processing units in SAA7113; you can configure the internal register through the I²C bus to set the chip working condition; brightness, chromaticity and saturation control can achieve inside the chip; output styles can be YUV411, YUV422, RGB565 and other digital image formats, in this case the system will meet the needs of a variety of situations.

D. Emulator

The function of an emulator is to connect the DSP development board with the PC machine, so that the written procedure can be read off or written onto the DSP chip, we can debug the DSP development board through the software (the CCS software) installed on the computer, we can download procedures and so on. Generally, emulator interfaces are USB interfaces nowadays, such as XDS510-USB2.0 TI DSP EMULATOR used in this paper.

The actual chart of image capture and processing module is shown in Fig. 2:

Fig. 2. The actual chart of image capture and processing module

4   The Principle of Image Capture

To express face images, this article uses MBLBP features which are the expansion of basic LBP features and have a stronger expressive ability[4]. At the same time, because the number of MBLBP features is fewer in 24*24 images, using MBLBP features can greatly reduce the time during the training stage. Considering the ultimate goal is to achieve real-time face detection, the time complexity of the algorithm needs to be as small as possible. The MBLBP feature example chart is shown in Fig. 3:

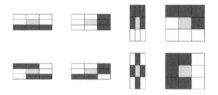

Fig. 3. MBLBP feature example chart

The training set uses 24*24 images, the total number of images is 12,788, for 4916 positive samples and 7872 negative samples. Using gentleboost algorithm selects the best MBLBP features. Each feature corresponds to a weak MBLBP classifier, the combination of all the optimal MBLBP characteristics constitute a strong classifier. Here, taking into account minimizing the processing time of each individual image, we use a cascade classifier (cascade) method. The basic idea of cascade classifier is as follows: we use a few weak classifies in the first level to filter out some sub-images which are obviously not the person face, the second level uses more weak classifiers to go on screening sub-images through the first level and then the third level uses some more weak classifiers to go on screening sub-images through the second level until the sub-images can get through from the strong classifier in the last level. At this time, the sub-images are the human face images.

A.   Gentleboost-based strong classifier construction

Here, a graphic method which is shown in Fig. 4 is used to explain the principle of a gentleboost-based strong classifier [5][8].
    The detailed process is as follows:

    1) A single weak classifier is used to classify the samples;
    2) The weight of the wrong classified samples will be promoted and the weight of the right classified samples will be reduced as a great importance;
    3) A second weak classifier is used to classify the samples;
    4) The weight of the wrong classified samples by the second weak classifier will be promoted and the weight of the right classified samples by the second weak classifier will be reduced;

N weak classifiers can be obtained when it repeats N times.
    When the N weak classifiers are combined together, you can get a strong classifier which can solve the linear non-separable problem that can't be solved by weak classifiers. The final strong classifier is shown in Fig. 5:

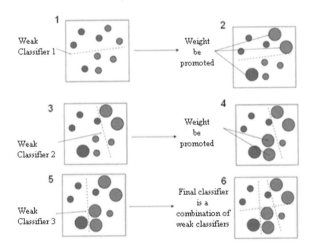

Fig. 4. Gentleboost principle chart

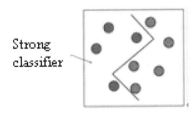

Fig. 5. The final strong classifier

B.   Strong classifier designing

Generally speaking, the construction of the strong classifier doesn't depend on the set threshold value, but on the set detection rate (true positive) and the set false detection rate (false positive) [6].

The number of positive samples has been identified by the strong classifier in all positive samples, we call this detection rate *tpr*, while the number of negative samples that has been identified by the strong classifier as positive samples, are called false detection rate *fpr*. We can use Table 1 to analyze classifier performance:

Table 1. Output of classifier outcomes

type of outcome	number
true positive	n_{tp}
false positive	n_{fp}
false negative	n_{fn}
true negative	n_{fn}
positive	$n_{tp} + n_{fp}$
negative	$n_{fn} + n_{tn}$

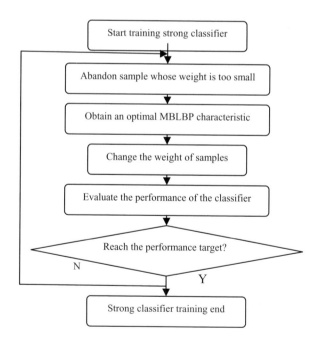

Fig. 6. The structure process of the strong classifier

$$tpr = n_{tp} / (n_{tp} + n_{fn}) \quad fpr = n_{fp} / (n_{fp} + n_{tn}) \tag{1}$$

From the above formula 1, we can see that *tpr* has a positive correlation with *fpr*, that is, the higher *tpr* is, *fpr* is often higher, and vice versa[7]. What we need to do is to choose a compromise target that means not only *tpr* can achieve the requirements but also *fpr* is in the affordable range. The structure process of the strong classifier is shown in Fig. 6.

C   Analysis of face detection experimental results

The operating environment in this paper includes two parts: hardware and software parts. Hardware parts include camera, DSP and emulator; software environments include CCS3.1 as well as windows XP system. The operating procedure programs by the C language.

Construction of the system trains the gentleboost-based strong classifier based MBLBP features. Output of the strong classifier is shown in Fig. 7 and Fig. 8. Fig. 7 shows that when we don't use cascade, this strong classifier's *tpr* is 1 and *fpr* is 0 in the training set; Fig. 8 shows that when we use cascade, this strong classifier's *tpr* is 0.9996 and *fpr* is 0.0022.

When we don't use cascade, *tpr* is high but the efficiency is too low. When we use the cascade, the efficiency is more than 10 times comparing with not using cascade while the detection rate is also in an ideal range and it meets the system's real time requirement, so we chose cascade classifiers.

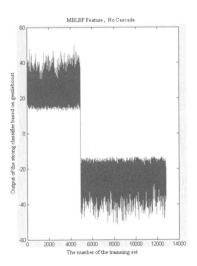

Fig. 7. Output of the strong classifier

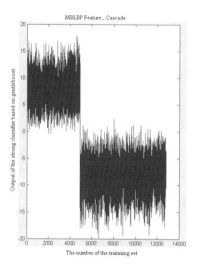

Fig. 8. Output of the strong classifier

Fig. 9. Detection results based on MBLBP characteristics

Using the strong classifier which is built basing on MBLBP features detects the classical image class57.jpg [8] which has 256 color grayscale and contains 57 individual face images whose angles are different from each other. At the same time, the image decoration patterns of human clothes are different too, so it is a good and standard image for algorithm checking. This system constructs three strong classifiers consisting of 60 weak classifiers which are based on MBLBP features and trained by gentleboost method. The first level has 10 weak classifiers, the second level has 16 weak classifiers and the third level has 34 weak classifiers, the experimental results are shown in figure 9. While in fatigue driving, in most cases it is to detect the driver's face in different frame images, the detection accuracy is higher than that shown in Fig. 9, so the experimental results meet the system requirements.

5   Conclusion

1) An image capture and processing system based on a high-speed digital signal processor DSP is designed and it can well complete real-time image capture and processing.

2) This system uses MBLBP features to express human face images, uses the way of cascade classifier and trains gentleboost-based strong classifiers based on MBLBP features in order to achieve real-time face detection.

3) Driver fatigue monitoring technology can be transplanted from the large volume PC to a small size, high stability and low power consumption embedded system (DSP). This system is small, easy installation, easy using and flexibility improves greatly.

Acknowledgment. We would like to thank our colleagues and academic predecessors whose academic papers and research results were quoted in this article.

References

1. Liu, Z.: Fatigue driving detection method based on vision machine. Manufacturing Information of China 35(2), 64–66 (2006)
2. Wang, Y., Liu, J.: TMS320DM642 DSP Application Design and Development, pp. 7–8. People's Posts and Telecommunications Press, Beijing (2009)
3. Tao, F.: Research and realization of all-weather fatigue driving monitoring system, pp. 37–48. Nanjing University. Master thesis (2009)
4. Zhang, L., Li, S.Z., et al.: Boosting Local Feature based classifiers for face recognition. In: Proc. of CVPR Workshop on Face Processing in Video (2004)
5. Ojala, T., Pietikinen, M., et al.: A comparative study of texture Measures with Classification based on Feature Distribution. Pattern Recognition 29, 51–59 (1996)
6. Freund, Y., Schapire, R.E.: A decision-theoretic generalization of on-line learning and an application to boosting. Computer and System Science
7. Ojala, T., Pietikanien, M., Maepaa, T.: Multiresolution gray-scale and rotation invariant texture classification with local binary patterns. Trans. on Pattern Analysis and Machine Intelligence 24(7), 971–987 (2002)
8. Yu, J.: Analysis of face detection based on Texture.Harbin Institute of Technology. BA thesis. pp. 6–20 (2010); Simpson, H. (ed.) Dumb Robots, 3rd edn. UOS Press, Springfield (2004)

A Novel Four-Dimensional Hyperchaotic System

Liangrui Tang, Lin Zhao, and Qin Zhang

School of Electric and Electronic Engineering
North China Electric Power University
Beijing, China
qinzhang2011@tom.com

Abstract. A novel four-dimensional hyperchaotic system is presented in this paper. The basic dynamic properties of the new system are investigated. First Lyapunov exponents and Lyapunov dimension are calculated, then Poincare diagrams, power spectrum, time domain chart and phase diagram are studied, furthermore, spectrum of Lypunov exponents and bifurcation diagram are analyzed. The numerical simulation results prove the feasibility and effectiveness of the proposed system.

Keywords: hyperchaotic system, Lyapunov exponent, Poincare diagram, bifurcation.

1 Introduction

Chaotic dynamics research in the field of non-linear has developed greatly since Lorenz discovered the first chaotic attractor accidentally in a three-dimensional system in 1963[1]. In recent years, many domestic and foreign scholars have studied on the characteristics of chaos and found many new chaotic systems, of which the more well-known systems are Chen system, Lü system[2], Rossler system[3], Chua's circuit [4]and so on. A common characteristic of these systems is that their structures are relatively simple and easy to achieve in physics. However, the effect of encryption is not very ideal because there is only one positive Lypunov exponent, and their confidentiality is weak and easy to decipher.

Hyperchaos was first reported by Rossler in 1979[3], and hyperchaotic Rossler system was presented. Such hyperchaotic systems are characterized by at least two positive Lyapunov exponents for trajectories in the arbitrarily high phase space, thus they have more complicated topological structures and dynamics than ordinary chaotic systems. Hyperchaotic systems can be widely used in the field of digital information such as secure communication and image encryption. Therefore, hyperchaotic system soon becomes an important aspect in non-linear dynamic research[4-6]. Recently, hyperchaos has attracted increasing attention from various scientific and engineering communities[7-8]. Chen, for instance, presented hyperchaotic Chen system on the basis of Chen system[9]. Another example is that Nikolov presented transformed hyperchaotic Rossler system[10]. However, it is well

J. Zhang (Ed.): ICAIC 2011, Part III, CCIS 226, pp. 392–401, 2011.
© Springer-Verlag Berlin Heidelberg 2011

known that most existing hyperchaotic systems have two obvious problems. Firstly, two positive LEs values are relatively small especially for the first one[9-11]. Secondly, the high-magnitude frequency bandwidths are not broad enough for many engineering applications.

A new four-dimensional hyperchaotic system is presented in this paper, the mathematical model and orbits of the system are proposed. Furthermore, basic dynamic properties of the new system are investigated via equilibria, dissipation, LEs and Lyapunov dimension, spectrum of LE and bifurcation diagram, Poincare diagrams. We found that the two positive LEs values are relatively larger than that of the commonly known hyperchaotic systems, and the new system has broader frequency bandwidths.

2 The Mathematical Model and Typical Attractor of the New Hyperchaotic System

The mathematical model of the new hyperchaotic system proposed is

$$\begin{cases} \dot{x} = a(-x+y) + yz; \\ \dot{y} = b(x+y) - xz; \\ \dot{z} = cx - dz + yu; \\ \dot{u} = ey - fu + xz. \end{cases} \quad (1)$$

Here, x, y, z, u are state variables and a, b, c, d, e, f are positive constant parameters. There are four nonlinear items in the system, when $a = 55, b = 25, c = 40, d = 13, e = 23, f = 8$, there is a typical chaotic attractor (shown in Fig.1).

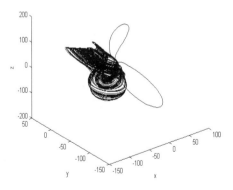

Fig. 1. Projection on the x-y-z plane

As shown in Fig.1, the degrees of disorder of the trajectories of this system are relatively high. The time-domain waveform of the system is non-cyclical (shown in Fig.2), and its frequency spectrums are continuous (shown in Fig.3). It can be seen from Fig.3 that the bandwidth of spectrum of variable x is located among about 0~30Hz. Thus, the attractor of the new chaotic system has wide spectrums, which is important to the real applications based on chaos, such as secure communications, hydromantic mixture, etc.

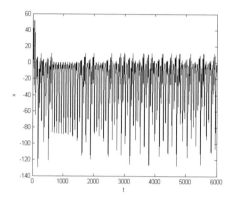

Fig. 2. The time response of state x of the new system

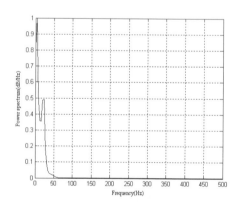

Fig. 3. Spectrum chart

3   Basic Dynamic Properties

A.   Equilibria

To analyze the system, a good start is to find its equilibriums, and then to characterize the local dynamical behaviors of the system orbits near these points. The spatial distribution and local dynamical characteristics of the equilibriums greatly influence the nonlinear dynamics of the system. The equilibriums of system (1) can be found by solving the following algebraic equations simultaneously:

$$\begin{cases} a(-x+y)+yz=0; \\ b(x+y)-xz=0; \\ cx-dz+yu=0; \\ ey-fu+xz=0. \end{cases} \quad (2)$$

Where $a=55, b=25, c=40, d=13, e=23, f=8$ five equilibriums are acquired by calculating formular (2) as follows:

$s_0 = (0,0,0,0)$,
$s_1 = (7.4753, 4.3487, 39.5436, 49.4525)$,
$s_2 = (-17.8690, -10.3951, 39.5436, -118.2115)$,
$s_3 = (-0.2703+3.4850i, 1.0222-13.1795i,$
$\qquad -69.5436, 5.2886-68.1862i)$,
$s_4 = (-0.2703-3.4850i, 1.0222+13.1795i,$
$\qquad -69.5436, 5.2886+68.1862i)$,

Linearize the system and its Jacobian matrix is obtained:

$$J_i = \begin{bmatrix} -a & a+z & y & 0 \\ b-z & b & -x & 0 \\ c & u & -d & y \\ z & e & x & -f \end{bmatrix}, i=0,1,2,3,4 \cdot \quad (3)$$

Let

$$\det(J_i - \lambda I) = 0. \quad (4)$$

The characteristic roots of the five equilibriums are solved (shown in Table 1). It is noticeable that the real parts of the eigenvalues $\lambda_1, \lambda_2, \lambda_3, \lambda_4$ of the equilibrium s_2 are all negative, implying that the equilibrium s_2 is a stable knot point according to Routh-Hurwitz conditions[12]. As for the other equilibriums, not all of their eigenvalues are negative real numbers, so they are unstable saddle points, which means there is a high possibility of the existence of chaos and even hyperchaos.

Table 1. The equilibriums and characteristic roots

Equilibriums	Characteristic roots	stability
S_0	$\lambda_1 = -13.0, \lambda_2 = -8.0,$ $\lambda_3 = -69.5436,$ $\lambda_4 = 39.5436$	unstable saddle point
S_1	$\lambda_1 = -51.4703,$ $\lambda_2 = 6.0538 + 32.0262i,$ $\lambda_3 = 6.0538 - 32.0262i,$ $\lambda_4 = -11.6372$	unstable saddle point
S_2	$\lambda_1 = -6.8256 + 39.8909i,$ $\lambda_2 = -6.8256 - 39.8909i,$ $\lambda_3 = -18.6744 + 24.0814i,$ $\lambda_4 = -18.6744 - 24.0814i$	stable knot point
S_3	$\lambda_1 = 13.0118 - 43.7463i,$ $\lambda_2 = -59.8946 + 1.5538i,$ $\lambda_3 = 3.9497 + 32.9737i,$ $\lambda_4 = -8.0668 + 9.2188i$	unstable saddle point
S_4	$\lambda_1 = -62.2224 - 9.1258i,$ $\lambda_2 = 8.4950 - 39.6559i,$ $\lambda_3 = 8.4552 + 39.6809i,$ $\lambda_4 = -5.7233 + 9.1008i$	unstable saddle point

B. Dissipation

As

$$\nabla V = \frac{\partial \dot{x}}{\partial x} + \frac{\partial \dot{y}}{\partial y} + \frac{\partial \dot{z}}{\partial z} + \frac{\partial \dot{u}}{\partial u} = -a + b - d - f \cdot \tag{5}$$

When $a - b + d + f > 0$, system (1) is dissipative and convergent:

$$\frac{dV}{dt} = e^{-(a-b+d+f)}. \tag{6}$$

That is volume element V_0 constringes to volume element $V_0 e^{-(a-b+d+f)t}$ at the time t. It means that each volume element including the system track constringes to zero at the exponent rate of $-a+b-d-f$ when $t \to \infty$. Therefore, all track lines of the system will eventually be limited to a collection with size zero, and the progressive movement will be fixed on an attractor, which indicates the existence of the attractor.

C. Lyapunov exponent and the Lyapunov dimension

In chaos, LE describes the sensitive dependence of the chaotic attractor on small disturbances or initial conditions. One positive LE $\lambda > 0$ shows separation of the trajectories, it is the sensitivity on initial values, which further demonstrates the existence of chaos.

The system has four LEs $\lambda_1 = 12.9338$, $\lambda_2 = 8.5521$, $\lambda_3 = -14.7593$, $\lambda_4 = -52.0815$ which are calculated by the method of the singular value decomposition (Where $a = 55$, $b = 25$, $c = 40$, $d = 13$, $e = 23$, $f = 8$). It can be verified that the system has two positive LEs, which demonstrates that it has the characteristic of hyperchaos. The largest Lyapunov exponent is bigger than that of the Qi system ($\lambda_1 = 3.3152$), which illustrates that the track of system (1) is more complicated than that of Qi system.

The Lyapunov dimension of system (1) is:

$$
\begin{aligned}
D_L &= j + \frac{1}{|\lambda_{j+1}|} \sum_{i=1}^{j} \lambda_i \\
&= 3 + \frac{(\lambda_1 + \lambda_2 + \lambda_3)}{|\lambda_4|} \\
&= 3 + \frac{(12.9338 + 8.5521 - 14.7593)}{|-52.0815|} = 3.1291
\end{aligned}
\tag{7}
$$

Evidently, the Lyapunov dimension of system (1) is fraction, which means that the system is a chaotic system.

D. The spectrum of Lyapunov exponent and bifurcation diagram

The dynamic properties of the system can be analyzed by the spectrum of Lyapunov exponent and bifurcation diagrams.

The spectrum of LE and bifurcation diagrams of the system are shown in Fig.4 when taking the parameters $a = 55, b = 25, c = 40, d = 13, e = 23$, and changing parameter f, $f \in [7,9]$. As showed in Fig.4, there are two positive Lyapunov exponents (LE1 and LE2) when $f \in [7.08, 8.26]$, and the system is in hyperchaotic state apparently. There is one positive Lyapunov exponent (LE1) when $f \in [0, 7.08) \cup (8.26, 9]$, and the system is in chaotic state. It can also be seen from Fig. 4(b) that the system is in either chaotic state or hyperchaotic state when $f \in [7,9]$, and there is no obvious boundary.

One can observe trajectories of the attractor in $x - y$ plane from Fig.5 when taking the parameter $f = 8$ and $f = 8.6$. When $f = 8$, as shown in Fig.5(a), the attractor of the system is hyperchaotic attractor. When $f = 8.6$, as shown in Fig.5(b), the attractor of the system is chaotic attractor. It is clear that the trajectories of the hyperchaos are more complicate than that of chaos.

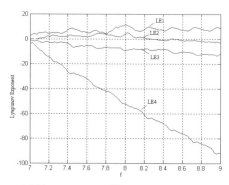

(a) The spectrum of Lyapunov exponent.

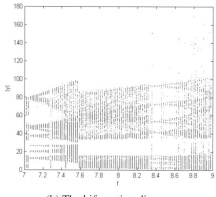

(b) The bifurcation diagram.

Fig. 4. The spectrum of Lyapunov exponent and the bifurcation diagram versus f

E.   The Poincare map

It is feasible to get stable images of the Poincare section with computer, and obtain the information about movement characteristic: the movement is cycle when there is only one fixed point or a few discrete points on Poincare section, the movement is quasi-cycle when there is a closed curve on Poincare section, the movement is chaos when there is a collection of distribution points along a segment of a line or a curve. There are Poincare maps of the system on several sections in Fig.6 when $a=55, b=25, c=40, d=13, e=23, f=8$. It can further indicate that the system is chaotic.

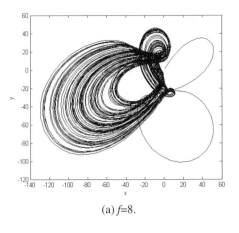

(a) f=8.

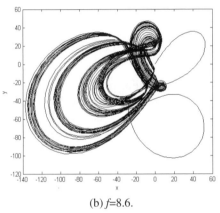

(b) f=8.6.

Fig. 5. Trajectories comparison charts versus f

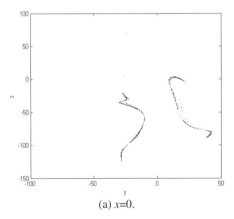

(a) x=0.

Fig. 6. Poincare maps of system (1)

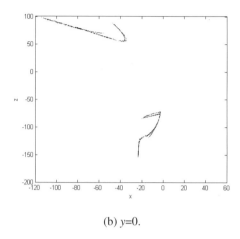

(b) y=0.

Fig. 6. *(continued)*

4 Conclusions

This paper presented a new four-dimensional hyperchaotic system. Some basic hyperchaotic characteristics and complex dynamical properties are studied. It has the common characteristics of all the hyperchaotic system, such as the sensitive dependence on initial value, long-term unpredictability, local instability but overall stability, has two positive LE, fractal structures with infinite self-similarity and continuous power spectrum in a certain range of frequency. It is believed that this kind of hyperchaotic system is very desirable for some engineering applications such as electronic measurement, secure communication and encryption. The techniques to control and synchronize this hyperchaotic system and its engineering application are worthy of deep research in the future.

References

1. Lorenz, E.N.: The Essence of Chaos. University of Washington Press, Washington (1993)
2. Chen, G.R., Lu, J.H.: Dynamics of the Lorenz System Family: Analysis, Control, and Synchronization. Science Press, Beijing (2003)
3. Rossler, O.E.: An equation for hyperchaos. Phys. Lett. 71, 155–157 (1979)
4. Kapitaniak, T., Chua, L.O.: Hyperchaotic attractor of unidirectionally-coupled Chua's circuit. Int. J. Bifurcat Chaos 4, 477–482 (1994)
5. Goedgebuer, J., Levy, P., Larger, L., Chen, C.C., Rhodes, W.T.: Optical Communications with synchronized hyperchaos generated electro-optical. IEEE J. Quant. Electr. 38, 1178 (2002)
6. Udaltsov, V.S., Goedgebuer, J.P., Larger, L., Cuenot, J.B., Levy, P., Rhodes, W.T.: Communicating with hyper-chaos: the dynamics of a DNLF emitter and recovery of transmitted information. Opt. Spectr. 95, 114–118 (2003)
7. Brucoli, M., Carnimeo, L., Grassi, L.: A method for the synchronization of hyper-chaotic circuit. Int. J. Bifurcat Chaos 6, 1673–1681 (1996)

8. Tsubone, T., Saito, T.: Hyperchaos from a 4-D manifold piecewisw-Linear system. IEEE Trans. Circ. Syst. I 45, 889–894 (1998)
9. Li, Y.X., Chen, G., Tang, W.K.S.: Controlling a unified chaotic system to hyperchaotic. IEEE Trans. Circ. Sys. II 52, 204–207 (2005)
10. Nikolov, S., Clodong, S.: Occrttence of regular, chaotic and hyperchaotic behavior in a family of modified Rossler hyperchaotic systems. Chaos, Solitons & Fractals 24, 407–431 (2004)
11. Cafagna, D., Grassi, G.: New 3D-scroll attractors in hyper-chaotic Chua's circuits forming a ring. Int. J. Bifurcat Chaos 13, 2889–2903 (2003)
12. Liu, Z.H.: Fundamentals and Applications of Chaotic Dynamics, p. 18. High Education Press, Beijing (2006)

Application of Association Rules in Analysis of College Students' Performance

Huiping Wang and Ruowu Zhong

Institute of Computer
Shaoguan University
Shaoguan, Guangdong Province, China
HuipingWang2011@126.com

Abstract. Association rules mining is an important part of research work in data mining field. In this article, Apriori association rule algorithm was applied to the analysis of college students' performance. First, the data were processed. Then, the relations which affect the students' performance were found out and the association rules were generated. This can be applied in guiding the studies and teaching.

Keywords: association rule; Apriori algorithm; college students' performance.

1   Introduction

With the rapid development of computer technology and Internet technology, data resources are becoming abundant. It has accumulated a large amount of student performance data in school's performance management system. The data is accumulated in the system, but has not been effectively utilized. Currently, teachers and administrators of college usually use Excel software to do the routine work of calculation and performance statistics. However, the analysis and evaluation of test papers is involved less. The calculation of correlation of different subjects in traditional statistical formula requires a normal distribution of performance, so that the evaluation has certain limitations. This article applies data association rule to the analysis of student performance and does association analysis of the result of data mining to provide decision support for college administrators and provide the basis for the guidance of teaching.

2   The Basic Concepts of Association Rules

Association rules mining is to find the relationship between data items in large amounts of data. It is a research hot in the field of data mining. The concept of association rules was first proposed by R. Agrawal, T. Imielinski and A. Swami. It was used in transaction database for the detection of the implied relationship, which is association rule, of the user to purchase goods in supermarkets. So that the basis was

J. Zhang (Ed.): ICAIC 2011, Part III, CCIS 226, pp. 402–408, 2011.

provided for decision making (such as: putting goods that user frequently purchased together).

Association rules problem can be divided into two processes:

(1) Finding all frequent itemsets, i.e., each of these sets will be occurred at least as frequently as a predetermined minimum support count, min_sup.

(2) Generating interesting association rules from the frequent itemsets, i.e., these rules must satisfy minimum support and minimum confidence. For each large itemset A, if $B \in A$, $B \neq \Phi$, and Support (A) / Support $(B) \geq$ min_conf, there are association rules $B => (A\text{-}B)$.

3 Apriori Algorithm

There are many algorithms about Association rules mining. The most classic is Apriori algorithm proposed by Agrawal and Srikant in 1993 [1] [2].

Apriori algorithm uses an iterative search method layer by layer: k - itemset used to search for $(k+1)$ - itemset. First, find the frequent 1 - itemset collection, denoted as L_1, L_1 is used to find the frequent 2- itemset L_2, and L_2 is used to find L_3, and so on , until we can't find the frequent k - itemset. Each time a search needs to scan database once. In order to improve the efficiency, traditional algorithm focused on reducing the number of database scans. We introduced the following properties:

Apriori property: All nonempty subsets of a frequent itemset must also be frequent [3] [4].

We do not derive them here, but use the property of data mining. By definition, if the itemset I does not meet the minimum support threshold min_sup, then I is not frequent, that is $P(I) <$ min_sup. If add item A to I, then the result set (that is $I \cup A$) does not appear more frequently than I. Therefore, $I \cup A$ is not frequent, that is P $(I \cup A) <$ min_sup.

Apriori algorithm consists of two parts:

(1) Using candidate itemset to find frequent itemset

How to find frequent k - itemset from frequent $(k-1)$ - itemset is the core of Apriori algorithm .This process uses Apriori property to compress space. In order to accumulate the speed of scanning database, this process can be divided into two steps:

① The join step

To find L_k, the join is performed to generate the collection of candidate k - itemset. The candidate itemset is denoted as C_k. Let l_1 and l_2 be itemset of L_{k-1}. Mark l_i [j] refers to the number j item of l_i (for example, l_1 [4] is the fourth item of l_1). Assume that the items in transaction and itemset are sorted by order of the dictionary, perform connection $L_{k-1} \times L_{k-1}$, if their first $(k-2)$ items are in common, then l_1 and l_2 in L_{k-1} are joinable. That is, if $(l_1 [1] = l_2 [1]) \wedge (l_1 [2] = l_2 [2]) \wedge ... \wedge (l_1 [k-2] = l_2 [k -2]) \wedge (l_1 [k-1] < l_2 [k-1])$, the itemset result of joining l_1 and l_2 is $l_1 [1] l_1 [2] ... - l_1 [k- 1] l_1 [k-1]$, where $l_1 [k-1] < l_2 [k-1]$ is the guarantee that it does not produce a simple repetition[3].

② The prune step

C_k is a superset of L_k. It means that itemsets in C_k may be frequent and may also be non-frequent, but all the frequent k-itemsets are included in C_k. By scanning the database, we calculate itemsets' support in Ck, and compared with the minimum support to determine the L_k. However, itemset C_k may contain a lot of itemsets, computation is very time-consuming. In order to compress C_k, we use Apriori property: if any $(k-1)$ - subset of a candidate k- itemset is not in L_{k-1}, then the candidate k- itemset can not be frequent, so the candidate k- itemset can be removed from C_k. This reduces the number of k- itemset in C_k, and reduces the times of scanning the database, so improves the efficiency of the algorithm.

According to the above two key steps, Apriori algorithm can be described as the specific process: first, find the frequent 1 - itemset collection of L_1 from the candidate 1 - itemset (C_1), then Use L_{k-1} join to generate candidate C_k, and in accordance with Apriori property, remove those candidate itemsets with non-frequent subsets. Next, we scan the database, statistic candidate itemsets count, compare it with the minimum support count, and then generate frequent itemset L_k.

(2) Generating association rules from the frequent itemset

For each frequent itemset l, generate all non-empty subset of l, if

$$\frac{support\_count(l)}{support\_count(s)} \geq min\_conf \tag{1}$$

Then output rule "s => (l-s)". Where, min_conf is the minimum confidence threshold [3].

4   Apriori Algorithm in Analysis of College Students' Performance

A.   Data Preprocessing

Data preprocessing is a very important part of the whole process of data mining. It usually needs to account for 70% workload of the mining process. Experience has shown that, if the data preparations work done in great detail, it will save a lot of energy in the process of model building.

1) Data integration

Data integration is to combine the data from multiple data sources. In this study, the database includes performance of regular assignments and course exams. This database is generated during teachers in the teaching process. Multiple database files are collected. We use database technology to generate the database – basic data for performance of student's exam papers. One grade students' performance of computer subjects (computer applications, computer programming language and design, database) is selected randomly, as shown in Table 1.

Table 1. Basic Data For Performance oF Students' Exam Papers

xh	k1	k2	k3
0912111001	98	87	65
0912111002	86	77	38
0912111003	60	73	66
0912111004	82	79	56
0912111005	77	97	54
0912111006	89	77	53
0912111007	69	77	77
0912111008	93	87	67
0912111009	70	60	78
…	…	…	…

Here, xh is student number, k1 is the performance of computer applications, k2 is the performance of computer programming language and design, k3 is the performance of database.

2) Data cleaning

The main job of data cleaning to fill the missing data values [5] [6]. In the database - basic data for performance of student's exam papers, we see that some of the properties we are interested in the lack of property values, for these vacancies can be filled with data cleaning techniques. There are many ways to fill vacancies for the property value, such as: ignore tuples, artificially filling vacancies, the use of a global constant value to fill vacancies. In this case, we use the method of ignoring tuples to delete records of quitting school, suspension from school, transferring, did not participate in exams or a large number of vacancies. For other individual vacancies, because the total number of records is not too much, and the vacancy is less, so artificially filling method is used. Filling principle is to use the average value of this record's other property to fill this vacancy.

3) Data conversion

Data conversion is the data normalized operation data, and converting the data into a uniform format, to fit the data mining.

Student scores on the association of mining papers, we need to type logic data. We should change the data to Boolean value. Because what we mining is the good relationship of the subjects, so more than 75 is "1", indicating the existence of the transaction; the other for "0" indicating that the transaction does not exist. TABLE I will be converted to facilitate the processing of Association Rules format, as shown in Table 2.

Table 2. Analytic Logic Data For Performance of Students' Exam Paper

xh	k1	k2	k3
0912111001	1	1	0
0912111002	1	1	0
0912111003	0	0	0
0912111004	1	1	0
0912111005	1	1	0
0912111006	1	1	0
0912111007	0	1	1
0912111008	1	1	0
0912111009	0	0	1
...	...	...	...

B. Apriori Algorithm performance analysis

Algorithm design: Improved Apriori Algorithm
Input:
D: a database of transactions;
min_sup: the minimum support count threshold.
Output:
L: frequent itemsets in D.
Method:
(1)for(i=0; i<=m; i++) //initialization
for(j=0; j<=n; j++)
(2)if($I_i \in T_j$){TDarray[i][j]=1;
(3)B[i]++;//count the transaction number which include item I_i}
(4)else TDarray[i][j] = 0;
(5)for(j=0; j<m; j++) //generate frequency 1- itemset L_1
(6)If(B[j]>=min_sup) $L_1 = L_1 \cup I_j$;
(7)else delete TDarray[i];//remove the row value of unfruitful item, packed array
(8)free(B); //saving space
(9) $C_1 = L_1$;
(10)for(k=2; | Ck | >2; k++){
(11)L_k=find_frequent_k_itemsets(C_{k-1},   TDarray[m][n],   min_sup);//generate frequent k- itemset
(12)for each itemset $c \in L_k$
(13)for each item $I_j \in c$
(14)$A_k[j]=I_j$.count++;//Counts the times that $I_j(I_j \in I)$appear in L_k and records the result in the array of $A_k[u]$
(15)C_k=TDarray_gen (L_k, A_k [m]) //prune step: call procedure TDarray_gen
(16)If(| Ck | <2)

(17)Return L_k-1;

(18)}

procedure find_frequent_k_itemsets(C_{k-1}, TDarray [m][n], min_sup)

(1)for each itemset $l_i \in C_{k-1}$

(2)for each itemset $l_j \in C_{k-1}${

(3)if($1_i[1]=l_j[1] \wedge 1_i[2]=l_j[2] \wedge 1i[3]=lj[3]...1i[k-2]=lj[k-2] \wedge 1_i[k-1]<l_j[k-1]$)

(4){c=$1_i \infty l_j$ //join setp:

(5) for(u =0; u<=n; u++)

(6)if(Iu$\in$c){C[n]= TDarray [u]; //copy the value of the first item to array C[n]

(7)break;}

(8)for(j=u+1; j<=n; j++)

(9)if(lj$\in$c)

(10)C[n]=C[n] $\wedge$ Vmatrix[j];

(11)d=support(C[n]);

(12)if(d>min_sup)

(13)L_k=c $\cup$ Lk ;//generate frequent k- itemset

(14)}

(15)else break;//stop Comparison and join

(16)}

procedure TDarray_gen(Ck, Lk , Ak[m])

(1)for(j=0; j< Ak .1egth; j++)

(2){If(A_k [j]<k)

(3)for each c$\in$Lk and Ij$\in$c

(4)$C_k = L_k - c$;

(5)return C_k;}

This transaction database has nine transaction records, association rules assume that the minimum support is 20%, minimum confidence is 70%. According to the definition of support and confidence, we can remove the subsets which are less than support, and then subsets are sorted from left to right in frequency ascending order. After the above treatment, we can get all the frequent itemsets. Because of the assumption that minimum support is 20% and minimum confidence is 70%, we get strong association rules which teachers can be of interest to be able to guide the teaching-- (k2, k1) => k3, where the minimum support is 30%, minimum confidence is 75%. This rule is explained as, when k1 is ecumenical and k2 is worse, k3 is also poor. Thus, learning the basics of computer is very important and the students should pay more attention to basics.

5   Conclusion

Association rules analysis is an important aspect in data mining field and is developing very quickly. This paper uses association rules of Apriori algorithm and analyzes performance of college students, then finds out strong association rules. In the future teaching work, if this method is applied to large amounts of data of different classes and different department, It will have more instructive meaning.

References

1. Agrawal, R., Imielinski, T., Swami, A.: Mining association rules between sets of items in large databases. In: Proc. of ACM SIGMOD Conference on Management of Data, pp. 207–216. ACM, New York (1993)
2. Agrawal, R., Srikant, R.: Fast algorithms for mining association rules in large databases. In: Proceedings of the 20th International Conference on Very Large Data Bases, pp. 487–499. Morgan Kaufmann Publishers Inc., San Francisco (1994)
3. Han, J., Micheline, K.: Data Mining Concepts and Techniques. Morgan Kaufmann Publishers, San Francisco (2001)
4. Wang, Y.: Data mining of association rules. Chengdu University of Information Technology 2(19), 173 (2004)
5. Kantardzic, M.: Data mining. Concepts, models, methods and algorithms. IEEE Press, Los Alamitos (2003)
6. Shao, J., Yu, Z.: Data mining principles and algorithms. China WaterPower Press, Beijing (2003)

Hybrid Controllers for Two-Link Flexible Manipulators

Yanmin Wang[1,2], HongWei Xia[1], and Changhong Wang[1]

[1] Department of Control Science and Engineering
[2] Department of Electrical Engineering
Harbin Institute of Technology
Harbin, Heilongjiang Province, China
ChanghongWang1@eyou.com

Abstract. A novel hybrid control scheme consisting of a fuzzy nonsingular terminal sliding mode (NTSM) controller and a genetic algorithm, is proposed for the tip-position control of an uncertain two-link flexible manipulator. By output redefinition, the whole system is decomposed into an input-output subsystem and a zero dynamic subsystem, aimed to solve the problem of non-minimum phase. By the designed fuzzy NTSM controller, the input-output subsystem is guaranteed of fast convergence, strong robustness and perfect capability of eliminating chattering. And simultaneously, by the designed genetic algorithm, the zero dynamic subsystem is guaranteed of convergence and good performance. The error range of tip-position output caused by system uncertainties is deduced by Lyapunov stability theorem.

Keywords: flexible manipulator, sliding mode control, fuzzy control, genetic algorithm.

1 Introduction

Flexible manipulators (FMs) are of great use, especially in some fields, e.g. outer space, because they possess such superior features as higher load-to-weight ratio, less energy consumption, higher speed. In this paper, the tip-position control is investigated. The major difficulty is the problem of non-minimum phase [1,2]. Until now, output redefinition has been regarded as an acceptable method to solve this problem, that is, by choosing a correct new output, minimum phase could be obtained around the equilibrium point. Some related results have been reported in [3-5]. However, the above researches were mainly concentrated on the existence of minimum-phase region or stability problem, and fewer on the convergence rates of tip-position control.

In order to realize fast convergence of tip-position control, a novel nonsingular terminal sliding mode (NTSM) is adopted in this paper [6]. Compared with traditional linear sliding mode and terminal sliding mode, NTSM is superior for finite-time convergence, strong robustness, global stability and better tracking precision. However, the chattering effect must be taken into account. Compared with the traditional boundary layer method [7,8] which may deteriorate system performance, the intelligent methods as fuzzy logic, neural network are regarded as satisfactory

J. Zhang (Ed.): ICAIC 2011, Part III, CCIS 226, pp. 409–418, 2011.

approaches to eliminate chattering [9-11].In this paper, by model decomposition with a new output, the problem of non-minimum phase is solved and the system is divided into an input-output subsystem and an internal subsystem. A fuzzy NTSM controller is designed to force the input-output subsystem to converge to zero fast and to eliminate chattering. Meanwhile, the internal subsystem is transformed into zero dynamic subsystem, whose performance is guaranteed by genetic algorithm (GA). Under the uncertain disturbances, the tip-position finally converges to a small region about equilibrium point by Lyapunov stability theorem. Simulation results are presented to validate the design.

2   Output Redefinition of an Uncertain FM

In this paper, model parameter uncertainties and external disturbances are both considered and an uncertain two-link FM system is constructed as[12]

$$
[M+\Delta M]\begin{bmatrix}\ddot{\theta}\\\ddot{q}\end{bmatrix}+\begin{bmatrix}E_1+\Delta E_1 & 0\\0 & E_2+\Delta E_2\end{bmatrix}\begin{bmatrix}\dot{\theta}\\\dot{q}\end{bmatrix}
$$
$$
+\begin{bmatrix}0 & 0\\0 & K+\Delta K\end{bmatrix}\begin{bmatrix}\theta\\q\end{bmatrix}+\begin{bmatrix}f_r+\Delta f_r\\f_f+\Delta f_f\end{bmatrix}=\begin{bmatrix}B+\Delta B\\0\end{bmatrix}u+\begin{bmatrix}\Delta f_1\\\Delta f_2\end{bmatrix}
$$
(1)

where $\boldsymbol{\theta}=[\theta_1\ \theta_2]^T\in R^2$ is the joint angle vector; $\boldsymbol{q}=[q_1\ q_2]^T\in R^4$, $\boldsymbol{q}_i=[q_{i1}\ q_{i2}]^T$ is the flexible mode vector of the ith flexible link, $i=1,2$; $E_1\in R^{2\times2}$ and $E_2\in R^{4\times4}$ are positive definite damping matrices; $K\in R^{4\times4}$ is positive definite stiffness matrix; $f_r(\boldsymbol{\theta},\ \boldsymbol{q})\in R^2$ and $f_f(\boldsymbol{\theta},\ \boldsymbol{q})\in R^4$ are terms related to gravity, Coriolis and centripetal forces; $B\in R^{2\times2}$ is the constant input effect matrix; $\boldsymbol{u}=[u_1\ u_2]^T\in R^2$ is the input torque vector; $\Delta f_1, \Delta f_2$ denote the external disturbances; other terms with 'Δ' denote the corresponding uncertainties; $M(\boldsymbol{\theta},q)\in R^{6\times6}$ is positive-definite mass matrix,   and is defined as

$$
M(\boldsymbol{\theta},\boldsymbol{q})=\begin{bmatrix}M_r(\boldsymbol{\theta},\boldsymbol{q}) & M_{rf}^T(\boldsymbol{\theta},\boldsymbol{q})\\M_{rf}(\boldsymbol{\theta},\boldsymbol{q}) & M_f(\boldsymbol{\theta},\boldsymbol{q})\end{bmatrix}
$$

where $M_r\in R^{2\times2}$, $M_{rf}\in R^{4\times2}$, $M_f\in R^{4\times4}$.

Removing all uncertain terms to the right-side of (1), we can get

$$
M\begin{bmatrix}\ddot{\theta}\\\ddot{q}\end{bmatrix}+\begin{bmatrix}f_r+E_1\dot{\theta}\\f_f+E_2\dot{q}+Kq\end{bmatrix}=\begin{bmatrix}B+\Delta B\\0\end{bmatrix}u+\begin{bmatrix}\varDelta_1\\\varDelta_2\end{bmatrix}
$$
(2)

where

$$
\varDelta_1=-\Delta M_r\ddot{\theta}-\Delta M_{rf}^T\ddot{q}-\Delta f_r-\Delta E_1\dot{\theta}+\Delta f_1
$$
$$
\varDelta_2=-\Delta M_{rf}\ddot{\theta}-\Delta M_f\ddot{q}-\Delta f_f-\Delta E_2\dot{q}-\Delta Kq+\Delta f_2
$$

Here assume $\|\varDelta_1\|\leq\varepsilon_1$, $\varepsilon_1>0$; $\|\varDelta_2\|\leq\varepsilon_2$, $\varepsilon_2>0$; $\|\Delta B/B\|<\varepsilon_3<0.5$, $\varepsilon_3>0$.

The tip-position of each link $y_i(L_i, t)$ $(i=1,2)$ can be expressed as[12]

$$y_i(L_i,t) = L_i\theta_i + \sum_{j=1}^{2}\phi_{ij}(x_i)q_{ij}(t) \tag{3}$$

where L_i is the length of the ith flexible link, $\phi_{ij}(x_i)$ is the corresponding flexible mode shape. In this paper, the control objective is to regulate the tip-position from any initial state $y_i(L_i, 0)\neq 0$ to converge to a small region around zero fast.

In order to solve the problem of non-minimum phase, output is redefined. Firstly, (2) is rewritten as the following form by defining state variables $x=[\,\theta^T \quad q^T \quad \dot{\theta}^T \quad \dot{q}^T\,]^T$

$$\dot{x} = f(x) + \big[g(x) + \Delta g(x)\big]u + \Delta f(x) \tag{4}$$

where

$$f(x) = \begin{bmatrix} \dot{\theta} \\ \dot{q} \\ -N_{11}(f_r + E_1\dot{\theta}) - N_{12}(f_f + Kq + E_2\dot{q}) \\ -N_{21}(f_r + E_1\dot{\theta}) - N_{22}(f_f + Kq + E_2\dot{q}) \end{bmatrix}, g(x) = \begin{bmatrix} 0 \\ 0 \\ N_{11}B \\ N_{21}B \end{bmatrix},$$

$$\Delta g = \begin{bmatrix} 0 \\ 0 \\ N_{11}\Delta B \\ N_{21}\Delta B \end{bmatrix}, \Delta f(x) = \begin{bmatrix} 0 \\ 0 \\ N_{11}\Delta_1 + N_{12}\Delta_2 \\ N_{21}\Delta_1 + N_{22}\Delta_2 \end{bmatrix}$$

Since the mass matrix M is positive definite, its inverse exists and is defined as

$$N(\theta,q) = \begin{bmatrix} N_{11}(\theta,q) & N_{12}(\theta,q) \\ N_{21}(\theta,q) & N_{22}(\theta,q) \end{bmatrix}$$

where $N_{11}\in R^{2\times 2}$, $N_{12}\in R^{2\times 4}$, $N_{21}\in R^{4\times 2}$, $N_{22}\in R^{4\times 4}$.

Then, a new system output is chosen as the linear combination of the joint angular position and mode function

$$z(t) = \lambda_0\theta(t) + \lambda_1 q(t) \tag{5}$$

where $z\in R^2$; design parameter $\lambda_0\in R^{2\times 2}$ is a diagonal matrix, $\lambda_1 = \text{diag}[\lambda_{11}^T \;\; \lambda_{12}^T]$ is a block diagonal matrix, with $\lambda_{1i}\in R^{2\times 2}$, $i=1,2$, and all diagonal elements of λ_0 and λ_{1i} are assumed nonzero. The selection of the six design parameters will be illuminated in Section IV.

Now perform input-output linearization on system (4),

$$\ddot{z}(t) = (\alpha + \Delta\alpha) + (\beta + \Delta\beta)u(t) \tag{6}$$

where

$$\alpha(\lambda_0,\lambda_1,x) = -(\lambda_0 N_{11} + \lambda_1 N_{21})(f_r + E_1\dot{\theta})$$
$$-(\lambda_0 N_{12} + \lambda_1 N_{22})(f_f + Kq + E_2\dot{q}) \tag{7a}$$

$$\Delta a(\lambda_0, \lambda_1, x) = (\lambda_0 N_{11} + \lambda_1 N_{21})\Delta_1 + (\lambda_0 N_{12} + \lambda_1 N_{22})\Delta_2 \qquad (7b)$$

$$\beta(\lambda_0, \lambda_1, x) = (\lambda_0 N_{11} + \lambda_1 N_{21})B \qquad (7c)$$

$$\Delta\beta(\lambda_0, \lambda_1, x) = (\lambda_0 N_{11} + \lambda_1 N_{21})\Delta B \qquad (7d)$$

The 4-dimensional flexible mode vectors construct the internal subsystem, obtained directly from (4) as

$$\ddot{q} = -N_{21}(E_1\dot{\theta} + f_r - \Delta_1) - N_{22}(E_2\dot{q} + f_f + Kq - \Delta_2) \\ + N_{21}(B + \Delta B)u(t) \qquad (8)$$

3   Fuzzy NTSM Control for Input-Output Subsystem

For the input-output subsystem (6), the upper bound of the uncertain term Δa in (7b) is easily calculated as

$$\| \Delta a \| = \left\| [\lambda_0 \ \lambda_1] \right\| \|N\| \left\| \begin{bmatrix} \Delta_1 \\ \Delta_2 \end{bmatrix} \right\| \le (\varepsilon_1^2 + \varepsilon_2^2)^{1/2} \left\| [\lambda_0 \ \lambda_1] \right\| \|N\| \le \sigma_1$$

and that of he uncertain term $\Delta\beta$ in (7d) is

$$g = 1 + 2\varepsilon_3 \ge 1 + \varepsilon_3 \ge \frac{\| \beta + \Delta\beta \|}{\| \beta \|} \ge 1 - \varepsilon_3 \ge \frac{1}{1 + 2\varepsilon_3} = \frac{1}{g}$$

with definition $g=1+2\varepsilon_3$.

A.   Design of NTSM Controller

Firstly, a NTSM manifold $l(t)$ is designed as

$$l(t) = z(t) + c^{-1}\dot{z}^{p/q}(t) \qquad (9)$$

where $l \in R^2$; design parameters $c=\text{diag}[c_1 \ c_2]$, with $c_i>0$, $i=1, 2$; p and q are all odd constants, and satisfy $p>q>0$, $1<p/q<2$.

Assume that the initial system state $\|l(0)\| \ne 0$. According to the convergence characteristic of NTSM, when $l(t)=0$, $\forall t \ge t_s$, the state variables of the input-output subsystem (6) will satisfy $l(t) = z(t) + c^{-1}\dot{z}^{p/q}(t) = 0$. Thus, by a proper control law, z and $\dot{z}$ can be driven to remain at the NTSM manifold $l(t)=0$. The dynamics of the input-output system is determined only by the design parameters c, p, q, and finally $z = \dot{z} = 0$ is realized in the finite time t_s along NTSM motion. The relevant control law is derived from the following theorem.

Theorem 1. For the input-output subsystem (6), if the NTSM manifold is chosen as (9), and if the control law is designed as (10)~(12), the subsystem is stable in finite time.

$$u(t) = u_{eq}(t) + u_n(t) \tag{10}$$

where

$$u_{eq}(t) = -\beta^{-1}\left(\alpha + \frac{q}{p}c\dot{z}^{2-p/q}\right) \tag{11}$$

$$u_n(t) = -\beta^{-1}\left[(g-1)\left\|\alpha + \frac{q}{p}\beta^{-1}\dot{z}^{2-p/q}\right\| + g(\sigma_1 + \eta)\right]\mathrm{sgn}(l(t)) \tag{12}$$

where design parameter $\eta = \mathrm{diag}(\eta_1, \eta_2)$, $\eta_i > 0$.

Proof. Consider the following Lyapunov function

$$V(t) = 0.5l(t)^T l(t)$$

$V(t)$ is differentiated with respect to time as

$$\dot{V}(t) = l^T \dot{l}$$

$$= l^T\left\{\dot{z} + \frac{p}{q}c^{-1}\dot{z}^{p/q-1}\left[(\alpha + \Delta\alpha) + (\beta + \Delta\beta)u(t)\right]\right\}$$

$$= l^T\left(\frac{p}{q}c^{-1}\mathrm{diag}\left(\dot{z}^{p/q-1}\right)\right)\left\{\left[1 - (\beta + \Delta\beta)\beta^{-1}\right]\left(\alpha + \frac{q}{p}c\dot{z}^{2-p/q}\right)\right.$$

$$-(g-1)(\beta + \Delta\beta)\beta^{-1}\left\|\alpha + \frac{q}{p}c\dot{z}^{2-p/q}\right\|\mathrm{sgn}(l(t))$$

$$\left. +\Delta\alpha - (\beta + \Delta\beta)\beta^{-1}g(\sigma_1 + \eta)\mathrm{sgn}(l(t))\right\}$$

$$\leq -l^T\frac{p}{q}c^{-1}\mathrm{diag}\left(\dot{z}^{p/q-1}\right)\eta\,\mathrm{sgn}(l(t))$$

According to [12], it can be proved that the above inequality is satisfied with the condition of Lyapunov stability and the system can reach the NTSM manifold $l(t)=0$ and later achieve stability in the finite time t_s. This completes the proof.

B.   Design of Fuzzy Controller

In theorem 1, (12) is the switching control term to trigger chattering. The bigger η is, the bigger the chattering is. Thus, in order to weaken chattering, it is necessary to decrease η. However, on the contrary, a big η is necessary in the process of reaching the sliding mode manifold $l(t)=0$ to provide strong robustness against system uncertainties and external disturbances. Thus, a fuzzy controller is designed in this paper to provide time-varying function $\eta(t)$ to adaptively balance system's robustness against the elimination of chattering.

The membership functions of input and output are shown in Fig. 1~2, respectively. The designed fuzzy controller is a single input and single output controller, and is parallelly applied to the two links.

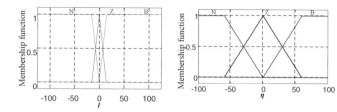

Fig. 1. Member functions of s   **Fig. 2.** Member functions of η

4   GA for Zero Dynamic Subsystem

When the output of the input-output subsystem (6) is zero, that is $\ddot{z}(t) = \boldsymbol{0}$, it has

$$u(t) = -\left(\boldsymbol{\beta} + \Delta\boldsymbol{\beta}\right)^{-1}\left(\boldsymbol{\alpha} + \Delta\boldsymbol{\alpha}\right) \tag{13}$$

After substituting $u(t)$ into (8), the internal subsystem is transformed into zero dynamic subsystem as

$$\ddot{q} = \left[-N_{22} + N_{21}\left(\lambda_0 N_{11} + \lambda_1 N_{21}\right)^{-1}\left(\lambda_0 N_{12} + \lambda_1 N_{22}\right)\right] \left(f_f + Kq + E_2\dot{q} - \Delta_2\right) \tag{14}$$

Now, linearization of the zero dynamic subsystem is done. Define Ω_1 as the neighborhood around $x=0$, and the matrix $N(\boldsymbol{\theta}, q)$ and $f_f(\boldsymbol{\theta}, q)$ is expanded by Taylor's Series respectively as [12]

$$N(\boldsymbol{\theta}, q)\big|_{x \in \Omega_1} = N_0 + f_{hot}(x) \tag{15}$$

$$f_f(\boldsymbol{\theta}, q)\big|_{x \in \Omega_1} = f_{hot}(x) \tag{16}$$

where the constant matrix N_0 is denoted as

$$N_0 = N(\boldsymbol{\theta}, q)\big|_{x=0} = \begin{bmatrix} N_{110} & N_{120} \\ N_{210} & N_{220} \end{bmatrix}$$

and $f_{hot}(x)$ is a matrix with high-order terms in x. Here assume $\| f_{hot} \| \leq \varepsilon_4$, $\varepsilon_4 > 0$.

Substituting (15)~(16) into (14), we can get

$$\ddot{q} = P_0(\lambda_0, \lambda_1)Kq + P_0(\lambda_0, \lambda_1)E_2\dot{q} + G_\Delta(\lambda_0, \lambda_1) \tag{17}$$

where

$$P_0 = -N_{220} + N_{210}\left(\lambda_0 N_{110} + \lambda_1 N_{210}\right)^{-1}\left(\lambda_0 N_{120} + \lambda_1 N_{220}\right)$$

$$G_\Delta(\lambda_0, \lambda_1) = P_0(\lambda_0, \lambda_1)\left[f_{hot}(x) - \Delta_2\right]$$

Define state variables $\boldsymbol{\Phi}=[\boldsymbol{q}^T, \dot{\boldsymbol{q}}^T]^T$, $G=[\boldsymbol{0}, \boldsymbol{G}_\Delta]^T$, and (17) can be rewritten as

$$\dot{\boldsymbol{\Phi}} = A(\lambda_0, \lambda_1)\boldsymbol{\Phi} + G(\lambda_0, \lambda_1) \tag{18}$$

where the state transfer matrix $A(\lambda_0, \lambda_1)$ is given by

$$A(\lambda_0, \lambda_1) = \begin{bmatrix} \boldsymbol{0} & \boldsymbol{I} \\ P_0(\lambda_0, \lambda_1)K & P_0(\lambda_0, \lambda_1)E_2 \end{bmatrix}$$

and the upper bound of disturbance term G is calculated as

$$\| G \| = \| P_0(f_{hot} - \Delta_2) \| \le (\varepsilon_4 + \varepsilon_2)$$

$$\left\| \left[-N_{220} + N_{210}(\lambda_0 N_{110} + \lambda_1 N_{210})^{-1}(\lambda_0 N_{120} + \lambda_1 N_{220}) \right] \right\| \le \varepsilon$$

A.   Design of GA

Parameters λ_0 and λ_1 determine control speciality of zero dynamic subsystem (18) on the premise that $A(\lambda_0, \lambda_1)$ is a Hurwitz matrix, whose eigenvalues are all strictly in the left-half complex plane. In order to optimize λ_0, λ_1 and realize the best performance of the zero dynamic subsystem, a genetic algorithm is designed.

Firstly, the six parameters of λ_0 and λ_1 are denoted as a chromosome (λ_{00}, λ_{01}, λ_{10}, λ_{11}, λ_{12}, λ_{13}) initialized with random selection to enlarge the searching space. $F = 1/J$ is adopted as the fitness function, and $J = 0.5 \int_0^\infty (\boldsymbol{x}^T \boldsymbol{Q}_1 \boldsymbol{x}) dt$ is the quadratic optimal performance of (4).

Under the restriction condition $\max_{1 \le j \le 8} \text{Re}(\lambda_j(A)) < 0$, three basic genetic operations, selection, crossover, and mutation, are performed to obtain the optimization solution. Selection is used to make individuals of the current population in pairs. The selection probability of the individual i is $p_i = f_i / \sum f_i$, in which f_i is the fitness function value of the individual i. In order to ensure the stability and global convergence, the stochastic remainder selection scheme is applied. In this paper, an adaptive probability of crossover P_c is given by [13]

$$p_c(i) = \begin{cases} k_1 \dfrac{F_{max}(i) - F_c(i)}{F_{max}(i) - F(i)} & F_c(i) \ge F(i) \\ k_2 & F_c(i) < F(i) \end{cases} \tag{19}$$

where i is the generation number; $F_{max}(i)$ and $F(i)$ are the maximum and the average fitness values of the population respectively; $F_c(i)$ is the fitness value to be crossovered; design parameters $0 \le k_1 \le 1$, $0 \le k_2 \le 1$. And arithmetic crossover operation is applied. Mutation is used to alter arbitrary genes in randomly selected chromosomes with a given probability to maintain diversity of the population. And uniform mutation operation is applied.

Error Calculation of Tip-position

Theorem 2. For the zero dynamic subsystem (18), since $A(\lambda_0, \lambda_1)$ is a Hurwitz matrix, there is a positive-definite matrix $P \in R^{4 \times 4}$, which satisfies the following equation $A^T P + PA = -Q$,where Q is a positive-definite matrix. Therefore, because of the existence of disturbance term G, the stability of the zero dynamic subsystem can be guaranteed within a region Ω_{2i}

$$\Omega_{2i} = \left\{ q_i \in R^2 : \|q_i\| \leq \| \Phi \| \leq \frac{2\varepsilon \|P\|}{\lambda_\Delta}, i = 1, 2 \right\} \qquad (22)$$

with the definition $\lambda_\Delta = \lambda_{min}(Q)$.

Proof. Choose a positive-definite Lyapunov function $V(\Phi) = \Phi^T P \Phi$, and differentiate $V(\Phi)$ with respect to time,

$$\dot{V}(\Phi) = \dot{\Phi}^T P \Phi + \Phi^T P \dot{\Phi}$$

$$\leq -\lambda_\Delta \| \Phi \|^2 + 2\varepsilon \| P \| \| \Phi \|$$

Thus , Eq. (22) exists.

Since $z(t) = \lambda_0 \theta + \lambda_1 q = 0$, we can further get the convergence region for θ in the neighborhood of equilibrium point $\theta = 0$

$$\Omega_{3i} = \left\{ \theta \in R^2 : |\theta_i| \leq \frac{2\varepsilon \| P \| \| \lambda_1 \|}{\lambda_\Delta \| \lambda_0 \|}, i = 1, 2 \right\} \qquad (23)$$

Thus, the error range of the tip-position can be approximately calculated as

$$\Omega_{4i} = \left\{ y_i : |y_i| \leq L_i |\theta_i| + \| \Phi_{ie} \| \| q_i \|, i = 1, 2 \right\} \qquad (24)$$

5   Simulations

The physical parameters of FM are shown in TABLE 1.

Table 1. Model Parameters of a Two-Link Flexible Manipulator

Model parameter	link 1	link 2
Length	L1=0.8m	L2=0.8m
Density	ρ1=1.1718kg/m	ρ2=0.5859kg/m
Flexural rigidity	E1I1=544.32Nm2	E2I2=68.04Nm2
Total moment of inertia	J1=2.0kgm2	J2=0.4kgm2
Load mass	Mt1=0.5kg	Mt2=0.25kg

Uncertainty in Eq.(3) is simulated with $\Delta_1 = [0.1\sin(t), 0.1\sin(t)]^T$, $\Delta_2 = [0.1\sin(t), 0.1\sin(t), 0.1\sin(t), 0.1\sin(t)]^T$. The initial values are assumed as $\theta_1(0) = 1$, $\theta_2(0) = 0.5$, and others are zeroes.

The parameters λ_0, λ_1 have been achieved by genetic algorithm with parameters chosen as: generation number is 200; individual number in one generation is 20; adaptive parameters are $k_1 = k_3 = 0.5$, $k_2 = 0.9$, $k_4 = 0.1$. The optimal parameters are obtained as $\lambda_0 = diag[3.9309, 4.9137]$, $\lambda_1 = diag[1.3045, 4.4845, 0.0806, 0.2164]$.

The parameters for NTSM manifolds are designed as $c=\text{diag}(2, 2)$, $p=5$, $q=3$. The scaling factors of the input variables l_1, l_2 for the fuzzy controllers are designed as $k_{l1}=500$, $k_{l2}=833$, and the scaling factors of the output variables η_1, η_2 are designed as $k_{\eta1}=0.216$, $k_{\eta2}=0.136$.

Fig.3 and Fig.4 show the control signals u_1, u_2 respectively, and no high-frequency chattering phenomena appear. Fig. 5 shows the tip-positions y_1, y_2, respectively, all of which become stable around their equilibrium points. Using Matlab/LMI toolbox, we can calculate $\|P\|=9.7279\times10^8$ and $\lambda_\Delta=1.6559\times10^{15}$ in Theorem 2. Thus, by (24), the tip-position error ranges for the two links are calculated as $\Omega_{41}=2.8707\times10^{-5}$rad and $\Omega_{42}=3.4363\times10^{-5}$rad, respectively. Therefore, the control objective is reached and the proposed control scheme is validated to be reasonable and effective.

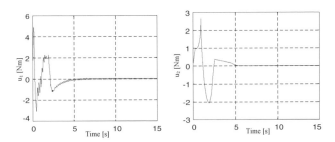

Fig. 3. Control signal u1   **Fig. 4.** Control signal u2

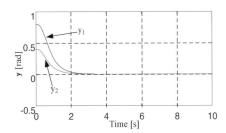

Fig. 5. Tip positions y_1 and y_2

6   Conclusions

In this paper, tip-position control of a two-link FM with model parameter uncertainties and external disturbances is investigated by a novel hybrid control scheme. The non-minimum phase problem and the robust control are the two emphases to be addressed. The prospective control objective is obtained, and the tip-positions of the two-link FM can converge quickly to a satisfying error range deduced by Lyapunov stability theorem. The proposed scheme can simplify the controller design, and is significant not only for theoretical study but for practical application of flexible manipulators.

References

1. Barichard, V.: Multiobjective Programming and Goal Programming: Theoretical Results and Practical Applications. LNEMS (2009)
2. Cao, H.J., Jin, H., Wu, S., et al.: ServiceFlow: QoS Based Service Composition in CGSP. In: Proceedings of the 10th IEEE International Conference on Enterprise Distributed Object Computing (EDOC 2006), Hong Kong, China, pp. 453–458 (2006)
3. Zhen, L., Chun, Y.F., Sen, S.: Fuzzy Multi-Attribute Decision Making-Based Algorithm for Semantic Web Service Composition. Journal of Software 20(3), 583–596 (2009)
4. Qin, F.X., Jun, J.C., Li, W.J., Chen, P.S.: Random-QoS-Aware Reliable Web Service Composition. Journal of Software 20(3), 546–556 (2009)
5. Canfora, G., Penta, M.D., Esposito, R., et al.: An approach for QoS-aware service composition based on genetic algorithms. In: Proceedings of the Genetic and Evolutionary Computation Conference (GECCO 2005), Washington, DC, USA, pp. 1069–1075 (2005)
6. Yuan, J.Z., Hong, H.J., Zhao, W.: An Optimization Model for Dynamic QoS-Aware Web Services Selection and Composition. Chinese Journal of Computers 32(5), 1014–1025 (2009)
7. Hong, X., Zhi, L.Z.: A Particle Swarm Optimization Algorithm for Service Selection Problem Based on Quality of Service in Web Services Composition. Journal of Beijing University of Posts and Telecommunications 32(4), 63–67 (2009)
8. Qing, Z., Rong, L.G., Qiang, L.G., Shan, W., Yong, D.X.: Dynamic service composition algorithms in grid. Journal of Huazhong University of Science and Technology (Nature Science) 34, 134–137 (2006)
9. Wei, W.C., Zhong, Q.X.: Application of ant colony algorithm in web services composition problem. Computer Engineering and Design 28(24), 5912–5914 (2007)
10. Ming, P.X., Xiang, H.Y., Jian, Z.B.: Application of Ant Colony Algorithm in Web Services Composition. Computer Engineering 35(10), 182–187 (2009)

Optimization Choice Algorithm for Composite Service Based on QoS Aggregation

Zhiwu Wang[1], Yu Wang[2], Liu Hong[3,*], and Xueguang Chen[3]

[1] Department of Computer Science and Engineering
Henan Institute of Engineering
Zhengzhou, 451191, P.R. China
[2] Department of Inforation Technology
Zoomlion Heavy Industry Science & Technology Development Co., Ltd
Changsha 410013, P.R. China
[3] Institute of System Engineering
Huazhong University of Science and Technology
Wuhan, 430074, P.R. China
XueguangChen@eyou.com

Abstract. Among a variety of composite services meeting functional demands, how to make optimization choice is a difficult problem faced by users whose QoS demand is a multidimensional objective, and QoS features are not interdependent. Therefore, the service choice based on QoS aggregation is a typical multi-objective optimization problem. By analyzing the existing optimization choice algorithm for composite service based on QoS aggregation, this paper has proposed an optimization choice algorithm for composite service based on cooperative evolutionary genetic algorithm; on the basis of defining service QoS attribute feature vector, it analyzes the strategy and mechanism influencing the efficiency and solution space of this algorithm and verifies the effectiveness and feasibility of this algorithm by comparison with the experiment on traditional single-species genetic algorithm.

Keywords: Composite service, The QoS aggregation, Service choice, Co-evolution genetic algorithm.

1 Introduction

Making evaluation on the non-function property QoS of composite service is the basis for users to make optimization choice for composite service. Users' QoS demand is a multidimensional objective and QoS features are not interdependent. Therefore, the service choice based on QoS aggregation is a typical multi-objective optimization problem. The current algorithms for solving the optimization problem of composite service based on QoS aggregation are divided into two categories: The first category adopts traditional multipurpose optimal methods such as Linear Programming[1], Analytic Hierarchy Process[2], TOPSIS[3], Markov chain[4] and so on to realize

---

* Corresponding author.

J. Zhang (Ed.): ICAIC 2011, Part III, CCIS 226, pp. 419–428, 2011.

research for optimum solution. When using this algorithm, we must obtain the optimum solution of the problem through exhaustive solution space, and the complexity of time computation will get great by exponent along with the increase of the number of candidate physical service in the efficient solutions of composite service, to make it difficult to meet the real-time demands. The other category adopts the intelligent optimization algorithms such as Traditional Genetic Algorithm [5][6], Swarm Optimization Algorithm[7], Simulated annealing Algorithm [8] and Ant Colony Algorithm [9][10] to solve the locally optimum solution of service composition, which realizes the multi-objective local optimization by establishing the Pareto optimal solution set of the problem and meets the needs of the optimization problem of physical composite service, but the problems such as convergence and solutions distribution must be solved for the algorithm. Based on the analysis for the above algorithms, this paper proposes an optimization choice algorithm for composite service based on cooperative evolutionary genetic algorithm to realize the optimization choice of the efficient solutions of composite service, regarding the feature vector of QoS aggregation as objective function.

In the second part, this paper has given a definition to the feature vector of service QoS; in the third part, this paper has proposed an optimization choice algorithm for composite service based on Improved Multi-Objective Cooperative Evolutionary Genetic Algorithm (IMOCEGA) and analyzed the strategy and mechanism influencing the efficiency and solution space of the algorithm; the fourth part has verified the effectiveness and feasibility of this algorithm through the analysis on the comparative trial of the algorithm mentioned in this paper and the traditional single-species genetic algorithm; the fifth part is a conclusion of the paper.

2   Definition and Pretreatment of QoS Feature Vector

This paper has proposed to regard feature vector of extensible multidimensional QoS as the multi-objectives decision variable of optimization algorithm of composite service.   Among the formula $V_{QoS=}\{V_P,V_{ST},V_A,V_{SR},V_R,V_S\}$. The six decision variables are price V_P, service-time V_{ST}, availability V_A, success ratio V_{SR}, reputation V_R and security V_S respectively.

Price: Price means the expenses shall be paid when the task is solved successfully by the service.

Service-time: Service-time means the total time used by the system from that the task is submitted to the service to that the service completes the execution and returns the results to users.

Availability: Availability means the current callable probability of physical services.

Success-ratio: Success-ratio means the probability of completing a task within a period of time after the service is established.

Reputation: Reputation means the users' trust and satisfaction for service and its values come from the evaluation of users about the practical result of called service.

Security: Security means the security class of the service, including the security of data resource access control policies adopted by the service and the security of data transmission encryption policies adopted by the service.

3   Optimization Choice Algorithm for Composite Service Based on QoS Aggregation

A.   Optimization Choice Algorithm for Composite Service Based on IMOCEGA

A typical optimization algorithm for composite service based on QoS aggregation is expressed as follows: Suppose if each efficient solution of composite service has n abstract services, then $ADSResult=\{ADS_1,ADS_2,....,ADS_n\}$ is one efficient solution of composite service, of which, ADS_j is an abstract service of $ADSResult$. Suppose if each abstract service has m physical services, which is $ADS_j=\{PDS_1,PDS_2,...,PDS_m\}$, then we can get the efficient solution set of physical composite service of DT: $PDSResultSet=\{PDSResult_1, PDSResult_2,..., PDSResult_t\}$, of which, $t=n^m$, means t efficient solutions of physical composite service can meet the functional requirements of task DT. To get the physical composite service with optimum QoS, we must calculate the QoS aggregation decision vector of the efficient solution of the tth physical composite service, and chose the efficient solution of physical composite service with optimum QoS aggregation decision vector. When n and m are small, this process can be obtained through exhaustion method, but when n and m get great rapidly, the time complexity for calculation will increase by exponent. Due to the real-time requirement for task solution, it is very important to rapidly find an efficient solution of local optimum physical composite service for the users' solution precision.

For this reason, this paper has proposed an optimization choice algorithm for physical composite service based on Improved Multi-Objective Cooperative Evolutionary Genetic Algorithm (IMOCEGA) to realize the optimum solution of Pareto. By dividing the multi-objective optimization problem into many sub-problems of single-objective optimization and producing one subspecies for each sub-objective, IMOCEGA adopts the cooperative evolution of many subspecies and completes the interactivity of many subspecies through the integration between individuals in the subspecies and the representatives in other species, to eventually get the optimum Pareto solution of the problem.

A typical optimization choice problem of physical composite service can be expressed with formula 1:

$$\left\{ \begin{array}{l} \min f_1((V_P)_{s1},(V_P)_{s2},...,(V_P)_{sn}) \\ \min f_2((V_{ST})_{s1},(V_{ST})_{s2},...,(V_{ST})_{sn}) \\ \max f_3((V_A)_{s1},(V_A)_{s2},...,(V_A)_{sn}) \\ \max f_4((V_{SR})_{s1},(V_{SR})_{s2},...,(V_{SR})_{sn}) \\ \max f_5((V_R)_{s1},(V_R)_{s2},...,(V_R)_{sn}) \\ \max f_6((V_S)_{s1},(V_S)_{s2},...,(V_S)_{sn}) \\ si \in ADS_i \end{array} \right. \tag{1}$$

Multi-objective optimization model includes six QoS decision objectives which correspond to the six QoS features of QoS aggregation decision vector, of which, to respectively are the calculation formulas for solving the QoS values of all QoS features in the efficient solutions of physical composite service. For consumptive QoS features such as service price and service response time, the optimum objectives of them are minimum values. For the efficient QoS features such as availability, success ratio, reputation and security, the optimum objectives of them are maximum values.

The basic process of the optimization choice algorithm for physical composite service based on improved multi-objective cooperative evolutionary genetic algorithm is as follows:

Step1: Initialization. Set the number of subspecies as N according to QoS decision objectives, randomly to create N initial subspecies with the scale of M; set the number of evolution generations as 1, set an external file of blank and set the maximum capacity of the external file as L, among which the external file is used to save the complete optimum Pareto solution obtained from the algorithm during the evolution;

Step2: Make orderly such genetic evolution operations as crossover operation and mutation operation for each subspecies, to obtain the filial generations of all subspecies; Choose different mutation probabilities according to the similarity of the individuals in the subspecies at the time of mutation;

Step 3: Make cooperative operation for each individual of all the subspecies to create complete solutions and get the completely evolved individuals of the whole subspecies; Estimate the adaptive value of the complete individual and determine whether this individual needs an update or abandonment of external file, till all the individuals in all subspecies are completely treated;

Step 4: If the actual number of the complete solutions in the external file is larger than the maximum value it stipulates, perform simplicity operation according to certain simplicity strategy;

Step 5: combine the corresponding component vectors of M individuals in the subspecies and all the T complete non-inferior solutions in the external file, and make calculation according to certain fitness function and choose M individuals as the final new generation of subspecies;

Step 6: determine whether the terminal conditions have been met, if met, the obtained external file is the optimum Pareto solution set of the algorithm; if not met, set the number of evolution generation plus 1 and transfer to step 2.

B.   Analysis on the Strategy and Mechanism Influencing the Efficiency and Solution Space of the Algorithm

1) Chromosome Coding Strategy

This algorithm adopts integer coding method to encode the individuals in the algorithm. First, sort the abstract member services in the efficient solutions of the abstract composite service, and the serial numbers of abstract member services are represented by integer element i; then sort the physical services in each abstract service and the serial numbers of the abstract services are represented by integer element j; the choice of physical services can be represented by a binary component (i,j). This chromosome coding strategy represents that the corresponding complete individuals of the efficient solutions of a physical composite service are composed of any one physical service option among each abstract services of the efficient solutions of abstract composite services.

2) Crossover Operator

This algorithm adopts the direct crossover of the corresponding gene segment between individuals. First randomly create crossover positions i and j which are the series numbers of the genes in the corresponding chromosome codes, then directly change over the corresponding positions in the gene segment from i to j of the gene series number in the two individual chromosome codes, to generate two new individuals.

3) Mutation Operator

This algorithm adopts simple mutation to realize the mutation of individuals. The method goes as follows: first, randomly produce mutation gene number i, and randomly choose a value in the available range of the corresponding variable values of the genes of this serial number to replace the original gene value.

It is found experimentally that the cooperative evolutionary genetic algorithm will rapidly get the local optimum solution when the genetic mutation is adopted with the single low mutation probability. Therefore, this algorithm adopts two kinds of mutation probabilities to realize the mutation of individuals, among which the mutation probability of 0.6 is used when there is super individual and the mutation probability of 0.1 under common conditions.

4) The Construction of Fitness Function

In the problem of multi-objective optimization, the fitness value of individual measures the performance of the solutions represented by the individuals. To estimate the fitness value of the individuals, a fitness function of individuals shall be constructed. The fitness functions of individuals of the optimization choice algorithm for physical composite service based on IMOCEGA can be divided into three types: fitness functions of sub-individuals, fitness functions of complete individuals and fitness functions with penalty variables.

(1)Standardization of QoS Aggregation Decision Variables

The fitness functions of individuals of the optimization choice algorithm for physical composite service are constructed through the values of QoS aggregation vector of individuals, so firstly, the standardization conversion for the original QoS aggregation vector of individuals shall be made. Suppose if all individuals' QoS vectors V^T_{QoS} compose a decision matrix $A=(a_{ij})_{n \times m}$, of which, a_{ij} represents the value of the jth QoS aggregation decision variable of the ith individual, $max(a_{ij})$ represents the maximum value of the jth QoS aggregation decision variable of all individuals and $min(a_{ij})$ represents the minimum value of the jth QoS aggregation decision variable of all individuals, then we can get the standardization decision matrix of QoS aggregation decision vector V_{QoS}, which is $D=(d_{ij})_{n \times m}$, according to the formula 2.

$$d_{ij} = \begin{cases} \dfrac{a_{ij} - min(a_{ij})}{max(a_{ij}) - min(a_{ij})} & a_{ij} \in \{V^T_A, V^T_{SR}, V^T_R, V^T_S\} \\[4mm] \dfrac{max(a_{ij}) - a_{ij}}{max(a_{ij}) - min(a_{ij})} & a_{ij} \in \{V^T_P, V^T_{ST}\} \end{cases} \tag{2}$$

(2)Fitness Function of Sub-individuals

The core concept of multi-objective cooperative evolutionary genetic algorithm is to divide the multi-objective optimization problem into many sub-problems of single-objective optimization and make cooperative evolution for each single objective generating one subspecies. Therefore, this paper adopts all the single-objective functions in formula 1 as the fitness functions of sub-individuals of corresponding subspecies so as to solve the subspecies representative of each heredity.

(3)Fitness Function of Complete Individual

The fitness function of complete individual adopts the weighing and construction of the QoS aggregation decision variables in QoS aggregation decision vectors. The five levels of fuzzy literals *VH(Very High)*, *H(High)*, *M(Middle)*, *L(Low)*, *VL(Very Low)* are used for users to set the weights of QoS features. The exact values of weights is calculated as shown in formula 3, of which, W_P, W_{ST}, W_A, W_{SR}, W_R and W_S respectively are the weights of V_P, V_{ST}, V_A, V_{SR}, V_R and V_S of QoS decision variables.

$$W_P, W_{ST}, W_A, W_{SR}, W_R, W_S \in \{VH, H, M, L, VL\}$$
$$W_P + W_{ST} + W_A + W_{SR} + W_R + W_S = 1 \tag{3}$$
$$\frac{H}{VH} = \frac{M}{H} = \frac{L}{M} = \frac{VL}{L} = \frac{3}{4}$$

The fitness function of complete individual f_{total} can be got by the formula 4 as shown.

$$f_{total} = W_P \times V_P + W_{ST} \times V_{ST} + W_A \times V_A + W_{SR} \times V_{SR} + W_R \times V_R + W_S \times V_S \tag{4}$$

(4)Fitness Function with Penalty Variables

When cropping the external file, eliminate the optimum pareto solutions with small fitness to maintain the predetermined scale of external file. When keeping the excellent quality of individuals in the external file, guarantee the uniform distribution of individuals in the solution space to prevent the individuals in the external file from getting into the local optimality of solution space. This algorithm adopts the mean value of Hamming distance   to determine the similarity between individuals and take it as the penalty variables to adjust the fitness function of complete individual.

The Hamming distance $p(i,j)$ between two individuals c_i and c_j can be solved with the formula 5, of which, $i,j=1,2,...,m$, c_{ik} represents the value of the kth gene value of solution c_i and n represents the number of genes.

$$p(i, j) = \sqrt{\sum_{k=1}^{n} (c_{ik} - c_{jk})^2} \tag{5}$$

Then the mean value $\overline{p}(i)$ of Hamming distance of a certain individual c_i in the external file can be solved with formula 6, of which, m represents the number of individuals in the external file.

$$\overline{p}(i) = \frac{1}{m-1} \sum_{j=1, j \neq i}^{m} p(i, j) \tag{6}$$

The fitness function f_{total} with penalty variables is established according to the formula 4 and formula 5, as shown in formula 7, of which, γ_{pen} is penalty coefficient.

$$f_{pen} = f_{total} + \gamma_{pen} \times \overline{p}(i) \tag{7}$$

(5)The Mode of Cooperation between Subspecies and the Estimation of Individual Fitness Value

This algorithm adopts the random and greedy choice as the cooperation mode between subspecies to estimate the fitness value of individuals. First, combine the representatives of all other subspecies and the sub-individual to be estimated in this subspecies to form a complete solution, and then randomly choose an individual from all other subspecies and combine it with the sub-individual to be estimated to form another complete solution candidate. If the former complete solution candidate can be Pareto-dominated by the latter solution for the total fitness function, reserve the solution candidate generated randomly; otherwise, reserve the solution candidate generated from the representatives.

(6)External Files Update

This algorithm adopts the complete solution candidate set generated from each generation of cooperative evolution to update the external files. Its updating process goes as follows: get all the complete solution candidate sets cooperatively generated from all subspecies, and if the solution candidates are not dominated by any existing solution candidate in external files, add it into the external file and delete all the existing solution candidates Pareto-dominated by this solution candidate; otherwise, the external file shall not be changed. The use of external file will quicken the algorithm convergence to the true Pareto optimum solution set of the problem.

(7)External File Cropping and Next Generation of Subspecies Constructing

If the number of the solutions in the external file exceeds the stipulated maximum value, calculate the fitness values of all individuals in the external file and sort them and remove the solution with minimum fitness value. Construct the next generation of subspecies with the same method. The external file cropping and the construction mechanism of next generation of subspecies can make the optimum Pareto solutions of external file evenly distribute in the Pareto optimum leading edge of problem of multi-objective composite optimization.

(8)Termination Criterion of Algorithm

This algorithm adopts two types of termination criterions: one is to set the maximum value of number of evolution generations, and terminate the algorithm when the species evolves to the maximum number of generations; the other one is to set the update cycle D of the external file, if the external file has not changed during the continuous D times of evolution, we can conclude that the subsequent evolution can not perform much update on the external file and we can terminate the algorithm.

4   Simulation Experiment and Analysis

The following will verify the effectiveness and feasibility of IMOCEGA in the optimization choice for the efficient solutions of QoS aggregation physical service.

The comparison algorithm is traditional single-species genetic algorithm (GA). The hardware conditions for the experiment are: Pentium Dual Core CPU 2.50GHz, memory 2GB; software conditions are: operating system Windows XP, programme software Matlab 7.

To compare the optimum Pareto solution values of IMOCEGA and GA and the convergence rate we can acquire at the same service composite scale, the common fitness function for both of IMOCEGA and GA must be determined. This paper adopts the gross mass of QoS based on weighted mean method shown in formula 4 as the fitness function of algorithm. Firstly, set the fuzzy weight {VH,H,L} and solve the weight of QoS features $W_P=0.615, W_A=0.307, W_S=0.078$ with formula 3, QoS decision variables V_P, V_A and V_S are generated from random numbers, and the fitness function of complete individual is shown in formula 8, which are used for the calculation of the fitness value of cooperative individuals in the IMOCEGA and the fitness value of single individual in GA; Set the penalty coefficient as 0.2.

$$f_{total}^{'} = W_p \times V_P + W_A \times V_A + W_S \times V_S \qquad (8)$$

The specific experiment parameters of this experiment are set as follows: besides the subspecies of multi-objective cooperative evolutionary genetic algorithm is set as 3, all the other parameters of the two comparative algorithms are the same, of which the population size is 50, the crossover probability is 0.7 and the mutation probabilities are 0.6 and 0.1, the number of genetic generations is 500, external file is 120 and the time unit is s. The experiment makes comparison for the statistical data from 50 times of operation, as shown in Table 1.

Table 1. The comparative experiment results on the fitness functions with weights

Algorithm comparison	Process number of composite service	Maximum Fitness Values	Average time	Average iteration
IMOCEGA	6	0.6574	42.98	75
GA		0.6496	39.36	156
IMOCEGA	15	0.6681	66.46	95
GA		0.6513	79.42	245
IMOCEGA	25	0.6757	133.94	124
GA		0.6593	184.11	340

This paper has further given the linear optimization results obtained by using the algorithms of IMOCEGA and GA when the process number of composite service is 15, of which, the relationship between maximum fitness value and iterations is shown in Fig.1 and the relationship between maximum fitness value and calculation time is shown in Fig.2. We can conclude from Fig.1 that solving the problem of optimization choice for the efficient solutions of physical composite service by IMOCEGA can obtain more convergence speed and better fitness value. IMOCEGA takes more calculation time than GA during single evolution, so in Fig.2, the maximum fitness value of IMOCEGA within the equal time at the initial stage is little smaller than that of GA. However, in the overall operation time, IMOCEGA spends less time than GA in obtaining the same fitness values.

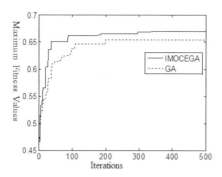

Fig. 1. The Evolution Cures (Maximum Fitness Values——Iterations) Comparison between the Optimum Solutions of IMOCEGA and GA

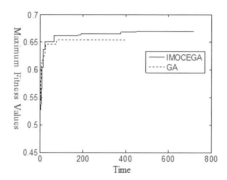

Fig. 2. The Evolution Cures (Maximum Fitness Values——Time) Comparison between the Optimum Solutions of IMOCEGA and GA

5   Conclusion

Through the analysis on the result of the above comparison experiment, we can conclude that the multi-objective cooperative evolutionary genetic algorithm has provided an efficient and practical method for solving the optimization choice problem of the efficient solution of physical composite service in the complex control flow model, and it has more convergence speed and better solution capability in comparison with the traditional intelligent optimization algorithms.

Acknowledgment. This work was supported by the Scientific Research Plan Projects of Zhengzhou (Grant. 10PTGS508-3), Doctoral Research Foundation of Henan Institute of Engineering, Fundation of Key Lab for Image Processing and Intelligent control (20093), Foundation (60773188, 2009B090300309, 2010MS017, 2010QN016).

References

1. Barichard, V.: Multiobjective Programming and Goal Programming: Theoretical Results and Practical Applications. LNEMS (2009)
2. Cao, H.J., Jin, H., Wu, S., et al.: ServiceFlow: QoS Based Service Composition in CGSP. In: Proceedings of the 10th IEEE International Conference on Enterprise Distributed Object Computing (EDOC 2006), Hong Kong, China, pp. 453–458 (2006)
3. Zhen, L., Chun, Y.F., Sen, S.: Fuzzy Multi-Attribute Decision Making-Based Algorithm for Semantic Web Service Composition. Journal of Software 20(3), 583–596 (2009)
4. Qin, F.X., Jun, J.C., Li, W.J., Chen, P.S.: Random-QoS-Aware Reliable Web Service Composition. Journal of Software 20(3), 546–556 (2009)
5. Canfora, G., Penta, M.D., Esposito, R., et al.: An approach for QoS-aware service composition based on genetic algorithms. In: Proceedings of the Genetic and Evolutionary Computation Conference (GECCO 2005), Washington, DC, USA, pp. 1069–1075 (2005)
6. Yuan, J.Z., Hong, H.J., Zhao, W.: An Optimization Model for Dynamic QoS-Aware Web Services Selection and Composition. Chinese Journal of Computers 32(5), 1014–1025 (2009)
7. Hong, X., Zhi, L.Z.: A Particle Swarm Optimization Algorithm for Service Selection Problem Based on Quality of Service in Web Services Composition. Journal of Beijing University of Posts and Telecommunications 32(4), 63–67 (2009)
8. Qing, Z., Rong, L.G., Qiang, L.G., Shan, W., Yong, D.X.: Dynamic service composition algorithms in grid. Journal of Huazhong University of Science and Technology (Nature Science) 34, 134–137 (2006)
9. Wei, W.C., Zhong, Q.X.: Application of ant colony algorithm in web services composition problem. Computer Engineering and Design 28(24), 5912–5914 (2007)
10. Ming, P.X., Xiang, H.Y., Jian, Z.B.: Application of Ant Colony Algorithm in Web Services Composition. Computer Engineering 35(10), 182–187 (2009)

Unidirectional Loop Facility Layout Optimization Design Based on Niche Genetic Algorithm

Lu Tong-Tong, Lu Chao, and Han Jun

College of Economy & Management
China Three Gorges University
YiChang 443002, China
lutongtong2011@eyou.com

Abstract. Based on the study of the unidirectional loop layout, this paper analyzed the necessity of genetic algorithm to the workshop layout optimization. To minimize transportation travel, the mathematical model of the unidirectional loop workshop facility layout was set up, using the niche genetic algorithm with introduction of penalty function and elite reservation strategy to accomplish the facility layout optimization. Through the calculation of the example, the feasibility and effectiveness of this algorithm in facility layout optimization design is verified.

Keywords: unidirectional loop layout, niche genetic algorithm, optimization design.

1 Introduction

The problem of the workshop facility layout is one of the most important topics which the modern industrial production confronts, and whether the facility layout is reasonable, scientific and refined or not will influent the development process of produce directly. As the development of the economy, every enterprise begins to realize that the reasonable workshop layout will not only reduce the cost of the transportation, but also improve the efficient of the process of the material, reduce the delay in product, improve the efficient of produce, so scientific and reasonable facility layout is very essential.

According to the different forms of things being conveyed, the workshop facility layout mainly includes three types that single layout, multiple layout, loop layout. Owing to unidirectional loop layout's simple structure and high soft, it is used widely in the system of manufacture. As for the workshop facility layout, ensuring the device's specific location is the key to the facility layout. Because workshop layout is a NP hard problem, traditional ways exist the limitation of complicated manipulation and low degree of accuracy, but genetic algorithm can solve this problem effectively. In view of practical situation of workshop layout, this paper adopts the niche genetic algorithm with introduction of penalty function to design unidirectional loop facility

J. Zhang (Ed.): ICAIC 2011, Part III, CCIS 226, pp. 429–436, 2011.

layout. Proved by practice, the measure taken by this paper is effective and is worth of being spread.

2   Design of Optimization Model for Unidirectional Loop Facility Layout

As shown in figure 1. In unidirectional loop facility layout, all devices are connected with the loop logistics path, and the materials move only in one direction (such as clockwise). Each component must pass by loading and unloading station when enter or leave the system, and its processing technique is known. When the processing of one component is completed, it is transported to the device where the next procedure needed by material handling device along the loop logistics path. If the device is currently busy, then the component is stored in the local buffer, waiting for the device for the idle state.

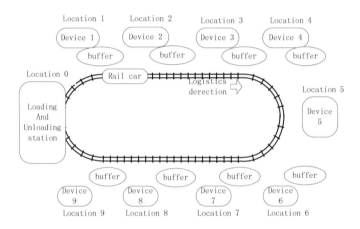

Fig. 1. Unidirectional loop workshop facility layout

In the loop rail there are $n+1$ locations, as shown in figure 1(assuming the loading and unloading station is fixed in location 0), the workshop has n devices, the logistics relationship between all these devices is known as: $w_{ij}, i, j = 1, \cdots, n, i \neq j$, and find the solution of how to put the n pieces of devices into the n locations (i.e. determine the optimal layout sequence), in order to minimum total expenses of material transporting among devices and time of delay.

Record $\alpha = (a(1), \cdots, a(i), \cdots a(j), \cdots a(n))$ as the location vector of all n devices, for example, $a(i)$ means the location of device i. If $a(i) < a(j)$, it means that device i is located in upstream, device j is located in downstream (as shown in figure 1 device 1 is located in upstream, device 2 is located in downstream), w_{ij} is the logistics volume between device i and device j , whose direction is from i to j . In design of facility layout, the main consideration are the indicators of the cost of system operation and the system residence time. While these indicators are relevant to system total travel, the smaller the total travel of transport is, the less the expenses is, and the shorter the system residence time is. So the goals of facility layout are turned into the pursuit of minimum total travel of transportation, thus the optimized target function can be simplified as [1, 2, 3]:

$$\min f(\alpha) = \sum_{i=1}^{n} \sum_{j=1}^{n} w_{ij} \times \max\left(0, \frac{a(i) - a(j)}{|a(i) - a(j)|}\right) \tag{1}$$

In this formula: $f(\alpha)$ represents the total travel in the planning production cycle, α represents the current sequence of facility layout.

3 Algorithm Theory and Design

Because traditional genetic algorithm exists characteristics of premature and falling easily into local convergence, therefore, the paper uses niche genetic algorithm to optimize design for workshop layout.

A. Basic Principles of Niche Genetic Algorithm with Introduction of Penalty Function and Elitist Strategy

The thoughts of that are as following: first, compare the distance between every two individuals in the group, if distance between two individuals is less than a pre-specified distance, then compare the fitness of the two individuals and impose a penalty in individual which has the lower fitness, making its fitness significantly reduced. Thus, in the pre-specified distance of L , the fitness of individual who has low fitness will become even lower after treatment, and this individual is more likely to be eliminated in the next evolutionary process, that is, there is only one good individual with the designated distance. Thus group keeps a certain distance between individuals and reduces the similarity degree, to maintain the diversity of population. At the same time, adopt elite reservation strategy[4], that is, in the evolutionary process of each generation, $N(N < M)$ best individuals are retained not to participate in selection, crossover and mutation operations, and are copied directly to the next generation group. This strategy can guarantee that the retained optimal individuals will not be damaged by crossover and mutation genetic algorithm, and have been preserved in groups; this also is an important guarantee condition of the convergence of genetic algorithm. Specific operation is: after evolutionary operation and eliminated operation of each generation are completed, sort the fitness of group based on descending order. Remember the former N individuals among the group, directly take niche eliminated operation with the already evolved individuals instead of participating in the selection, crossover and mutation.

B. Crossover Operator

Individuals of group which have M individuals forms $M/2$ individual groups in the way of randomly paired. If adopt conventional single-point crossover operator, it will produce a large number of infeasible solutions. Therefore, the paper has to design a new crossover operator [2, 5]. Supposing there are nine devices' vector location is the corresponding gene number. Here crossover operator used is as follows. Parent one randomly passes half of number of its genes to allele seat of child one, then according to order of parent two, genes that child one lacks will in turn assign to the empty locus, and produce child two in the same way. Basic operation is as shown in figure 2.

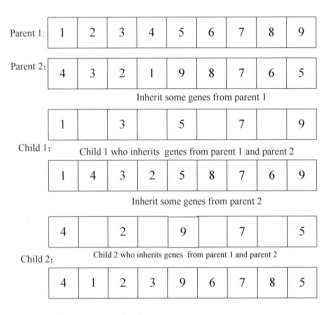

Fig. 2. Schematic diagram of crossover operator

C. Mutation Operator

If adopt the traditional mutation operator, it will produce infeasible solutions, therefore, this paper adopts transposition mutation that exchanges randomly two gene bits selected. Basic operation is as shown in figure 3.

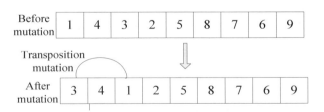

Fig. 3. Schematic diagram of mutation operator

D. Steps of Algorithm

1) Generate Initial Population: Randomly arrange n devices in order to obtain M types of equipment layout.

2) Sequence: According to their individual fitness, sort individuals based on descend and remember former N individuals, in order to preserve individuals that have higher fitness in the population. $(N < M)$

3) Select Options: Obtain new population by roulette wheel selection from the population.

4) Crossover and Mutation operator: According to the method of this paper, carry out crossover and mutation operation.

5) Niche Crowding Operator: Get $M + N$ individuals from step (4), and take any two individuals X_i and X_j from the $M + N$ individuals to calculate the Euclidean distance as following formula:

$$\left\| X_i - X_j \right\| = \sqrt{\sum_{i=1}^{M} \left(X_{ik} - X_{jk} \right)^2} \tag{2}$$

Among: $i = 1,2,\cdots,M + N - 1$, $j = i+1, i+2, \cdots, M + N$.

When $\left\| X_i - X_j \right\| < L$, compare fitness of individual X_i and X_j , and impose a strong penalty function on the individual that has the lower fitness: $F_{\min}\left(X_i, X_j \right) = penalty$, in order to greatly reduce the fitness.

6) Elitist Strategy: According to the fitness of individuals sort the order based on descend, and remember former individuals.

7) Termination Condition: Determine whether meet the condition of the termination, if it does not meet, update the evolutionary algebra counter $gen = gen + 1$, and former N individuals of step (6) will be as the next generation population, then go to step (3); if it meets condition of termination, output results.

4   The Illustration Results

In order to complete a project, an enterprise builds up a unidirectional loop facility layout section, and the workshop needs processing nine kinds of components. According to craft of components that need processing, purchase nine pieces of devices, and represent respectively as $m1, m2, \cdots m9$. In a unidirectional loop layout, processing device is placed in accordance with the order of process, and logistics relationship of the nine pieces of devices $w_{ij}, i, j = 1,\cdots,9, i \neq j$ see Table 1 as below.

Table 1. Logistic diagram between devices

device	m1	m2	m3	m4	m5	m6	m7	m8	m9
m1	0	0	40	2	17	40	0	19	0
m2	28	0	19	0	32	0	0	0	17
m3	39	62	0	40	0	0	0	0	0
m4	19	0	4	0	30	12	0	0	0
m5	0	17	22	0	0	42	0	28	0
m6	0	0	0	19	0	0	2	0	0
m7	0	0	0	0	22	19	0	0	2
m8	0	55	32	0	0	0	22	0	0
m9	0	0	0	0	0	0	17	0	0

Adopt niche genetic algorithm as above to optimize and calculate the facility layout. Take initial population $M = 50$, crossover probability is 0.8, mutation probability is 0.05, penalty function value is $10^{(-30)}$, and the distance's parameters of the niche is 0.5. The number of former N individuals is $N = M / 2$, and the maximum number of iterations is 500. Results of calculation are as shown.

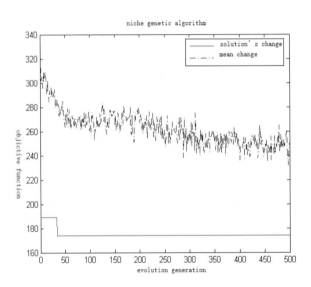

Fig. 4. Performance chart of niche genetic algorithm

As can be seen from figure, adopt niche genetic algorithm with penalty functions to optimize unidirectional loop facility layout, which gets the better solutions. And compare before and after optimization of facility layout, as following table.

As we can see from Table 2, before optimization the location of facility layout is $(2,7,6,9,5,8,4,3,1)$, which means device $m1$ arranges in location 2, device $m2$

Table 2. Comparison table before and after optimization

Device name	m1	m2	m3	m4	m5	m6
Location before optimization	2	7	6	9	5	8
Location after optimization	7	4	2	3	8	9

Device name	m7	m8	m9	The optimal solution $f(\alpha)$		
Location before optimization	4	3	1	232		
Location after optimization	6	1	5	174		

arranges in location 7, ... device $m9$ arranges in location 1, and the calculated corresponding solution is $f(\alpha) = 232$. After optimization the optimal layout is $(7,4,2,3,8,9,6,1,5)$, which means device $m1$ arrange in location 7, device $m2$ arranges in location 4, device $m3$ arranges in location 2, ... device $m9$ arranges in location 5, and the calculated optimal solution is $f(\alpha) = 174$. Through comparative analysis as above, it can be seen that adopting niche genetic algorithm with introduction of penalty function and the elitist strategy calculates model of facility layout, which can optimize workshop layout, reduce greatly logistics capacity of workshop, reduce operating cost of workshop, and bring benefits to enterprises. At the same time, also further confirm the feasibility and effectiveness of the niche genetic algorithm.

5   Conclusion

Optimal design of workshop layout is very important for improving productivity and reducing transportation costs, and mainly the workshop layout of unidirectional loop layout is studied and its mathematical model is established. Through adopting niche genetic algorithm with introduction of penalty function and the elite reservation strategy, the unidirectional loop facility layout optimization problem is solved .The feasibility and validity of this algorithm is proved through calculation, and there are good practical value and popularized significance for solving this kind of problem such as workshop layout.

References

1. Li, Z., Zhong, Y., Liu, J.: Machine Layout Design in a Unidirectional Loop Manufacturing System. Jouranal Of Computer-Aided Design & Computer Graphics 17(7), 818–822 (2003)
2. Qi, J., Zhu, C., Zeng, Y.: Genetic Algorithm in Facility Layout Design. China Plant Engineering, 4–6 (2005)

3. Zhu, C., Qi, J., Zeng, Y.: Study on machine layout problem based on genetic algorithm and Tabu search hybrid algorithm. Systems Engineering And Electronics 28(4), 630–632 (2006)
4. Wang, Y.: Rough Set Attribute Reduction Algorithm Based on Niche GA. Computer Engineering 34(5), 66–68 (2008)
5. Han, W.-m., Fan, J.-w.: Based on an Improved Genetic Algorithm for Flexible Job Shop Scheduling Problem. Science Technology and Engineering 8(22), 6315–6317 (2008)

Hyperchaotic Attractors Generated from Nadolschi Chaotic System*

Ruochen Zhang[1] and Yan Zhao[2]

[1] Department of Electronic Engineering, Engineering Faculty,
The Chinese University of Hong Kong, New Territories, Hong Kong, China
[2] Department of Automatic Control Engineering, Shenyang Institute of Engineering,
Shenyang, Liaoning Province, China
s0761080@ee.cuhk.edu.hk

Abstract. This paper presents several novel hyperchaotic systems generated from Nadolschi chaotic system. The dimension of the considered Nadolschi chaotic system is increased from three to four by introducing a new variable. Then, the evolving law of the new variable is designed appropriately to realize the hyperchaotification. There are two positive Lyapunov exponents in the generated hyperchaotic systems. Finally, a variety of novel hyperchaotic attractors are presented in the simulation results.

Keywords: hyperchaos, Nadolschi chaotic system, hyperchaotic attractor, Lyapunov exponent.

1 Introduction

In recent years, the suppression and synchronization of hyperchaotic systems have become a hot research topic in the field of nonlinear science [1-7]. Meanwhile, many novel hyperchaotic systems were found or created constantly in the last few years [8-13]. It should be noted that the presence of more than one positive Lyapunov exponent clearly improves the security by generating more complex dynamics [14]. For hyperchaos, some basic properties are described as follows [15]. (i) Hyperchaos exists only in higher-dimensional systems, i.e., not less than four-dimensional (4D) autonomous system for the continuous time cases. (ii) It was suggested that the number of terms in the coupled equations that give rise to instability should be at least two, in which one should be a nonlinear function.

Inspired by the above ideas, the hyperchaotification problem of a class of well-known chaotic systems named Nadolschi chaotic system is investigated in this paper. For this purpose, a new variable is introduced into the considered chaotic system and the dimension of the chaotic system is increased from three to four. Then, the evolving law of the new variable is designed appropriately to realize the hyperchaotification. By calculation, there are two positive Lyapunov exponents in the constructed 4D systems. Therefore, hyperchaos is generated. The hyperchaotic attractors are presented in the simulation results.

---

* This work is partially supported by the Scientific Research Fund of Liaoning Provincial Education Department under Grant #2009A544 to Y. Zhao.

J. Zhang (Ed.): ICAIC 2011, Part III, CCIS 226, pp. 437–444, 2011.

2   Problem Statement

Consider the following Nadolschi chaotic system [16]:

$$\begin{cases} \dot{x}_1(t) = -x_2(t)x_3(t) + ax_1(t), \\ \dot{x}_2(t) = x_1(t)x_3(t) + bx_2(t), \\ \dot{x}_3(t) = x_1(t)x_2(t)/3 + cx_3(t), \end{cases} \tag{1}$$

where $x_1(t)$, $x_2(t)$ and $x_3(t)$ are state variables, a, b and c are system's parameters. As is well-known, the above system are chaotic when the parameters are chosen appropriately. For example, when the parameters are chosen as $a = 5$, $b = -10$ and $c = -3.8$, the considered system is chaotic. The corresponding chaotic attractor is shown as Fig. 1 (The initial conditions are chosen as $x(0) = (-6, 3, -2)^T$).

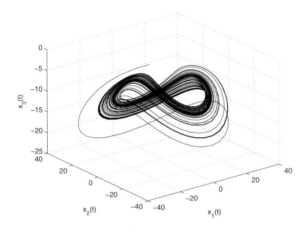

Fig. 1. The chaotic attractor of the Nadolschi chaotic system

It is obvious that there are three coupled terms in the above Nadolschi chaotic system. Our goal is to introduce a new variable into the chaotic system (1) and choose appropriate evolving law of the new variable to make the constructed 4D system generate hyperchaotic behavior.

3   Hyperchaotic Attractors Generated from Nadolschi Chaotic System

Firstly, we introduce a new variable $x_4(t)$ and construct the following four-dimensional system:

$$\begin{cases} \dot{x}_1(t) = -x_2(t)x_3(t) + ax_1(t), \\ \dot{x}_2(t) = x_1(t)x_3(t) + bx_2(t) + x_4(t), \\ \dot{x}_3(t) = x_1(t)x_2(t)/3 + cx_3(t), \\ \dot{x}_4(t) = dx_2(t) \end{cases} \tag{2}$$

where $x_1(t)$, $x_2(t)$, $x_3(t)$ and $x_4(t)$ are state variables, a, b, c and d are system's parameters.

For the above system, it holds that

$$\Delta V = \frac{\partial \dot{x}_1(t)}{\partial x_1(t)} + \frac{\partial \dot{x}_2(t)}{\partial x_2(t)} + \frac{\partial \dot{x}_3(t)}{\partial x_3(t)} + \frac{\partial \dot{x}_4(t)}{\partial x_4(t)} \tag{3}$$
$$= a + b + c$$

Obviously, the above system (2) is dissipative when the system's parameters are chosen as $a = 5$, $b = -10$ and $c = -3.8$. In fact, while the last parameter d is chosen as $d = -15$, there are two positive Lyapunov exponents in the above 4D system which are described in Fig. 2 ($\lambda_1 = 1.2798$, $\lambda_2 = 0.15518$). Therefore, hyperchaos is generated in this condition. The corresponding hyperchaotic attractor is given in Fig. 3 and Fig. 4. The state evolving curves of the hyperchaotic system are presented in Fig. 5.

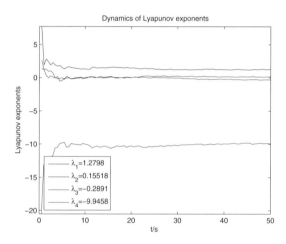

Fig. 2. The dynamics of Lyapunov exponents

Next, we introduce the new variable $x_4(t)$ in the following form and then the constructed four-dimensional system is given as follows:

$$\begin{cases} \dot{x}_1(t) = -x_2(t)x_3(t) + ax_1(t), \\ \dot{x}_2(t) = x_1(t)x_3(t) + bx_2(t), \\ \dot{x}_3(t) = x_1(t)x_2(t)/3 + cx_3(t) + x_4(t), \\ \dot{x}_4(t) = dx_3(t) \end{cases} \tag{4}$$

where $x_1(t)$, $x_2(t)$, $x_3(t)$ and $x_4(t)$ are state variables, a, b, c and d are system's parameters.

It can be seen that the above system (4) is also dissipative when the system's parameters are chosen as $a = 5$, $b = -10$ and $c = -3.8$ since $\Delta V < 0$. In fact, while the last parameter d is chosen as $d = -20$, there are two positive Lyapunov exponents

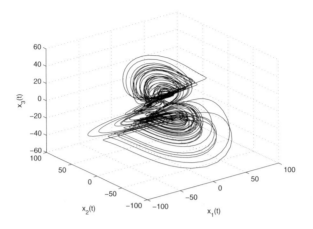

Fig. 3. The hyperchaotic attractor of the hyperchaotic system (i)

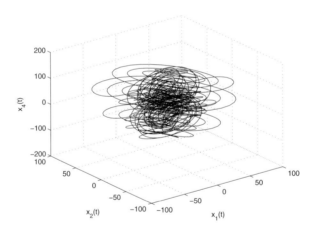

Fig. 4. The hyperchaotic attractor of the hyperchaotic system (ii)

in the above 4D system which are described in Fig. 6 ($\lambda_1 = 2.1658$, $\lambda_2 = 0.015528$). Therefore, hyperchaos is generated in this condition. The corresponding hyperchaotic attractor is given in Fig. 7 and Fig. 8. The state evolving curves of the hyperchaotic system are presented in Fig. 9.

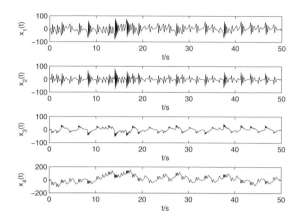

Fig. 5. The state evolving curves of the hyperchaotic system

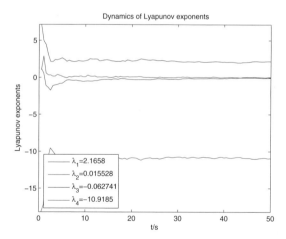

Fig. 6. The dynamics of Lyapunov exponents

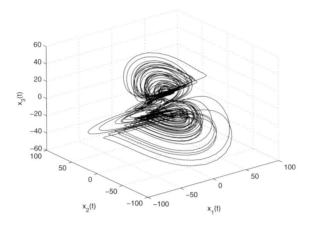

Fig. 7. The hyperchaotic attractor of the hyperchaotic system (i)

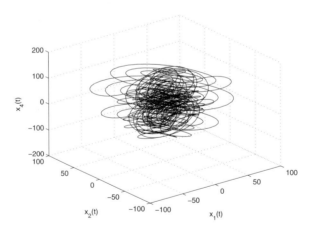

Fig. 8. The hyperchaotic attractor of the hyperchaotic system (ii)

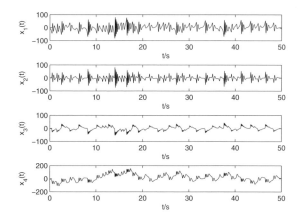

Fig. 9. The state evolving curves of the hyperchaotic system

4   Conclusions

In this paper, the novel hyperchaotic systems generated from Nadolschi chaotic system are proposed. By introducing a new state variable into the considered Nadolschi chaotic system, the corresponding four-dimensional systems are constructed. When the evolving laws are chosen properly, there are two positive Lyapunov exponents in the constructed four-dimensional systems and therefore hyperchaos is generated. The future work should be to investigate the properties of the proposed novel hyperchaotic systems and the bifurcation analysis with respect to the system's parameters.

Acknowledgment. The authors would like to thank the constructive advises of the reviewers. This work is supported by National Nature Science Foundation under Grant 60972164, 60804006 and the Scientific Research Fund of Liaoning Provincial Education Department under Grant 2009A544.

References

1. Huang, J.: Chaos synchronization between two novel different hyperchaotic systems with unknown parameters. Nonlinear Analysis 69(11), 4174–4181 (2008)
2. Li, Y.-X., Liu, X.-Z., Zhang, H.-T.: Dynamical analysis and impulsive control of a new hyperchaotic system. Mathematical and Computer Modelling 42(11-12), 1359–1374 (2005)
3. Yang, C.-D., Tao, C.-H., Wang, P.: Comparison of feedback control methods for a hyperchaotic Lorenz system. Physics Letter A 374(5), 729–732 (2010)
4. Zheng, S., Deng, G.-G., Bi, Q.-S.: A new hyperchaotic system and its synchronization. Applied Mathematics and Computation 215(9), 3192–3200 (2010)
5. Xue, Y.-J., Yang, S.-Y.: Synchronization of generalized Henon map by using adaptive fuzzy controller. Chaos, Soliton & Fractals 17(4), 717–722 (2003)
6. Yanchuk, S., Kapitaniak, T.: Chaos-hyperchaos transition in coupled Rössler systems. Physics Letter A 290(3-4), 139–144 (2001)

7. Guo, R.-W.: A simple adaptive controller for chaos and hyperchaos synchronization. Physics Letter A 372(34), 5593–5597 (2008)
8. Gao, T.-G., Chen, Z.-Q., Gu, Q.-L., et al.: A new hyperchaos generated from generalized Lorenz system via nonlinear feedback. Chaos, Soliton & Fractals 35(2), 390–397 (2008)
9. Wang, G.-Y., Zhang, X., Zheng, Y., et al.: A new modified hyperchaotic Lü system. Physica A 371(2), 260–272 (2006)
10. Yang, Q.-G., Liu, Y.-J.: A hyperchaotic system from a chaotic system with one saddle and two stable node-foci. Journal of Mathematical Analysis and Applications 360(1), 293–306 (2009)
11. Ahmad, W.-M.: A simple multi-scroll hyperchaotic system. Chaos, Soliton & Fractals 27(5), 1213–1219 (2006)
12. Xue, Y.-J., Yang, S.-Y.: Synchronization of generalized Henon map by using adaptive fuzzy controller. Chaos, Soliton & Fractals 17(4), 717–722 (2003)
13. Deng, H.-M., Li, T., Wang, Q.-H., et al.: A fractional-order hyperchaotic system and its synchronization. Chaos, Soliton & Fractals 41(2), 962–969 (2009)
14. Zhang, H.-G., Zhao, Y., Yu, W., et al.: A unified approach for fuzzy modeling and robust synchronization of different hyperchaotic systems. Chinese Physics B 17(11), 4056–4066 (2008)
15. Chen, Z.-Q., Yang, Y., Qi, G.-Y., et al.: A novel hyperchaos system only with one equilibrium. Physics Letter A 360(6), 696–701 (2007)
16. Li, R.-H., Xu, W., Li, S.: Linear state feedback control for a new chaotic system. Acta Physica Sinca 17(2), 598–606 (2006)

Satellite Attitude Determination Using Space Camera and Gyros' Information

Peijun Yu[1], Keqiang Xia[2], and Jiancheng Li[2]

[1] Northwestern Polytechnical University,
[2] State Key Laboratory of Astronautic Dynamics
PeijunYu2011@163.com

Abstract. A new algorithm of satellite attitude determination is put forward which uses the information of camera's measurements. The relationship of attitude angle and position of image spot was derived from imaging principle. According to the imaging character of CCD the measurement residual model of CCD camera represented by quaternion error was deduced, and the model was linearized in the case of small attitude angle. An attitude determination system was made up by gyros and camera, and the state error equation and measurement equation of the system were presented. Kalman filter was adopted to accomplish the attitude determination system. The conditions of attitude determination using camera were derived by analyzing the observability of the system. Results of simulation indicate that the high resolution of camera photo ensures that the system is capable of high accuracy and convergence speed. The offered algorithm is simple and effective.

Keywords: Attitude Determination, Camera, Error Quaternion, Kalman Filter.

1 Introduction

Space camera possesses of large filed of view and high resolution which is used to take the photos of ground and stars. For this reason the approaches of exploring information from space camera to estimate attitude are investigated gradually. The approach of tracking three characteristic spots in camera image to estimate spacecraft attitude is investigated in reference [1][2], and it demands not only the assurance of tracking three spots but also the height of space camera which is hardly to satisfy. A new approach of using space camera and gyros to estimate attitude is presented for three-axis stable satellite in this paper, which doesn't demand the height of camera and has lower computation with respect to the approach mentioned in reference[1][2].

The measurement residual model expressed by error quaternion is deduced from imaging principle of space camera. According to the model of space camera a method of satellite attitude determination which uses space camera and gyros is derived. The basic principle of the method is using camera and gyros separately as short period attitude reference and long period attitude reference. Gyros can sense the angular velocity and continuously provide the attitude of satellite by integrating angular velocity, but the attitude error increases with the time going because of the gyro inherent drift. The measurement of high resolution camera which includes accurate

J. Zhang (Ed.): ICAIC 2011, Part III, CCIS 226, pp. 445–453, 2011.
© Springer-Verlag Berlin Heidelberg 2011

attitude information can be used to revise the drift of gyro. Kalman filter can be adopted to accomplish the attitude determination. The frame of attitude determination system composed by space camera and gyros is shown in Fig.1.

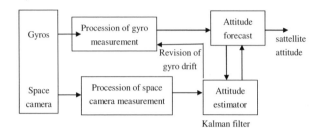

Fig. 1. Frame of attitude determination

2   Attitude Measurement Model of Space Camera

Define image of landmark on camera photo as reference image spot during the stage of ground imaging, and the position of reference image spot in photo varies with satellite attitude. According to the light path of space camera shown in Fig.2[3], the relation of the position of reference image spot and attitude angles can be deduced.

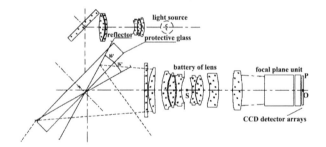

Fig. 2. Light path of space camera

Before investigating the relation, it is necessary to introduce the coordinates involved and the installation of space camera. The coordinates are as follows: $OX_oY_oZ_o$, $OX_bY_bZ_b$ and OX_pY_p where the subscripts o, b, p denote respectively orbit, body, photo. The installation of space camera is, the normal direction of photo P parallels OZ_b, and the initial spot of OX_pY_p is the intersecting point of lens optical axis and photo P, OX_p parallels OX_b, and OY_p parallels OY_b. The distance between projective center S and origin O of photo is focal length of lens f. $OX_bY_bZ_b$ and $OX_oY_oZ_o$ match together on condition that the satellite observes earth stably, and define the position of reference image spot as $a(x_0, y_0)$. Then the relation of the position of reference image spot and attitude angles can derive from optical geometry theory. They are as follows,

(a) Define the geometry position of image spot as $a_\psi (x_\psi, y_\psi)$ when satellite takes on the attitude of yaw ψ only, then the relation is

$$x_\psi = x_0 \cos(\psi) + y_0 \sin(\psi) \tag{1-a}$$

$$y_\psi = y_0 \cos(\psi) - x_0 \sin(\psi) \tag{1-b}$$

(b) Define the geometry position of image spot as $a_\varphi(x_\varphi, y_\varphi)$ when satellite takes on the attitude of roll φ only, then the relation is

$$x_\varphi = \frac{fx_0}{y_0 \sin(-\varphi) + f \cos(-\varphi)} \tag{2-a}$$

$$y_\varphi = f \frac{y_0 \cos(-\varphi) - f \sin(-\varphi)}{y_0 \sin(-\varphi) + f \cos(-\varphi)} \tag{2-b}$$

(c) Define the geometry position of image spot as $a_\theta (x_\theta, y_\theta)$ when satellite takes on the attitude of pitch θ only, then the relation is

$$x_\theta = f \frac{x_0 \cos(\theta) - f \sin(\theta)}{x_0 \sin(\theta) + f \cos(\theta)} \tag{3-a}$$

$$y_\theta = \frac{fy_0}{x_0 \sin(\theta) + f \cos(\theta)} \tag{3-b}$$

Because the space camera images in the form of digital and each CCD cell matches one image spot, so define the size of CCD cell d as the unit length of OX_pY_p. Then the relation of coordinate (X, Y) of image spot in photo and geometry position (x, y) is

$$x = X \cdot d, \quad y = Y \cdot d \quad (X, Y \in N) \tag{4}$$

and the coordinate of image spot in photo changes from (x_0, y_0) to (X_0, Y_0) accordingly. The rest is deduced by analogy. The relation of attitude and image position can be derived in term of 3-1-2 Euler transformation by executing (a)(b)(c) step by step, which is the measurement model of space camera. Substitute (3) by (1)(2)(4) and reform, then the camera measure model is

$$X_3 = \frac{[C_1 \cos(\theta) - C_2 \sin(-\varphi) \sin(\theta) - C_3 \sin(\theta)] f}{dC_4} + v_{Cx} \tag{5-a}$$

$$Y_3 = \frac{[C_2 \cos(-\varphi) - f \sin(-\varphi)] f}{dC_4} + v_{Cy} \tag{5-b}$$

Where

$C_1 = d[X_0 \cos(\psi) + Y_0 \sin(\psi)]$, $C_2 = d[Y_0 \cos(\psi) - X_0 \sin(\psi)]$, $C_3 = f \cos(-\varphi)$,
$C_4 = C_1 \sin(\theta) + C_2 \sin(-\varphi) \cos(\theta) + C_3 \cos(\theta)$,and v_C is noise which is influenced by

448   P. Yu, K. Xia, and J. Li

fix error, lens error, image acquisition panel error, orientation error of image recognition and so on, and the influence can be equal to Gauss white noise. Equation(5) indicates the relation of coordinate of image spot and attitude is independent of the height of camera.

When the attitude angles are small ($|\psi| \le 1°$, $|\varphi| \le 1°$, $|\theta| \le 1°$),the relations exist:

$$q_0 \approx 1, \quad q_1 \approx 0.5\varphi, \quad q_2 \approx 0.5\theta, \quad q_3 \approx 0.5\psi \tag{6}$$

$$\sin(\varphi) \approx \varphi, \quad \cos(\varphi) \approx 1, \quad \sin(\varphi)\sin(\theta) \approx 0 \tag{7}$$

When the attitude angles are zero $X_3 = X_0$, $Y_3 = Y_0$. The definitions of the attitude errors are

$$\Delta\varphi = \varphi - \hat{\varphi}, \quad \Delta\theta = \theta - \hat{\theta}, \quad \Delta\psi = \psi - \hat{\psi} \tag{8}$$

According to definitions of attitude errors the relation of quaternion is $q = \hat{q} \otimes \Delta q$. And by (6) there is

$$\Delta q_0 \approx 1, \quad \Delta q_1 \approx 0.5\Delta\varphi, \quad \Delta q_2 \approx 0.5\Delta\theta, \quad \Delta q_3 \approx 0.5\Delta\psi \tag{9}$$

Define the measurement residual of space camera as the difference of measurement and estimated value, there are

$$\Delta X_3 = X_3 - \hat{X}_3, \quad \Delta Y_3 = Y_3 - \hat{Y}_3 \tag{10}$$

Substitute (10) by (6)(7)(8)(9) and Taylor series expansion of (5) on the estimated value $\begin{bmatrix} \hat{\varphi} & \hat{\theta} & \hat{\psi} \end{bmatrix}^T$, and reform it to derive the measurement residual model(11):

$$\Delta X_3 = h_{Cx} \begin{bmatrix} \Delta q_1 \\ \Delta q_2 \\ \Delta q_3 \end{bmatrix} + v_{Cx} \tag{11-a}$$

$$\Delta Y_3 = h_{Cy} \begin{bmatrix} \Delta q_1 \\ \Delta q_2 \\ \Delta q_3 \end{bmatrix} + v_{Cy} \tag{11-b}$$

where

$$h_{Cx} = 2f \begin{bmatrix} \dfrac{Y_0(dX_0 + 2dY_0\hat{q}_3 - 2f\hat{q}_2)}{(2dX_0\hat{q}_2 - 2dY_0\hat{q}_1 + f)^2} \\ -\dfrac{f(f - 2dY_0\hat{q}_1) + d^2(X_0 + 2Y_0\hat{q}_3)X_0}{d(2dX_0\hat{q}_2 - 2dY_0\hat{q}_1 + f)^2} \\ \dfrac{Y_0}{2dX_0\hat{q}_2 - 2dY_0\hat{q}_1 + f} \end{bmatrix}^T$$

$$h_{Cy} = 2f \begin{bmatrix} \dfrac{f(2dX_0\hat{q}_2 + f) + d^2(Y_0 - 2X_0\hat{q}_3)Y_0}{d(2dX_0\hat{q}_2 - 2dY_0\hat{q}_1 + f)^2} \\[3mm] -\dfrac{(dY_0 - 2dX_0\hat{q}_3 + 2f\hat{q}_1)X_0}{(2dX_0\hat{q}_2 - 2dY_0\hat{q}_1 + f)^2} \\[3mm] -\dfrac{X_0}{2dX_0\hat{q}_2 - 2dY_0\hat{q}_1 + f} \end{bmatrix}^T$$

and

$$\hat{X}_3 = \frac{f}{d}\left(\frac{dX_0 + 2dY_0\hat{q}_3 - 2f\hat{q}_2}{2dX_0\hat{q}_2 - 2dY_0\hat{q}_1 + f} \right) \tag{12-a}$$

$$\hat{Y}_3 = \frac{f}{d}\left(\frac{dY_0 - 2dX_0\hat{q}_3 + 2f\hat{q}_1}{2dX_0\hat{q}_2 - 2dY_0\hat{q}_1 + f} \right) \tag{12-b}$$

And in (11)(12), $\hat{q}$ is the estimated value which derives from attitude estimator, and d is the unit length of OX_pY_p, and f is the focal length of space camera which is determined by the tusk of camera. The calculation formula of f [4]is

$$f = d \cdot H / R_p \tag{13}$$

where R_p is the resolution of camera, d is the size of CCD cell, H is altitude of orbit. The usual size $d = 13\, \mu$ m.

3   Attitude Determination System Composed of Gyros and Space Camera

A.   State Equation and Measurement Equation

Attitude determination system is composed of gyros and space camera whose frame is shown in figure 1, so the states selected are[5]

$$X = \begin{bmatrix} \Delta q_{13}^T & \Delta b^T \end{bmatrix}^T \tag{14}$$

The state equation is

$$\begin{bmatrix} \Delta \dot{q}_{13} \\ \Delta \dot{b} \end{bmatrix} = \begin{bmatrix} -[\hat{\omega}_{bi} \times] & -\dfrac{1}{2}I_{3\times3} \\ 0_{3\times3} & 0_{3\times3} \end{bmatrix} \begin{bmatrix} \Delta q_{13} \\ \Delta b \end{bmatrix}$$
$$+ \begin{bmatrix} -\dfrac{1}{2}I_{3\times3} & 0_{3\times3} \\ 0_{3\times3} & I_{3\times3} \end{bmatrix} \begin{bmatrix} v_{g(3\times1)} \\ v_{g2(3\times1)} \end{bmatrix} \tag{15}$$

In order to simplify representation, equal

$$A(t) = \begin{bmatrix} -[\hat{\omega}_{bi} \times] & -\dfrac{1}{2}I_{3\times3} \\ 0_{3\times3} & 0_{3\times3} \end{bmatrix},$$

$$F(t) = \begin{bmatrix} -\dfrac{1}{2}I_{3\times3} & 0_{3\times3} \\ 0_{3\times3} & I_{3\times3} \end{bmatrix}, \quad w(t) = \begin{bmatrix} v_{g(3\times1)} \\ v_{g2(3\times1)} \end{bmatrix}$$

then the system state equation can be simplified as (16)

$$\dot{X}(t) = A(t)X(t) + F(t)w(t) \tag{16}$$

The the measurement residual of i landmark image spot is $z_i = [\Delta X_i \quad \Delta Y_i]^T$, and the system measurement is $Z = \begin{bmatrix} z_1^T & \cdots & z_i^T & \cdots & z_n^T \end{bmatrix}^T$ where n is the number of spot images. According to (11) the system measurement equation is

$$Z(t) = H(t)X(t) + L(t)v(t) \tag{17}$$

where is

$$H(t) = \begin{bmatrix} h_{C1(2\times3)} & 0_{2\times3} \\ \vdots & \vdots \\ h_{Ci(2\times3)} & 0_{2\times3} \\ \vdots & \vdots \\ h_{Cn(2\times3)} & 0_{2\times3} \end{bmatrix}_{2n\times6},$$

$$v(t) = \begin{bmatrix} v_{c1}^T & \cdots & v_{ci}^T & \cdots & v_{cn}^T \end{bmatrix}_{2n\times1}^T, \quad L(t) = I_{2n\times2n}$$

B. Analysis of Model Error and Filter Convergence

In order to guarantee the filter precision and convergence of attitude estimation, have to take the model error and filter observation into account. They are discussed separately. The model error comes from two aspects. One is the selection of reference image spot, the other is the measurement error. If the image spot of landmark selected is near the origin of coordinate OX_pY_p, the motion of image spot is not sensitive to the attitude during the satellite rotates within tiny angle , and if the image spot of landmark selected is far, the image spot is probably out of the photo that will lead tracking lost. So the selection of reference image spot should follow the rule that the image spot is neither too near nor too far from the origin of coordinate OX_pY_p .Judging from (5), measurement error v_c relates to four factor. (a) Installation error of space camera which includes projective center installation error and image plate installation error. (b) Lens error which includes focal length error, geometric distortion. (c) Image collection plate error which includes A/D error and resolution. (d) Identification error of reference image spot. All the error can be approximated by white Gauss noise. According to (12), attitude angular of 0.01deg can cause about $4d$ to $6d$ motion of image spot. And the motion magnitude is decided by the reference spot coordinates (X_0,Y_0). Here regard the space camera measurement noise standard variance as $5d$.

Obviously the attitude determination system which is made up of (16)(17) is a time-varying linear system. But it can be dealt as linear system in little time interval because angular velocity change very slowly, so the time-varying system can be dealt as sectionalized constant system[6]. Use Meskin method to analyze the observability and the SOM matrix shows that the system can be observed. For the (16)(17), apply extended Kalman filter, and on each step reset the states as zero after updating the estimated value of attitude [7] in order to keep filter convergence.

Something special need to pay attention to is that the model of camera is only applied in attitude holding stage due to assumption of small angle. In the stage of attitude maneuvering only the gyros can be utilized.

4   Simulation

Situation of simulation is as follows, the initial position of landmark image in digital photo $(X_0,Y_0)=(1000,1000)$ on the geostationary satellite, $H=35800$ km, $R_p=1$ km, the constant drift of gyro is $5(\deg/h)$ whose initial value estimated is $4(\deg/h)$, and the constant bias of earth sensor measurement is $0.1\deg$ whose initial value estimated is $0.05\deg$. The variance of gyro noise, camera noise, are respectively $(0.1\deg/h)^2$ and $(5d)^2$. The results are shown in the Fig.3 and Fig.4.

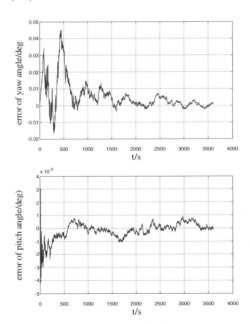

Fig. 3. Attitude estimation errors

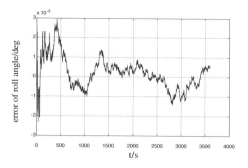

Fig. 3. (*continued*)

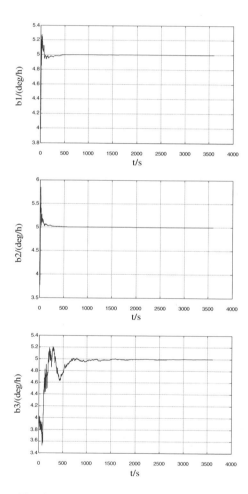

Fig. 4. Gyro fixed drifts estimation time history

The results of simulation illustrate that the attitude determination system made up of space camera and gyro is able to estimate the drift of gyro and the satellite attitude quickly and accurately. It is also to say that the measurement model of space camera is effective.

5   Conclusions

The measurement model of space camera is explored to estimate the satellite attitude. Basing on the model an attitude determination system is built which is composed of gyro and space camera. The simulation results illustrate the model above is effective and the system is able to estimate satellite attitude quickly and accurately. Further more the model of camera not only can estimate the satellite attitude effectively combining gyros but also can improve the precision and the convergence speed of the attitude estimation by introducing the camera model into other attitude determination system. With the development of digital imaging technology, the camera model will play more and more important role in the satellite attitude determination and the precision of the attitude determination will also be improved greatly.

References

1. Misu, T., Hashimoto, T., Ninomiya, K.: Optical Guidance for Autonomous Landing of Spacecraft. IEEE Transactions on Aerospace and Electronic Systems 35(2), 459–473 (1999)
2. Huang, X.-y., Cui, H.-t., Cui, P.-y.: Autonomous Optical Navigation for Probe s Landing on Small Body. Acta Electronica Sinica 31(5), 659–661 (2003)
3. Lin, D.-l.: Development of the CCD Camera for CBERS-1 Satellite. Spacecraft Recovery & Remote Sensing 21(3), 4–8 (2001)
4. Yang, X.-m.: Ground Resolution Measurement and Radiometric Characteristic Analysis of CBERS-1 Satellite CCD Camera. Spacecraft Recovery & Remote Sensing 23(4), 47–51 (2002)
5. Zhang, C.-q., Li, Y., Liu, L.-d.: Research On Information Fusion Method In Satellite Multi-sensor Attitude Determination Systems. Journal of Astronautics 26(3) (2005)
6. Liu, Z.-j., Wu, M.-p., Hu, X.-p.: Kalman Filter Design for Multi-sensors Satellite Attitude Determination. Journal of National University of Defense Technology 23(6), 28–32 (2001)
7. Leffets, R.J., Markley, E.L., Shuster, M.D.: Kalman Filtering for Spacecraft Attitude Estimation. Journal of Guidance Control and Dynamics 5(5), 417–429 (1982)

Data Association Rules in Analyzing Performance Level of College Students

Ruowu Zhong and Huiping Wang

Institute of Computer
Shaoguan University
Shaoguan, Guangdong Province, China
huipingwang2011@sina.com

Abstract. Relation itemsets can be found by association rules of data mining. This article uses association rules of Apriori algorithm and analyzes performance levels of college students. Valuable rules and information are obtained, so a fundamental improvement is made in students' study.

Keywords: association rule, performance level, Apriori algorithm.

1 Introduction

With the rapid development of computer technology and Internet technology, data resources are becoming abundant. It has accumulated a large amount of student performance data in school's performance management system. The data is accumulated in the system, but has not been effectively utilized. Currently, teachers and administrators of college usually use Excel software to do the routine work of calculation and performance statistics. However, the analysis and evaluation of test papers is involved less. The calculation of correlation of different subjects in traditional statistical formula requires a normal distribution of performance, so that the evaluation has certain limitations. This article applies data association rule to the analysis of student performance and does association analysis of the result of data mining to provide decision support for college administrators and provide the basis for the guidance of teaching.

2 The Basic Concepts of Association Rules

Association rules mining is to find the relationship between data items in large amounts of data. It is a research hot in the field of data mining. The concept of association rules was first proposed by R. Agrawal, T. Imielinski and A. Swami. It was used in transaction database for the detection of the implied relationship, which is association rule, of the user to purchase goods in supermarkets. So that the basis was provided for decision making (such as: putting goods that user frequently purchased together).

J. Zhang (Ed.): ICAIC 2011, Part III, CCIS 226, pp. 454–458, 2011.

Association rules problem can be divided into two processes:

(1) Finding all frequent itemsets, i.e., each of these sets will be occurred at least as frequently as a predetermined minimum support count, min_sup.

(2) Generating interesting association rules from the frequent itemsets, i.e., these rules must satisfy minimum support and minimum confidence. For each large itemset A, if $B \in A$, $B \neq \Phi$, and Support (A) / Support $(B) \geq$ min_conf, there are association rules $B \Rightarrow (A\text{-}B)$.

3   Apriori Algorithm

There are many algorithms about Association rules mining. The most classic is Apriori algorithm proposed by Agrawal and Srikant in 1993 [1] [2].

Apriori algorithm uses an iterative search method layer by layer: k - itemset used to search for $(k+1)$ - itemset. First, find the frequent 1 - itemset collection, denoted as L_1, L_1 is used to find the frequent 2- itemset L_2, and L_2 is used to find L_3, and so on , until we can't find the frequent k - itemset. Each time a search needs to scan database once. In order to improve the efficiency, traditional algorithm focused on reducing the number of database scans. We introduced the following properties:

Apriori property: All nonempty subsets of a frequent itemset must also be frequent [3] [4].

We do not derive them here, but use the property of data mining. By definition, if the itemset I does not meet the minimum support threshold min_sup, then I is not frequent, that is $P(I) <$ min_sup. If add item A to I, then the result set (that is $I \cup A$) does not appear more frequently than I. Therefore, $I \cup A$ is not frequent, that is P $(I \cup A) <$ min_sup.

Apriori algorithm consists of two parts:

(1) Using candidate itemset to find frequent itemset

How to find frequent k - itemset from frequent $(k-1)$ - itemset is the core of Apriori algorithm .This process uses Apriori property to compress space. In order to accumulate the speed of scanning database, this process can be divided into two steps:

① The join step

To find L_k, the join is performed to generate the collection of candidate k - itemset. The candidate itemset is denoted as C_k. Let l_1 and l_2 be itemset of L_{k-1}. Mark l_i [j] refers to the number j item of l_i (for example, l_1 [4] is the fourth item of l_1). Assume that the items in transaction and itemset are sorted by order of the dictionary, perform connection $L_{k-1} \times L_{k-1}$, if their first $(k-2)$ items are in common, then l_1 and l_2 in L_{k-1} are joinable. That is, if $(l_1 [1] = l_2 [1]) \wedge (l_1 [2] = l_2 [2]) \wedge \ldots \wedge (l_1 [k-2] = l_2 [k-2]) \wedge (l_1 [k-1] < l_2 [k-1])$, the itemset result of joining l_1 and l_2 is $l_1 [1] l_1 [2] \ldots - l_1 [k-1] l_1 [k-1]$, where $l_1 [k-1] < l_2 [k-1]$ is the guarantee that it does not produce a simple repetition[3].

② The prune step

C_k is a superset of L_k. It means that itemsets in C_k may be frequent and may also be non-frequent, but all the frequent k-itemsets are included in C_k. By scanning the database, we calculate itemsets' support in Ck, and compared with the minimum support to determine the L_k. However, itemset C_k may contain a lot of itemsets, computation is very time-consuming. In order to compress C_k, we use Apriori property: if any $(k-1)$ - subset of a candidate k- itemset is not in L_{k-1}, then the candidate k- itemset can not be frequent, so the candidate k- itemset can be removed from C_k. This reduces the number of k- itemset in C_k, and reduces the times of scanning the database, so improves the efficiency of the algorithm.

According to the above two key steps, Apriori algorithm can be described as the specific process: first, find the frequent 1 - itemset collection of L_1 from the candidate 1 - itemset (C_1), then Use L_{k-1} join to generate candidate C_k, and in accordance with Apriori property, remove those candidate itemsets with non-frequent subsets. Next, we scan the database, statistic candidate itemsets count, compare it with the minimum support count, and then generate frequent itemset L_k.

(2) Generating association rules from the frequent itemset

For each frequent itemset l, generate all non-empty subset of l, if

$$\frac{support\_count(l)}{support\_count(s)} \geq min\_conf \qquad (1)$$

Then output rule "s => (l-s)". Where, min_conf is the minimum confidence threshold [3].

4   Mining Association Rules Using Apriori Algorithm

A.   Data Preprocessing

We randomly select 401 questionnaires as a data table to gather statistics of college student learning factors. Gender, identity, daily study time will be layered and entered into database, the layers if property are determined [6-8] as follows:

Gender: Male (A1), Female (A2).
Identity: specialty students (B1), undergraduate students (B2).
Daily study time :2-4 hours (C1) ,4-8 hours(C2) ,8-12 hours (C3), 12 hours or more (C4).
Grade: Excellent (D1), well (D2), middle (D3), poor (D4).

After gender, identity, daily study time, performance levels are entered into database, association rules can be found by data mining. We use Apriori association rule mining algorithm. Input: transaction database D and the minimum support count threshold min_sup, output: the frequent itemsets L in transaction database D. We take 5 records from the database to show. Transaction database is as shown in Table 1.

Table 1. Transaction Database D

	Gender	Identity	Daily study time	Grade
1	A1	B1	C2	D2
2	A2	B1	C3	D1
3	A2	B1	C2	D1
4	A2	B1	C2	D3
5	A2	B1	C2	D1

B. Find frequent itemsets

Apriori algorithm is used to find frequent itemsets in D [5-6]:

(1) L_1 generation. Candidate frequent 1- itemsets is generated and by scanning the database the support counts are calculated. $C_1 = \{(A1, 1), (A2, 4), (B1, 5), (C2, 4), (C3, 1), (D1, 3), (D2, 1), (D3, 1)\}$, we select the set of items whose minsup_count is 2 to generate frequent 1 – itemsets $L_1 = \{A2, B1, C2, D1\}$.

(2) L_2 generation. Candidate frequent 2- itemsets is generated from L_1 and by scanning the database the support counts are calculated. $C_2 = \{(A2B1,4), (A2C2,3), (A2D1,3), (BIC2,4), (B1D1,3), (C2D1,3)\}$, we select the set of items whose minsup_count is 2 to generate frequent 2 – itemsets $L_2 = \{A2B1, A2C2, A2D1, B1C2, B1D1, C2D1\}$.

(3) L_3 generation. Candidate frequent 3- itemsets is generated from L_2 and by scanning the database the support counts are calculated. $C_3 = \{(A2B1C2, 3), (A2B1D1, 3), (A2C2D1, 2), (B1C2D1, 2)\}$,we select the set of items whose minsup_count is 2 to generate frequent 3 – itemsets $L_3 = \{A2B1C2, A2B1D1, A2C2D1, B1C2D1\}$.

(4) L_4 generation. Candidate frequent 4- itemsets is generated from L_3 and by scanning the database the support counts are calculated. $C_4 = \{(A2B1C2D1, 2)\}$, we select the set of items whose minsup_count is 2 to generate frequent 4 - itemsets $L_4 = \{A2B1C2D1\}$.

(5) L_5 generation. Generated from the L_4, frequent 5 - itemsets $C_5 = \Phi$, $L_5 = \Phi$, so the process is stop and we find all the frequent itemsets.

C. Analysis of association rules generated by using Apriori algorithm

In Table 1, the maximum frequent itemsets is $\{A2B1C2D1\}$, tracking the implementation process of Rule_generate [5, 8] (set min_confidence = 60%), association rule generation process is as shown in Table 2.

By using mining association rules technology, we can get some useful model rules. For example, female specialty students spend 4-8 hours a day to ensure the study time, and the performance level is excellent. This shows us that female specialty students have a reasonable allocation of time, they can fully ensure the study time, so the performance level is higher. At the same time, schools should pay attention to train male students' interests, and help them arrange their study time reasonably.

Table 2. Association Rules Generated by Apriori Algorithm

	Rules	Confidence (%)	Support (%)
1	D1 $\Rightarrow$ A2B1C2	67%	40%
2	A2C2 $\Rightarrow$ B1D1	67%	40%
3	A2D1 $\Rightarrow$ B1C2	67%	40%
4	B1D1 $\Rightarrow$ A2C2	67%	40%
5	C2D1 $\Rightarrow$ A2B1	100%	40%
6	A2B1C2 $\Rightarrow$ D1	67%	40%
7	A2B1D1 $\Rightarrow$ C2	67%	40%
8	A2C2D1 $\Rightarrow$ B1	100%	40%
9	B1C2D1 $\Rightarrow$ A2	100%	40%

5 Conclusion

This article focuses on mining association rules of performance level of college students. It uses the classic Apriori algorithm to mine associate factors related to student ferformance levels from massive data, and obtains valuable rules and information, so a fundamental improvement is made in students' study.

References

1. Agrawal, R., Imielinski, T., Swami, A.: Mining association rules between sets of items in large databases. In: Proc. of ACM SIGMOD Conference on Management of Data, pp. 207–216. ACM, New York (1993)
2. Agrawal, R., Srikant, R.: Fast algorithms for mining association rules in large databases. In: Proceedings of the 20th International Conference on Very Large Data Bases, pp. 487–499. Morgan Kaufmann Publishers Inc., San Francisco (1994)
3. Han, J.-w., Micheline, K.: Data Mining Concepts and Techniques. Morgan Kaufmann Publishers, San Francisco (2001)
4. Wang, Y.: Data mining of association rules. Chengdu University of Information Technology 2(19), 173 (2004)
5. Mao, G., Duan, L., Wang, S., Shi, Y.: Data mining principles and algorithms, pp. 68–72. Tsinghua University Press, Beijing (2007)
6. Xu, L.: The practical application of association rules Apriori algorithm. Computer Knowledge and Technology, 862–864 (2008)
7. Dong, P.: Association rules in student achievement. Sanmenxia Vocational and Technical College 8(4), 117M20 (2009)
8. Zheng, C., Han, C., Dong, J.: Association Rules in the teaching evaluation. Computer Technology and Development 19(9), 215–217 (2009)

Design and Implementation of Scenario Production System for Sea Battlefield Situation Analysis

Yang Lujing, Hao Wei, and Niu Xiaobo

Department of Command Automation
Electronic Engineering College, Naval Engineering University
Wuhan, Hubei Province, 430033, China
YangLujing2011@163.com

Abstract. Situation analysis is a key technology in the battlefield situation surveillance system. It can explain the battlefield picture and judge the offensive intention of the enemy in the sea battlefield. The design and implementation of scenario production system for sea battlefield situation analysis is discussed in the paper. It aims to produce scenario for the sea battlefield situation analysis system. Firstly, some motion models for single target and formation target are created. Based on the models, a scenario production system for sea battlefield situation analysis is developed. Then a scenario is produced to be applied to a function clustering algorithm for maneuvering target. The simulation result shows that the algorithm can distinguish target function clustering and discover the enemy's offensive intention correctly.

Keywords: situation analysis, scenario production, military simulation, target function clustering.

1 Introduction

Situation Analysis and Threat Assessment (STA) is a key technology in the battlefield situation surveillance system. Situation Analysis belongs to the secondary level of the data fusion. Its goal is to assess, accurately and completely, the battlefield situation, such as all quarters' strength deployment, operational ability, combat intentions and so on. It is based on the first level fusion and analysis of all combat objectives' behavior, state, event, relation[1].

At present, domestic research on the sea battlefield situation analysis is in the elementary stage. To do research on the situation analysis requires sea battlefield situation scenario, which can be used for examination of battlefield situation analysis process. In the paper, the design and implementation of scenario production system for sea battlefield situation analysis is discussed.

Firstly, some motion models of single target and formation target are created. Then the related parameters are discussed. Based on them, a sea battlefield situation analysis scenario production system is developed. It can simulate following events:

J. Zhang (Ed.): ICAIC 2011, Part III, CCIS 226, pp. 459–467, 2011.

discovering new targets; targets vanishing; turning on and turning off of radiant source(radar, radio station, countermeasure,...); target maneuvering rapidly(speed up, in turn, ascent, dive,......) ; fleet batching/ grouping; and so on. Then it can input scenario data for the sea battlefield situation analysis system. Finally, a scenario is prouced, which includes three scripts. It is applyed to a clustering algorithm for maneuvering target. The simulation result shows that the algorithm can distinguish target function clustering and discover the enemy's offensive intention correctly.

2   Target Motion Model

A.   Single Target Motion Model

Compared with formation motion target, single motion target can move flexibly, change speed significantly. Therefore the description of curvilinear motion is complicated. For the reason, we supply complicated parameters to the curvilinear motion in the design of motion model. It can describe every times of maneuvering at any curvature radius, any angle and any variable acceleration of circular motion. Based on the differential thinking, the whole track of single motion target is divided into several linear motion segments and circumference motion segments which are linked through maneuvering points. The accuracy of simulation track can be improved by refining each maneuvering segments.

The linear motion model of single target is as Fig. 1.

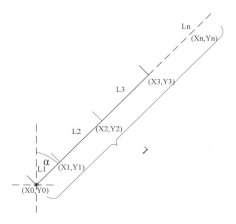

Fig. 1. The linear motion model of single target

Suppose that L is a linear linked by maneuvering segment $(L1, L2,......, Ln)$, which is with different state parameters. The maneuvering points are $(X1, Y1),(X2, Y2)......(Xn, Yn)$ .A maneuvering segment can be described as uniform acceleration linear motion, in which

V_i ——initial velocity;

a_i ——acceleration;

α ——heading angle;

Δt_i ——time length of ith maneuvering segment;

V_{max} ——the max speed of target;

a_{max} ——max acceleration of target.

Taking into account the influence of natural condition to ship movement, such as sea area, storm ocean current and visibility in the sea battlefield environment:

1) Sea area condition: it mainly influences the maneuvering of target. β is defined as factor of sea area influence,

Open sea area: $\beta = 1$;

More narrow sea area: $\beta = 0.8$;

Most narrow sea area: $\beta = 0.5$;

Under the influence of sea area, the maximum navigation speed of ship is: $v'_{max} = v_{max} \times \beta$

*2)*Storm, ocean current condition: they influence the maneuvering of ships more greatly and the speed of ships.

Suppose that the speed of storm is $\vec{v}^w(v_l^w, v_f^w)$, where v_l^w is in the tangent direction, v_f^w is in the normal direction of ship navigation. v_l^w can speed-up or decelerate the ships in the navigation direction, while v_f^w change navigation direction.

The two influences of storm to the maneuvering of ships sum up as follows:

$$\begin{cases} v_l^{pw} = v_l^p + v_l^w \\ v_f^{pw} = v_f^w \\ \delta = \arctan(v_f^{pw} / v_l^{pw}) \\ \alpha^{pw} = \alpha + \delta \end{cases}$$

In which, v_l^{pw} is the real navigation speed of ship in the tangent direction and v_f^{pw} is in the normal direction under the influence of storm, ocean current. δ is the change of navigation direction in unit time. α^{pw} is the real navigation direction of ship under the influence of storm, ocean current.

*3)*Visibility condition: it infuences maneuvering performance of ship to a certain extent. η is defined as visibility factor:

High visibility: $\eta = 1$;

Middle visibility: $\eta = 0.8$;

Low visibility: $\eta = 0.4$

Under the influence of visibility factor, the maximum navigation speed of ship is:

$$v''_{max} = v_{max} \times \eta$$

Sum up, under the influences of above natural conditions, the maneuvering points linking model of linear motion is as follows:

$$
\begin{cases}
L = \sum_{i=1}^{n} Li \; \dots \dots \dots \dots \dots \dots \dots \quad 1 \\[2mm]
Xi = X0 + \sum_{j=1}^{i-1} Lj \times \sin \alpha_j^{pw} \\[2mm]
Yi = Y0 + \sum_{j=1}^{i-1} Lj \times \sin \alpha_j^{pw} \\[2mm]
Lj = v_j^{pw} \times \Delta t_j + \frac{1}{2} a_j \times \Delta t_j^2 \dots \dots \quad .2 \\[2mm]
\delta = \arctan(v_f^{pw} / v_l^{pw}) \\[2mm]
\alpha_j^{pw} = \alpha_j + \delta \\[2mm]
v_j^{pw} = \sqrt{(v_{jl}^{pw})^2 + (v_{jf}^{pw})^2} \\[2mm]
v_l^{pw} = v_l^{p} + v_l^{w} \\[2mm]
v_f^{pw} = v_f^{w} \\[2mm]
v_j < v_{max} \; \dots \dots \dots \dots \dots \dots \dots \quad .3 \\[2mm]
v_j^{pw} < \sqrt{(v_{max})^2 + (v_{jf}^{pw})^2} \times \beta \times \eta \dots \dots \quad 4 \\[2mm]
a_j < a_{max}
\end{cases}
$$

In the above equations, formula 1 expresses the accumulation link of all maneuvering segments through maneuvering points; formula 2 is the length of every maneuvering segment with same parameters; formula 3 is the power restrictions of ship itself, which limit its maximum speed under no impact state; formula 4 is the environment and ship capacity constraints, which limit its maximum speed in particular circumstances for equipment capacity and security considerations.

Fig.2. shows the curved motion model, which can also be taken as any link combination of some circle maneuvering segments through maneuvering points.

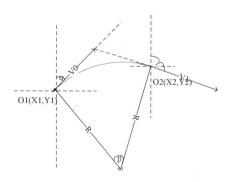

Fig. 2. Curved motion model

If affected by the natural environment, the target curved motion model is as follows:

$$
\begin{cases}
V1^{pw} = V0^{pw} + a \times t \\
\beta = a/R \times t \\
X2 = X1 + R*[\sin\gamma - \sin\alpha] \\
Y2 = Y1 + R*[\cos\gamma - \cos\alpha] \\
\gamma = \alpha^{pw} + \beta \\
\alpha^{pw} = \gamma + \delta \\
V0 < v_{max} \\
V1 < v_{max} \\
V1^{pw} < \sqrt{(v_{max})^2 + (v_{jf}^{pw})^2} \times \beta \times \eta \\
a < a_{max}
\end{cases}
$$

Where, V0,V1 are respectively the starting speed and ending speed of circle motion some segment. β is steering angle, α is initial heading angle, γ is heading angle after steering, and a is line acceleration. O1,O2 are respectively the starting point and ending point.

B. Formation Target Motion Model

In combat, in order to effectively organize forces to enhance combat efficiency, the combat intentions of groups often have to be implemented by effective collaboration of all members. These collaboration often have fixed pattern. The order of combat groups, which often reflects the combat intention, identity and threat, is a practical embodiment of the pattern in the space layout. It is of great significance to situation assessment on the battlefield and military decision-making. Moving formation target can be taken as combination of several single moving targets. Its features are: parallel moving cause mutual restraints between targets, so that its mobility is degraded. The movement is simple, and the description of curve motion is simple. Every formation has a capital ship, which commands the combat maneuvering of whole formation. Based on the features of formation moving targets, a formation motion model is suggested. The formation relative position is fixed. Controling the motion state of the capital ship, and calculating the motion state of other ships in the formation through certain conversion relation. Next, simplifing the track of formation moving targets as link combination of several line maneuvering segments and turning around at any angle. The set of capital ship motion state is the same as single moving target model(formation moving is restrained as turning around).

The motion state calculation of any ships controlled by capital ("Herringbone team" and "Diamond teams") is as Fig.3.

The model of "Herringbone team" is

$$
\begin{cases}
X2 = X1-6*\cos(\alpha-30); Y2 := Y1-6*\sin(\alpha-30); \\
X3 = X1-12*\cos((\alpha-30); Y3 = Y1-12*\sin(\alpha-30); \\
X4 = X1+6*\cos(\alpha+30); Y4 = Y1-6*\sin(\alpha+30); \\
X5 = X1+12*\cos(\alpha+30); Y5 = Y1-12*\sin(\alpha+30);
\end{cases}
$$

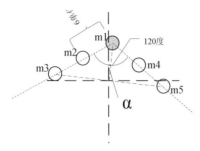

Fig. 3. (a)"Herringbone team" model
Note: "o" represents a ship, and blue "o" represents capital ship

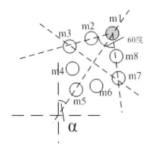

Fig. 3. (b)"Diamond teams" model

The model of "Diamond teams" is

$$
\begin{cases}
X2 = X1 - 6*\sin(\alpha + 30); Y2 = Y1 - 6*\cos(\alpha + 30); \\
X3 = X1 - 12*\sin(\alpha + 30); Y3 = Y1 - 12*\cos(\alpha + 30); \\
X4 = X3 - 6*\sin(\alpha - 30); Y4 = Y3 - 6*\cos(\alpha - 30); \\
X5 = X1 - 20.784*\sin\alpha; Y5 = Y1 - 20.784*\cos\alpha; \\
X6 = X5 + 6*\sin(\alpha + 30); Y6 = Y5 + 6*\cos(\alpha + 30); \\
X7 = X1 - 12*\sin(\alpha - 30); Y7 = Y1 - 12*\cos(\alpha - 30); \\
X8 = X1 - 6*\sin(\alpha - 30); Y8 := Y1 - 6*\cos(\alpha - 30);
\end{cases}
$$

3   Sea Battlefield Situation Analysis Scenario Production System

Based on above models, a sea battlefield situation analysis scenario production system is developed. It aims to produce scenario for the sea battlefield situation analysis system, which has following functions:

1) *S*ingle targets are produced. The amount, origin position, the moving rule of targets can be set and revised through HCI;

2) The appearance and disappearance of target can be simulated;.

3) Formation moving of targets can be simulated, which forms various formation teams. For example, single-column formation, parallelogram formation, fan-shaped formation, ring formation, trapezoid formation and so on.

4) The battlefield situation can be simulated, which can simulate situation change. That is change of space group and function group.

The structure of sea battlefield situation analysis Scenario production system is as Fig.4.

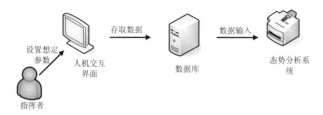

Fig. 4. The structure of sea battlefield situation analysis Scenario production system

The process inference is mainly based on target motion models and combat scenario, such as time scheduling based on event or time step.

It needs setting time, step length, data store method and representation method to drive the models realizing simulation and process inference, preparing simulation data. Manual intervention can be realized in the process inference. The situation producing interface is as Fig.5.The parameters of moving targets are defined in the interface, which can set maneuvering points and maneuvering segments.

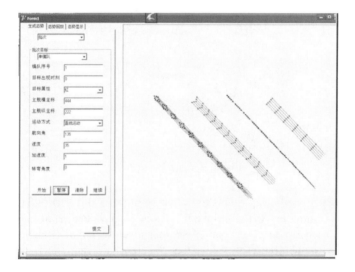

Fig. 5. The interface of single target and formation target

A scenario is produced in the system, which includes three scripts. In the scenario, red and blue sides composite combat situation. Five space groups of blue side attack three targets of red side. The scenario is as table 1 and Fig.6.

Table 1. A scenario

Situation Elements Constitution	Origin Situation	Script Representation
blue side: five space groups (X1~X5); red side: three targets (O1~O3)	blue side has four function groups: {X1},{X2,X3},{X4} attack red targets(O1~O3); {X5}is an independent function group	Script S1.1: Origin function groups don't change; Script S1.2:{X5} and {X1} function merge; Script S1.3:{X2,X3} function separate,{X2} retains riginal intention, {X5} and{X1} function merge; {X3}is an independent function group

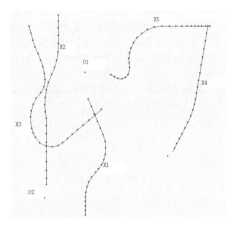

Fig. 6. A scenario situation

In the fig.6, script S1.1 represents the situation of frame 1-10,script S1.2 represents the situation of frame 11-20,and script S1.3 represents the situation of frame 21-30.

Apply the scenario to a sea battlefield maneuvering targets function clustering algorithm. The simulation result shows that the algorithm can realize target function clustering and discover the enemy's offensive intention correctly.

4   Conclusion

The design and implementation of sea battlefield situation analysis scenario production system is discussed in the paper. It aims to produce scenario for the sea battlefield situation analysis system. The main design requirements have been completed. The results can be used as the battlefield situation analysis system for the front-end input. But it still requires the following aspects of work:

1) Introduce electronic charts as battlefield background for call at any time.

*2)*Establish operational goals inherent attribute parameter database to provide the basis for simulating the reality of the simulative scenario.

*3)*Introduce the tactical rules so as to fit the reality of battlefield situation.

*4)*Build knowledge-based systems and improve the movement parameters, movement state so that the system can simulate various complex environment.

References

1. Wang, B., Shentu, X.: Study and Implementation of Situation Assessment Models. Computer Enngineering 30(6), 125–127 (2004)
2. Carl, G.L., Lily, R.L.: Cognitive Situation and Threat Assessments of Ground Battle Spaces. Information Fusion 4(4), 297–308 (2003)
3. Guo, N., Wang, J., Lei, Y.: A Simulative 3D Model of Target's Trail in the Military Training Supposition. Journal of System Simulation 14(4), 534–535, 538 (2002)
4. Wang, h., Tian, k.: Realization Method for Real-time Radar Intelligence Simulation. Journal of Air Force Radar Academy 16(4), 34–42 (2002)
5. Zou, W., Wei, J., Sun, N.: Inform Technology for Intelligence Simulation based on Scenario. Computer & Digital Engineering 27(4), 32–36, 26 (1999)

Research on Sea-Battlefield Perception Capability of the Naval Fleet

Luo Bing[1], Li Zhong-Meng[2], Li Ya-Nan[1], and Feng Kun[1]

[1] College of Electronic and Engineering
[2] Equipment Department
[1,2] Naval University of Engineering
[1,2] Wuhan, China
liyanan_2011liyanan_2011@sina.com

Abstract. To assess the perception of the sea-battlefield formation, the paper analyzed the capacity from both the sensor detection range and detection probability. And we focus on the multi-sensor network model of the battlefield awareness based on the features of multi-sensor. Then an application is given and the effectiveness of the algorithm is illustrated by the numerical example.

Keywords: perception of the battlefield, Probability of Target Detection, Multi-sensor.

1 Introduction

The formation of joint operations at sea-battlefield has become the main operational mode under information. Through network, information sharing and coordinated control, the formation of the overall capacity of the sea can outstrip the ability of a single ship [1]. The advantage of overall capacity of the formation is reflected in many aspects, which the perception of the battlefield is the most significant. The battlefield awareness can be analyzed through the sensor coverage, detection probability and the effect of multi-sensor network [2]. Thus we can effectively assess the perception battle fleet at sea-battlefield.

2 Sensors Detect Coverage

We have the intuition that the sensor probe farther and higher, stronger the ability of its detection. For ease of comparison, we propose the concept of sensor detection coverage ξ, which is defined as the total range of sensors to detect the percentage of designated airspace operations, such as coverage of 70% indicated that the sensor cannot fully scan combat zone, and 30% of the combat airspace undetectable.

J. Zhang (Ed.): ICAIC 2011, Part III, CCIS 226, pp. 468–476, 2011.
© Springer-Verlag Berlin Heidelberg 2011

Firstly, according to the different areas of detection, sensor detection coverage of the battlefield can be classified as detected by air coverage (O_{sky}), surface detection coverage (O_{water}) and coverage of underwater detection ($O_{underwater}$). For example, O_{water_i} is the ith team organization of surface detection range of sensors, $i = 1,\ldots,n$, where n is the number of sensors. Let R_i be the ith sensors of the effective detection radius, and O_{water_i} can be expressed as $O_{water\_i} = \pi R_i^2$. Similarly, O_{sky_i} denotes the ith sensors detecting air targets, because the detection space is a hemisphere, so $O_{sky\_i} = \frac{2}{3}\pi R_i^3$. In addition, let Ω be the fight allegations of airspace. For example, when target detection in air, then $O_{sky\_i} = \frac{2}{3}\pi R_i^3$, where, R is the radius of the specified operational airspace.

If there are multiple sensors in the fleet operations region and Ω^* be the detection range of the sensor system, then $\Omega^* = O_1 \cap O_2 \cap \cdots O_n$ denotes the intersection of n combat zone coverage. Thus, the corresponding capacity of the detection coverage could be

$$\xi = \left\| \frac{\Omega^*}{\Omega} \right\| \tag{1}$$

3   Probability of Target Detection Sensor System

Many scholars has analyzed the target detection model from different research aspects, such as [1] gave two kinds of detectors for optical and radar target detection probability respectively, but the method described for target detection probability model is too simple, and cannot be applied in practice because of the lack of more factors.

Walter Perry et.al proposed the reliability model in the Rand report submitted to the U.S. Department of Defense [3], where they map the time variable into the distance variables, and the reliability function was expressed by the probability of detection of not more than R .The disadvantage of the method is that the failure rate function by drawing the target detection probability curve detection distances in a short drop rate curve too fast, and the real target detection probability curve there is a big deviation.

In this paper, we give the radar target detection probability model based on the radar sensors. Typically, the target detection can use the binary decision under the condition that the radar in the NP criterion. The detection performance can be described by the false alarm probability and detection probability description. The calculation process shown in Figure 1:

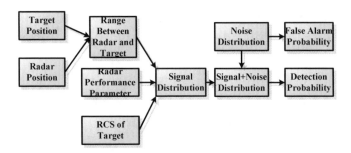

Fig. 1. Flow chart of radar target detection probability

Radar detection probability and false alarm probability is calculated as follows:
Detection probability:

$$P_d = \int_{V_T}^{\infty} f_{sn}(v)dv \qquad (2)$$

False alarm probability:

$$P_{fa} = \int_{V_T}^{\infty} f_n(v)dv \qquad (3)$$

where $f_n(v)$ is the noise distribution, and $f_{sn}(v)$ is the distribution of the noise characteristics of the target.

Assuming that the distribution of the noise is Gaussian noise, then the envelope detector noise n can be considered subject to Rayleigh distribution in the absence of clutter into the case:

$$f(x) = \begin{cases} \dfrac{x}{\sigma^2}\exp(-\dfrac{x}{2\sigma^2}), & x \geq 0 \\ 0, & x < 0 \end{cases} \qquad (4)$$

Where σ is the model parameter. Then we can get the average power of Rayleigh distributed clutter from the above equation:

$$P_c = \int_0^{\infty} x^2 \frac{x}{\sigma^2}\exp(-\frac{x}{2\sigma^2})dx = 2\sigma^2 \qquad (5)$$

When considering the colored noise or clutter comes, we can use Log-Normal distribution or Weibull distribution model to describe (more details see [4]).

When the target has the character of non-rolling, the probability distribution of a single pulse echo $r = s + n$ is:

$$f(r) = \frac{r}{\sigma^2}I_0(\frac{rA}{\sigma^2})\exp(-\frac{r^2 + A^2}{2\sigma^2}) \qquad (6)$$

where $I_0(\beta) = \dfrac{1}{2\pi}\int_0^{2\pi} e^{\beta\cos\theta}d\theta$.

When the signal-to-noise ratio is large enough, the signal plus noise is approximately Gaussian distribution:

$$f(r) = \frac{1}{\sqrt{2\pi\sigma^2}} \exp(-\frac{(r-A)^2}{2\sigma^2}) \tag{7}$$

When the target has the character of up-down, we can calculate the distributions function:

$$f(r) = \int f(r/\sigma)f(\sigma)d\sigma \tag{8}$$

where $f(\sigma)$ denotes the up-down function. The complete analytical expression is derived from [5] which present the parts of model.

For the detection probability and false alarm probability calculation, we give the target detection probability calculation process while take a single pulse detection, non-fluctuating target as the background.

①Calculate the distance between target and radar R

In the Cartesian coordinate, let radar coordinates and the target coordinates be the (x_r, y_r, z_r) and (x_t, y_t, z_t) respectively, then the distance between target and radar is:

$$R = \sqrt{(x_t - x_r)^2 + (y_t - y_r)^2 + (z_t - z_r)^2} \tag{9}$$

②Calculate the signal noise ratio from the radar equation

$$SNR = \frac{P_t G_T G_R \lambda^2 D n^{\frac{1}{2}} RCS}{(4\pi)^3 kT_0 B_n F_n L_s L_a R^4} \tag{10}$$

where P_t denotes the peak power for the transmitter; G_T denotes antenna gain; G_R denotes antenna gain; λ denotes the signal wavelength; D denotes the pulse pressure ratio; n denotes the accumulation of the number of pulses; RCS denotes target radar cross section; $k = 1.38 \times 10^{-23}$ denotes the Boltzmann constant; T_0 denotes the absolute environmental temperature; B_n denotes the receiver bandwidth; F_n denotes the receiver noise coefficient; L_s denotes the system insertion loss; L_a denotes insertion loss of the atmosphere.

For simplicity, the relevant factors about radar can be removed in (10), there are:

$$SNR = K \Box RCS / R^4 \tag{11}$$

where K denotes the factors associated with the radar power of regular factors in (10), which include radar target detection reflect the power of the underlying factors. And

$$K = \frac{P_t G_T G_R \lambda^2 D n^{\frac{1}{2}}}{(4\pi)^3 k T_0 B_n F_n L_s L_a} \tag{12}$$

③Calculate the probability of false alarm P_{fa} in the case of setting the detection threshold T_{CFAR} and detection probability P_d

$$P_{fa} = \int_{T_{CFAR}}^{\infty} \frac{x}{\sigma^2} \exp(-\frac{x^2}{2\sigma^2}) dx$$
$$= \exp(\frac{-T_{CFAR}^2}{2\sigma^2}) \tag{13}$$

$$T_{CFAR} = \sqrt{-2\sigma^2 In(P_{f_a})} \tag{14}$$

$$P_d = \int_{T_{CFAR}}^{\infty} \frac{r}{\sigma^2} I_0(\frac{rA}{\sigma^2}) \exp(-\frac{r^2 + A^2}{2\sigma^2}) dr \tag{15}$$

The computation is too complex, but there are many simplified method. Assuming that the radar signal s is a sine wave, amplitude is A, then its power $P_s = A^2/2$. For the single pulse echo, let the Rayleigh distribution of the noise n is $\sigma = \sigma_0$, then

$$SNR = P_s/P_0 = A^2/2\sigma_0^2 \tag{16}$$

With Eq (12) and (14), (13) can be rewritten as

$$P_d = \int_{\sqrt{2\sigma_0^2 In(1/P_{f_a})}}^{\infty} \frac{r}{\sigma^2} I_0(\frac{rA}{\sigma^2}) \exp(-\frac{r^2 + A^2}{2\sigma^2}) dr$$
$$= Q\left[\sqrt{2\square SNR}, \sqrt{2In(1/P_{f_a})}\right] \tag{17}$$

where Q is the Marcum's Q-function,

$$Q[\alpha, \beta] = \int_{\beta}^{\infty} \zeta I_0(\alpha\zeta) e^{-(\zeta^2 + \alpha^2)/2} d\zeta \tag{18}$$

When P_{fa} is small and P_d is relatively large, then the threshold is large, and equation (17) can be approximately expressed as:

$$P_d \approx F(\frac{A}{\sigma} - \sqrt{2In(\frac{1}{P_{fa}})}) \tag{19}$$

where the function $F(\square)$ is

$$F(x) = \int_{-\infty}^{x} \frac{1}{\sqrt{2\pi}} e^{-\zeta^2/2} d\zeta \tag{20}$$

Assume the parameters of a radar is as follows:

Table 1. Parameters of Radar

NO	Parameter
Transmit power /W	1.0×105
Antenna gain launched /dB	35
Antenna receiving gain /dB	35
Radar wavelength /m	0.03
Receiver Bandwidth /Hz	5.0×106
Pulse compression ratio	1
number of pulses accumulated	30
Ambient temperature /K	293
Noise coefficient /dB	3
Loss /dB	8

Then we can calculate the radar regularization factor 1.79662×1019 according to (12). Figure 2 shows 10m2 and 1m2 target detection probability under different radar detection range in accordance with the simulation of the radar parameters set to 1.0×10-6 radar false alarm probability.

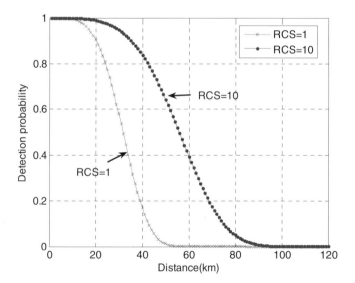

Fig. 2. False alarm probability of 10^{-6}, the probability of radar detection under different distance

4   Multi-sensor Configuration

The radar target detection model based on radar equation, radar parameters and detection probability not only can be used to describe the single radar target detection

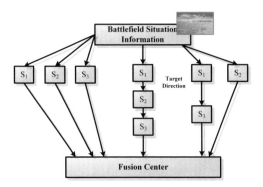

Fig. 3. Multi-sensor configuration mode

power, and also for the radar network [6,7,8]. In order to obtain better detection performance, the process of formation of operations at sea-battlefield often combines the different sensors to form the sensor network. Typical configurations include: independent configuration, target configuration, and mixed configurations, which shown in Figure 3.

Independent configuration means that a sensor detects the operational area independently. The detection probability is:

$$P_{DS} = 1 - (1 - P_{D1})(1 - P_{D2})(1 - P_{D3}) \qquad (21)$$

Target configuration means that a target indicator sensor detects the target firstly, and then notifies the other sensors to search for and capture the information of the prior target caught by the first sensor, and sent the results to the fusion center. The probability of detection is

$$P_{DS} = P_{D1} \square P_{D2} \square P_{D3} \qquad (22)$$

Mixed configuration is the mixture of independent configuration and target configuration. The detection probability depends on the structure of the sensor system. The probability of detection of a mixed configuration is

$$P_{DS} = 1 - (1 - P_{D1}P_{D3})(1 - P_{D2}) \qquad (23)$$

Assuming that the radar network size R is 300km * 300km, and the radar network consists of five identical radar (radar parameters shown in table 1, and the location of each radar shown in Table 2).

Table 2. Radar location

	Radar	Radar	Radar	Radar	Radar
Abscissa /km	50	50	150	180	250
Ordinate /km	50	250	250	150	100

Assuming five radar uses Independent configuration, then the radar network consists of the five radar network for RCS = 10m^2 target detection power shown in Figure 5. The color shades shows the different power of detection sizes. From Figure 4, we can find that the above target detection model can be more reasonable to show the detection power of the radar network. The power of the each radar begins with detection radar center of symmetry coordinates, while the detection power decreases with the increase of distance.

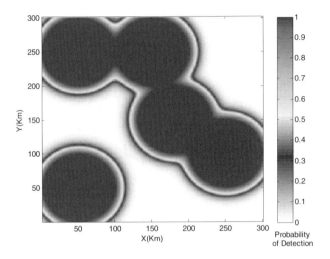

Fig. 4. The power of Radar network at RCS=10m^2

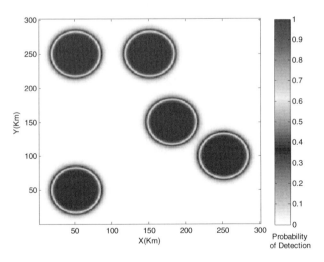

Fig. 5. The power of Radar network at RCS=1m2

The simulation results shows that the target detection model can describe the single radar or radar network for target detection capability, and can be effectively used to quantify the battlefield awareness model.

Figure 5 shows the detection power of the radar network when the target RCS = $1m^2$. Compared with Figure 12, there is a clear gap and has a blind spot detection, while the blind can be utilized as the enemy penetration channel.

The simulation results shows that the target detection model can describe the single radar or radar network for target detection capability, and can be effectively used to quantify the battlefield awareness model.

5 Conclusions

Formation of joint operations at sea-battlefield awareness capabilities under information is an important part of overall performance. The paper analyzes the power of detection from the coverage of sensor, detection accuracy and multi-sensor networks. The conclusion is that we can quantitatively assess the battlefield awareness. Moreover, sensor networks can significantly improve the formation of the battlefield awareness. Based on the sensor configuration schemes, formation of battlefield awareness is also somewhat different.

References

1. Chen, L.-x., Yin, X.-l., Chen, W.-c.: Analyzing the effectiveness of network centric operating system in information domain. Systems Engineering and Electronics 26(7), 918–923 (2004)
2. Que, W., Peng, Y.N., Lu, D.J., et al.: An approach to radar netting. In: CIE International Conference of Radar Proceedings. IEEE Press, Beijing (1996)
3. Walter, P., David, S., John, B.: Exploring Information Superiority-A Methodology for Measuring the Quality of Information and its Impact on Shared Awareness 1467(2003)
4. Huang, P.-k., Yin, H.-c.: Radar Target Signature. Electric Industure Publish, Beijing (2004)
5. He, Y., Guan, J.: Automatic Radar Detection and CFAR Processing. Tsinghua University Press, Beijing (1999)
6. Fang, X.-l., Yang, Y.-x.: Radar Target Detection Range Model Based on Detection Probability. Modern Radar 30(7), 18–20 (2008)
7. Yang, D.-z., Ding, J.-j., Xie, C.: Modeling and Simulation of Detection Probability Based on Distributed Detection in Netted Radar System. Modern Radar 30(12), 24–27 (2008)
8. Mahafza, B.R.: Radar systems analysis and design using Matlab. Chapman & Hall/CRC (2000)

Design and Analysis of Outer Baffle of Space Telescope[*]

Yingjun Guan[1], Deqiang Mu[1], and Zhilai Li[2]

[1] School of Mechatronic Engineering,
Changchun University of Technology,
Changchun, Jilin Province, China
[2] Department of Space Optics,CIOMP,
Changchun, Jilin Province, China
zhilaili@sina.cn

Abstract. Stray light prevention of space telescope to improve the imaging quality plays a vital role. Through the outer baffle is properly set can effectively restrain the stray light. In order to satisfy the requirements of lightweight, high stiffness, high strengthen and high dimensional stability, carbon fiber composite material was selected as the outer baffle of space telescope materials. A design idea of independent installation of outer baffle and main support structure of space telescope was proposed, thus the influence on the optical elements by outer baffle was reduced extremely. By adopting finite element analysis technique, thermal and dynamic characteristics of outer baffle were analyzed detailed and the structure parameters were optimized. The final design scheme shows that the mass is 5.2 kg and the first order natural frequency is 113 Hz. Dynamic test results indicate that the first order natural frequency is 106.8 Hz, the magnification of acceleration response is less 10 times and the maximum stress is **86.6MPa in the sinusoidal and random vibration test, which meet the design requirements.**

Keywords: space telescope, TMA, outer baffle, finite element method, dynamic experiment.

1 Introduction

Stray light prevention has become one of the key technologies of space telescope development and can or not effectively control of stray light of space telescope directly concerns the imaging quality. By properly designing lens and outer baffle of space telescope is the most effective method on Stray light prevention, which can directly keep out part reflex from the earth and other miscellaneous light into the space telescope mirror and using its surface material properties and the aperture installed in the outer baffle absorbs stray light entering the outer baffle, thereby enhancing the signal-to-noise ratio (SNR) of the space telescope [1-4]. In recent years, the off-axis three-mirror space optics system is concerned highly by developed countries around the world because of advantages of its large field of view, large

---

[*] This work is partially supported by National high technology research development plan(No. 863-2-5-1-13B).

J. Zhang (Ed.): ICAIC 2011, Part III, CCIS 226, pp. 477–485, 2011.
© Springer-Verlag Berlin Heidelberg 2011

relative aperture and optical system without center block. Compared with coaxial system, the irregular shape of the outer baffle of the off-axis three-mirror space telescope has brought great difficulty to opto-mechanical engineers [5-7]. From the standpoint of improving transfer function, the length of the outer baffle should be as long as possible. But longer outer baffle makes the weight increased, dynamic stiffness lower and destroy easily in the launch vehicle dynamics environments. The shorter outer baffle will not restrain stray light effectively.

In this paper, material selection, structure layout, installation pattern and structural parameters optimization are took into account in the designing of outer baffle of off-axis three-mirror space telescope. By using the finite element method and optimal design theory, the outer baffle was designed and analysed detailed. Through optimal design, the outer baffle structural pattern meeting design parameters are obtained, and the dynamic test is done. Test results show that the structure of the outer baffle meet space application requirements and the analysis model is accurate and valid.

2   Structural Design of Outer Baffle

A.   Material selection of the outer baffle

Material selection should be considered firstly on the structure design of the outer baffle. In order to meet the mass, stiffness, strength and thermal characteristics requirements, the material of outer baffle should be low density, high elastic modulus, high heat conductivity and low coefficient of expansion.

Considering the material properties, at present the optimal material is carbon fiber/epoxy reinforced polymer. This material has the characteristics of low density, high intensity, high elastic modulus and fatigue resistance, excellent thermal performance and vibration absorbing damping and molding process, spatial dimensional stability and lower environmental pollution and so on a series of advantages. The properties of carbon fiber/epoxy reinforced polymer were shown in Table 1.

Table 1. Material properties of carbon fiber composite

material	ρ $10^{-6} kg.mm$	E/GPa	α $10^{-6} / \ °C$	Poisson's ratio/ μ
T700	1.6	60	1	0.28

B.   Structure pattern of the outer baffle

The structure pattern of the outer baffle is shown in figure 1. According to the requirements put forward by the optical system, the configuration layout of the main structure of outer baffle was designed.

The main structure of outer baffle is composed of space telescope external skin, the entrance of the light and internal aperture. The size of the outer baffle is 820mm×805mm×550mm. Through setting reinforced ribs in its internal, on the one hand, structure strength and rigidity has been enhanced, on the other hand, reinforced ribs restrained stray light entering the outer baffle effectively. The outer baffle and the main structure of space telescope are connected by screws in initial design scheme, but through the finite element analysis, when the temperature changes in the outer baffle, the distortion of the outer baffle itself will influence surface figure accuracy of the optical elements and the imaging quality of space telescope will degraded greatly. In order to avoid the deformation of the outer baffle components generated by own temperature change will influence the optical elements, a kind of structure which space telescope outer baffle and the main structure are installed independently was put forward in this paper, thus the influence which the deformation of the outer baffle on the main structure of the space telescope was reduced.

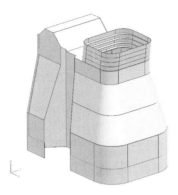

Fig. 1. Structure of outer baffle

The outer baffle connected with the back frame of space telescope only in bottom position, and other parts don't connect with the main structure of space telescope. But this installation pattern will cause the overall rigidity of the outer baffle reduced and local stress of the connecting parts is excessive in dynamic environment, so in order to ensure its strength and rigidity requirement, we must do full of engineering analysis and dynamical experiment and the reasonable structure parameters should be optimized.

3 Finite Element Analysis and Structural Optimization design

Mass, strength and stiffness of the outer baffle are strictly limited in the system. Overall mass of the outer baffle is not more than 6kg, the first-order natural frequency is more than 100Hz. The structure in the dynamic environment shouldn't be destroyed in the process of overload, and low frequency sinusoidal and random vibration. This series of design parameters can be guaranteed fast and reliably only through scientific and accurate finite element analysis and structural optimization design.

A. Establishment of the finite element model

The outer baffle structure is the thin shell structure. The mesh is divided by shell element in MSC/Patran. The finite element model is shown in figure 2. The material properties of carbon fiber/epoxy reinforced polymer T700 are shown in table 1.

Boundary condition is defined as the connection position with back framework of the space telescope 6 DOF constraints. Based on this model the modal analysis and the strength analysis was done.

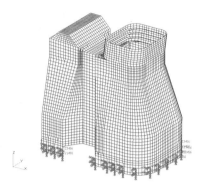

Fig. 2. Finite element model of outer baffle

B.   Structural parameters optimization of outer baffle

Structural optimization essentially belongs to the mathematical programming; the mathematical expression of the structure optimization is [8]:
    Find X to minimize (or maxmize)

$$F(X) \text{ objective} \tag{1}$$

subject to

$$g_j(X) \leq 0 \quad j = 1, \cdots, n_g \text{ inequality constraints} \tag{2}$$

$$h_k(X) = 0 \quad k = 1, \cdots, n_h \text{ equality constraints} \tag{3}$$

$$x_i^L \leq x_i \leq x_i^U \quad i = 1, \cdots, n \text{ side constraints} \tag{4}$$

where:

$$X = (x_1, x_2, \cdots, x_n) \text{ design variables} \tag{5}$$

In this notation, items that are in upper case and bold are vectors while members of the vectors are designated using a lower case symbol with a subscript to indicate the member. The objective function is the scalar quantity to be minimized. It is a function of the set of design variables. (Although we stated the problem as a minimization task, we can easily maximize a function by minimizing its negative.) Side constraints are placed on the design variables to limit the region of search, for example, to plate thicknesses that are nonnegative or tubes whose wall thicknesses are less than one-tenth of the outer radii. The inequality constraints are expressed in a less than or equal to zero form by convention; that is, a constraint is satisfied if its value is negative.

In mathematical description of the optimized design structure, three elements mainly involve design variables, constraint conditions and objective function.

The structure configuration of outer baffle of the space telescope studied in this paper has been determined according to the basic structure of space telescope already, the design variables optimized is mainly the sectional dimensions, namely the shell thickness of the outer baffle and internal aperture ($X = (x_1, x_2)$).Constraint conditions is defined as the first-order natural frequency of outer baffle and the thickness range of the shell, is specifically: $1mm \leq x_1 \leq 6mm$; $0.5mm \leq x_2 \leq 4mm$; $100Hz \leq f_1 \leq 150Hz$. Objective function is defined as the components mass is the lightest, namely $Min \psi(X,Y)$. Among them, x_1, x_2 is respectively the thickness of the outer baffle and internal aperture plate, f_1 is first-order natural frequency of the outer baffle. Through multiple iterative optimization, and the final optimization results obtained are as follows: the thickness of connection section between the outer baffle and space telescope back framework is 5mm, the body thickness of the outer baffle is 2.5 mm, the thickness of entrance is 2mm, the thickness of all aperture plates are 1mm. The structure weight obtained of the outer baffle components is 5.2 kg.

C. Modal Analysis

Modal analysis is the main method to evaluate dynamic stiffness of the structure which is to extract low order natural frequency and vibration model, thereby find the weak link of the structure.

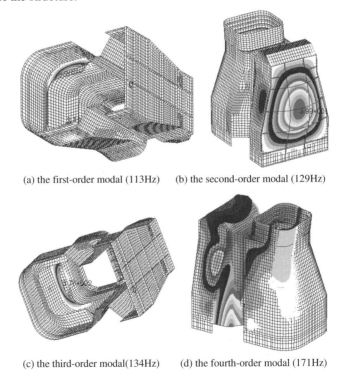

(a) the first-order modal (113Hz)   (b) the second-order modal (129Hz)

(c) the third-order modal(134Hz)   (d) the fourth-order modal (171Hz)

Fig. 3. The first 4-order modes of outer baffle component

We can see from the first 4-order modal of the outer baffle as shown as figure 3, the first-order natural frequency of component is 113Hz and its vibration mode is local vibration of aperture plate in the outer baffle, the second and the third order is local vibration of side plate and internal aperture plate, the fourth-order natural frequency is 171Hz, and the vibration mode is overall vibration modal of the outer baffle, so it can be seen that the dynamic stiffness of the outer baffle is high enough.

D.   Strength analysis

Due to the fundamental frequencies of the outer baffle structure along the three axial are far higher than 100Hz, so the resonance can't occur in sinusoidal vibration and stress response of the overload is only considered in the strength analysis. The experimental conditions of the components acceleration are shown as table 2.

Table 2. Conditions of overload test

Test item	acceleration	remarks
z axis	16g	Vertical direction is launch direction
x, y axis	2g	Horizontal direction is vertical with launch direction
Velocity of load		0.5~1.0g/s
Holding time	5 minutes	This is time after overload value reaches requirement

To be on the safe side, 10g input was analysed in crosswise. The overload analysis results of outer baffle structure are shown as table 3.

Table 3. Analysis results of overload test

direction	The maximum stress (MPa)	Coefficient of safety	locality
Z axis (16g)	34.6	18.3	Connection point
X axis (10g)	7.7	78.9	Connection point
Y axis (10g)	5.2	127.2	Connection point

Analysis results show that the maximum stress under the action of three directions overload of outer baffle structure is 34.6 MPa and far less than 877MPa tensile strength of T700 , so overload working condition can't be destroyed and have enough safety margin.

4   Dynamic Test

For adjusting finite element analysis model, also to test the ability of outer baffle structure resisting to dynamics interference, the dynamic test is doing in V946 vibration machine. Dynamic test items include: 0.2g sine frequency characteristic scanning in the range of 0~2000Hz frequency, low frequency sinusoidal vibration test

(a) Outer baffle on the shaker

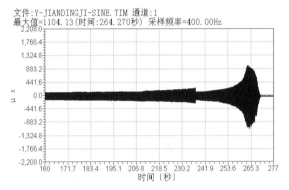

(b) Response curves of stress under sinusoidal vibration

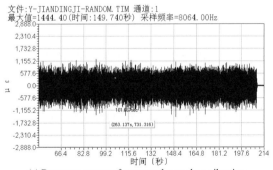

(c) Response curves of stress under random vibration

Fig. 4. Dynamic experiment of outer baffle component

of 0 ~ 100Hz and random vibration test of 10 ~ 2000Hz. In order to test all frequency characteristics of outer baffle component in the frequency range of 0~2000Hz, 0.2g sine frequency characteristics scan is done, we can preliminary get a few resonance frequency of component and the magnification multiple of the power acceleration response of structure. Sinusoidal vibration test mainly examines acceleration and stress response level of structure under the condition of low frequency sinusoidal vibration, The random vibration test mainly simulates the influence of the noise vibration to structure during the period of launch and examine the acceleration response(g_{rms}) and the stress response.

0.2g characteristic frequency scanning test results show that the first-order resonant frequency of outer baffle components is 107 Hz, finite element analysis result is 113 Hz, analytical error is 5.8% and in allowing range. In the random vibration acceleration response, the output g_{rms} is 49g, relative to the input of 8.2g, its magnification is 5.97 times, meet the requirements of acceleration magnification less than 10 times. As shown as stress test results of the low frequency sinusoidal vibration and random vibration, in the course of low frequency sinusoidal vibration, because the first-order natural frequency of outer baffle component is higher than 100Hz, the structure didn't resonate within 0 ~ 100Hz, the maximum stress occurred when frequency reached 100Hz the specific location is the structure part of outer baffle of light entrance and body outer baffle. The maximum stress level was calculated according to $\sigma = E \cdot \varepsilon$, for the maximum micro strain is 1104 $\mu\varepsilon$ and the elastic modulus is 60GPa, so the maximum stress is 66.2 MPa, while in the process of random vibration of the maximum stress as shown in figure 4 (c) is 86.6 MPa, far less than 800MPa T700 tensile strength. After the vibration at the outer baffle no damage or local tear phenomenon, prove the structure strength is high enough to adapt to the dynamics environment of launch.

5   Conclusion

In the process of outer baffle design, material selection, structure parameter optimization, finite element analysis and dynamic test were studied detailed in this paper. Got a outer baffle structure with the carbon fiber/epoxy reinforced polymer, by adopting independent installation between outer baffle and the space telescope body, the surface figure accuracy of optical elements can be improved greatly. Analysis and test results indicate that the first-order natural frequency of the outer baffle is 107Hz, analysis error is 5.8%, meet the requirement of analytical precision. The maximum stress in overload condition is 34.6 MPa; the maximum stress of structure in sinusoidal and random vibration is 86.6 MPa, the acceleration response magnification is less than 10 times, the structure has high stiffness, strength and dimensional stability. The final designed mass of structure is 5.2 kg, meet the requirement of lightweight that the structure mass should less than 6kg. The outer baffle has been applied on a certain type of space telescope successfully.

References

1. Sheng, L., Chen, P., Sun, D.-h.: Development of Light Baffle of Space telescope. Spacecraft Recovery & Remote Sensing 27(2), 41–45 (2006)
2. Li, Y., Xiang, L.-b., Li, L.-b.: Design and Simulation of the Baffle of a New Type Space telescope. Opto-Electronic Engineering 37(7), 41–44 (2010)
3. Chen, L.-h., Wu, Q.-w.: FEA of structure parameters of baffle for high-resolution space telescope. Optical Technique 34(3), 445–448 (2008)
4. Yan, C.-x., Xu, J., Peng, Y.: Stray light suppression of three-mirror off-axis space optical telescope. Optics and Precision Engineering 18(2), 289–293 (2010)
5. Liu, L., Gao, M.-h., Li, L.-f., Chen, W., Ren, J.-y.: Development of light baffle of space telescope with large field of view. Optical Technique 35(6), 822–824 (2009)
6. Stephen, M.P.: A stray light analysis of the apache point observatory 3.5-meter telescope system, vol. 4842, pp. 128–138. SPIE, San Jose (2003)
7. Sholl, M.J., Grochocki, S., Fleming, J.C., et al.: Stray light design and analysis of SNAP telescope, vol. 6675, p. 66750C. SPIE, San Jose (2007)
8. Jia, X.-z., Jin, G., Zhang, L.: Design and optimization of lightweight outer baffle for space telescope. Optics and Precision Engineering 16(8), 1560–1565 (2008)

The Research of the Command and Control Model for the Naval Battle Groups with Multi-agent Theory

Ji-Jin Tong[1], Zhong Liu[1], Li Duan[1], and Li-Mei Xu[2]

[1] Department of Command and Control, Naval Univ. of Engineering,
Wuhan, Hubei Province, China
[2] The Command Automation Workstation, The 92919 Force of Chinese PLA,
Ningbo, Zhejiang Province, China
jijintongjijintong@sina.com

Abstract. How to effectively disseminate the information flow and command instruction among the platforms of naval battle groups (BG) is one of the key-problems for the cooperative engagement. In order to evaluate and analyze the command and control model quantitatively, a multi-agent model about command and control system is proposed firstly. Then the typical constitution of the BG and topology of the BG organization are presented. Finally, a simulation example is given, which analyze the method of how to distribute the information flow and command instruction in detail. The simulation results show that the method is reasonable and effective. This paper has some reference value to the assessment and evaluate of the command and control model for the naval battle groups.

Keywords: multi agent, naval battle groups (BG), command and control model, information flow, command instruction.

1 Introduction

In modern naval warfare, there are a lot of battlefield perceptive information flow and command instructions among the BG's platforms. How to disseminate information timely, accurately and reliably is the precondition of forming the consistent battlefield situation and cooperative operation. It is one of the key problems to disseminate large information and command flow reasonably, which need to be considered during the battle process of BG with carrier.

The essence of the problem is how to find the optimization organization structure of BG's platforms in modern networking combat conditions. Many researchers pay more attention to the study of the coupled network of information network and command network [1] [2] [4], and the multi-agent modeling method proposed by Georgiy M. Levchuk etc is the most influential.

J. Zhang (Ed.): ICAIC 2011, Part III, CCIS 226, pp. 486–494, 2011.
© Springer-Verlag Berlin Heidelberg 2011

In this paper, a model of command and control is proposed based on multi-agent theory, which analyzes the U.S. BG with carrier from the topological structure and internal relations. Final, the model is used to analyze in one specific case. The simulation results prove that this method is effective. Furthermore, some useful revelation in the analysis of carrier can be drawn from the simulation.

2 The Model of Command and Control Based on the Multi-agent

The typical process of the command and control of BG can be described in this way: Firstly, carrier and its member-ships make reconnaissance of the operation area in real time, if some targets are detected, the special member-ships will be send to fulfill target recognition (identification, type identification) task through the command and control system, and the recognized information should be disseminated to the right member ships, which used these information to update the battlefield situation. Then, the information will be processed and converted into command instruction (some corresponding decisions coming into being), and the command instruction will be distributed to other platforms. Finally, those platforms execute the allocated decision-making tasks (warn, expel or carry out attacks).

A. Task analysis of the Agent
Agent is a circumstance-resident entity, which can work continuously and independently in certain environment, and having the character of autonomy, reactiveness, proactivity and the ability of interaction with other Agent. The agent can not only has the function of knowledge solution, but also can acquire knowledge timely in dynamic and uncertain environment [3]. Therefore, agent can be used as a process unit to distribute and process the battlefield perceptive information and command instruction.

The function performed by of the member-ship entity can be imitated by the agent. And in the operation of BG with carrier, these agents answer for distribute and process the battlefield perceptive information and command instruction, which constitute a Multi-Agent System (MAS).

In the system of command and control, MAS have the function of information distribution, information processing (converts information into command), command instructions distribution, command processing (accomplish task), which need to perform eleven tasks [4].

As a result, we can view an agent as having the following responsibilities:

(1) Monitoring (observe external environment information event);
(2) Decision-making (internal information to command conversion);
(3) Processing (execute tasks from command);
(4) Communication (receive/send information and command).

B. Agent parameters and constraints of the command and control model based on MAS

According to agent responsibilities outlined above, the following parameters can be defined for each agent of MAS:

(1) Information monitoring parameters: Maximal Monitoring capacity m_i^{max} and monitoring efficiency g_i^{M}.

(2) Information communication parameters: Maximal Received information capacity $r_i^{I,max}$, Maximal Received command capacity $r_i^{C,max}$, Maximal Sent information capacity $s_i^{I,max}$ and Maximal Sent command capacity.

(3) Information processing parameters: Maximal Information processing capacity $p_i^{I,max}$, Maximal Command processing capacity $p_i^{C,max}$, Information processing efficiency g_i^{I}, and Command processing efficiency g_i^{C}.

(4) Information events distribution parameters:

Event-to-agent assignment，$u_{n,i} \in \{0,1\}$，where $\sum_{i=1}^{M} u_{n,i} = 1$，these parameters define the observers or sources of the flow in the organization.

(5) Link constraint parameters:

Information link constraints $x_{i,j}^{I} \le c_{i,j}^{I}$ and Command link constraints $x_{i,j}^{C} \le c_{i,j}^{C}$.

(6) Workload constraints parameters:

The monitoring, infovdrmation and command processing capacities defined above usually refer to the trade-off that an agent exercises in dedicating its time to internal information (information and command processing capacities) and external information (monitoring capacity).

Let Ω be the total workload capacity of agent, then $\Omega = m_i^{max} + p_i^{I,max} + p_i^{C,max}$，(for simplicity, we assume all agents have identical workload capacities).

C. Objectives:

The objective of designing model is to finding the optimal routing of information and command flow in the network, which can achieve the optimal target what we care. Various objective functions might be considered: maximization of reward from information and command processing, minimization of information delay, etc.

In this paper, the whole gain of observation, information and command is used to evaluate the performance of network.

Then, objective function may express as following:

Objective function:

$$\text{MAX}\{\sum_{i=1}^{M} g_i^{M} m_i + \sum_{i=1}^{M} g_i^{I} p_i^{I} + \sum_{i=1}^{M} g_i^{C} p_i^{C}\}$$

Constraint:

$$\begin{cases} m_i + \sum_{j=1}^{n} x_{ji}^I + \sum_{j=1}^{n} x_{ji}^C = \sum_{j=1}^{n} x_{ij}^I + \sum_{j=1}^{n} x_{ij}^C + p_i^C \\[2mm] m_i + \sum_{j=1}^{n} x_{ji}^I = \sum_{j=1}^{n} x_{ij}^I + p_i^C \\[2mm] \sum_{i=1}^{n} m_i = M; \quad m_i \le m_i^{\max}; \sum_{j=1}^{n} x_{ji}^I \le r_i^{I,\max} \\[2mm] \sum_{j=1}^{n} x_{ji}^C \le r_i^{C,\max}; \sum_{j=1}^{n} x_{ij}^I \le s_i^{I,\max}; \sum_{j=1}^{n} x_{ij}^C \le s_i^{C,\max} \\[2mm] p_i^I \le p_i^{I,\max}; \quad p_i^C \le p_i^{C,\max}; \quad c_{i,j}^{I,\min} \le x_{i,j}^I \le c_{i,j}^{I,\max} \\[2mm] c_{i,j}^{C,\min} \le x_{i,j}^C \le c_{i,j}^{C,\max}; \sum_{i,j=1}^{n} c_{i,j}^I + \sum_{i,j=1}^{n} c_{i,j}^C \le C; \\[2mm] m_i + p_i^I + p_i^C \le \Omega; \quad x_{ij}^I \ge 0, x_{ij}^C \ge 0 \\[2mm] p_i^I \ge 0, p_i^C \ge 0, m_i \ge 0 \end{cases}$$

Here: $\sum_{i=1}^{M} g_i^M m_i$ is observation gain, $\sum_{i=1}^{M} g_i^I p_i^I$ is information gain, $\sum_{i=1}^{M} g_i^C p_i^C$ is command gain.

3 Organizational Network Based on MAS

In this section, combining with the model of command and control discussed above, we present an example of aerial-defense in the backdrop of USA BG with single carrier, and then design the network of command and control based MAS.

A. Typical constitution of BG

Background: a BG with single carrier sail for an appointed ocean area to execute mission, now the BG are in a highly uncertain environment, one of its mission is to ensure that the BG arrive in the destination in security. Firstly, the BG needs to monitor environment and search the unidentified object by the radar. Furthermore, the BG should allocate different warships with different mission to complete warn, expels or attack task.

Constitution and Mission: a defined BG consists of at least one carrier (CV) together with several escorting platforms (ships, submarines, and aircraft). And the platforms which can be assigned to complete aerial defense consist of one carrier, two anti-aircraft cruisers, two universal destroyers, two anti-aircraft frigates, one battleship and one fighter plane which are dispatched to guard.

The CV is core entity of BG, and the CV's and their platforms contain a wide variety of sensors and weapon systems which allow the BG to carry out defensive and offensive missions. In order to enlarge reconnaissance range and ensure the security, commonly BG will dispatch several battle ship and fighter plane spread out across the operation area. The hostile objects should be engaged (or destroyed) before they can threaten the BG. Which can be shown as follows(see Fig.1).

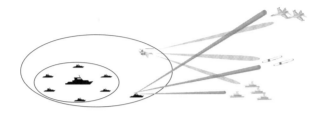

Fig. 1. The BG's constitution schemes

B.   BG's structure analysis [5]

Through the analysis above, in this sub-section, we assume that every platform(battleship or fighter plane) is an agent, then typical constitution of BG can be regard as a network of 9-node organization, and the organization is hierarchical, information flow is from the lower to the top levels, in contrast with the command flow(see Fig.2). The network composed of information sub-network and command sub-network, information and command flows are decomposed into the two independent networks, which can be considered as networks in two dimensions. The information flow in the information network, the command flow in the command network, and information flow can leave information network and enter command network, but not other way around. So we can call the network of MAS as coupled information-command networks. The flowing analysis is on the basis of the coupled information-command networks.

We start with the definition of hypothetical agents' efficiency parameters. In this case, we use the characteristics of typical hierarchical organizations. The agents of CV being in the top levels of this organization, which have highest efficiency, all the information will be processed through it. The coupled network is divided into five layers according to the process information efficiency of each platform.

The agents in the top levels of this organization have the highest efficiency in decision-making (due to high generalization capability), but lower efficiency in task

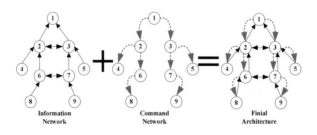

Fig. 2. Organization's topology of BG given above

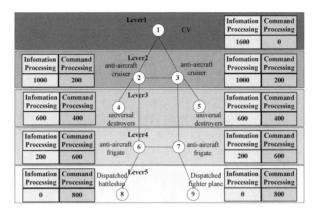

Fig. 3. Agent's efficiency and gain parameters

processing. On the contrary, the agents in the bottom level have higher task processing efficiency (due to high specialization capability). The efficiency/gain parameters for BG are illustrated in Fig. 3.

4   Example of Application

The processing capacity of each platform in the BG is limited, for example, the amount of receiving the perceptive information, the capability of processing information and the capability of converting information into command instruction, the capability of processing command and executing tasks from the command, etc. Excessive tasks can not be dealt with efficiently and timely.

The process capacity of the platforms is equal to the process capacity of agents. For the sake of analyzing the problem, we explore the behavior of optimal routing strategy of the organization when the agents' information and command processing capacities are decreased from ∞ to 0, corresponding the MAS model, the process capacities of agent also decreased from ∞ to 0. At the same time, we assume that the link costs are zero, and the link capacities are unlimited.

This problem is NP-hard problem. Considering the software of Lingo has the superiority to solve NP-hard problem [6], we use Lingo software to simulation the problem. Assuming other parameters in the model of command and control are fixed, but the processing capacity constraints of agent can be adjusted. The optimal routing strategy of the organization in different instance are depicted in Fig.4 (in certain instance, there are several optimal routing strategies, but only one optimal solution is present). Meanwhile, the effects trend-line of BG processing capacity can be got by simulation (see Fig.5).

Some conclusions can be drawn from the results of simulation:

Firstly, when the platform processing capacity is reduced, the flow of information and command in the network are also reduced. This is due to the fact that the total event flow can no longer be processed by single agent, and must be shared among organizational nodes for processing. But when the processing capacity larger than a certain threshold value (this threshold is decided by the platforms quantity of network, the quantity of external information events and the capacity of platform processing), all the external event information can also be responded and dealt with in the network.

Secondly, when processing capacity less than a certain threshold value, not all the external event information can be responded timely in the network. Meanwhile, the important information which we concerned should be selected to process firstly.

Thirdly, The mission gain decrease with decrease in the platform processing capacities (see Fig.5). In [1, 5] range the gain exhibits sharp decrease with non-linear. Whereas, in [12,∞] range (this range is decided by the quantity of external information event), the gain is constant since all event flow can be processed at a single node.

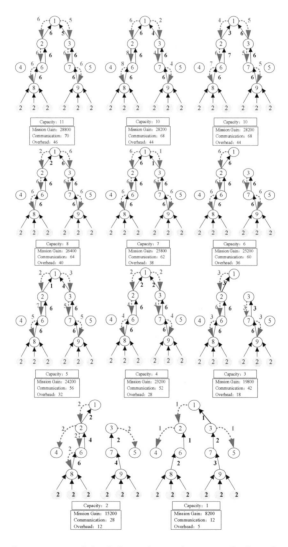

Fig. 4. Optimal routing strategy of the information and command when the platform of BG process information and command capacity is restrained

Some useful revelation can be elicited by the results of simulation:

Firstly, in order to guarantee the information of hostile objects can be processed timely and the command instruction can be executed efficiently, the process capacities of battleship and fighter plane must arrive at a certain basic threshold (the threshold is determined by the process capacities of the platforms, the topology of the military organization and the contemplated process capacities of hostile targets in the battlefield). Otherwise, the efficiency of campaign would descend obviously. So we should try to enhance the basal capacity of the platform of BG.

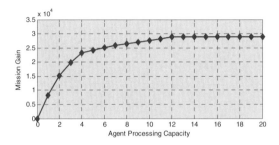

Fig. 5. Effects of BG processing capacity

Secondly, when there are a mass of hostile objects appear in the same time and the quantity of hostile objects have exceeded the threshold given above, but the capacities of platform of BG are immovable, we should sort the threatening degree of the objects firstly, then processing the objects according to the threatening degree.

5   Complimentary

In modern battlefield, each platform of BG will face with the amount of battlefield perceptive information and command instruction, how to effectively disseminate information to keep the BG to arrive at the supreme campaign efficiency has aroused much attention of many scholars. In this paper, a model of information and command based on MAS is proposed to analyze the distribution of information and command. And with a typical case in BG battle, the method of how to distribute the flow of information and command is analyzed, and some useful revelation can be elicited from the simulation.

Acknowledgment. This work was supported in part by National Social Science Foundation of China under Grant 09GJ322-050 and Natural Science Foundation of Hubei Province of China under Grant 2009CDB334.

References

1. Yang, C., Chen, H., Luo, X.: Evaluating the C2 organization structure based on information flows. Systems Engineering and Electronics, 574–578 (April 2007)
2. Zhang, Y., Zhang, A., Li, X.: Modeling and analysis of tactical information distributive process based on network-centric warfare. Systems Engineering and Electronics, 108–111 (January 2008)

3. Michael, W.: And interpret by SHI chunyi. An Introduction to Multi-agent System. Publishing house of electronics industry, Beijing (2003)
4. Levchuk, G.M., Yu, F., Levchuk, Y., Pattipati, K.R.: Networks of Decision-Making and Communicating Agents: A New Methodology for Design and Evaluation of Organizational Strategies and Heterarchical Structures
5. Levchuk, G.M., Feili, Y., Pattipati, K.R., Levchuk, Y.: From Hierarchies to Heterarchies: Application of Network Optimization to Design of Organizational Structures. In: Proceedings of the CCRTS 2003, Washington, DC (June 2003)
6. Wan, b.: LINGO8.0 for windows software and its application (2004)

The E-Learning System Model Based on Affective Computing

Zhiling Li

College of Computer and Information Engineering
Tianjin Normal University
BinShuiXi Road, XiQing District, Tianjin, China
Zhiling@nankai.edu.cn,
zhilingli2011@sina.cn

Abstract. In accordance with affective deprivation in e-learning system, based on affective computing theory, this system uses learners' affection such as expression, positions and time of reading, etc as feedbacks to adjust teaching tactics, effectively personalized the interaction of perception and affection.

Keywords: e-Learning; affective computing; electronic emotion portfolio.

1 Introduction

E-Learning is a brand-new way of learning that provides ideal academic environment, conditions of learning not restricted to time and space, and fully reflects the principal role of the student by effectively integrating information technology and academic programs. But compared with routine forms of instruction, the only shortcoming of e-Learning is affective deprivation. Current teaching system lacks the capability of understanding and adapting human sentiment and mind. When learners are confronted with an unsentimental computer for long-term and cannot feel interactive interest and emotional inspiration, it will result in an aversion, which will affect learning efficiency. According to cognitive science theory, learning process is always accompanied by the occurrence and changes of sentiment, which will in turn influence learning efficiency. In reality, it is the interaction of learning cognition and sentimental cognition process. Thus affective interaction is a vital component of computed and personalized system.

2 Application of Affective Computing in e-Learning

Currently, researches and discussions about "affectionizing" the computer and make it understandable and sentimental has aroused the interests of all walks of life. In 1997, Professor Picard of MIT Media Lab published a monograph entitled Affective

J. Zhang (Ed.): ICAIC 2011, Part III, CCIS 226, pp. 495–500, 2011.

Computing, giving definition and systematic introduction of the research on affective computing. The objective of the system is to provide the computer with high sentimental intelligence to make it capable of human-like emotions, so as to have contextualized interaction with human beings.

Applying affective computing in e-Learning is helpful for the instructors adjust their actions and teaching tactics based on learner's status and sentimental changes. It will increase study efficiency and bring satisfactory teaching results. When the system receives the users' affective signals, it will provide comprehensive analysis and judgment on it. Once perceived their sentiment, it will adjust program process to provide personalized learning environment.

3   E-Learning on Affective Computing System Model Frame

This system can realize personalized online teaching by cognitive and sentimental interaction; acquire students' learning mood and cognitive effects at any moment; provide personalized instruction; create synchronized electronic emotional files; record and update learners' sentiment status; and regularly conclude their sentimental changes at a certain period of time.

This model improves the traditional e-Learning system frame with affective computing as the core technology. The basic frame is shown as Figure 1. It has three functions: ① capture and recognize students' sentimental information in real-time and treat it as an important ground of adjusting teaching tactics dynamically to provide personalized instructing services for the students; ② realize emotional interaction between the students and computer through personalized teaching assistance; ③ create electronic emotion portfolio to keep learners' personal affective information during learning process and adjust and conclude the status accordingly.

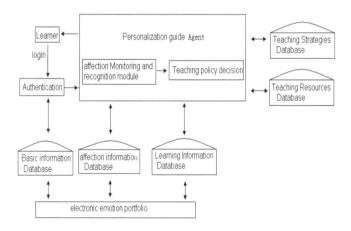

Fig. 1. Basic model frame of the system

4   Learners' Emotional Inspection and Recognition

When students log on the system, it retrieves student's facial expressions and body gestures through a sensor and inspects their study process. Also it obtains their learning mood by comprehensive analysis according to correspondent models. Currently lot s of scholars regard affective communication as one problem in e-Learning system. The researches mostly include inspecting learners through effective sensors (like camera, etc.) and acquiring effective sentimental signals by relevant techniques such as facial detection, expression, vocal and gesture recognition, etc.

Human's sentiments are complex and diversified, which has a number of ways to categorize. Based on the concept of emotional space and in order to clearly indicate students' study status, this system defines the sentiments in three dimensions: to create an affective space with degrees of approach-avoidance, concentration and understanding. As Figure 2 shows. Any normal emotions can be represented by 3D vector quantities (Ex, Ey, Ez).

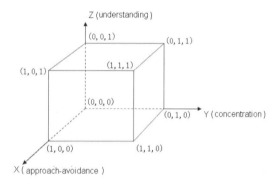

Fig. 2. Learning affective space

Body languages such as expressions and gestures are display of one's thoughts. So it is in learning. When the learner has interest or determination and motivation for the content, his body will lean forward unconsciously with widened eyes; when he feels bored or wants to avoid, the body will move backward without control, eyes closely or completely shut. Through facial recognition, the degree of approach-avoidance uses the proportion of learners' face area and the whole window as the distance of the head from the monitor. The bigger the proportion value is, the closer the head from the monitor and more interest he has. Besides, by facial expressions retrieval and recognition, the value of concentration degree can be achieved. When the learner is focused on the content, distance between the eyes will be longer, and otherwise shorter.

Firstly, collect data of learners' sample icons and input around 60 icons different distance from the monitor. Inspect the image by complexion and binarize the selected area of the face by calculating skin color density. Then by retrieving eye, mouth and profile characteristics to match and finally detect human face and eyes. Then receive the data on the foundation of the ratio of height and width of the face and compare the predefined interest value. At last, through function transformation and normalization, we get learning interest affective recognition model based on facial degree of approach-avoidance.

Set the equation of the function transformation as (1)

$$e_x = \left\{ \left(\frac{\sqrt{x} - \sqrt{x_{fmin}}}{\sqrt{x_{fmax}} - \sqrt{x_{fmin}}} \right)^{\frac{1}{2}} \mid x_{fmin} < e_x < x_{fmax} \right\} \tag{1}$$

In the equation, X stands for the actual facial area detected; xfmax is the maximum; xfmin is the minimum area.

Accordingly, we get concentration detection model of the distance between eyes, whose results has relevance with those of degree of approach-avoidance. The influence of this degree on the sample data of concentration should be weakened.

Then, we get the concentration detection model as (2)

$$e_y = \left\{ \left(\frac{\frac{Y}{P_1} - y_{emin}}{y_{emax} - y_{emin}} \right)^{\frac{1}{2}} \mid y_{emin} < e_y < y_{emax} \right\} \tag{2}$$

In the equation, X is the actual distance between eyes detected; xemax is the maximum average value; xemin the minimum; P1 is the degree of approach-avoidance under such state.

In e-Learning system, if study tactic and process are able to adapt to students' learning ability, learners will finish reading of a point in the webpage during a certain period of time. But if being confronted with difficulties, the period will be prolonged that some may even lose the patience to continue and keep switching the web pages or shut it down directly. So it is vitally important of supervising students' learning process to inspire and help before they give up and adjust instruction tactics to finish established learning smoothly.

The periods spend on a point of the knowledge are varied from person to person. Besides, there is a difference in people's cognition. We form a team of learners with similar knowledge background and capabilities who may have little difference in length of study instead of setting a specific value. As a result, a reasonable value range can be achieved with the help of large amounts of learners. Such value can be regarded as normal period of study. When difficulties in studying occur, repeatedly reading or switching pages are relevant to students' personality. But under such circumstances as higher as or lower than the normal value, it reflects learning difficulty. This system normalizes the length of reading each knowledge point after calculation, as in (3).

$$e_z = \frac{1}{z_{ever} + |z - z_{ever}|} \tag{3}$$

In the equation, Zever is the weighted mean value of the length of reading time in one point among the group.

Due to the variance in accuracy of the three items in detection, and in the imbalance of approach-avoidance, concentration and understanding degree in affective evaluation, weights are provided in comprehensive evaluation, which is acquired by the form of questionnaires and professional advice. The weights are reflected by fuzzy vector, namely (a, b, c). We get a comprehensive evaluation value of learning affection by synthesis, as in (4).

$$\gamma = \sqrt{ae_x^2 + be_y^2 + ce_z^2} \tag{4}$$

In the equation (4), a+b+c=1, γ, module of the vector stands for sentimental strength, vector angle θ is sentimental approach degree.

5 Personalized Instruction Facilities

Personalized instruction agents determine effective teaching tactics and content to meet learners' personalized long-distance education needs, depending on their current sentimental status and past study history with corresponding strategic solutions in the database. When there is any changes of their learning process and capabilities in receiving knowledge, the system is able to analyze the causes in real-time and adjust teaching tactics and content accordingly, such as encouragement, criticism or personalized guidance like web page recommendation, teaching tactics update, and design virtual images to increase vividness.

6 Creation of Electronic Emotion Portfolio

Electronic emotion portfolios keep learners' personal sentimental information which clearly shows the status and development during the whole learning process. It mainly includes learners' basic information, affective changes and their study information. The system saves learners' study status and emotional changes in the electronic folder of affective files as the basis of analyzing their sentiment. The learners' themselves and the instructor may refer to the analysis immediately and adjust and improve accordingly. Besides, it is accompanied by staged evaluation during the learning process so as to create active emotional inspiration for further study.

7 Conclusion

It has become an important issue worth further studying of evaluating learners' cognition and affection while being educated in e-Learning system and realizing harmonious sentimental interaction. This system, based on affective computing theory by treating learners' expressions and gestures and emotional expressions during learning process as feedbacks, can adjust teaching tactics immediately and create personalized study environment for its users. Future researches will further provide information integration of multiple affective characteristics and improving detection accuracy of human faces. Also on the basis of this study, affection interactive information system in e-business can be developed and applied, so as to provide wider application of "Man-computer Interaction."

Acknowledgment. This study is sponsored by The National Natural Science Foundation of China (60970060/F020508); Natural Science Foundation of Tianjin (08JCYBJC13700).

References

1. Wang, Z.: Artificial emotion. Machinery Industry Press (2009)
2. Ekman, P.: An Argument for Basic Emotions. Cognition and Emotion 6, 169–200 (1992)
3. Shute, V., Psotka, J.: Intelligent Tutoring System: past, present and future. In: Jonassen, D. (ed.) Handbook of Research for Educational Communications and Technology, pp. 570–600. Macmillan, New York (1996)
4. Meng, X.-y., Wang, Z.-l., Wang, L.-j.: Teaching Assistant System Based on Affective Modeling. Application Research of Computers (4), 74–76 (2007)
5. Zhang, X.-y.: Framework of an E-Learning System based on Affective Computing. Journal of Hunan Institute of Science and Technology (Natural Sciences) (12), 51–54 (2009)

A Novel Immune-Inspired Method for Malicious Code Extraction and Detection*

Yu Zhang[1], Liping Song[2], and Yuliang He[2]

[1] College of Information Science and Technology
Hainan Normal University, Haikou 571158, China
[2] Zhejiang Key Laboratory of Information Security
Zhejiang Testing Institute of Electronic Products
LipingSong2011@163.com

Abstract. Malicious code has been generally accepted as one of the top security threats to computer information systems around the world for several years. Malicious code is changing more rapidly; it has become modular in design and propagates using new and novel methods. The roorkit techniques that malicious code uses to hide itself in the operating system kernel make the traditional antivirus difficult to extract its signature, not to mention detect it. Inspired by the biological immune system, we proposed a novel immune-inspired method for malicious code extraction and detection---IMCD. The IMCD extracts the I/O Request Packets (IRPs) sequence produced by the process running in kernel mode as antigen, defines the normal benign programs as self programs, and defines the malicious codes as nonself programs. By the process behavior monitoring and the family gene analysis, the method can monitor the evolution of malicious code. The method generates the immature antibodies by vaccination, produces mature antibodies by clonal selection and gene evolution, and then learns and evolutionary identifies the unknown malicious codes by the mature antibodies. Theoretical analysis and experiments show that the proposed method for unknown malicious code detection has high detection rate, low false-positive rate, and low omission rate.

Keywords: Malicious code, Artificial immune system, IRPs sequence, Anti-malware, Signature extraction.

1 Introduction

Internet technology and the hacker industrial chain promote the malicious code technology with two remarkable characteristics as follows: (1) the increasing number of unknown malicious codes; (2) the gradual rootkits techniques used by malicious codes. The former leads to update frequently the malicious codes database, while the latter results in malicious codes hidden in the system kernel, which will steal user

---

* This work was supported by Hainan Natural Science Foundation (610220), Project of Zhejiang Key Laboratory of Information Security (2010ZISKL007) and the Science and Technology Project of Hainan Normal University (00203020214).

J. Zhang (Ed.): ICAIC 2011, Part III, CCIS 226, pp. 501–509, 2011.

sensitive data, monitor user network behavior and attack the networks. The traditional signature antivirus technology is difficult to effectively respond to the challenges of malicious codes of new generation [1]. Therefore, how to effectively deal with such challenges of malicious codes has become an important and urgent problem to resolve [2, 3].

Human immune system with the characteristic of robustness, adaptability, scalability, and efficiency, has the similar functions with the information security system, which brings inspirations for the design of the information security system [4]. Inspired by the biological immune system, researchers have proposed a variety of algorithms and models of artificial immune system that focus on malicious code detection. Forrest et al. [5] for the first time applied the immune principle to information security systems, and proposed a general-purpose artificial immune system model named ARTIS. Kephart et al. [6] in IBM corporation proposed a digital immune system---DIS. Harmer et al. [7] proposed a computer immune system model called CDIS. Tao Li [8] presented a dynamic immune-based model for computer virus detection. These artificial immune systems draw inspirations from the biological immune system and have some similar features in functions that regard the normal programs as Self, suspicious programs as Nonself, malicious code detectors as antibodies or immune cells, all procedures in the network system as antigen. Moreover, These artificial immune systems generate qualified malicious code detectors by negative selection mechanism, clonal selection mechanism and genetic evolution mechanism, and detect malicious codes by detectors/antigens matching.

However, the immune systems above still have some shortcomings: (1) the definitions of Self and Nonself lack flexibility, which do not reflect the dynamic evolution of network environment; (2) low generation efficiency of antibody (detector), which do not make use of the reservation of the best antibody genes; (3) insufficiency of antibody diversity; (4) antigen extraction method is simple and does not reflect the process behavior. These deficiencies led to the big cost of antibody (detector) generation, long detection time, and high false-positive rate.

We proposed a novel immunity-inspired method for malicious code detection named IMCD. The method extracts the I/O Request Packets (IRPs) sequence produced by the process running in kernel mode as antigen, defines the normal benign programs as Self, and defines malicious code as Nonself. Moreover, the IMCD can monitor the evolution of malicious code by the process behavior monitoring and genetic analysis of family genes of malicious code, learn and evolutionary identify the unknown malicious codes through vaccination, clonal selection, genetic evolution, and afterwards extract the malicious codes genes to update the antibody genes pool. Both theoretical analysis and experiments show that the proposed model has high detection rate and low false-positive rate for unknown malicious codes.

2   Theory of Proposed Method

A.   Proposed Architecture

The proposed model architecture is shown in Figure 1. First, the model forms immature antibody set (immature detectors) by both some new antibodies vaccinated with vaccines extracting from the antibody genes pool and some randomly generated antibodies. Second, the immature antibody set will be divided into two groups by undergoing self-tolerance (negative selection). Those who endure the self-tolerance will evolve into mature antibody set (mature detectors), while those who fail to pass through the self-tolerance (or match one of self) will be removed. Third, some of the mature antibodies will be activated and evolve into memory antibody set (permanent detectors) if they match enough antigens (learning process) in their life cycle, otherwise some mature antibodies will be apoptosis. During this learning process, mature antibodies could cause initial response if they detect and identify malicious codes antigen. These memory antibodies that evolved from the mature antibody set have infinite length of life cycle, during which they will be immediately activated once matching any antigen, resulting in secondary response. In addition, part of memory antibodies will go through high-frequency variation and clonal expansion to produce new next generation immature antibodies. Finally, the model will extract malicious code gene by antigen-presenting from these detected malicious codes to form the antibody gene pool. Moreover, the memory antibody set used to detect known malicious codes and the mature antibody set used to unknown malicious code have different activation threshold values, respectively.

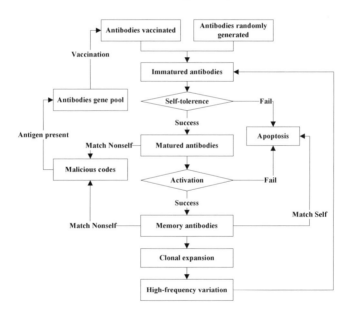

Fig. 1. The Proposed Model Architecture

B. Definitions in the Model

1) Antigen
The proposed model uses IRPs (I/O Request Packets) sequence created by the process running in the kernel mode as antigen based on the following reasons. First, all user mode or running time API functions eventually execute the kernel mode

504 Y. Zhang, L. Song, and Y. He

system calls through the system call gate (INT 2E or SYSENTER). Second, those malicious codes that use rootkits techniques running in kernel mode will directly or indirectly call or hook the kernel mode system calls. Third, the I/O (input and output) operations conducted by the kernel mode system calls eventually complete by passing corresponding IRPs created by I/O Manager to the device driver. Finally, the process dynamic behavior can be acquired by intercepting its IRPs [9] sequence whether generated by user mode API or kernel mode API. Therefore, the antigen extraction method used in this model reflects the essential characteristics of running process, and thereby overcomes traditional artificial immune system defects in antigen-extracting.

The commonly used IRPs types are fifteen or more. For the sake of simplicity, we have encoded these IRPs with hexadecimal characters from 0 to F, respectively, and the others are encoded with character "*". The commonly used IRPs types and their corresponding codes are shown in Table 1.

Table 1. IRPs types and the corresponding codes

IRPs types	Corresponding codes
IRP_MJ_CREATE	0
IRP_MJ_READ	1
IRP_MJ_WRITE	2
IRP_MJ_CLEANUP	3
IRP_MJ_CLOSE	4
IRP_MJ_SHUTDOWN	5
IRP_MJ_PNP	6
IRP_MJ_POWER	7
IRP_MJ_FLUSH_BUFFERS	8
IRP_MJ_QUERY_INFORMATION	9
IRP_MJ_SET_INFORMATION	A
IRP_MJ_DEVICE_CONTROL	B
IRP_MJ_INTERNAL_DEVICE_CONTROL	C
IRP_MJ_SYSTEM_CONTROL	D
IRP_MJ_QUERY_VOLUME_INFORMATION	E
IRP_MJ_SET_VOLUME_INFORMATION	F
Others	*

Definition 1. *Antigen space* is an IRPs sequence set generated by the running processes, which can be expressed as $A = \bigcup_{i=1}^{\infty} H^i$,where H={0,1,2,3,4,5,6,7,8,9, A,B,C,D,E,F,*}, and i is a positive integer.

Definition 2. The *antigen* is an IRPs sequence created by the running process expressed as $Ag = \{x \mid x = $ IRPs sequence created by the running process, $x \in A\}$

Definition 3. *Self* are benign Windows system files and application programs in computer, indicted as $N = \{x \mid x = $ IRPs sequence created by the malicious codes, $x \in A\}$.

Definition 4. *Nonself* are the files and processes with unusual suspicious behavior in a computer system, expressed as $N = \{x \mid x = \text{IRPs sequence created by the malicious codes,}, x \in A\}$.

The above *Self* and *Nonself* meet these conditions as follows: $S \subset Ag$, $N \subset Ag$, $S \cup N = Ag, S \cap N = \phi$.

 2) Antibody

Definition 5. Antibody is the malicious code detector extracted from IRPs sequence of *Nonself*, expressed as $Ab = \overset{\infty}{\underset{j=1}{\cup}} H^j$, in which $j < i$ is a positive integer and $Ab \subset N$.

The antibodies in the biological immune system must endure a succession of processes to become eligible immune cells. First, newly generated antibodies enter the central immune organs for self-tolerance (negative selection), in which those who successfully undergo self-tolerance will distribute in various lymph nodes. Then, with the help of immune helper cells, these antibodies are activated to be mature immune cells. Finally, parts of mature immune cells evolve into memory cells only after matching a large number of antigens.

As presented in the literature [1], a negative selection algorithm based on self-tolerance was designed to establish the model ARTIS. Although this elegantly simple algorithm seemed to make a lot of sense, it had problems in training costly the eligible antibodies. To address this problem, we propose a novel negative selection algorithm that creates eligible antibodies based on both *Self* and *Nonself*. The reason we propose such idea is that *Self* and *Nonself* in the process antigen space exist intersection. To specifically speaking, some *Self* programs (benign codes) may be refer a certain technology of *Nonself* programs (malicious codes), and vice versa.

To better simulate real biological functions of antibody in the immune system, the model has establish corresponding antibody evolutionary mechanism as follows.

$$Ab(t) = \begin{cases} Ab_{initial} & , t = 0 \\ Ab(t-1) + Ab_{new}(t), t \geq 1 \end{cases} \tag{5}$$

$$Ab(t-1) = Ab_{immature}(t-1) + Ab_{mature}(t-1) + Ab_{memory}(t-1) \tag{6}$$

$$Ab_{immature}(t-1) = Ab_{new}(t-1) + Ab_{vaccination}(t-1) \tag{7}$$

$$Ab_{mature}(t-1) = \{v \mid v \in Ab_{immature}(t-1) \wedge \forall y \in N \wedge affinity(v, y) \geq \beta\} \tag{8}$$

$$Ab_{memory}(t-1) = \{v \mid v \in Ab_{mature}(t-1) \wedge \forall y \in N \wedge affinity(v, y) \geq \delta\} \tag{9}$$

As shown in above equations, $Ab(t), Ab(t-1) \subset A$ represent the antibody set at time t and t-1, respectively. $Ab_{immature}(t-1), Ab_{mature}(t-1), Ab_{memory}(t-1) \subset A$ mean the immature antibody set, the mature antibody set, and the memory antibody set at time t-1, respectively. $Ab_{new}(t-1)$ stands for the newly random generated antibodies at time t-1. $Ab_{vaccination}(t-1)$ represents the antibodies vaccinated by the vaccines from the antibody genes pool at time t-1. *affinity* ( ) is the affinity function.

3   Experiments and Results

A.   Experiment Environment

The experimental environment of this study is shown in Table 2.

Table 2. Experimental environment

Experimental Platform	IRP Trace Tool	Malicious Code Number	Malicious Codes Source
VMWare 5.5 Windows XP	IRPTrace 1.00.007	1000	WildList [11] VX Heavens [12]

Due to the specificity of malicious codes detection, the experiments were carried on in an isolated environment or a virtual environment. This study was tested in such virtual environment as VMWare 5.5. The antigen in the model is defined as IRPs sequences created by the processes running in the system kernel-mode, so we use the tool IRPTrace to capture IRPs sequence.

B.   Experimental Procedure

The Experimental data shown in Table 3 were divided into two groups of which one is for learning and the other is for testing.

Table 3. Experimental sample classification

Self		Malicious Codes	
Self-tolerance (for learning)	*Immune Recognition (for testing)*	*Antibody gene pool*	*Immune Recognition (for testing)*
500	500	400	600

The experimental parameters are deployed as follows. The antibody length l is variable, ranging from 4 to 8; the self-tolerance threshold value α =0.1; the mature antibody matching threshold value β =0.4; the memory antibody matching threshold value δ =0.5; the malicious codes detection threshold value ε =0.5. We use detection rate, false-positive rate, and omission rate to assess the proposed detection model performance.

The experimental results are shown in Table 4.

Table 4. The experimental results

Antibody Length l	Detection Rate	Omission Rate	False-positive Rate
4	94.35%	5.65%	1.58%
5	97.56%	2.46%	1.25%
6	95.82%	4.18%	1.42%
7	92.68%	7.32%	3.18%
8	85.12%	14.82%	2.46%

4   Comparisons with Related Study

In order to test the proposed model performance, the model ARTIS by Forrest et al. was chosen as a comparative experimental object. The ARTIS is a typical model of artificial immune system, which has a significant impact on the design and application of intrusion detection and virus detection.

The comparison items include antibody generation time, self-tolerance time, scanning time, and detection rate. The comparison experimental results are shown in Figure 3 to Figure 6.

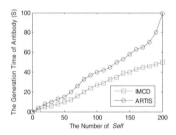

Fig. 2. The relationship between the generation time of antibody and the number of self

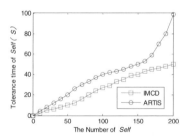

Fig. 3. The relationship between tolerance time of self and the number of self

As shown in Figure 3, the generation time of antibody exponentially increase with the increase of *Self* for ARTIS model, while the generation time of antibody is linear with the *Self* for the proposed IMCD model. The reason is that the IMCD creates the qualified antibody by vaccination with the malicious codes gene in the antibody gene pool, while the ARTIS generates the eligible antibody by random method which will cost much time.

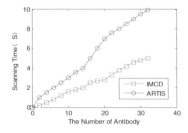

Fig. 4. The relationship between scanning time and the number of antibody

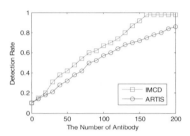

Fig. 5. The relationship between detection rate and the number of antibody

From Figure 4, we see the similar graphics as shown in Figure 3. The reason is that the IMCD self-tolerance is based on both *Self* and *Nonself* which evolve dynamically during the self-tolerance, while the ARTIS self-tolerance is based only on *Self* which is static during the self-tolerance.

As expressed in Figure 5, the scanning time of ARTIS is much more than that of IMCD. The reason is that the IMCD uses a novel r-step-matching algorithm instead of r-bit-contiguous-matching algorithm used by ARTIS. The r-step-matching algorithm uses some gene fragments to detect malicious codes thus to save scanning time.

From Figure 5, we see that the detection rate of IMCD is higher than that of ARTIS. Comparative to ARTIS, IMCD takes some measures including vaccination, clonal expansion, and high-frequent variation to improve the detection efficiency.

5   Conclusions

Malicious codes have been becoming invisible in our computer systems when using rootkits and thus making traditional antivirus difficult to detect. Fortunately, artificial immune system has brought a ray of hope for network security community.

However, traditional artificial immune system has problems of *Self* integrity and detector completeness, which lead to high training costs and difficult to expand. We present a novel immunity-inspired model for malicious code detection---IMCD. We propose the IRPs sequence as the antigen for the first time, and present *Self*/*Nonself* evolutionary equations, antibody gene pool evolutionary equation, and antibody evolutionary equation which can improve the efficiency of mature antibody generation. By vaccination, self-tolerance, and clonal selection, IMCD could dynamically monitor malicious codes evolution, which also improved the detection rate and lower the false-positive rate. The main innovations of the paper are as follows. First, a novel antigen extraction method was proposed which extracts the IRPs sequence of the process running the system kernel-mode as antigen. Second, a novel immature antibody generation method that vaccinates the randomly created antibody was presented. Third, a new self-tolerance method that is based on both *Self* and *Nonself* to produce mature antibody was proposed. Finally, a new antibody/antigen matching algorithm called r-step-matching algorithm was presented.

References

1. Wulf, W.A., Jones, A.K.: Reflections on Cybersecurity. Science 13 26(5955), 943–944 (2009)
2. Ford, R., Spafford, E.H.: Happy birthday, dear viruses. Science 13 317(5835), 210–211 (2007)
3. Chang, F.R.: Is Your Computer Secure? Science 31 325(5940), 550–551 (2009)
4. Li, T.: Computer Immunology. Publishing House of Electronics Industry, Beijing (2004)
5. Forrest, S., Perelson, A.S., Allen, L., et al.: Self-Nonself Discrimination in a Computer. In: Proceedings of the IEEE Symposium on Research in Security and Privacy, Oakland, USA (1994)
6. Kephart, J.O.: A Biologically Inspired Immune System for Computers. In: Proceedings on the 4th International Workshop on the Systhesis and Simulation of Living Systems and Artificial Life, pp. 130–139. MIT Press, Cambridge (1994)
7. Harmer, P.K., Williams, P.D., Gunsch, G.H., et al.: An artificial immune system architecture for computer security applications. IEEE Transactions on Evolutionary Computation 6(3), 252–280 (2002)
8. Li, T.: Dynamic Detection for Computer Virus based on Immune System. Science In China Series F: Information Science 51(10), 1475–1486 (2008)
9. IRP (2010), http://en.wikipedia.org/wiki/I/O_request_packet
10. Sproul, T.W., Cheng, P.C., Dykstra, M.L., Pierce, S.K.: A role for MHC class II antigen processing in B cell development. International Reviews of Immunology 19(2-3), 139–155 (2000)
11. The WildList Organization International (2010), http://www.wildlist.org
12. VX Heavens (2010), http://vx.netlux.org

Study on the Effectiveness of the TCP Pacing Mechanism

Xinying Liu, Fenta Adnew Mogus, and Lei Wang

School of Information and Communication Engineering
Beijing University of Posts and Telecommunications
No.10 Xitucheng Road Haidian District Beijing China
xinyingliu2011@sina.com

Abstract. The key idea proposed in this paper is to evaluate the effectiveness of TCP pacing mechanism minimizing the buffer requirements by routers. Based on references related to TFRC, buffer size needed in the bottleneck link, and analysis of the queue length in the router, the assumption that the router just needs less packets as buffer size, if the TCP traffic was paced than regularly TCP traffic in the bottleneck link shared by TCP and TFRC was made. Analysis of the queue length in the router was made. Simulation results show that the router can save at least 50% buffer size in the bottleneck link shared by pacing-based TCP and TFRC than in the bottleneck link shared by regular Reno TCP and TFRC, and when the utilization of the bottleneck reaches 90%, the loss rate hardly changes. The experiments are performed in both over-provisioned and under-provisioned network situations.

Keywords: Paced-TCP, TFRC, congestion control mechanism, buffer size.

1 Introduction

Nowadays, the streaming media usage is in a rapid growth. RTP (Real-Time Transport Protocol) is the Internet standard protocol for the transport of real-time data, which is used extensively in communication and entertainment systems that involve streaming media. TCP protocol is not appropriate for applications such as real-time stream transfer. Typically, RTP runs on top of the UDP protocol. Simply using UDP to transmit streaming media will cause TCP to hunger for bandwidth, and even lead for the collapsing of the network. An End-to-End congestion control of best-effort traffic is required to avoid the congestion of Internet. Therefore a relatively smooth transmission rate is very important. It's also necessary to find a good transport protocol which makes it more suitable for applications like video telephony or streaming media which is TCP friendly. TCP-Friendly Rate Control (TFRC) [1] is such a congestion control mechanism designed for the transmission of streaming media with TCP traffic.

Delay and delay variance are the important factors to influence the quality of the transmission of the media. Buffers cause queuing delay and delay variance. Many researches are done regarding the buffers size of a router. Villamizar and Song [2] proposed the well known rule-of-thumb, $B = \overline{RTT} \times C$ rule, where B is the buffer size

J. Zhang (Ed.): ICAIC 2011, Part III, CCIS 226, pp. 510–518, 2011.

needed by the link, $\overline{RTT}$ is the average round-trip time of a flow passing across the link, and C is the data rate of the link. Appenzeller [3] argues that the rule-of-thumb is outdated and incorrect for backbone routers as the number of flows enter a single backbone link is increasing. So they proposed that a link with n flows requires no more than $B = (\overline{RTT} \times C)/\sqrt{n}$. Then Enachescu [4] argued that if the TCP source are not overly burst, then $O(\log W)$ buffers is enough for high throughput, where W is the window size of each flow.

This paper focuses on how to get the less buffer size in the bottleneck link shared by TCP and TFRC flows. If the TCP source sends "pacing" packets into the link, the number of packets needed as buffer size in router by the link shared by TCP and TFRC flows is also argued in this paper. The rest of the paper is organized as follows. Section 2 provides a description of the ideas and advantages of the Pacing-based flows in reducing buffer size. The simulation modeling design, results from simulations and experiments are presented and discussed in section 3. Section 4 is the conclusion part of the paper followed by references.

2   Description

A. Motivation

According to RFC3448 [1], TFRC is designed to be reasonably fair when competing for bandwidth with TCP. The throughput of TCP flow is calculated according to the parameters from the receivers and the data send by using the throughput equation.

There are many researches in TFRC [4], [5], [6], the disadvantage of TFRC is that while competing for available bandwidth, its response is slower than TCP. So it needs smoother throughput of TCP Reno and less packet drop. Adding "pacing" into TCP Reno can realize the transmission of the packets into link smoothly [7].

Enachescu [8] proposed and verified it through experiments, that a router needs about ten packets as buffer size when the TCP packets are sent smoothly.

From the above, there is an assumption that a router needs less buffer size to get a high throughput, if a sender sends the TCP flows smoothly into the bottleneck link shared with TFRC flows, than in the bottleneck link shared by TCP Reno and TFRC.

B. Histogram of the Queue Length in Router

To verify the above assumption, the Fig.1 is used as simulation topology. In this paper, the TCP Reno and TFRC on the basis of RFC3448's TCP throughput model equation are used. In the simulation, the number of TCP and TFRC flows is variable, and the buffer size is not limited. The queue length is recorded as a function of time, and then "pacing" is added into the TCP, which allows TCP sender to send the packet in a rate of CWND/RTT Smoothly, so that the frequency of queue length can be calculated and its variation can be spotted. (CWND is the congestion window and RTT is the round-trip time).

The simulation result show that (Fig.2 and Fig.3) the frequency of the queue length changes a little in the bottleneck link shared by TCP Reno and TFRC flows. The frequency of the queue length with a constant buffer size is higher than other buffer size in the bottleneck link shared by Paced TCP (adding "pacing to TCP Reno) and TFRC flows.

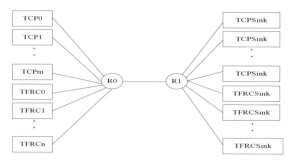

Fig. 1. Simulation Topology

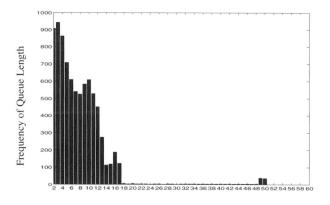

Fig. 2. The frequency of queue length in router when the bottleneck link is shared by TCP Reno and TFRC flows

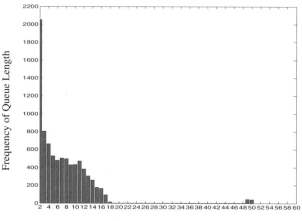

Fig. 3. The frequency of queue length in router when the bottleneck link is shared by Paced TCP and TFRC flows

C. One TCP and one TFRC Flow in the Network

Using the topology of Fig.1, the throughputs and loss rates of the bottleneck link are studied. At first, the variation of throughput and loss rate are recorded as a function of buffer size (the buffer size is from 2 to 100 packets) when the source sends one TCP flow (TCP Reno) and one TFRC flow into bottleneck link. Then the source sends packets smoothly using the pacing-based algorithm. The "pacing" allows TCP to pace the packet in a rate of CWND/RTT. The variations of throughput and loss rate recorded are compared with the shared link by TCP Reno and TFRC flows. The result proved that 75% buffer size can be saved (Fig.5 and Fig.6) by "pacing" TCP in the shared bottleneck link, and the loss rate is better. For further investigation, other simulations are done in both over-provisioned and under-provisioned network conditions.

D. Over-Provisioned Network

In this section, the bottleneck link C is 10Mbps and RTT is 200ms.The source sends 4 TCP (TCP Reno) and 4 TFRC flows into the link. The maximum congestion window size is 32 packets, and the size of the packets is 1,000 bytes. Thus the maximum congestion offered load is (maximum of CWND × packet size × number of traffics) / RTT, which is about 10Mbps, it shows that the TCP and TFRC flows are in the over-provisioned network. The throughput and loss rate are recorded while changing the buffer size from 2 to 10, and when the "pacing" is added into TCP. Comparing the results of the two conditions, it can be found that the link shared by paced TCP and TFRC flows can save about 50% buffer size than the link shared by regularly TCP and TFRC flows with the same utilization of throughput and little difference in loss rate.

E. Under-Provisioned Network

In this network, the bottleneck link C is 10Mbps and RTT is 200ms. The source sends 8 TCP (TCP Reno) and 8 TFRC flows into the link. The maximum congestion window size is 32 packets, and the size of packets is 1,000 bytes. The maximum congestion offered load is 20Mbps, which shows that TCP and TFRC flows are in the under-provisioned network. The throughput and loss rate are recorded while changing the buffer size from 2 to 10, and the same too when "pacing" is added into TCP. The comparison result of the two shows that the link shared by paced TCP and TFRC flows can save about 50% buffer size compared to the link shared by regularly TCP and TFRC with same utilization of throughput and little difference in loss rate.

3 Simulation

To investigate the influence of "pacing" on the buffer size in the router, bottleneck link utilization and loss rate in the shared link, an experimental simulation is done based on NS, by using Fig.1 topology . The capacity of the bottleneck link is 10Mbps, and the average RTT is 200ms. The simulation is run for 100 seconds, and the data is recorded after 20 seconds.

A. Single TCP and TFRC Flows

The simulation scenario model is based on one TCP and TFRC flow shared the same link. Fig.3 shows the bottleneck link utilization as a function of the buffer size used in the router; one TCP and one TFRC flow share the link. The solid line shows the throughout utilization when the TCP source sends paced packets into the link, and the dot line show the throughout utilization when the TCP source sent packets with no pacing. The maximum congestion window size is 32 packets, and the size of packets is 1,000 bytes, and thus the maximum congestion offered load is about 1.25Mbps.

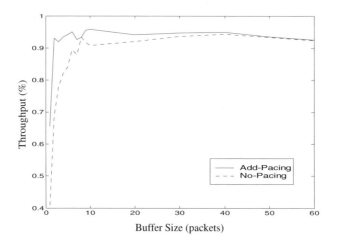

Fig. 4. The relative of bottleneck link utilization and buffer size when buffer size is set from 1 to 100

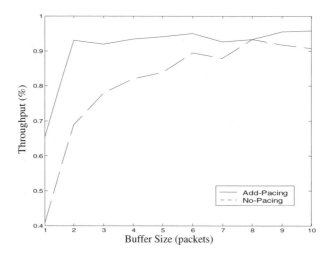

Fig. 5. The relative of bottleneck link utilization and buffer size when buffer size is set from 1 to 10

Fig.4 shows the bottleneck link utilization when the router buffer size is from 1 to 100 and both situations can gain a very high throughput when the buffer size is above 10 packets. Fig.5 shows when the buffer size is from 1 to 10 packets in details. It shows that if the sender sends TCP packets smoothly, the bottleneck link utilization is around 90% when the buffer size is 2. For TCP Reno link to gain the same bottleneck link utilization, it needs 8 packets buffer size. Fig.6 shows that the loss rate in pacing-based link is better than regular link, and from these we can conclude that by adding "pacing" into the shared link, it can save 75% buffer size with better loss rate.

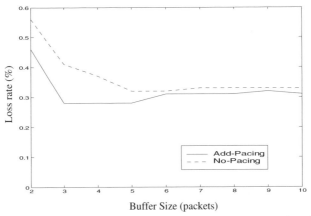

Fig. 6. The loss rate variation when the buffer is set 2-10 packets in the bottleneck link shared by 1 TCP and 1 TFRC flows

B. Over-Provisioned Network

In this part, the source sends 4 TCP and 4 TFRC flows into the bottleneck link. The maximum congestion window size set is 32 packets, and the size of packets is 1,000

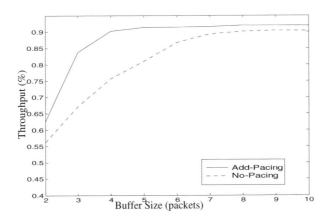

Fig. 7. The relative of bottleneck link utilization and buffer size when 4 TCP and 4 TFRC flows were sent into shares link

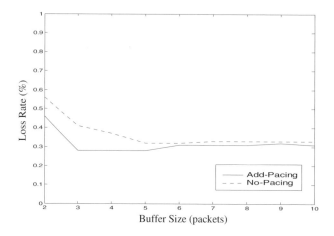

Fig. 8. The loss rate variation when the buffer is set 2-10 packets in the bottleneck link shared by 4 TCP and 4 TFRC flows

bytes, so the maximum congestion offered load 10Mbps. Fig.7 depicted the bottleneck link utilization as a function of the buffer size in the router. The x-axis represents the buffer size, while the y-axis represents the bottleneck utilization. The solid line represents the bottleneck link utilization of 4 paced Reno and 4 TFRC flows that can achieve 90% with just 4 packets buffer. The smoother dashed line shows the link utilization of 4 unmodified TCP (Reno) and 4 TFRC flows that achieved 90% with at least a buffer size of 8 packets. From Fig.8, we can generalized that the loss rate in the link shared by Paced TCP and TFRC is better than the link shared by TCP Reno and TFRC, so it saves 50% buffer size with better link utilization and loss rate adding "pacing" into the over-provisioned network.

C. Under-Provsioned Network

For this network, the sender sends 8 TCP and TFRC flows each in the shared link. The maximum congestion window size is 32 packets, and the size of packets is 1,000 bytes, that makes the maximum congestion offered load 20Mbps. Fig.9 depicts that the link utilization as a function of the buffer size used in the router. Solid line represents the link utilization of 8 modified TCP (paced Reno) and 8 TFRC flows that achieve 90% with a buffer size of 4. The dashed line shows the bottleneck link utilization of 8 unmodified TCP (Reno) and 8 TFRC flows with a 90% throughput with at least a buffer size of 8. From this we can conclude that the modified TCP and TFRC have a high gain throughput with much smaller buffers in the over-provisioned network. From Fig.10,we can see that in the bottleneck shared by Paced TCP and TFRC the loss rate (about 0.5%) is a little higher when the buffer size is from 2 to 6, and is a little lower when the buffer size is from 7 to 10 packets. To generalize we can save 50% buffer size with almost the same link utilization and loss rate by adding "pacing" into the under-provisioned network.

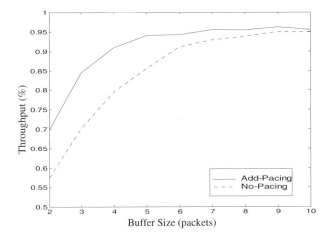

Fig. 9. The relative of bottleneck link utilization and buffer size when 8 TCP and 8 TFRC flows were sent into shares link.

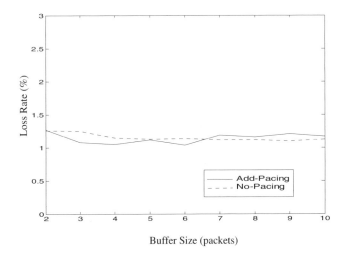

Buffer Size (packets)

Fig. 10. The loss rate variation when the buffer is set 2-10 packets in the bottleneck link shared by 8 TCP and 8TFRC flows

4 Conclusion

In this paper, a pacing-based congestion control algorithm technique added into the bottleneck link shared by TCP and TFRC is presented. The simulation results show that by using this technique, less buffer size is in need for the bottleneck link shared by Paced TCP and TFRC. It can achieve about 90% throughput utilization of bottleneck link when the buffer size is from 2 to 4 packets, keeping the loss rate and make the link in a good condition. This is a remarkable result compared to Villamizar and Song [2]'s 63 packets and Appenzeller [3]'s 16 packets as a buffer size.

References

1. Handley, M., Floyd, S., Padhye, J., Widmer, J.: TCP Friendly Rate Control (TFRC): Protocol Specification. In: RFC, vol. 3448 (January 2003)
2. Villamizar, Song, C.: High performance tcp inansnet. ACM Computer Communications Review 24(5), 45–60 (1994)
3. Appenzeller, G., Keslassy, I., Mckeown, N.: Sizing Router Buffers. In: ACM SIGCOMM Computer Communication Review, ACM, New York (2004)
4. Padhye, J., Firoiu, V., Towsley, D.F., Kuose, J.F.: Modeling TCP Reno Performance: A simple Model and its Empirical Validation. IEEE/ACM Transactions on Networking 8(2) (April 2000)
5. Floyd, S., Handley, M., Padhye, J., Widmer, J.: Equation-Based Congestion Control for Unicast Applications: the Extended Version. ICSI tech report TR-00-03 (March 2000)
6. Padhye, J., Firoiu, V., Towsley, D., Kurose, J.: Modeling TCP Throughput: A Simple Model and its Empirical Validation. In: Proc. ACM SIGCOMM (1998)
7. Aggarwal, A., Savage, S., Anderson, T.: Understanding the performance of TCP Pacing. In: Proc. of the IEEE INFOCOM 2000 Conference on Computer Communications, INFOCOM 2000 (2000)
8. Enachescu, M., Ganjali, Y., Goel, A., Mckeown, N., Roughgarden, T.: Routers with Very Small Buffers. In: Proceedings of 25th IEEE International Conference on Computer Communications, INFOCOM 2006 (2006)

Research on the Architecture of Cloud Computing

Jun Wu, Jing Yang, Xisi Tu, and Guangling Yi

School of Economics and Management
Beijing University of Posts and Telecommunications
Beijing, China
junwu2011@sina.com

Abstract. Cloud computing is a paradigm that focuses on sharing data and computations over a scalable network of nodes. In this paper, we propose five-layer architecture to illustrate their interrelations as well as their inter-dependency on preceding technologies.

Keywords: Cloud computing, five layer architecture.

1 Introduction

Cloud computing can be considered a new computing paradigm that allows users to temporary utilize computing infrastructure over the network, supplied as a service by the cloud-provider at possibly one or more levels of abstraction. Consequently, several business models rapidly evolved to harness this technology by providing software applications, programming platforms, data-storage, computing infrastructure and hardware as services. While they refer to the core cloud computing services, their inter-relations have been ambiguous and the feasibility of enabling their inter-operability has been debatable.

At the same time, the current cloud computing research lacks the understanding of the classification of the cloud systems, their correlation and inter-dependency. In turn, this obscurity is hindering the advancement of this research field. As a result, the introduction of an organization of the cloud computing knowledge domain, its components and their relations is necessary to help the research community achieve a better understanding of this novel technology.

In this paper, we present a five-layer architecture abstraction of cloud computing, with a classification of its components, and their relationships as well as their dependency on some of the prior concepts from other fields in computing. In addition, we highlight some of the technical challenges involved in building cloud components in each layer of our proposed architecture, and how these challenges were addressed in the predecessor areas of computing research. We also underline the constraints associated with specifying a user interface for each layer.

The rest of this paper is organized as follows. Section 2 discusses the research status quo in light of the limitations and imperfections of current cloud systems. Section 3 examines each layer of the architecture, elaborating on its composition, limitations, and correlation with other layers. We conclude our paper with a

J. Zhang (Ed.): ICAIC 2011, Part III, CCIS 226, pp. 519–526, 2011.

discussion on several challenges for cloud computing research, and the various hinders delaying its wide adoption in application area.

2 Research Motivation

The recent evolution of cloud computing has borrowed its basics from several other computing areas and systems engineering concepts. Cluster and Grid Computing on one hand, and virtualization on the other hand are perhaps the most obvious predecessor technologies that enabled the inception of cloud computing. However, several other computing concepts have indirectly shaped today's cloud computing technology, including peer-to-peer (P2P) computing [1], SOA [2] and autonomic computing [3].

In order to comprehend the impact of those various concepts on cloud computing, our approach is to determine the different layers and components that make the cloud, and study their characteristics in light of their dependency on the other computing fields and models. Therefore, it was important to define the constituents of cloud computing in order to define its strengths and imperfections with respect of its adoption of previous technological concepts.

Besides, an architecture of cloud computing will allow better understanding of the inter-relations between the different cloud components, enabling the composition of new systems from existing components and further re-composition of current systems from other cloud components for desirable features like extensibility, flexibility, availability or merely optimization and better cost efficiency.

3 The Cloud Architecture

Cloud computing systems fall into one of five layers: applications, software environments, software infrastructure, software kernel, and hardware. Obviously, at the bottom of the cloud stack is the hardware layer which is the actual physical components of the system. Some cloud computing offerings have built their system on subleasing the hardware in this layer as a service, as we discuss in subsection III-E. At the top of the stack is the cloud application layer, which is the interface of the cloud to the common computer users through web browsers and thin computing terminals. We closely examine the characteristics and limitations of each of the layers in the next five subsections.

A. Cloud Application Layer

The cloud application layer is the most visible layer to the end-users of the cloud. Normally, the users access the services provided by this layer through web-portals, and are sometimes required to pay fees to use them. This model has recently proven to be attractive to many users, as it alleviates the burden of software maintenance and the ongoing operation and support costs. Furthermore, it exports the computational work from the users' terminal to data centers where the cloud applications are deployed. This in turn lessens the restrictions on the hardware requirements needed at the users' end, and allows them to obtain superb performance to some of their cpu-intensive and memory-intensive workloads without necessitating huge capital investments in their local machines.

As for the providers of the cloud applications, this model even simplifies their work with respect to upgrading and testing the code, while protecting their intellectual property. Since a cloud application is deployed at the provider's computing infrastructure (rather than at the users' desktop machines), the developers of the application are able to roll smaller patches to the system and add new features without disturbing the users with requests to install major updates or service packs. Configuration and testing of the application in this model is arguably less complicated, since the deployment environment becomes restricted, i.e., the provider's data center. Even with respect to the provider's margin of profit, this model supplies the software provider with a continuous flow of revenue, which might be even more profitable on the long run. This model conveys several favorable benefits for the users and providers of cloud applications, and is normally referred to as Software as a Service (SaaS). Salesforce Customer Relationships Management (CRM) system [4] and Google Apps [5] are two examples of SaaS. As such, the body of research on SOA has numerous studies on composable IT services which have direct application to providing and composing SaaS.

Despite all the advantageous benefits of this model, several deployment issues hinder its wide adoption. Specifically, the security and availability of the cloud applications are two of the major issues in this model, and they are currently avoided by the use of lenient service level agreements (SLA). Furthermore, coping with outages is a realm that users and providers of SaaS have to tackle, especially with possible network outage and system failures. Additionally, the integration of legacy applications and the migration of the users' data to the cloud is another matter that is also slowing the adoption of SaaS. Before they can persuade users to migrate from desktop applications to cloud applications, cloud applications' providers need to address end-users' concerns about security and safety of storing confidential data on the cloud, users authentication and authorization, up-time and performance, as well as data backup and disaster recovery and provide reliable SLAs for their cloud applications.

B. Cloud Software Environment Layer

The second layer in our proposed cloud architecture is the cloud software environment layer (also dubbed the software platform layer). The users of this layer are cloud applications' developers, implementing their applications for and deploying them on the cloud. The providers of the cloud software environments supply the developers with a programming-language-level environment with a set of well-defined APIs to facilitate the interaction between the environments and the cloud applications, as well as to accelerate the deployment and support the scalability needed of those cloud applications. The service provided by cloud systems in this layer is commonly referred to as Platform as a Service (PaaS). One example of systems in this category is Google's App Engine [5], which provides a python runtime environment and APIs for applications to interact with Google's cloud runtime environment. Another example is SalesForce Apex language [6] that allows the developers of the cloud applications to design, along with their applications' logic, their page layout, workflow, and customer reports.

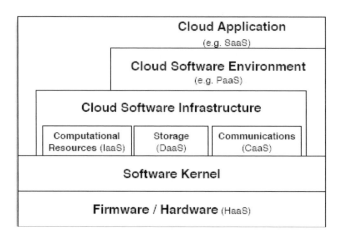

Fig. 1. Our Proposed Cloud Computing Architecture

Developers reap several benefits from developing their cloud application for a cloud programming environment, including automatic scaling and load balancing, as well as integration with other services (e.g. authentication services, email services, user interface) provided to them through the PaaS-provider. In such a way, much of the overhead of developing cloud applications is alleviated and is handled at the environment level. Furthermore, developers have the ability to integrate other services to their applications on-demand. This in turn makes the cloud application development a less complicated task, accelerates the deployment time and minimizes the logic faults in the application. As such, cloud software environments facilitate the process of the development of cloud applications.

C. Cloud Software Infrastructure Layer

The cloud software infrastructure layer provides fundamental resources to other higher-level layers, which in turn can be used to construct new cloud software environments or cloud applications. Our proposed architecture reflects the fact that the two highest levels in the cloud stack can bypass the cloud infrastructure layer in building their system. Although this bypass can enhance the efficiency of the system, it comes at the cost of simplicity and development efforts.

Cloud services offered in this layer can be categorized into: computational resources, data storage, and communications

1) Computational Resources:

Virtual machines (VMs) are the most common form for providing computational resources to cloud users at this layer, where the users get finer-granularity flexibility since they normally get super-user access to their VMs, and can use it to customize the software stack on their VM for performance and efficiency. Often, such services are dubbed Infrastructure as a Service (IaaS). Virtualization is the enabler technology for this cloud component, which allows the users unprecedented flexibility in configuring their settings while protecting the physical infrastructure of the provider's data center. Recent advances in OS Virtualization have made the concept of IaaS plausible. This was specifically enabled by two virtualization technologies: paravirtualization and hardware-assisted virtualization. Although both virtualization technologies have addressed performance isolation between virtual machines contending on common resources, performance interference between VMs sharing the same cache and TLB hierarchy cannot yet be avoided [7]. Further, the emergence of multicore machines into mainstream servers exacerbate this performance interference problem. In turn, the lack of strict performance isolation between VMs sharing the same physical node has resulted in the inability of cloud providers to give strong guarantees for performance to their clients. Instead, they offer them unsatisfactory SLAs in order to provide a competitive pricing for the service. Such weak guarantees, unfortunately, can inject themselves up the layers of the cloud stack, and affect the SLAs of the cloud systems built above the IaaS's SLAs.

2) Data Storage:

The second infrastructure resource is data storage, which allows users to store their data at remote disks and access them anytime from any place. This service is commonly known as Data-Storage as a Service (DaaS), and it facilitates cloud applications to scale beyond their limited servers. Data storage systems are expected to meet several rigorous requirements for maintaining users' data and information, including high availability, reliability, performance, replication and data consistency; but because of the conflicting nature of these requirements, no one system implements all of them together. For example, availability, scalability and data consistency can be regarded as three conflicting goals. While those features are hard to be met with general data storage systems, DaaS-providers have taken the liberty of implementing their system to favor one feature over the others, while indicating their choice through their SLA. These implementations have borrowed their fundamental ideas from proceeding research and production systems. Some examples of data storage systems are: distributed file systems (e.g., GFS [8]), replicated relational databases (RDBMS) (e.g., Bayou [9]) and key value stores (e.g., Dynamo [10]). RDBMS, for example opt to present a stricter consistency model at the cost of the availability of the data, while key-value stores have placed more importance on the availability of the data while relaxing the consistency model for the storage. In this respect, the cloud DaaS has inherited the different characteristics of today's data storage systems. Example of commercial DaaS-systems are Amazon's S3 [11] and EMC Storage Managed Service [12].

3) Communication:

As the need for a guaranteed quality of service (QoS) for network communication grows for cloud systems, communication becomes a vital component of the cloud infrastructure. Consequently, cloud systems are obliged to provide some communication capability that is service oriented, configurable, schedulable, predictable, and reliable. Towards this goal, the concept of Communication as a Service (CaaS) emerged to support such requirements, as well as network security, dynamic provisioning of virtual overlays for traffic isolation or dedicated bandwidth, guaranteed message delay, communication encryption, and network monitoring. Although this model is the least discussed and adopted cloud service in the commercial cloud systems, several research papers and articles [11], [12], [13] have investigated the various architectural design decisions, protocols and solutions needed to provide QoS communications as a service. One recent example of systems that belong to CaaS is Microsoft Connected Service Framework (CSF) [14]. VoIP telephone systems, audio and video conferencing as well as instant messaging are candidate cloud applications that can be composed of CaaS and can in turn provide composable cloud solutions to other common applications.

D. Software Kernel

This cloud layer provides the basic software management for the physical servers that compose the cloud. Software kernels at this level can be implemented as an OS kernel, hypervisor, virtual machine monitor and/or clustering middleware. Customarily, grid computing applications were deployed and run on this layer on several interconnected clusters of machines. However, due to the absence of a virtualization abstraction in grid computing, jobs were closely tied to the actual hardware infrastructure and providing migration, checkpointing and load balancing to the applications at this level was always a complicated task.

E. Hardware and Firmware

The bottom layer of the cloud stack in our proposed architecture is the actual physical hardware and switches that form the backbone of the cloud. In this regard, users of this layer of the cloud are normally big enterprises with huge IT requirements in need of subleasing Hardware as a Service (HaaS). For that, the HaaS provider operates, manages and upgrades the hardware on behalf of its consumers, for the life-time of the sublease. This model is advantageous to the enterprise users, since they do not need to invest in building and managing data centers. Meanwhile, HaaS providers have the technical expertise as well as the cost-effective infrastructure to host the systems. One of the early examples HaaS is Morgan Stanley's sublease contract with IBM in 2004 [14]. SLAs in this model are more strict, since enterprise users have predefined business workloads whose characteristics impose strict performance requirements. The margin benefit for HaaS providers materialize from the economy of scale of building huge data centers infrastructures with gigantic floor space, power, cooling costs as well as operation and management expertise.

HaaS providers have to address a number of technical challenges in operating and managing their services. Efficiency, ease and speed of provisioning such large scale systems, for example is a major challenge. Remote scriptable boot-loaders are one solution to remotely boot and deploy complete software stacks on the data centers. PXE [15] and UBoot [16] are examples of remote bootstrap execution environments that allow the system administrator to stream a binary image to multiple remote machines at boot-time. One example of such systems is IBM Kittyhawk [17], a

Table 1. Summary of examples of some commercial cloud computing systems in our proposed cloud computing Architecture

Cloud Layer	Examples of Commercial Cloud Systems
Cloud Application Layer	Google Apps and Salesforce Customer Relation Management (CRM) system
Cloud Software Environment	Google App Engine and Salesforce Apex System
Cloud Software Infrastructure	*Computational Resources:* Amazon's EC2, Enomalism Elastic Cloud.
	Storage: Amazon's S3, EMC Storage Managed Service.
	Communication: Microsoft Connected Service Framework (CSF).
Software Kernel	Grid and Cluster Computing Systems like Globus and Condor.
Firmware / Hardware	IBM-Morgan Stanley's Computing Sublease, and IBM's Kittyhawk Project.

research project that uses UBoot to script the boot sequence of thousands of remote Bluegene/P nodes over the network. Other examples of challenges that arise at this cloud layer include data center management, scheduling, and power-consumption optimizations.

Table 1 exemplify some of the commercial cloud systems discussed earlier in our proposed architecture.

4 Conclusions

In this paper, we proposed a detailed architecture for the cloud in an attempt to establish the knowledge domain of the area of cloud computing and its relevant components. We used composability as our methodology in constructing our cloud architecture which allowed us to capture the inter-relations between the different cloud components. We presented our proposed architecture as a stack of cloud layers, and discussed each layer's strengths, limitations as well as dependence on preceding computing concepts. Few recent online articles attempt to establish a similar structure for cloud computing and its components [16], [17], [18]. Although they attain some valuable understanding of several cloud services and components, they tend to be more general classifications. They neither went to the level of detail in the analysis as we did, nor they included all the cloud layers we captured in our model. Their main end-goal is to classify the commercial cloud offerings in order to analyze the cloud computing market opportunities. As such, they do not address the specific potentials or limitations of the several cloud layers, nor the research opportunities associated with each cloud layer. We believe our proposed cloud architecture is more comprehensive, and encompass more detailed analysis of the cloud computing knowledge domain.

References

1. Androutsellis-Theotokis, S., Spinellis, D.: A survey of peerto- peer content distribution technologies. ACM Comput. Surv. 36(4), 335–371 (2004)
2. Papazoglou, M.P., Heuvel, W.-J.: Service oriented architectures: approaches, technologies and research issues. The VLDB Journal 16(3), 389–415 (2007)
3. Jin, X., Liu, J.: From individual based modeling to autonomy oriented computation. In: Nickles, M., Rovatsos, M., Weiss, G. (eds.) AUTONOMY 2003. LNCS (LNAI), vol. 2969, pp. 151–169. Springer, Heidelberg (2004)
4. Olston, C., Reed, B., Srivastava, U., Kumar, R., Tomkins, A.: Pig latin: a not-so-foreign language for data processing. In: SIGMOD 2008: Proceedings of the 2008 ACM SIGMOD International Conference on Management of Data, pp. 1099–1110. ACM, New York (2008), http://dx.doi.org/10.1145/1376616.1376726
5. Koh, Y., Knauerhase, R.C., Brett, P., Bowman, M., Wen, Z., Pu, C.: An analysis of performance interference effects in virtual environments. In: ISPASS, pp. 200–209. IEEE Computer Society, Los Alamitos (2007)
6. Ghemawat, S., Gobioff, H., Leung, S.-T.: The google file system. SIGOPS Oper. Syst. Rev. 37(5), 29–43 (2003)

7. Petersen, K., Spreitzer, M., Terry, D., Theimer, M.: Bayou: replicated database services for world-wide applications. In: EW 7: Proceedings of the 7th Workshop on ACM SIGOPS European Workshop, pp. 275–280. ACM, New York (1996)
8. DeCandia, G., Hastorun, D., Jampani, M., Kakulapati, G., Lakshman, A., Pilchin, A., Sivasubramanian, S., Vosshall, P., Vogels, W.: Dynamo: amazon's highly available key-value store. In: SOSP 2007, pp. 205–220. ACM, New York (2007)
9. Hanemann, A., Boote, J.W., Boyd, E.L., Durand, J., Kudarimoti, L., Łapacz, R., Swany, D.M., Trocha, S., Zurawski, J.: PerfSONAR: A service oriented architecture for multi-domain network monitoring. In: Benatallah, B., Casati, F., Traverso, P. (eds.) ICSOC 2005. LNCS, vol. 3826, pp. 241–254. Springer, Heidelberg (2005)
10. Smr, P., Novek, V.: Architecture acquisition for automatic building of scientific portals. In: SOFSEM 2006: 32nd Conference on Current Trends in Theory and Practice of Computer Science, pp. 493–500. Springer, Heidelberg (2006), http://www.fit.vutbr.cz/research/viewpub.php?id=8004
11. Chau, M., Huang, Z., Qin, J., Zhou, Y., Chen, H.: Building a scientific knowledge web portal: the nanoport experience. Decis. Support Syst. 42(2), 1216–1238 (2006)
12. Christie, M., Marru, S.: The lead portal: a teragrid gateway and application service architecture: Research articles. Concurr. Comput.: Pract. Exper. 19(6), 767–781 (2007)
13. Plale, B., Rossi, A., Simmhan, Y., Sarangi, A., Slominski, A., Shirasauna, S., Thomas, T.: Building grid portal applications from a webservice component architecture. Proceedings of the IEEE (Special issue on Grid Computing) 93(3), 551–563 (2005)
14. Stanley, M.: IBM ink utility computing deal, http://news.cnet.com/2100-7339-5200970.html
15. Appavoo, J., Uhlig, V., Waterland, A.: Project Kittyhawk: building a global-scale computer: Blue Gene/P as a generic computing platform. SIGOPS Oper. Syst. Rev. 42(1), 77–84 (2008)
16. Deelman, E., Singh, G., Livny, M., Berriman, B., Good, J.: The cost of doing science on the cloud: the montage example. In: SC 2008: Proceedings of the 2008 ACM/IEEE Conference on Supercomputing pp. 1–12. IEEE Press, Piscataway (2008)
17. Defogging Cloud Computing: A Taxonomy (June 16, 2008), http://refresh.gigaom.com/2008/06/16/defogging-cloud-computing-a-taxonomy/
18. Cloud Services Continuum (July 3, 2008), http://et.cairenene.net/2008/07/03/cloud-services-ontinuum/

Multi-objective Optimization Using Immune Algorithm[*]

Pengfei Guo, Xuezhi Wang, and Yingshi Han

School of Civil and Architectural Engineering
Liaoning University of Technology
Jinzhou, Liaoning Province, China
feiguo.peng@sohu.com

Abstract. Immune algorithm is kind of intelligent optimization algorithm which simulates the biology immunity system, and has potential to provide novel method for solving problem. From the basic principle of biological immune system, an immune algorithm based on complete biological immune system is proposed for finding Pareto-optimal solutions to multi-objective optimization problems. The technical problems of this algorithm are discussed: calculation of accessible degrees and expectation, maturation, inhibition, clonally selection and regeneration. The program flow of the immune algorithm was designed and the computer program was compiled. The correctness and effectiveness of the algorithm are verified by the test equations and multi-objective truss-structure sizing optimization with discrete variables.

Keywords: immune algorithm, multi-objective optimization, biological immune system.

1 Introduction

The optimization is the process of searching for one or more feasible solutions which correspond to extreme values of one or more objectives in a problem until no other superior solution can be found. When an optimization problem modeling a physical system considering only one objective, the task of finding the optimal solution is referred to as single-objective optimization problems or SOOPs. There exist single-objective optimization methods that work by using calculus-based or deterministic search principles such as gradient-based and heuristic-based techniques and stochastic search principles, which allow optimization method to find globally optimal solutions more reliably including. Evolutionary algorithm and simulated annealing are two of such stochastic methods. While an optimization problem involves more than one objective, the task of finding one or more solutions is known as multi-objective optimization problems or MOOPs. Much of the current focus is on single-objective engineering optimization, even though most real-world problems require that several

---

* This work is partially supported by the National Science Foundation of China (No.50709013).

J. Zhang (Ed.): ICAIC 2011, Part III, CCIS 226, pp. 527–534, 2011.
© Springer-Verlag Berlin Heidelberg 2011

objectives be satisfied simultaneously. A challenging MOOPs-related problem concerns the goodness of fit of a solution, since all solutions have their own range of fitness values. Trade-offs are common, since any solution may be good for some objectives but not for others. The frequency of conflicting objectives has made multi-objective optimization an important aspect of engineering and design.

Even though, genetic algorithms are considered powerful in terms of global optimization, but they have several drawbacks regarding local searches. A number of researchers have experimented with optimization approaches inspired from biological immune system to overcome these particular drawbacks implicit in genetic algorithms. Biological immune system (IS) is responsible for protecting the living body against the foreign antigens and other toxins that may be harmful. It exhibits abilities to specificity, learning and memory, and adaptation and discrimination, and presents as a remarkable natural defence mechanism. The immune system eliminates the harmful materials or foreign antigens mainly by producing soluble antibodies, which recognize and then bind the molecules of foreign antigens. In addition, the immune system is capable of remembering infection, hence, a second exposure to identical or similar antigen is deal with more efficiently. For these reasons, and many others, the biological immune system can be viewed as a mechanism of vast potential for inspiration in variety of domains. Based on the features of a biological immune system, a new biologically inspired technique, so-called artificial immune system (AIS), has been developed for a computational tools and applied to a myriad of computational scenarios during the recently years.

To highlight the significant features of immune systems, a novel immune algorithm based fully on imitating of biological immune system has been developed in this dissertation for the purpose of optimal searching in the various optimization fields for multi-objective, and multi-modally optimizations. Via using several performance metrics and comparison with different evolutionary approaches, the results indicated that the proposed immune algorithm in the field of multi-objective optimization (named MOIA) generally performs better than SPEA (strength Pareto evolutionary algorithm), MOGA (multi-objective genetic algorithm), NPGA (niche Pareto genetic algorithm), and NSGA (non-dominated sorting genetic algorithm) for these test functions.

2   Immune Algorithms

A novel scheme–Immune Algorithm (IA) based on emulating a biological immune system is developed to solve the optimization problems. Analogous to the biological immune system, the proposed immune algorithm has the capability of seeking Pareto-optimal solutions while maintaining a high-level of diversity in the search space. Corresponding to the optimization problem, the antigens and antibodies serve as objectives and associated solutions in a computational model, respectively, and are expressed as follows:

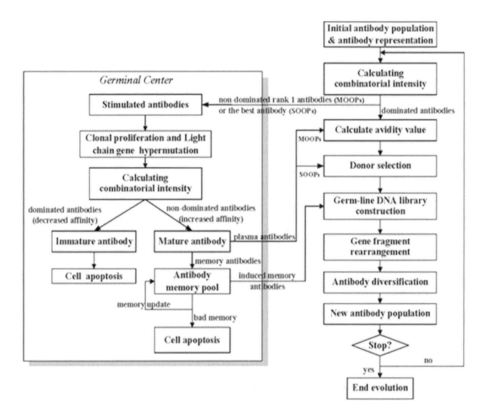

Fig. 1. Immune algorithm flowchart

3 Multi-objective Immune Algorithm

A. Unconstrained Test Functions

(1) Test function $F_1(x) = \left(f_1(x), f_2(x) \right)$ *(with convex Pareto-optimal front)*

$$f_1(x_1) = x_1$$

$$f_2(x) = g(x_1, \cdots, x_n).h(f_1(x_1), g(x_2, \cdots, x_n))$$

and $\quad g(x_2, \cdots, x_n) = 1 + \dfrac{n}{n-1} x_i$

$$h(f_1, g) = 1 - \sqrt{f_1 \big/ g}$$

where $x = (x_1, \cdots, x_n)$, $n = 30$, and $x_i \in [0,1]$, the Pareto-optimal front is formed with $g=1$. The results are given in Fig. 2.

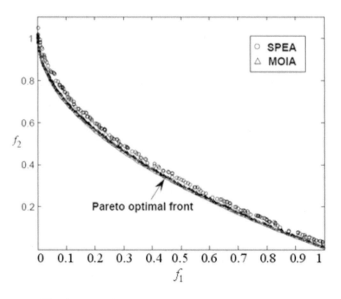

Fig. 2. Simulation results for test function F_1 (convex)

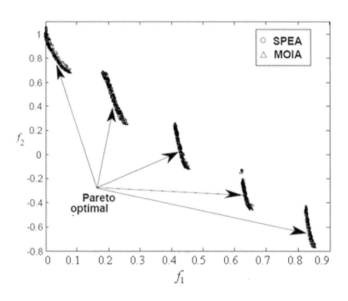

Fig. 3. Simulation results for test function F_2 (discrete)

(2) Test function $F_2(x) = \left(f_1(x), f_2(x)\right)$ *(with several non-continuous convex parts)*

$$f_1(x_1) = x_1$$

$$f_2(x) = g(x_1, \cdots, x_n).h(f_1(x_1), g(x_2, \cdots, x_n))$$

and $g(x_2, \cdots, x_n) = 1 + \dfrac{n}{n-1} x_i$

$$h(f_1, g) = 1 - \sqrt{f_1\big/g} - \left(f_1\big/g\right)\sin(10\pi f_1)$$

where $x = (x_1, \cdots, x_n)$, $n = 30$, and $x_i \in [0,1]$, the Pareto-optimal front is formed with $g=1$. The results are given in Fig. 3.

B. Constrained Test Functions

Two constrained test functions were employed in this study to assess the performance of the constrained multi-objective immune algorithm. In addition, these test functions were designed to cause two different kinds of tun able difficulties in a constrained multi-objective optimization algorithm:

(1) The difficulty in the vicinity of the Pareto-optimal front

$$\min f_1(x) = x_1$$

$$\min f_2(x) = (1\text{-}x_2)\left(1 - \frac{f_1(x)}{1\text{-}x_2}\right)$$

$$s.t.\ c(x) = \cos\theta(f_2(x) - e) - \sin\theta f_1(x) \geq$$

$$a\left|\sin(b\pi(\sin(\theta)(f_2(x) - e) + \cos(\theta)f_1(x)^c)\right|^d$$

where $\theta = -0.2\pi$, $a=0.2$, $b=10$, $c=1$, $d=6$, $e=1$. The decision variable x_1 is restricted in [0, 1]. The results are given in Fig. 4.

(2) The difficulty in the entire search space

$$\min f_1(x) = x_1$$

$$\min f_2(x) = g(x)\left(1 - \frac{f_1(x)}{g(x)}\right)$$

$$s.t.\ c(x) = \cos\theta(f_2(x) - e) - \sin\theta f_1(x) \geq$$

$$a\left|\sin(b\pi(\sin(\theta)(f_2(x) - e) + \cos(\theta)f_1(x)^c)\right|^d$$

where $g(x) = 11 + x_2^2 - 10\cos(2\pi x_2)$, $\theta = 0.1\pi$, $a=40$, $b=0.5$, $c=1$, $d=2$, $e=2$. The decision variable x_1 is restricted in [0, 1]. The results are given in Fig. 5.

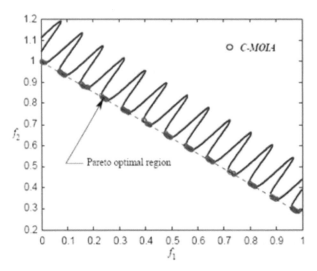

Fig. 4. Simulation results

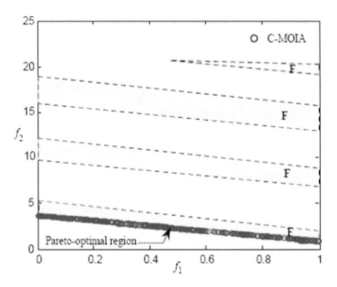

Fig. 5. Simulation results

C. Multi-objective Truss-Structure Sizing Optimization

A 10-bar plane truss with the node and element numbering illustrated in Fig.6 is adopted to evaluate the performance of the proposed C-MOIA approach. The objective is to minimize the volume of the structure and the vertical displacement at node 6 simultaneously using the cross-sectional areas of the ten truss numbers as design variables with pre-defined allowable on maximum (extension) and minimum (compression) stresses. Such objectives are conflicting in nature since reducing the displacement will increase the cross-sectional area, consequently increasing the volume of the structure. The upper and lower boundaries of each truss element are 0.1 and 30 in^2, respectively. The location of external load is shown in Fig. 6 with F = 100,000 lb. Material properties are taken as modulus of elasticity E= 1×10^4 ksi. Constraints on the truss limit σ_j in each element below the maximum allowable stress, σ_a of ±25 ksi. In this dissertation, normalized constraint function is expressed as following:

$$g_j = \frac{|\sigma_j|}{\sigma_s} - 1 \le 0 \quad (j=1,\ldots,10)$$

Note that the cross-sectional areas are assumed to be continuous numbers in this case.

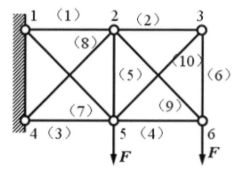

Fig. 6. 10-bar plane truss structure

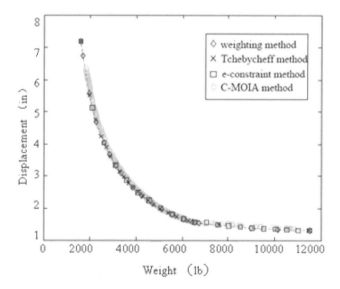

Fig. 7. Feasible Pareto solutions of 10-bar plane truss

For 10-bar plane truss problem, the Pareto-optimal front with 474 feasible solutions is presented in Fig. 7. The two extreme objective values are [108413.542, 1.3611] and [17935.1162, 6.3562], respectively. It is important to emphasize that only 21 solutions were derived for these methods since they employed weighting-based method with 21 fixed and uniform-distributed weighting ratio values. The extreme values of these weighting ratios were (0.0, 1.0) and (1.0, 0.0) with interval 0.05. Obviously C-MOIA is capable of finding much more satisfactory non-dominated solutions excluding the two extreme objective values.

4 Conclusions

The proposed immune algorithm was implemented to several test functions considering with/without constraints and truss-structure sizing problems with continuous variables for the purpose of determining constrained Pareto-optimal solutions. Overall results indicate that the proposed immune algorithm is capable of quickly determining accurate and diverse Pareto-optimal solutions to multi-objective optimization problems. It is suggested that this capability is due to the combination of diversification immune operators, the construction of germ-line library equivalents, and a process of gene fragment recombination, they are all the features in the immune system. The key natural selection components (gene fragments) are similar to the building blocks of genetic algorithms associated with stimulus antibodies and memory cell pools. In this particular immune algorithm, the antibodies (solutions) are the direct products of gene fragment combinations (schemata), rather than the antibody (analogy to the role of individual in genetic algorithms) itself. This explains the need for several diversification schemes to prevent the premature effect of proposed immune algorithm.

References

1. Guo, P., Han, Y.: Chaotic genetic algorithm for structural optimization with discrete variables. Journal of Liaoning Technical University 26(1), 68–70 (2007)
2. Guo, P., Han, Y.: An imitative full-stress design method for structural optimum design with discrete variables. Engineering Mechanics 16(5), 95–99 (2003)
3. Guo, P., Han, Y., Wei, Y.: An Imitative Full-stress Design Method for Structural Optimization with Discrete Variables. Engineering Mechanics 17(1), 94–98 (2000)
4. Guo, P., Wang, X., Han, Y.: The Enhanced Genetic Algorithms for the Optimization Design. In: IEEE BMEI 2010, pp. 2990–2994 (2010)
5. Coello Coello, C.A., Christiansen, A.D.: Multiobjetive optimization of trusses using genetic algorithms. Computers and Structures 75(6), 647–660 (2000)
6. Deb, K.: Multi-objective genetic algorithms: Problem difficulties and construction of test problems. Evolutionary Computation 7(3), 205–230 (1999)
7. Deb, K., Gulati, S.: Design of truss-structures for minimum weight using genetic algorithms. Finite Elements in Analysis and Design (37), 447–465 (2001)
8. Fourie, P.C., Groenwold, A.A.: The particle swarm optimization algorithm in size and shape optimization. Structural Multidiscipline Optimization (23), 259–267 (2002)
9. Luh, G.-C., Chueh, C.-H.: Multi-objective Optimal Design of Truss Structure with Immune Algorithm. Computers and Structures (82), 829–844 (2004)

A Wireless Water Quality Monitoring System Based on LabVIEW and Web[*]

Ziguang Sun, Chungui Li, and Zengfang Zhang

Department of Computer Engineering
Guangxi University of Technology
Liuzhou 545006, P.R. China
ziguangsun@sina.com

Abstract. A wireless water quality monitoring system had been developed with LabVIEW and Web Technology. GPRS had been adopted for data transmission of water parameters. A virtual instrument panel for data display had been designed and published.

Keywords: wireless, GPRS, LabVIEW, water quality monitoring, VI.

I Introduction

Surface water environment plays a vital role in human lives as fresh water source, transportation media, and recreation location. Also coastal waters and freshwater coasts are home of natural resources and are rich with diverse species. Hence, surface water environment has been attracting people since the human history began. As water quality perturbations related to escalating human population growth and industry pressures continue to increase in coastal and inland areas.

The impact of pollution on Chinese surface waters has being serious since the end of the 1970s. In fact, industrial discharges of toxic substances have been increased over the past 30 years with the fast-paced economic growth. A similar trend is also observed in most other developing countries. The government should implement stricter regulations and develop cleaner technologies [1]. This is becoming urgent, as governments are becoming aware of threats associated with climate change to the supply of clean drinking water all around the world. It is important for the success of any legislation and associated actions, such as withdrawal of particularly harmful anthropogenic pollutants, improvements in the treatment of waste waters, and remediation campaigns, that good water quality data are available. This information is needed to assess the extent of any problems, the associated risks, the impact of remedial measures and any trends in water quality in space and time. The problems are further compounded by the continuing introduction of new substances (sometimes referred to as emerging pollutants of concern), often with little available toxicological information.

[*] This work is partially supported by 2010 Guangxi Science Research and Technology Development Project Grant.

J. Zhang (Ed.): ICAIC 2011, Part III, CCIS 226, pp. 535–540, 2011.

Currently, spot (bottle or grab) sampling is the most commonly used method for monitoring water quality. This has limitations when used to obtain a representative picture of water quality across a wide area and over time. An extensive range of alternative methods is becoming available. Some of these may be able to provide more representative information, but, for them to be widely adopted, further work is needed to establish their reliability, reproducibility and sensitivity for a range of substances of concern [2].

Remote Web-based virtual instrument technology in the Internet, Web development, leading to B/S model of the new popularity of software applications, B/S model is the traditional C/S model of derivative, this new thin client model to pursue fat server concept, the main application in the data collection side (server), the control side (client) only needs a browser environment, can be downloaded from the server as needed to complete the corresponding application task.   This makes application maintenance easier, the main effort focused on the server side, the workload of the smaller, lower cost, and the Web has a friendly interface and convenient operation.

2   Overview of the System

A. Alternative Strategies

A range of alternative strategies is available for monitoring biological and chemical water-quality parameters. These methods can be classified in a number of different ways. One useful approach is to distinguish them on the basis of the relationship between the sampling and analytical processes. The three main categories are in situ, on-line and off-line [3].

1) In situ: These generally involve the use of a sensing device directly immersed in the water body. The data are collected automatically, and either recorded for later retrieval or transmitted telemetrically to a distant laboratory for interpretation.

2) On-line: Here, the analytical instruments are located near to the water body being monitored. The sample is drawn into a system that processes it and feeds it into the analytical instrumentation. Both discrete and continuous measurements are possible, depending on the analytical method employed.

3) Off-line: This method requires that a sample of water is taken and transported to the analytical system. The distance between the sampling site and analytical device can vary between a few metres for on-site instruments to long distances where transport to a central laboratory facility is necessary. We select this way in our system.

B. Our Approach

Water quality online monitoring and wireless transmission systems consist of hardware and software of two major components, its composition shown in Figure 1. The main hardware devices are sampling pumps, water quality monitoring instrumentation, distributed I/O modules, data acquisition computer and power supply center and safety equipment; wireless data transmission system is responsible for raw water monitoring data received. We used LabVIEW to realize the data collection, transmission, storage, query and report generation and display.

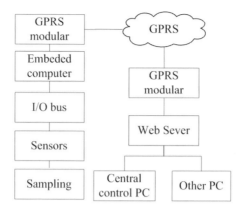

Fig. 1. Architecture of the system

3 Data Acquisition and Transmission

A. Data Acquisition Hardware

The sampling system is mainly including sampling pumps, filters and pipes. We have installed some instruments which can monitor dissolved oxygen, conductivity, PH, ORP, temperature, turbidity, ammonia nitrogen, total phosphorus earth illumination and so on. All instruments are with 0~20mA analog signal output which is convenient for data collection and analog-digital conversion. Data acquisition system can uses universal modular I/O system. By RS-232/RS-485 serial interface, the measurement data can be economically connected to the embedded computer in the sampling site for data storage, processing and transmission.

B. Data Transmission

GPRS (General Packet Radio Service) is short for General Packet Radio Service, is the increase in the existing GSM network, the gateway support node (GGSN), Service Support Node (SGSN) and packet control unit (PCU) to provide wireless packet switched services including point to point and multipoint data services data services. Because of the GPRS network a "virtual" connections possible, in both ends of the system has time to re-use on-line features MODEM, and computer interface with USB, no external power supply, built-in mobile operators to bind IP address the SIM card, to ensure that monitoring data be stable, reliable and secure transmission.

4 The Software of the System

Water quality remote monitoring software is based on the GPRS network for remote monitoring of multiple indicators of raw water, virtual instrument, the data source is from the GPRS network terminal. Remote monitoring system can be set up two network models: C/S or B/S. C/S model is most for the case of large amount of data transfer and high efficiency, reliable data integrity, compatibility and other characteristics. As for the little amount of data transfer, the situation need remote simulation can use B / S mode, so the demand for the client to be low, without the client install the appropriate client software, the browser will only need to log in server monitor remote testing. The relatively small flow of monitoring data, is appropriate for the B/S mode.

A. LabVIEW Introduction

LabVIEW is a graphical programming environment used by millions of engineers and scientists to develop sophisticated measurement, test, and control systems using intuitive graphical icons and wires that resemble a flowchart. It offers unrivaled integration with thousands of hardware devices and provides hundreds of built-in libraries for advanced analysis and data visualization – all for creating virtual instrumentation. The LabVIEW platform is scalable across multiple targets and OSs, and, since its introduction in 1986, it has become an industry leader [4].

LabVIEW contains a comprehensive collection of drag-and-drop controls and indicators so you can quickly and easily create user interfaces for your application and effectively visualize results without integrating third-party components or building views from scratch (as Figure 2 shown). The quick drag-and-drop approach does not come at the expense of flexibility. Power users can customize the built-in controls via the Control Editor and programmatically control user interface (UI) elements to create highly customized user experiences.

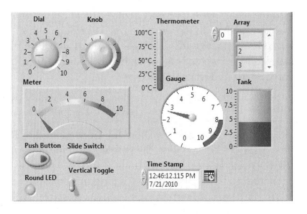

Fig. 2. Engineering Controls and Indicators

B. Designing the Software Using LabVIEW

In our system, the LabVIEW Web Server had been adopted to implement network publishing. The Web-Publishing Tool in LabVIEW facilitates publishing a VI on the Internet while granting and denying access to certain computers. The following steps are necessary for publishing a VI to the Web.

1. Run the VI to make sure it is working as required. The VI must stay open on the main computer. The server will not recognize a closed VI.

2. Go to "Tools" and click on "Options". This will lead to a pull down menu where both configuration of the web server and browser access can take place.

3. Go through the pull down menu and click on "Web Server Configuration."

4. In this screen, click on "Enable Web Server" to start up the server.

5. After clicking OK head back to "Tools" and click on "Web Publishing Tool."

6. On this screen, choose the VI to be published. Choose the embedded label, and type any text that is needed on the Web page. Once this is accomplished click on "Save to Disk". A screen will pop up with a URL address. Copy this address and paste it into either Netscape's or Internet Explorer's address bar.

Once the above steps are completed, the VI should be seen on the web site. The main server can grant anyone to take control of the VI but it also has the ability to regain control at any time. Denying access to a VI can be accomplished as follows. Go to the LabVIEW screen and click on "Tools – Options" as noted before, but this time click on "Web Server Browser Access". Here you are given the options to allow viewing and controlling, only viewing, or to deny access. In the small window above these choices, type the Internet Provider's address of any computers that should not have access to this VI, and click OK. This will forbid any user at those computers from opening up the Web site.

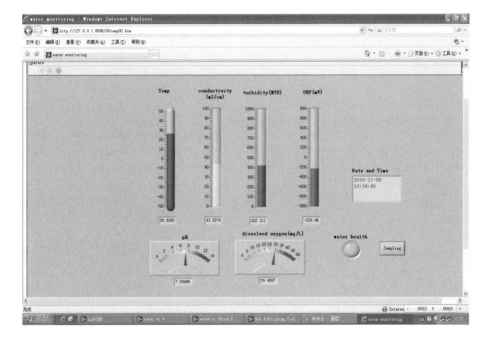

5   Conclusion

With the virtual instrument technology and network technology, based on web sever technology to build a remote monitoring system will be more widely used. This achieved a network of Web-based Distributed Control System in practice and achieved good effect is easy client to connect to the Internet via remote measurement system that can very well interact with the remote monitoring and control of resources, but also have very good real-time, remote water quality parameters to meet the measurement and control system requirements.

References

1. Howells, J.M.: China's Water Quanlity, Environmental Mangement Issues And The Effectiveness of Government-Imposed Solutions: An Analysis From Thirty Thousand Feet, degree paper of Bachelor, pp. 3–10. University of Pittsburgh (2010)
2. Zhua, X., Li, D., Heb, D., et al.: Remote wireless system for water quality online monitoring in intensive fish culture. Computers and Electronics in Agriculture 71, s3–s9 (2010)
3. Glasgow, H.B., et al.: Real-time remote monitoring of water quality: a review of current applications, and advancements in sensor, telemetry, and computing technologies. Journal of Experimental Marine Biology and Ecology 300, 409–448 (2004)
4. Bitter, R.: LabVIEW Advanced Programming Techinques. CRC Press, LLC, Boca Raton (2001)

Piezoelectric Pulse Diagnosis Transducer of 9x9 Sensing Arrays and Pulse Signal Processing

Hung Chang and Jia-Xu Chen[*]

Department of Traditional Chinese Medicine Diagnosis
Beijing University of Chinese Medicine
Chaoyang, Beijing City, 100029, China
HungChang@163.com, chenjx@bucm.edu.cn

Abstract. Purpose: To propose the fabrication of pulse transducers of a 9x9 sensing array, and the strategies for collecting pulse patterns and studying these patterns with Fourier analysis. There will be 9 sensing probes on each location to attain pulse information from 27 locations of entire pulse holography.

Methodology: Our pulse transducers will be composed of 9 sensing probes in 1.5×1.5mm², which are integrated according to the array utilized in pulse diagnosis in Traditional Chinese Medicine (TCM). These probes will be separated by 0.1mm in rows and 0.3mm in columns, and therefore, the fabrication of the proposed transducers will be mainly based on microfabrication techniques. The piezoelectric material will be soft PVDF (Polyvinylidene Fluoride), which will be processed into sensor arrays using a PDMS (Polydimethylsiloxane) mold. All pulse information will be digitized and saved into a computer. MATLAB programs will be created to analyze the 243 signals that are output from the three partitions (Cun, Guan and Chi) of pulse holography with mathematical methods, such as Fourier analysis and transformations of matrix.

Conclusion: We expect the following research outcomes by the end of this project: (1) Design of the transducer; (2) Fabrication of the transducer; (3) Test of the transducer; (4) Composition of MATLAB programs; (5) Acquisition and analysis of pulse patterns in large numbers; (6) Establishment of a database for pulse patterns. Standardization and normalization of pulse patterns will be realized. As a result, our project will be helpful to manage the variations of pulses, and will provide an efficient approach for non-invasive and early diagnosis.

Keywords: pulse diagnosis, transducer, signal analysis, Traditional Chinese Medicine (TCM).

1 Introduction

Research related to standardization and normalization of pulse diagnosis in TCM is a conspicuous topic in contemporary pulse research. This kind of research topics can be classified into three categories by their characteristics: research and development

---

[*] Corresponding author.

J. Zhang (Ed.): ICAIC 2011, Part III, CCIS 226, pp. 541–548, 2011.

(R&D) of pulse instrumentations; clinical research; statistical analysis. R&D of pulse instrumentations is the most significant among the above categories seeing that it is the groundwork for normalization of clinical pulse diagnosis.

Pulse diagnosis is one of the major diagnostic techniques in TCM. The theory of pulse diagnosis is to apply the speed and the status of pulses to examine physiological and pathological conditions of patients. Pulse diagnosis is simple, highly accurate, and easy to operate. Consequently, it is vastly valuable in TCM. However, the shortcoming of pulse diagnosis is hard to learn. This technique relies on apprenticeship to pass through generations. This drawback thus leads pulse diagnosis to erroneousness and subjectiveness, and brings about results of pulse diagnosis varying from person to person. To address this problem, researchers in TCM have made efforts to standardize and normalize pulse diagnosis for decades.

Back to 1885, Marey (French pathologist) utilized levers and springs to measure waveforms of patients' pulses. This instrument was the earliest mechanical pulse diagnosis device. Over a century, scientists have invented numerous pulse diagnosis devices employing mechanical, optical, and electronic approaches. Along with these devices, transducers have been made as well to convert pulse information to electronic signals for analysis. In recent two decades, the key research topics relevant to pulse transducers are presented as the followings: (1) Piezoelectric; (2) Electro-optical; (3) Capacitive; (4) Resistive; (5) Doppler ultrasonic. Among these methods, piezoelectric technique is the mostly used. For example, ZM-I, ZM-III pulse diagnosis device in Shanghai; MXY-II pulse diagnosis device in Shandong; model TP-CBS pulse holography device in Beijing, and model BYS-14 cardio-pulse device in Hunan. Additionally, hydraulic pulse transducers using mercury were reported. The named product was model MX-811 pulse diagnosis device in Jiangxi.

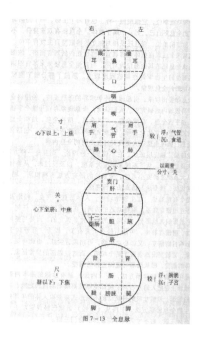

Fig. 1. The scheme of pulse holography [2]

Conventional piezoelectric transducers are categorized into four types based on the number of sensing probes: a. Single probe; b. Double probes; c. Triple probes; d. Multiple probes. The design of transducers with single and double probes is simple, yet their capability of acquiring pulse information is inadequate. In general, transducers with triple and multiple probes are more practical, because three probes may be compatible to the three partitions of pulse holography, Cun, Guan and Chi. For that reason, three probes are able to obtain pulse information more completely than single and double ones. Recent transducers with three probes have nine measuring points on each probe, which are able to gain nine sets of pulse information on each partition of pulse holography. Another product with three probes has 3x4 measuring points on each probe for gauging the three partitions of pulse holography (Fig. 1) [2]. Nevertheless, this 3x4 array is solely able to measure one point on each location shown in Fig. 1. The accuracy could be insufficient for practical use.

As described above, researchers have developed pulse diagnosis devices with various numbers of probes in these few decades, and pursued standardization and normalization of pulse patterns with investigating time domain, frequency domain and wavelet transform of pulse signals, and applying mathematical models and chaotic analysis. Still, pulse diagnosis devices principally record the waveforms of pulses at Cun area, regardless of single probe and multiple probes. The results present the activity traces of micro-area at the recorded point, such as projection of pulse waveforms-pulse locations, projection of pulse rate, and waveforms of pulses. Moreover, the pulse analysis exclusively studies elasticity of blood vessels, composition of blood, viscosity of blood, structures of tissues surrounding blood vessels, and peripheral vascular pressure, etc. The aforementioned information is beneficial to understand the pressure applied to vascular walls, the effects of heartbeats to pulses, and analysis to cardiac function derived from pulses. This research direction highlights the study of pathogenesis in some parts of human body from the view of traditional biology, and is incapable of delivering abundant messages that can be offered in pulse diagnosis in TCM.

In this report, we suggest the fabrication of pulse transducers in a 9x9 sensing array, and the methodology to acquire pulse patterns and to investigate the patterns with Fourier analysis. Our design will have 3 transducers, 243 sensing probes, to obtain pulse information from entire pulse holography. This design will achieve more accurate and more complete acquisition of pulse holography. The proposed pulse transducers will be a breakthrough in the area of pulse standardization, and will further enhance standardization and normalization of pulse diagnosis in TCM.

2 Material and Methods

A. Design

The three partitions in pulse holography, Cun, Guan and Chi, are so small that traditional multiple sensing probes are unable to mount on the small areas, as shown in Fig. 2. The transducers proposed in this paper will resemble to traditional transducers, but the improvement of our transducers is to utilize microfabrication technologies. Consequently, the size of our sensing probes may be as small as 50 to 100μm. If there are 81 probes in Cun, Guan and Chi, respectively, there will be 9 probes distributed on each locations of one partition (one partition has 9 locations). The total area occupied by the 81 probes will be around 5 mm², which is slightly smaller than Cun, Guan and Chi. These 9 sensing probes will be able to precisely acquire pulse information on each location. They will be more sensitive and more thorough than the 3x4 transducers mentioned in the last section, as the 3x4 transducers are distributed only one sensing probes on each location.

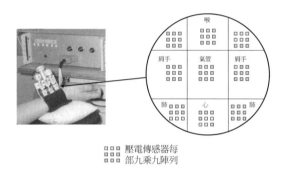

Fig. 2. The hypothetical diagram of our pulse transducers

The proposed design will integrate 9 sensing probes of 1.5×1.5mm² based on the array utilized in pulse diagnosis in TCM. These micro-transducers will be separated by 0.1mm in rows and 0.3mm in columns.

All pulse information will be output in electronic signals to a computer. We will write a MATLAB program to process the 243 signals from the three partitions of pulse holography. These signals will be handled with mathematical methods, such as Fourier analysis and transformations of matrix. Similarities and differences of pulses from different partitions will be studied. Additionally, experienced TCM physicians will be invited to join this project for normalizing pulse patterns. A database may be accordingly established upon the experiences of these TCM experts. Namely, we will be able to combine the experiences of TCM experts and the analysis of electronic signals to realize standardization and normalization of pulse diagnosis.

B. Fabrication

The fabrication of the transducers will be mainly based on microfabrication technologies. A soft piezoelectric material, PVDF, will be deployed in the transducers. This material is both highly sensitive and elastic. Consequently, the device will properly fit patients' wrist when being used on their wrist, and discomforts caused by solid materials will be avoided. The process flow is shown in Fig. 3. An oxidized silicon wafer will be employed as a substrate, and then gold will be evaporated for common grounds. After that, PVDF sensing units in pillars will be fabricated using a PDMS mold (Fig. 4)[3]. Atop these pillars, individual pads will be created with optical lithography and lift-off. Finally, the metal pads for outputs will be manufactured, and transducers will be cut into dies utilizing a dicing saw.

The cost of our device will be low. There will be 200 to 300 transducers produced on a 4 inch wafer, and each transducer will have 81 sensing probes. It will cost around

500 dollars to manufacture one wafer, which has 200 to 300 transducers. In other words, one pulse diagnosis device needs 3 transducers for Cun, Guan and Chi, so it will cost around 6 dollar to manufacture one device. If this diagnosis device is successfully developed, it will be fabricated in mass production, which will greatly reduce the cost. The proposed pulse transducers of a 9x9 sensing array will be a breakthrough for pulse research, and also it will be a useful and cheap diagnosis device in TCM.

(a) An oxidized silicon wafer will be used as a substrate

(b) Gold will be evaporated on the wafer as an electric ground.

(c) PVDF pillar structures will be fabricated on the substrate.

(d) Electric pads will be placed atop the pillars.

(e) The substrate will be diced into individual transducers.

Fig. 3. The process flow of our transducers

C. Acquisition and Analysis of Pulses

Our transducers are piezoelectric transducers, so the pulse signals will be output in voltage, as shown in Fig. 5. Fig. 5(a) may be the pressure of pulse detected by our transducers, and the pressure may then be output as fluctuations in voltage. To enhance the output signals, differential amplifiers may be added to amplify the signals. All signals will be digitalized and saved into a computer, and will be processed with Fourier analysis. Fourier analysis is a commonly used method for function analysis. It decomposes a function into sine and cosine functions of multiple frequencies, such as $\sin(x),\cos(x),\sin(2x),\cos(2x),\sin(3x),\cos(3x),\sin(4x),\cos(4x)$, etc. A function is thus able to be characterized with the compositions of trigonometric polynomials.

Fig. 4. PVDF pillar structures made with a PDMS mold [3]

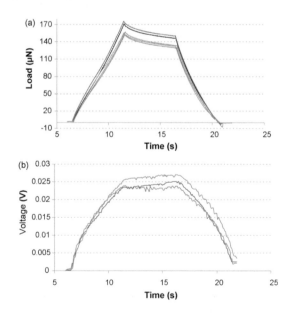

Fig. 5. The hypothetical charts for output signals [3]

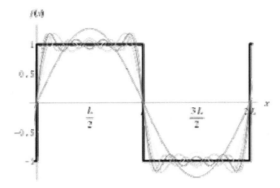

Fig. 6. A square wave function can be decomposed into numerous trigonometric polynomials [4]

Fig. 6 illustrates an example for Fourier analysis. A square wave function is able to be decomposed into numerous sine and cosine functions of multiple frequencies. The composition is $4/\pi(\sin(\pi x/L) + 1/3\ \sin(3\pi x/L) + 1/5\ \sin(5\pi x/L) + 1/7\ \sin(7\pi x/L) +...)$, where $4/\pi,1/3,1/5,1/7$ are Fourier coefficients, which represent the weight of each trigonometric function in the analysis. These trigonometric polynomials can specifically correspond to the characteristics of the evaluated functions. On the other hand, the combination of these trigonometric polynomials with Fourier coefficients will be exactly a square function. By this technique, we will record various pulse patterns, and decompose the patterns into a series of trigonometric polynomials with MATLAB written programs. We will be then able to identify the characteristics of every pulse patterns, and compare among these patterns for discovering their similarities and differences. The findings described in the above may be employed in two directions: (1) To define trigonometric polynomials for 28 pulse patterns with the assistance of experienced TCM physicians for establishing a standard database; (2) To investigate physiological and pathological conditions of patients in depth with trigonometric polynomials for digitalizing symptoms.

3 Conclusion

This work has been partially accomplished, and has been granted one national patent (The device for pulse examination, patent number: ZL200510115279.9). Five technical reports related to this work have been published [5-9].

The following outcomes will be obtained by the end of this project: (1) Design of the transducer; (2) Fabrication of the transducer; (3) Test of the transducer; (4) Composition of MATLAB programs; (5) Acquisition and analysis of pulse patterns in large numbers; (6) Establishment of a database for pulse patterns.

Although the research and development of pulse transducers have been done for several decades; however, there is no ideal transducer reported up to date. It is hopeful that the results from this project will promote research and development of pulse transducer. At the same time, we expect when this report is published to academia, it will be able to inspire our colleagues to make use of our transducers to carry out clinical trials in large numbers. Afterwards, normal pulse pattern and 28 abnormal pulse patterns may be quantitated, and sensitive indicators for these abnormal patterns will be created. These works will be significant to normalization of pulse diagnosis and pulse research in TCM.

Types of pulse are the characteristics of pulse when palpation is performed at wrist area. Types of pulse are directly associated with heartbeats, smoothness of channels and collaterals, and sufficiency and deficiency of Qi and blood. Heartbeats drive blood in blood vessels, and therefore, generate pulsations. Flows of blood in vessels and its distribution in body require not only heartbeats, but also harmonies of organs. Pulses may demonstrate abnormal even before our body appears unwell. As a result, realizing standardization and normalization of pulses and managing variations of pulses are advantageous to achieve non-invasive and early diagnosis.

Acknowledgment. This work was supported by China National Funds for Distinguished Young Scientists (No. 30825046) and Hi-Tech Research and Development Program of China (863 Program) (No. 2008AA02Z406) to Prof. J.X. Chen.

References

1. Tang, W.-c.: Seminar for Pulse Diagnosis Research. TCM Engineering Laboratory of Shanghai University of Chinese Medicine
2. Chen, J.-x.: Study of TCM Diagnosis, p. 122. High Education Press, Beijing (2008)
3. Xu, J., Dapino, M.J., Gallego, D., Hansford: Microphone based Polyvinylidene Fluoride (PVDF) micro-pillars and patterned electrodes. Sensors and Transducers A: Physical 153, 24–32 (2009)
4. http://mathworld.wolfram.com/FourierSeriesSquareWave.html
5. Chen, J.-x., Liu, F.: Research on Characteristics of Pulse Delineation in TCM & Omnidirectional Pulse Detecting by Electro-Pulsograph. In: 2008 IEEE International Symposium on IT in Medicine & Education (ITME 2008), Xiamen, China, December 12-14 (2008)
6. Liu, F., Chen, J.-X.: A new method and implementary scheme of pulse signal analysis. Chinese Archives of TCM 24(12), 2217–2218 (2006)
7. Liu, F., Chen, J.-X.: Study on reproducibility of pulse tracings detection in TCM. Acta Chinese Medicine and Pharmacology 35(1), 35–36 (2007)
8. Liu, F., Chen, J.-X.: Study on Objective Pulse Tracing in TCM from Whole-Dynamic State. Chinese Journal of Basic Medicine in Traditional Chinese Medicine 13(4), 249–250 (2007)
9. Liu, F., Chen, J.-X.: The Design of a New-Style All-Round Electro-Pulsograph. Modern Scientific Instruments (4), 40–42 (2007)

OFDM Channel Estimation for Broadband Wireless Based on Fractal Interpolation and Adaptive Filtering

Bing Qi, Ya-Wei Li, Yi Sun, and Liang-Rui Tang

School of Electric & Electronic Engineering
North China Electric Power University
Changping District, Beijing, China
tangliangrui12@sina.com

Abstract. Channel estimation which utilizes OFDM is one of the key issues to be resolved in broadband wireless access. A channel estimation algorithm is proposed on account of the fast time-varying characteristics in wireless channel. Firstly, the rough estimation to the pilot frequency information is acquired by LS algorithm. Then fractal interpolation is applied to the impulse response of the pilot frequency point channel estimated. Finally the accurate estimation results are received by adaptive filtering. Simulation results illustrate that the algorithm can estimate the properties of wireless channel effectively, and reduce the error rate. So this algorithm has a good channel estimation performance.

Keywords: OFDM, channel estimation, fractal interpolation, adaptive filtering.

1 Introduction

To meet the gradually increasing demand for data transmission in wireless applications of the public and industry users, domestic and foreign-related institutions are actively developing a new generation of wireless communications technology in recent years. Broadband wireless access is the technology that the transmission equipments access by means of broadband wireless, while the transmission equipments are between the switching node of the telecommunication network to the CPN (Customer Premises Network) or the user terminal. Namely the access network is all or part of instead of broadband wireless transmission to provide telephone or data services to user terminal [1]. As a strong anti-interference technology, OFDM can effectively overcome the affect of multipath, time-varying, frequency selective fading and other characteristics in wireless channel, and achieve high-speed data transmission [2-3]. Therefore, new generation of wireless technologies such as LTE, WiMax, McWiLL, etc commonly use OFDM as physical layer core algorithm.

When the data go through frequency selective wireless environment, the signal distortion occurs. It needs to balance signal so as to demodulate better in the receiver and reduce error rate [4-5]. In order to balance signal, accurately estimating the transmission characteristics of wireless channel is seen as a key technology in OFDM system. According to whether there are pilot symbols or not, channel estimation

J. Zhang (Ed.): ICAIC 2011, Part III, CCIS 226, pp. 549–557, 2011.

algorithm can be divided into the pilot estimation, blind estimation and semi-blind estimation. Pilot estimation roughly estimates the known pilot channel signal that is inserted in the first .Then it obtains the full response of the channel through some means of disposing, so that the received signal is equalized and the system performance is improved. Blind estimation does not need to insert the pilot symbols, and there are blind channel estimation algorithms based on sub-space and second order statistics properties. However, the calculation in blind estimation is too large, so it has been limited in the practical application. Half-blind estimation is the blind estimation which is combined with training sequence, so it obtains a part of the features of pilot channel estimation algorithm and blind channel estimation algorithm. It has certain applications, but there are still some problems such as large computation, poor real-time. All of these channel estimation algorithms have their own advantages, while there are also some limitations.

In order to estimate the wireless channel characteristics effectively, accurately transmit information and reduce the error rate, an adaptive channel estimation method based on fractal interpolation is presented. This method firstly estimates the pilot information once, and then combines with fractal interpolation method in order to obtain the overall channel response rough estimation. Finally, the obtained estimation results are adaptively filtered and then the final accurate results are obtained. Simulation results show that the algorithm can estimate the wireless channel characteristics. In the same SNR, the algorithm achieves a lower bit error rate.

The rest of this paper is organized as follows. In section 2, the OFDM channel estimation and the wireless channel properties are introduced in brief. In section 3, the channel estimation based on fractal interpolation and adaptive filtering is explained. In section 4, simulation results are provided. Finally, conclusion is drawn in section 5.

2   OFDM Channel Estimation Techniques and the Wireless Channel Properties

A.   OFDM Channel Estimation Techniques Outlined

OFDM system is a multi-carrier transmission technology. Its core is the flow of data to be transmitted through the S / P conversion and IFFT modulation, and transform into the low-speed data streams on multiple orthogonal narrowband sub-channels. Over each OFDM symbol is modulated and the sub-carrier signal, which can be different of each sub-carrier modulation [6-7]. In OFDM system, as the transmission characteristics of the channel estimation are obtained, frequency domain can achieve attenuation, and the part of high SNR has a higher rate of sub-carrier transmission, so as to achieve the optimal transmission. OFDM system block diagram is shown in Figure 1.

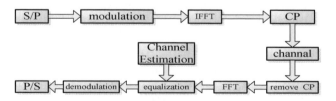

Fig. 1. Block diagram of the OFDM system

The function of channel estimation is to estimate the frequency response which the information goes through from the sending end to receiving end in the channel. For OFDM systems, it's to estimate the value of the frequency response $\hat{H}_k$ of each sub carrier, $k = 0, 1, 2 \ldots N\text{-}1$. Channel estimation is a mathematical representation affected by the channel input signal. Channel estimation algorithm can be divided into three categories: pilot estimation, blind estimation and semi-blind estimation. In all of three algorithms, because of its less computation and good accuracy, pilot estimation is widely used in OFDM systems.

The basic idea of the pilot estimation is first calculated at the pilot sub-carrier frequency response $H^*(k)$ ($k = mL$, m=1,2,3, ..., M, M=N/L, L is the pilot interval, M is the number of pilot symbol) as following:

$$H^* = | \frac{r^*(1)}{s^*(1)} , \frac{r^*(2)}{s^*(2)} , \ldots , \frac{r^*(M)}{s^*(M)} | \qquad (1)$$

Here s is the launch pilot sequence, and r is the received one correspondingly. Then calculate the frequency response of transmission channel $H(k)$ by interpolating. Interpolation algorithm, which is commonly used, is first-order linear interpolation, Lagrange interpolation and interpolation-based LMMSE filter [8-9]. Those interpolation algorithms are usually simple, which could not reflect the characteristics of actual wireless channel effectively. There would be poor performances in channel estimation when channel impulse response have great diversification in the poor condition of channel characteristics. So the requirements of the wireless channel estimation can not be satisfied with those algorithms.

B. Wireless Channel Environment

In the wireless signal transmission process, electromagnetic wave propagates mainly in three ways [10], reflection, refraction and scattering, which brings three kinds of effect on the propagation of signal by the channel: (1) Transmission losses, which exhibits that the signal intensity varying with distance in large scope. (2) Shadow fading, which is the value of the signal level varying slowly in middle scope. (3) Multi-path fading, which means the instantaneous value of the receiving signal intensity varying fast in small scope, and it is also called fast fading, short-term fading and Rayleigh fading. What is more, multi-path transmission will cause the expansion of the signal in time, space and frequency, which will affect the signal transmission obviously. The actual received signal losses can be described as $P(d) = |d^{-n}| s(d) R(d)$,

Here d is the distance from the base station to the mobile terminal, $|d^{-n}|$ is transmission losses, $s(d)$ is shadow fading and $R(d)$ is multi-path fading. In the real system, the path losses $\overline{PL}(d)$ of the wireless channel can be expressed as $\overline{PL}(d) \propto (\frac{d}{d_0})^n$. The shadow fading approximately subjects to lognormal distribution, its probability density function is as following

$$p(x) = \begin{cases} \dfrac{1}{\sqrt{\pi}\sigma x} \exp[-\dfrac{(\log x - \mu)^2}{2\sigma^2}], & x > 0 \\ 0, & x \leq 0 \end{cases} \tag{2}$$

Where x is the random variable of the slow disturbance of the signal level, the standard value of σ is 8 dB. Multi-path fading, also called fast fading or short-term fading, its probability density function subjects to the Rayleigh distribution as following

$$p(r) = \begin{cases} \dfrac{r}{\sigma^2} \exp[-\dfrac{r}{2\sigma^2}], & r \geq 0 \\ 0, & r < 0 \end{cases} \tag{3}$$

Here σ^2 is the time-average power of the received signal before envelope detection.

Taking the relevant characteristics of the computer simulation platform and the difference from the real environment, it is usually carried out using white noise as the noise modelling to simulation [11-12]. Figure 2 shows a simplified wireless channel model.

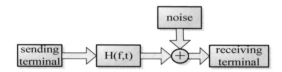

Fig. 2. Simplified model of wireless channel

3   Channel Estimation Algorithm Based on Fractal Interpolation and Adaptive Filtering

Channel estimation algorithm system flowchart presented in the paper is shown as Figure 3, on the basis of traditional pilot estimation, it analyses the estimated value of each pilot point, the crude estimated value of the response to the entire channel is obtained according to the interpolation of fractal interpolation function, then the fined estimated value is obtained by using of the adaptive filtering method to filter the crude estimated value above.

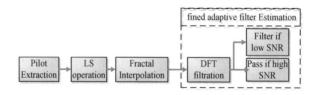

Fig. 3. Flow chart of the channel estimation algorithm in this paper

A. Fractal Interpolation

Fractal generally refers to "a rough or fragmented geometric shape that can be divided into several parts and each part is (at least roughly) the shape of the overall reduced size", this property is called self-similarity. Fractal interpolation is a method to construct Fractal -curve, proposed by MFBarnsley on the basis of the iterated function system. The principle is to construct the corresponding IFS (Iterated Function System) of a set of given interpolation points, making the IFS attractor be the function diagram of this group of interpolation points [13]. The traditional interpolation methods emphasize the smoothness of the data, that is, when local line is fully zoomed the graph still looks like a line, which is far from ideal to describe a very irregular curve. Channel environment is a curve of high degree of variability and sharp shock, traditional methods can not be used to track the channel change ideally. As a generalized form of spline interpolation, fractal interpolation is very suitable for the situation with highly discreteness and fine structure.

Let the N pilot estimation be $H_1, H_2, \ldots\ldots, H_N$. Let the coordinates of each point be (n, Hn), where, $n \in \{1, 2, \ldots\ldots N\}$, Hn is the estimated value of the pilot points to form two-dimensional sequence. According to fractal theory, IFS affine transformation constructed by these points is shown as figure 4.

$$W_n \begin{pmatrix} x \\ f(x) \end{pmatrix} = \begin{pmatrix} a_n & 0 \\ c_n & d_n \end{pmatrix} \begin{pmatrix} x \\ f(x) \end{pmatrix} + \begin{pmatrix} e_n \\ f_n \end{pmatrix} \tag{4}$$

Let $xn = n$, $f(n) = Hn$, substituted in equation (5) to determine the IFS. The d_n value can be set according to the circumstances.

$$\begin{cases} a_n = \dfrac{x_n - x_{n-1}}{x_N - x_1} \\ c_n = \dfrac{f(n) - f(n-1)}{x_N - x_1} - \dfrac{d_n (x_n - x_{n-1})}{x_N - x_1} \\ e_n = \dfrac{x_N x_{n-1} - x_1 x_n}{x_N - x_1} \\ f_n = \dfrac{x_N f(n-1) - x_1 f(n)}{x_N - x_1} - \dfrac{d_n (f(1) x_N - x_1 f(N))}{x_N - x_1} \end{cases} \tag{5}$$

According to the identified IFS, using fractal interpolation method, the response of the entire channel and the crudely estimated value can be obtained, the result is shown as figure 4. As can be seen from the figure, the results of fractal interpolation can track the subtle changes of the curve better.

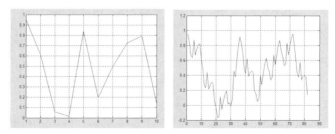

Fig. 4. The contrast between linear interpolation and fractal interpolation

B. Fined Adaptive Filter Estimation

Though the result by fractal interpolation can acquire the channel frequency response characteristics fairly correctly, the channel estimation error is still relatively high. In order to obtain more accurate channel estimation value, optimizing the channel estimation is needed. A filter to implement adaptive filter according to the different signal to noise ratio is presented.

The optimal policy will do as follows when SNR is lower than the set threshold. First of all, the DFT filter is applied to the treatment of filtering waves for the channel estimation value obtained by fractal interpolation , the detail step is that, initially the IDFT transformation is implemented for the values H obtained by fractal interpolation, then according to the characteristics that impulse response length is less than the cyclic prefix of OFDM symbol in the time domain channel, part of the time domain signals achieved from IDFT transformation shall revert to zero, subsequently the channel estimation value H in frequency domain is regained by the DFT transformation to finish the filter.

After the completion of DFT filter, it is processed as the equation (6).

$$\hat{H}_F = R_{HH} (R_{HH} + \frac{\beta}{SNR} I)^{-1} \hat{H} \tag{6}$$

Here $R_{HH} = E[H.H^H]$ is the self-correlation matrix of the channel response, which can be measured by sending training sequences or pre-statistics. $SNR = E|X_P(k)|^2 / \sigma_n^2$, it is SNR of the signal ($X_P(k)$ is the date which need to send, σ_n^2 is the noise power). SNR can be measured at the receiving terminal. $\beta = E|X_P(k)|^2 \cdot E|1/X_P(k)|^2$ is a constant which dependent on the modulation, here for QPSK modulation $\beta = 1$. $\hat{H}$ is the estimation result by DFT filtered And $\hat{H}_F$ is the fined estimation result.

When SNR is higher than the threshold set by the system, the final detailed estimated values of channel will be obtained by the DFT filter rather than processed by the equation (6).

4 Simulation Results and Discussion

Based on the multipath propagation characteristics of the wireless channel, the multipath propagation channel with Doppler frequency shift is selected in simulation of this paper, and additive white Gaussian noise is adopted. The longest time-delay is $1.5\mu s$, guard interval is usually 2-4 times the longest time-delay, the guard interval $T_g = 3\mu s$, in this case, the multi-path interference on the wireless channel can be eliminated. Generally in OFDM systems, we set $T_g \leq T/4$, so we can get $T \geq 12 \ \mu s$. IFFT sampling frequency $f = 8.8MHZ$, set the number of data sub carriers N as 110, and the number of pilot sub carriers as 12. Pilot interval is 10 data sub carrier. The period of the symbol is $T = N / f = 12.5 \mu s$, the interval of the neighbouring sub carriers is $\Delta f = 80 kHZ$, and QPSK is chosen as the modulation. Figure 5 shows the bit error rates of the LS algorithm, LMMSE filtering algorithm and the algorithm proposed in this paper under different SNR respectively.

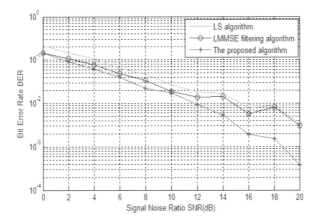

Fig. 5. Bit error rate curves of different algorithms

Figure 5 shows that in LS algorithm the channel frequency response between the two pilot symbols has been seen as a simple linear relationship, without taking into account the actual situation of the sudden the channel, so its estimation result has the maximum channel bit error rate and the worst channel estimation performance. This algorithm fully considers the randomness of the channel changes. Each time computing a sub-carrier frequency response, not only two adjacent pilot symbols for frequency response are used, all the pilot sub-carrier frequency response in a symbol are used in the light of the characteristics of self-similarity. This approach makes the sign of the frequency response of each sub carrier related to each other, and track the change of the channel. Therefore, the algorithm in the same SNR estimated channel bit error rate is lower than the LS. At the same time as the algorithm in adaptive filtering part of the traditional LMMSE filter has been improved with the method of fractal LMMSE, overcomes some shortcomings, therefore, this algorithm is also better than LMMSE algorithm.

As the application of fractal interpolation method in this algorithm, computation has a certain increase than the LMMSE algorithm, but still within an acceptable range. This experimental platform environment: windows XP SP3 installation MATLAB 7.1, processor Intel Core Duo T2350, clocked at 1.86G, the memory is 1G. In this environment, averaged over 10 calculations, the results show the time used LMMSE algorithm was 3.9 seconds, the time used the algorithm of 5.8 seconds. Since this algorithm uses adaptive technology, if channel environment changed better, the system will choose the efficient algorithms automatically, reduce complexity, only in poor channel environment and low signal to noise ratio, it will significantly enhance the computational complexity, so the complex of the proposed algorithm increase limited compare with LMMSE algorithm. This algorithms can contented the real time requirements in broadband wireless access systems.

5 Conclusion

Aiming at fast changeable characteristics of a radio channel, channel estimation algorithm is proposed based on fractal interpolation and adaptive filter combination in the OFDM system. This algorithm first made rough estimates by fractal interpolation of channel frequency response, utilized the adaptive filter to revise the estimate, completed fine estimate of channel characteristic. The algorithm in the frequency response calculation of arbitrary symbols every sub-carrier, utilized frequency response of the two adjacent pilot sub-carrier, and used all frequency response estimate in one OFDM symbol , according to self-similarity of the channel impulse response, interpolate the response of each sub-carrier by applied pilot information overall trend, therefore can follow the channel of slow change. At the same time it optimized channel estimation by applying the autocorrelation matrix of channel response, improved the system performance in antioxidant ISI and noise. The simulation results show that the proposed channel estimation algorithm greatly reduced channel estimation error and had better performance, compared with traditional interpolation algorithm. It was an effective method of wireless channel estimation in the OFDM system.

References

1. Ren, Z., Li, Z.: Simulation and Analysis of Modulation Algorithm for Broadband Wireless OFDM System. China New Telecommunications 17, 188–193 (2009)
2. Hirakawa, T., Itami, M., Itoh, K.: An Iterative Scheme to Reduce Influence of Impulse Noise in OFDM Transmission. In: International Conference on Consumer Electronics, ICCE 2007. Digest of Technical Papers, pp. 1–2 (2007)
3. Yin, C.-c., Luo, T., Le, G.-x.: Multi-carrier broadband wireless communication technology. Beijing University of Posts and Telecommunications Press, Beijing (2004) (in Chinese)
4. Yu, X., Lin, P., He, Z., et al.: OFDM Channel Estimation with Impulse Noise Cancellation. In: International Conference on Wireless Communications, Networking and Mobile Computing, WiCom 2007, vol. 9, pp. 330–333 (2007)
5. Wang, Y.-m.: OFDM key technologies and application. Machine Press, Beijing (2006) (in Chinese)
6. Zhou, E., et al.: The next generation broadband wireless communications technology of OFDM and MIMO. People Post Press, Beijing (2008) (in Chinese)
7. Yu, H.-y., Mao, D.-x.: Research on applying OFDM to high data rate communication in low voltage power line. Relay 31, 23–25 (2003)
8. Bai, Y.: Channel estimation technique in MIMO-OFDM system, vol. 2, pp. 37–41. Xidian University, Xian (2006) (in Chinese)
9. Duan, F., Liu, Y., Chen, J.: Channel estimation technique in OFDM communication system. China Patent, 1437338A (August 20, 2003)

10. Coleri, S., Ergen, M., Puri, A.: Channel estimation techniques based on pilot arrangement in OFDM systems. IEEE Trans. Broadcast 48, 223–229 (2002)
11. Haghighi, S.J., Primak, S., Wang, X.: Effects of Side Information on Complexity Reduction in Superimposed Pilot Channel Estimation in OFDM Systems. In: IEEE 71st Vehicular Technology Conference (VTC 2010-Spring), vol. 5, pp. 1–3 (2010)
12. Hu, M.-k., Chen, X.-h., Dong, S.-q.: An Improved SVD Estimation Algorithm for OFDM. Electrical Measurement & Instrumentation 8(524), 56–58 (2009)
13. Sha, Z., Ruan, H.-j.: Fractal and fitting. Zhejiang University Press, Hangzhou (2005) (in Chinese)

Design of the Mass Customization Strategy for Special Purpose Vehicles

Jianzhong Li

College of Economics and Management
Hubei University of Automotive Technology
Shiyan, Hubei, China
jianzhongli2011@sohu.com

Abstract. As a personalized production model, mass customization can have both characteristics of low costs and differentiation, so it is more suitable for the car market where demand differentiation is significant. In the field of special-purpose vehicles, mass customization achieves economies of scale and market effects through modularization, differentiation and other ways. It combines advantages of the two modes of mass production and customized production, and also reflects a way of thinking that is to think from the view of customers.

Keywords: special purpose vehicles, mass customization, modularization, differentiation.

1 Introduction

Special purpose vehicle is a joint name of special trucks, such as dump trucks, semi-trailer towing vehicles, vans, tank trucks, lift trucks, special construction vehicles, stake trucks, etc. Special purpose vehicle industry in China started in the late 1950s, which now has a certain market size after 40 years of development. At present, there are approximately 5,000 special purpose vehicle varieties in China, whose production has accounted for about 40% of the production of commercial vehicles, so they have become an important part in China's automobile industry. Demands from users of special purpose vehicles have a very strong characteristic of individuality. In order to meet this demand characteristic, special purpose vehicle enterprises must choose a right development model. As a personalized production model, mass customization can have both characteristics of low costs and differentiation, so it is more suitable for the special purpose vehicle market.

2 The Design Background of the Mass Customization Strategy

From the perspective of the total market demand, special purpose vehicles have a broad market prospect in China. Currently, China is in a development stage of the synchronous acceleration of industrialization and urbanization, which is characterized

J. Zhang (Ed.): ICAIC 2011, Part III, CCIS 226, pp. 558–564, 2011.

by its large investment scale, long industry chain, high degree of processing, more intermediate products, and long growth duration. Also, due to the very uneven distribution of resources, high output of raw coal in central China, high yields of steel in the east, and the still very high transport intensity, the development of the special purpose vehicle industry is facing lots of opportunities. Some experts predict that by 2020 the commercial vehicle market in China will maintain an average annual growth rate of about 9%, which thus provides good development space for special purpose vehicles. Large infrastructure projects will bring great demands and market growths to engineering special purpose vehicles. The total of the high grade highway construction is still very huge, which promotes the rapid development of engineering vehicles for highway construction, special operating vehicles for highway maintenance and operating vehicles on highways. Meanwhile, due to the huge amount of energy consumption, the transport of energy and materials will also expand the total demand for special purpose vehicles. The acceleration of urbanization and the improvement of urban functions will produce a greater demand for special purpose vehicles in urban construction and services such as construction, environmental sanitation, gardens, power, communications, public security, justice, airports, and various commercial transports. The rapid development of the logistics industry will also greatly promote the rapid development of vans, refrigerated trucks, semi-trailer vans, and other special purpose vehicles.

Seen from the characteristics of market demand, multiple varieties and small batch are truly reflected in the current production and demand of special purpose vehicles. The development and production of special purpose vehicle modification enterprises have lots of characteristics including multiple varieties, serialization and diversification. Aiming to different needs, enterprises adjust the output proportion of different series of products. This feature may significantly distinguish special purpose vehicles from cars and ordinary trucks. Generally speaking, there is a large annual demand for van transporters, semi-trailer towing vehicles and other special purpose vehicles, up to tens of thousand or more, while dump trucks can reach hundreds of thousand. The demand for most of special purpose vehicles is only several hundred to a few thousand, some even a few or a few dozen.

As can be seen from the above two points, special purpose vehicle is a typical personalized product, which is characterized by its special functions, special users, special structural requirements, special shapes and other features. The special purpose vehicle enterprises in China generally have a small production scale and more manufacturers. To win a success in the competition and meet the personalized requirements of special purpose vehicle users, mass customization can be used in the production of special purpose vehicles.

3 Design of the Mass Customization Strategy

Mass customization is a strategic thinking based on customer value innovation, which is also a portfolio competitive strategy integrating mass production with customized production, integrating economies of scale with economies of scope, integrating costs and product diversities with speed. Mass customization is different from mass production. The main difference between the two is shown in Table 1. The mass customization strategy is a marketing strategy for a personalized product based on differences in customer demand, thus, it is suitable to adopt a mixed strategy combining modularization with differentiation in the specific implementation.

Table 1. Differences between mass customization and mass production

category	mass customization	mass production
objective	To design, manufacture and sell products at a reasonable cost, which satisfies different needs of each customer	To design, manufacture and sell products at the lowest possible cost, which enables as many customers as possible can afford products
methods	Differentiated and personalized product design, quick response, CAD/CAM modular design, multiple marketing tools and methods	Standardized product design The mode of flow line production The scale of marketing tools and marketing networks
major features	Differentiated demand Heterogeneous market Low cost, scope economy High degree of customer satisfaction Customized products Short life cycle	Stable market demand Homogeneous market Low cost, economy of scale Standardized products Long life cycle

A. The Idea of Mass Customization

Mass customization is a production model, where enterprises use modern technologies and management tools to achieve customization for each customer, and its cost and time are consistent with those in mass production. Mass customization integrates enterprises, customers, suppliers, employees, and environment. Guided by the system thought, with the total optimization point of view, enterprises make full use of various resources. Under the support of standard technologies, modern design methods, information technologies and advanced manufacturing technologies, according to customers' personalized requirements, enterprises provide customized products and services in low-cost, high-quality and high-efficiency mass production. This mode of production ultimately achieves each customer's specific needs, and offers customized products with the efficiency and benefits of large-scale production. It combines advantages of the two modes of mass production and customized production, and also reflects a way of thinking that is to think from the view of customers.

The basic idea of mass customization is through the reconstruction of product structure and manufacturing process, and the use of a series of high and new technologies such as modern information technology, new materials technology, and flexible manufacturing technology, customized production is completely or partly transformed into mass production. With the costs and speed in mass production, any number of products is customized for a single customer or a multivariety-small batch market.

B. Means of Implementation of Mass Customization

(1) Modularization

The so-called modularization is to create multiple modules, and each module has other modules which can mutually coordinate. Each module is restricted to coordinate with several optimum modules. When a user is buying a car, he can select these modules within the prescribed limits according to his own needs. The combination of these modules is the car type he needs (see Figure 1). The main purpose of modularization is to partly meet a customer's need for customization, and meanwhile to ensure the products' optimization match in the customization process.

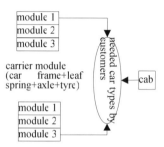

Fig. 1. The diagram of modularization

It can be seen from the figure that the basic idea of the modular design is to obtain customer information in the marketing department, to design modules in the product development department, to customize and package modules in the production department, and to provide convenience in after-sales service. The marketing department and the product development department jointly make a study to build module groups according to the configuration favored by most users. These module groups are based on the current configuration modes for further standardization, and combine some items to reduce the complexity and irrationality in the configuration process. In the modules after being standardized, a cooperative relation between modules is established based on technical requirements, and each module is named. The after-sales service department and the production department make suggestions for the establishment of modules, which enables modules to obtain convenience in production and after-sales service.

(2) Differentiation

The differentiation strategy, also known as the unique strategy, is to differentiate products or services offered by enterprises, in order to form some products with unique features in the industry range. Now products have a high degree of homogenization, and a buyer's market has obvious characteristics among the major manufacturing enterprises of professional automotive products. In this situation, market profits can be won only through earlier and faster discovering sub-product demands and fast launching products which meet market demands. In this market, taking the follow-up strategy means passive. Enterprises only adopt the differentiation strategy to change those products with the same property, and to enable products to form different preferences in the minds of users. Then, business will win a success.

As a special purpose vehicle enterprise, it can create marketing competitive advantages from the following aspects.

① Product differentiation. For competitors in the same industry, the core value of products is basically the same, and their differences lie in performance and quality. Under the circumstance of meeting the basic needs of customers, to provide unique products for customers is a goal pursued by the differentiation strategy. As a special purpose vehicle enterprise, in order to win more market shares, it should offer different products and services aiming to different markets, and carry out targeted marketing campaigns.

② Image differentiation. Through strong band awareness, successful CI strategy and the media publicity, the enterprise establishes a superior image in the minds of consumers, so that consumers may have a preference for this enterprise's products. Once a consumer has a consumption demand, he will not hesitate to choose the enterprise's products.

③ Regional differentiation. Based on geographical conditions, economic conditions and road transport conditions in different regions, special purpose vehicles should be put on the market differently, and different effective marketing strategies should be implemented. For example, for the characteristics in the western region of China such as the backward economy, poor road conditions and more coal transport enterprises, automotive products should be purposefully launched to meet the road conditions in the western region.

④ After-sale service differentiation. The new market competition will mainly lie in service competition. With the arrival of a buyer's market and the homogenization of the core functions of products, the added value generated from the differences in after-sale services will be a principle way to promote product differentiation. Special purpose vehicles are considered as means of production, so customers will require more for after-sale services of special purpose vehicles than those of other products. To do well in after-sale services and highest possibly occupy the values produced from the after-sale service market have become a common view and act of special purpose vehicle enterprises.

4   The Implementing Measures of the Mass Customization Strategy

A.   To Establish a Flexible Automobile Production Technology Platform

As the mass customization strategy, its core is the large scale and customization, whose smooth implementation needs to rely on a certain technology platform. To achieve the large scale, enterprises must use a certain platform technology, which can greatly reduce manufacturing difficulties, shorten the manufacturing cycle and reduce costs in design, development and procurement. Meanwhile, the use of a certain platform technology can also greatly shorten the development and production cycle of special purpose vehicle products, and fully improve cost performance of products. In order to achieve customization, enterprises must adopt flexible production technologies and intelligent production equipment, which enable the manufacturing technologies to adapt to the multivariety-small batch characteristic of special purpose vehicles. For special purpose vehicle enterprises, the market they face has a large demand difference and a wide demand range, so they produce more than one type of special purpose vehicle products to meet the market's demand for varieties of special purpose vehicles. On the one hand, they should make full use of the platform technology to carry out a modular design; on the other hand, they need flexible production.

B. To Establish a Management Information System

The key issue on the implementation of mass customization lies in customers' waiting time. If special purpose vehicle enterprises cannot shorten the time when customers are offered products and services, they also cannot achieve full competitive advantage. Therefore, in order to realize the mass customization strategy, it is very essential to establish a computer-based information system in enterprises, which should be able to completely record information about the needs of various customers, and quickly transmit it to all the concerned departments. Managers can make use of this information system to check working conditions of all working groups, departments and production units and to control the overall progress of work, so as to control the enterprise's overall costs. The enterprise management information system can be established from the following aspects: (1) Create an organic organization. Establish a temporary inter-departmental working group in the enterprise. Such an organic organization can quickly transmit information, give full play to employees' enthusiasm and creativity, and quickly respond to the needs of customers. (2) Use advanced production technologies. Enterprises establish a flexible manufacturing system and the computer integrated manufacturing system, which allows the same equipment to produce different types of products, shortens production cycle, improves product quality, reduces production costs, and thus greatly improves the enterprise's response speed to customers' personalized needs.

C. To Establish a Supply Chain System with Special Purpose Vehicle Enterprises at the Core

Special purpose vehicle enterprises have core business and non-core business. For core business, enterprises need to concentrate on to do a good job, while for non-core business, they can be completely undertaken by other supporting enterprises in the way of outsourcing. For special purpose vehicles, the customer needs are constantly changing, so enterprises must promptly meet the changing customer needs. It is far from enough and unnecessary to only rely on the ability of special purpose vehicle enterprises. Under the production mode of mass customization, different automotive parts should be manufactured by different enterprises, so as to achieve reasonable social division of work. Therefore, the development of specialized automotive parts enterprises is of great importance to the implementation of mass customization in China's special purpose vehicle industry. Only when the automotive parts enterprises achieve division of labor based on specialization can it be possible for China's special purpose vehicle enterprises facing mass customization to outsource a lot of automotive parts to professional automotive parts enterprises, so as to improve productivity. Under the mass customization mode, special purpose vehicle enterprises facing mass customization should serve as the core of the supply chain. With a rational division of work, other automotive parts enterprises jointly participate to meet customer needs. Special purpose vehicle enterprises, which are regarded as the core, should coordinate each side of suppliers and strengthen supply chain management, so that the supply chain can respond quickly to customer needs.

In conclusion, mass customization means that under the guidance of the system thinking, a view of overall optimization is used to achieve each customer's specific needs, which combines advantages of the two modes of mass production and customized production, and also reflects a way of thinking that is to think from the view of customers.

References

1. Yi, H.-y., Liu, W.: Product family size optimization method for on-line mass customization. Computer Integrated Manufacturing Systems 15(12), 2370–2398 (2009)
2. Xu, J.-p., Luo, Y.: Research on production planning based on mass customization. Machinery (1), 37–40 (2010)
3. Xu, J.: BOM Research for Modular Manufacturing Based on Large-scale Customization. Construction Machinery and Equipment 40(6), 1–5 (2009)
4. Liu, C.: Performance Evaluation of Mass-customization Supply Chain Cooperation. Logistics Technology 29(5), 107–111 (2010)
5. Wang, J.: Research on the model of mass customization's applicability. Science and Technology Management Research 29(4), 176–178 (2009)

Improved Feature for Texture Segmentation Using Gabor Filters[*]

Chuanzhen Li and Qin Zhang

Information Engineering School
Communication University of China
Chaoyang District, Beijing, China, 100024
chu.anzhenli@sohu.com

Abstract. The local structure of texture can be obtained by transforming a texture image to new basis given by convolving it with Gabor filters in order to segment images contain multiple textures. In recent years, some features have been proposed, but the segmentation performance can still be improved. In this paper, an improved energy feature, which using variable window size decided by scale of Gabor kernel, has been proposed. So the local properties in an appropriated neighbourhood can been captured better. Since we focus on observing the performance of new features, we use PCA (principal component analysis) as the dimension reduction method and K-means algorithm as clustering algorithm for simplicity. From the experimental results using several features, it can be seen that our feature can improve the separability of texture boundaries and irregular textures.

Keywords: Gabor filters, texture, segmentation, variable size window, energy.

1 Introduction

In the primary visual cortex (V1) of mammal, the receptive fields exhibit orientation, phase, and frequency tuned properties. This mechanism plays an important role in texture processing, since image textures generally consist of organized patterns of quite regular subelements. Moreover, Gabor function has been demonstrated to characterize a signal simultaneously in the temporal and frequency domains. Therefore the local structure of the image can be obtained by transforming an image to the new basis given by convolving it with Gabor filters.

For the above reasons, Gabor filters are widely applied in texture segmentation [1-9], edge detection [9-12] and face recognition 13. Among the three, texture segmentation is a very fundamental problem in computer vision and image processing. The researches about texture segmentation mainly focus on three areas. The first area focuses on designing optimal filters 6712, such as the parameter selecting and Gabor kernels selecting. The second area focuses on the fast algorithm

---

[*] This work is supported by a grant from the Key Programs of NSFC (No. 60832004) and XNG project of CUC (No. 0917).

J. Zhang (Ed.): ICAIC 2011, Part III, CCIS 226, pp. 565–572, 2011.

1315 of Gabor filters. The third area focuses on the features extraction and features fusion 2616, since features are one of the most important factors in texture segmentation.

In recent years, some features have been proposed for texture segmentation using Gabor filters. Simona E. Grigorescu et al. 16compared texture features based on Gabor filters including Gabor energy features, complex moments features, and grating cell operator features. Among the three categories, grating cell operator gave the best segmentation results. Mittal N. et al. **4** and Huang C. et al. 2 obtained similar segmentation results with grating cell operator features using textures features described as " energy measure", and the calculation of the features was simply and convenient. However, segmentation performance was seriously affected by the size of the window, since the energy feature was calculated in a window. According to the existing literature, the size of the window was generally set to a fixed value to tradeoff between reliable measurement and texture boundary or between large scale texture and small scale texture. When the window size was too large, the computed value of each point would contain the points in an inappropriate neighbourhood. When the window size was too small, the computed value of each point would lose some points in the appropriated neighbourhood. In other words, the size of window was incapable of matching the corresponding scales of Gabor kernels.

In this paper, we propose an improved energy measure feature which using variable window size decided by scales of Gabor kernels. That is, after transforming a texture image to the new basis given by convolving it with Gabor filters, we calculate the energy in a variable size window, and the size of windows are related with Gabor filters' scales. From the experimental results using several features, it can be seen that our feature can improve the separability of texture boundaries and irregular textures. The remainder of the paper is organized as follows. After describing the improved feature in Section 2, we introduce the dimension reducing and clustering algorithm for integrity of this paper in section 3. In section 4, experiments comparing the proposed approach against the method proposed in reference **21018** are presented. Finally, conclusions are given in section 5.

2   GABOR Filters Designing and Feature Extracting

A. Gabor Filters Designing

A Gabor filter is obtained by modulating a sinusoid with a Gaussian. Then the sinusoid becomes spatially localized. For 2D signals, the sinusoid, Gaussian, and a Gabor filter are shown in Fig. 1**17**.

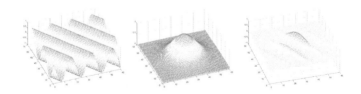

Fig. 1. Gabor filter composition: (a) 2D sinusoid oriented at 30°with the x-axis, (b) a Gaussian kernel, (c) the corresponding Gabor filter

A Gabor filter is mathematically given by 10:

$$G_{\theta,\phi,\sigma,\omega}(x,y) = \exp^{-(x^2+\gamma y^2)/2\sigma^2} \cos(2\pi\omega x'+\phi)$$

where, $x' = x\cos\theta + y\sin\theta$, $y' = -x\sin\theta + y\cos\theta$, $\omega = 1/\lambda$.

The parameter λ represents the wavelength of the sinusoidal signal. Generally, λ is a constant no less than 2, and less than 1/5 of input image. σ represents the standard deviation of Gaussian factor and constitutes the linear size space of receptive field. θ represents the orientation of the sinusoidal signal. Φ represents the phase offset of cosine function (- $\pi <\Phi ⩽\pi$). γ represents the aspect ratio of Gaussian factor. An example map of a receptive field function with a particular position, size, orientation, and symmetry is shown in Fig. 2. Fig .2 (a) shows the Gabor filter constituted by 18 kernels (γ=0.5, b=1, Φ=0). Fig.2 (b) shows another Gabor filter constituted by 18 kernels (γ=1, b=1, Φ=0).

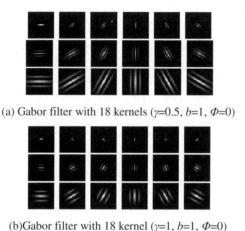

(a) Gabor filter with 18 kernels (γ=0.5, b=1, Φ=0)

(b)Gabor filter with 18 kernel (γ=1, b=1, Φ=0)

Fig. 2. Gabor filters constituted by 18 Gabor kernels with three wavelengths and six orientations. (a)The first Gabor kernel (γ=0.5, b=1, Φ=0), (b) The second Gabor kernel (γ=0.5, b=1, Φ=0).

B. Feature Extracting

Typically, an input image $I(x,y) \in \Omega$ is convolved with a 2-D Gabor function to obtain a Gabor feature image as follows:

$$r(x,y) = \iint_{\Omega} I(\xi,\eta)G(x-\xi, y-\eta)d_\xi d_\eta$$

In reference 10, the outputs of a symmetric and an antisymmetric kernel filter in each image point can be combined in a single quantity that is called the Gabor energy. This feature is related to the model of a specific type of orientation selective neuron in the primary visual cortex called the complex cell. In reference **18**, the mean value and variance of wavelet coefficients has been applied to extract the features of a grey-scale image. In reference 2, "energy measure"(similar to texture energy proposed by Laws) has been used to detect texture primitives. But some properties in the appropriated neighbourhood are lost for the size of window is fixed. In our experiments, variable size windows are applied to calculate the texture feature measurement in the appropriated neighbourhood. The proposed feature is mathematically given by:

$$e(x, y) = 1 / (2n+1)^2 \sum_{i=x-n}^{x+n} \sum_{j=y-n}^{y+n} |r(i, j)|,$$

$$n = S \times \lambda.$$

The parameter λ represents the wavelength of the sinusoidal signal. The parameter S represents the scaling of windows. The n represents the size of windows. $e(x,y)$ represents the energy in a variable size window, and the size of a window is adjusted with the wavelength of Gabor wavelet. The improved feature reflects the nonlinear characteristics of the visual system, and is ability to detect the texture primitive more clearly.

In our experiments, we use the filter banks with 24 symmetric Gabor kernels. The application of such a filter bank to an input image results in a 24-dimensional feature vector for each point of that image. The feature vector is represented by:

$$\mathbf{O} = (O(0,0)^T, O(0,1)^T, \cdots, O(x, y), \cdots, O(N_\lambda, N_\theta)^T)^T$$

where $O(x,y)$ is the column vector constituted by $O_{\lambda^i,\theta^j}(x, y)$.

3   Feature Reduction and Clustering

In order to ensure the integrity of this paper, the dimension reduction method and clustering method used in the paper will be introduced briefly.

For the size of feature vector $\mathbf{O}$ is too large to cluster efficiently, we must obtain a smaller set of features that "accurately represents" the feature vector $\mathbf{O}$. It's important that the new set of features should capture as much of the old vector's variance as possible. In reference 13, Independent Component Analysis of Gabor features is used for texture segmentation. ICA captures both second and higher-order statistics and projects the input data onto the basis vectors that are as statistically independent as possible. In reference 2 18, Principal Component Analysis is applied to obtain a smaller set of features. PCA [2] finds a set of the most representative projection vectors such that the projected samples retain the most information about original samples. Easy to understand and achieve, we choose PCA as the feature reduction method, since we focus on observing the performance of new features. The PCA basis vectors are represented as eigenvectors of the scatter matrix S_T defined as:

$$S_T = \sum_{i=1}^{M} (x_i - \mu) \cdot (x_i - \mu)^T$$

where μ is the mean of all feature images and x_i is the i-th feature image with its columns concatenated in a vector.

Then we need to determine the intrinsic grouping in a set of unlabeled feature data. There are a lot of clustering algorithms, such as K-means, Fuzzy C-means, Hierarchical clustering, Mixture of Gaussians and so on. K-means is one of the simplest unsupervised learning algorithms that solve the clustering problem. The K-means algorithm aims at minimizing an objective function, in this case a squared error function. The objective function:

$$J = \sum_{j=1}^{k} \sum_{i=1}^{n} \left\| x_i^{(j)} - c_j \right\|^2$$

$\left\| x_i^{(j)} - c_j \right\|^2$ is a chosen distance measure between a data point $x_i^{(j)}$ and the cluster centre c_j, is an indicator of the distance of the n data points from their respective cluster centers.

4 Experimental Results

In this paper, all images come from brodatz database. We evaluate the performance of the proposed feature presented in Section II using K-means clustering algorithm and PCA dimension reduction algorithm. The test images are shown as Fig.3 (a).

For the Gabor filters, we use N_λ scales and N_θ orientations (N_λ=4, N_θ=6). They are described as:

$$\lambda_i = \sqrt{2} \times 2^{(i-1)}, \text{ where } i=1,2...N_\lambda.$$

$$\theta_j = (j-1)\pi / N_\theta, \text{ where } j=1,2...N_\theta.$$

In order to improve computing speed, we use FFT instead of convolution. Then the filtered image can be described as:

$$r_{\lambda^i,\theta^j}(x, y) = F^{-1}[F(I(x, y) \bullet G_{\lambda^i,\theta^j}(x, y)]$$

The parameter n of proposed improved energy feature is set to:

$$n=floor((N_\lambda +1) \lambda_i).$$

The improved energy feature is described by:

$$(O(0,0)^T, O(0,1)^T, \cdots, O(x,y), \cdots, O(N_\lambda, N_\theta)^T)^T,$$

where $O(x,y)$ is the column vector constituted by $O_{\lambda^i,\theta^j}(x, y)$. Then Principal Component Analysis is applied to obtain a smaller set of features. The chosen features make great contributions (ratio=0.9) to segment the input texture images. At last, K-means clustering algorithm is applied to obtain the segmented images.

Fig. 3 shows the segmentation results obtained with PCA algorithm and K-means classification algorithm for texture images containing two, four, and five textures. Fig.3 (a) shows three test images containing two, four, and five textures chosen from

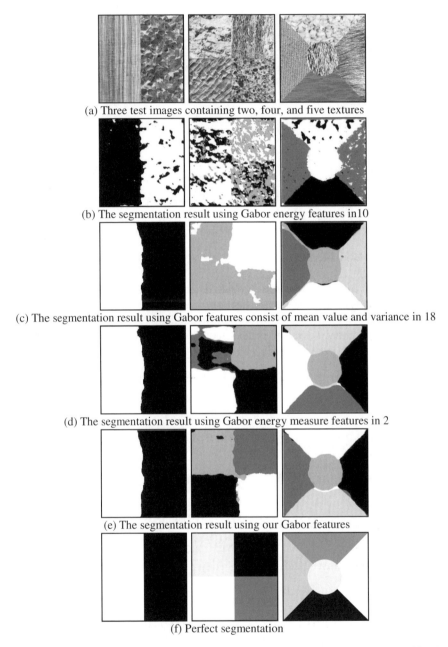

(a) Three test images containing two, four, and five textures

(b) The segmentation result using Gabor energy features in10

(c) The segmentation result using Gabor features consist of mean value and variance in 18

(d) The segmentation result using Gabor energy measure features in 2

(e) The segmentation result using our Gabor features

(f) Perfect segmentation

Fig. 3. Segmentation results obtained with PCA algorithm and K-means classification algorithm for texture images containing two, four, and five textures.(a) Three test images containing two, four, and five textures, (b) The segmentation result using Gabor energy features in 10,(c) The segmentation result using Gabor features consist of mean value and variance in 18,(d) The segmentation result using Gabor energy measure features in 2,(e) The segmentation result using our Gabor features,(f) Perfect segmentation.

brodatz database. Fig.3 (f) shows the perfect segmentation. Fig.3 (b) shows that the results using the Gabor energy features 10. It can be seen that the results are far away from perfect segmentation because the Gabor energy features are calculated by independent points. Fig.3 (c) shows the segmentation results using Gabor features consist of mean value and variance 18. The boundaries difficult to distinguish are segmented incorrectly. Especially, the result is so bad when the textures (e.g. texture image with four textures) are difficult to distinguish by human visual. Fig.3 (d) shows the segmentation results using Gabor energy measure features in 2. The results at boundaries are improved, but irregular texture is segmented incorrectly. Notice upper left corner of the texture images containing four textures. Fig.3 (e) shows the results using the proposed method. It can be seen that our feathers improve the separability of the boundaries (regardless of whether the textures' boundaries are easy to distinguish by human visual), and improve the separability of irregular textures as well.

5 Conclusions

Image textures are generally consist of organized patterns of quite regular subelements. Gabor function has been demonstrated to characterize a signal simultaneously in the temporal and frequency domains. This mechanism is similar to the primary visual cortex (V1) of mammal. Features are one of the most important factors in texture segmentation performance, so an improved energy feature using variable window size decided by scales of Gabor kernels has been proposed in this paper. Since we focus on observing the performance of new features, we use PCA as the dimension reduction method and K-means algorithm as clustering algorithm for simplicity. The experimental results show the improvement we have obtained. The reason is that the local properties in an appropriated neighbourhood can be captured better. Further research focus may be on testing the efficacy of this method on natural texture images. Moreover, how to improve the segmentation accuracy is a crucial problem to be investigated.

References

1. Chen, Y., Wang, R.-s.: A Method for Texture Classification by Integrating Gabor Filters and ICA. Chinese of Journal Electronics (Febrauary 2007)
2. Huang, C., Yang, G.: Texture Image Segmentation Based on Gabor Wavelet and Principle Component Analysis. Modern Electronics Technique (2005)
3. Chen, Y., Wang, R.: Texture Segmentation Using Independent Component Analysis of Gabor Features. In: 18th ICPR (2006)
4. Mittal, N., Mital, D.P., Chan, K.L.: Features for texture segmentation using Gabor filters, Image Processing And Its Applications (1999)
5. Wang, H., Wang, X.-H., Zhou, Y., Yang, J.: Color Texture Segmentation Using Quaternion-Gabor Filters. In: IEEE International Conference on Image Processing (2006)
6. Sandler, R., Lindenbaum, M.: Gabor Filter Analysis for Texture Segmentation. In: Conference on Computer Vision and Pattern Recognition Workshop (2006)
7. Basca, C.A., Brad, R.: Texture Segmentation. Gabor Filter Bank Optimization Using Genetic Algorithms. In: The International Conference on Computer as a Tool, EUROCON (2007)

8. Dunn, D., Higgins, W.E.: Optimal Gabor filters for texture segmentation. IEEE Transactions on Image Processing, 947–964 (1995)
9. Ma, L., Zhu, L.: Integration of the Optimal Gabor Filter Design and Local Binary Patterns for Texture Segmentation. In: IEEE International Conference on Integration Technology (2007)
10. Petkov, N., Subramanian, E.: Motion detection, noise reduction, texture suppression and contour enhancement by spatiotemporal Gabor filters with surround inhibition. Biological Cybernetics (September 2007)
11. Jiang, W., Lam, K.-M., Shen, T.-Z.: Edge detection using simplified Gabor wavelets. In: International Conference on Neural Networks and Signal Processing (2008)
12. Jiang, H., Cheng, Q., Zhang, Y., Liu, H., Wang, B.: An Adaptive Gabor Filtering Method and Its Application in Edge Detection. In: 2nd International Congress on Image and Signal Processing (2009)
13. Yang, Y., Sun, J.: Face Recognition Based on Gabor Feature Extraction and Fractal Coding. In: Third International Symposium on Electronic Commerce and Security, ISECS (2010)
14. Chen, X.G., Feng, J.-F.: Fast Gabor Filtering. ACTA Automatic SINICA 33(5) (May 2007)
15. Feichtinger, H.G.: Optimal iterative algorithms in Gabor analysis. In: Proceedings of the IEEE-SP International Symposium on Time-Frequency and Time-Scale Analysis (1994)
16. Grigorescu, S.E., Petkov, N., Kruizinga, P.: Comparison of Texture Features Based on Gabor Filters. IEEE Transactions On Image Processing 11(10) (October 2002)
17. Prasad, V.S.N., Domke, J.: Gabor Filter Visualization. Technical Report. University of Maryland (2005)
18. Zhang, M., Xu, T.: Novel method of target recognition based on Gabor wavelet texture feature. Physics Experimentation 24(4) (April 2004)

A Micro-Grid Communication Mechanism in Distributed Power System[*]

Hongbin Sun[1] and Xue Ye[2]

[1] School of Electrical Engineering and Information
Changchun Institute of Technology
Changchun, 130012, China
[2] Department of Electro-Mechanical Engineering
China Water Northeastern Investigation, Design & Research Co., Ltd
Changchun, 130012, China
binsun.hong@sohu.com

Abstract. In this paper, this paper proposes scalable communication mechanism for micro-grid of islanded power systems based on multi-agent system. Distributed intelligent multi-agent technology is applied to make the power system more reliable, efficient and capable of exploiting and integrating alternative sources of energy. we propose a scalable communication system within frequently agents migration and failure, it includes distribution and parallelization of message propagation method, a token-ring protocol that considerably improves the performance of, and failure detection mechanisms. We prove the correctness of the protocol and discuss the performance evaluation results obtained from simulations.

Keywords: scalable communication, micro-grid, protocol, agent.

1 Introduction

The Micro-grid (MG) concept assumes a cluster of loads and micro-sources operating as a single controllable system that provides both power and heat to its local area. [1,2] The intelligent grid achieves operational efficiency through distributed control, monitoring and energy management. [3]. A micro-grid can be regarded as a controlled entity within the power system that can be operated as a single aggregated load and as a small source of power or ancillary services supporting the network. Concurrently, the power system researchers focus on the potential value of multi-agent system (MAS) technology to the power industry [4–8]. Coordinating behavior of autonomous agents is a key issue in agent-oriented technique, which leads the MAS towards the system goal.

* This work is supported in part by the Key Project of the National Nature Science Foundation of China (No. 60534020), the National Nature Science Foundation of China (No. 60975059), the Cultivation Fund of the Key Scientific and Technical Innovation Project from Ministry of Education of China (No. 706024). A Project Supported by Scientific Research Fund of Jilin Provincial Education (20080202). A Project Supported by Scientific and Technological Planning Project of Jilin Province (20100565).

J. Zhang (Ed.): ICAIC 2011, Part III, CCIS 226, pp. 573–580, 2011.

A fundamental issue in the platform is how to support fault-tolerance communication for the agents. Micro-Grid Communication (MGC) means that, a group of mobile agents, no matter how frequently agents migrate, messages still need to be routed to all active and connected agents of Micro-Grid. Clearly, in scenarios that fully exploit mobility, their migration is not as tightly controlled, most of the conventional group communication techniques are inapplicable. Cao [9] proposed a generic mailbox-based scheme for the design of flexible and adaptive mobile agent communication protocols. Xu [10] presented a group communication system GCS-MA. Nevertheless, the support for reliable MEC has not been addressed. An efficient communication mechanism can considerably improve performance of the agent control of Micro-Grid. A series of implementation basic strategies have been proposed in our previous work [11], such as the RMI-IIOP-based transport mechanism. In this paper, we propose an MC system for agent Communication, which includes data structures, token-based message algorithm, token-based recover protocol, the agent membership migration algorithm and efficient distributed failure detection mechanism.

2   Micro-Grid Communication Mechanism Based on the Agents

A. Micro-Grid Communication Scheme

We have designed agent Communication in Fig.1 [11]. Agent's communications are constrained according to predefined speech act-based messages, which make up a agent communication language (ACL). FIPA ACL has been reused to design a high-level language called biological network communication language. A message payload contains one or more parameters that can be arranged randomly in the message. RMI-IIOP, an application-level protocol on the top of TCP has been used as the transport protocol for the messages. To ensure the interoperability among agents in wide-area environments, a sequence of interactions (actions and communications) between two agents (a community can also be viewed as a high-level agent) is defined by a interaction protocol (BIP). The BIP provides a reusable solution for various message sequences between agents.

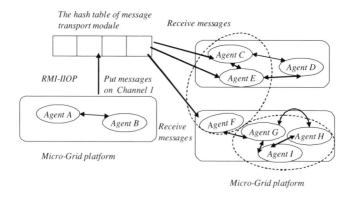

Fig. 1. Micro-Grid Communication Scheme

However, these researches are not always suitable for mobile agent community in Micro-Grid systems. Since migration path to agent is in no way limited and the migration speed of agents is decided by the network links. The asynchronous way of message passing and agent migration may cause the loss of messages during its migration. agents should be able to reliably send messages to all the Micro-Grid members and to react consistently upon failures of some of the members.

B. Protocol for Micro-Grid Communication

In order to support scalable Micro-Grid communication, we design the agent clusters, each of which is a collection of agents that reside on the same Micro-Grid platform. For every agent cluster, a special communication manager (SCM) is designed to manage the local agent cluster and provides community communication services. Then all SCM construct a ring-based overlay network [12, 13] for exchanging messages between clusters [Fig.2]. In the Micro-Grid platform, one ring is built for one group. The system is asynchronous. It implements reliable multicast communications and make up a fault-tolerant membership management sub-system.

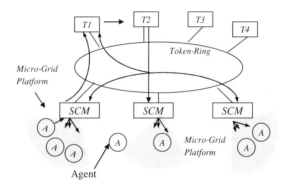

Fig. 2. Micro-Grid Communication Network

1) Data structures.
To broadcast messages on the ring, an SCM must hold the token. The token contains the following fields:

$$T = (EID, BID, Aru, Aru\_cr, Aru\_pr) \tag{1}$$

Where *EID* is the *ID* of Micro-Grid community, *BID* is the identifier of the ring on which the token is circulating. *Aru* is a sequence number used to determine if all SCMs on the ring have received all messages with sequence numbers less than or equal to this sequence. *Aru_cr* is the maximum sequence number of messages that have been delivered by all agents in the current rotation of token T. *Aru_pr* is assigned with the value of the *Aru_cr* in the previous rotation of token *T*.

Each SCM maintains a cluster view CV for local agent cluster.

$$CV = (EID, BID, MBList, M_{bur}^{seq}, M_{bur}^{rev}, Aru\_cv, \\ Aru\_pv, Aru\_sr) \tag{2}$$

Where *EID* is the ID of community, *BID* is the ID of the ring. *MBList* is the list of agents in the local agent cluster. M_{bur}^{seq} buffers messages that have been sent by agents, but not been multicast to BID. M_{bur}^{rev} buffers multicast messages received from BID. These messages are ordered by their sequence numbers in M_{bur}^{rev}. *Aru_cv* is the maximum sequence number of messages that have been delivered by local agents, *Aru_pv* is assigned with the value of the *Aru_cv* in the previous visiting of token T. *Aru_sr* is the safe sequence number. In M_{bur}^{rev}, messages whose sequence numbers are less than or equal to the *Aru_sr* can be safely released.

$$MBList = (Bio\_ID, L\_AD, Seq\_M, Sta\_M) \tag{3}$$

MBList is the list of agent in the local cluster. Bio_ID the ID of the agent; L_AD is the address of coordinator for the previous agent cluster where the agent resided; Seq_M is the maximum sequence number of messages that have been delivered by the agent; Sta_M is the status of the agent, *Ar* indicates arriving , *Le* is leaving , and *Re* is residing in current agent cluster.

A multicast message is MM.

$$MM = (MID, BID, Seq, Sender, Con) \tag{4}$$

Where *MID* is the ID of SMC originating the message, *BID* is the ID of the community. *Seq* is the sequence number of message *MM*. *Sender* is the ID of the agent sending message *MM*. *Con* is the content of message *MM*.

2) Micro-Grid communications Protocol and Algorithm

The protocol supports high-performance fault tolerant distributed systems. The mechanism provides totally ordered message delivery with low overhead high throughput and low latency using a logical token passing ring imposed on a broadcast domain, the key to its high performance is an effective control mechanism and protocol. We provides rapid the token-based algorithm, recover protocol, migration algorithm and failure detection mechanism.

(1) Token-based message algorithm

```
BEGIN
  If T.Aru >My_Aru
  then T.Aru= My_Aru
  Gettoken():
  End If
    GetSCM();
    C.getCV(T.BID);
        While ( M_bur^seq is not empty)
        Multicast Message MM □
        M_bur^seq.GetMessage();
        AssignSequenceNumber(MM, T.Aru+1);
        T.Aru=T.Aru+1;
        Send (MM, All SMC);
        SMB.removeMessage(MM);
      End
```

Min $(T.Aru\_cr, CV.Aru\_cv)$;
Minimum $(CV. M_{bur}^{rev})$;
$RMB.realseMessage(CV.Aru\_sr)$;
END

(2) Token-based membership protocol
BEGIN
    A SMC.buffers ( )
    //a message for retransmission until the message has been acknowledged by the other SMCs on the ring
    If a SMC. fails $=True$
      //fails to receive a particular message then other SMC.buffer
        //the other SMCs buffer until that message is received
        If $Token.loss\_timeout=True$ (foreign of join message received)
      Then SMC.collect
      // SMC information broadcasts that information in Join messages.
    SMC.updates $(My\_proc\_set, My\_fail\_set)$
      If My_proc_set and My_fail_set have changed,
    SMC.abandons $(membership)$,
    SMC.abandons.broadcast
    SMC. Reset
   End if
   Commit.token()
   //All of the members whose identifiers appear are committed to the membership.
   If receive Commit token$=True$
   Then convert (Commit token, regular token)
   \\ regular token for the new ring.
END

(3) The agent membership migration algorithm
E1 is the SMC of agent cluster BC1. E2 is the SMC of agent cluster BC2. CV1 is the cluster view for BC1. CV2 is the cluster view for BC2. R is the record of agent in CV1. R' is a copy of R, supposing a agent B_n migrates from BC1 to BC2.

BEGIN
 Send $(NOTIFY, EID, BID, Bio\_ID)$ to E1
 If (Authorized)
 Then E1.set $(R. Sta\_M=Le, R'.copy=E1)$
  B_n.Migrate $(BC2)$
   $E2$ inserts R' into the $CV2$, MBlist sets $R'. Sta\_M =Ar$.
   If $R'.Seq\_M < CV2.Aru\_cv$,
     E2.send $(push, EID, BID, Seq\_M)$
    Set $R'.Seq\_M= CV2.Aru\_cv$
    $R'. Sta\_M =Ar$
  $E2$ .send $(NOTIFY, EID, BID, Bio\_ID)$ to $E1$.
  End if
 END

(4) Efficient Distributed Failure Detection Mechanism

A randomized distributed failure detector algorithm must satisfy the speed and accuracy requirements, namely, every member failure is detected by some non-faulty group member within T time units after its occurrence; at any time instant, for every non-faulty member B_i(agent) not yet detected as failed, In this section, We present the detector algorithm for EC(Fig3).

Begin
$pr = pr + 1$,
Select (B_i)
Send a ping $(B_i; B_j ; pr) \rightarrow B_j$
GetAck $(B_i;B_j ; pr)$\\Wait for the worst-case message round-trip time for an Ack
                    $(B_i;B_j ; pr)$ message
If (not received Ack $(B_i;B_j ; pr)$)
  Select (K) \\Select k members randomly from view
  Send a ping $(B_i; B_j ; pr) \rightarrow K$ \\ Send each of them a ping-req($B_i;B_j$, pr) message
     GetAck $(B_i;B_j ; pr)$ \\Wait for an Ack $(B_i;B_j$, pr) message
                    until the end of period pr
     If (have not received Ack($B_i; B_j$, pr) message)
     Declare B_j as failed
     End if
End if
End

3 Simulation and Discussion

In previous work [11], we have implemented the prototype of agent simulation platform, including software, general objects and simulators in java. It supports pluggable functions and provides a generic easy-to-use programming API. The communication mechanism is implemented with modifications of functions and behaviours.

The simulation experiment is constructed on Windows 2000 operation system with Intel Pentium 4 processor (2.4 GHz) and 512 MB RAM. The developed simulator has the capabilities of evolution state management agent. A simulated network is an 18×24 topology one with 432 network hosts, and agents are deployed on the platform. The platform is initialized on all network hosts.

Table 1. The throughout with the increase of the agent

	FIPA Throughs	MGC Throughs
100 (agent)	1831	3000
200(agent)	1834	2910
300(agent)	1921	3012
400(agent)	1842	2870
500(agent)	1872	3100
600(agent)	1901	3005
700(agent)	1904	2950
800(agent)	1910	2890

Table 2. Migration frequency in different communication

	FIPA	MGC
0	54	54
20	37	30
40	29	21
60	25	18
80	25	15
100	22	15

Table 3. Response time in different communication

	FIPA	MGC
0	650	700
20	520	450
40	370	260
60	300	200
80	247	175
100	232	150

As Table 1 shows, with the MGC, two agents running on different platforms can send approximately 1,800 messages (i.e. 900 roundtrip interactions) per second with each other. This result is lower than communication with previous FIFA ACL, and we believe the message transport with MGC is efficient enough. Table 1 also shows that the throughput remains mostly constant as the number of agents grows up to 800, indicating that the bio-network platform has the perfect scalability.

The design of MGC can improve the adaptability, as in Table 3. Response time represents the efficiency of service, the simulation presents comparison between two experiment settings. In all 100 minutes, response time decrease slowly in the mechanism of EC. At the beginning, response time reaches 700ms. When the request is changed, the agents start operations, communication-driven control service as natural selection mechanism is used to choose useful and survivable agents from diverse ones.

Service is the cooperation among micro-grid with MGC. Each agent should negotiate with others based on the capabilities that can be executed. With the time passing by, the high effective services are presented in MGC. Finally, the response time decreases dramatically, until it reaches the minimum value to be about 150 ms. The design of EC can decrease the response time. Comparing the migration frequency in two experiment settings, as in Table 2, we can see that the excessive migration behaviours decrease for the agents of MGC, it exhibits the less cost.

4 Conclusion

We have designed and implemented the Micro-Grid mechanism. A series of protocol and algorithm are proposed, the experimental results on the throughput of the communication implementations, response time and migration frequency indicate their efficiency and scalability. The next work includes the improvement of dynamic multicast management protocol of the agent. It is necessary to increase the efficiency during problem solving. More experiments will be designed to evaluate the design in Micro-Grid service and management.

References

1. Lasseter, R.: Microgrids (distributed power generation). In: IEEE Power Engineering Society Winter Meeting, vol. 1, pp. 146–149 (2001)
2. Lasseter, R.: Microgrids. In: IEEE Power Engineering Society Winter Meeting, vol. 1, pp. 305–308 (2002)
3. Rahman, S., Pipattanasomporn, M., Teklu, Y.: Intelligent Distributed Autonomous Power System. IEEE Power Engineering Society General, 1–8 (2007)
4. Dimeas, A.L., Hatziargyriou, N.D.: Agent based control of Virtual Power Plants. In: IEEE International Conference on Intelligent Systems Applications to Power Systems, pp.1–6 (2007)
5. Nagata, T., Nakayama, H., Sasaki, H.: A multi-agent approach to power system normal state operations. In: IEEE Power Engineering Society General Meeting, pp. 1582–1586 (2002)
6. Logenthiran, T., Srinivasan, D., Wong, D.: Multi-agent coordination for DER in MicroGrid. In: IEEE International Conference on Sustainable Energy Technologies, pp. 77–82 (2008)
7. Shrestha, G.B., Kai, S., Goel, L.K.: An efficient power pool simulator for the study of competitive power market. In: Power Engineering Society Winter Meeting, 1365–1370 (2000)
8. Solanki, J.M., Khushalani, S., Schulz, N.N.: A multi-agent solution to distribution systems restoration. IEEE Transactions on Power System, 1026–1034 (2007)
9. Cao, J.N., Feng, X.Y., Lu, J.: Design of adaptive and reliable mobile agent communication protocols. In: Proceedings Of The 22nd International Conference on Distributed Computing Systems, pp. 427:471–427:478. IEEE, Vienna (2002)
10. Xu, W., Cao, J.N., Jin, B.H.: GCS-MA: A group communication system for mobile agents. Journal of Network and Computer Applications 30(3), 1153–1172 (2007)
11. Ding, Y.S., Gao, L., Ruan, D.: Communication mechanisms in ecological network-based grid middleware for service emergence. Information Sciences 177(3), 722–733 (2007)
12. Murphy, A., Picco, G.P.: Reliable communication for highly mobile agents. In: Proceedings of the 1st International Symposium on Agent Systems and Applications And The 3rd International Symposium on Mobile Agents, California, pp. 141–150 (1999)
13. Gupta, I., Chandra, T.D., Goldszmidt, G.S.: On scalable and efficient distributed failure detectors. In: Proceedings of the 20th Annual ACM Symposium on Principles of Distributed Computing, New York, USA, pp. 170–179 (2001)

A New Time-Delay Compensation Method in NCS Based on T-S Fuzzy Model[*]

Xiaoshan Wang and Yanxin Zhang

School of Electronics and Information Engineering
Beijing Jiao Tong University
Beijing, China
xiaoshanwang2011@sohu.com

Abstract. The end-to-end time-delay induced by the network is one of the main issues in Networked Control Systems (NCS). In order to compensate the delay more effectively, this paper presents a novel approach to predict it on line using the T-S fuzzy method. The basic idea of this method is to assume that the system dynamics can be described by a set of rules rather than a single one, and the final output is given by a combination of the estimates according to all these fuzzy rules. GK fuzzy clustering will be used in the process of building the T-S fuzzy model and generating the predicted values. By numerical simulations, it is proved that the T-S fuzzy method can predict and compensate the time delay effectively.

Keywords: networked control system, round trip time, T-S fuzzy model, GK fuzzy clustering, delay compensator.

1 Introduction

The network time-delay is often a key parameter in Networked Control Systems (NCS), which directly affects the control performance and even the stability of control systems. So it is significant to investigate the characteristics of it.

Generally speaking, the research on network delays can be divided into two categories:

One category is to investigate the entire or marginal distribution of delays using statistical theory. In this aspect, Pareto distribution with a heavy tail [1], Weibull distribution [2], and the shifted Gamma distribution [3, 4] all have been put forward. However, because of the self similarity nature and the random nature of the network traffic, Poisson distribution is proved that it is not suitable to model the network delay effectively [5].

The other category is to model the end-to-end time-delay based on system identification and time series analysis. In this aspect, both linear and nonlinear models have been proposed, including the linear autoregressive (AR) models [6], and the nonlinear functional networks [7].

* This paper was supported in part by National Natural Science Foundation (79970114).

J. Zhang (Ed.): ICAIC 2011, Part III, CCIS 226, pp. 581–590, 2011.
© Springer-Verlag Berlin Heidelberg 2011

In this paper, we develop a novel approach to predict the end-to-end delay using the T-S fuzzy method. The basic idea of this method is to assume that the system dynamics can be described by a set of rules, each of which corresponds to a linear AR model. And the final output is given by a combination of the estimates from all the AR models. Both in the process of model building and prediction calculating, GK fuzzy clustering plays a key role.

The rest of this paper is organized as follows: In Section 2, a brief description of the end-to-end delay data collected and some results from preliminary data analysis are given. In Section 3, the T-S fuzzy method based on a set of fuzzy rules is presented. Numerical results using real measurement data are given in Section 4. And Section 5 concludes the paper.

2 RTT Data Analysis

In the NCS, the time-delay consists of three parts: 1) from sensor to controller τ_{sc}; 2) from controller to actuator τ_{ca}; 3) calculating time of controller τ_c. τ_{sc} and τ_{ca}, which compose the main part of the time-delay are both one-way transmission time (OTT). However, as the end-to-end round trip time (RTT) can be conveniently measured by Ping Program only, it is used here to study as a first step, and the next step is to study the OTT later.

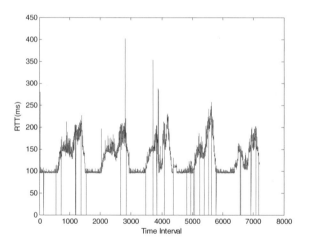

Fig. 1. The RTT sequence collected for 5 days

Using the ping program PingTesterPro, we collected the RTT data as a time series. In our experiment, the source host is set in the dormitory of Beijing Jiao Tong University, and the destination host is the Google server. The ping program is configured to send the probing packet of 32 bytes at a constant time interval 1ms, because in control applications, signals are often being sent at regular time intervals between the controller, sensors and actuators. If one probing packed is lost in the experiment, the measured value of this interval will be set to zero. The measurement is carried out for 5 days, and the whole RTT sequence is shown in Fig 1. We can find that the RTT process is relatively periodical and slow-varying intuitively. The average of the RTTs is 129.1046ms and the packet loss rate is 0.0046. It is shown that the packet loss rate is very small.

3 The Fuzzy T-S Method

A. Description of the Fuzzy T-S Model

In the T-S fuzzy method, a set of rules is assumed to represent the typical system patterns or structures. Each of the rules corresponds to an AR model. Fig.2 shows the framework of the whole T-S fuzzy model.

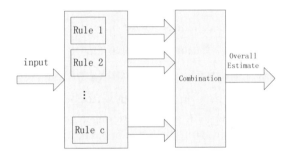

Fig. 2. The whole T-S fuzzy model

In this model, the $i-th$ rule is as follows:

R_i : If $y(t-1)$ is A_{i1},..., $y(t-n)$ is A_{in} ,

$$\text{then } y^i(t) = \sum_{j}^{n} a_{ij} y(t-j). \tag{1}$$

where A_{ik} is a fuzzy set ($i = 1, 2,...,c$, $k = 1, 2,...,n$) whose membership function is $\mu_{A_{ij}}$, a_{ij} is the consequent parameter, $y(t)$ is the RTT at t , n is the order of the input vector, and $y^i(t)$ is the output of the consequent function, i.e. the estimated RTT at t according to the $i-th$ fuzzy rule.

For convenience, note that

$$\begin{cases} x_1 = x_1(t) = y(t-1) \\ x_2 = x_2(t) = y(t-2) \\ \vdots \\ x_n = x_n(t) = y(t-n) \end{cases} \tag{2}$$

Choosing x_1, x_2, $\cdots$, x_n as the input vectors, the T-S fuzzy model (1) can be transformed by fuzzy clustering into the following form:

R_i: If z is $\overline{z}_i$, then $y_i = \theta_i^T z$,

$$i = 1, 2, \cdots, c, \ k = 1, 2, ..., N . \tag{3}$$

where z is the input vector, $z_k = [x_1, \cdots x_n]^T \in R^n$, N is the number of input vectors. $\overline{z}_i$ is the central vector of the $i-th$ cluster, $\overline{z}_i = [\overline{x}_{i1}, ... \overline{x}_{in}]^T \in R^n$, μ_i is the fuzzy membership of input vector belonging to the $i-th$ cluster, y_i is the consequent output of the $i-th$ fuzzy rule, θ_i is the consequent parameter vector of the $i-th$ fuzzy rule, $\theta_i = [a_{i1}, \cdots, a_{in}]^T \in R^n$, and c is the number of fuzzy rules.

In order to determine the parameter vector θ_i of the $i-th$ fuzzy rule, we must determine the central vector $\overline{z}_i$ and the membership μ_i of each input vector first. From the view of fuzzy clustering, $\overline{z}_i$ can be taken as the center of the fuzzy cluster, and μ_i can be taken as the membership of input vector belonging to the cluster. Both of them can be obtained via GK fuzzy clustering algorithm, which expands the adaptive distance dynamic clustering algorithm in the fuzzy field [8].

B. G-K Fuzzy Clustering

The aim of fuzzy clustering is to get the membership matrix $U = [\mu_{ij}]_{c \times N}$ and the clustering center matrix $\overline{Z} = [\overline{z}_1, \overline{z}_2, \cdots \overline{z}_c]^T$ by seeking the minimum of the cost function, where c is the number of fuzzy rules, and N is the number of vectors to be clustered. The cost function of GK fuzzy clustering algorithm is:

$$J(Z, V, U) = \sum_{i=1}^{c} \sum_{j=1}^{N} (\mu_{ij})^m \left\| z_j - \overline{z}_i \right\|_A^2 \tag{4}$$

where Z is a set consists of the vectors to be clustered, $z_j \in Z$ is the factor of Z, $j = 1, 2, ..., N$, $U = [\mu_{ij}]_{c \times N}$ is a fuzzy membership matrix of Z, $\overline{Z} = [\overline{z}_1, \overline{z}_2, \cdots \overline{z}_c]^T$, $\overline{z}_1, \overline{z}_2, \cdots \overline{z}_c$ are central vectors of GK fuzzy clustering, μ_{ij} is the membership of z_j belonging to the $i-th$ cluster, $\mu_{ij} \in [0, 1]$, $\sum_{i=1}^{c} \mu_{ij} = 1$, and $m \in [1, +\infty)$ is a adjustable parameter, which is often chosen as $m = 2$.

The specific steps of GK fuzzy clustering are as follows:

1) Choose the number of fuzzy clusters c, fuzzy index m, and iterative termination condition $\varepsilon > 0$. Initialize the fuzzy membership matrix U, and let iterative time $l = 0$.

2) Renew v_i as

$$z_i = \frac{\sum\limits_{j=1}^{N}(\mu_{ij})^m z_j}{\sum\limits_{j=1}^{N}(\mu_{ij})^m} \tag{5}$$

3) Calculate the clustering covariance matrix F_i as

$$F_i = \frac{\sum\limits_{j=1}^{N}(\mu_{ij})^m (z_j - \overline{z}_i)(z_j - \overline{z}_i)^T}{\sum\limits_{j=1}^{N}(\mu_{ij})^m} \tag{6}$$

4) Calculate the distance norm as

$$D_{ij}^2 = (z_j - \overline{z}_i)^T A_i (z_j - \overline{z}_i) \tag{7}$$

where A_i is a positive definite matrix

$$A_i = \det(\rho_i F_i)^{\frac{1}{d+1}} F_i^{-1} \tag{8}$$

ρ_i is constant for a certain clustering.

5) Renew the fuzzy membership matrix U as

$$\mu_{ij} = \frac{1}{\sum\limits_{k=1}^{c}(\frac{D_{ij}}{D_{kj}})^{\frac{2}{m-1}}} \tag{9}$$

6) If $\left\| U^{(l+1)} - U^l \right\| < \varepsilon$, then stop, otherwise let $l = l+1$, and then return to step 2).

Following the above steps, we can get all the central vectors and the memberships of each input belonging to different clusters. Based on them, the parameters of each fuzzy rule can be estimated, and then the whole T-S fuzzy model can be built.

C. Parameter Estimation

Given the input and output data $\{z_j, y_j\}$, $j = 1, 2, \cdots, N$, N is the number of the data vectors used for model building, z_j is the $j-th$ input,

$z_j = [x_{1j}, x_{2j}, \cdots, x_{nj}]^T \in R^n$, which composes the observation matrix Z_e . Each

row vector of Z_e is z_j^T , $Z_e \in R^{N \times n}$. And the weight of each fuzzy rule μ_{ij}

($i = 1, 2, \cdots, c$, $j = 1, 2, \cdots, N$) composes a diagonal matrix Γ_i , $\Gamma_i \in R^{N \times N}$,

$diag\{\Gamma_i\} = \{\mu_{1i}, \mu_{2i}, ..., \mu_{Ni}\}$, $i = 1, 2, \cdots, c$. Thus a new matrix Z can be
obtained.

$$Z = [\Gamma_1 Z_e, \Gamma_2 Z_e, \cdots, \Gamma_c Z_e] \tag{10}$$

In addition, the estimated parameter vector θ is $\theta = [\theta_1^T, \theta_2^T, \cdots, \theta_c^T]^T$, where

$\theta_i = [a_{i1}, a_{i2}, ..., a_{in}]^T$. Thus, the model (3) can be formulated as follows:

$$Y = Z \cdot \theta + e \tag{11}$$

where $Y = [y_1, y_2, ..., y_N]^T$, e is the approximation error. In order to estimate the
parameter vector θ of the T-S fuzzy model, the recursive least squares method with
forgetting factor is used here, because the forgetting factor can overcome the data
saturation in the process of estimation.

D. Calculating the Prediction Delay

According to the above methods and steps, After the T-S fuzzy model for prediction
is built as described from 3.1 to 3.3, the future delays over K intervals can be
predicted on line based on the model. The specific steps are as follows: Given a new
input vector $z_j = [x_{1j}, x_{2j}, \cdots, x_{nj}]^T \in R^n$, which consists of the latest n real RTT
data that are already known. $j = N + 1, N + 2, ...$.

1) Let $l = 1$.

2) Calculate the distance norm by (7), as the $\bar{z}_i$ and A_i have already be obtained
in the model building.

3) Calculate the fuzzy membership matrix $U = [\mu_{ij}]$ for the new input vector by (9).

4) Calculate the output of the T-S fuzzy model as

$$y_j = \sum_{i=1}^{c} \mu_{ij} z_j^T \theta_i \tag{12}$$

The $j - th$ y_j is the latest prediction of RTT.

5) Let $j = j + 1$, $z_j = [x_{2j}, \cdots, x_{nj}, y_j]^T$.

6) If $l = K$, then stop, otherwise let $l = l + 1$, and then return to step 2).

Following the above steps, the future RTT over K intervals can be predicted in
order on line.

4 Numerical Results and Simulations

The RTT data described in Section 2 are used to implement our T-S fuzzy method. We cut the RTT sequence collected into two parts: RTT data of the first 3 days for training model, and the other RTT data of the other 2 days for testing the prediction error.

According to the discussion in [9], the order of AR models was chosen fixed at 4. Let the predicting horizon K is 1, we can get the sequence of predicted RTT over 1 interval using the T-S fuzzy method. The real RTT data and the predicted sequence are shown in Fig.3 together.

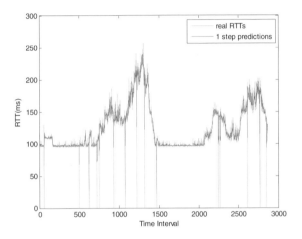

Fig. 3. RTT sequence

The number of fuzzy rules c can also be chosen for different values. In this paper, we **build** the T-S fuzzy model from $c = 2$ to $c = 6$. We compare the T-S fuzzy method with the method based on the linear AR model, which can be taken as the fuzzy model for $c = 1$. The expection and variance from different models are shown in Table 1.

The time-delay compensator which is based on the T-S fuzzy method proposed in this paper, can be applied to a servo motor control system which is described in [10], the model of the plant was identified as:

$$G(z^{-1}) = \frac{B(z^{-1})}{A(z^{-1})} = \frac{0.05409z^{-2} + 0.115z^{-3} + 0.0001z^{-4}}{1 - 1.12z^{-1} - 0.213z^{-2} + 0.335z^{-3}}$$

where the input is the voltage applied to the dc motor, and the output is the voltage sampled from an angle sensor. The sampling time is $0.1s$. When the communication time delay is not considered, a controller is designed as:

$$u(t) = \frac{D(z^{-1})}{C(z^{-1})} = \frac{0.502 - 0.5z^{-1}}{1 - z^{-1}}$$

The step response of the closed-loop control system without network time-delay is shown in Fig.4, which indicates that the control performance is good.

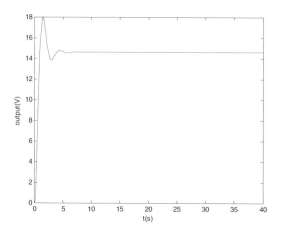

Fig. 4. Simulation of networked control system without time delays

However, as is shown in Fig.5, the system will be no longer stable if the RTT delays collected exist in the network communication. The simulation result confirms that the performance of the closed-loop control system degrades rapidly with network delays.

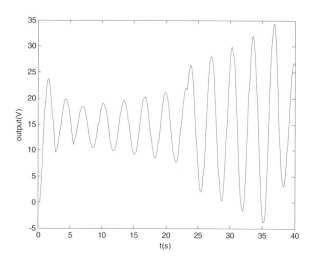

Fig. 5. Simulation of networked control system with time delays

In order to compensate the time-delays, a compensator based on the T-S fuzzy method is adopted. As is shown in Fig.6, the closed-loop control system is stable with the compensator. It confirms that, the T-S fuzzy method can compensate the network time-delay of the servo motor control system effectively.

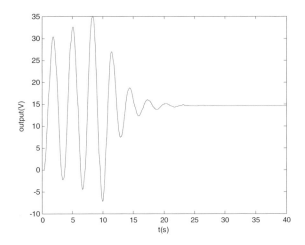

Fig. 6. Simulation of networked control system with compensator

5   Conclusion

In this paper, a novel approach using the T-S fuzzy method is proposed to predict time-delay in NCS. The basic idea of this method is to assume that the system dynamics can be described by a set of rules rather than a single one, and the final output is given by a combination of the estimates according to all these fuzzy rules. As a future work, the T-S fuzzy method will be used to predict delays for different network communication environments, especially for those of high packet loss rate. And we also try to use this method to predict packet losses as well as time delays. Based on the predictions, new compensators can be designed and applied in networked control systems.

References

1. Wei Zhang, J.H.: Modeling end-to-end delay using pareto distribution. In: Second International Conference on Internet Monitoring and Protection, ICIMP 2007, pp. 21–27 (2007)
2. Hernandez, J.A., Phillips, I.W.: Weibull mixture model to characterise end-to-end Internet delay at coarse time-scales. IEEE Proceedings: Communications 153(2), 295–304 (2006)
3. Bolot, J.-C.: End-to-end packet delay and loss behavior in the internet. Journal of High Speed Networks 2, 305–323 (1993)
4. Mukherjee, A.: On the dynamics and significance of low frequency components of internet load. Internetworking Chichester 5(4), 163–205 (1994)

5. Paxson, V.: Wide-area traffic: the failure of Poisson modeling. IEEE/ACM Transactions on Networking 3(3), 226–244 (1995)
6. Hong, W., Chao, G.: Internet Time-delay Prediction Based on Autoregressive and Neural Network Model. In: Proceedings of International Conference on Communications, Circuits and Systems, ICCCAS, vol. 3, pp. 1758–1761 (2006)
7. Zhu, C., Pei, C., Li, J.: Functional Networks Based Internet End-to-End Delay Dynamics. In: Proceedings - International Conference on Advanced Information Networking and Application (AINA), vol. 2, pp. 540–543 (2004)
8. Gustafson, D.E., Kessel, W.C.: Fuzzy clustering with a fuzzy covariance matrix. In: Proceedings of the IEEE Conference on Decision and Control, pp. 761–766 (1978)
9. Hu, W., Liu, G., Rees, D.: Event-Driven Networked Predictive Control. IEEE Transactions on Industrial Electronics 54(3), 1603–1613 (2007)

Web Data Extraction Based on Structure Feature[*]

Ma Anxiang, Gao Kening, Zhang Xiaohong, and Zhang Bin

College of Information Science and Engineering
Northeastern University
Shenyang, China
maanxiang2011@sohu.com

Abstract. Most existing methods of Web data extraction realize goals based on DOM tree analysis or wrapper building. However, applicability and efficiency of these methods need to be further improved. According to the amount of information, Web pages will be divided into two structure types which are 1:1 and 1:N type respectively. As same type of Web pages has similar structure features, the paper proposes an approach of two-phase Web data extraction base on structure feature. In the phase of samples learning, structure feature and depository rules of Web pages are obtained according to the text feature of sample pages. In the phase of information extraction, Web data extraction is implemented by matching the page to be extracted with depository rules in knowledge base. Experimental results show that the approach proposed in the paper has well applicability and high efficiency.

Keywords: Web data extraction, structure feature, text feature, depository rules.

1 Introduction

With the rapid development of World Wide Web, users can access a variety of information. However, users have to spend a lot of time to find what they really want from the vast amount of information. In this case, it is necessary to design an efficient method of Web data extraction [1].

At present, there are a number of Web data extraction tools which are based on the sample learning to generate extraction rules [2,3], or based on the HTML tag structure of the page [4-9]. Although these methods can achieve semi-automatic or automatic data extraction, applicability and efficiency need to be further improved.

According to the amount of information carried by Web pages, the Web pages will be divided into two structure types which are 1:1 and 1:N respectively. The type of 1:1 refers to the page that contains only a logical record, such as news pages. The type of 1:N refers to the page that contains multiple logical records, such as notebooks quote pages or query result pages from search engine. As same type of Web pages has similar structure features, the paper proposes an approach of Web data extraction base

---

[*] This work is supported by "The Fundamental Research Funds for the Central Universities" (N100304003), "National Natural Science Foundation of China" (61073062), and "Natural Science Foundation of LiaoNing Province" (20102060).

J. Zhang (Ed.): ICAIC 2011, Part III, CCIS 226, pp. 591–599, 2011.

on structure feature. In the phase of samples learning, structure feature and depository rules of Web pages are obtained according to the text feature of sample pages. In the phase of data extraction, Web data extraction is implemented by matching the page to be extracted with depository rules in knowledge base. In this way, the flexibility of the wrapper is greatly improved.

2   Related Researches

There are a number of semi-automated or automated Web data extraction tools. References [2-5] get the extraction rules by learning hand-marked sample pages. These methods obviously require lots of human intervention which make the generation and maintenance of wrapper extremely complex.

References [4] [5] separate the data records by DOM tree structure and visual information of Web page. Reference [6] uses open source software supporting Deep Web information extraction. In fact, it only simplifies workload and complexity of basic work. References [7] [8] obtain data records only by DOM tree structure information. Since a large number of Web pages do not follow W3C's HTML specification and DOM tree building is very complex, methods mentioned above have poor applicability.

Reference [9] completely uses visual information of Web page such as location, layout and appearance characteristics to locate and extract data records. Although this method doesn't rely on the DOM structure of Web page, it is very difficult to get accurate visual information because of semi-structure of Web data.

In summary, it is necessary to improve applicability and efficiency of Web data extraction methods.

3   Web Data Extraction Based on Structure Feature

Through studying a large number of Web pages, we find that same type of Web pages has similar structure features. For example, notebooks quote pages usually use table which consists of rows and columns to store Web data. The tables are divided into horizontal and vertical cases. For the horizontal table, "row" means one record, "column" means an attribute and the number of attributes means the width of table. Another example is that news pages usually include structural features such as title, time, source, author and body. Whether news pages or notebooks quote pages, the structure feature can be obtained through analysis of text feature of the data of sample pages such as data type, string length and special string.

The process of Web data extraction based on structure feature is shown in figure 1. The approach includes two phases which are samples learning and data extraction respectively.

In the phase of samples learning, structure feature and depository rules of Web page which are the basis of processing similar pages are obtained by sample pages learning. When giving a sample page, since Web page usually consists of many parts such as navigating segment, text segment and advertising segment, text segment of Web pages is firstly identified and obtained through page segmenting algorithm [10].

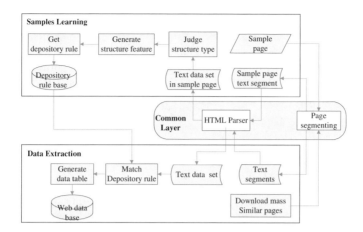

Fig. 1. Web data extraction mechanism based on structure feature

Then text data in HTML tags are obtained by analysis of HTML source file of text segment. Finally, structure feature and depository rule of sample page are obtained according to text features of text data.

In the phase of data extraction, firstly, the Web pages similar to sample page are downloaded. Then the text data in text segments of Web pages are extracted through segmenting processing. Finally, without analysing the structure feature of Web page, the text data can be directly stored into relational database by matching depository rules in knowledge base.

4 Samples Learning

A. Judging Structure Type

Given the text segment of sample page, we need to extract the text data in text segment. By analysing a large number of Web pages, we find that most text data is stored in "*<td>*" or "*<div>*" tags. For example, the title in a piece of news is usually stored between *<td>* tag and *</td>* tag. Therefore the paper uses HTML Parser tool to filter *<td>* and *<div>* tags, and get the text data in sample page.

Through studying number of pages, we get a conclusion that the structure type of Web page can be identified by analysing the statistical characteristics of text data. Here are the statistical characteristics used in the paper:

[1] The total number of text data item in text segment of sample page called *TotalItemCount*;

[2] The number of digital text data item in text segment of sample page called *DigitItemCount*;

[3] The total number of HTML tags in text segment of sample page called *AllTagCount*;

[4] The number of hyperlink tags in text segment of sample page called *HrefTagCount*;

When *TotalItemCount* and *DigitItemCount* both have high values, the structure type of sample page is judged as 1:1.

For the result page from search engine, since the number of hyperlink tags is higher than other page, we judge this kind of pages by the proportion of hyperlink tags. When satisfying $RATE\_LOW \leq HrefTagCount/AllTagCount \leq RATE\_HIGH$, the structure type of sample page is judged as 1:N. In the experiment, we set maximum value $RATE\_HIGH=0.25$ and minimum value $RATE\_LOW=0.18$ respectively.

B. Generating Structure Feature

1) Generating Structure Feature of 1:1 type

We take news page as example to illustrate how to get the structure feature of 1:1 type. The text segment of news page usually consists of six attributes, namely: title, time, author, source, source URL and body. The composition of news page is usually fixed, only some of the news sites may miss several attributes. Therefore, according to the feature of each attribute, we design related heuristic rules. Heuristic rules can help to judge the content of text data item by analysing the text feature of text data.

Here are heuristic rules to judge whether text data item Ψ is news title.

- The position of Ψ in all text data items is below a value. In the experiment, we set the value *TotalItemCount*/2;
- The number of characters in Ψ is within the range interval. Letters γ denotes the minimum of range, and v denotes the maximum. In the experiment, we set $\gamma=5$ and $v=30$. Note that an English word is a character.

News time is identified by matching regular expression ($yyyy[/|-|,|.|]mm[/|-|,|.]dd$).

Similarly, through the text feature text data items can be identified whether is belong to other attributes such as author, source and source URL. For the news page missing some attributes, the content of missing attribute is set null.

2) Generating Structure Feature of 1:N type

The pages which use table to store data records are called table page. We take table page as example to illustrate how to get the structure feature of 1:N type. For the table page, we need to judge whether the table is horizontal case or vertical case. For multiple records in table, the contents of the same attribute have the same format. For example, the format of attribute "price" contents of two different data records are both digital. According to this feature, it will be convenient to identify the structure feature of the table without involving natural language analysis.

Given two text data items with digital characters α and β, three factors are given as basis to judge whether text features of α and β is similar. When satisfying any of the following factors, α and β are similar.

- The string length of α and β are equal;
- Special character such as "$", "%", "@", "¥", "‰", "℃", "m²" etc. appears in both α and β;
- Decimal appears in both α and β.

When satisfying any of the following factors, α and β are not similar.

- Chinese characters only appear in one of α and β;
- English characters only appear in one of α and β.

Based on the above analysis, given the text data items in   table page, this paper gives the following steps to generate structural features of 1:N type.

Step1: Judge whether there are the text data items including date. If having, record the position of these text data items, and store them in array *DateItemPosition*[]. Goto Step5.

Step2: Judge whether there are the text data items including digit. If having, goto Step3, else goto Step4.

Step3: Find text data items including digit whose text features are similar with each other. Record the position of these text data items, and store them in array *DigitItemPosition*[]. Goto Step5.

Step4: Judge the similarity of text data items by calculating the number of Chinese characters or English words. Record the position of similar text data items, and store them in array *StringItemPosition*[].

Step5: If the position information of similar text data items satisfy arithmetic sequence, we use β to denote interval of arithmetic sequence. If $\beta>1$, then the table is horizontal case, each row means one record, and each record has β attributes. If $\beta=1$, then the table is vertical case, and each column means one record. If $\beta(\beta>1)$ is less than *DigitItemPosition*[0], then the first β items in all text data items are table header, else the table has not table header.

3) Getting Depository rule

Depository rule is used to store text data of Web page into relational database. Based on structure features of sample page, we can get depository rule described by XML. Because the depository rule of 1:1 type is relatively simple, the paper will take ticket list page from *southwest.com* as example to illustrate how to describe the depository rule of table page.

Depart	Arrive	Flight # (% ontime)	Routing	Travel Time (hh:min)	Business Select $444	Anytime $419	Senior $257	Wanna Get Away $271 - $380
8:00 AM	12:30 PM	5018 / 3999	1 stop Change Planes LAS	7:30	○ $444	○ $419	Available	○ $271 Web Only!
11:20 AM	4:20 PM	654 / 1884	1 stop Change Planes PHX	8:00	○ $444	○ $419	Available	○ $271 Web Only!
3:05 PM	7:30 PM	1121 / 1680	1 stop Change Planes LAS	7:25	○ $444	○ $419	Available	○ $271 Web Only!
5:25 PM	10:00 PM	878 / 822	1 stop Change Planes MDW	7:35	○ $444	○ $419	Sold Out	○ $380

Fig. 2. Ticket list page from *southwest.com*

Through structure type judging and structure feature generating, we know the ticket list page is horizontal case, the table has header and each record has nine attributes.

In order to describe depository rule of Web page, we need to get table header as custom tags of XML document. In addition, a *<interval>* tag which means the number of attributes in each record is needed. In each pair of attribute name tags, fill in the starting position of the corresponding data. We can locate the data concern and the structure of related table by the starting position of attribute and interval value. Thus, a XML document to descript depository rule is automatically generated and stored in the knowledge base.

Base on the above analysis, depository rule of ticket list page shown in figure 2 can be described as following.

```
<southwestticketbooking>
        <depart name="depart">9</depart>
        <arrive name="arrive">10</arrive>
        <flight name=" flight ">11</flight>
        <routing name=" routing ">12</routing>
        ......
        <interval    name="number    of    attributes    per
record">9</interval>
        </wangbayonghuliebiao>
```

The name of XML document is composed of Web site name and domain name. The domain name refers to semantic category or navigating category of the page belonging to. For example, depository rule document of ticket list page from *southwest.com* is named as *southwest_ticketbooking*. The naming method of database tables in the phase of data extraction is similar with repository rule document.

5 Data Extraction

In the phase of data extraction, Web pages similar with sample page are processed according to structure features and depository rules obtained in the phase of samples learning. Data extraction mainly includes three modules which are depository rules matching, database tables generating and data storing.

Depository rules matching module is used to find related depository rule in knowledge base according to the site name and domain name of Web pages. If having not related depository rules in knowledge base, we should obtain structure feature and depository rule by sample learning, else we can directly stored data into database table according to depository rule.

Contents of Web pages of 1:1 type are relatively fixed. For example, news pages are usually composed of six parts which are title, time, author, source, source URL and body respectively. For most pages of 1:N type, table headers are different from each other. Therefore, we dynamically create database table according to depository rules. Given depository rule, corresponding XML document is parsed to get attribute name, start position of attribute contents and interval value, then database table can be created.

Based on the above work, we can store the text data in array into relational database table according to depository rule. Because array is a linear list, the paper converts the text data into two-dimensional array in order to consistent with database table. The algorithm of data storing is shown as following.

Algorithm 1. Text data storing algorithm
Input: array[](meaning the array storing text data), depository rule
Output: True (meaning that text data was successfully stored into the database table) or False
1.   Delete the table header in array[], and keep the contents of attributes
2.   Parse depository rule, namely XML document, to get interval value
3.   Set "row" counter i=1 and "column" counter j=1 for two-dimensional array result[][]
4.   Set variable v=1
5   While (not reaching the end of array[]) do
6.   for (j; j<interval; j++) do
7.   text data in array[v] is assigned to result[i][j]
8.   v++
9.   end for
10   j:=1
11.   i++
12. end while
13. Generating SQL statement according to result[i][j]
14. if (SQL statement is not successfully executed) then
15.   return False
16   else return True
17. end if

6   Performance Evaluation

In the experiment, we use recall and precision to evaluate performance of data extraction. For the five data sources of 1:N type (DS$_1$: http://biz.finance.sina.com.cn/stock/; DS$_2$: http://quotes.stock.163.com/order_list.jsp?type=0; DS$_3$: http://quote2.eastmoney.com/external_rank_list1.html; DS$_4$: http://quote.stock.hexun.com/urwh/ggph/h_a_rise.shtml; DS$_5$: http://stock.business.sohu.com/t/sort.php?sh_sz=0&isB =0), performance test is conducted, and the result is shown in table 1. In table 1, "#ap" and "#ar" mean the number of pages and records respectively, "#ep" and "#er" mean the number of pages and records extracted respectively, "#cp" and "#cr" mean the number of pages and records correctly extracted respectively.

After generating structure features and depository rules, above experiment is conducted immediately. The result in table 1 shows that the approach proposed in the paper has well performance. However, after a period of time, structure feature of Web page may be changed. If depository rules in knowledge base are not timely updated, performance of data extraction will be affected. Related experiment result is shown in table 2.

Table 1. Performance of data extraction for 1:N pages

DS	#ap	#ar	#ep	#er	#cp	#cr	recall (%)	precision (%)
DS$_1$	17	1602	17	1602	17	1590	100	99.25
DS$_2$	17	806	16	755	15	698	93.67	92.45
DS$_3$	41	830	40	803	37	730	96.75	90.91
DS$_4$	32	789	31	744	29	689	94.3	92.6
DS$_5$	54	807	49	732	45	666	90.7	90.98

Table 2. Performance of data extraction for 1:N pages after a period of time

DS	after one day(%)		after one month(%)		after one year (%)	
	recall	precision	recall	precision	recall	precision
DS$_1$	100	98.45	98.3	95.37	93.75	89.46
DS$_2$	93.67	92.45	90.8	88.75	85.45	83.75
DS$_3$	96.75	90.91	95.25	87.9	90.7	82.9
DS$_4$	94.3	90.18	90.27	88.6	86.3	83.27
DS$_5$	90.7	90.98	88.9	88.1	83.26	84.5

In order to improve the performance of data extraction, we need to set a time threshold by analyzing varying pattern of Web pages, then update structure features and depository rules according to time threshold.

7 Conclusion

The paper proposes the approach of Web data extraction based on structure feature. In the phase of sample learning, structure features and depository rules can be automatically generated by analysing the text feature of data. It reduces the human intervention during the extraction rules generating. In the phase of data extraction, Web data can be directly stored into relational database according to depository rule. It improves the efficiency of data extraction.

References

1. Aykut, F., Stuart, M.E., Nor, A.Y., et al.: Information Aggregation Using the Caméléon# Web Wrapper. In: Proceedings of the 6th International Conference on E-Commerce and Web Technologies, Copenhagen, Denmark, pp. 76–86 (2005)
2. Pinto, D., McCallum, A., Wei, X.: Table Extraction Using Conditional Random Fields. In: Proceedings of the 26th Annual International ACM SIGIR Conference on Research and Development in Information Retrieval, pp. 235–242. ACM Press, New York (2003)
3. Wang, Y., Hu, J.: A Machine Learning Based Approach for Table Detection on the Web. In: Proceedings of the 11th International World Web Conference, pp. 242–250. ACM Press, New York (2002)
4. Zhai, Y., Liu, B.: Web Data Extraction Based on Partial Tree Alignment. In: Proceedings of the 14th International Conference on World Wide Web, pp. 76–85. ACM Press, New York (2005)
5. Zhao, H., Meng, W., Wu, Z., et al.: Fully Automatic Wrapper Generation for Search Engines. In: Proceedings of the 14th International Conference on World Wide Web, pp. 66–75. ACM Press, New York (2005)
6. Baumgartner, R., Ceresna, M., Ledermuller, G.: Deep Web Navigation in Web Data Extraction. In: Proceedings of the International Conference on Intelligent Agents, Web Technology and Internet Commerce, pp. 698–703. IEEE Press, Los Alamitos (2005)
7. Liao, T., Liu, Z.T., Sun, R.: Research and Implementation of Web Table Positioning Technology. Computer Science 36(9), 227–230 (2009)

8. Ren, Z.S., Xue, Y.S.: Structured Data Extraction Based on Web Page Tags. Computer Science 34(10), 133–136 (2007)
9. Liu, W., Meng, X., Meng, W.: Vision-based Web Data Records Extraction. In: Proceedings of the 9th SIGMOD International Workshop in Web and Databases, pp. 20–25 (2006)
10. Gao, K.: Technology and Application of Web Information Reorganization Based on Visual classifying Schema (Ph.D. Thesis). Northeastern University, Shenyang (2006)

Decoupling Control for DACF Pressure Based on Neural Networks and Prediction Principle*

Dengfeng Dong, Xiaofeng Meng, and Fan Liang

School of Instrument Science and Opto-electronics Engineering,
Beihang University, Beijing 100191, China
dengfengdong@tom.com

Abstract. Overcoming the coupling impact is the premise to achieve rapid, precise and especially independent control for the two concatenate pressures of the double-level air current field (DACF) system. Due to the nonlinearity, time lag, and strong coupling characteristics of the system, a decoupling method based on neural networks and prediction principle is presented in this paper. With the neural networks, a nonlinear mathematical model of the relationship describing air flow rate and other variations including the upstream pressure, the downstream pressure and valve opening is developed. With the prediction principle, the predicted pressure state formula is derived. On the basis of them, the predictive expressions of disturbances between the upstream and downstream pressure are obtained by the ideal gas equation. Thereby the controller outputs are regulated on line properly in advance, and the coupling disturbances and time lag effect are weakened notably. Experimental results show the method is effective to achieve the system decoupling.

Keywords: Decoupling, Neural network, prediction.

1 Introduction

Rapid, precise and especially independent control for the two concatenate pressures of the double-level air current field (DACF) system is the key and difficulty of humidity generation technology based on the principle of "two-pressure" or "two-pressure and two-temperature". Decoupling control of the DACF pressure has two steps: firstly to divide the strong coupling system into two single-input single-output (SISO) systems, and then to achieve independent parameters setting and precise control for the two SISO systems. If the pressures of the system cannot be decoupled effectively, they are not only to delay to reach steady state, but also not to achieve independent control at all. The traditional way to decouple a multi-input multi-output (MIMO) system is mainly represented by the full decoupling state space approach based on exact cancellation and modern frequency domain method based on diagonal dominance [1]. However, both the two class methods need accurate system model, thus their

---

* This work is partially supported by a special key project of National Public Sector of China (Grant No. GYHY2007060003).

J. Zhang (Ed.): ICAIC 2011, Part III, CCIS 226, pp. 600–607, 2011.

applications are limited to a certain extent. With the development of the decoupling and control theory, many other methods are proposed in recent years, for example: adaptive decoupling [2], fuzzy decoupling [3], disturbance decoupling [4], neural networks decoupling [5,6], prediction decoupling[7,8], etc. Neural network can approximate a nonlinear function with arbitrary accuracy in a specified compact set and have learning and adaptive abilities, so it can deal with system's nonlinear property. Multi-step prediction can expand amount of information to reflect future trend, thus it is helpful to overcome the impacts of complex change and uncertainty [9]. Hence the combination of the neural networks and the prediction principle is a powerful tool to solve the coupling problem for a nonlinear and time lag system.

2 Proposal of Decoupling Method

A. System Constitution and Control Structure of DACF

The DACF system is mainly constituted of four parts: the air source system, the upstream pressure control system, the downstream pressure control system, and the vacuum system. The air source system and vacuum system supply stationary pressure source and vacuum environment. The DACF system diagram is showed as Fig.1

The agents to adjust the DACF pressure adopt parallel structure combining rough and fine regulation. At the stage of the upstream and downstream pressure switching from one to another state, the rough valves are applied to achieve rapid regulation of the pressure. In the steady state, the pressure is regulated by the fine ones. So the parallel structure is helpful to give consideration to both the rapid and precise control of the DACF pressure.

Assumed that $G_H(s)$ and $G_L(s)$ are the transfer functions of the upstream and downstream pressure control system respectively. $L_H(s)$, $L_L(s)$ are the controller functions. The control structure of the DACF system is showed as Fig.2.

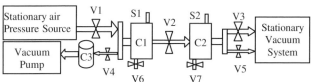

C1/C2: Upstream/downstream pressure chamber; C3: Vacuum chamber;
V1-V3: Rough regulating control valve; V4/V5: Fine regulating control valve; V6/V7: Discharge valve; S1/S2: Pressure sensor.

Fig. 1. Parallel structure of the double-level air current field

In Fig.2, the $R_H(s)$ and $R_L(s)$ represent the upstream and downstream pressure step transfer functions; the $E_H(s)$, $E_L(s)$ represent error functions; the $U_H(s)$, $U_L(s)$ represent controller outputs; the $Y_H(s)$, $Y_L(s)$ represent actual outputs; the $d_{pH}(s)$ represents the downstream pressure disturbance caused by $U_H(s)$; the $d_{pL}(s)$ represents the upstream pressure disturbance caused by $U_L(s)$.

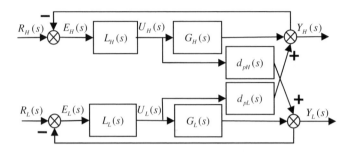

Fig. 2. Control structure of the double-level air current field

B. Decoupling Method Analysis

In theory, if all the transfer functions in Fig.2 could be gotten accurately, the disturbance effect would be eliminated in advance by traditional decoupling method. But each pressure is adjusted by a rough regulating control valve and a fine one, and the air passing through a control valve are divided into the choked flow case and the non-choked flow case, so the control of the two pressures have eight models altogether. Considering the complexity of control valve's structure and uncertainty of pressure loss caused by pipelines and tee tubes, it is very difficult to build even one accurate mathematical model, not to mention eight models in all.

In fact, from Fig.2, it can be seen the pressure coupling is caused essentially by the flow rate changing of air passing through the control valve V2. According to the restriction characteristic of the control valve, the air flow rate Q is written as:

$$\begin{cases} Q = N_a K_V P_1 Y \sqrt{\dfrac{X}{M_a T_a Z_a}} \\ Y = 1 - (X / 3F_K X_T), X = (P_1 - P_2)/P_1 \end{cases} \tag{1}$$

Where N_a is the numerical constant to take care of units, K_V is the flow coefficient, P_1, P_2 is the upstream and downstream pressure, X is the ratio of the pressure drop($P_1 - P_2$) to the upstream pressure, M_a is the air's molecular weight, T_a is the air temperature, Z_a is the compressibility factor, as the air absolute pressure less than 150kPa, the factor is near to 1, X_T is the terminal pressure drop ratio, for a specific control valve it is constant, F_K is the ratio of specific heat factor, for the air it is 1.

From (1), it can be concluded the flow rate is determined by four factors P_1, P_2, T_a and K_V (other factors are approximately constant). However, the flow coefficient K_V is depending on not only the physical properties of the air and control valve but also the opening percentage of the control valve (O). So the general expression of the relation between flow rate and the four factors can be given in a comprehensive function as:

$$Q = f(P_1, P_2, T_a, O) \tag{2}$$

Equation (1) and (2) tell us the function relation is nonlinear. Moreover, considering other factors, such as: the large volume of the chamber and the complexity of the control structure, the time lag characteristic of the coupling system is distinctive.

According to the characteristics of the coupling system, if the nonlinear models of (2) are captured with the neural networks and the pressure estimation formulas at the next moment is established with the multi-step prediction method, the predictive expressions of disturbances between the upstream and downstream pressure can be obtained by the ideal gas equation. Thus the coupling system can be divided into two SISO systems with the known disturbances. By adjusting the controller outputs on line properly in advance, the disturbance and time lag effects would be restricted.

3 Implementation of Pressure Decoupling

A. Flow Rate Estimation Based on Neural Networks

Neural network has strong ability to approximate a nonlinear function. The expression of a three layers neural network can be written as:

$$z_k = f_z(\sum_{j=1}^{j=J} y_j w_{ojk} + c_k) \tag{3}$$

$$y_j = f_y(\sum_{i=1}^{i=I} x_i w_{hij} + b_j) \tag{4}$$

Where z_k is the output of neural network model, representing the flow rate Q, y_j is the output of hidden layer neuron, x_i is the input of the model, representing P_1, P_2, T_a and O. i, j and k are the indices of the neurons in each layer, and I, J and K are the total number of neurons in each layer. w_{ojk} is the weight connecting from jth neuron in hidden layer to kth neuron in output layer. w_{hij} is the weight connecting from the ith neuron in input layer to the jth neuron in hidden layer. b, c are the biases of neurons in the hidden and output layers. $f(\cdot)$ is the activity function. In this paper, a three layers BP neural networks with 18 hidden neurons is built.

B. Pressure State Prediction Based on Multi-step Prediction

Assumed that the pressure sample values at the current time $T(n)$, the last time $T(n-1)$ and the time before the last $T(n-2)$ are P_{S1}, P_{S2} and P_{S3} respectively; and the predictive pressure value of the next sample time $T(n+1)$ is P_0; the sample period is T_s. Considering the variation of pressure is smooth, the multi-step prediction formula is expressed as:

$$[(P_0 - P_{S1}) - (P_{S1} - P_{S2})]/T_s = [(P_{S1} - P_{S2}) - (P_{S2} - P_{S3})]/T_s \qquad (5)$$

Then P_0 can be derived:

$$P_0 = 3(P_1 - P_2) + P_3 \qquad (6)$$

Assumed that P_{H1}, P_{H2}, P_{H3} and, P_{L1}, P_{L2}, P_{L3} are the upstream and the downstream pressure sample values at $T(n), T(n-1), T(n-2)$ respectively. By (6), at the next sample time $T(n+1)$, P_{H0} and P_{L0} are predicted as:

$$P_{H0} = 3(P_{H1} - P_{H2}) + P_{H3} \qquad (7)$$

$$P_{L0} = 3(P_{L1} - P_{L2}) + P_{L3} \qquad (8)$$

C. Pressure Disturbance Prediction

According to the biases and weights in table 1, the flow rate difference ΔQ_H (sL/min) between $T(n+1)$ and $T(n)$ caused by the upstream pressure variation is:

$$\Delta Q_H = f_z (\sum_{j=1}^{j=J} w_{oj1} * [f_y(\sum_{i=1}^{i=I} w_{hij} x_i + b_j)] + c_1)|_{x_1 = P_{H0}; x_2 = P_{L1}; x3 = O}$$
$$-f_z (\sum_{j=1}^{j=J} w_{oj1} * [f_y(\sum_{i=1}^{i=I} w_{hij} x_i + b_j)] + c_1)|_{x_1 = P_{H1}; x_2 = P_{L1}; x3 = O} \qquad (9)$$

Meanwhile, the flow rate difference ΔQ_L (sL/min) caused by the downstream pressure variation is:

$$\Delta Q_L = f_z (\sum_{j=1}^{j=J} w_{oj1} * [f_y(\sum_{j=1}^{i=I} w_{hij} x_i + b_j)] + c_1)|_{x_1 = P_{H1}; x_2 = P_{L0}; x3 = O}$$
$$-f_z (\sum_{j=1}^{j=J} w_{oj1} * [f_y(\sum_{i=1}^{i=I} w_{hij} x_i + b_j)] + c_1)|_{x_1 = P_{H1}; x_2 = P_{L1}; x3 = O} \qquad (10)$$

According to the ideal gas equation, when the air temperature and volume keep the same, the pressure variation ΔP_c (kPa) in the sample time is proportional to the difference between the air mass flow rates in and out in the meantime, that is:

$$\Delta P_c = R_a T_a (m_{ai} - m_{ao})/M_a V \qquad (11)$$

Where m_a is the air's mass, Kg; R_a is the air constant, J/mol·K; T_a is the air temperature, K; M_a is the air's molecular weight, g/mol; V is the chamber's volume, m^3 .

According to (9), (10) and (11), during the next sample time T_s the predictive expressions of the disturbance to the downstream pressure d_{pH} (kPa) caused by the upstream pressure and the disturbance to the upstream pressure d_{pL} (kPa) caused by the downstream pressure are expressed as:

$$d_{pH} = R_a T_a \rho_a \Delta Q_H T_S / 120000 M_a V \tag{12}$$

$$d_{pL} = R_a T_a \rho_a \Delta Q_L T_S / 120000 M_a V \tag{13}$$

4   Experimental Results

4.1   Experimental Result without Decoupling Procedure

Firstly, the experiments without the decoupling procedure are carried out. One group of result is showed as Fig.7

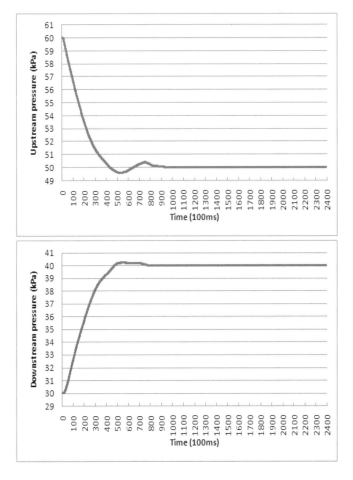

Fig. 3. Pressures step from 60/30kPa to 50/40kPa before decoupling

From Fig.3 it can be seen: during the period from about 580th to 730th sample time, the downstream pressure is supposed to fall from peak value if there is no coupling disturbance influence. However, it remains the same at that period, disturbed by the raise of the upstream pressure from the bottom value with much more overshoot.

B. Experimental Result with Decoupling Procedure

After introducing the decoupling procedure, the results are showed as Fig.4.

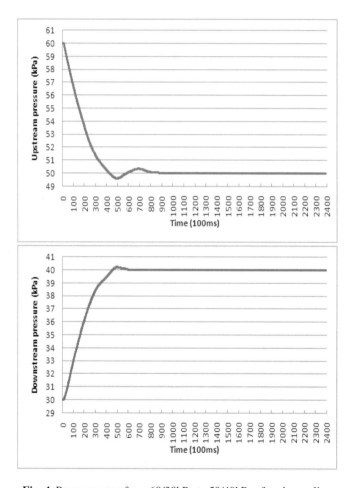

Fig. 4. Pressures step from 60/30kPa to 50/40kPa after decoupling

Compared Fig.4 with Fig.3, it is clear to see that: (1) the time of the upstream and downstream pressures approximating steady state is reduced to about 87 and 60 from 93 and 76 seconds respectively; (2) the downstream pressure is hardly disturbed by the upstream pressure raise, which fall to the steady state from peak value directly.

5 Conclusion

The predictive expressions of the disturbances caused by the upstream and downstream pressure variations are derived by the neural networks, the multi-step prediction and the ideal gas equation. After introducing the predictive expressions to the control loop, the pressure step process is speeded up and becoming relatively independent. It indicates the time lag and coupling effects are obviously weakened. Thus the combination of the neural networks and prediction principle is an effective way to achieve decoupling.

References

1. Ma, P., Fang, J., Cui, C., Hu, S.: Current situation and development of decoupling Control. Control Engineering of China 12(2), 97–100 (2005)
2. Sang, B., Xue, X.: A Summary of multivariable decoupling methods. Fire Control and Command Control 32(11), 13–16 (2007)
3. Lee, T., Nie, J., Lee, M., et al.: A fuzzy controller with decoupling for multivariable nonlinear servo mechanisms, with application to real-time control of a passive line-of-sight stabilization system. Mechatronics 7(1), 83–104 (1997)
4. Zheng, Q., Chen, Z., Gao, Z.: A practical approach to disturbance decoupling control. Control Engineering Practice 17(9), 1016–1025 (2009)
5. Jin, Q., Zeng, D., Wang, Y., Gu, S.: New Decoupling Method Based on Neural Network for Multivariable System. Journal of Northeastern University (Natural Science) 20(3), 250–253 (1999)
6. Li, H.: Design of multivariable fuzzy-neural network decoupling controller. Control and Decision 21(5), 593–596 (2006)
7. Chai, T., Mao, K., Qin, X.: Decoupling design of multivariable generalized predictive control. IEE Proceedings-Control Theory and Application 141(3), 197–201 (1994)
8. Su, B., Chen, Z., Yuan, Z.: Multivariable Decoupling Predictive Control with Input Constraints and Its Application on Chemical Process. Chinese Journal of Chemical Engineering 14(2), 216–222 (2006)
9. Li, J., Yang, M., Jiang, P.: Multivariable dynamic matrix decoupling control for strong coupling temperature object. Control Engineering of China 13(5), 423–425 (2006)

A Multipath Routing for Mobile Ad Hoc Networks

Sihai Zheng and Layuan Li

School of Computer Science and Technology
Wuhan University of Technology
Wuhan, China
ZhengSihai2011@163.com

Abstract. With the development of mobile Ad Hoc networks, it is more impor-tant to provide QoS guarantee for multimedia application. QoS-based routing is an available method to do that, whereas most of the QoS-based routing are based on single path, which do not take full advantage of network resources. This paper puts forward a QoS-based multipath routing called QMPSR. QMPSR takes bandwidth and delay constraint into account, it can find several paths to provide QoS guarantee. Also, it can simultaneously use the node disjoint paths to transmit application data stream. The results of simulation show QMPSR routing is better than QoS-MSR.

Keywords: Ad Hoc; QoS; Routing overhead; Multipath.

1 Introduction

QoS is defined as a non-functional characteristic of the system. In computer networks, the QoS goal is to get the communication behavior in order to be more secured and reliable protection of information carried by the network and more efficient to make use of network resources. Specifically, QoS is a set of service parameters can be pre-dicted, which is provided by the network, including delay, delay jitter, bandwidth and packet delivery ratio, it also can be seen as an agreement between user and network, which requires both sides to comply with [1]. The QoS ability will directly affect the network service.

At present, some papers on multipath routing show that providing more than one path can better support high mobility network with low end-to-end delay, high packet delivery ratio and lower control overhead. Ref. [2] proposes a QoS metric called end-to-end reliability with multipath discovery (MP- DSR), but it is not defined for real-time traffic with QoS constraints. Ref. [3] proposes an interfering-aware QoS multipath routing for QoS multimedia applications in Ad Hoc network (IMRP). Though it can compute disjoint paths based on bandwidth availability and the link stability computed by the nodes, it has not mentioned about the method used for esti-mation of bandwidth and stability values. Ref. [4] proposes a distributed multi-path dynamic source routing protocol (QoS-MSR) to improve QoS support with respect to end-to-end reliability. In a sort of ideal model, but it doesn't consider the congestion of nodes to QoS routing.

J. Zhang (Ed.): ICAIC 2011, Part III, CCIS 226, pp. 608–614, 2011.

The main contributes of this paper are as follow. We have in-depth researched on multipath routing and QoS routing, propose a QoS multipath source routing protocol (QMPSR). It takes bandwidth and delay constraints into account. It can find several paths to provide QoS guarantee. Also, it can simultaneously use the node disjoint paths to transmit application data stream. Finally, the simulation analysis is completed. Experiments show the performance of QMPSR is better than some other QoS routing protocols.

In the rest of this paper, we first research on QoS model in section 2. QMPSR routing algorithm is analyzed in section 3. The results of simulation are shown in Section 4. At last, we offer conclusions in Section 5.

2   QoS Model and Parameter Calculation

A. Multiple QoS Model

Multi-QoS routing problem is to find a feasible path to meet multiple independent constraints, it is a NP-complete problem. That is, it will lead to significant computation to meet the conditions for the optimal solution of these restrictions simultaneously. This paper will adopt a simplified QoS model, which can not only achieve certain QoS guarantee, but also easy to be implemented. From the perspective of queuing theory, network bandwidth is more than the required bandwidth means the arrival ratio equal to the service ratio, in theory there are no packets waiting in the queue of delay. A routing meeting the bandwidth requirement can provide lower delay for data stream. In addition, the routing with minimum hops can also provide lower delay. Therefore, routing selection standard of QMPSR can be simplified as: the shortest routing to meet the bandwidth condition. The bandwidth is used as the main conditions for access to the data stream; protocol will try to find the shortest routing with the delay constraints. If protocol finds a routing to meet the required bandwidth, it will access the data stream, otherwise reject it.

B. Bandwidth Calculation

The channel idle time of nodes is a very important parameter for bandwidth calculation. It is determined by the amount of business between the nodes and the neighbor nodes, during the time, the node can transmit data successfully. Therefore, the node idle time reflect the available bandwidth [5]. We can use (1) to calculate the available bandwidth.

$$B_{available}(i) = B(i) \times T_{idle}/T_{interval} \qquad (1)$$

$B_{available}(i)$ is the available bandwidth of node n_i, $B(i)$ is the maximum transmission bandwidth of node n_i, $T_{interval}$ is the observation interval, T_{idle} is the channel idle time during the time $T_{interval}$. According to (1), the main difficulty to measure $B_{available}(i)$ is how to calculate T_{idle}. After many experiments, $T_{interval}$ time is set to 2 seconds in this paper. If T_{idle} is too much, it can not promptly reflect the changes in available bandwidth, T_{idle} is too little will cause too much overhead.

C. Delay Estimation

End to end delay is used as another QoS parameter in QMPSR. When source node receives a routing reply from destination nodes, we can calculate the two-way delay T_r according to the current time and the time of required routing. And compare it with the maximum delay data stream can bear, finally decide on whether the routing can be used to transfer data stream [6]. That has been optimized in this paper: when RREQ packets arrive at destination nodes, if downlink delay T_{down} has exceeded T, i.e. $T_{down} > T$, then the routing is not satisfied with the delay required, discard the RREQ packets directly.

3   Routing Algorithm

QMPSR routing is divided into three parts. The first is routing discovery; The second is to calculate node disjoint path; The third is load distribution.

A. Routing Discovery

When data need to be transmitted, the source node checks whether if there are feasible paths in routing cache, if there are not such paths, then broadcast RREQ packets to its neighbor nodes. The format of RREQ packet is as follow:.

S_A	D_A	R_ID	R_Record	Hops	B	Delay	Bth	Tth

S_A is the address of source node; D_A is the address of destination node; R_ID is the sequence number of routing request packet; R_Record is the routing record, it is used to record the address of intermediate nodes from the source node to destination node. $Hops$ is the number of the hops from source node to current node, it can increase the routing load. B is the minimum available bandwidth from source nodes to current nodes; $Delay$ is the cumulative delay of current path. B_{th} and D_{th} are the threshold searching bandwidth and delay. They can prevent routing requests from flooding in the whole network. The intermediate nodes maintain the list of sequence (S_A, R_ID), it is used to uniquely identify a routing request packet.

B. Node Disjoint Path

After the destination node receives a multiple QoS routing record, QMPSR will start the routing recovery mechanism. The destination node replies multipath record to source node using the path with the least delay, after source node receives the RREP packet returning from destination node, it will get several records of QoS routing, then it can construct a directed graph $G<V,E>$. The bandwidth is used as the first criteria to select; QMPSR will choose a main path in graph G. If bandwidths are the same, then choose the path with lower delay. Remove the intermediate nodes in this path and their links in G, construct a new graph G'. There are no more than three node disjoint paths in QMPSR. The algorithm is as in table 1.

C. Load Distribution

If the weight of load distribution in k-path is W_k, then,

$$W_k \propto B_k \quad (k=1,2,3,\ldots,n) \tag{2}$$

B_k is the available bandwidth in k-path. In addition,

$$B_U = B_1 + B_2 + \ldots + B_n \tag{3}$$

$$W_k = B_k / B_U \tag{4}$$

Load distribution algorithm is as follow,

$$W_k = \min([B_k / B_U], M) \times R \tag{5}$$

M is the maximum value of W_k, Its role is to limit W_k, if W_k is over the range, multipath would degenerate into single path. R is used to the granularity of load distribution on each path. When the load is distributed to the multipaths, *Round Robin Scheduling Algorithm* [7] is used.

Table 1. The Main Algorithm

```
while(construct a directed graph G){
max_num(Path)=3;
MP₀=φ;
num_MP₀=0;
search a QoS path p from S to D in G;
if(P){
     MP₀= MP₀+{P};
     num_MP₀☐ num_MP₀+1; }
if(num_MP₀< max_num(Path)){
     Remove the intermediate nodes in path P and their links in G;
     Construct a new graph G';
     Continue ;}
else {break;}
}
```

4 Simulation Analysis

In order to fully examine the performance of QMPSR, we had conducted two sets of simulation experiment. In the first set, the scene is 500m × 500m; there are 30 nodes in the scene, they are randomly distributed. The connections are ten pairs. Nodes can randomly move, its maximum speed is 10m/s; Data source is CBR, packet size is 512 bytes, the speed of sending packets is 200.0. In the second set, the scene is 1000m × 1000m; there are 50 nodes, they are also randomly distributed. The connections are ten pairs. Nodes can randomly move. Its maximum speed is 15m/s; Data source and packet size are the same as the first set, but the speed of sending packets is 300.0.

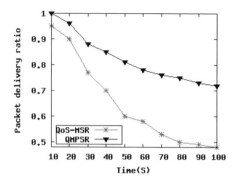

Fig. 1. Average packet delivery ratio of 30 nodes

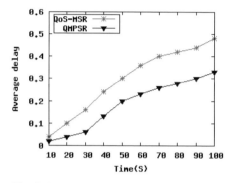

Fig. 2. Average end to end delay of 30 nodes

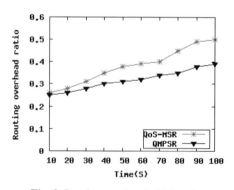

Fig. 3. Routing overhead of 30 nodes

Fig.1, Fig.2 and Fig.3 show the results of the first set of simulation.

Fig.1 shows the packet delivery ratio of QMPSR has been significantly improved, the probability of successful transmission is much higher than that of QoS-MSR.

Fig.2 shows the average delay of QMPSR is less than that of QoS-MSR. It can find several suitable QoS paths, which speed up the transmission of data.

Fig.3 shows routing overhead of QMPSR is significantly less than that of QoS-MSR. It indicates QMPSR can effectively prevent the routing request packets overly forwarding. Meanwhile, the principle of bandwidth separation in QMPSR plays an important role, which can reduce the amount of routing.

Fig.4, Fig.5 and Fig.6 show the results of the second set of simulation.

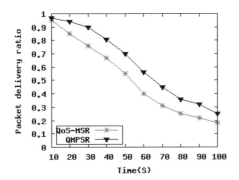

Fig. 4. Average packet delivery ratio of 50 nodes

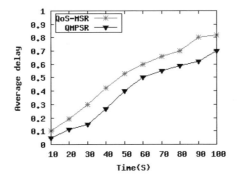

Fig. 5. Average end to end delay of 50 nodes

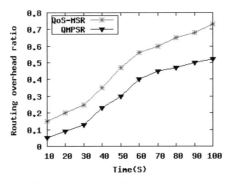

Fig. 6. Routing overhead of 50 nodes

Fig.4 shows packet delivery ratio of QMPSR is about 5% higher than that of QoS-MSR, but that is about 15% higher in first set. There are more nodes and connections in the second set, the communication between nodes is very frequent, it is more difficult to choose multipath, therefore, the difference is not much obvious.

Fig.5 shows the delay of QMPSR is less than that of QoS-MSR. It indicates QMPSR can speed up the delivery of data and reduce the delay. However, the delay increases too much in the second set. The hops of communication links are more, therefore, it has a corresponding increase in average delay. But the advantage of QMPSR is still very clear.

Fig.6 shows the routing overhead of QMPSR is less than that of QoS-MSR. But overhead of the two protocols are more than that of the first set. It indicates the performance have declined with the expansion of the network.

5   Conclusion

This paper proposes a QoS multipath routing protocol (QMPSR). It takes bandwidth and delay constraints into account, it also can find several QoS paths to transmit data stream. The results show the performance of QMPSR is better than some other protocols. Author will focus on how to load balance more effectively in future work, which can solve the problem of out of order caused by multipath.

Acknowledgment. This paper is supported by National Natural Science Foundation of China(No: 60672137, 60773211, 60970064), Open Fund of the State Key Laboratory of Software Development Environment(No: SKLSDE-2009KF-2-02), New Century Excellent Talents in university(No: NCET-08-0806), Specialized Research Fund for the Doctoral Program of Higher Education of China(Noȵ 20060497105).

References

1. Yang, Y.-M., Han, W.-D.: A QoS routing protocol for mobile ad hoc networked control systems. In: NSWCTC 2010 - The 2nd International Conference on Networks Security, Wireless Communications and Trusted Computing, vol. 2, pp. 89–92 (2010)
2. Sarma, N., Nandi, S.: Route Stability based QoS Routing (RSQR) in MANETs. In: Proc. of the 10th International Symposium on Wireless Personal Multimedia Communications (WPMC 2007), pp. 770–773 (December 2007)
3. Wang, Y.-H., Tsai, C.-H., Lin, H.-Z.: Interference-aware QoS Multipath Routing for Ad Hoc Wireless Networks. International Journal of Computers and Applications 29(4) (2007)
4. Sambasivam, P., Murthy, A., Belding-Royer, E.M.: Dynamically Adaptive Multipath Routing based on AODV. In: Proc. of the 3rd Annual Mediterranean Ad Hoc Networking Workshop (MedHocNet), Bodrum, Turkey (June 2008)
5. Lei, C., Wen, d.: QoS-aware routing based on bandwidth estimation for mobile Ad Hoc networks. Journal on Selected Areas in Communications 23(3), 561–572 (2005)
6. Wu, H., Jia, X.: QoS multicast routing by using multiple paths/trees in wireless ad hoc networks. Ad Hoc Networks 5(5), 600–612 (2007)
7. Wajahat, M., Saqib, R.: Adaptive multi-path on-demand routing in mobile ad hoc networks. In: Proceedings of ISORC, pp. 237–244 (2005)

Method of Light-Spot Subpiexl Center Orientation Based on Linear CCD in Fiber Sensing System[*]

Jun Tao[1] and Xia Zhang[2]

[1] Physics School of Science, Wuhan University of Technology
[2] Digital Engineering Research Center,
Huazhong University of Science and Technology
Zhangxia_2011@126.com

Abstract. In the CCD of Fiber sensing measurement system, the orientation of light-spot pixel position which decides the accuracy of the entire system is very important. Based on the traditional center of gravity algorithm, a new algorithm which adopts weight nonlinearity and linear interpolation is proposed. And it is compared the precision of system using two algorithm under different noise level. The simulation result shows that the new algorithm can reach 0.05 pixel of orientation precision, it is much more precise and stable.

Keywords: Intensity peak orientation, Filtering, Linear interpolation, Weight nonlinearity.

Fiber sensing system which is based on linear CCD can realize the static or dynamic measurement of the external physical quantities, through measure the position change of the light spot in CCD. The accurate location of the center of CCD light spot guarantees the improvement of the reliability and stability of Fiber sensing measurement system. The measurement accuracy of peak value of light spot's intensity is limited due to low resolution of CCD. And it leads to decrease resolution of the whole measuring system. In order to achieve higher resolution, the direct way is to choose the CCD which pixel is smaller as possible. But reducing the size will impact the sensitivity of the CCD and the technology requirement of small pixel is higher. And because of the limitation of the import high intensity CCD, it's very hard to induce the pixel of CCD without restriction. Another way is to improve the optical imaging part in sensing system to satisfy the requirement of sensitivity. But this solution will make the whole system more complex and the added optical element will impact the integration of the system. So we propose a solution, called sub pixel level location method, which based on the current low intensity CCD. There are several sub pixel level location methods, the normal methods of extraction light intensity curve peak are Gravity method [1], Extreme value method [2], Fitting method[3]. Fitting method use the polynomials to fit the light intensity curve. Extreme value method is to extract the max gray value. Gravity method is to calculate the gravity of the light intensity which

---

[*] Supported by "the Fundamental Research Funds for the Central Universities" 2010-Ia-035.

precision is much higher than Extreme value method and the calculation is easier than Fitting method. In the article, we provide an improved resolution method which combines the gray gravity method and linear interpolation. Compared to traditional gray gravity method, this solution has the improvement in both sub pixel location sensitivity and reliability.

1 Current Algorithm Analysis

The ideal optical system can make the parallel light focus on one pixel of CCD to form the gray image signal. Due to the limitation of CCD resolution, the sensitivity of resolution can just reach one pixel.

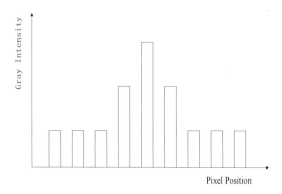

Fig. 1. The CCD image of the ideal optical system

In the measurement application especially dynamic, in order to achieve the real time response, the processing speed should be quick enough and the transformation and processing of the signal should be completed during the integral time of CCD. One of the effective methods to improve the processing speed is to reduce the amount of data processing, which means only process the data in the area of the light spot imaging. The center of light spot through gray gravity method is showed as below:

$$N = \frac{\sum_{i=1}^{n} N_i B(N_i)}{\sum_{i=1}^{n} B(N_i)} \tag{1}$$

N is the pixel coordinate of the light spot centre, N_i is pixel coordinate, $B(N_i)$ is the grey value of pixel in i point. The serial number of CCD pixel is from 1 to n. From equation 1, we can see that the effect of pixel to the light spot center location is liner to its gray intensity. The gray intensity is bigger in the actual processing, the effect of the light spot center location is more obvious.

2   Practical Improvement of Light Spot Center Location

In the measurement process of CCD Fiber sensing, the final imaging light spots are always irregular because of the stray light caused by the spectroscopic device, uselss signal caused by secondary spectrum, electrical noise and thermal noise caused by quantization errors from CCD. Using the gravity method above directly cannot find the peak position of the light intensity distribution curve of light spot. So we need to find a method which can realize the quick actual location in the practical application.

2.1   The Confirmation of the Scope of the Light Spot Centre

Firstly using the 1×3 sliding window to slide in the image line, calculate the gray sum of three pixel which satisfy the requirement in gray distribution in sliding window according to the threshold value and other constraint conditions. The gray sum of three pixel in sliding window is the got according to the center position of the maximum value which is the rough position of the light spot center in that line. For the one-dimensional gray pictures $B(N_i)$, i=1...n, 1×3 sliding windows is from column i=1 to column i=n-2, calculate the gray sum of the three pixels in the sliding window. To avoid the interference from white noise and high intensity light spot and reduce the calculation amount, only process calculation of gray value and S(i) when gray threshold and gray distribution satisfy the equation 2 at the same time.

$$S(i) = B(N_{i-1}) + B(N_i) + B(N_{i+1})$$
and
$$B(N_i) > B_{low}, \quad \left| B(N_i) - B(N_{i-1}) \right| < B_{high}, \quad \left| B(N_i) - B(N_{i+1}) \right| < B_{high} \quad (2)$$

The position of i, the maximum of S(i), is the rough position Ci in the one dimensional   picture light spot center. B_{low} is threshold, its value is less than the minimum grey values in light spot area and more than background grey value outside light spot area. Setting B_{low} condition can reduce the calculation in the picture background area and focus on the higher gray value area. Imaging light spot has the pixel width and the gray distribution is like Gaussian distribution. The light spot area, especially in the light spot center area, the gray value of the adjacent pixels will not change extraordinarily. Setting B_{high} can prevent one single or two successive high gray value positions will be set as the rough position of the light spot by mistake outside the light spot area. The conditions above improve the calculation efficiency and robustness during abstracting the rough position of light spot centre.

2.2   Noise Elimination in Light Spot Area

Process the low-pass filter for the picture data in rough light spot area to reduce the effect from the high frequency noise. The normalized cutoff frequency in the low-pass filter is 0.15. The length of filter is 5, order is 3. The factor of the filter and original picture make convolution operation and get the picture data after filtering. Set the $B_f(N_i)$ as the picture data after low-pass filter

$$B_f(N_i)=K_0B(N_i)+K_1[B(N_{i-1})+B(N_{i+1})]+K_2[B(N_{i-2})+B(N_{i+2})],$$

and

$$i=C_i-L,\cdots,C_i+L \tag{3}$$

The factor of the filter is:

$$K_0=0.370286, K_1=0.271843, K_2=0.095016$$

In this article, the light spot width is $15\sim20$ pixels in the fiber sensing measurement system. After get the rough position of light spot center C_i, set the area L pixels in left and right sides from C_i as the rough area in that line. $L\in[8,10]$ can guarantee all the light spots are included in that area. After filtering, the signal noise especially high frequency noise's amplitude will reduced extraordinarily and the gray curve will become smooth.

Process power transformation for the filtering picture data $B_f(N_i)$

$$\hat{B}_f(N_i)=B_f(N_i)^{0.25} \tag{4}$$

$\hat{B}_f(N_i)$ is the transformed picture date.

As showed in Figure 2, The change of the original gray picture data $B_f(N_i)$ is bigger, the smaller of the value after the power transformation. This will make the curve of $\hat{B}_f(N_i)$ become flat. The aim of this target is to reduce the noise in the light

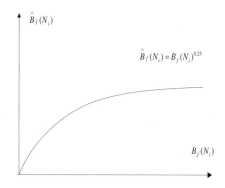

Fig. 2. The relationship curve of image data power transformation

spot area in original picture and the effect from gray non-normal distribution to the abstracting of the peak value in light spot center.

2.3 The Improvement of the Nonlinear Weight

In order to highlight the effect of pixels which gay value is big to the center location, improve the weight ratio and change the traditional gray gravity method to the nonlinear relationship. If assume that the nonlinear function is $S = \hat{B}_f{}^m(N_i)$, the gravity method will be showed as below:

$$N = \frac{\sum\limits_{i=1}^{n} N_i \hat{B}_f{}^m(N_i)}{\sum\limits_{i=1}^{n} \hat{B}_f{}^m(N_i)} \tag{5}$$

When m is different, the gray weight is different. When m=0, $\overline{N} = \sum\limits_{i=1}^{n} N_i /(n-1)$ which is mean method. It didn't consider the value of the gray value of each pixel and used the mean value of the position of the pixels to get the peak position of the light spot center. When m=1, (2) is equal to (1), and it is the traditional gravity method. when m = ∞, it is extreme value method, the peak position of the light spot is decided by the biggest pixel without any other pixels. It is obvious that the location precision of the extreme value can only achieve one pixel. So the value of m will affect the precision of the peak location. When m > 1, it will improve the weight of the pixels which gray value is bigger. In this condition, the pixels which gray value is bigger will have more effect to the light spot center location. On the contrary, When 0 < m <1, the pixels which gray value is smaller will have more effect to the light spot center location and., the result is different from the location requirement. In the actual system measurement, we should choose m > 1 and get the best m value through several times of experiment.

2.4 Linear Interpolation Method

The location precision of the peak value of the light spot center depends on the light distribution curve in the imaging CCD and signal noise ratio of the CCD output signal. Linear interpolation method can be adopted to increase the used spots to get sub-pixel level location precision of the peak value. There're many linear interpolation methods, such as nearest neighbor interpolation, liner interpolation, cubic spline interpolation. Compared to other methods, liner interpolation method has the advantages such as simply, strong practicality, good inhibition for the noise and high picture quality.

We adopt liner interpolation in this article, set the interpolation point as u, the gray value of the two adjacent points are $\hat{B}_f(N_i)$, $\hat{B}_f(N_{i+1})$

$$\hat{B}_f(u) = \hat{B}_f(N_i) + a[\hat{B}_f(N_{i+1}) - \hat{B}_f(N_i)], \ a = \frac{N_u - N_i}{N_{i+1} - N_u} \tag{6}$$

After interpolation calculation, the peak value of the light spot center is

$$N = \frac{\sum_{i=1}^{n} N_i \overset{m}{\hat{B}_f}(N_i) + \sum_{u=b_1}^{b_2} N_u \overset{m}{\hat{B}_f}(N_u)}{\sum_{i=1}^{n} \overset{m}{\hat{B}_f}(N_i) + \sum_{u=b_1}^{b_2} \overset{m}{\hat{B}_f}(N_u)} \tag{7}$$

b_1 and b_2 are the serial number of the interpolation pixel, N_u is interpolation unit coordinate.

3   Experiment and Application

The light intensity of the light spot distribution likes Gaussian distribution, the light intensity of the light spot imaging in the CCD can be showed as:

$$I_s = I_0 \exp\left[\frac{-2(x-30)^2}{225}\right] \tag{8}$$

The spatial distribution of the light intensity is showed as Figure 3.

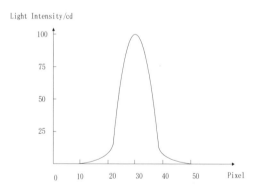

Fig. 3. The distribution curve of image light spot intensity

In the experiment, set the peak value of the light spot center as 30, the maximum light intensity is 100. As we calculated before, the non-liner gray weight values is 2. In the ideal condition, the light spot imagining in the CCD will not be affected by the noise, peak value is 30. 00 through improved gray gravity method and peak value is 30. 00 through traditional gravity method. There is the same between two methods. If we add some noise interference which accord s with normal distribution and increases gradually. The table below shows the peak positions through two different algorithms.

Table 1. The comparison of mean square error of two algorithms

Added Noise n	Traditional gravity method		Improved gravity method	
	N/Pixel	Deviation /%	N/ Pixel	Deviation /%
n(0,1)	30.01	1	30.00	0
n(0,2)	30.02	2	30.00	0
n(0,3)	30.05	5	30.01	1
n(0,4)	30.06	6	30.01	1
n(0,5)	30.08	8	30.01	1
n(0,6)	30.09	9	30.02	2
n(0,7)	30.09	9	30.02	2
n(0,8)	30.11	11	30.02	2
n(0,9)	30.13	13	30.02	2
n(0,10)	30.14	14	30.03	3
n(0,11)	30.15	15	30.03	3
n(0,12)	30.16	16	30.03	3
n(0,13)	30.18	18	30.03	3
n(0,14)	30.19	19	30.03	3
n(0,15)	30.21	21	30.03	3
n(0,16)	30.21	21	30.03	3
n(0,17)	30.22	22	30.04	4
n(0,18)	30.24	24	30.04	4
n(0,19)	30.27	27	30.04	4
n(0,20)	30.28	28	30.04	4

Compare two different algorithms, when the added gaussian noise is small, the result error of gravity method and improved gravity method are very small, the target can be located in the sub-pixel level. With the increase of the added gaussian noise, when the noise added to N(0, 10),the error of gravity method is big and the target location accuracy decreased to under 0.1.The improved gravity method has good interference ability. When the noise is N(0,20), the target location accuracy can reach 0.05 pixel with high precision.

4 Conclusions

Based on the imaging characteristics of the light intensity peak value location in liner CCD measurement system, the article propose an improved gravity method for sub-pixel abstracting of light spot center, This method use the sliding window as the light spot center abstracting area, adopt the low-pass filter power transformation to smooth filter the light spot image data to reduce the effect from the noise, improve the nonlinearity of the weight in the gravity method, increase the effect from the pixel which the gray value is big in light spot center location. Using the linear interpolation method, add the imaging points. The result of the experiment shows that the algorithm has the advantages such as high abstracting precision for the light spot center, good anti-noise performance and robustness. It can abstract the peak value location of the light spot center even under greater noise.

References

1. Wu, S., Su, X., Li, J.: A New Method for Extracting the Centre-line of Line Structure Light-stripe. Journal of Sichuan University (Engineering Science Edition) 39(4), 151–155 (2007)
2. Zhang, Y., Huang, Y., Jiao, J.: Detection Technique for Circular Parts Based on Machine Vision. Computer Engineering 34(19), 185–186, 202 (2008)
3. Ding, Y., Li, C., He, Y.: Subdivision Algorithm for n Order Uniform B-spline Curves. Computer Engineering 34(12), 58–60 (2008)

AlphaBeta-Based Optimized Game Tree Search Algorithm

Xiao-Bin Yang and Wen Li

School of Computer Science
Sichuan University
Chengdu, China
yangxiaobin2011@tom.com

Abstract. Analog Drosophila plays an important role in the genetics, Man-machine Game has become a classic topic in Artificial Intelligence field since computer come out. These have important and profound effects on Artificial Intelligence. This paper analyze the Man-machine Game core technology in-depth. Then presents a optimal search algorithm of Game -tree based on classic AlphaBeta pruning, aspiration search, interactive deepening, transposition table and heuristic technologies—ABOS. The algorithm analysis and experiment shows that the time efficiency of ABOS increased more than 10 fold while ensuring the search quality.

Keywords: Man-machine Game, AlphaBeta Pruning, Aspiration Search, Iterative Deepening, Transposition Table, History Heuristic.

1 Introduction

Game theory between human and computer is described in the literature as the drosophila of artificial intelligence. With excellent data structure and algorithm, an accurate grasp of game theory and computer high-speed large-scale computing power, human-computer program has won the game ability rivals human intelligence. But with the increasing demand for machine intelligence, the whole game tree search depth increases, the number of nodes in the search and the time complexity of the way to exponentially increase, resulting in a combinatorial explosion problem. Although there are many scholars put forward many ideas and optimized algorithms, such as AlphaBeta pruning, transposition table, history heuristic and so on, but the effect of unilateral optimization is no longer obvious, and in-depth analysis and optimized algorithms has become a combination is the main work of this paper.

2 Core Technology of Human-Computer Game

In the game machine system, we follow the high principles of cohesion low coupling module division by function. Move generation: Depending on the rules of the game determine which moves are legal, all produced on the current situation and the

J. Zhang (Ed.): ICAIC 2011, Part III, CCIS 226, pp. 623–631, 2011.

organization of legal moves in a queue for the search module; Board evaluation: Based on the current state of the initiative to the board on the current state quantitative evaluation of the current situation is good or bad. Search engine: In the game, don't choose the most beneficial moves of the current state at every step, that is not a simple sense of the greedy, the whole game tree to start looking forward few steps, the search select the most beneficial step for the long-term moves. Minimax search is basic process [1], it's a depth-first algorithm, but with the search depth increased, the time complexity increases exponentially, resulting in combinatorial explosion.

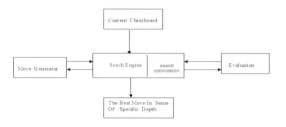

Fig. 1. Calls between each module diagram

The current situation using a specific algorithm for in-depth search, game tree search using the search space describe. Game tree diagram as follows:

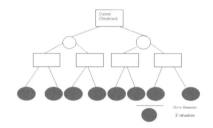

Fig. 2. Game tree diagram (search deep is three)

In figure each rectangle and circle represents the situation, each connection is a move of a game, the two connected mean the situation represented by the connection moves the situation into each other. For simplicity, assume that each situation in the diagram moves only two choices, the generation module is responsible for the moves, while in the game of chess leaves surfaces nodes need to be evalued, their evaluation module is responsible for the chess side.

Assuming all the nodes in the corresponding game tree of chess in the form of judgments of the merits of the perspective of standing on the computer. Then if the evaluation of the computer module enabling the board to return the value is positive, beneficial to the board if the evaluation of the module on the return value is negative. According to game theory, called the leaf nodes of the game the evaluation module, and for other non-leaf node if the initiative should be chosen by the computer accounts for the largest value of all child nodes as its value, if the initiative should be accounted by the people select all the child nodes as the minimum value of the value . This leaf node up from the bottom and finally get the optimal value of the root node moves, it is the most basic minimax search process.

3   Optimization Algorithm and ABOS

A.   AlphaBeta Prune Algorithm

With the depth of game tree search increases exponentially expand the minimax tree search process is a blind search the entire time-consuming work, its time complexity is $O(b^d)$, where b representative of the average non-leaf node bifurcation number, d means that the search depth. The Chinese Chess, for example, in the game every move about 40 or so, that is, the search 4 layers need to check the 2,500,000 possible, search 5 layers 100,000,000 possible need to check, search the 6 layers 4,000,000,000 may need to check, home PC usually can not search the game tree of more than 6 layers, otherwise it will cause big time waiting for the computer's move to the unbearable point[3]. Three scientists from the University of Pittsburgh, Newell, Shaw and Simon in 1958's AlphaBeta pruning algorithm based on the characteristics of game-tree search to optimize the operation, cut off a branch of meaningless, AlphaBeta pruning of its principles are as follows:

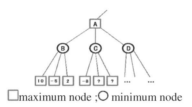

□maximum node ;O minimum node

Fig. 3. AlphaBeta prune diagram

In Figure 3, node A on the root of the game tree, the search depth is 2, followed by the first visit of each child node B node. Since it has to the maximum search depth, called the evaluation of the valuation module, get the value series: 10,-5,2. Because node B is a minimum node, it selects the minimum value -5.Then analyzes the second node C, node C and node B belong to the same level, and then click view results point C, the scores of each child node. The first child node returned -8, it's not necessary to continue to search the rest children node of C, regardless of node C, what the score the remaining child nodes has, it can only return -8, B and C nodes after node A as compared to the node will not greatly will choose node C, also lost the necessary game-tree search which C as the root.

Another way to understand, you can assume that the value of the node A in the interval [- ∞, + ∞], with their first son, the return value -5 node B because node A to request the node is the maximum of his son, Therefore, the son of the node in the following only the value in the interval [-5, + ∞] where it makes sense, that is, the value of the node C in the interval [-5, + ∞] where it makes sense, and because node

C is whichever is the son of the minimum node, C value of the node first son the value of -8 C in the interval led to [- ∞, -8] where, $[-5, +\infty] \cap [-\infty, -8] = \varnothing$, C node can not generate meaningful value fo the node A, so you can do the C node son node pruning. Implementation of the algorithm in the form of coding, in the initial, $\alpha = -\infty$, $\beta = +\infty$.

Kunth, and Moore made in 1975 improved the negative maximum value search form [2], stood on the situation in possession of the initiative in the evaluation side, shielding the great difference between maximum node and minimum node. Not only saves a great summary operations which determine node type , but also code simple and beautiful. At the same time more efficient.

According to the negative maximum value of the search recursively pruning algorithm given in the form AlphaBeta pseudo code:

```
Input:
        p:The current situation in the game tree for the
corresponding node
        depth:Search deepth
        alpha:Low bound of search process
        beta:High bound of search process
Output:
        The evaluation of node p in sense of depth

int AlphaBeta(node p,int depth,int alpha,int beta){
        if(depth > MaxSearchDepth OR GameOver)
            return Evaluation(p);
        for(each move in MoveQueue Q){
            Accoring to the move change node p to new node
p';
            value= -AlphaBeta(p',depth+1,-beta,-alpha);
            Accoring to the move recovery node p' to old
node p;
            if(value > alpha){
            alpha=value;
            }
            if(alpha >= beta)
                break;
        }
        return alpha;
}
```

The following theoretical analysis of AlphaBeta pruning: the traditional minimax search procedure for the search nodes is

$$N_d = 1 + b + b^2 + ... + b^d = b^d \frac{1 - 1/b^{d+1}}{1 - 1/b} = O(b^d)$$

Kunth and other[2] evidence in the best cases, the use AlphaBeta pruning the number of nodes generated

$N_d = 2b^{d/2} - 1$, D is even

$N_d = b^{(d+1)/2} + b^{(d-1)/2} - 1$, D is odd

Comparison shows that the order of moves sorted enough Ideally, at the same time AlphaBeta pruning minimax search depth process than doubled.

A. Optimization Strategy

In fact the efficiency of pruning AlphaBeta most cases could not be ideal, AlphaBeta pruning the order of the node pair production efficiency is extremely sensitive to one of the main algorithm is to adjust the order of child nodes generated; AlphaBeta pruning process of pruning the smaller the interval will likely lead to more pruning, the main direction of the second algorithm is managed to reduce the pruning interval $[\alpha, \beta]$. To maximize the performance of AplapaBeta pruning, many scholars put forward the following optimization strategy:

- **Aspiration search**

Initialization $[\alpha, \beta]$ is set to a very small range, large-scale complete game tree pruning operations. Two cases, when the search is successful, the return value $v \in [\alpha, \beta]$, then the rapid completion of the game tree search; when the search fails, the return value $v \notin [\alpha, \beta]$, if $v < \alpha$, then use the $[-\infty, \alpha]$ re-search, and if $v > \beta$, the $[\beta, +\infty]$ use of re-search.

- **Iterative deepening[4]**

In the study show that the depth-1 search depth of only a depth game-tree search time under 1 / 15 to 1 / 5, game tree can be a range from low to high search and information obtained by the search to adjust the root node in the order of the children , that they begin the search to get the most low-level or sub-optimal moves have to do efficient pruning done then complete the iterative deepening process.

- **Transposition Table**

In the process of game-tree search may be encountered in different nodes of the situation the same chess game, chess game after the evaluation value of the depth of the search after the *vaule*, the best moves *move*, the initiative *right*, *depth* and the depth of chess game search feature descriptive information into the transposition table, and then experience the same chess game is to get directly from the transposition table and avoid search process again. In the actual coding, the use of technology as a solution is hash, reduce the time complexity and space complexity, while there may be some conflict, but after carefully designed to ensure that the probability of conflict is small enough, the use of Zobrist's chess game in 1970 with the replacement of fast mapping table records Zobrist hashing techniques[5], chess game table in the transposition table position *logId* with 32bits, chess game features infomation *boradId* with 64bits, in the calculation of *logId* and *boradId* calculated using the incremental mode, further reducing the amount of computation.

- **History Heuristic[6]**

When a multiple searches specific move to go for the best move, it's reasonable to believe that the moves of the chess game again in the future was identified as the probability of the best moves are relatively large, each time the search moves to a time optimal the weight given to a history of its points, when the nodes of the game tree search when the first moves to get all the weight of its history points and descending order, in accordance with the sorted sequence of moves will lead to greater search pruning possible.

B. ABOS Search Algorithm

Optimization strategy increased Aplahbeta pruning the search efficiency in varying degrees, but the difficulty of a single optimizing is growing and no longer significant performance improvement, in-depth analysis of our optimization strategy thinking, based on AlphaBeta purune will be aspiration   search, iterative deepening, transposition table technology, history heuristic technology to combine became our ABOS (AlphaBeta Based Optimized Search) algorithm aims to resolve these problems.

```
Input:
        p:The current situation in the game tree for the
corresponding node
        maxSearchDepth:The max search depth  allow
Output:
        The bestMove after   deep search
MoveStruct  ABOS(node p){
        Backup the node p to node q;
        Initialize Transposition Table T;
        Initialize History  Heuristic Table H;
        Initialize alpha= −∞ ,beta= +∞ ;

for(maxDepth=1;maxDepth<=maxSearchDepth;maxD
epth++)

/ /Interative   Deep{
                result=THAlphaBeta(q,1,alpha,beta);
//Aspiration
                if(reslut<alpha)
                    result=THAlphaBeta(q,1, −∞ ,alpha);
//Aspiration
                else    if(result > beta)
                    result=THAlphaBeta(q,1,beta, +∞ ) ;
//Aspiration
                if(result  ==  TIMEOUT)
//Interative  Deep    timeout
                    break;
                else{
                        alpha=result-
MinimumWindowSize/2;

beta=result+MinimumWindowSize/2;
                Backup  bestMove  to backupMove;
```

```
                }
            }
        Use node q  cover node q;
        backupMove cover bestMove;
        return   bestMove;
}
```

```
Input:
     p:The current situation in the game tree for the
corresponding node
     depth:Search deepth
     alpha:Low bound of  search process
     beta:High  bound  of  search process
Output:
     The  evaluation of  node p  in  sense of  depth

int  THAlphaBeta(node p,int depth, int alpha, int beta){
    if( GameOver ){
        if(Achieve the goal for  positive side)
             return  +∞
        else
             return   −∞
    }
    if( Search node p information in T)
//Transposition   Table
         return  corresponding value in T;
    if(depth  > maxDepth{
        Result=Evaluation(p);
        Insert the node p, result, depth etc into T;
        return result;
    }
    Generator the move queue Q of node  p;
    Get  all history weight  in  Q from H;//History
Heuristic
    According  history weight of  moves merge sort
them in descending order ;
//History Heuristic
    Initialize best= −∞ ;
    for(each move in  MoveQueue Q){

        if( TimeOut() )
             return  TIMEOUT;
        Accoring to the move change node p to new
node p';
        score=-THAlphaBeta(p',depth+1,-beta,-
alpha);   //recursive call
```

```
            Accoring to the move recovery node p' to
old node p;
            if(score > best){
                best=score
                if (depth = = 1) {
                    bestMove=move;
                }
                if(best > alpha){
                    alpha=best;
                }
                if(alpha >= beta){
                    break;
                }
            }

    }
        Insert the node p, result, depth etc into T;
//Transposition  Table
        Increase the  history  weight  of  bestMove  in
H;  //History Heuristic
        return  best;
}
```

ABOS algorithm to achieve the two functions are ABOS and THAlphaBeta , which function ABOS in the main application of the Aspiration Search and Interactive Deep optimization, and then in the ABOS in turn called by the Transposition Table and History Heuristic optimized THAlphaBeta function. In ultimately better the Aspiration Search, Interactive Deep, Transposition Table and History Heuristic combined with AlphaBeta pruning achieve our ABOS algorithm.

4 Comparative Experiment

To verify the ABOS algorithm, we implement ABOS algorithms on Chinese Chess game platform. Main experimental environment is as follows: Operating system Microsoft Windows XP Professional Service Pack 3, processor Intel (R) Pentium (R) 4 CPU 3.06 GHz, memory 1024MB RAM, to develop software for the Microsoft Visual C + +6.0, comparing results as shown in Figure 4, Figure 5 below:

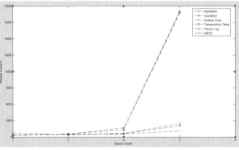

Fig. 4. Comparison of time efficiency by step

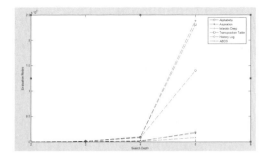

Fig. 5. Comparison of number of search nodes by step

Easy to see from the results with the search depth increases with each algorithm takes time, the evaluation number of nodes increases exponentially, ABOS algorithm in the variety of algorithms showed good performance, its time complexity and the number of nodes are valued the least. Compared with AlphaBeta prune algorithm and depth in case of 5 layers AlphaBeta the time required is about 23 times the ABOS, the need evaluate nodes number is about 76 times the ABOS.

5 Conclusion

After analyzing Alphabeta pruning and various game-tree optimal search algorithm, this paper proposes and implements ABOS. ABOS is better optimization strategy that combines the different advantages and characteristics of other strategy. The time efficiency of ABOS increased more than 10 fold while ensuring the search quality. Comparative test data from Chinese Chess Man-human platform makes the case. Man-machine has a long way to go. The net step of Man-machine will be focused on intelligent game program ability to learn. Using modifying valuation module of neural network to achieve more powerful intelligence.

References

1. Shannon, C.E.: Programming a computer for playing chess. Philosophical Magazine 41, 256 (1950)
2. Knuth, D.E., Moore, R.W.: An analysis of Alpha-Beta pruning. Aritificial Intelligence 6, 293 (1975)
3. Wang, X.-c.: PC game programming (Human-computer game), pp. 1–170. Chongqing University Press, Chongqing (2002)
4. Frayn, C.: Computer chess programming theory (EB/OL) (November 08, 2008), http://www.frayn.net/beowulf/theory.html
5. Zobrist, A.: A New Hashing Method with Application forGame Playing. Technical Report 88, Computer Science Department, University of Wisconsin, Madison (1970)
6. Schaeffer, J.: The history heuristic and Alpha-Beta Search enhancements in practice. IEEE Transactions on Pattern Anlysis and Machine Intelligence 11, 1203 (1989)

Color Image Segmentation Based on Learning from Spatial and Temporal Discontinuities

Chen Pan and Feng Cui

College of Information Engineering, China Jiliang University,
Hangzhou, Zhejiang, China
chenpan_2010@sogou.com

Abstract. This paper presents a coarse-to-fine learning method based on Extreme Learning Machine (ELM) for color image segmentation. Firstly, we locate a part of the object and background as candidate regions for sampling. By sampling from high gradient pixels (spatial discontinuity) and learning by ELM, we can extract object roughly. Due to ELM could produce different models by training with same data, the difference of their segmentation results shows some flicker in temporal feature (temporal discontinuity). So we can resampling from spatial and temporal discontinuities, and then produce a new classification model. The new model could extract object more accurately. Experimental results in natural image segmentation demonstrate the proposed scheme can reliably extract the object from the complex scenes.

Keywords: Image segmentation, ELM, Learning by sampling.

1 Introduction

Image segmentation is to separate the desired objects from the background. It is one of the most basic and key step in the automatic image analysis system. It's also a difficult and challenging problem owing to the complexity and the uncertainty of image. Image data is typically unstructured. Learning by sampling from data is an effective strategy to modeling unstructured data. However, how to selecting the learning algorithm and sampling from data are very critical in practice.

In past decade, supervised learning algorithm such as neural network (NN) and support vector machine (SVM) have been successfully applied to image segmentation [1]. Both of them have excellent ability of nonlinear approximation to provide models that are difficult to handle using classical parametric techniques. However, training is seldom in real-time due to time cost, so that few algorithms can generate segmentation model on-line adaptively. For examples, the training algorithms of conventional NN typically iteratively optimize the input and output weight vectors and the neuron biases, especially gradient descent techniques such as back-propagation (BP) methods are often used in training. That may result in long training time and lead overfitting. SVM is particularly attractive for its good generalization ability. However, training of SVM needs tune SVM kernel parameters carefully, that is not an easy job and time-consuming.

J. Zhang (Ed.): ICAIC 2011, Part III, CCIS 226, pp. 632–639, 2011.

Recently, Huang et al.[2] proposed a novel machine learning algorithm namely Extreme learning machine (ELM) that can significantly reduce the training time of a NN. The ELM theory shows that the hidden nodes of the "generalized" single-hidden layer feed forward networks (SLFNs), which need not be neuron alike, can be randomly generated and the universal approximation capability of such SLFNs can be guaranteed. ELM can analytically determine all the parameters of SLFNs instead of adjusting parameters iteratively.

For a given set of training samples $\{(\mathbf{x}_i, \mathbf{t}_i)\}_{i=1}^{N} \subset R^n \cdot R^m$, the output of an SLFN with L hidden nodes can be represented by

$$f_L(\mathbf{x}_j) = \sum_{i=1}^{L} \beta_i K(\mathbf{a}_i, b_i, \mathbf{x}_i) = t_j, \ j = 1, ..., N. \tag{1}$$

where $\mathbf{a}_i$ and b_i are the parameters of hidden node which could be randomly generated. $K(\mathbf{a}_i, b_i, \mathbf{x})$ is the output of the ith hidden node with respect to the input $\mathbf{x}$. And β_i is the weight connecting the ith hidden node to the output node. Equation (1) can be written compactly as

$$\mathbf{H\beta} = \mathbf{T} \tag{2}$$

After the hidden nodes are randomly generated and given the training data, the hidden-layer output matrix $\mathbf{H}$ is known and need not be tuned. Thus, training SLFNs simply amounts to getting the solution of a linear system (2) of output weights $\boldsymbol{\beta}$. According to Bartlett's theory [3] for feedforward neural networks, in order to get the better generalization performance, ELM not only tries to reach the smallest training error but also the smallest norm of output weights.

$$\text{Minimize: } \|\mathbf{H\beta} - \mathbf{T}\|$$
$$\text{and Minimize: } \|\boldsymbol{\beta}\| \tag{3}$$

Under the constraint of equation (3), a simple representation of the solution of the system (2) is given explicitly by Huang et al. [2] as

$$\hat{\boldsymbol{\beta}} = \mathbf{H}^{\dagger}\mathbf{T} \tag{4}$$

where $\mathbf{H}^{\dagger}$ is the Moore–Penrose generalized inverse of the hiddenlayer output matrix $\mathbf{H}$. When $L < N$,

$$\mathbf{H}^{\dagger} = (\mathbf{H}^{\mathbf{T}}\mathbf{H})^{-1}\mathbf{H}^{\mathbf{T}} \tag{5}$$

The number of hidden nodes of ELM is the only factor that need be set by user. Huang [2] proved if the number of hidden nodes of ELM is large enough, ELM always tends to minimize the training error as well as the norm of the output weights. So the performance of ELM depends on the training samples actually.

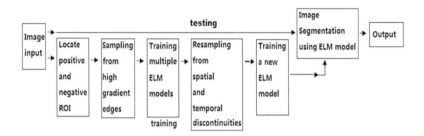

Fig. 1. The framework of the learning based image segmentation

It is worth to note that ELM is a SLFN with randomly generated hidden nodes. The model of ELM trained with same training data at different times may be slightly different. So the object extracted by those models may be different in the details. The difference could create a flickering effect in perception. This phenomenon is very interesting that means a kind of temporal discontinuity, which may provide some useful samples to improve segmentation result in the details.

This paper proposed a multiple learning strategy by sampling data from coarse-to-fine for complex image segmentation. In coarse stage, firstly we locate the region of interesting (ROI) as a part of the object and background. The high gradient pixels of object and background (which represents spatial discontinuity) are sampled to train several two-class classification models, which then extract object preliminarily. In fine stage, based on the first segmentation result, we re-sample the object region to group new positive samples, both spatial and temporal discontinuities could be considered in this stage. A new classification model could be trained finally, and then extracts entire object from the image.

2   Proposed Method

The framework of the method is shown in Fig.1. To segment entire multi-color object, we firstly uniform sampling from the edges within the ROIs, and then construct a classification model with ELM to make a CLUT in RGB color space for image segmentation. The key steps of training are to find the pixels with "saliency" in spatial and temporal domains in order to guide sampling or resampling.

A.   Locate the positive and negative regions of interesting

Learning by sampling strategy needs to locate the positive and negative ROIs to prepare training samples firstly. Many approaches could be used for this goal. For instances, we can indicate the location and region of the object and background by a few markers using strokes [4], give some initial points for clustering by mean shift [5], or over-segment image into homogenous subregions with watershed [6]. It is worth to note that the ROI is just a part of regions of object, so over-segmentation technique may be good at to make ROI, since it can produce pure samples without noise or outliers.

B. Sampling based on entropy in spatial domain

Shannon entropy of local attributes is often used to define saliency in terms of local signal complexity or unpredictability [7]. We note that the entropy of edge (spatial discontinuity) within a region in some gradient level is always higher than that of the original region. It means that edges could have higher "information content" in some scale to form a peak of entropy. So the aim of sampling in our method is the high gradient pixels in the region with the maximum entropy rather than all pixels.

Given an original region, a gradient threshold s is used to select high gradient pixels to form a new region R(s), and a descriptor D that takes on values $\{d_1,...,d_r\}$ (e.g. in an 8 bit grey level image D would range from 0 to 255), local entropy is defined as a function of s:

$$H_{D,R}(s) = -\sum_i P_{D,R}(s,d_i)\log_2 P_{D,R}(s,d_i) \tag{6}$$

where $P_{D,R}(s,d_i)$ is the probability of descriptor D taking the value d_i in the local region R with s gradient level (or scale). In order to determine where edge (high gradient pixels) should be sampled, the optimal gradient threshold is

$$s = \arg\max H_{D,R}(s) \tag{7}$$

In order to determine the number of sampling, the Nyquist–Shannon sampling theorem is applicable in our method.

$$N_{sample} > 2C_{object} \tag{8}$$

where N_{sample} is the number of sampling from an object, and C_{object} is the number of color in the object, which is regard as the frequency of color. In this paper, C_{object} is a range value of color distribution of an image in hue histogram.

C.   Sampling based on difference in temporal domain

We train at least two models of ELM with same training set, but randomly generated hidden nodes to each model. So those two models may be slightly different. Using different models, we can extract same object repeatedly and easily find out the difference about the object by comparison.

In order to avoid noise, we focus on the changes of the main connected part of object, rather than external difference far away the object. The difference of object region represents some temporal discontinuity which is salient in temporal feature due to its flicker. These salient pixels in temporal feature are usually the details of the object in spatial domain, which could be sampled as temporal information to complement spatial samples. Thus the final training samples of our method can be grouped with spatial and temporal information. Fig.2 shows an instance of the proposed method.

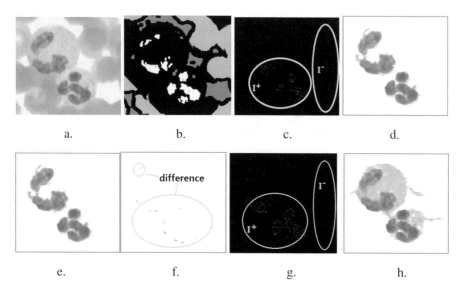

a.   b.   c.   d.

e.   f.   g.   h.

Fig. 2. An instance for leukocyte image segmentation. a).Original image. b). ROIs of object and background found by mean shift algorithm. c). Positive samples (I+) and negative samples (I-) after uniform sampling from high gradient pixels. d). Result 1. e). Result 2. f). The difference between segmentation result 1 and 2. g). New training set grouped by re-sampling in (b) and (f). h).Final segmentation result.

3   Experimental Results

Three segmentation error measures such as over-segmentation rate (OR), under-segmentation rate (UR), and overall error rate (ER) are applied to evaluate the ability of the segmentation method. Let Q_p is the number of pixels that should be included in the segmentation result but are not, U_p is the number of pixels that should be excluded in the segmentation result but are included, and D_p is the number of pixels that are included in the desired objects generated by manual cutting. OR, UR and ER can be described as:

$$OR = \frac{Q_P}{U_P + D_P},$$

$$UR = \frac{U_P}{U_P + D_P},$$

$$ER = \frac{Q_P + U_P}{D_P} \tag{9}$$

We had test 65 complex leukocyte images with ELM-based models trained with spatial information and both spatial and temporal information, respectively. The comparison results are shown in Fig.3.

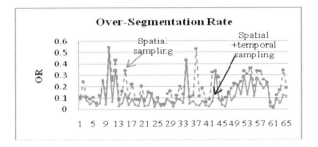

a.

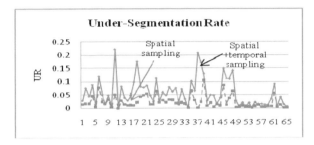

b.

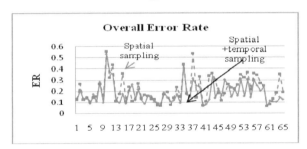

c.

Fig. 3. Comparison performance curves of two sampling strategies. The dotted curve denotes performance of the model trained with spatial information only. The solid curve denotes performance of the model trained with spatial and temporal information.

From the Fig.3, the proposed method could sharply reduce the over-segmentation rate to most images. Although the under-segmentation rate of the new sampling strategy slightly increase compare to the conventional sampling strategy, the overall error rate is reduced indeed. These results demonstrate that the effect of performance improvement is obvious.

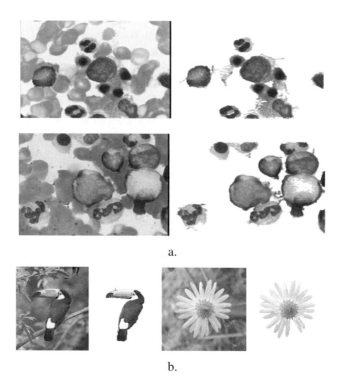

Fig. 4. Examples of the proposed method segments images. a). Leukocyte images. b).Natural bird and flower images.

4 Conclusions

This paper presents a novel framework for color image segmentation with learning by multiple classifiers. This idea has been less studied in literature, probably due to the large time needed in training. However, based ELM, supervised algorithm can generate segmentation model on-line adaptively. We present an effective resampling strategy focus on the spatial and temporal discontinuities, and use entropy criterion and the segmentation difference of ELM models to locate the most effective samples automatically. Experimental results in natural image segmentation demonstrate the proposed scheme can reliably extract the object from the complex scenes.

Acknowledgment. This work was supported by the Natural Science Foundation of Zhejiang Province of China (No. Y1091039).

References

1. Cheng, H.D., Jiang, X.H., Sun, Y., Wang, J.L.: Color image segmentation: advances and prospects. Pattern Recognit. 34, 2259–2281 (2001)
2. Huang, G.-B., Zhu, Q.-Y., Siew, C.-K.: Extreme learning machine: theory and applications. Neurocomputing 70(3), 489–501 (2006)

3. Barlett, P.L.: The sample complexity of pattern classification with neural networks: The size of the weights is more important than the size of the network. IEEE Trans. on Information Theory 44(2), 525–536 (1998)
4. Ning, J.F., Zhang, L., Zhang, D., et al.: Interactive image segmentation by maximal similarity based region merging. Pattern Recognition 43(2), 445–456 (2010)
5. Pan, C., Fang, Y., Yan, X., Zheng, C.: Robust segmentation for low quality cell images from blood and bone marrow. International Journal of Control, Automation, and Systems 4(5), 637–644 (2006)
6. Hengen, H., Spoor, S., Pandit, M.: Analysis of Blood and Bone Marrow Smears using Digital Image Processing Techniques. In: SPIE Medical Imaging, San Diego, vol. 4684, pp. 624–635 (February 2002)
7. Kadir, T., Brady, M.: Saliency, Scale and Image Description. IJCV 45(2), 83–105 (2001)

Wisdom Logistics Based on Cloud Computing

Zhiying Zhou and Dandan Lv

Modern Logistics School
Zhejiang Wanli University
Ning bo, Zhejiang Province, China, 315100
DandanLv2011@163.com

Abstract. Wisdom logistics is considered as modern logistics service system based on intelligent transportation systems and relevant information technology. It is eager for wisdom logistics to integrate IT resources in logistics industry. Previous technologies such as grid computing can not help wisdom logistics achieve this goal without appropriate business model and cloud computing can. With cloud computing network service-providers can deal with hundreds of millions of information at one moment just as using super computers with strong computing capability. Meanwhile, users can use of these resources and services on demand to achieve the dream of using of computing as public utilities. Based on analyzing the demand of logistics for cloud computing, this paper constructed logistics cloud computing platform solution. And cloud computing implement architecture consisting of infrastructure layer, application layer and service provider layer was set up. This model has expedited new market and new services for logistics.

Keywords: Cloud Computing, Wisdom Logistics, Platform, Implement Architecture.

1 Wisdom Logistics Introduction

IBM CEO proposed "Wisdom Earth" in 2008 and the China premier proposed "Experience China" in 2009. Logistics industry is the earliest one to contact with "Internet of Things" and to achieve intelligent and atomized logistics. So China Logistics Technology Association of Information Center and Chinese Internet of Things first proposed the concept of "Wisdom Logistics". Wisdom Logistics is considered as modern logistics service system of electronic commercialized operation based on intelligent transportation systems and relevant information technology[1]. Wisdom Logistics mainly includes the following four sides. The first is intelligently traceable network system based on RFID. The second is visually management network of intelligent distribution, which can real-timely schedule and manage logistics vehicle distribution on line based on GPS. The third is building fully automated logistics network distribution center based on advanced technologies of sound, light, machines, electricity and mobile computing. It will realize logistics intelligent and network automatic operation. The fourth is logistics network public information platform based on intelligent distribution. Wisdom Logistics needs more

J. Zhang (Ed.): ICAIC 2011, Part III, CCIS 226, pp. 640–646, 2011.

thoroughly aware, more comprehensive Unicom, more deep intelligence and more advanced platform[1].

2 Cloud Computing Overview

Cloud computing is a convenient and flexible calculation mode. And it is a shared pool of resources and computers which are on-demand, accessed and used through network. Cloud computing achieves to quickly configure and launch kinds of computing resources at the least management payment and minimal interaction with service providers. Cloud computing is the further development and Commercial implementations of distributed processing, parallel processing, grid computing, network storage and large data centers[2]. Such as power plant provides measurable power resources to users, cloud computing can package the abstract resources into measurable service to users. Cloud computing is considered as a big resources pool, in which resources can be accessed by abstract interface and general standards[3]. As new network technology, cloud computing is a complex of many technologies including virtualization, distributed mass data storage and distributed parallel programming[4].

Cloud computing has many advantages. In cloud computing computer users will not depend on one specific computer to access and deal with owner data. And it will improve the use mobility of computers resources. Computers will be smaller, lighter and less energy consumption. It brings new opportunities for multiple people collaboration[5].

Service model of cloud computing includes three levels of "end", "pipe", "cloud", shown in Fig 1. The "end" means the terminal equipments for users' access to the "cloud". The "pipe" means network channels of information transmission. The "cloud" means the resources pool of infrastructure center, platforms and application servers supplying ICT resources and information service. Cloud computing provides infrastructure, platform and application. "Cloud" consists of three layers: Infrastructure layer such as kinds of servers, databases, storage devices, parallel and distributed computing systems and so on; platform layer consisting of operations, support and development platform; application layer providing application such as software, data and information[6].

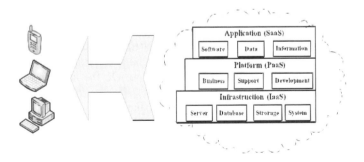

Fig. 1. "End"- "pipe"-"cloud" service model of cloud computing

Cloud computing and Internet of Things complete each other. One side cloud computing needs development from concept towards application, the other side Internet of Things needs strong support platform to meet the scale[7].

3   The Demand for Cloud Computing of Logistics Industry

China's logistics proportion of GDP has remained high. Logistics market is small and scattered. China has no logistics informatization long-strategy system because of the low total planning capability in Chinese logistics enterprises. The difficulty in information communication led to large storage and transport capacity waste in the links. The information degree is low in many logistics enterprises, which have backward information technology and logistics devices. Many information system functions have not played the important role, in which the logistics information platform is most significant. The former logistics information platform has the dispersed logistics information and the recourses can't be integrated. Many information islands come into being. How to improve industry efficiency and logistics service quality to reduce logistics costs becomes the urgent problem. Integrating current logistics resources in society is an effective way, in which resources can be shared and information network will be one. And some challenges are faced with. The first is information technology how to spread, information coordination how to improve, how to reduce the waste from asymmetric information. The second is how to build and optimize logistics network. The third is financial logistics how to reduce cash flow cycle. The fourth is how to share and train logistics knowledge. The fifth is how to plan urban transportation and protect environment by technology. The sixth is how to improve government service by more convenient electronic government service. How do we achieve these targets but do not increase investment in hardware and software? Cloud computing can help it.

Smarter logistics operation is the key to be stronger for logistics enterprises.

Among operating links, cost optimization, collaboration and visualization are the most important. In modern logistics especially in modern supply chain, collaboration is very extensive. How to form effective coordination mechanism is an urgent problem. The visualization of the logistics chain and supply chain can bring thorough insight for enterprise development. Cost is always the focus of logistics and customers. Analysis and optimization can bring the logistics cost reduced. Logistics visualization is the basis to achieve the high quality logistics service and Internet of Things is the basis of logistics visualization. By embedding sensors into various public facilities, Internet of Things is integrated with current internet. In the integration, there are super-powerful central computers group able to control the personnel, machinery, equipment and infrastructure. On the basis wisdom logistics come true, shown in Fig2.

In wisdom logistics, 3PL, bank, government and mobile communication are the basis guaranty. The logistics business includes TMS(Transportation Management System), WMS(Warehouse Management System), EMS(Express Management System) and logistics coordination. Logistics tracking and traceability system makes it possible to solve problems at first time. Logistics analyzing and optimization services bring higher quality.

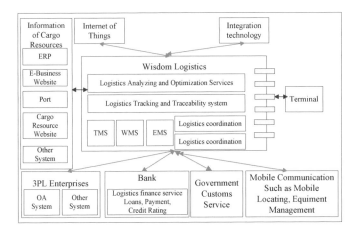

Fig. 2. Wisdom logistics architecture

Cloud computing can combine high internet, high-performance computers, large databases, sensors and remote devices into one. In cloud computing resources, storage resources, information resources and knowledge resources etc can be shared so that it can eliminate the information islands and resources inlands. It has its unique advantages in resources integration. In cloud computing logistics resources will be integrated on the basis of current software and hardware to reduce the logistics cost by sharing logistics resources.

4   Cloud Computing in Wisdom Logistics

Cloud computing can effectively reduce IT investment and risk, can get IT service in less investment and shorter cycle to improve enterprises' responsiveness to business changes. Meanwhile enterprises can achieve more professional IT solution more fit to develop.

A.   Logistics cloud operation platform solution, shown in Fig3

The solution provides total solution for platform planning, designing and implementing. It combines the most advanced concept and logistics statue to help customers analyze and know Chinese logistics statue and development from total and strategy. It builds the logistics public information service platform.

This platform is based on cloud computing concept. It builds high stability and strong expansion basic framework by using data management virtualization technology, calculation virtual technology and application service virtual technology. It creates reusable, loosely coupled SOA application architecture.

In this solution, there are eleven kinds of service providers supporting varieties of special services for logistics service platform. They are government support from government agencies, information services from platform operators, logistics consulting services from logistics consulting business, software technical support from logistics ISV/SI, industry knowledge training from training institutions, financial support from banks, new technologies form research institutions, logistics insurance from insurance industry, mobile information network support from mobile providers, network hardware services from network hardware providers, improving equipment from logistics equipment suppliers for logistics service platform.

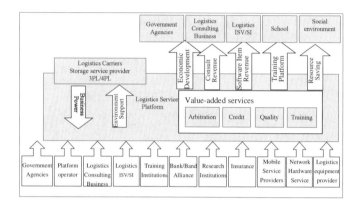

Fig. 3. Logistics cloud operation platform solution

B. The cloud computing implement architecture of wisdom logistics, shown in Fig 4

The architecture is composed of three layers.

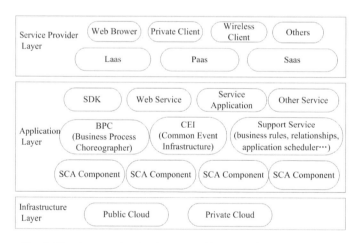

Fig. 4. Cloud computing implement architecture of wisdom logistics

1) Infrastructure Layer: In this layer, there are hardware resources and software resources which support the platform. Hardware resources include computers, storage devices, net devices etc. Software resources include storage services, queue services, application services and logistics management business services. These resources are managed by distributed computing system and it external offers unique computing services. According to the different confidentiality of resources, different resources are deployed in public cloud and private cloud. For big logistics enterprises, cloud computing platform can be set up in their own internal. This is private cloud which can offer services for production management within the enterprise or some high security data. For most SME(small and median enterprises) or some low security data, their resources can be deployed in public cloud. Public cloud deployed on internet provides special services for permission users. These services are usually deployed in the hosting place. Service software and database are maintained by operators. Public cloud well solves the problem of data islands and information asymmetric. System integration is easily achieved. The public can avoid duplication development and waste of resources; can enhance the information level of SME.

2) Application Layer: It is necessary to construct software infrastructure to meet enterprise application on infrastructure layer if cloud computing wants to play advantage and provide enterprise-class services of external. The software infrastructure is just operating environment, by which users can design and operate service in cloud computing. Operating environment should meet the requirement from service definition, service management and service call. Users can define service to meet business by the support of service definition from operating environment. Service assembling, service arrangement and service regulation are offered by service management to meet the definition of specific business processes. And service call provides the unified interface for the service call of users. And it is convenient for users to use the services in cloud computing platform.

3) Service Provider Layer: As a new business model cloud computing is provided to users in the way of IT as a service. IT as a service includes IaaS(Infrastructure as a Service), PaaS(Platform as a Service) and SaaS(Software as a Service).

The demand for IT of enterprises is flexible. Those three ways offered by cloud computing can meet enterprises' demand in different applications levels. IaaS provides infrastructure to meet the enterprises' demand for hardware resources. PaaS provides users with the basic runtime environment for application to support enterprises designing on the platform. The platform adaptation will be stronger. SaaS provides software supporting enterprises to operate. In this environment enterprises can achieve faster software delivery and get professional software services at lower cost. In the mode of IT as a service, service providers offer users hardware, software service and consulting service through network. Users can customize services in the cloud according to their actual needs. Then users can pay to cloud computing provider by the number of service and the length of time. Thus logistics enterprises don't need to maintain software because the service provider of cloud computing platform does it.

As an innovation of technology concept and business models, cloud computing play more influence on people's thinking way and information development. Just as what Deyi Li said: cloud computing can bring the socialization of information service. It has changed and refined popular demands. And it has expedited new market and new services. The application of cloud computing in logistics will bring more wisdom logistics.

Acknowledgment. R.B.G. thanks the reference authors for helps in my paper.

References

1. Wu, S., Yan, G.: Wisdom City—Technology Leading Harmony, pp. 215–221. Zhejiang University Press, Hang Zhou (2010)
2. Zhang, J.: The Concept and Impact Analysis of Cloud Computing. Telecom Network Technology (1), 55–58 (2009)
3. Yang, S., Liu, Y.: Comprehensive Comparison of Grid Computing and Cloud Computing. Digital Communications (6), 32–36 (2009)
4. Xiao, Y., Liu, Y.: Key Technology and Application Outlook of Cloud Computing. Digital Communications (6), 29–31 (2009)
5. Xu, L.: Application and Research Cloud Computing Technology in IT Industry. Computer Study (6), 8–10 (2010)
6. Liu, Y.: Reviews of Cloud Computing and Research on the Application of Mobile Cloud Computing. Computing, Information Communication Technology (2), 14–20 (2010)
7. Zhu, J.: Wisdom Cloud Computing—the Basis of Internet of Things Development, pp. 156–159. Electronic Industry Press, Beijing (2010)

The Research of Multi-pose Face Detection Based on Skin Color and Adaboost[*]

Ran Li, Guang-Xing Tan, and Sheng-Hua Ning

Department of Electronic Information and Control
Engineering, Guangxi University of Technology
Liuzhou, Guangxi, China
tanguangxing12@tom.com

Abstract. According to the situation of the traditional Adaboost algorithm can't effectively detect multi-pose, skin color segmentation and Adaboost used to detect face is presented in this paper. First, the general face region-Region of interesting (ROI) is detected with skin color segmentation to divide face and background, and then Adaboost detector is used to detect this region. The experiment result shows multi-pose face can be well detected by the algorithm combing color segmentation and Adaboost.

Keywords: Adaboost, face detection, skin color segmentation, multi-pose.

1 Introduction

Face detection is the process of determining the location of all the face, size, and posture in the image or video. Frontal face is the main aspect of study in early, there has several mature algorithms been prospected [1]; but few achievements in multi-pose face detection. Recently, the algorithm research of multi-pose face detection are mainly focused on multi-pose templates[2], Adaboost algorithm [3] with new Haar-like features added in, the improved boosting algorithm-FloatBoost [4]. These methods are sensitive for face pose; the detection rate will come down with the variation of poses.

Face detection based on skin color as a rough detection has advantages of computing speed, gesture, size, cover with robust for the multi-pose face color image. Face color most gathered in a region, so skin color can be used on face detection. Research[5] indicates skin color in Cb-Cr plane of color space YCbCr gathered in an ellipse region. Ten pieces in different sizes and luminance of different facial images has been collected as the specimens downloaded from internet to projection, skin color pixels are in a cabined region, and experimental results demonstrate the skin color has a well clustering property in YCbCr color space.

In this paper, the image has been transformed from RGB to YCbCr, obtained the binary image after segmentation using simple Guassian model and improved OSTU algorithm, then to calculate the candidate region of face using projection, and then used Adaboost algorithm to detect this candidate region, last the result of detection has been exported. It not only solves face detection in multi-pose solution, but also shorts time by using fast locating face region. Through the experiments of testing vast multi-pose

J. Zhang (Ed.): ICAIC 2011, Part III, CCIS 226, pp. 647–654, 2011.
© Springer-Verlag Berlin Heidelberg 2011

faces in different environments, the experiments indicate the algorithm in this paper has a well performance in multi-pose face detection, and it has higher detection rate than Adaboost.

2 Face Location Based on Skin Color

A. Skin Color Segmentation

Currently there are many color spaces applied to skin color detection, such as RGB, YCbCr, YIQ, HSV, etc. RGB space is the most common color space; it adopts the different mixing ratio of red, green, blue three basic colors to characterize different colors. In skin color of face analysis, RGB color space is not suit to apply in skin color detection as its three basic weights all containing luminance information, and having overwhelmingly correlation with it. Literature[6] takes a clustering comparisons with skin color and non-skin color in RGB, YcbCr, YIQ, HSV color spaces, the weight SV of HSV color space has a scattered distribution in non-skin color specimens, the distributions of the weight CbCr of YcbCr color space and the weight I of YIQ color space both in skin color specimens and non-skin color specimens have well gathered together. And YcbCr space has good discreteness, Separation of luminance and chrominance and color clustering features, so we use YcbCr space as our color space. We randomly download 10 picture containing faces from internet; project the segmented skin color regions to the Cb-Cr plane. The total pixels number is 480647, the projection figure is follow:

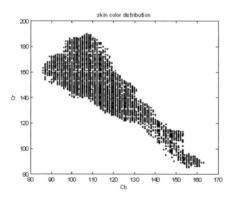

Fig. 1. Distribution of skin color in Cr-Cb

As can be seen from Figure 1, the distribution of skin color mainly is in the narrow region of Cb: [90, 160], Cr: [80, 190]. The equation of conversion from RGB color space to YcbCr color space is as follow:

$$
\begin{bmatrix} Y \\ Cb \\ Cr \end{bmatrix} = \begin{bmatrix} 16 \\ 128 \\ 128 \end{bmatrix} + \begin{bmatrix} 0.257 & 0.504 & 0.098 \\ -0.148 & -0.291 & 0.439 \\ -0.439 & -0.368 & -0.071 \end{bmatrix} \cdot \begin{bmatrix} R \\ G \\ B \end{bmatrix} \tag{1}
$$

Commonly used color models are regional models, histogram model, Gaussian model, based on neural network model etc. The simple Gaussian model and improved OSTU algorithm are used skin color segmentation in this paper. By the formula (2) ~ (4) determine Gaussian model G(m, C) of color pixels in Cb-Cr space is:

$$m = (\overline{Cb}, \overline{Cr}) \tag{2}$$

$$\overline{Cb} = \frac{1}{N} \sum_{i=1}^{N} Cb_i \tag{3}$$

$$\overline{Cr} = \frac{1}{N} \sum_{j=1}^{N} Cr_j \tag{4}$$

$$C = E[(x-m)(x-m)^T] = \begin{bmatrix} \sigma_{CrCr} & \sigma_{CrCb} \\ \sigma_{CbCr} & \sigma_{CbCb} \end{bmatrix} \tag{5}$$

which $\overline{Cb}$, $\overline{Cr}$ is average value of Cb, Cr; C is covariance matrix. Statistics 10 face images are m, C as follows:

$$m = [111.7394, 141.0289]^T,$$

$$C = \begin{bmatrix} 168.2083 & 179.6752 \\ 179.6952 & 324.8560 \end{bmatrix}.$$

Converting every pixel of color image from RGB color space to YCbCr color space, and then calculating the probability of the pixel belonged to the face region, that is to get the similarity of the pixel to the center of Gaussian distribution. The formula is:

$$P(Cb, Cr) = \exp[-0.5(x-m)^T C^{-1}(x-m)] \tag{6}$$

P(Cb, Cr) reflects the degree of similarity between each pixels and skin color, the greater its value, the greater the likelihood that skin color is, the smaller the contrary.

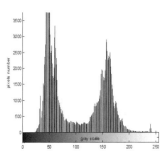

Fig. 2. Histogram of likelihood

Through formula (5) calculated the probability of skin area of pixels in image, the range of face color probability is 05-0.7, so the corresponding to the skin color range of skin color likelihood image is [127.5, 178.5]. The range of classical OSTU algorithm is [0, 255], the improved range is [127.5, 178.5].

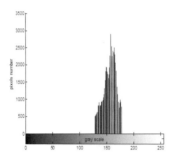

Fig. 3. Histogram of ROI

Figure 2 is the histogram of skin color likelihood image; Figure 3 is the histogram of face candidate region (ROI). Using the improved OSTU algorithm to calculate the ROI can get the threshold k, if the value of pixel is greater than threshold k, the value of pixel is 255, and otherwise the value is 0. At last, the binary image of original image segmented can be calculated.

a. original   b. likelihood   c. binary image

Fig. 4. Process of skin color segmentation

Figure 4 shows the processing of skin color segmentation, Fig 4.a is the original image, Fig 4.b is the likelihood image of the original image, it calculated from Gaussian model, Fig 4.c is the binary image of segmentation, using improved OSTU from the likelihood image to get the binary image.

B. Morphology Processing and Face Location

Due to the effect of noise, the binary image of after skin color segmentation usually has a few isolated pieces, or missed hole as the unbalance illumination in the face region. Therefore, we preprocess the image using morphological before the further detection. In order to eliminate small noise in skin areas, the 3*3 structuring element selected in the paper used to calculate opening operation for the skin color segmented binary image, removed the isolated noise and the protruding part of face. Using 2*2 structure elements operates the expansion treatment for the image after corrosion to eliminate the smaller holes in the region. Projection the image after morphological processing to determine the left-right borders and the upper-lower border of face region, we can get the region of interesting (ROI).

3 Adaboost Detection

After face region location based on skin color, a more accurate position of face by using Adaboost[7] algorithm detecting face can be reveived. Adaboost is an iterative algorithm, the basic idea is to cascade a large number of weak classifiers to be a strong classifier which has a strong ability to classify.

Adaboost algorithm is based on the Haar-like rectangular, some simple characters of face can be described by these simple rectangular features, and the feature value is defined as the difference of the white pixel and the black pixel.

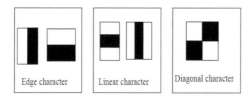

Edge character   Linear character   Diagonal character

Fig. 5. Haar-like characters

For the point A in graphics, the definition of integral image is the sum of all pixels of the top left.

$$ii(x, y) = \sum_{x \le x', y \le y'} i(x', y') \tag{7}$$

Calculate the sum of all pixels in the line:

$$s(x, y) = \sum_{y' \le y} i(x, y') = s(x, y-1) + i(x, y) \tag{8}$$

Traversing the image using above formulas once can calculate the integral image. Adaboost algorithm is described as follow:

a)   Given n training samples $(x_1, y_1), \cdots, (x_n, y_n)$ as a training set, which $y_i = 0$ or 1, $(i = 1, 2, \cdots n)$ 0 indicates that the sample doesn't contain a face, 1 means containing face.

b)   Initialize the weight of the sample:

$$\omega_1(x_i) = \frac{1}{n}, i = 1, 2, \cdots, n \tag{9}$$

c)   Training T round, $t = 1,2,\cdots,n$, normalized sample weights:

$$\omega_t(x_i) = \frac{\omega_t(x_j)}{\sum\limits_{j=1}^{n}\omega_t(x_j)} \tag{10}$$

d)   For each characteristic j, train a simple classifier $h_j(x)$:

$$h_j(x) = \begin{cases} 1, & p_j f_j(x) < p_j \theta_j \\ 0, & other \end{cases} \tag{11}$$

which, θ_j is a threshold, $p_j = \pm 1$ control the direction of inequation, then calculate classification error rate of each characteristic j:

$$\varepsilon_j = \sum_{i=1}^{n}\omega_i(x_i)\left|h_j(x_i) - y_i\right| \tag{12}$$

Selected the lowest error classification is used as a simple classification of the weak classifier $h_t(x)$, mark the error rate as ε_t , adjust the weights of all samples:

$$\omega_{t+1}(x_i) = \begin{cases} \omega_t(x_i)\beta_t & classifiered \\ \omega_t(x_i) & other \end{cases} \tag{13}$$

which $\beta_t = \dfrac{\varepsilon_t}{1-\varepsilon_t}$.

Through the analysis of positive and negative samples, select the number T of lowest error rate weak classifier optimization into a strong classifier.

The final strong classifier is:

$$H(x) = \begin{cases} 1, & \sum\limits_{t=1}^{T}\alpha_T h_t(x) \geq \dfrac{1}{2}\sum\limits_{t=1}^{T}\alpha_t \\ 0, & \end{cases} \tag{14}$$

which $\alpha_t = -\log\beta_t$

To find the minimum error rate weak classifier on the probability distribution of each iterations, and then adjust the probability distribution, reduction the value of current weak classifiers to classify the right samples in order to highlight the error classified samples, so that the next iteration point to this error classification, that is making the error classified samples getting more training. Thus, the weak classifier followed extraction will train more the error classified samples.

4 Experiment

This algorithm is divided into two stages: skin color segmentation and Adaboost detection. Algorithm achieves on the Matlab7.0. The experimental samples are 108 frontal face images and 72 multi-pose images. The system processing described as Figure 6.

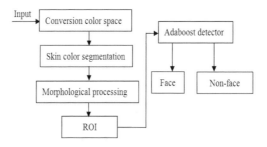

Fig. 6. System processing image

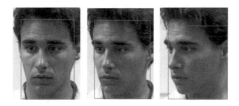

Fig. 7. Multi-pose pose detection

The Figure 7 is partial results of multi- pose detection, this algorithm compared with Adaboost, and the result is as Tab1, Tab2:

Table 1. Result of algorithm in paper

Result	Algorithm in paper	
	Front face	Muti-pose
No. sample	108	72
Correct	102	64
Error detect	6	8
Detect rate	94.4	88.9

From the Tab.1 and Tab.2, it can be found the detect rates are almost the same when using the algorithms proposed in this paper and Adaboost detecting the front faces, and the Adaboost algorithm has lower detection rate detecting the multi-pose faces. At the same time, it can be found both the detectors will lose function if the face rotation over 60 degree.

Table 2. Result of Adaboost

Result	Adaboost	
	Front face	Muti-pose
No. sample	108	72
Correct	102	64
Error detect	7	22
Detect rate	93.5	69.4

5   Conclusions

To solve the lower detection rate of Adaboost algorithm for multi-pose face detection, a novel algorithm of combined skin color model and Adaboost algorithm for multi-pose face detection has been proposed in this paper. The experiments show this algorithm is better than single Adaboost algorithm in multi-pose face detection.

References

1. Yang, M.-H., Kriegman, D., Narendra, A.: Detecting faces in images: A survey. IEEE Tran. on Pattern Analysis and Machine Intelligence 4(1), 34–58 (2002)
2. Shao, P., Yang, L.-m., Huang, H.-b., Zeng, Y.-r.: Rapid Face Detection with Multi-pose Knowledge Models and Templates. Journal of Chinese Computer Systems 2(2), 346–350 (2007)
3. Liu, X.-k., Sun, X.-h., Zhou, Y.-x.: Multi- angle Face Detection Based on New Haar-like Feature. Computer Engineering 35(19), 195–197 (2009)
4. Li, S.Z., Zhang, Z.-q.: Floatboost learning and statistical face detection. IEEE Trans. on Pattern Analysis and Machine Intelligence 26(9), 1112–1123 (2004)
5. Bojic, N., Pang, K.K.: Adaptive skin segmentation for head and shoulder video sequences. In: Visual communications 8th Image Processing, vol. 4067, pp. 704–711. SPIE, San Jose (2000)
6. Hsu, R.-L., Mohamed, Jain, A.K.: Face detection in color images. IEEE Trans. on Pattern Analysis and Machine Intelligence 24(5), 696–706 (2002)
7. Viola, P., Jones, M.: Rapid object detection using a boosted cascade of simple features. In: Proc. of Conf. on Computer Vision and Patten Recognition, Kauai, Hawaii, USA, pp. 511–518 (2001)
8. Comaniciu, D., Ramesh, V.: Robust Detection and Tracking of Human Faces with an ActiveCamem. In: IEEE Int. Workshop on Visual Surveil-lance, Dublin, Ireland, pp. 11–18 (2000)
9. Jones, M.J., Rehg, J.M.: Statistical Color Models with Application to Skin Detection. Technical Report Series, Cambridge Research Laboratory 46(1), 81–96 (1998)

Research and Implementation of 3D Interactive Digital Campus Based on Spatial Database[*]

Libing Wu, Tianshui Yu, Kui Gong, Yalin Ke, and Peng Wen

School of Computer
Wuhan University
Wuhan, China
shuiyu.tian22@sogou.com

Abstract. Immersion and interactivity are the main characteristics of virtual reality technology. It gives the user the real world experience beyond the two-dimensional. This article focuses on the key technologies involved and their principles and applications in the process of establishing a dynamically modified to in-depth 3D interactive of Digital Campus System. These technologies include modeling, scene generation technology and interactive technology. Their interaction with the system features and user experience are closely related.

Keywords: BS Contact, VRML, interactive technology, 3D scene, Spatial Database.

1 Introduction

The traditional 3D model is completed by the modeler. If you want to modify it, the source file must be changed. It can't be easily and fast dynamic changes. And the static 3D scene just shows us the 360 degrees scene. It is lack of interaction with the user and realism is not strong. The 3D scene based on spatial database can open the information automatically generated according to the database file each time, and all nodes in the scene changes are saved to the database. It can be modified to facilitate a dynamic scene. The BS SDK provides the 3D scene of VRML powerful interactive capabilities, allowing us to easily control the 3D scene through the pages to the behavior, allowing us to multi-angle, more 3D observation of 3D scene [1].

A. VRML

VRML (Virtual Reality Modeling Language) is a language of establishing a model of a real-world scenarios or an imaginary scene modeling 3D world, and it is independent of platform. It is the mainstream language of WWW-based 3D interactive website that was produced in the Internet. VRML 2.0 standard, known as the second generation of Web language, it changed the WWW on the monotonous, poor interaction weaknesses,

---

* Supported by National Natural Science Foundation of China (Grant No. 61070010), National Science Foundation for Post-doctoral Scientists of China, the Natural Science Foundation of Hubei Province and the Fundamental Research Funds for the Central Universities.

J. Zhang (Ed.): ICAIC 2011, Part III, CCIS 226, pp. 655–662, 2011.

which will act as viewed topics and all with the performance of all acts of the operator is changed. VRML create an accessible and participated world. You can see site vivid, lifelike 3D world on a computer network and you can roam free inside. You can be the popular MUD games on the network into 3D graphic world. You can adapt your company's home page into 3D home page, enabling visitors to experience the actual appearance of your company and not just simple text or tables.

VRML is essentially a modeling language for the web and 3D object-oriented, and it is an interpretive language. VRML objects called nodes and child nodes can constitute a complex set of features. Nodes can be reused by an example and after they assigned the name defined you can create dynamic virtual world.

B. BS Contact

BS Contact player is developed by Bitmanagement Software GmbH of Germany. It implements most of the node of the x3d standard of web3d Union, but also expanded the number of application nodes. Good graphics rendering system for the development of virtual reality x3d provides programming interfaces and it greatly improved the efficiency of construction x3d virtual reality system.

The 3D digital campus system researched in this paper is based on VRML, BS Contact and JavaScript. The relationship between them is shown in Fig.1.

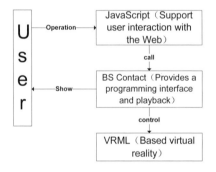

Fig. 1. Sketch of Technical Relationship

Based on the above-mentioned tools and technology, this paper divides technologies of 3D digital campus system into three key technologies. They are modeling, scene generation technology and interactive technology. Let's elaborate the followings one by one.

2   Modeling

The modeling of 3D model, including buildings, trees, ponds, terrain and so on need professional modelers working with professional tools. These model node file called the original model node and it is simply used to display. If you want to interact with 3D scene and may be able to achieve a variety of operations, it must be controlled outside of its statement and created a powerful new node, called the initial node.

However, the initial node has an obvious drawback, many control statements, complex structure, it is not in our habit of software development and not conducive to the development and maintenance. To solve this problem is the prototype node, the function of the prototype node in an external file can be defined, leaving only a very simple form of expression, such node is simple and effective.

The significance of the definition of a prototype node is that we can set a uniform format, a unified control and management (such as the explicit-implicit control, pan control) for all nodes in the VRML source code level. A simple and efficient format of nodes is very good for us to achieve functional. It can greatly simplify the control of our outer code, improve the efficiency of the system and conducive to future maintenance. The node relationship is shown in Fig. 2.

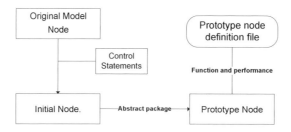

Fig. 2. Node Relationship diagram

Create prototyping nodes which according to the function we want to achieve; the control function we want to implement corresponds to a field of prototype node.

The prototype node of this system is as follows.

EXTERNPROTO   OMProto;

[

exposed Field SFInt32 show   ;

exposed Field SFBool   enableR ;

exposed Field SFBool   enableXZ ;

exposed Field SFBool   enableY ;

exposed Field SFVec3f translation;

exposed Field SFRotation   rotation;

exposed Field MF String urlModel;

];

Explain:

Show field was used to control hidden. 0 stands for display and -1 stands for occultation.

EnableR field was used to control the rotation. TRUE stands for open and FALSE stands for close.

EnableXZ field was used to control the Translation. TRUE stands for open and FALSE stands for close.

EnableY field was used to control the Lifting. TRUE stands for open and FALSE stands for close.

Translation field was used to indicate the location.

Rotation field was used to indicate the angle.

urlModel field was used to store the link building.

Note: This is only the manifestation of the prototype nodes and specific function in the prototype node should be defined in definition file.

3   Scene Generation Technology

A.   Spatial database

Spatial database is the basis for the entire 3D scene and the scene dynamically generated based on spatial data in the database. There are several nodes in the scene and their purpose, requirements are different. So the data table must be reasonable and simple[2].

Different types of nodes as shown in Fig. 3.

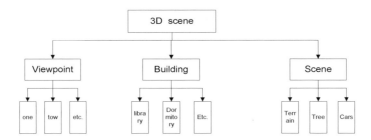

Fig. 3. Schematic diagram of the node type

Viewpoint may place in a separate data table because of the role of viewpoint and the model nodes are different and the data stored in the table are different. Model nodes such as buildings, trees, terrain and cars can be placed in a same table because the information they contain is about the same. Data table should include 3DID, location information (*DX*, *DY* and *DZ*), the angle information (*EX*, *EY*, *EZ* and *Angle*) and other 3D information. It also needs to increase the corresponding fields according to the function.

In addition, it need to create a main table to store the 3D scene model (Model table model does not necessarily in the scene). Dynamic adding or removing models in the scene is just need add or delete a record in the main table.

B.   Dynamic composite scene

The traditional 3D scene in 3D digital systems is built by modeler. The model of the scene can't be added or deleted dynamically. And Interactivity is very limited. If we want to be able to dynamically change the scene and to retain this change, the result of the operation must be stored in the database. Afterwards, it changes composites scene according to the spatial database each time. This is very easy to implement user control of 3D scene and modify the 3D scene model is no longer required to re-modelers.

The whole process is shown in Fig. 4.

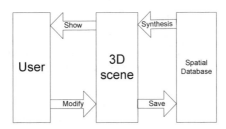

Fig. 4. Schematic generated scene

The principle of dynamic synthetic scenes is relatively simple. Using C# to create a file and then write the required VRML code into the file. A function can generate a class of nodes

A simple code to create the prototype of the node is as follows.

string strNode = "";

strNode += "Group {;

strNode += "children [;

strNode+= "DEF" + strName + " OMProto {;

strNode += "show 0;

strNode += "enableR   FALSE;

strNode += "enableXZ FALSE;

strNode += "enableY   FALSE;

strNode += "translation   " + dx + " " + dy+ " " + dz + ";

strNode += "rotation   " + ex + " " + ey + " " + ez + " " + angle + ";

strNode += "urlModel \"" + strUrl + "\"\n};

strNode += "];

strNode += "};

Key segments (such as *strName*, *dx*, *ex* and *strUrl*) are obtained from the database and they constitute a particular model node. Write all nodes in the main table into file as this, the scene is completed.

So each time the system starts, the scene database is dynamically generated according to the latest, which implements the dynamic updates.

4 Interactive Technology

Interactive technology of 3D scene is an important way to improve the user experience. Through interaction, the user can easily access more information and better control the behavior of 3D scene. This was more realistic 3D scene, more attractive to users. VRML provides a lot of support for interactive technology [3], which involves interaction of the nodes as follows.
Anchor: This node can add descriptions and hyperlinks for the model nodes.

Group node: *Group node* organizes the scene orderly. The *renmovechildren* field and *addchildren* field are mainly used in their interaction. Can be used to dynamically add or remove nodes.

Viewpoint: Including roaming events pre-defined. We mainly use its *set_bind* field to dynamically switch node or start with the suspension of roaming events.

Switch: Used to dynamically control the explicit-implicit.

Sensor node: There are three kinds of detectors. Touch Sensor detector is used to capture mouse click events or suspended, and as the initiator of the event. Plane Sensor node is used to implement the drag plane. Cylinder Sensor node is used to adjust the orientation.

Script: It is the executor of the event. Many functions need to be processed by *Script*, and it can also call a function in web pages. It is often used in conjunction with the detection node.

Interactive technology is divided into web-to-scene interaction and scene-to-web interaction. Relationship between two kinds of interaction is shown as Fig. 5 [4].

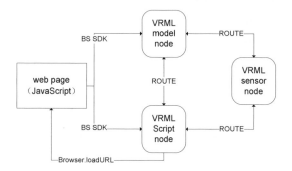

Fig. 5. Schematic diagram of interactive technology

A. Web-to-scene interaction

Web-to-scene interaction mainly used the function provided by BS SDK. It can easily control the behavior of 3D scene, or to obtain some parameters of 3D scene.
     Some most commonly used and most representative function in BS SDK is as follows.
     setNodeEventIn ()

The function is used to assign node. Many functions can be done by this function. For example, switch to Viewpoint_1

can use the statement as following:

document.CC3D.setNodeEventIn('Viewpoint_1','set_bind','true');

getNodeEventOut ()

The function is used to obtain the value of the node. It can be used to obtain the coordinates, angle, name, etc.

createVrmlFromString ()

The function is used to add model to the scene dynamically.

setViewpointByValue ()

The function is used to positioning viewpoint to the specified location.

B. Scene-to-web interaction

This system used JavaScript code in the future, so it is lack of control. Many functions are difficult to complete. Adequate support needs to be given though VRML. Fortunately, the Script node can give this support.

We can call JS code in the front though the function Browser. *LoadURL* and its format are as follows.

Browser.loadURL('javascript:closedis('+\'''+discrip+\'''+'); ',' ');

Note: *closedis()* is a function which is defined ourselves.And *discrip* is the parameter of function.

Browser object refers to BS contact the player itself. Its identity the whole 3D scene and provide more programming interface for Script node. The meaning of this code is to call the function closedis () in the front.

5 Conclusion

This article focuses on the key technologies in the process of establishing a dynamically modified to in-depth 3D interactive of Digital Campus System. They are the basis to complete a powerful interactive foundation. We have real ability to complete its function when we have good prototype nodes and databases and understanding of the interactive technology and scene generation technology.

The 3D technology is more realistic and easy-to-transmission characteristics of the network. It is showing its unique advantages and potential. In the future there will certainly be more 3D world in many application areas which emphasis on user experience.

Acknowledgment. This work is supported by National Natural Science Foundation of China (Grant No. 61070010), National Science Foundation for Post-doctoral Scientists of China, the Natural Science Foundation of Hubei Province and the Fundamental Research Funds for the Central Universities.

References

1. Zhang, x., Wu, c.: Hierarchy-invariant interactive virtual maintenance model and its VRML-based simulation. In: 2009 WRI World Congress on Computer Science and Information Engineering, CSIE 2009, vol. 2, pp. 115–120 (2009)
2. Zhang, w.: Virtual Campus System Design and Development. Computer and Digital Engineering (4), 181–183 (2010)
3. Qi, a.: VRML-based virtual scene seitching system design and implementation. Excellent Master Thesis of Jilin University (2007)
4. Li, h., Yin, g., Peng, b.: X3D-based interactive information visualization management system for substation. Computer Engineering (2), 265–267 (2007)
5. Zhang, T.K., Wang, C.S.: Product's Level Construction Tree Model and the Method of Generating Disassembly Sequence. Machinery Engineer 2, 78–80 (2005)
6. Liu, J.H., Ning, R.X., Yao, J.: Research on Assembly Task Based Virtual Assembly Process Model. Journal of System Simulation 7(9), 2163–2170 (2005)
7. Fan, J., Ye, Y., Cai, J.-M.: Multi-level Intelligent Assembly Sequence Planning Algorithm Supporting Virtual Assembly. In: 2004 IEEE International Conference on Systems, Man and Cybernetics, pp. 3494–3499 (2004)
8. Lei, W.: Collaboration in 3D shared spaces using X3D and VRML. In: 2009 International Conference on CyberWorlds, pp. 36–42 (2009)
9. Qi, L.: Function-based shape modeling and visualization in X3D. In: 2006 Web3D Symposium Proceedings, pp. 131–141 (2006)
10. Wu, J.: 3D interactive simulation of Arma-Brown gyrocompass based on VRML. In: 2010 International Conference on Mechanic Automation and Control Engineering, pp. 2465–2469 (2010)
11. Min, Y., Li, Y.: Research on the interaction of VRML and external program. Jisuanji Gongcheng/Computer Engineering 31(19), 82–84 (2005)
12. Zhou, Z.: Interactive processing methods of real-time VRML modeling in a Web-based virtual design system. Jisuanji Fuzhu Sheji Yu Tuxingxue Xuebao/Journal of Computer-Aided Design and Computer Graphics 17(6), 1371–1377 (2005)
13. Hung, S.-s.: Hierarchical distance-based clustering for interactive VRML traversal patterns. In: Proceedings of ITRE 2005 - 3rd International Conference on Information Technology: Research and Education, vol. 2005, pp. 485–489 (2005)
14. Korošec, D.: Building interactive virtual environments for simulated training in medicine using VRML and Java/JavaScript. Computer Methods and Programs in Biomedicine 80(suppl. 1), 61–70 (2005)

Joint Pricing and Replenishment Policies for a Deteriorating Inventory Model with Stochastic Demand[*]

Ying Feng and Yanzhi Zhang

School of Management
China University of Mining and Technology
Xuzhou, Jiangsu, 221116, P.R. China
Ying_f@126.com

Abstract. This paper developed an on-going deteriorating inventory model for a single item. Stochastic fluctuating demand patterns is concerned which decreases with the price of items. Deteriorating rate is constant and replenishment rate is infinite. Replenishment lead time is a constant. Continuous review (s, S) inventory policy is adopted which means an order to replenish the inventory to S is placed when current inventory level drops to s. Demand in each replenishment cycle forms a regenerative process. Our objective is to find the joint optimal pricing and replenishment policies to maximize the expected total average profit of the system. This problem can be simplified as a deterministic problem which can be solved by genetic algorithms. The detailed procedure of algorithm is listed. Finally, a numerical example is given which is simulated by Matlab 7.0.

Keywords: deteriorating inventory model, stochastic demand, price and replenishment policies, genetic algorithm.

1 Introduction

Inventory models considering deteriorating items with deterministic demand have been discussed for many years. There exists a large number of literatures considering deteriorating inventory model which adopt various patterns of demand rate and deteriorating rate. Also, they assumed finite or infinite replenishment rate, single or multi-item, single or multi-replenishment cycle and so on. The detailed classification and review of these literatures can be found in Goyal and Grir [1] while this introduction just focus on some works related closely with our research.

Ghare and Schrader [2] first derived an economic order quantity model (EOQ) for the on-going deteriorating items when demand is constant and inventory items decay exponentially with time. Pricing policy for deteriorating items is first considered by Cohen [3] who assumed deterministic and constant demand and simultaneously set price and order level for exponentially decaying items. Kang and Kim [4] extended Cohen's model to considering finite replenishment. Wee [5] dealt with a deteriorating inventory model in a finite planning horizon where demand decreases linearly with

---

[*] This work is partially supported by Youth Research Fund of China University of Mining and Technology#2008A029 to Y. Feng.

J. Zhang (Ed.): ICAIC 2011, Part III, CCIS 226, pp. 663–671, 2011.
© Springer-Verlag Berlin Heidelberg 2011

time and cost of items. However, all above models are limited to deterministic demand patterns. Shah and Jaiswal [6] first developed an order level deteriorating inventory model with probabilistic demand, constant deteriorating rate and zero lead time. Shah [7] considered an order level deteriorating inventory model allowing delay in payment with probabilistic demand and zero lead time. Dave [8] developed a probabilistic inventory model for deteriorating items with lead time equal to one scheduling period. Deterministic lead time was taken into account by Dave [9] which assumes no shortages and a general deterioration function. A very limited literatures are referred to the on-going deteriorating inventory model with stochastic demand and lead time. Aggoun et al. [10] developed a continuous time stochastic inventory model for deteriorating items in which demand rate and deteriorating rate are assumed to have N possible scenarios and lead time is stochastic. They found the optimal (r, Q) policies to minimize the total expect cost per unit time.

This paper is an extension of Aggoun et al. [10]. Unlike [10], we adopted the stochastic fluctuating demand patterns affected by selling price and our objective is to find the joint optimal pricing and replenishment policies to maximize the expected total average profit of the system.

2 Notations and Assumptions

A. Notations

Parts of notations to be used in this paper are listed as follows, while others will be defined in the text following closely behind the symbols for convenience. T Stochastic replenishment cycle length; L :Constant replenishment lead time; p :Unit selling price; $D(p)$:Demand rate at price p ; θ :Constant deteriorating rate; $I(t)$:Inventory level at time t ; Q :Ordering qualities; t_1 :The time when inventory level drops to zero; t_2 :The time to place an order; K :Fixed replenishment cost per order; c_1 :Constant purchase cost per unit; c_2 :Inventory holding cost per unit per unit time; c_3 : Backlogged shortage cost per unit; $\pi(p,s,S)$:Expected total average profit.

B. Assumptions

Some assumptions that will be used in this paper are listed as follows,

1) A single item is considered which is subjected to a constant rate of deterioration.
2) Continuous review (s, S) inventory policy is adopted which means an order to replenish the inventory to S is placed when current inventory level drops to s.
3) Demand rate is the multiple of a stochastic variable and a constant decreasing with the selling price of the item. $D(p)=(a-pb)\cdot x$, where a denotes a "market base", b measure the responsiveness of the demand to selling price, x is a random variables with p.d.f. $f(x)$ and 1 as its mean. Note that the selling price satisfies $p < a/b$ to ensure demand is positive and $p > c_1$ to ensure the profit is positive, thus $p \in (c_1, a/b)$.

4) Replenishment rate is infinite and replenishment interval is stochastic.
5) Replenishment lead time is a known constant.
6) Shortages are allowed and are completely backordered in the following cycle.
7) There is no replacement or repair of deteriorated items.

3 Mathematic Model

Fig. 1 shows the changes of the inventory level with time. Assume that the initial inventory level of the first cycle is S units, i.e. $I(0)=S$, then it decreases due to demand and deterioration. An order is placed when the current inventory level drops to s and it arrives after L time units, which also means the second cycle begins.

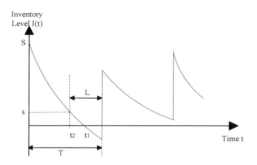

Fig. 1. Curves of inventory level

Define T_i as the cycle length of the i th replenishment cycle and $S_n = \sum_{i=1}^{n} T_i . T_i$ are i.i.d., then the sequence $S = \{S_n, n = 1, 2, \cdots\}$ forms a renewal process [10]. According to renewal reward theory [11], the expected total average profit during the whole time horizon can be obtained by simply computing the expected total average profit of the first cycle. Thus,

$$\pi(p, s, S) = \frac{E[profit \quad for \quad the \quad first \quad cycle]}{E[length \quad of \quad the \quad cycle]} \tag{1}$$

The expected total average profit of the first cycle is equal to the expected total revenue subtract the expected total cost which consists of fixed ordering cost, purchase cost, holding cost and shortage cost in the first cycle.

$$\pi(p, s, S) =$$
$$\frac{pD(p)T - K - E[c_1 Q + c_2 \int_0^T I^+(t)dt + c_3 \int_0^T I^-(t)dt]}{E[T]} \tag{2}$$

where $I^+(t) = \max\{0, I(t)\}$ and $I^-(t) = \max\{0, -I(t)\}$. Define p^*, s^*, S^* as the optimal solutions which can maximize expected total average profit π and π^* as the maximum of π.

Due to the difficulty of solving stochastic differential equations, we still adopt the method proposed by Aggoun [10]. That is to look at each realization of the process on each possible path in order to reduce this stochastic problem to a deterministic pattern. Define x as a realization of ε and its p.d.f. is $f(x)$. Similarly, y is a realization of L and its p.d.f. is $g(y)$. Define $I_x(t)$ as a realization of $I(t)$ when demand is $(a - pb) \cdot x$.

The inventory system in Fig. 1 can be depicted by the following differential equations

$$\frac{dI_x(t)}{dt} + \theta I_x(t) + (a - pb) \cdot x = 0, \quad 0 \le t \le t_1 \tag{3}$$

and

$$\frac{dI_x(t)}{dt} + (a - pb) \cdot x = 0, \quad t_1 \le t \le T \tag{4}$$

Note (4) expresses the case when shortage exists, while (4) doesn't exist when $t_1 \ge T$. With the boundary condition $I_x(0) = S$ the solutions of (3) can be obtained as

$$I_x(t) = \exp(-\theta t)\left[S - \frac{(a - pb)x}{\theta}(\exp(\theta t) - 1)\right], 0 \le t \le t_1 \tag{5}$$

And using the boundary condition $I_x(t_1) = 0$, the solution of (4) can be obtained as

$$I_x(t) = (a - pb)x \cdot (t_1 - t), \quad t_1 \le t \le T \tag{6}$$

Taking $I_x(t_1) = 0$ and $I_x(t_2) = s$ into (5) and (6), we can get

$$t_1 = \frac{1}{\theta}\ln\frac{S\theta + (a - pb)x}{(a - pb)x} \tag{7}$$

$$t_2 = \frac{1}{\theta}\ln\frac{S\theta + (a - pb)x}{s\theta + (a - pb)x} \tag{8}$$

Property 1. Shortages are not exist when

$$0 < x \le \frac{s\theta}{(a - pb)[\exp(\theta L) - 1]}.$$

Proof. According to (5), we must have $I_x(T) \ge 0$ in order to ensure that shortages do not occur. Then, we have $(a - pb)x[\exp(\theta T) - 1] \le S\theta$.

Substituting T with $t_2 + L$ and simplifying this quadratic inequation, we have

$$[(a - pb)x + S\theta] \cdot [(\exp(\theta L) - 1)(a - pb)x - s\theta] \le 0.$$

Then, property 1 is hold by solving this in equation.

Define $A = \dfrac{s\theta}{(a-pb)[\exp(\theta L)-1]}$, this problem will be discussed by two sub-cases

1. $0 < x \leq A$ and 2. $x \geq A$.

Note that $0 < x \leq A$ means shortages do not exist while $x \geq A$ means shortages occur.

Case 1: $0 < x \leq A$

1) Expected total revenue

$$RV1 = p \int_0^A \int_0^T D(p)f(x)dtdx = (a-pb)\int_0^A Tf(x)dx \tag{9}$$

2) Expected total ordering cost including the setup cost and purchase cost

$$OD1 = [K + c_1(S-s)]\int_0^A f(x)dx \tag{10}$$

3) Expected total inventory cost

$$IN1 = c_2 \int_0^A \int_0^T \exp(-\theta t)\left[S - \frac{(a-pb)x}{\theta}(\exp(\theta t)-1)\right]f(x)dtdx$$

$$= \frac{c_2}{\theta}\int_0^A \left\{S(1-\exp(-\theta T)) - \frac{(a-pb)x}{\theta}(\exp(-\theta T)+\theta T -1)\right\}.$$

$$f(x)dx \tag{11}$$

Case 2: $x \geq A$

1) Expected total revenue

$$RV2 = p \int_A^\infty \int_0^T D(p)f(x)dtdx = (a-pb)\int_A^\infty Tf(x)dx \tag{12}$$

2) Expected total ordering cost including the setup cost and purchase cost

$$OD2 = [K + c_1(S-s)]\int_A^\infty f(x)dx \tag{13}$$

3) Expected total inventory cost

$$IN2 = c_2 \int_A^\infty \int_0^{t_1} \exp(-\theta t)\left[S - \frac{(a-pb)x}{\theta}(\exp(\theta t)-1)\right]f(x)dtdx$$

$$= \frac{c_2}{\theta}\int_A^\infty \left\{S - \frac{(a-pb)x}{\theta}\ln\left[1+\frac{s\theta}{(a-pb)x}\right]\right\}f(x)dx \tag{14}$$

4) Expected total backordered cost

$$BO2 = c_3 \int_A^\infty \int_{t_1}^{t_2+L}[-(a-pb)x(t_1 -t)]dtdx$$

$$= \frac{c_3}{2} \int_A^\infty (a-pb)x \left[L - \ln\left(1 + \frac{s\theta}{(a-pb)x}\right)\right]^2 f(x)dx \qquad (15)$$

The total expected revenue

$$RV = RV1 + RV2 = p(a - pb)E(T) \qquad (16)$$

The total expected cost of the system
$$TC = OD1 + OD2 + IN1 + IN2 + BO2$$

$$= K + c_1(S-s) + \frac{c_2}{\theta} \int_0^A \{S(1 - \exp(-\theta T)) - \frac{(a-pb)x}{\theta}$$

$$(\exp(-\theta T) + \theta T - 1)\} f(x)dx +$$

$$\frac{c_2}{\theta} \int_A^\infty \left\{ S - \frac{(a-pb)x}{\theta} \ln\left[1 + \frac{s\theta}{(a-pb)x}\right]\right\} f(x)dx +$$

$$\frac{c_3}{2} \int_A^\infty (a-pb)x \left[L - \ln\left(1 + \frac{s\theta}{(a-pb)x}\right)\right]^2 f(x)dx \qquad (17)$$

This problem can finally be formulated as:

$$\text{Maximize: } \pi(p, s, S) = \frac{RV - TC}{E(T)} \qquad (18)$$

Subject to: (16), (17);

$$c_1 < p < a/b;$$

$$T = \frac{1}{\theta} \ln \frac{S\theta + (a-pb)x}{s\theta + (a-pb)x} + L.$$

Our objective is to find the joint optimal values p^*, s^*, S^* in order to maximize the expected total average profit π.

4 Solution Procedure

The objective function (18) is too difficult to handled for the existence of some exponential and logarithmic functions, therefore, we use the Taylor series forms of them to simply the function and ignore the terms   with the second and higher order powers of θ. Two assumptions are given for the feasibility of Taylor expansion.

Assumption 1. To satisfy the convergence condition of Taylor series, θ satisfies
$\theta L < 1$ and $\frac{S\theta}{(a-pb)B} < 1$.

Let $M = a - pb$ for writing complicity. Then, expression (18) can be simplified as,

$$\pi(p, s, S) = pM - \{K\theta + c_1\theta(S - s) + c_2 \times$$

$$\int_0^B \left[S - s + s\theta L - \frac{M\theta L^2}{2} x \right] f(x)dx - c_2 \times$$

$$\int_0^B \frac{Mx}{\theta} \ln \frac{S\theta + Mx}{s\theta + Mx} f(x)dx + c_2 \int_B^\infty \frac{S^2\theta}{2Mx} f(x)dx$$

$$+ \frac{c_3}{2} \int_B^\infty ML^2 x\theta f(x)dx\} /$$

$$\left\{ \int_0^B \ln \frac{S\theta + Mx}{s\theta + Mx} f(x)dx + \int_B^\infty \left[\frac{(S - s)\theta}{Mx} - \frac{(S^2 - s^2)\theta^2}{2M^2 x^2} \right] f(x)dx + \theta L \right\}$$

(19)

where

$$B = \frac{s(L - \theta L^2 / 2)}{M}.$$

Expression (19) still has two logarithmic functions after Taylor series expansion. These two items are nonintegrable functions. Therefore, we can use numerical method to derive their approximate values. Here, we use the complex formula of Simpson.

The analytical solution of this problem is difficult to derive for its' complexity, so we will solve this problem by genetic algorithms. The algorithm in this paper uses genetic algorithms with the chromosome of real number type. The procedure of algorithm will follow as:

Step1: Adopting floating-point encoding method with the solution precision of 10^{-6}.

Step2: Generating reasonable initial population randomly with the pop-size of 25.

Step3: Using the classical penalty function method to transform the original problem in order to change the constrained nonlinear programming problems into unconstrained extremum problem.

Step4: A selection based on Roulette Wheel picks up two candidates from population.

Step5: A crossover, by taking the average of two candidates to produce child 1, is taken under a given probability .

Step6: Mutation is taken under a given probability with randomly initiating two random numbers to mutate child2 from child1 by

$$child2 = \alpha * child1 + (1 - \alpha)\omega, 0 \le \alpha, \omega \le 1$$

Step7: Only the best according to its fitness to the objective function is kept to maintain the population sizes constant.

Step8: Repeat Step4 to Step7 until the termination criterion of maximal iterations has achieved.

5 Numeric Example

For illustrative purpose, a simple numerical example is tested under the operation environment of Windows XP Professional with AMD Turion (tm) 64 X2, 512M RAM and encoding with MATLAB 7.0. Some parameters are selected randomly, as $L = 5$, $a = 100$, $b = 0.5$, $\theta = 0.08$, $K = 100$, $c_1 = 20$, $c_2 = 5$, $c_3 = 12$, population size = 25, probability of crossover = 0.8, probability of mutation =0.08, and the maximal iterations is 1000. To simplify the calculation, we let

$$f(x) = \begin{cases} \frac{1}{6} x^2 \exp(-x), & x \geq 0 \\ 0, & otherwise \end{cases}.$$

Using genetic algorithms according to the steps listed in section IV, we can finally get the joint optimal pricing and replenishment policies as follows, $p^* = 47.365$, $S^* = 1.875 \times 10^3$, $s^* = 0.428 \times 10^3$. Then, the maximal expected total average profit of the system can be calculated by (19).

$$\pi^* = 1.273 \times 10^7 .$$

6 Conclusion

In this paper, an on-going deteriorating inventory model with stochastic demand was developed. The problem was formulated as a nonlinear programming which contains some exponential and logarithmic functions in its objective functions. Then, it was simplified by using Taylor series expansion and numerical integration. Finally, a numerical example was given and the joint optimal pricing and replenishment policies were calculated by genetic algorithms. The main innovation is that we first proposed a stochastic inventory model for the deteriorating item by adopting continuous review (s, S) inventory policy. As we just consider a special case, lots of extensions can be done to this problem. For example, the replenishment lead time L can also be a stochastic variable and the probability density function $f(x)$ can take other forms. These problems will be solved in our later research.

References

1. Goyal, S.K., Giri, B.C.: Recent trends in modeling of deteriorating inventory. European Journal of Operational Research 134, 1–16 (2001)
2. Ghare, P.M., Schrader, S.F.: A model for exponentially decaying inventory. Journal of Industrial Engineering 14, 238–243 (1963)
3. Cohen, M.A.: Joint pricing and ordering policy for exponentially decaying inventory with known demand. Naval Research Logistic 24, 257–268 (1977)
4. Kang, S., Kim, I.: A study on the price and production level of the deteriorating inventory system. International Journal of Production Research 21, 449–460 (1983)

5. Wee, H.M.: Joint pricing and replenishment policy for deteriorating inventory with declining market. Int. J. Production Economics 40, 163–171 (1995)
6. Shah, Y.K., Jaiswal, M.C.: An order-level inventory model for a system with constant rate of deterioration. Operations Research 14, 174–184 (1977)
7. Shah, N.H.: Probabilistic order level system when times in inventory deteriorate and delay in payments is permissible. Asia-Pacific Journal of Operational Research 21, 319–331 (2004)
8. Dave, U.: A probabilistic inventory model for deteriorating items with lead time equal to one scheduling period. European Journal of Operational Research 9, 281–285 (1982)
9. Dave, U.: A probabilistic scheduling period inventory model for deteriorating items with lead time. Mathematical Methods of Operations Research 30, 229–237 (1986)
10. Aggoun, L., Benkhrouf, L., Tad, L.: On a stochastic inventory model with deteriorating items. International Journal of Mathematics and Mathematical Sciences 25, 197–203 (2001)
11. Ross, S.H.: Stochastic processes. Wiley press, New York (1995)

Application of Wireless Sensor Network in Farmland Data Acquisition System[*]

Bei Wang[1], Xiaona Guo[2], Zhiqi Chen[2], and Zhaoqian Shuai[2]

[1] Department of Science and Technology
[2] Department of Information
[1,2] Zhejiang Gongshang University
[1,2] Hangzhou, Zhejiang Province, China
bei___w@tom.com

Abstract. With the development of agricultural production technology, characteristics that appear in the farmland information such as diversity, polytropy and dispersity. In order to solve the problems of obtaining quickly and long-distance transmission the farmland information, the paper proposes a farmland data acquisition system based on the GPRS technology. The system exerts GPRS network of the china mobile communications and combines integrated circuits, sensors and GPRS communication modules on data transmission, and establishes the whole crop monitoring system. Through the Internet, GPRS and field monitoring communications, the data center can finish a complete record, the curve showing and query of field data, meanwhile it can detect equipment remotely. These instructions give you the basic guidelines for preparing papers for WCICA/IEEE conference proceedings.

Keywords: Wireless Sensor Network, GPRS, Data Acquisition, Precision Agriculture, Internet of Things.

1 Introduction

The traditional farmland information monitoring depends mainly on technical person collecting data on the field, A/D transform, and the method of preserving and analysing the data by PC achieves the data transmission. These patterns are not good. Because of farming bad environment, the weather factors of cold and high temperature easily lead to the PC can't work properly, PC for their bulky, and the high cost lead to a low price performance ratio, and unable to achieve a remote monitor. Even using digital radio station will also be limited by the state of the ground, and the distance with dozens of kilometers will not achieve in a real-time monitoring 24h[1].Therefore, remote real-time monitoring of agricultural environmental should solve quickly.

Wireless Sensor Network is a hot research spot in information technology, it has been integrated with study of sensor, computer science, signaling and information

---

[*] This work is partially supported by Zhejiang Science and technology projects (2009C34015) and the Xinmiao Project of Zhejiang Province (2007R408067).

J. Zhang (Ed.): ICAIC 2011, Part III, CCIS 226, pp. 672–678, 2011.

processing, communications, and so on, and integrated information collection, data transmission, data processing and data management of the main features, and widely applied to meteorological, geography, natural and man-made disasters monitoring and big area surface monitoring [2-6]. But agriculture is one of   potential important fields of WSN applications, it has not yet received sufficient attention. In   precision agriculture applications, lots of sensors nodes can be made by the monitoring network, through gathering information, coordination with many routings, ad hoc network and information exchange, and row and to the real-time publishing information and achieve automation, intelligent and remote control.

The technology of WSN composed of the microcomputer technology, the embedded space technology, network and wireless communications technology together. It is the sensor node by the wireless connection from the organization into a network system [7], the sensor nodes are much lower costs, low power consumption, a perception, data processing and wireless communications capacity. Sensors nodes can complete in collaboration with real-time monitoring and gather the monitoring object information, which will be treated and sent to observer [8].

2   The Design of WSN Node

Wireless Sensor Networks with sensing, signal processing and wireless communication function, and it can transmit or format the packet information. They send data gateway through network self-organization and multiple hops routing. Gateways can use various ways to communicate external network, such as Internet, satellites or mobile communications network and so on. Large-scale application may use multiple gateways.

Although wireless sensor node design varies among different applications, their basic structure is the same as them. The typical hardware structure includes battery and power circuit, sensor, signal regulate circuit, AD transform device, storage, microprocessors and radio frequency module and so on. In order to maximize the save of electricity, trying to use low-power devices and cut off the radio frequency module when under no communication tasks in the hardware design. Meanwhile, each layer of communication protocol should be save energy for the center, and in order to obtain higher power efficiency may, if necessary, sacrifice some other network performance index, in the software design.

The paper designs the structure of WSN nodes is figure 1. It is mainly composed of the data collection subsystem, data processing subsystem, wireless communications subsystem and the power of the subsystem. When designing WSN nodes, we can solve the key problem of the WSN nodes in energy consumption, robustness, and computation and communication capability, cost and volume of the general is improving.

1) Data collection subsystem is responsible for perceiving and getting information of the area of monitoring, and converts them to signs of figure, it contains the sensor, A/D converters and supporting circuits.

2) Data processing subsystem is the core components WSN nodes, it takes charge of data processing, storage, battery energy monitoring, systems task scheduling, the

communications protocol (including the MAC or routing protocols) and the nodes scheduling management.

3) Wireless communications subsystem is responsible for among WSN nodes and between WSN nodes and gateway exchanging control communication and getting and sending collected information.

4) The power of the subsystem is composed of lithium battery(capacity at 1200 mAh), intelligence battery monitoring and chips(DS2762), battery protection of the chip(R5426), cell battery management chip(BQ2057), power and the external interface with the electrical circuits. It will provide intelligent charging circuit and the short circuit protection for WSN node and ensure the requisite energy for WSN node in the normal work.

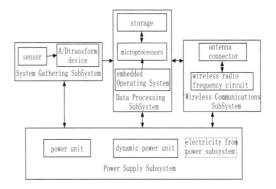

Fig. 1. Configuration of nodes for WSN-CWSM system

3   The Characteristics of Farm Data Acquisition

Gathering quickly and efficiently, describing all kinds of variables information of crops and its growth conditions are important foundation of realizing precision agriculture. At present, the research of field gather rapidly information technology has been lagging behind the technology of supporting other agricultural. Precision agriculture is actually a agricultural management system based on information, using sensors and monitoring technologies can gather field of information Conveniently, accurately and fast, then along with the factors of the control or influence the crops growth find out correlations between these factors and crops, and make scientific management decision and control the crops investment or adjust your homework.. Therefore, the information collected is very important.

The data collection of field information is different from the industrial data collection, which are particularities. Main aspects as follows:

1. Much more kinds of information, the widely measuring range and the large of information. The samples collection is the first step of analysis the fields of information, the samples must have adequate representation and can be a true reflection of realities in the field of information.

2. Field operations, the power, volume and weight for data collection system have special requirements.

3. More channels are necessary for measurement, they can measure and deal with many signs. In the agricultural machinery of variable work, it also requires immediate measure, and according to measuring results to control variables.

Because of the specialization and complexity of the field information collection, it is difficult to have a unified data collection method, and now there are many data collection models to meet different demands of the field information collection in precision agriculture. The platform of field data collection is figure 2:

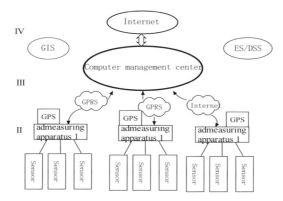

Fig. 2. The general structure of farmland data collection system

First, there are many sensors. Measuring field information needs the various, the precision of measurement system generally depends on the performance of the sensor. In order to choose the sensors, you should follow the practical, economical, standards and durability, etc.

Second, it is the most important in system, including integration GPRS receiver and GPRS terminal module. Not gathering the information of the below various sensors, and also needs to sort and deal with the information simply, at the same time, needs to sent the data to the base station of GPRS.

Third, the computer remote control center which may be called a data center. All data will be collected here, the main work is to receive and show all kinds of data, of course users can carry out all the senior management and operation.

Forth, the collect data can be to publish by Internet.

4 The Design of Field Information Collection System

The cropland data collecting system consists of three parts: Remote control terminal system, communication links and collection terminal. The remote control terminal is a PC machine connected to the Internet. It communicates with GPRS by binding Network IP address; In Addition, the PC machine interior is running the historical database of data collection, the geographic information system, the decision support system and the agricultural expert, to store, process and make a decision support to the data that was sent from the collection module. Communication links is the Internet network and the mobile communication networks. Mobile company assigns the remote control terminal a fixed IP address to connect with the GPRS network. The terminal collection integrate follow parts: the soil humiture sensor, the soil moisture sensor, the juice speed of flow sensor, the air humiture sensor and the soil pH value sensor. It can measure multiple parameters of cropland simultaneously. Figure 3: the system block diagram of cropland information collection system based on GPRS. The cropland information collection system will be integrated in the system as a part of the subject to collection data.

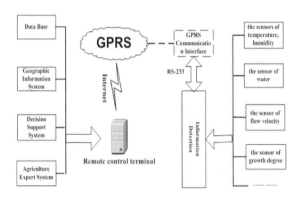

Fig. 3. The system framework of GPRS-based farmland information collection system

The major function of the data collection control is to open the GPRS service, use the GPRS Network and the INTERNET to issues the collection control commands and accept the data of the sensor terminal and the state data of the terminal collection, closing the GPRS service.

The technical superiority of GPRS mainly manifests in two aspects: First, it is able to make the data of users and the wireless network combine perfectly. Thus, it has guaranteed the cost benefit of the grouping pattern data application and the effective use of wireless network resource; Secondly, it has realized the transparent transmission on IP protocol. The GPRS based on the standard data protocol, so it supports all applications that based on the TCP/IP protocol, and guarantees the applications which based on GPRS that can realized the Interaction with the Internet.

The communication module of GPRS connects with the serial port of the embedded CPU, so that it can realize the data transmission. The embedded CPU accepts the data of sensor and sends the data into GPRS modules through the serial port. The control center accepts the data sent by GPRS modules through GPRS network.

The data collection terminal mainly completes the following two functions: First, the real-time monitor serial port which receives and processes request from the monitor center; Secondly, collecting data according to these requests, and sending the data packed into GSM modules through the serial port. The flowchart of main program is showed in Figure 4.

In the figure 4, the collection request of monitor center includes disposable collection and regular collection. When the collection request is the regular collection, it can achieve the function of regular collection. The collection task is completed on the terminal program. Because the main program contains operations of monitoring time serial requirements port, and the operation has the certain succession request. When the serial port has stored some data, if these data are not read within the prescribed time, they will be eliminated. Therefore, if it is be interrupted when reading data on the serial port, and it is complex to process the interrupt, the data will be eliminated. In order to prevent the data missing, it may use the pre-definition to express whether to have the bit variable of collection task. In the interrupt program, we only to complete the operation of this bit variable, and the actual collection task is completed in the main program.

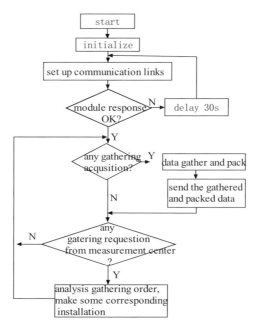

Fig. 4. Main flow chart of data collection system

5 Summary

Collecting the fields of agriculture information accurately, timely and reliable is the prerequisite for achieving precision agriculture. The system achieves the accurate position-setting, the remote transport for the field of information, the farmland data collection platform finishing the field data collection, transporting and achieving the basic requirements of the field data collection, and it provides an effective basis for agricultural policy. Getting the field information accurately and real-time is an effective way for making decision accurately and increasing agricultural produce Owing to Our geographical situation is complex and varied. With the development of GPRS technology, the farmland information remote monitoring system based on GPRS will further improved and mature, and the system has broad prospects.

Acknowledgment. This research is supported by Zhejiang Science and technology projects (2009C34015) and Xinmiao Project of Zhejiang Province.

References

1. Wang, Q., Sun, Z., Li, X., et al.: The design of agricultural environmental monitoring system based on the embedded system. Microcomputer Information 22(8), 38 (2006)
2. Wang, S., Yan, S., Hu, F., et al.: Wireless sensor network theory and application. Beijing aerospace university press, Beijing (2007)
3. Ji, J.: The application of ZigBee wireless sensor networking to an industrial automatic monitor system. Industrial Instrumentation and Automation (3), 71–76 (2007)
4. Guo, S., Ma, S., Wu, P., et al.: Pulse wave measurement system based on Zigbee wireless sensor network. Application Research of Computers 24(4), 258–260 (2007)
5. Liu, H., Wang, M., Wang, Y., et al.: Development of farmland soil moisture and temperature monitoring system based on wireless sensor network. Journal of Jilin University: Engineering and Technology Edition 38(3), 604–608 (2008)
6. Qiao, X., Zhang, X., Wang, C., et al.: The application of Wireless sensors network in agriculture. Agricultural Engineering Journal 21(2), 232–234 (2005)
7. Sun, L., et al.: Wireless sensors network. Tsinghua university press, Beijing (2005)
8. Lu, D., Xu, W., Wang, L.: Wireless sensors network. Industrial Control Computer 18(4), 24–25 (2005)

Research on Optimization Algorithm of TCP Reno Based on Wireless Network

Chun Bai[1], Jin Liu[2], and Hong Deng

[1] College of Computer and Automatic Control
Hebei Polytechnic University
Tangshan, Hebei, China
[2] Shijiazhuang Railway Institute
Shijiazhuang, Hebei, China
Ch_Bai@126.com

Abstract. The high error rate of wireless link result in most of Packet loss rate that is caused by error of the wireless link, The standard TCP network will start congestion control before congestion, result in the sharp decrease of performance. In this paper, we propose an idea that adjust dynamic the size of TCP segment according to the error rate, and modify the tcpreno.cc function to implement this algorithm to improve the overall performance of TCP.

Keywords: error rate, retransmission rate, TCP segment size, throughput, Reno algorithm improved.

1 Introduction

Wireless network is a high error rate, low bandwidth, high latency, with mobile network terminals. Wireless channel error rate and high mobility terminals frequent cause interruption of transmission. Link layer error control will lead to relatively large packet delay ,more powerful delay jitter, which are easy to make the traditional retransmission timer early time-out, lead to decreased throughput.

Since wireless networks only involves the MAC layer and physical layer protocol. Above the IP layer protocols are still used in traditional TCP / IP model, from view of network layer. Assuming that the loss of packet is caused by the congestion, Obviously, This approach is appropriate in the wired environment that the link quality is well. However, congestion in the wireless network is not the only reason of packet loss, the high error rate of wireless link is caused by error of the wireless link. There is no appropriate mechanism to distinguish reason that congestion or wireless link error which lead to packet loss. If the packet loss which is caused by error of wireless link also taken to reduce the sending rate to congestion control that is bound to reduce the bandwidth utilization, resulting in TCP performance declining.

In order to enhance the performance of TCP in the wireless network environment, this paper proposes a new scheme based on end to end performance algorithms.

J. Zhang (Ed.): ICAIC 2011, Part III, CCIS 226, pp. 679–685, 2011.

2 Improvement Program of Wireless Network TCP Performance

In wireless networks, the main reason of packet loss is miss code. The traditional TCP only due packet loss to network congestion, so that it worsens TCP performance in the wireless environment. In the wireless environment, in order to reduce error of TCP segments, reducing the TCP segment size is an effective method. But reduction of the TCP segment size will result in lower utilization of data channel or waste of bandwidth. According the probability theory, We can get relationship of the size of TCP segment (segment_size), segment_loss (segment_loss) and error rate (pe), Shown as 2.1-style:

$$segment\_loss = 1 - (1 - Pe)^{segment\_size} \qquad (2.1)$$

From the above equation we know: the TCP segment size is much smaller, the TCP segment damage rate is much less, and thus packet loss due to errors would be less. On the contrary ,if the error rate is too large, the segment size is not adjust accordingly, section of the failure rate will increase rapidly , result in massive data re-transmit, not only waste bandwidth ,but also reduces the throughput.

As the actual wireless network is vulnerable to all kinds of interference, the bit error rate is in a constant process of change .This article on the optimization of TCP congestion control algorithm is based on the concept of dynamic changes of BER dynamic adjustment of TCP segment size.

When the network becomes very bad, we can properly adjust the TCP segment size to be able to maximize use of limited resources. Experiments show that: for each state of the bit error rate, with only one TCP segment size which can achieve maximum performance of network transmission, We can get the best TCP segment size through the simulation experiments in the condition of different bit error rate, so that the TCP segment size can be changed according to the error rate dynamically, its performance would be improved.

3 Dynamically Adjust the TCP Segment Size to Improve TCP Performance

In this paper the network simulation software we use is NS (Network Simulator), NS is a open source software based on the Linux, it can be used easily to simulate the operation of the network, verify the improved network algorithm, test improved network algorithm.

A. Analysis of TCP segment the best size in the condition of each steady-state error rate

In order to measure the bit error rate in the steady state of optimal TCP segment size, we set up a simulation scene shown in Figure 1, in a variety of error conditions, TCP segment size increased from 100byte to 1000byte, every other 20S increases one time. Observe the throughput per unit time to get the best size of TCP segment in the steady-state error rate. In the paper, the reason that maximum segment is set to 1000byte is to keep consistent with TCP segment the default size.

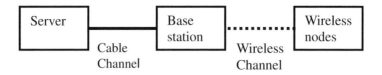

Fig. 1. Wireless network simulation environment

In order to analyze the relation of error rates and best segment size, in the course of TCP segment size increasing form 100byte to 1000byte, we simulate the instance of 10^{-5}, $5*10^{-5}$, 10^{-4} bit error rate, then we get the best segment size is 100byte, 1000byte, 1000byte, 1000byte. We can get a relation of error rates and best segment size, the relation is shown in Figure 2.

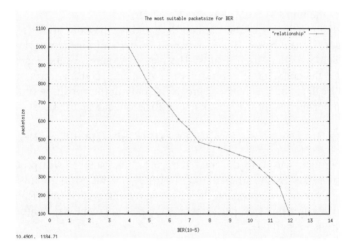

Fig. 2. Relationship of error rates and best segment size

From Figure 2, it is can be observed that We can get the best performance on 1000byte when the bit error rate is less than $4*10^{-5}$; but we can but get the best performance when the bit error rate is larger than $1.5*10^{-5}$ by setting segment size l00byte; the best segment size decrease with the bit error rate increasing when the bit error rate is in the range of $4*10^{-5}$-$1.5*10^{-4}$. From the above dates we can get a computation formula for best segment when the bit error rate is changing from $4*l0^{-5}$ to 10^{-4}. Shown as 2.2-style:

$$Packetsize = 10^7 * (BER - 4)(4*10^{-5} < BER < 10^{-4}) \qquad (2.2)$$

From the simulation experiment of TCP segment size in range of 100byte-1000byte, we can get a segment size of the best throughput for TCP in the same bit error rate circumstance, for instance $Pe=5*10^{-5}$, the best segment size is 800byte; but when it is in high bit error rate circumstance as $Pe=1.2*10^{-4}$, then TCP can not run normally if the segment size larger than 500byte. The reason is the larger segment size the higher possibility of packet loss in bad error code circumstance, packet loss lead retransmission date increased consequentially, and then the throughput performance is badly decreased; in the circumstance of $5*10^{-5}$ and 10^{*-4} bit error rate, the throughput is visible higher than it is in $1.2*10^{-4}$ bit error rate, and variety curve change different too. Under these two bit error rates, we select segment size 800byte and 400byte respectively, the throughput can achieve the best results. In low bit error rate circumstance, the throughput increase with the segment size increasing, so we can set the segment size 1000byte; in bad bit error rate circumstance, as bit error rate is greater than 10^{-4} ,we can set the segment size 100byte.

From the experiment, we get the following simulation results: In different bit error rates circumstances, select the data segment size need to consider the actual environment, can not choose blindly. It can be seen from the formula 2.1, in the condition of certain error rate, the size of segment directly affects the Packet loss rate. The segment size and packet loss rate determine the size of the throughput, when we choose TCP segment size, the TCP segment loss probability should be considered, and consider the impact on the channel utilization.

Though the possibility of the segment loss and the cost of various retransmissions can be reduce, if the amount of data transmission per unit time is very low, throughput would not achieve the desired results. The method to improve the channel utilization is to reduce the amount of retransmission data and consider proportion between amount of the data and the head of agreement, only in the condition of the best match relationship between them, which channel utilization, can be used best.

B.   Analysis on segment retransmission rate of different bit error rate

Different segment sizes and different bit error circumstances will produce different retransmission rate. By the simulation test of the same bit error circumstances, can be obtained for different segment size range of the retransmission rate (Rmin, Rmax), by comparing their transmission performance, the best segment size can be found in the range of retransmission rate.

In the same way, it can obtain the range of retransmission rate of corresponding different bit error circumstances and the best segment size. In the same bit error environment, different segment size can produce different retransmission rate, and there is a segment size of the best transmission performance. Experiments show that in the different bit error circumstances, no matter how chosen segment size, resulting in the retransmission rate range basically do not cross.

In different bit error rates circumstances, as 10^{-4}, $5*10^{-5}$, 10^{-5}, variety curve of retransmission rate in different TCP segment size is shown in Figure 3. Every segment would be simulated for 20s, and then we record the retransmission.

It can be seen from the simulation results, retransmission rate, bit error rate and the segment size has a direct relationship:

Under the same segment size, the higher bit error rate, the greater the retransmission rate. For example, the retransmission rate measured in 200S, At this point the size of TCP segment is 1000byte, retransmission rates measured were 0,2%, 11% under the 10^{-5}、 $5*10^{-5}$、 10^{-4} bit error rate. Under the same bit error rate, the larger segment size, the greater the retransmission rates. For example, the bit error rate of 10-4 circumstances, the process of the segment size increased from 500byte to 1000byte, retransmission rate from less than 2% increased to nearly 11%.

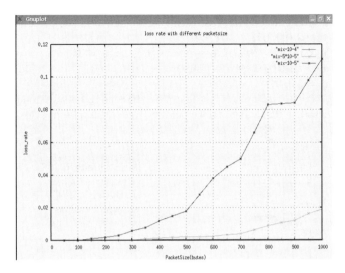

Fig. 3. Relationship of retransmission rate and segment size in different bit error circumstances

The retransmission rate increases are not the same in different bit error circumstances. Retransmission rate increases faster under high bite error circumstances. For each bit error rate, no matter how the TCP segment size, there is a non-overlapping range of retransmission rate, which provides a basis for us through the retransmission rate to estimate bit error rate. According to the conclusions of the previous section, bit error rate in each case there is only one segment size of TCP who can make the best throughput. TCP segment size dynamically set through measuring retransmission rate, making TCP performance improvement.

4 Improved Algorithm of TCP Reno

Through the above discussion, according to the retransmission rate of TCP segment size dynamically change to improve the overall performance of TCP. The algorithm is achieved by modifying function tcpreno.cc in this paper. The main flowchart is shown in Figure 4.

The relevant pseudo-code below of each main module expressed as:
Initialization:

```
init i;                 // Initialized to the 20S, every 20S measured once
double loss_rate;       // Packet loss rate, initialized to 0
double current_time;    // reading the current package
int total_sent;         //total sent package
int total_ret;          //total retransmission package
// judgment of the current time:
if(current_time>i)
```

// Read the retransmission rate within 20S, according to retransmission rate updating segment size of TCP:

loss_rate=(double)total_ret/total_sent; //retransmission rate calculated every 20S
if(loss_rate<=0.0005)   size_=1000;
else if(loss_rate>0.0005&&loss_rate<=0.02) size_=800;
else if(loss_rate>0.02&&loss_rate<=0.11)size_=400;
else size_=100;
total_ret=0;   //calculated per loss_rate, the total retransmission packet to 0
total_sent=0;   //calculated once per loss_rate, the total sent packet to 0
i+=20;   //read the next moment loss rate

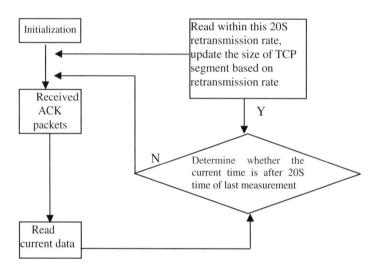

Fig. 4. Improved Algorithm Flowcharts

Every 20S measured the current retransmission rate. Retransmission rate can be calculated by sending data packets and retransmission data packets. According to the retransmission rate to determine the next 20S TCP segment size, and the relationship between retransmission rate and segment size has been discussed in the previous section, the section data can be quoted directly. Then according to the new segment size to send data, so you can according to different network environment to choose the best segment size sending data, and then get the best performance.

5 Conclusion

The simulation results show that the TCP performance has significantly improved with improved algorithm in high error rate of wireless network environment. The throughput of wireless networks can maintain the performance of the original in relatively low bit error rate environment. It can be concluded that the improved Reno algorithm enhanced TCP throughput compared to traditional algorithm.

References

1. Ron, P., Ran, X., Wang, B., Wang, F.: Principles and Applications of Wireless Networks, pp. 32–58. Tsinghua University Press, Beijing (2008)
2. Rackley, S., Yi, W.: Principles and Applications of Wireless Network Technology, pp. 81–98. Electronic Industry Press, Beijing (2008)
3. Pahlavan, K., Krishnamurthy, P.: Principles of wireless networks, pp. 93–121. Science Press, Beijing (2003)
4. Stallings, W.: Wireless communications and networks, pp. 98–109. Tsinghua University Press, Beijing (2003)
5. Cormen, T.H., Leiserson, C.E., Riverst, R.L.: Introduction to Algorithms, 2nd edn. The MIT Press, McGraw-Hill book company (2001)

Author Index

Aijun, Luo   IV-298
An, Shi   V-367
An, Xie   II-113
An, Zhanfeng   II-677
Anhui, Wang   I-207
Anning, Zhou   I-134
An-Song, Feng   III-215
Anxiang, Ma   III-591

Bagchi, Satya   V-643
Bai, Chun   III-679
Baihua, Mu   IV-613
Bei, Wang   IV-374
Bian, Yinju   II-280
Bin, Liu   I-418
Bin, Shen   V-290
Bin, Yu   IV-186
Bin, Zhang   II-397, II-439, III-591
Bing, Luo   III-468
Bitao, Ma   IV-430
Bo, Fang   IV-588
Bo, Lei   I-1
Buxin, Su   IV-449

Cai, Lianhong   II-186
Cai, Qiang   IV-32
Cao, Minnian   V-574
Cao, Wenlun   III-360
Cao, Yuhui   IV-98
Cen, Qin   IV-388
Chai, Yanyou   IV-678
Chang, Hung   III-541
Chang, Jiang   II-287
Chang, Li   II-455
Chang, Zhang   I-93
Changyun, Miao   II-140
Changzheng, Qu   IV-82
Chao, Bu   II-727
Chao, Lu   III-429
Chen, Bei   III-360
Chen, Changjia   II-614
Chen, Chan-juan   II-384
Chen, Chaoxia   IV-150
Chen, Chuanhe   I-705

Chen, Dongqu   I-38
Chen, Feng   II-19
Chen, Gang   II-600
Chen, Hua   I-397
Chen, Jian   IV-304
Chen, Jian feng   IV-330
Chen, Jianyun   II-669
Chen, Jia-Xu   III-541
Chen, Jie   II-715
Chen, Jing   II-600
Chen, Jinshan   II-430
Chen, Jinxiu   IV-9
Chen, Lei   V-359
Chen, Li-Hui   III-152
Chen, Lingling   V-239
Chen, Menglin   V-54
Chen, Na   II-708
Chen, Peng   III-239
Chen, Ping   II-236
Chen, Qing   I-315
Chen, Shaoxiong   IV-354
Chen, Shian   IV-204
Chen, Taisheng   V-54
Chen, Wei   I-113, I-156
Chen, Wei-yi   V-230
Chen, Xiao   II-105
Chen, Xiaojing   II-523
Chen, Xiaoying   II-446
Chen, Xinmiao   V-260
Chen, Xin sheng   I-734
Chen, Xiqu   V-298
Chen, Xueguang   III-419
Chen, Yan   V-581
Chen, Yibo   IV-1
Chen, Yichun   IV-526
Chen, Yijiang   IV-143
Chen, Yingwu   IV-282
Chen, Yinyan   II-280
Chen, Yizhao   III-182
Chen, Yongen   IV-220
Chen, Yuchen   V-574
Chen, Zhibo   IV-291
Chen, Zhiqi   III-672
Cheng, Bo   I-412

Cheng, Chuan   V-94, V-421
Cheng, Hui   II-352
Cheng, Jing   III-189
Cheng, Jun   V-196
Cheng, Zhang   II-531
Cheng, Zhong-kuan   I-338
Chenxiao, Qu   V-666
Chuan, He   V-467
Chun, Xiao   IV-298
Chun-Hong, Bao   II-479
Chunling, Wang   IV-648
Chunsen, Xu   I-121
Chunyuan, Gao   IV-374
Ci, Hui   IV-463, V-70
Cong, Nie   IV-641
Congfa, Cai   V-666
Cui, Feng   III-632
Cui, Helin   IV-253
Cui, Jianjun   I-248, I-254
Cui, Jianqun   I-705
Cui, Rong-yi   II-538, II-546, II-555
CuiHong, Wu   I-507
Cunjiang, Yu   IV-613

Dai, Jiayue   III-1
Dai, Kuobin   IV-598
Dai, Shuguang   II-464
Dai, Xue-zhen   I-682
Dai, Yanqing   I-456
Dakun, Zhang   I-93
Dang, Hongshe   IV-627, IV-633
Danni, Zhai   III-312
daqing, Li   I-202
Da-zhi, Pan   I-424
Deng, Guangqing   II-614
Deng, Hong   III-679
Deng, Juan   IV-497, V-522
Deng, Yanfang   III-321
Deng, Zongquan   IV-178
Deqiu, Fan   IV-449
Dey, Lakshmi Kanta   V-643
Ding, Rui   II-586
Ding, Sheng   V-102
Dingjun, Chen   IV-483
Dong, Dengfeng   III-600
Dong, Ji-xian   II-384
Dong, Wen-feng   I-338
Dong, Wenyong   I-573
Dong, Xingye   II-236
Dou, Chunhong   I-74

Du, Jia   II-97
Du, Jiaxi   III-125
Du, Minggang   V-77
Du, Wencai   I-663
Du, Wen-xia   I-286
Duan, Li   III-486
Duan, Lianfei   II-677
Duan, Zhimin   II-316

Fan, Boyuan   IV-337
Fan, Dazhao   I-59
Fan, Wenbo   V-437
Fang, Chaoyang   V-384
Fang, Debin   IV-282
Fang, Luebin   IV-246
Fang, Yadong   V-405
Fang, Zhang   IV-443
Fang, Zhiyang   IV-664
Fang-ying, Yuan   IV-25
Fei, Peng   I-566
Fei, Shumin   V-445
Fen, Rao   IV-618
Feng, Dapeng   II-311
Feng, Gefei   V-70
Feng, Li   II-131
Feng, Ying   III-260, III-663
Feng, Yu   I-202
Fenghui, Niu   I-672
Feng-ju, Kang   V-150
Fengrong, Zhang   II-25
Fu, Rong   I-602
Fu, Sufang   V-298

Gang, Huang   IV-588
Gang, Liu   II-1
Gao, Chunxiao   IV-538
Gao, Fei   I-262
Gao, Jun   I-691
Gao, Meifeng   V-390
Gao, Ming   I-127
Gao, Qinquan   II-487
Gao, Rui   III-111
Gao, Shengying   III-383
Gao, Xiaoqiu   IV-368
Gao, Yan   IV-472
Gaobo, Yang   V-566
Geng, Ruiping   V-493
Ghosh, Debashis   V-643
Gong, Chang-Qing   I-321
Gong, Kui   III-655

Gong, Neil Zhenqiang   I-38
Gong, Yadong   V-196
Gu, Jianlong   I-127
Guan, Heshan   II-593
Guan, Yingjun   III-477
Guan, Yuzhuo   I-726
Guanglin, Xu   II-330
Gui, Jiaping   III-167
Guiqing, Zhang   V-290
Guiyuan, Jiang   I-93
Guo, Chun juan   I-639
Guo, Erfu   II-708
Guo, Hongbin   II-171
Guo, Hongwei   IV-122, IV-178
Guo, Jie   V-109
Guo, Jinliang   I-87
Guo, Jun   IV-497, V-522
Guo, Pengfei   III-527
Guo, Qin   IV-633
Guo, Xiaojun   IV-1
Guo, Xiaona   III-672
Guo, Xiaoshan   II-700
Guo, Yubin   IV-122
Guo, Zailin   II-155
Guo-Feng, Zhang   I-418
Guojin, Chen   III-267, III-273
Guomei, Shi   IV-274
Guo-qiang, Xue   II-82
Guoqiang, Xue   III-10
Guoqing, Wei   II-504
Guoqing, Wu   IV-259
Guoxin, Li   IV-613

Hai, Lan   III-221
Hai, Zhao   IV-505
Haibin, Wu   II-131
Haibo, Zhang   I-202
Haisheng, Li   I-672
Haiyang, Yu   II-413
Han, Chunyan   I-223
Han, Lian-shan   II-9
Han, Ningqing   I-522
Han, Wenzheng   V-581
Han, Yingshi   III-527
Hang, Yin   III-221
Hanyu, Li   V-21
Hao, Hu   IV-555
Hao, Juan   IV-381
Hao, Wu   IV-259
Hao, Yuan   II-571

Haohua, Zhang   IV-505
He, Changyu   IV-170
He, Fanguo   IV-598
He, Hai-ran   I-532
He, Hui   V-413
He, Jun   I-734
He, Pengfei   II-344
He, Ping   II-361
He, Tongxiang   I-522
He, Yanwei   II-88
He, Yanxiang   III-189
He, Yuliang   III-501
He, Yuyao   III-360
He, Zhengwei   II-271
Heng, Wu   II-644
Heng-shen, Yao   I-215
Hong, Liu   III-419
Hong, Xia   IV-706
Hong, Zheng   IV-555
Hongjun, Xue   II-496
Hongmei, Wang   IV-641
Hongqing, Zheng   II-131
Hongwei, Guo   IV-449
Hongwei, Yang   III-282, III-344
Hou, Yibin   IV-238
Hou, Yunhai   II-407
Hu, Fengye   III-49, III-58
Hu, Gang   IV-354
Hu, Mingdu   I-611
Hu, Tao   V-549
Hu, Xiaoling   IV-66
Hu, Xiaoming   IV-170
Hu, Xiaoqing   I-46
Hu, Ye   V-549
Hu, Yongqin   II-586
Hua, Lin   IV-405
Hua, Zhang   I-356
Huaibin, Zhu   IV-298
Huaishan, Liu   I-654
Huang, Bing   II-59
Huang, Hanming   II-280
Huang, Houkuan   II-236
Huang, Jiasheng   III-182
Huang, Jiejun   V-165
Huang, Jing   IV-57
Huang, Lei   IV-227
Huang, Min   I-8, I-469, I-484
Huang, Qinghua   I-16
Huang, Tao   II-337
Huang, Ting   II-579

Huang, Wei he   IV-330
Huang, Weijie   I-432
Huang, Yong   IV-157
Huang, Zhangqin   IV-238
Huang, Zhongming   V-346
Huang, Zitong   II-593
Huanqi, Tao   V-124
Hui, Bu   IV-74
Huidan, Gao   I-566
Huiling, Zhou   III-304
Huo, Dongfang   III-376
Huo, Jiayu   IV-122
Huo, Linsheng   IV-489

Ji, Hua   V-62
Ji, Jian-Wei   III-152
Ji, Song   I-59
Ji, Weiyong   I-248, I-254
Jia, Keming   I-705
Jia, Lan Hong   IV-550
Jia, Songhao   I-87
Jiajia, Li   II-439
Jian, Chang   IV-449
Jian, Mao   II-50
Jian, Wei   I-179
Jianchen, Hu   II-504
Jiang, Haixia   V-223
Jiang, Jiang   IV-282
Jiang, Libiao   III-383
Jiang, Miao   II-41
Jiang, Min   III-297
Jiang, Pengfei   III-88
Jiang, Siyu   III-383
Jiang, Xiubo   IV-246
Jiang, Yunchen   V-269
Jianguo, Cheng   I-202
Jiangyu, Yan   IV-706
Jian-hai, Wang   V-189
Jian-Hui, Liu   III-175
Jianliang, Zhang   IV-449
Jianming, Yang   II-131
JianWang,   V-452
Jian-Xiang, Wei   V-1
Jiao, Runhai   V-628
Jia-shan, Jin   V-323
Jiashi, Yang   V-282
Jiaxi, Yu   II-504
Jia-xin, Wu   V-189
Jiayin, Peng   IV-397
Jichang, Guo   II-124

Jin, Tao   I-156
Jin, Xiaochen   IV-122
Jin, Xue-bo   I-532
Jin, Zhang   I-654
Jing, Chen   IV-298
Jing, Fu xing   I-734
Jing-Jing, Bai   II-479
Jingjing, Liu   IV-671
Jingping, Jia   IV-706
Jingyun, Liu   III-304
Jinhang, Li   IV-588
Jinhui, Li   III-282, III-344, IV-443
Jinlei, Ding   I-1
Jinling, Li   III-160
JinPing, Li   III-103
Ju, Xiaona   IV-291
Jun, Han   III-429
Jun, Wang   II-669
Jun, Yan   IV-555
Junhai, Ma   V-606, V-614
JunYong, Liu   V-282
Junyong, Liu   III-141

Ke, Yalin   III-655
Ke, Zhang   III-344
ke, Zhang   IV-641
Ke, Zongwu   II-700
Kening, Gao   III-591
Kumar, Ghosh Debabrata   V-638
Kun, Feng   III-468
Kuo, Yonghong   IV-304

Lai, Mincai   I-705
Lan, Jian   IV-405
Lan, Yihua   I-582
Le, Chen   IV-82
Lei, Rong   I-59
Lei, Zhang   I-647
Li, BaoHong   V-549
Li, Cai   IV-437
Li, Changqing   I-714
Li, Chao   III-289
Li, Chuanxiang   IV-422
Li, Chuanzhen   III-565
Li, Chungui   III-535
Li, Cunhua   I-582
Li, Dan   III-252
Li, Dancheng   I-223, I-378
Li, Dong   IV-49
Li, Ershuai   II-407

Li, Ganhua   IV-49
Li, Guangxia   II-287
Li, Guofeng   III-49, III-58
Li, Guoqiang   V-70
Li, Haisheng   IV-32
Li, Hao   II-205
Li, He   V-437
Li, Honglei   I-663
Li, Hongnan   IV-489
Li, Hui   I-404
Li, Jiancheng   III-445, IV-49
Li, Jianlong   III-182
Li, Jianwu   II-32
Li, Jianzhong   III-558
Li, Jinfeng   IV-40
Li, Jing   IV-304
Li, Jinlong   II-186
Li, Jun   V-102
Li, Kun   IV-211
Li, Layuan   III-608
Li, Lingling   V-337, V-503
Li, Longji   V-205
Li, Luan   III-26
Li, Lun   II-660
Li, Man   II-73
Li, Miaoying   III-26
Li, Ming   I-286
Li, Nan   III-26, III-33
Li, Pan   II-361
Li, Peng   I-522
Li, Ping   IV-693, V-109
Li, Qi   IV-32
Li, Qian   II-88
Li, Qiang   V-359
Li, Qin   IV-170
Li, Qinzhen   III-376
Li, Ran   III-647
Li, Ruitai   I-79
Li, Shasha   III-49, III-58
Li, Taijun   I-663
Li, Wei   V-196
Li, Wen   III-239, III-623
Li, Xiang   I-25
Li, Xiaoping   IV-686
Li, Xin   II-255
Li, Xin-e   IV-415
Li, Xinhui   II-487
Li, Xinyur   IV-700
Li, Xuan   IV-282
Li, Yafeng   I-726

Li, Yan   III-1, III-312
Li, Yangzhi   II-287
Li, Yanping   IV-656
Li, Yanxi   III-111
Li, Ya-Wei   III-549
Li, Yong   II-513
Li, Yu   V-298
Li, Zengxue   I-560
Li, Zengzhi   V-205
Li, Zhang   IV-483
Li, Zhi   II-700
Li, Zhigang   V-337
Li, Zhihua   I-113, I-156
Li, Zhijiang   V-86
Li, Zhilai   III-477
Li, Zhiling   III-495
Li, Zongying   I-270
Lian, He   V-566
Liang, Dakai   IV-211
Liang, Fan   III-600
Liang, Fan Yuan   IV-550
Liang, Hui   I-330
Liang, Jun   II-218
Liang, Kai   II-464
Liang, Shuang   I-143
Liang, Yujing   V-165
Lian-jiong, Zhong   V-150
Liao, Ling-zhi   II-631
Liao, Qin   IV-321
Liao, Shengbin   II-684
Lie-hui, Zhang   I-215
Lihua, Chen   IV-641
Lijuan, Du   I-179
Lijuan, Wu   IV-505
Lijun, Zhang   III-221
Li-li, Zhang   I-278
Lin, Aidi   I-573
Lin, Jinshan   I-478
Lin, Junxiao   III-88
Lin, Ruqi   IV-9
Lin, Wenshui   II-638
Lin, Yuan   V-493
Lin, Zhang   V-290
Lin, Zhenshan   V-239
Linfei, Wang   I-654
Ling, Minhua   IV-17
Ling, Weiqing   V-452
liping, Ma   IV-513
Liu, Baozhong   V-589
Liu, Binsheng   I-378

Liu, Bo   II-73
Liu, Chanjuan   III-95
Liu, Cheng   I-223, I-378
Liu, Dafu   IV-664
Liu, Gang   II-178
Liu, Guangyu   I-541
Liu, Guoqing   V-252
Liu, Haiyan   I-560
Liu, Hongyun   I-165
Liu, Hongzhao   I-611
Liu, Huining   I-233
Liu, Jianhua   I-172
Liu, Jie   I-439
Liu, Jin   III-679
Liu, Jing   IV-627
Liu, Jingbiao   II-422
Liu, Jingzheng   I-432
Liu, Kai   V-474
Liu, Liandong   IV-113
Liu, Lingxia   I-190
Liu, Lixin   V-337, V-503
Liu, Mao   V-133, V-429
Liu, Mei   III-252
Liu, Nian   II-430
Liu, Nianzu   II-105
Liu, Peiqi   V-205
Liu, Ping   IV-163
Liu, Qian   IV-238
Liu, Quan   I-338
Liu, Rongqiang   IV-178
Liu, Sanming   III-18
Liu, Shuai   I-639
Liu, ShuMin   II-473
Liu, Songyuan   I-143
Liu, Ting   V-359
Liu, Wei   IV-220
Liu, Wenxia   II-430
Liu, Xiang   I-270
Liu, Xiaohua   III-337
Liu, Xiaolin   II-487
Liu, Xiaoxia   I-87
Liu, Xin   III-197
Liu, Xingliang   IV-627
Liu, Xinying   III-510
Liu, Yanfen   I-33
Liu, Yang   I-299
Liu, Yanping   V-413
Liu, Yanxia   III-376
Liu, Yi   IV-128
Liu, Ying-Ji   III-152

Liu, Yintian   IV-227
Liu, Yixian   I-223
Liu, Yong   V-376
Liu, Yuanchao   IV-40
Liu, Yue   IV-170
Liu, Yueming   V-196
Liu, Yuewu   IV-32
Liu, Zhaoxiang   II-178
Liu, Zhigang   II-715
Liu, Zhiliang   I-378
Liu, Zhong   I-698, III-486
Liwen, Cai   I-202
Lixiao, Zhang   III-82
LiYing, Ren   III-103
Li-Yu, Chen   I-590
Long, Wang   I-418
Long, Zhang Xiao   I-356
Lou, Zhigang   I-611
Lu, Dianchen   III-131
Lu, Guonian   IV-463
Lu, Wei   I-33
Lu, Yali   I-631
Lu, Yuzheng   V-397
Lujing, Yang   III-459
Luo, Caiying   II-622
Luo, Hong   II-430
Luo, Qi   V-54
Luo, Zhifeng   II-487
Lv, Cuimei   IV-17
Lv, Dandan   III-640
Lv, Dawei   I-560
Lv, Tao   III-260

Ma, Guang   I-541
Ma, Lijie   V-298
Ma, Lixin   III-297
Ma, Wenqiang   II-178
Ma, Xiao-Yu   III-66
Ma, Xiuli   V-352
Ma, Zhi   IV-90
Ma, Zhiqiang   II-369
Mai, Qiang   V-367
Manjusri, Basu   V-638
Mao, De-jun   V-230
Mao, Xie   IV-483
Matsuhisa, Takashi   V-647
Mei, Qun   I-348
Meng, Hua   V-367
Meng, Xianglin   IV-422
Meng, Xiaofeng   III-600

Miao, Huiyi   IV-163
Miaofen, Zhu   III-267, III-273
Min, Zhang   IV-374
Min, Zhifang   I-582
Min, Zou   V-124
Ming, Li   IV-456
Ming, Wang   V-290
Ming, Zhao   I-179
Mingche, Su   V-21
Minjun, Chen   II-124
Mogus, Fenta Adnew   III-510
Mou, Ying   V-173
Mu, Deqiang   III-477
Mu, Zhichun   V-479

Na, Li   IV-443
Na, Xiaodong   I-66
Nannan, Zhou   II-82, III-10
Nianzu, Liu   II-330
Nie, Guihua   III-73
Ning, Sheng-Hua   III-647
Ning, Tao   I-113, I-156
Ning, Xin   III-125
Ning, Xu   V-142
Ning, Xueping   II-378
Ning, Zhou   V-189
Niu, Xinxin   II-397

Ouyang, Minggao   IV-337

Pan, Chen   III-632
Pan, Cunzhi   II-708
Pan, Xuezeng   IV-157
Pan, Zi-kai   I-338
Pei, Xiao-fang   II-631, III-26, III-33
Peilin, Zhang   II-50
Peng, Junjie   V-413
Peng, Pengfei   I-698
Peng, Xiong   III-246
Peng, Xiuyan   IV-678
Peng, Ying-wu   V-230
Peng, Zhou   IV-274
PingRen, Hou   V-316

Qi, Bing   III-367, III-549
Qi, Min   IV-253
Qi, Qiaoxia   III-131
Qi, Xin   IV-135
Qi, Yongsheng   II-324
Qi, Zhou Ru   V-142

Qian, Feng   II-352
Qian, Ying   II-212
Qiao, Yan   V-290
Qi-Min, Zhang   I-590
Qin, Xiaoyan   IV-128
Qin, Xuan   V-260
Qin, Ya   IV-128
Qin, Yong   IV-463, V-70
Qin, Zheng   III-197
Qing'an, Li   IV-268
Qing-Hui, Wang   III-215
Qingwei, Luan   III-160
Qingxiang, Meng   V-666
Qiu, Weidong   V-109
Qiuping, Tao   IV-618
Qiuyuan, Huang   IV-274
Qiya, Zhou   V-566
Qiyan, Wu   II-140
Qu, Xiaolu   III-297
Qun, Miao Yi   IV-550

Ran, Liu   IV-74
Ren, Haozheng   I-582
Ren, Shuming   V-30
Ren, Yafei   IV-122
Ren, Zhaohui   II-571
Rui, Peng   I-356
Rui, Wang   V-323
Ruifan, Li   V-467
Ruixia, Yang   V-544
Rui-Zhao,   IV-415

Satya, Bagchi   V-638
Sen, Liu   I-278
Shang, Gao   V-316
Shang, Wei   II-361
Shao, Yunfei   IV-361
Shao, Yuxiang   I-315
Shaohui, Su   III-267, III-273
Shaolei, Liu   IV-588
Shaopei, Lin   IV-555
She, Chundong   IV-664
She, Wei   II-316
Shen, Hong   III-125
Shen, Jian   V-275
Shen, Luou   I-469, I-484
Sheng, Yehua   IV-463
Sheng, Zheng   I-207
Shengbin, Liao   II-691

Shenyong, Gao   I-202
Shi, Guoliang   IV-150
Shi, Hongmei   I-514
Shi, Jingjing   V-346
Shi, Jiuyu   IV-678
Shi, Junping   I-150
Shi, Ke   V-260
Shi, Liwen   V-215
Shi, Minyong   I-330
Shi, Weiya   II-563
Shi, Yanling   I-172
Shichao, Chen   IV-186
Shi-Guang, Feng   II-479
Shrestha, Gyanendra   III-221
Shu, Donglin   II-163
Shuai, Zhaoqian   III-672
Shulun, Wang   I-654
Shunxiang, Wu   III-82
Shu-yong, Hu   I-215
Sihai, Zheng   III-608
Siyou, Tong   I-654
Song, Baowei   II-148
Song, Changping   II-299
Song, Feng   I-541
Song, Gangbing   IV-489
Song, Jinguo   IV-633
Song, Kai   V-413
Song, Liping   III-501
Song, Lixiang   V-558
Song, Li-xin   IV-415
Songquan, Xiong   II-653
Su, Chang   IV-143
Su, Guoshao   I-365
Su, Jian   I-233
Su, Jianxiu   V-298
Su, Kehua   II-271
Sui, Xin   III-41
Sui, Yi   III-152
Sun, Chao   II-487
Sun, Chongliang   II-97
Sun, Guang-Zhong   I-38
Sun, Guodong   I-448
Sun, Guo-qiang   II-9
Sun, Hongbin   III-573
Sun, Hongwei   II-294
Sun, Huiqi   II-361
Sun, Jianfeng   I-25
Sun, Jing   III-111
Sun, Maoheng   II-88
Sun, Shihua   II-407

Sun, Xiaohan   I-373
Sun, Xin   IV-526
Sun, Yajin   V-589
Sun, Yi   III-367, III-549
Sun, Yuxin   V-86
Sun, Ziguang   III-535

Tan, Guang-Xing   III-647
Tan, Li   I-439
Tan, Shanshan   V-54
Tan, Siyun   II-600
Tan, Wuzheng   III-252
Tan, Xiong   I-432
Tan, Yuan   IV-526, IV-538
Tan, Yunmeng   II-684
Tang, Gang   I-456
Tang, Kai   I-573
Tang, Liang-Rui   III-367, III-392,
     III-549
Tang, Liu   IV-238
Tang, Lu-jin   II-59
Tang, Shoulian   V-275
Tang, Xiaowen   II-446
Tang, Xiaowo   IV-361
Tao, Cuicui   I-726
Tao, HaiLong   IV-686
Tao, Jiang-Feng   I-541
Tao, Jun   III-615
Tao, Liu   IV-618
Tao, Xing   II-504
Tao, Zhang   IV-483
Taorong, Qiu   IV-618
Tian, Dake   IV-178
Tian, Hongli   V-46
Tian, Jinwen   V-421
Tian, Ran   V-215
Tian, Shiwei   II-287
Tian, Xiang   II-287
Tianen, Zhu   II-413
Tianwei, Li   I-179
Tie, Liu   IV-274
Tiejun, Jia   III-246
Tong, Hengqing   III-321
Tong, Ji-Jin   III-486
Tong, Xiaolei   III-1
Tong-Tong, Lu   III-429
Tongyu, Xu   III-282
Tu, Qixiong   I-602
Tu, Xisi   III-519

Wan, Shanshan   V-269
Wan, Yuan   III-321
Wang, Baojin   I-127
Wang, Bei   III-672
Wang, Bin   II-614
Wang, Bingcheng   II-571
Wang, Changhong   III-409
Wang, Changjiang   IV-195
Wang, Chungang   III-376
Wang, ChunHua   IV-381
Wang, Dandan   V-30
Wang, Dehua   I-299
Wang, Desheng   V-13
Wang, Enhua   IV-337
Wang, Fei   II-205
Wang, Feng   V-397
Wang, Hong   V-77
Wang, Hongjing   V-30
Wang, Hong-li   II-538
Wang, Hongtao   III-230
Wang, Hongxia   V-352
Wang, Huaibin   IV-40
Wang, Hui   I-307
Wang, Huiping   III-402, III-454
Wang, Huirong   III-383
Wang, Jian   II-88
Wang, Jiancheng   II-369
Wang, Jiandong   II-638
Wang, Jianyu   II-344
Wang, Jing   II-677
Wang, Juanle   II-97
Wang, Jun   I-113
Wang, Junfeng   IV-664, V-173
Wang, Kuifu   III-119
Wang, Lei   I-619, II-228, III-510
Wang, Li   V-246
Wang, Liwen   II-306
Wang, Longjuan   I-663
Wang, Lu   I-439
Wang, Mei   II-316
Wang, Meige   II-608
Wang, Mingpeng   V-581
Wang, Ping   II-41
Wang, Pu   II-324
Wang, Qian   IV-195
Wang, Rifeng   III-352
Wang, Rui   V-230
Wang, Shilin   III-167
Wang, Shui-ping   II-631, III-33
Wang, Siyuan   IV-538

Wang, Songxin   V-459
Wang, Taiyue   I-456
Wang, Wan-sen   I-639
Wang, Weidong   I-165
Wang, Weihong   IV-98
Wang, Weiming   I-127
Wang, Wenqi   II-513
Wang, Xi   V-94
Wang, Xianchao   V-413
Wang, Xiaochun   II-294
Wang, Xiaoshan   III-581
Wang, Xin   II-205
Wang, Xinchun   II-390
Wang, Xiuqing   V-38
Wang, Xue   IV-497, V-522
Wang, Xuejie   IV-220
Wang, Xuezhi   III-527
Wang, Ya-ming   I-532
Wang, Yanmin   III-409
Wang, Yi   V-474
Wang, Ying   III-289
Wang, Yisong   V-655
Wang, Yong   V-376
Wang, Yonggang   V-275
Wang, Yongqiang   V-529
Wang, Yu   III-419
Wang, Yuchun   V-558
Wang, Zequn   I-663
Wang, Zhankui   V-298
Wang, Zhengzhi   IV-422
Wang, Zhenzhen   V-529
Wang, Zhijie   III-18
Wang, Zhiwu   III-419
Wang–qun, Xiao   V-662
Wanping, Hu   I-386
Wei, Da-kuan   II-59
Wei, Fang   V-421
Wei, Fangfang   III-111
Wei, Gong   IV-437
Wei, Haizhou   II-32
Wei, Hao   I-654, III-459
Wei, Qiang   I-378
Wei, Ting   II-614
Wei, Wu   IV-268
Wei, Xianmin   I-109
Wei, Ying   I-294
Wei, Zhang   IV-82
Wei, Zhi-nong   II-9
Weidong, Huang   III-312
Weiguo, Zhang   IV-513

Wei-Li, Jiang   I-493
Weixin, Tian   I-207
Wen, Bangchun   V-437
Wen, Hao   II-194
Wen, Peng   III-189, III-655
Wen, Qingguo   II-148
Wen, Wushao   IV-388
Wen, Youkui   II-194
Wenbo, Guo   III-10
Wenhui, Yu   IV-582
Wenpei, Zhuang   IV-519
Wensheng, Cao   I-463
Wu, Chanle   IV-1
Wu, Danping   IV-66
Wu, Demin   I-573
Wu, Dengrong   II-614
Wu, Hanwei   I-663
Wu, Jingjing   IV-405
Wu, Jun   III-519
Wu, KaiXing   IV-381
Wu, Libing   I-705, III-189, III-655, IV-1
Wu, Lihua   V-513
Wu, Min   IV-346
Wu, Mingguang   V-54
Wu, Shaopeng   II-163
Wu, Wei   III-197
Wu, Xinyou   II-638
Wu, Yingshi   V-252

Xia, HongWei   III-409
Xia, Jiang   V-544
Xia, Jingming   II-41
Xia, Keqiang   III-445
Xia, Pan   III-205
Xian, Li   II-504
Xian-feng, Ding   I-424
Xiang, Lili   I-691
Xiangjun, Li   IV-618
Xiang-yang, Liang   V-150
Xiao, Min   IV-135
Xiao, Nan   II-218
Xiao, Rui   III-367
Xiao, Wen   V-529
Xiao, Xiang   IV-204
Xiao, Yong   II-246
Xiaobo, Niu   III-459
Xiaodong, Huang   V-323
Xiaofeng, Xu   III-141
Xiaogang, Hu   IV-605
Xiaogang, Wang   III-246

Xiaohang, Zhang   V-21
Xiao-hong, Zhang   II-1
Xiaohong, Zhang   III-591
Xiaohua, Wang   II-439
Xiaojia, Wu   II-124
Xiaoliang, Zhu   II-691
Xiaolong, Zhou   III-103
Xiaoluo, Jiang   II-455
XiaoMin, Ge   I-507
Xiaoming, Guo   III-141
Xiaopeng, Cao   I-386
xiaoyan, Chen   I-560
Xiao-Yu, Ge   III-215
Xie, Charlene   IV-66
Xie, Chuanliu   V-173
Xie, Jianmin   IV-361
Xie, Ming   IV-1
Xie, Qingsen   V-215
Xie, Tian   V-558
Xie, Xiang-Yun   I-262
Xie, Yongquan   III-252
Xieyong, Ruan   V-331
Xigui, Ding   I-560
Xi-lin, Hou   I-278
Xin, Yang   II-397
Xi-nan, Zhao   I-278
Xing, Jianping   I-299
Xing, Jun   I-698
Xing, Lei   I-682
Xinjian, Dong   V-606, V-614
Xinquan, Xiao   V-282
Xinwei, Xiao   II-25
Xiong, Jiping   II-337
Xiong, Weicheng   IV-1
Xiu, Li   II-82, III-10
Xu, Ao   III-189
Xu, Bugong   I-46
Xu, Guang-yu   II-555
Xu, Haifei   IV-227
Xu, Jinping   II-638
Xu, Lian-Hu   I-619
Xu, Li-Mei   III-486
Xu, Liufeng   IV-678
Xu, Shangying   III-73
Xu, Wei-ya   V-62
Xu, Xinwei   IV-354
Xu, XuJuan   II-473
Xu, Yang   IV-128
Xu, Zhang   I-179
Xuan, Lifeng   II-337

Xuan, Wang   IV-430
Xuan, Wenling   V-536, V-596
Xue, Haiyan   I-241
Xue, Wu   IV-298
Xunquan, Yu   V-566

Yadong, Yu   V-331
Yajun, Guo   I-566
Yan, Dong-xu   V-62
Yan, Hongjin   V-619
Yan, Huiqiang   V-46
Yan, Jingfeng   II-171, III-119
Yan, Lin   V-666
Yan, Liubin   I-365
Yan, Wu   V-282
Yan, Xiaohui   III-41
Yan, Zhang   I-121
Yan, Zhuang   II-669
Ya-Nan, Li   III-468
Yang, Bo   II-586
Yang, Cai   I-87
Yang, Chunwen   V-337, V-503
Yang, Enlong   V-346
Yang, Guo-qing   II-546
Yang, Hongwu   II-186
Yang, Huan   V-581
Yang, Hui   IV-463, V-70
Yang, Jing   III-519
Yang, Jingyuan   V-384
Yang, Jun   V-421
Yang, Lisheng   IV-321
Yang, Luyi   II-677
Yang, Shaopu   II-708
Yang, Xiao-Bin   III-239, III-623
Yang, Xiaofang   IV-9
Yang, Xiaoqing   IV-627
Yang, Xulei   II-246
Yang, Ya-Hui   I-321
Yang, Yanlan   V-445
Yang, Zuquan   II-155
Yanjuan, Zhao   I-121
Yanjun, Li   IV-641
Yanqing, Weng   II-700
Yanxi, Li   III-160
Yanxiang, He   IV-268
Yao, Gang   V-376
Yao, Xiaoming   I-663
Ye, Fang   II-9
Ye, Fei   II-413
Ye, Hua   V-445

Ye, Jimin   II-579
Ye, Ning   V-376
Ye, Xi   IV-388
Ye, Xue   III-573
Ye, Yiru   IV-388
Yi, Guangling   III-519
Yi, Hehe   IV-90
Yi, Liu   I-134
Yichun, Luan   II-496
Yimin, Guo   I-566
Yiming, Qin   V-21
Yin, Tianyi   I-223
Yin, Xinke   I-397
Yin, Ying   V-486
Ying, Lu   V-150
Ying, Yue   I-386
Yingchao, Zhang   IV-671
Yinghong, Wan   I-386
Yixin, Zhong   V-467
Yong, Chen   IV-268
Yong, Peng   II-644
Yong, Zhu   III-344
Yongchang, Liu   II-330
You-jun, Chen   I-424
Youping, Gong   III-267, III-273
Youxin, Yuan   IV-298
Yu, Bin   IV-113
Yu, ChongChong   I-439
Yu, Feng   III-304
Yu, Haibin   II-422
Yu, Hanghong   IV-312
Yu, Hua   II-163
Yu, Kangkang   IV-686
Yu, Le   II-264
Yu, Pei   V-346
Yu, Peijun   III-445
Yu, Tianshui   III-655
Yu, Xuchu   I-432
Yu, Zhenwei   II-212
Yuan, Dong-Xia   III-66
Yuan, Gannan   V-306
Yuan, Huang   V-282
Yuan, Kaiguo   II-397
Yuan, Kefei   V-306
Yuan, Li   IV-82
Yuan, Liu-qing   I-286
Yuan, Meng-yang   I-532
Yuan, Shengchun   IV-567
Yuan, Yi-Bao   I-619
Yuan, Youxin   II-600

Yuan, Yuanlin   V-384
Yuanping, Jing   I-1
Yuansheng, Qi   II-439
Yue, Qiangbin   IV-700
Yue-Hong, Sun   V-1
Yufeng, Li   IV-648
Yujie, Yan   IV-430
Yun, Ju   IV-706
Yun, Wang   V-116
Yuren, Zhai   IV-505
YuXiang, Jiang   III-103

Zang, Shuying   I-66
Zang, Yujie   V-513
Zeming, Fan   II-113
Zeng, Guohui   V-574
Zeng, Jie   IV-211
Zhai, Pei jie   I-734
Zhan, Yuan   I-25
Zhan, Yunjun   V-165
Zhang, Baoyin   I-254
Zhang, Bin   II-397, IV-472, V-486
Zhang, Bo   I-682
Zhang, Chengke   IV-368
Zhang, Chi   II-246
Zhang, Chunfang   I-79
Zhang, Chunxia   V-38
Zhang, Denghui   II-264
Zhang, Enhai   IV-656
Zhang, Fengyu   I-127
Zhang, Hailiang   II-422
Zhang, Haiqing   IV-227
Zhang, Haiyan   V-474
Zhang, Hang-wei   II-384
Zhang, Hong   IV-573
Zhang, Hongguang   IV-337
Zhang, Hongwei   V-306
Zhang, Hui   V-133
Zhang, Huibing   IV-238
Zhang, Jie   II-73
Zhang, Jing   V-157, V-182
Zhang, Jiwei   II-218
Zhang, Jun   IV-312
Zhang, Kang   IV-472
Zhang, Lei   III-260, V-405
Zhang, Ling   IV-107
Zhang, Lisheng   IV-98
Zhang, Liyi   V-359
Zhang, Man   II-178
Zhang, Mang   I-714

Zhang, Mingyi   V-655
Zhang, Na   IV-656
Zhang, Peng   II-228
Zhang, Qian   I-348
Zhang, Qikun   IV-526, IV-538
Zhang, Qin   III-392, III-565
Zhang, Qi-wen   I-286
Zhang, Quangui   II-324
Zhang, Ruochen   III-437
Zhang, Shaohua   I-248
Zhang, Shilin   I-307
Zhang, Shun   IV-113
Zhang, Siping   II-316
Zhang, Sujuan   II-390
Zhang, Tao   II-344, IV-246
Zhang, Tianming   III-289
Zhang, Wei   IV-57, IV-90
Zhang, Weigong   II-586
Zhang, Weizhao   II-186
Zhang, Wenhua   II-563
Zhang, Xia   III-615
Zhang, Xian   V-38
Zhang, Xiaoping   III-330
Zhang, Xiaoyan   I-502
Zhang, Xing-jin   II-660
Zhang, Xiwen   III-73
Zhang, Xizhe   V-486
Zhang, Xueping   II-228
Zhang, Yan   I-365
Zhang, Yang   IV-253
Zhang, Yanxin   III-581
Zhang, Yanzhi   III-260, III-663
Zhang, Yonglin   V-619
Zhang, Yu   III-501
Zhang, Yuanliang   II-299
Zhang, Yuanyuan   II-212
Zhang, Yumei   I-514
Zhang, Zengfang   III-535
Zhang, Zhengbo   I-165
Zhang, Zhian   II-600
Zhangxin, Pan   V-331
Zhao, Chuntao   V-503
Zhao, Daxing   I-448
Zhao, Guangzhou   II-246
Zhao, Hongdong   V-46
Zhao, Jie   IV-195
Zhao, Jun-xia   II-660
Zhao, Liang   V-252
Zhao, Lin   III-392
Zhao, Meihua   III-330

Zhao, Ming   V-86
Zhao, Minghua   II-715
Zhao, Qingzhen   IV-693
Zhao, Rongyong   V-452
Zhao, Xiang   IV-700
Zhao, Xiaoming   IV-567
Zhao, Xuefeng   I-582
Zhao, Yan   III-437
Zhao, Ying-nan   II-631
Zhao, Zengliang   I-602
Zhao-Ling, Tao   V-1
Zhao qian, Shuai   IV-374
Zhen, Huang   V-316
Zheng, Jiachun   I-550
Zheng, Jianzhuang   V-223
Zheng, Jun   IV-526, IV-538
Zheng, Wen-tang   V-62
Zheng, Yu   II-88
Zheng, Zhi-yun   II-660
Zhengping, Shu   IV-82
Zhengping, Zhao   V-544
Zhengyong, Duan   II-644
Zhi-bin, Liu   I-424
Zhifeng, Luo   III-82
Zhigang, Wu   II-140
Zhiguo, Zhang   V-544
Zhihong, Feng   V-544
Zhili, Gu   IV-605
Zhong, Guanghui   I-79
Zhong, Kai   V-13
Zhong, Ruowu   III-402, III-454
Zhong, Weimin   II-352
Zhong, Xiaoqiang   I-38
Zhong, Xu Li   IV-550
Zhong-Meng, Li   III-468
Zhou, Changle   IV-143

Zhou, Chao   I-573
Zhou, Haijun   II-280
Zhou, Haiying   V-479
Zhou, Jianjun   IV-227
Zhou, Jianzhong   IV-497, V-522, V-529,
    V-558
Zhou, Ming   III-337
Zhou, Shucheng   II-622
Zhou, Wei   III-152
Zhou, Xiaodong   II-593
Zhou, Xiaoyuan   IV-567
Zhou, Xin   I-404
Zhou, Xuan   II-88
Zhou, Yafei   V-429
Zhou, Yifei   IV-211
Zhou, Yinkang   IV-195
Zhou, Zhiying   III-640
Zhu, Guangxi   V-13
Zhu, Huainian   IV-368
Zhu, Wanzhen   II-446
Zhu, Wei   II-614
Zhu, Wenbing   V-346
Zhu, Yancheng   II-608
Zhu, Yunlong   III-41
Ziwen, Yuan   II-50
Zi-Xian, Zhao   II-479
Zongyuan, Yang   IV-430
Zou, Hailin   III-95
Zou, Hongbo   IV-211
Zou, Lixia   I-241
Zou, Qiang   V-558
Zou, Qing-hua   I-100
Zou, Shuliang   II-593
Zou, Wenping   III-41
Zou, Zhi-jun   II-205
Zulong, Lai   II-531